The
SECURITY SERVICE
1908–1945

Portrait of John Curry by Nadia Benois, wife of Jona 'Klop' Ustinov.

The
SECURITY SERVICE
1908–1945

The Official History

Introduction by
Christopher Andrew

PUBLIC RECORD OFFICE

Public Record Office
Ruskin Avenue
Kew
Surrey
TW9 4DU

© Crown Copyright 1999

ISBN 1 873162 79 0

A catalogue card for this book
is available from the British Library

Photographs from the Public Record Office
except frontispiece and back cover, which are courtesy of the Security Service

Printed by Redwood Books Ltd, Trowbridge

CONTENTS

Publisher's note   vi

Introduction   1
Christopher Andrew

The Documents   29
The Security Service: Its Problems and
Organisational Adjustments 1908–1945
John Curry

Index   431

PUBLISHER'S NOTE

This publication brings you the official internal history of the Security Service as completed by John Curry in 1946. A more comprehensive modern index replaces Curry's original; otherwise the documents are reproduced in full. The history – and accompanying minutes not included here – can be consulted at the Public Record Office, Kew, in files KV 4/1–3.

Our intention is to reproduce the material as faithfully as possible without compromising the integrity of the original. This means that the occasional error survives from Curry's text.

The symbol [...] is used in the small number of instances where the original text cannot be deciphered.

INTRODUCTION
Christopher Andrew

Origins of Curry's History

On 3 October 1944 Sir David Petrie, Director-General of the Security Service (better known as MI5), informed his divisional heads that a top-secret wartime history of the Service was to be written 'for future guidance'.

> Heads of Divisions should therefore begin to:
>
> (a) Review the work of the Divisions and define those subjects of which an account should be given.
> (b) Appoint a suitable Officer, or Officers, to assemble the requisite material bearing on each of the subjects selected, and to prepare rough drafts.

The 'rough drafts', Petrie ordered, were to form the basis both of detailed accounts of the wartime work of each division and of a short general history to be written by John Court ('Jack') Curry, a fifty-seven-year-old MI5 officer who was nearing retirement.[1]

Petrie and Curry were veterans of the Indian Police. Before the First World War they had served in its Criminal Investigation Department (CID), from which emerged between the wars the Intelligence Bureau of the Home Department of the Government of India.[2] Both also had some experience of writing official histories. As Assistant Director of the CID in 1911, Petrie had won the gold medal of the United Service Institution of India for an essay on 'The maintenance of law and order in India considered in relation to the mutual cooperation of the civil and military power in the country'. While Director of the Intelligence Bureau from 1924 to 1931, Petrie was responsible for the production of a classified official history, *Communism in India, 1924–1927*, whose sources included the intercepted correspondence of both Indian Communists and the Communist International.[3]

After a quarter of a century in India, Curry joined the Security Service in 1934.[4] He probably owed his appointment, a decade later, as MI5's wartime historian to his experience in writing several studies of the Indian Police which had impressed Petrie. The volume which Curry produced in 1946, however, was rather different from what the Director-General had in mind. Petrie, who retired shortly after Curry completed his work, had wanted a 40,000-word short history which his successor 'could quickly ... assimilate'. This could be used to impress other government departments and the armed services when requesting 'the many-sided assistance he will undoubtedly require from them'.[5]

Curry's volume was much longer than the Director-General had intended. His explanation for its length is reminiscent of the possibly apocryphal letter attributed to several well-known authors when writing to their publisher, 'I apologise for sending you a long book. I did not have time to write a short one.' Curry had had remarkably little time to digest the histories of MI5 divisions, most of which were delayed by pressure of wartime and immediate post-war work. He wrote to Petrie in March 1946:

> ... As late as October 1945 I had no idea of the quantity of material I was going to receive from the sections or of the significance of much of the detail ... Many of the more important sectional histories did not come in until December or January, and even February 1946 ... As they came in I found that nearly every one of the sectional histories was full of facts with which, in many cases, I had only a slight or incomplete previous acquaintance...[6]

Though sympathising with Curry's problems, Petrie was plainly disappointed by the book that he produced:

> The thing that still worries me about it is its length, for people in these days find it very hard to cope with very lengthy documents. The tempo of official life is not likely to get any slower in the years to come.[7]

In the summer of 1946, Curry produced a 15,000-word summary of his History 'with a view to its being shown to Permanent [U]nder Secretaries and Directors of Intelligence'. He was disappointed to be told subsequently that it was unsuitable for this purpose but could be used 'for instructional purposes in the case of new officers'.[8]

Curry's 'Note on completion of the "History"' conveys some sense of resentment at Petrie's unenthusiastic reception of his work. He claims, probably with a good deal of exaggeration, that he and Petrie had not merely different but 'incompatible views' of MI5's record under his leadership:

> As far as I understand him, I think he feels that this office, after his reorganisation, has worked so successfully that it would be impossible for me to show that it had defects which should be avoided in future (as he directed me to do ...), whereas, as I see it, it has been highly successful in spite of the gravest defects which have caused a very serious amount of friction (especially internally and in our relations with S.I.S.), mental confusion and waste of effort and expense.[9]

Most of the account in Curry's History of Petrie's term as Director-General lays rather less emphasis on 'mental confusion and waste of effort and expense'. It also places most of the blame for wartime friction with the Secret Intelligence Service on SIS rather than on grave defects in MI5.

The contents of the Curry History, which was not declassified until January 1999, overlap with those of the official history of British wartime security and counter-intelligence by the late Sir Harry Hinsley, Emeritus Professor of the History of International Relations at Cambridge University and former Vice-Chancellor, and

Anthony Simkins, Deputy Director-General of MI5 from 1965 to 1971, which was published in 1990.[10] Each volume, however, contains important material missing from the other. Though hastily assembled and less impressive than the official wartime history as a work of historical scholarship, the Curry History seems at times closer to the working experience of MI5 officers. A majority of the officers referred to by Curry are not identified by Hinsley and Simkins.[11] Intelligence historians will henceforth need to take account of both volumes.

The First World War and its Aftermath

Curry devotes more space than Hinsley and Simkins to MI5's pre-war history. Petrie, however, had not intended him to pay serious attention to the period before the Second World War:

> Indeed my idea was that no more would be required than what would serve as an introduction to what we did from 1939 throughout the recent war ... Too much of a past that is now remote can help but little with useful lessons. It was a reproach levelled against our Army that in 1914 it was perfectly trained and equipped to fight the Boer War, and in 1939 to fight the first World War. The same tendencies may beset a counter-intelligence organisation.[12]

Petrie failed to see the contradiction in his own argument. It was precisely the study of past conflicts which had helped to identify 'useful lessons' such as the tendency of generals to enter new wars expecting to refight the battles of a previous generation. MI5's main successes and failures during the Second World War are also far more comprehensible when seen in the historical perspective which Petrie failed to appreciate. Its success in tracking down enemy agents during the First World War provided an important precedent for, and probably helped to inspire, the operations in the Second World War which once again demolished the German spy network in Britain.[13] Curry notes that during the First World War, MI5's work 'gradually broadened from the detection of espionage to the impersonation of hostile agents for the purpose of feeding the enemy with misleading information'. One of those whom MI5 impersonated was a German agent who had been captured and shot. Unaware of his fate, German intelligence continued to send large sums for a series of bogus reports concocted in his name by MI5.[14] There, in microcosm, was the spectacularly successful Double Cross system of the Second World War.

Curry's brief account of MI5's origins and of its operations up to 1919 mostly summarises a story told in much greater detail in the 'historical reports' compiled shortly after the First World War, which were declassified in 1997. The material on the inter-war years is of much greater interest. During the 1920s MI5 was a small section of the War Office under General Staff control. Its operations were hampered both by drastic post-war staff reductions and by the division of responsibility for monitoring Communist activities between itself and the Special Branch at Scotland Yard. While MI5 was responsible for counter-espionage on British territory and for detecting Communist and other 'seditious movements' within the armed forces, the

Postcard image of Mata Hari (Margaretha Zelle), who was executed in France on February 13 1917 for spying for the Germans, although there was little real proof of espionage (KV 2/2).

Special Branch was charged with the surveillance of civilian 'revolutionary movements'. The Secret Service Committee, composed of the Cabinet Secretary and the Permanent Under-Secretaries of the Treasury, Foreign and Home Offices, set up after the First World War to advise ministers on the organisation and functions of the intelligence agencies, met too rarely during the 1920s to resolve such demarcation problems. Meeting in 1925 for the first time since 1921, however, it noted some of the problems caused by the cumbersome division of labour between MI5 and the Special Branch:

> ... A Communist, working in naval or military circles at Portsmouth or Aldershot, may spend his Sundays making revolutionary speeches in Hyde Park. The former of these occupations is a matter for research by MI5; his week-end relaxations bring him into the preserve of the Special Branch.[15]

Curry draws briefly but interestingly on Special Branch files on Communist surveillance in the 1920s, which were later transferred to MI5, as well as on the Security Service's own records. He confirms the importance of Soviet diplomatic telegrams decrypted by the Government Code and Cypher School (GC&CS), forerunner of today's Government Communications Head-Quarters (GCHQ), as a source for monitoring both Soviet espionage and Moscow's relations with the British Left. Signals intelligence (SIGINT) from the decrypts provided evidence of secret Soviet funding for the socialist *Daily Herald*, and revealed that Lev Kamenev, head of the

Soviet trade mission to Britain in 1920, had secretly encouraged plans to prevent British intervention (which, in reality, was never likely) in the Russo-Polish War. The decrypts also disclosed official Soviet funding for strike action by British miners in 1925–6.[16]

In addition to the SIGINT which they received from GC&CS, MI5 and the Special Branch also had access to a regular flow of intercepted communications of the Communist International (Comintern), containing exhortations and instructions to foreign Communist parties. Petrie's *Communism in India, 1924–1927* contains a number of references to such intercepts, and Curry had doubtless seen many examples while serving in India. These intercepts, however, unlike the diplomatic decrypts, were an intelligence source which from time to time was polluted by forged documents. Recent research in still classified intelligence files by the Foreign Office historian, Gill Bennett, has established that the celebrated 'Zinoviev Letter' to the Communist Party of Great Britain (CPGB), dated 15 September 1924, was one such forgery.[17] Curry, on the basis of less comprehensive research, concludes only that the Zinoviev letter was 'possibly a forgery', but reasonably adds that it 'contained nothing that had not been seen in intercepted correspondence as going from the Berlin Bureau of the Comintern to the C.P.G.B. or the National Minority Movement [Communist-led trade-union organisation]'.[18]

The Zinoviev Letter epitomised the problems caused by the fragmentation and inadequate coordination of the British intelligence service during the 1920s. Those parts of it which instructed the CPGB to put pressure on Labour sympathisers and generally to prepare for the coming of the British Revolution concerned the Special Branch, while the passage which ordered intensification of 'agitation-propaganda work in the armed forces' was the responsibility of MI5. The fact that SIS, though a foreign intelligence service, also ran some agents in the United Kingdom caused further confusion. As well as providing the text of the Zinoviev Letter, SIS also provided confirmation, based on a report from an agent inside the British Communist Party, that the letter had been received and discussed by the CPGB leadership. Though the Foreign Office accepted the reliability of this corroboration, the Special Branch – and probably MI5 – were less convinced. Appearing before the Secret Service Committee in 1925, the head of the Special Branch, Sir Wyndham Childs, disputed the SIS corroboration and declared, 'I could produce from equally reliable sources evidence to the exact opposite'. His scepticism was well founded. Recent research by Gill Bennett in classified SIS files probably unavailable for Curry's History has revealed that its agent had, in reality, made no reference to the receipt by the CPGB of the Zinoviev Letter but had merely referred to a discussion by the Party's Central Committee of issues which resembled some of those mentioned in the Letter.[19] The episode provides further justification for Curry's criticism both of the lack of any adequate liaison between SIS and MI5 during the 1920s, and of the inadequate resources available to SIS to monitor the international Communist movement.

The 1920s were MI5's least influential decade. At the end of the First World War its total staff had numbered 844, of whom 133 were listed as 'officers and civilian officials'. By 1929 there were no more than 16 'officers and civilian officials', all but one of them male.[20] As Curry acknowledges:

The pay was small and the prospects such as to make no appeal except to a small number of officers with private incomes. The work itself was light and no one in authority in the War Office or elsewhere was closely interested.

On a number of occasions during the 1920s there were proposals to abolish MI5. Curry credits its survival largely to the personality of its Director-General, Sir Vernon Kell. First appointed as chief on the foundation of MI5 as the home department of the newly-created Secret Service Bureau in 1909, Kell continued in office until 1940, thus becoming the longest-serving head of any British government department in the twentieth century.[21]

Reorganisation as the Security Service

MI5's fortunes revived in 1931, paradoxically as a result of a dispute with SIS. Following complaints by both MI5 and the Special Branch that SIS was continuing operations against Communist targets within the United Kingdom, the Secret Service Committee reconvened in an overdue attempt to resolve demarcation disputes between the intelligence agencies. It was agreed that SIS confine itself strictly to operations at least three miles away from British territory, and that the domestic agencies operate only within this limit. The Committee also sought a solution to the impracticable division of duties between MI5 and the Special Branch which it had identified, but not resolved in 1925. 'Intelligence operations connected with civil security', chiefly involving the Communist Party, were transferred to MI5 from the Special Branch, which, however, retained responsibility for 'Irish and anarchist matters'. As part of the transfer of responsibilities, MI5 acquired Scotland Yard's leading experts on 'subversion'. Chief among them was Guy Liddell, later wartime head of B Division (counter-espionage).

MI5's official title henceforth became the Security Service.[22] It ceased to be a section of the War Office and acquired an enhanced but ill-defined status within Whitehall as an interdepartmental intelligence service working for the Home, Foreign, Dominion and Colonial Offices, the service departments, Committee of Imperial Defence, Attorney General, Director of Public Prosecutions, and Chief Officers of Police at home and throughout the Empire.[23] While writing his History, Curry was told by A. W. A. ('Jasper') Harker, then Deputy Director-General, that service chiefs and the Chief of the Imperial General Staff had given verbal approval to MI5's change of status, but he discovered no evidence that their consent had been given in writing.

For at least two years there was some confusion about the 1931 reorganisation, stemming partly from the fact that the Security Service was still also known by its old title, MI5, thus appearing to imply that it remained a department of military intelligence (MI). Kell's deputy, (Sir) Eric Holt-Wilson, noted in 1933 that the War Office Directorate of Military Intelligence was 'only aware in a vague way' of what had happened two years earlier, and that even MI5 had no accurate written record of the changes. He therefore drew up a memorandum whose purpose, according to Curry, was 'to make it clear that the Security Service was no longer in any sense a part of the Directorate of Military Intelligence'.[24] Curry says little about the Security Service's enhanced status in the Empire as a result of the reorganisation. Holt-Wilson, however, claimed proudly in a classified lecture not quoted by Curry:

> Our Security Service is more than national, it is Imperial. We have official agencies cooperating with us, under the direct instructions of the Dominion and Colonial Offices and the supervision of the local Governors, and their chiefs of police, for enforcing local Security Laws in every British Community overseas.
>
> These all act under our guidance for Security duties. It is our duty to advise them, when necessary, on all security measures necessary for defence and civil purposes; and to exchange information regarding the movement within the Empire of individuals who are likely to be hostile to its interests from a Security point of view.[25]

As part of the 1931 reorganisation, SIS established a new Section V (Counter-intelligence) under Valentine Vivian (later Deputy Chief of SIS), which liaised with MI5. According to Curry, the liaison worked well until the outbreak of war, due largely to 'the goodwill and readiness for give and take between the officers concerned at all levels' in SIS and the Security Service. In 1935 intelligence from Section V derived from the interception of Comintern radio messages led to the discovery of a secret wireless used by the CPGB for communications with Moscow. These communications revealed much about Moscow's policy directives and secret subsidies to the British Communist Party. After the 1931 reorganisation, MI5 also took over from SIS an agency, renamed M Section, which had run agents inside the CPGB.[26] M was Maxwell Knight, later to achieve fame as a writer and broadcaster on natural history, presenting a BBC children's programme under the name 'Uncle Max'. One of his most successful penetration agents was Olga Gray, who exposed a Soviet spy ring inside the Woolwich Arsenal. It was run by Percy Glading, a leading British Communist who was arrested and found guilty of espionage in 1938.[27] Ms Gray is not identified by name in the declassified version of the Curry History. Both MI5 and SIS continue to take the view that the traditional promise to their agents and informants that their identities will not be revealed extends indefinitely, save when they choose to identify themselves. To break this undertaking, they believe, would undermine the confidence of their current sources.

When Curry wrote his History at the end of the Second World War, MI5 was still unaware of its most important failure during the 1930s. Though, particularly in view of its limited resources, it was well informed about Soviet influence within the CPGB and labour movement, it was unaware of Soviet intelligence recruitment at Cambridge and other universities. The KGB considered five of the young Cambridge graduates recruited in the mid-1930s – Kim Philby, Donald Maclean, Guy Burgess, Anthony Blunt and John Cairncross (later dubbed 'The Magnificent Five') – as possibly the ablest group of foreign agents in its history.[28] MI5's inter-war horizons may well have been limited by its lack of contact with higher education. Until the recruitment in 1935 of Dick White, who had graduated in history from Christ Church, Oxford, MI5 had not a single university graduate on its staff. (White, later knighted, went on to become the only man ever to head both MI5 and SIS.)[29] Before the Second World War, Soviet intelligence had more British graduates working for it than MI5 and SIS combined. Soviet penetration was facilitated by the general lack of security in Whitehall. Until the Second World War, the Foreign Office had not a single security officer, let alone a security department.

The Growing Nazi Threat

Before Hitler came to power in 1933, MI5 paid 'practically no attention' to Nazism. Curry, who joined the Security Service in the following year, is said to have been among the first of its officers to grasp the magnitude of the Nazi threat. Early in 1934, Kell asked the Permanent Under-Secretary at the Home Office, Sir Russell Scott, 'whether he expected the Security Service to take any special steps about Nazis in this country'. According to Curry, Scott appeared entirely unconcerned, and replied that 'unless we discovered in the ordinary course of our work any case of subversive propaganda or other inimical steps against the interests of this country we were to leave them alone'. In April 1934, however, MI5 began investigating the links of the British Union of Fascists (BUF) with German Nazism and Italian Fascism.[30] Though the declassified version of Curry's History does not identify any of the MI5 agents in the BUF, they included James McGuirck Hughes, who, remarkably, succeeded in becoming BUF head of intelligence under the pseudonym P. G. Taylor.[31] In October 1935 MI5 discovered that Mussolini had secretly agreed to pay the BUF £3,000 a month.[32] It also identified a number of leading BUF members with strong pro-Nazi sympathies – among them William Joyce, later better known to the British public as 'Lord Haw-Haw', who broadcast German propaganda to Britain for most of the Second World War.[33]

Among MI5's greatest successes during the 1930s was its penetration of the German embassy. It is possible, once again, to identify some of the names of the MI5 sources within the embassy which have been excised from the declassified text of the Curry History. All were probably motivated by opposition to the Nazi regime. They included Jona 'Klop' Ustinov (father of Peter), the press attaché; Theodor Kordt, embassy counsellor; and Wolfgang zu Putlitz, junior embassy secretary.[34] After leaving the London embassy in 1935, 'Klop' Ustinov, continued to provide valuable intelligence from his contacts in both Germany and the embassy. Dick White, who became Ustinov's case officer, later described him as 'the best and most ingenious operator I had the honour to work with'.[35] Curry, whose main pre-war responsibilities were the investigation of German espionage and Nazi policy, also worked with Ustinov. The portrait of Curry reproduced in the frontispiece to this volume was painted by Ustinov's wife, Nadia Benois.

The substantial flow of intelligence provided by MI5 from Ustinov and its embassy sources included 'numerous reports' on Joachim von Ribbentrop, German ambassador in London from 1936 to 1938 (later Hitler's foreign minister from 1938 to 1945). By a curious chance, the sons of Ribbentrop and Ustinov spent the academic year 1936–7 in the same class at Westminster School, sitting at neighbouring desks. Peter Ustinov's first success as a budding journalist was to earn seven shillings and sixpence from the *Evening Standard* for his lurid description of an artwork by the young Ribbentrop entitled 'Armed Strength', which depicted warfare, murder and mayhem.³⁶

Ribbentrop *père*, whose grasp of British policy was clouded by conspiracy theories, was said to have informed Berlin that the abdication of Edward VIII was 'the result of the machinations of dark Bolshevist powers against the Führer-will of the young King'. MI5 also reported that Ribbentrop had said that Hitler's main aim, which he was dictating to 'a reluctant Reichswehr and Foreign Office', was war with Russia, during which he hoped Britain would stay neutral. Curry claims that in September 1938 the Security Service provided 'a clear forecast of the line which Hitler subsequently developed during the Munich Crisis'. After the crisis, MI5 reported that Hitler had 'referred to Mr Chamberlain in terms of school-boyish obscenity'. According to Curry, this made, as MI5 had intended, 'a considerable impression on the Prime Minister'.³⁷

Before the Second World War, MI5 obtained intelligence on the actual or attempted recruitment of thirty German agents in Britain, twenty-one of whom were British subjects. Eleven of those approached by German intelligence reported the fact to the authorities. Nine agents were identified by MI5 from the interception by HOW (an acronym used by Curry to refer to Home Office warrants) of correspondence at addresses already under surveillance. Of the remainder, five were reported by 'private people whose suspicions had been aroused, one by an immigration officer, and one by "an anonymous informant"'. Two 'came to notice adventitiously'.³⁸

The pre-war German espionage detected by MI5 was, Curry concludes, 'run on a very crude basis'. Many of the agents provided 'information of no importance in order to extract the maximum of reward for the minimum of effort'. The Security Service, however, remained worried, unnecessarily as it later transpired, that 'a cloud of agents of low quality served to hide a few good ones', which it had failed to detect. It was deeply conscious that there was much it did not know about German foreign intelligence operations.³⁹ Until 1939 both MI5 and SIS were unaware either of the name of the *Abwehr*, the German espionage agency, or of the identity of its head, Admiral Wilhelm Canaris.⁴⁰

In the summer of 1938 the Security Service sought the advice of the former Director of the Indian Wireless and Telegraph Service, Lieutenant Colonel Simpson, on arrangements for monitoring radio messages sent by spies stationed in Britain and other 'illicit transmissions'. Simpson reported in October that radio interception was so inadequate that trained agents in wartime would be able to send radio messages with little chance of detection; indeed, they might already be doing so.⁴¹ A meeting in the War Office in December 1938 agreed to set up a new agency, later known as the Radio Security Service (RSS), to intercept 'illicit transmissions'. MI5 was pressed to take responsibility for the new agency, but refused to do so because of the financial and administrative burdens which would be involved. Curry blames this decision, which he likens to a 'Greek tragedy', on an outmoded bureaucratic mindset in MI5's inter-war leadership (and, by implication, the fact that Kell had been Director-General for almost thirty years) which had 'produced failures in organisation and planning and an absence of thinking on sufficiently big lines'. The RSS was to prove a crucial weapon both in the detection of wartime German agents and in the running of the Double Cross System. Originally run by the War Office with the assistance of the GPO, the RSS was transferred in May 1941 to the control of SIS.[42]

The Second World War

The Security Service on the eve of the Second World War was still a comparatively small organisation. At the end of 1938, according to Curry, it had 30 officers with 103 secretaries and Registry staff.[43] Despite an expansion in its personnel after the outbreak of war, the dramatic growth in the demands placed on the Security Service brought it close to collapse by the time Hitler ended the Phoney War and launched his attack on France and the Low Countries on 10 May 1940. Kell had failed to heed the warning contained in an MI5 report at the end of the First World War that, in the event of another war, it would be deluged with 'a flood of paper'.[44] The subsequent expansion of government bureaucracy ensured that the flood would be even greater than had been predicted after the Armistice. Even had Kell been more farsighted, however, his pre-war budget was too small to have funded adequate preparations for wartime conditions. During the second quarter of 1940 MI5 was receiving, on average, 8,200 requests a week from newly security-conscious government departments for the vetting of individuals and the issue of exit permits. Curry describes some of the excessive demands made on it as 'almost Gilbertian' in their bureaucratic absurdity. They were increased still further by the ill-advised mass internment of mostly anti-Nazi 'enemy aliens' from May to July 1940.[45]

MI5 found the enormous volume of alarmist reports from the public even more difficult to cope with than the demands of government departments. The

Suspicion of fifth column activities meant that strange markings on the ground, on paper and on telegraph poles, which it was feared might be related to German invasion plans, had to be investigated. The cross on this Cornwall field turned out to be heaps of lime for agricultural uses (KV 4/11).

extraordinary rapidity of Hitler's conquest of France and the Low Countries in less than six weeks was widely, though mistakenly, ascribed to the assistance given to German forces by large 'fifth columns' working behind the lines. Many, probably most, of the British population, jumped to the conclusion that a similar fifth column was at work in Britain, preparing the way for an invasion. A Home Intelligence report to the Ministry of Information concluded on 5 June, 'Fifth Column hysteria is reaching dangerous proportions'. Marks on telegraph poles were frequently interpreted as elaborate codes designed to guide a German invasion; some were discovered to be the work of boy scouts and girl guides who, after questioning, 'readily agreed to refrain from the practice'.[46] Pigeons were also widely suspected of secret intercourse with the enemy; counter-measures included the recruitment of British birds of prey to intercept suspicious pigeons in mid-air.[47] 'None of these numerous reports' notes Curry, '... led to ... the uncovering of any real "Fifth Column" activities or even to the detection of a single enemy agent'. MI5, however, was overwhelmed by the sheer number of non-existent fifth columns it was called upon to investigate.

The Security Service's lack of preparedness to deal with public wartime paranoia about German-inspired subversion reflected a failure, once again, to learn the lessons of the First World War. In the autumn of 1914, wrote Sir Basil Thomson, head of the Special Branch, spy mania 'assumed a virulent epidemic form accompanied by delusions which defied treatment':

> It attacked all classes indiscriminately and seemed even to find its most fruitful soil in sober, stolid, and otherwise truthful people.[48]

Many of the 'delusions' which wasted the time of the Special Branch and MI5 at the outbreak of the First World, such as reports of signalling at night to German submarines – sometimes from locations far inland – and the use of carrier pigeons to send secret messages to Germany, recurred in almost identical form during the fifth column hysteria of 1940.

As in 1914, the hysteria affected some in high places and government departments as well as the general public. Curry notes a 'report sponsored from a very high quarter ... that trees had been felled in a wood so as to make an arrow pointing to a neighbouring aerodrome'.[49] Though not identified by Curry, the highly-placed alarmist may well have been Field Marshal Sir Edmund (later Baron) Ironside, who, shortly before being replaced as C-in-C Home Forces in July 1940, issued an extraordinary warning that there were 'people quite definitely preparing aerodromes in this country' for use by the Luftwaffe.[50] One of the lessons later drawn by Petrie from the experience of 1940 was:

> ... the need to have people ready to deal with alarmist rumours about wireless, lights, pigeons and so on; in fact all the scare stories that are bound to descend like a flood. Such material must be kept away from and not allowed to clog the wheels of the real counter-intelligence machinery.[51]

One MI5 dossier (KV 4/10) documents the use of pigeons by both sides for intelligence and even counter-intelligence during the Second World War. *Clockwise from top:* British parachutist's device for carrying up to six pigeons; British press cutting; map of pigeon lofts in Western Germany; British falcon trained to intercept enemy pigeons.

The crisis in MI5 during 1940 led to three top-secret official enquiries and to the dismissal of both Kell and his deputy. The first of the enquiries was conducted from March to May 1940 by Lord Hankey, Minister without Portfolio in Chamberlain's War Cabinet and previously Cabinet Secretary for the record period of twenty-two years from 1916 to 1938. Curry is scathing about Hankey's failure to grasp the serious problems which confronted the Security Service: 'So far from reporting on the breakdown he referred in eulogistic terms to the efficiency of the Registry which he said he had visited.'[52] Petrie thought much of Currie's criticism would have been better omitted from the History, but was himself privately dismissive about Hankey's report:

> [Hankey] was not a trained Intelligence officer and his report was largely descriptive, even if too approving. He could not be expected to cut very deep, and it was perhaps as much as could be expected from anyone so indifferently equipped.[53]

Hankey's report was swiftly followed by a further investigation of MI5 by Lord Swinton, the former Secretary of State for Air, who on 28 May was made head of a newly-founded Security Executive, charged by Churchill with sorting out what he called 'the overlaps and underlaps' in dealing with espionage and subversion. Swinton proved as abrasive as Hankey had proved emollient. He was probably largely responsible for persuading Churchill that, after thirty-one years under Kell, MI5 needed new leadership. On 10 June Kell wrote in his diary, 'I get the sack from Horace Wilson [permanent head of the civil service]', added his dates of service '1909–1940', and drew a line beneath them.[54]

Though implicitly accepting that it was time for Kell to go, Curry is even more critical of Swinton than of Hankey. His chief criticism is that Swinton 'helped to reduce B Branch [counter-espionage] to a state of chaos and ... seriously damaged the morale of its officers' by appointing a solicitor, William Crocker, as joint head of B Division but leaving undefined both his powers and those of the other joint head, Guy Liddell. By August Liddell and other B Division officers were seriously considering resignation, but with the war at a critical stage decided that it was their duty to stay. In September, however, Curry records that 'the position was cleared up by Mr Crocker's departure'. Liddell was appointed sole head of B Division, which then had ninety officers, and Curry became his deputy.[55] Though vulnerable in his private life and incautious in some of his friendships (with, among others, Guy Burgess), Liddell went on to win a reputation as one of the War's outstanding intelligence officers. Hugh Trevor-Roper (later Lord Dacre), a wartime recruit to SIS, who got to know him well, found Liddell 'a remarkable and very charming man who gave the B Division its special character: open, genial, informal, but highly professional'.[56]

In July 1940 Swinton was given 'executive control' over MI5 and its new Director-General, 'Jasper' Harker, Liddell's predecessor as head of B Division. Though Curry does not criticise Harker directly, it is clear from his short tenure that he was not a success. One of MI5's wartime recruits, (Sir) Ashton Roskill (later a well-known QC), compared him to 'a sort of highly-polished barrel which, if tapped, would sound hollow (because it was). Swinton saw through him in a flash'.[57] In November, with morale in MI5 still at a low ebb, Sir David Petrie, then serving with the Intelligence Corps in Cairo, was summoned to London to carry out a further investigation. A minute by Petrie on Curry's history implies that he was also approached at this stage to succeed Harker as Director-General. But, wrote Petrie, 'I refused outright to take charge until I had examined things for myself'.[58]

For reasons which remain unclear, Curry did not have access to Petrie's report,[59] which was completed on 13 February 1941. Petrie concluded, unsurprisingly, that

Documents from the MI5 file on Duncan Alexander Croall Scott-Ford, a British merchant seaman who supplied the Germans with information on British shipping. He was executed for treason on 3 November 1942. *Clockwise from top:* identity card (KV 2/57); News Chronicle cutting, 4 November 1942 (KV 2/59); Scott-Ford with an unnamed woman friend (KV 2/59); and incriminating notes (KV 2/59) found in his wallet.

the rapid wartime expansion of the Security Service (which in January 1941 numbered 234 (almost entirely male) officers and 634 (mostly female) support staff) had caused organisational breakdown and confusion in the chain of command. He concluded that Crocker's appointment as joint head of B Branch and, by implication, Swinton's 'executive control' had been an unfortunate mistake. Outside interference had lowered MI5 morale.[60] Before becoming Director-General in April

1941, wrote Petrie later, 'I got the principle of the D.G. being master in his own house recognised and endorsed'.⁶¹

Dick White, assistant director of B Division when Petrie took over, later described the new Director-General as 'one of the best man managers I ever met'.⁶² Ashton Roskill agreed:

> Solid in appearance and in mind, [Petrie] made it his business to know the essentials of his job, but did not hesitate to delegate. I doubt if he had more than a B + mind but he used it, made few – if any – mistakes, and combined courtesy with firmness.⁶³

According to Curry, Petrie 'restored confidence – almost immediately internally and more gradually among the officers and Departments with whom [MI5] was in external relation'.⁶⁴

Despite his hostility to Swinton, Curry concludes that his period of 'executive control' had brought some benefits. Swinton brought in a business efficiency expert, Reginald Horrocks, to modernise MI5's antiquated filing system, introduce a Hollerith punch-card system, and assimilate a large number of untrained Registry staff. Horrocks, in Curry's view, 'brought about a great improvement in the mechanics of the Office and gradually introduced order where there had been disorder and confusion'. There was, however, a good deal of opposition to the new methods from Security Service veterans who had grown accustomed to old ways and had become expert in operating the traditional filing system. Controversy over the new methods 'was only brought to an end by Sir David Petrie's decision in favour of Mr Horrocks's scheme'.⁶⁵ Petrie seems to have resented Curry's suggestion that he had inherited some of Swinton's reforms, commenting acerbically:

> Actually Lord Swinton did very little until after my report which Mr Curry has not seen. It was completely independent ... What I adopted I did because I approved thereof ... Similarly with the Registry. The basic "mechanical" [Hollerith punch-card sorter] idea was not the patent of Mr Horrocks, or me, or anyone else, and I had anyhow tried out that system in India. Mr Horrocks deserves the fullest credit for perfecting the machine, but various other things, such as making officers responsible for carding and speeding up the connection of papers, were introduced at my instance. If such things are worth mentioning at all, and I hardly think they are, they had better be correctly stated.⁶⁶

Petrie's appointment as Director-General followed hard on the heels of a major break-through in MI5's investigation of enemy espionage. In August 1940 *Abwehr* radio transmissions dealing with intelligence operations against Britain began to be intercepted by the Radio Security Service (RSS); some were decrypted by GC&CS at its wartime home in Bletchley Park. By this time, unknown to the *Abwehr*, four of its agents operating against Britain had been turned into double agents working for MI5. This combination of SIGINT and double agents led to the complete failure of the first major *Abwehr* offensive from September to November 1940. Of the twenty-one agents landed in Britain during this period, one committed suicide and the remainder were either captured or quickly surrendered.[67] Three joined the ranks of the double agents, feeding disinformation back to Germany. The same pattern recurred in subsequent German attempts to infiltrate agents into wartime Britain. All were executed, imprisoned or became part of the Double Cross system.

In December 1940 the *Abwehr* section at Bletchley succeeded in breaking the main hand cipher used for *Abwehr* radio messages; the decrypts were known henceforth, in honour of the GC&CS section head, as ISOS (Intelligence Service Oliver Strachey). Once the RSS passed under the control of SIS in May 1941, however, immediate problems arose over MI5's access to the decrypts. B Division found the wartime head of SIS Section V, Felix Cowgill, who controlled the distribution of ISOS material, far less easy to deal with than his predecessor, Valentine Vivian. Curry recounts a series of 'instances in which Colonel Cowgill attempted to prevent the Security Service from obtaining information which was essential to the proper discharge of their responsibilities'.[68] Kim Philby, who was put in charge of the Iberian sub-section of Section V in 1941, believed that, 'Cowgill revelled in his isolation. He was one of those pure souls who denounce all opponents as "politicians"':

> MI5 argued that counter-espionage was indivisible, and that they were entitled to all information on the subject available to Section V. Cowgill, speaking for Section V, rejected that view, maintaining that MI5 were entitled only to information bearing directly on the security of British territory, with the implicit rider that he himself was sole judge of the relevance of information to British security.[69]

Moscow was probably shocked by one of Philby's reports which contained a politically incorrect comparison between Cowgill and the founder of Communism: 'He drinks very little, but smokes pipe tobacco in prodigious quantities, like Karl Marx.'[70]

Though disputes over the distribution of ISOS material continued throughout 1941 and much of 1942,[71] Curry reports that various methods were discovered of circumventing Cowgill's restrictions:

> ... Great benefits accrued when, without his knowledge or contrary to his intentions, different recipients got in touch with one another and exchanged views on the nature of the material and the possibilities of exploiting it.[72]

While Petrie was privately critical of Cowgill's narrowmindedness, he was unhappy that such criticisms should appear in Curry's History:

> All this, in my view, had better be forgotten and omitted from our manual for reasons other than shortage of space. The personal aspects are of no lasting interest or value, however true it may be, as it is, that the outlook of this particular officer [Cowgill] is neither wide nor catholic.

What it is essential to lay down, as objectively and as firmly as possible, is what in *fact* were the disabilities imposed on us, and consequently on our work, from this grudging and inadequate sharing of this vital material. This is what needs to be clearly pointed out, so that it may be remedied now and avoided for the future.[73]

The Double Cross System

MI5's wartime collaboration with the rest of the intelligence community, however, was more notable for its successes than for its failures.[74] The most striking of those successes was the Double Cross system. In order to use its double agents to deceive the enemy, MI5 needed a plentiful supply of bogus intelligence. The intelligence was supplied by the interdepartmental Twenty Committee (so called because the Roman numeral for 'twenty', XX, was a double cross), chaired by the Oxford historian, J. C. Masterman, former tutor to Dick White and a wartime recruit to MI5. During weekly meetings which began in January 1941, the committee considered what information was safe for the double agents to pass on to the *Abwehr*, a process likened by Masterman to handling dynamite. Initially, the Twenty Committee feared that there might be an undetected German espionage network at work in Britain. It was quickly reassured, however, by both the success of the double agents in deceiving the enemy and the evidence provided by SIGINT. The Twenty Committee rapidly came to the astonishing conclusion that, in Masterman's words, *'We actively ran and controlled the German espionage system in this country'*.[75] That conclusion was slightly exaggerated. Curry reveals that a small number of German agents were operating under diplomatic cover in neutral embassies outside MI5 control. All, however, appear to have been under close surveillance, and it is unlikely that any provided the Germans with intelligence of real significance.[76]

Curry's History adds only modestly to what has already been published on the working of the Double Cross system. Masterman's in-house history of the double agent sub-section, B1a, on which Curry based much of his own briefer account, was published in the United States in 1972 – to the considerable annoyance of Whitehall.[77] Curry's account of the double agents, however, also draws on a number of other sources – in particular the account of the GARBO case by his case officer, Tomas Harris, an art dealer bilingual in English and Spanish.[78] Juan Pujol Garcia, codenamed GARBO, was one of the most successful double agents in the history of espionage.[79] No-one in Curry's History receives higher praise than Harris and Pujol:

> GARBO is described as working with passionate and quixotic zeal for many hours a day to produce voluminous reports from a network of imaginary or "notional" agents which was eventually composed of no less than twenty-eight members, covering a considerable part of the British Isles with out stations in North America, Canada and Ceylon. The transmission of the numerous reports which resulted involved immense labour by GARBO himself and Mr Harris. The case was worked out by both with extraordinary devotion and skill over a long period.[80]

Curry's judgment was endorsed by Sir Michael Howard's official history of wartime strategic deception published in 1990. Though Sir Michael did not identify Harris by name, he described his collaboration with GARBO as 'one of those rare partnerships between two exceptionally gifted men whose inventive genius inspired and complemented one another'.[81] At 1 a.m. on D Day, 6 June 1944, GARBO radioed to his *Abwehr* controller that Allied forces had embarked for Normandy. The message arrived too late to be of practical use but raised still higher GARBO's reputation with German intelligence. On 9 June, at a time when the Allied assault could still have been pushed back into the sea, GARBO radioed, '... It is perfectly clear that the present operation, though a large-scale assault, is diversionary in character'. At a crucial moment he thus powerfully reinforced the Allied deception operation designed to convince the Germans that the main attack would come in the Pas de Calais. The 1st SS and 116th Panzer divisions, which were on their way to Normandy, were stopped in their tracks and ordered to head for the Calais region. On 29 July GARBO was informed by his controller, 'With great happiness and satisfaction I am able to inform you that the Führer has conceded the Iron Cross to you for your extraordinary merits'. GARBO replied, 'I cannot at this moment, when emotion overwhelms me, express in words my gratitude'.[82]

On 26 June 1944 Petrie wrote to the Foreign Secretary, Anthony Eden, who had been given ministerial responsibility for the Security Service in December 1943. Petrie claimed that, since becoming Director-General in 1941, he had 'perhaps said more hard things of the Service than almost anyone else'. He now wanted, however, to pay tribute to MI5's remarkable accomplishments:

> It is now considered by the Imperial General Staff that there is clear evidence to show that 'the timing of our attack on Normandy was a complete surprise to the enemy'. This has resulted from the combined efforts of the various Services and Agencies which have been working hard and long on the security side of the operation. The role of the Security Service has been particularly important and particularly difficult.
> ... Whatever innovations may be thought of after the war, it should not be forgotten that the Service, throughout a long period of national emergency, has done the work for which it exists and done it with complete success.

Curry endorsed 'the validity of these general conclusions'.[83] So did X-2, the counter-intelligence section of the wartime American intelligence agency, the Office of Strategic Services (OSS).[84]

Soviet Espionage

If MI5's greatest wartime successes were its total defeat of German espionage in Britain and its major contribution to the Double Cross system, its greatest failure was inadequate surveillance of Soviet espionage. The Security Service, however, was not solely to blame. In 1943 D.F. Springhall, the National Organiser of the

Communist Party, was sentenced to seven years' imprisonment for obtaining classified information from the Air Ministry, including details of a top-secret radar-jamming device, which he had intended to pass on to Moscow. Subsequent MI5 enquiries showed that Springhall's other contacts included Desmond Uren, a staff officer in the Special Operations Executive (SOE), who also received a seven-year prison term. MI5 drew up a list of fifty-seven other Party members 'known to be engaged in the Services or in Government Departments or in the aircraft or munitions industries on work of some secrecy'. In most cases they had gained their jobs because the departments concerned had no coherent vetting procedures for Party members and had failed to follow Security Service guidelines. MI5's proposal for the introduction of uniform procedures was turned down and a secret Whitehall panel which contained no Security Service representative was given responsibility for examining all cases of Communists in government departments.[85] The Security Service believed, probably correctly, that the panel was not up to its job.[86]

A further serious obstacle to MI5's attempts to investigate Soviet espionage was the attitude of the Foreign Office. The best way for the Security Service to have discovered the extent of Soviet espionage would have been to penetrate the Soviet Embassy and Trade Delegation, both of which contained Soviet intelligence officers under diplomatic or official cover, seek to recruit agents in both locations and bug their premises. Similar methods used against Communist Party headquarters had already yielded valuable intelligence. The Foreign Office, however, refused to allow such methods to be employed against Britain's wartime allies – despite the fact that it did not forbid the penetration of some neutral embassies and legations.[87]

In the wake of the arrest of Springhall and Uren, MI5 discovered one Communist in its own ranks and one (a secretary) in those of SIS, both of whom were dismissed.[88] The Security Service was well aware that the Soviet espionage it had uncovered represented only the tip of an iceberg. Curry's History reaches 'two main conclusions':

> The first is that counter espionage measures are not easily taken with success in time of peace or against the Secret Intelligence Service of a country with which we are at peace or in alliance; and that this is particularly so in the case of Russia. The second conclusion is that the cases which have been detected can only represent a small part of the effective work done by the Soviet Military Intelligence against us in any one period. The Soviet Military Intelligence Service has a great advantage compared with any normal state in virtue of the fact that it has so many opportunities of exploiting the position created by the existence of numerous British Communists and Communist sympathisers. Many of these individuals are in positions of confidence and trust and feel a greater obligation of loyalty to the Union of Soviet Socialist Republics than to their own country, or even to oaths by which they have been bound.[89]

The success of wartime Soviet espionage in Britain also owed much to weaknesses in MI5's own security of which Curry seemed unaware. Both MI5's lack of awareness of the Soviet recruitment of high-flying ideological agents from the mid-1930s onwards, and its hasty expansion after the outbreak of war left it vulnerable to Soviet penetration. Early in the war, for example, 'Jasper' Harker asked a young Oxford graduate in the Home Office, Jenifer Fischer Williams, to recommend the names of suitable recruits to MI5. He was blithely unaware that Ms Fischer Williams had until recently been a secret member of the CPGB, and that the NKVD (predecessor of the KGB) had tried unsuccessfully to recruit her as a Soviet agent. Harker appears to have assumed that her family background, Oxford education and employment by the Home Office were sufficient evidence of her reliability.[90]

A similar laxity was evident in the recruitment of the art historian and Soviet agent, Anthony Blunt, to B Division. Though expelled from a military intelligence training course in September 1939 when evidence emerged of his past Communist associations, Blunt succeeded in talking his way back into military intelligence and thence, a few months later, into MI5.[91] Once inside the Security Service, Blunt proved adept at cultivating his fellow officers. As Sir Dick White was later to acknowledge:

> He made a general assault on key people to see that they liked him. I was interested in art and he always used to sit down next to me in the canteen and chat. And he betrayed us all.[92]

Curry records that in 1941 Blunt was made head of a newly-created 'special section' of B Division, responsible for the surveillance of neutral embassies, some of which were regarded as 'possible sources of leakage to the enemy about important political and military matters' and even as possible bases for German agents. One of Blunt's first priorities was to gain access to the 'voluminous material' on foreign diplomats in London which was in SIS files.

Curry refers to three important sources of intelligence of a 'highly secret nature' on neutral embassies, 'wrapped in complicated prohibitions', which were supplied to Blunt's section by SIS. The declassified version of his History, however, identifies only two: diplomatic traffic decrypted by GC&CS and forwarded by SIS; and bugged telephone conversations by embassy staff.[93] The third 'highly secret' source, though still officially classified, can be clearly identified from material already in the public domain, in particular from a wartime report by Blunt to his Soviet controller which refers to the surreptitious opening of diplomatic bags by censorship staff working on SIS instructions. Blunt explains that the interception of diplomatic traffic, the bugging of embassy telephones and the opening of diplomatic bags were the responsibility of SIS rather than MI5 because 'SIS is technically under the Foreign Office and diplomats are supposed to be primarily of interest to the Foreign Office'.[94]

To supplement the intelligence obtained from SIS, MI5 succeeded in recruiting agents in, or inserting agents into, a series of London embassies. Some were anti-Nazi diplomats from neutral countries who 'were prepared to work as far as it lay in their power to help the Allied cause'.[95] Other agents included housemaids and other servants supplied to diplomatic missions by a domestic service agency working for Maxwell Knight. According to Blunt's report to his Soviet controller:

> Our best agent of all, who is a secretary ... in the Spanish embassy, gets us cipher tape, clear versions of cipher telegrams, drafts of the ambassador's reports, private letters, notes on dinner parties and visitors, and general gossip about members of the embassy.[96]

Blunt's section identified German agents in both the Spanish and Portuguese embassies. There was particular anxiety early in 1944 that these agents might succeed in providing advance warning to the Germans of the D Day landings. According to Curry, it was largely as a result of pressure from the Security Service that, from 15 March 1944 onwards, the Cabinet decreed that foreign diplomatic missions in London were not to be allowed to send cipher telegrams or uncensored diplomatic bags out of the country.[97] The only exceptions were to be the embassies of the United States and the Soviet Union. NKVD and GRU (Soviet military intelligence) residencies in London, operating under diplomatic cover, were thus able to continue communicating freely with Moscow about their operations in Britain.

MI5's greatest single wartime handicap in attempting to uncover Soviet penetration, apart from the fact that it was penetrated itself, was a lack of Soviet SIGINT. Curry emphasises the crucial importance of decrypted *Abwehr* communications in defeating German espionage.[98] GC&CS, however, did not decrypt the communications of Soviet intelligence agencies. The striking difference which SIGINT on Soviet espionage would have probably made to MI5 wartime operations was demonstrated when it became available early in the Cold War. During the late 1940s and early 1950s American codebreakers, with some help from their British allies, succeeded in decrypting in whole or in part almost 3,000 Soviet telegrams mostly dating back to the Second World War. In the spring of 1951 the decrypt of an NKGB telegram of June 1944 identified Agent HOMER as the British diplomat, Donald Maclean, one of the Magnificent Five from Cambridge recruited in the mid-1930s.[99] With the unmasking of HOMER, the Five quickly began to unravel. In May 1951 Maclean and Burgess fled to Moscow. Suspicion quickly fell on Philby, then SIS liaison officer in Washington; on American insistence he was withdrawn to London and retired from SIS after a 'judicial enquiry' at MI5 headquarters. Incriminating evidence against Cairncross found in Burgess's flat, though insufficient for a prosecution, led to his forced resignation from the civil service. As a close friend of Burgess, with whom he had shared a flat while working for MI5, Blunt also came under suspicion for the first time.[100] Had Soviet decrypts been available to MI5 during the Second World War, the careers of the Magnificent Five would surely have been much curtailed.

During the Second World War Soviet intelligence was baffled by MI5's failure to unmask Blunt and the rest of the Five. Their Communist sympathies while Cambridge students, it believed, must surely have led the Security Service to identify them as potential Soviet agents. Moscow's bafflement turned gradually to deep suspicion. In 1943 NKGB headquarters bizarrely informed its London residency that the Five were double agents, working on the instructions of MI5 and SIS. While at Cambridge, it concluded, all had probably been instructed by British intelligence to infiltrate the student Left before making contact with Soviet

Images from MI5 files on German agents captured and executed in the Second World War. *Clockwise from top:* Josef Jakobs (KV 2/26) – the cardboard code (KV 2/27) was an exhibit in his trial; Josef Jan Van Hove (KV 2/55); Karel Richter, his miniature wireless set and the recovery of his parachute in Hertfordshire (KV2/32).

intelligence. Only thus, Moscow reasoned, was it possible to explain why both MI5 and SIS were currently employing in highly sensitive jobs Cambridge graduates with a Communist background. Not till after D Day did Soviet intelligence abandon its own conspiracy theory and recognise that the Five were, in reality, among its most committed and valuable agents.[101]

In the spring of 1943 collaboration between MI5 and SIS in the surveillance of Communism and Soviet espionage entered what appeared to be a new era. The head of F Division ('subversive activities'), Roger Hollis (later knighted and Director-General of MI5 from 1956 to 1965), was impressed by the intelligence potential of intercepted radio transmissions between Moscow and the British Communist Party, and appears to have urged SIS to set up a new section to specialise in international Communism and its links with Moscow.[102] The Chief of SIS, Sir Stewart Menzies, and the Deputy Chief, Valentine Vivian, pre-war head of Section V, agreed that 'the subject of Communism required to be handled by an officer who was not trammelled by the urgent needs of the Section V staff in connection with the war'. In May 1943 Curry was 'lent' by Petrie to SIS to found a new department, Section IX, for this purpose.

Curry writes scornfully of what he found in SIS: '... Section V had been unable to cope with current information on Communism which had been coming into S.I.S. and ... the S.I.S. Registry was inadequate for the purpose'.[103] Cowgill, predictably, was equally critical of Curry. Philby reported to his Soviet controller in May 1944:

> Cowgill is seizing every opportunity to disparage Curry's work, on the grounds that, at the moment, it is a study of purely academic interest. Vivian, though in principle willing to support Curry's efforts, realises that Curry is totally lacking in the force necessary to pursue the study with success. The result is that, whereas Curry constantly attempts to put questionnaires on Communist problems to Section V representatives abroad, Cowgill consistently blocks these enquiries on the grounds that his officers have more immediate problems on hand.[104]

As the time for Curry's return to MI5 late in 1944 approached, Cowgill seems to have hoped to merge Section IX under his leadership with Section V. Moscow, however, informed Philby through his controller, that 'I must do everything, but *everything*, to ensure that I became head of Section IX ... They fully realised this meant that Cowgill must go'. By a classic piece of bureaucratic backstabbing, in which he was assisted by Vivian, Cowgill's mortal enemy, Philby got the job and Cowgill resigned.[105] Thus it was that Curry's last assignment before beginning work on his History, the establishment of Section IX in SIS, accidentally paved the way for a spectacular Soviet intelligence success. Philby's wartime colleague in SIS, Robert Cecil, wrote later:

> Philby at one stroke had got rid of a staunch anti-Communist [Cowgill] and ensured that the whole post-war effort to counter Communist espionage would become known in the Kremlin. The history of espionage records few, if any, comparable masterstrokes.[106]

The Second World War had seen a number of unprecedented intelligence triumphs. Britain discovered more about Germany than any power had ever known about a wartime enemy. The Soviet Union, though less well-informed about its enemies, gained more intelligence about its wartime allies than any state had ever done before. Curry's History provides important insights into both of these remarkable achievements.

Notes

Document references PRO unless stated otherwise. *The Security Service* page references from this volume.

1. Director-General's Circular, 3 Oct 1944, annex 13a to minutes in Curry History file (KV 4/1). Petrie had originally wanted work on the history to begin in 1941, but, according to Curry, 'this proved not to be a workable proposition' doubtless because of MI5's pressure of current business at a critical stage in the War. Curry, 'Note on completion of the "History"', 29 July 1946, annex 28a (KV 4/3). My information on Curry's career comes from a retired intelligence officer who prefers not to be identified.
2. On the development of the Indian intelligence system, see Richard J. Popplewell, *Indian Intelligence and Imperial Defence: British Intelligence and the Defence of the Indian Empire, 1904–1924* (London: Frank Cass, 1995). On Petrie's career, see also his entry in E.T. Williams and C.S. Nicholls (eds), *The Dictionary of National Biography, 1961–1970* (Oxford: Oxford University Press, 1981), pp. 837–8.
3. The classified 1927 edition of Sir David Petrie, *Communism in India, 1924–1927*, discovered in Indian archives after Independence, was published in Calcutta in 1972, edited by Mahadevaprasad Saha. Decrypted Soviet telegrams referring to India were evidently considered too secret for inclusion even in the classified edition.
4. Curry joined the Indian Police in 1907 at the age of twenty, retiring in 1932.
5. Minute by Petrie, 2 February 1945; minute 20 in Curry History file (KV 4/1). Curry, 'Note on completion of the "History"', 29 July 1946, annex 28a to minutes in Curry History files (KV 4/3).
6. Currie to Petrie, 29 March 1946; minute 25 in Curry History file (KV 4/3).
7. Petrie to Curry, 29 March 1946; minute 26 in Curry History file (KV 4/3).
8. Curry, 'Note on completion of the "History"', 29 July 1946, annex 28a to minutes in Curry History file (KV 4/3).
9. Curry, 'Note on completion of the "History"', 29 July 1946, annex 28a to minutes in Curry History file (KV 4/3).
10. Sir F.H. Hinsley and C.A.G. Simkins, *British Intelligence in the Second World War*, vol. 4: *Security and Counter-Intelligence* (London: HMSO, 1990). Though an important work of intelligence history, largely based on classified files, volume 4 fails to reach the magisterial standards of Hinsley's previous volumes; Sir Harry, who died in 1998, told Christopher Andrew in 1990 that he was not wholly satisfied by it.
11. Even the co-author of the official wartime history, C.A.G. Simkins, though a former Deputy Director-General of MI5, is identified only as formerly 'attached to the War Office and the Ministry of Defence'.
12. Minute by Petrie, 29 March 1946; minute 26 on Curry History (KV 4/3).
13. Christopher Andrew, Introduction to *MI5: The First Ten Years, 1909–1919* (Kew: PRO Publications, 1997). Most MI5 documents for this period (class KV 1) are available on a PRO CD-ROM also entitled *MI5: The First Ten Years, 1909–1919*.
14. *The Security Service*, p. 76.
15. Report of the Secret Service Committee, 1 December 1925, published as Annex E in Gill Bennett, *'A most extraordinary and mysterious business': The Zinoviev Letter of 1924*, FCO History Note 14 (London: FCO, 1999). The Secret Service Committee does not seem to have met again until 1931.
16. *The Security Service*, pp. 93–4. In keeping with the mildly eccentric terminology in use in the 1920s, Curry refers to the decrypts as 'BJs' (or 'Blue jackets'). The chronology of Curry's discussion of Soviet SIGINT contains one error. He writes that, 'About this time [1925] Lord

Curzon started his famous series of notes making disclosures about Soviet intrigues all over the world'. Curzon had ceased to be Foreign Secretary in January 1924. Curry's reference is probably to the 'Curzon ultimatum' of May 1923, which quoted from a number of Soviet decrypts. On British interception of Soviet communications in the 1920s, see Christopher Andrew, *Secret Service: The Making of the British Intelligence Community*, paperback edition (London: Sceptre, 1986), chs. 9,10.

17 Bennett (see no. 15).

18 *The Security Service*, p. 93.

19 Bennett, pp. 36–8 (see no. 15).

20 Curry identifies as the 'officers and civilian officials' in 1929: the 'Chief', Colonel (later Major-General) Sir Vernon Kell; his deputy, Lieut.-Colonel (later Brigadier Sir) Eric Holt-Wilson; three officers in A Branch (administration and preventive security) under Major Phillips; six officers in B Branch (investigations) under Mr (later Brigadier) Harker; and a staff of three in the 'Observation' section, responsible for shadowing suspects and making 'confidential' enquiries. Curry's statistics are somewhat ambiguous. It is not clear whether his figures for officer numbers in A and B Branches include or exclude Phillips and Harker, or whether the 'Observation' staff had officer/official rank. *The Security Service*, p. 99.

21 *The Security Service*, p. 99.

22 MI5 had previously been known, since the late 1920s, as the Defence Security Service. *The Security Service*, p. 99.

23 Hinsley and Simkins, vol. 4, p. 8 (see no. 10).

24 *The Security Service*, pp. 101–2.

25 Holt-Wilson, 'Security Intelligence in War', notes for classified lecture in 1934, Kell MSS, Imperial War Museum.

26 *The Security Service*, pp. 103–8.

27 Andrew, *Secret Service*, pp. 474, 520–5 (see no.16). Anthony Masters, *The Man Who Was M* (Oxford: Blackwell, 1984).

28 On the Cambridge Five, see, inter alia, Christopher Andrew, 'Cambridge Spies: the Magnificent Five, 1933–45', in Sarah J. Ormrod (ed), *Cambridge Contributions* (Cambridge: Cambridge University Press, 1998).

29 On White's career, see Tom Bower, *The Perfect English Spy: Sir Dick White and the Secret War* (London: Heinemann, 1995).

30 *The Security Service*, pp. 109–10.

31 On MI5 penetration of the BUF, see, inter alia, Richard Thurlow, *The Secret State: British Internal Security in the Twentieth Century* (Oxford: Blackwell, 1994); and John G. Hope, 'Surveillance or Collusion?: Maxwell Knight, MI5 and the British Fascisti', *Intelligence and National Security*, vol. 9 (1994), no. 4.

32 The brief reference in Curry's History to the discovery of Mussolini's secret subsidies to the BUF is amplified in a number of declassified MI5 reports. See 'Home Office information concerning the present source of BUF funds', 27 November 1936; Kell to Home Office, 27 November 1936; minute by Liddell, 10 December 1936; HO144/20162.

33 Andrew, *Secret Service*, pp. 527–8 (see no. 16).

34 All had been among the German sources cultivated by the Permanent Under-Secretary at the Foreign Office, Sir Robert Vansittart–a group known within Whitehall as Van's 'private detective agency'; Andrew, *Secret Service*, pp. 540–2 (see no. 16). Putlitz, who joined the East German foreign service after the Second World War, may also have been providing intelligence to the Russians.

35 Bower, p. 29 (see no. 29).

36 Geoffrey Williams, *Peter Ustinov* (London: Peter Owen, 1957), pp. 39–41.

37 *The Security Service*, pp. 118–22.

38 *The Security Service*, pp. 124–7. Curry's figures do not quite add up. He claims to provide details of how all the cases of actual or attempted recruitment of German agents came to light, but gives no information on one of the thirty cases.

39 *The Security Service*, pp. 124–6.

40 They also did not know until 1939 that the *Abwehr* was subordinate to the Armed Forces Supreme Command (OKW). Hinsley and Simkins, vol. 4, pp. 11–12 (see no.10).

41 Hinsley and Simkins, vol. 4, pp. 13–14 (see no.10). In keeping with their usual practice, Hinsley and Simkins do not mention Simpson (who is identified by Curry) by name.

42 *The Security Service*, pp. 143–4, 177–9.

43 *The Security Service*, p. 142. There is a minor apparent discrepancy between Curry's figures and those of the official history of wartime intelligence, which says that in September 1938 MI5 had 33 officers and 119 'supporting staff'. Hinsley and Simkins, vol. 4, p. 69n (see no. 10).

44 *The Security Service*, pp. 160.

45 *The Security Service*, ch. 4.

46 Curry's summary account of telegraph pole hysteria draws on the detailed 'Summary of the work of B3 sections during the war 1939–1945. An investigation of markings on telegraph poles for suspected codes'; KV 4/12.

47 'Report on the use of Carrier Pigeons by the German Intelligence Service, 1940–1941'; 'Report on the operations of B3 C in connection with suspected communication with the enemy by the use of carrier pigeons, during 1939–1945'. KV 4/10.

48 Andrew, *Secret Service*, pp. 264ff (see no. 16).

49 *The Security Service*, p. 168.

50 Andrew, *Secret Service*, p. 667 (see no. 16).

51 Minute by Petrie, 13 April 1946; minute 27 on Curry History (KV 4/3).

52 *The Security Service*, p. 158.

53 Minute by Petrie, 13 April 1946; minute 27 on Curry History (KV 4/3).

54 Kell Diary (microfilm), 10 June 1940, Imperial War Museum.

55 *The Security Service*, pp. 145–7, 168–73.

56 Hugh Trevor-Roper, 'The man who put intelligence into spying', *Sunday Telegraph*, 9 April 1995 (Review section).

57 Interview by Christopher Andrew with the late Sir Ashton Roskill in 1984.

58 Minute by Petrie, 13 April 1946; minute 27 on Curry History (KV 4/3).

59 Minute by Petrie, 13 April 1946; minute 27 on Curry History (KV 4/3).

60 Hinsley and Simkins, vol. 4, p. 69 (see no. 10).

61 Minute by Petrie, 13 April 1946; minute 27 on Curry History (KV 4/3). Petrie was responsible through the Security Executive to the Lord President of the Council (then Sir John Anderson) for the running of MI5 but free from interference in staff matters and its day-to-day work.

62 Interview by Christopher Andrew with the late Sir Dick White in 1984.

63 Interview by Christopher Andrew with the late Sir Ashton Roskill in 1984.

64 *The Security Service*, p. 199.

65 *The Security Service*, pp. 168–71.
66 Minute by Petrie, 13 April 1946; minute 27 on Curry History (KV 4/3).
67 The MI5 files on nine of the German agents, all executed or imprisoned, were declassified in January 1999; KV 2/11–23.
68 *The Security Service*, pp. 206–212.
69 Philby's view of Cowgill was endorsed by his fellow SIS officer, Graham Greene. Kim Philby, *My Silent War*, with introduction by Graham Greene, paperback edition (London: Panther Books, 1969), pp. 8, 52–3.
70 Nigel West and Oleg Tsarev, *The Crown Jewels: The British Secrets at the Heart of the KGB Archives* (London: HarperCollins, 1998), appendix 2, p. 310.
71 Details of the disputes and attempts to reach a *modus vivendi* are given in Hinsley and Simkins, vol.4, ch.8 (see no. 10), which, however, does not refer to Cowgill by name.
72 *The Security Service*, p. 206.
73 Minute by Petrie, 13 April 1946; minute 27 on Curry History (KV 4/3).
74 There was also collaboration between MI5 and Irish military intelligence in the detection of German espionage in Eire and the surveillance of German contacts with the IRA. Curry gives much of the credit for this collaboration to the good personal relations ('far beyond the normal scope of an intelligence liaison') established between the head of MI5's Irish section, B1h, Cecil Liddell (brother of Guy), and Colonel Liam Archer of Irish military intelligence. *The Security Service*, pp. 277–81.
75 J.C. Masterman, *The Double Cross System in the War of 1939 to 1945*, paperback edition (London: Sphere Books, 1973), p. xii.
76 See below, p. **21**
77 The first edition of Masterman, *The Double Cross System in the War of 1939 to 1945*, was published in 1972 by Yale University Press. The original typescript was declassified in January 1999, along with appendices not included in the published version–among them messages sent and received by the double agents; KV 4/5.
78 Harris's 'Summary of the Garbo Case', declassified in January 1999, consists of a substantial typed volume with thirty appendices; KV 2/41.
79 Pujol's own account of his career as a double agent appears in Juan Pujol and Nigel West, *GARBO* (London: Weidenfeld and Nicolson, 1985).
80 *The Security Service*, p. 254.
81 Sir Michael Howard, *British Intelligence in the Second World War*, vol. 5: *Strategic Deception*, appendix 2, p. 231. The accounts of GARBO's career in Masterman (see no. 77), and Hinsley and Simkins, vol.4 (see no.10), also fail to identify Harris by name.
82 Among the MI5 files declassified in January 1999 were a substantial series of German intercepts and other important documents on GARBO's role in FORTITUDE, the deception operation which helped to ensure the success of the Normandy landings; KV 2/39, 40, 42.
83 *The Security Service*, pp. 400–402.
84 Christopher Andrew, *For the President's Eyes Only: Secret Intelligence and the American Presidency from Washington to Bush* (London: HarperCollins, 1995), pp. 139–40.
85 *The Security Service*, pp. 346–8. Desmond Morton, Churchill's intelligence adviser, commented dismissively, 'MI5 tends to see dangerous men too freely and to lack that knowledge of the world and sense of perspective which the Home Secretary rightly considers essential'. Hinsley and Simkins, vol.4, p. 288 (see no. 10).
86 Hinsley and Simkins, vol.4, p. 288 (see no. 10).

87 *The Security Service*, p. 364.

88 *The Security Service*, p. 357.

89 *The Security Service*, pp. 363. Though Curry refers to 'Soviet Military Intelligence', he seems to have had in mind Soviet intelligence as a whole, rather than simply the GRU.

90 Interview by Christopher Andrew with Jenifer Hart (née Fischer Williams) in 1983. In 1941 Ms Fischer Williams married the MI5 officer, Herbert Hart, later Professor of Jurisprudence at Oxford University and Principal of Brasenose College.

91 West and Tsarev, pp. 134–45 (see no. 70). The discussion of MI5's response to Soviet penetration in Hinsley and Simkins, vol.4 (see no. 10), is disappointingly superficial. Although the authors were given unrestricted access to MI5 files, there is, for example, no mention of the Blunt case.

92 Barrie Penrose and Simon Freeman, *Conspiracy of Silence: The Secret Life of Anthony Blunt* (London: Grafton Books, 1986), p. 251.

93 *The Security Service*, p. 260.

94 The text of much of Blunt's report to his Soviet controller is published in West and Tsarev, pp. 138ff (see no. 70).

95 *The Security Service*, pp. 260.

96 West and Tsarev, pp. 140–1 (see no. 70).

97 *The Security Service*, pp. 259–61.

98 In addition to producing ISOS decrypts of *Abwehr* hand-cipher communications, Bletchley Park also succeeded in December 1941 in breaking the *Abwehr* variant of the Enigma machine cipher, used for communications between its headquarters and controlling stations in occupied and neutral countries. The Enigma decrypts were known as ISK (Intelligence Service Knox), in honour of 'Dilly' Knox, head of the Bletchley Park section which produced them. Hinsley and Simkins, vol.4, p. 108m (see no.10).

99 On the Soviet decrypts (codenamed VENONA), see, inter alia, Roger Louis Benson and Michael Warner (eds), *VENONA: Soviet Espionage and the American Response, 1939–1957* (Washington, D.C.: National Security Agency/Central Intelligence Agency, 1996); and Christopher Andrew, 'The VENONA Secret', in K.G. Robertson (ed), *War, Resistance and Intelligence: Essays in Honour of M.R.D. Foot* (Barnsley: Pen and Sword, 1999).

100 Christopher Andrew and Oleg Gordievsky, *KGB: The Inside Story of its Foreign Operations from Lenin to Gorbachev*, paperback edition (London: Sceptre, 1991), pp. 402–8.

101 Genrikh Borovik, *The Philby Files* (London: Little, Brown, 1994), pp. 216–18. Andrew, 'Cambridge Spies', pp. 220–3 (see no. 28).

102 There is no truth to claims by Peter Wright and others that Hollis was a Soviet agent. Andrew and Gordievsky, pp. 27–8 (see no. 100).

103 *The Security Service*, pp. 358.

104 West and Tsarev, appendix 2, pp. 327–8 (see no. 70).

105 Philby, pp. 92–102 (see no. 69). In Philby's memoirs, Curry appears as 'Currie'. His wartime reports to Moscow, however, spelled Curry's name correctly.

106 Robert Cecil, 'The Cambridge Comintern', in Christopher Andrew and David N. Dilks (eds), *The Missing Dimension: Governments and Intelligence Communities in the Twentieth Century* (London: Macmillan, 1984), p. 179.

THE DOCUMENTS

TOP SECRET

THE SECURITY SERVICE

ITS PROBLEMS AND ORGANISATIONAL ADJUSTMENTS
1908-1945

March 1946.

TOP SECRET

THE SECURITY SERVICE

ITS PROBLEMS AND ORGANISATIONAL ADJUSTMENTS
1908-1945

VOL. I. (CHAPTERS I TO IV.)

MARCH 1946

VOLUME I

NOTE

This history of the Security Service is prepared exclusively for the use of the Directorate of the Service and it is not intended that it should go out of the Office in its present form. It contains references to Cabinet papers which cannot be quoted or referred to in communications going to any other office. The same may apply to certain references to opinions expressed by various high officials at different times. It is essential to include these matters in such a report because they are cardinal factors in the development of the organisation and its constitutional position which cannot be correctly appraised without taking them into consideration.

It is a matter for decision whether an abridged version, from which these more secret references should be excluded, should be prepared for wider circulation within the Office for instructional and similar purposes or for any distribution outside it.

	Page
CHAPTER I: FUNCTIONS AND STRUCTURE	**41**

PART 1: INTRODUCTORY 41

PART 2: FUNCTIONS OR RESPONSIBILITIES AND POWERS 41

    (i) General principles and their application to the Security Service 41
    (ii) Responsibilities 42
    (iii) General nature of the organisational structure 47
    (iv) Powers 51
    (v) Action in an advisory capacity 52
    (vi) Liaison with other Departments and Authorities in the United Kingdom; with Dominions and Colonies; and with Allies 53
    (vii) Functional relations with S.I.S. 55
    (viii) Functional relations with Service Intelligence Staffs in London and in Operational Zones 58
    (ix) The scope of the Security Service 58

CHAPTER II: REACTIONS TO FOREIGN DEVELOPMENTS IN PEACE AND WAR   **63**

NOTE 63

PART 1: THE GERMAN THREAT 1908-1914 63

    (i) The origins of M.I.5. - in the War Office and the Admiralty in 1908 63
    (ii) The origins of M.I.5. - proceedings of the Committee of Imperial Defence 1909 65
    (iii) The creation of the Special Intelligence Bureau in 1909 67
    (iv) Developments from 1910-1914 67

PART 2: THE GERMAN ESPIONAGE SYSTEM IN WAR - 1914-1918 69

    (i) The Special Intelligence Bureau becomes M.0.5. under the Directorate of Military Operations 69
    (ii) Creation of the Directorate of Military Intelligence - M.0.5. becomes M.I.5 70
    (iii) The history of M.I.5. as compiled after the War of 1914-1918 72
    (iv) The dawning recognition of the concept of 'total war' under modern conditions 77

PART 3: DEVELOPMENTS IN GERMANY - 1918-1931 80

	Page
PART 4: COMMUNISM AND THE U.S.S.R. - 1917-1931	82

(i) General Introduction (1917-1945) — 82
(ii) The Russian Revolution of 1917 — 86
(iii) The foundation of the Comintern and its early stages — 90
(iv) Counter measures — 92
(v) Developments in Russia: a change of policy — 95
(vi) The development of the Comintern machinery — 95
(vii) Soviet Espionage — 96

PART 5: INTERNAL ORGANISATION AND STAFF OF THE SECURITY SERVICE — 98

CHAPTER III: REACTIONS TO DEVELOPMENTS ON THE 'RIGHT' AND 'LEFT' IN INTERNATIONAL AFFAIRS 1931-1939 — 101

PART 1: COMMUNISM AND THE U.S.S.R. 1931-1939 — 101

(i) Changes of function as the result of re-organisation affecting the Security Service, S.I.S. and Scotland Yard — 101
(ii) Results of the changes: collaboration between the Security Service and S.I.S. — 103
(iii) Light thrown on the C.P.G.B. as a Section of the Comintern by information obtained by S.I.S. in other countries — 104
(iv) Comintern communications with the Communist Parties in Great Britain and other countries: information regarding Comintern finance and subsidies to its 'Sections' — 105
(v) Soviet Espionage 1931-1939 — 107

PART 2: THE NAZI THREAT 1933-1939 — 109

(i) The problems presented by Germany — 109
   (a) The NSDAP (Nazi Party) and its Auslands Organisation — 109
   (b) The Nazi Party and its relations with the Fascist Movement in England — 115
   (c) General intelligence regarding Hitler's policy and preparation for war — 116
   (d) German Espionage 1933-1939 — 124
(ii) Preventive action suggested by the Security Service — 129
(iii) Liaison with the Eire Authorities — 134
(iv) Liaison with the American Authorities — 135

	Page
PART 3: ITALIAN AND JAPANESE AGGRESSIVENESS	138

    (i)   The Italian Secret Intelligence Service and the Italian Partito Nazionale Fascista   138
    (ii) Japanese   140

PART 4: INTERNAL ORGANISATION AND STAFF OF THE SECURITY SERVICE   141

CHAPTER IV: REACTIONS IN THE SECOND WORLD WAR - FIRST PHASE   145

INTRODUCTORY NOTE   145

PART 1: THE 'PHONEY' WAR BEFORE THE FALL OF FRANCE   147

    (i)   Developments immediately before the outbreak of war   147
    (ii) The outbreak of war   149
    (iii) Preventive or security investigations by B. Branch   151
    (iv) The establishment of travel control   156
    (v) The breakdown in the Registry   157
    (vi) Lord Hankey's Report   158
    (vii) The breakdown in the Security Service   160
    (viii) Attempts to develop B Branch   161

PART 2: THE CRISIS FROM THE FALL OF FRANCE TO THE GERMAN ATTACK ON THE U.S.S.R.   163

    (i)   The retirement of Major-General Sir Vernon Kell and Lt.-Colonel Holt-Wilson   163
    (ii) Preventive measures taken by the internment of enemy aliens and British subjects   164
    (iii) The appointment of Lord Swinton and the Security Executive   168
    (iv) Developments during the summer of 1940   169
    (v) Developments from October 1940 to June 1941   176

PART 3: COMMUNISM AND THE U.S.S.R. - 1939-1941   182

    (i)   The outbreak of war and Comintern policy   182
    (ii) The C.P.G.B. adopts the Comintern policy : "revolutionary defeatism"   183
    (iii) The German attack on the U.S.S.R.   184

(iv) Alien Communists in the United Kingdom 1939-1941   184
(v) B Branch policy in regard to Communism   185
(vi) Soviet Espionage   189

END OF VOLUME I

CHAPTER I: FUNCTIONS AND STRUCTURE

Part 1: Introductory

The history of an organisation cannot be properly understood unless we have before us a clear account of its functions and structure; of what it does or is intended to do and how it is shaped and adapted to meet what is required of it. In the case of the Security Service, formerly known as M.I.5., experience, from the time when it was first formed in 1909 onwards, has shown that while the essential functions have been recognised from the beginning and have remained constant, the internal structure of the organisation has been frequently changed. The changes have been due, almost entirely, to the necessity of development and adaptation to meet changing circumstances.

For present purposes it will be convenient in the first place to glance at certain general principles which govern the work of the Security Service and then to consider their application to its present and past circumstances.

The object in view is to put on record for future use an account of the experience gained, of the problems which presented themselves, of the machinery devised to deal with them and of the measure of success or failure obtained in practical working.

Part 2: Functions or Responsibilities and Powers

(i) General principles and their application to the Security Service.

Every organ of government has certain functions, i.e. powers and responsibilities. If these are not clearly defined confusion inevitably results internally, i.e. inside the office concerned as well as externally, i.e. in relations with other offices.

Under the British constitutional and administrative systems, with their lack of logical finish, an exact definition of functions is often impossible. The resultant confusion sometimes has consequences seriously detrimental to the public interest, but it may at times lead to flexibility and facilitate the cutting away of dead wood; and thus help the development of new growth.

If an organ of government has powers without corresponding responsibility an abuse of power is liable to result. If it has responsibilities without the power to discharge them inefficiency and confusion are inevitable. Good organisation, therefore, implies a proper balance of powers and responsibilities.

Functions may be administrative, executive or advisory. Where the functions are purely advisory there are no powers of an executive nature and the responsibilities are limited to giving advice to the authorities which have executive powers and responsibilities.

Responsibility for the King's Peace, for the maintenance of Law and Order including the detection and prevention of crime rests with the Home Secretary and with the Police Forces working under the general supervision of the Home Secretary. Responsibility for the detection and prevention of a specialised form of crime, espionage and sabotage by the agents of a foreign power, falls to the Security Service working in close co-operation with the police. All these responsibilities are derived from that part of the Royal Prerogative which concerns the keeping of the King's Peace.

The position does not admit of an exact definition of relative responsibilities, but it is clear that the operative words in regard to these relations are "co-operation" and "goodwill"; and that the responsibility of the Security Service in matters of espionage and sabotage embrace a wider field than that of the police as a whole or of any single Police Force limited as it is to its own jurisdiction.

The Police Forces of England are essentially a part of that system of local autonomy which is the free English heritage; but the Home Secretary has a co-ordinating authority over the whole country. The prerogative powers of the Crown are exercised by him, or on his advice, and the King is bound by the decisions of the Courts of Law under precedents which go back through the Bill of Rights and Magna Carta to the Norman who agreed to maintain the "good laws of Edward the Confessor", and beyond that to the coronation customs of the Saxons according to which the King bound himself to maintain certain specified laws and thus to that extent limited the power of the executive.

These precedents form the basis of the Rule of Law which is of the essence of our constitutional and administrative systems, in which may be found both a cause and an effect of the empirical workings of the pragmatical English mind. Here, then, are the circumstances in which the Security Service works and adapts itself to the changing conditions imposed by German aggressiveness, by Nazism and Fascism or by international Communism. Here is the antithesis of both these over-logical extremes and here is the reason for the frequent difficulties in the way of an exact definition of functions.

To say this does not mean that a definition of functions should not be attempted. On the contrary it is important that it should be restated from time to time - as the organisation adapts itself to changing conditions - if only to remove confusion of thought wherever possible and to indicate the lines along which fresh developments may be usefully directed.

(ii) Responsibilities

The primary functions of the Security Service are the detection and prevention in peace and in war of espionage and sabotage by the enemy. In the phraseology current inside the Service, detection is enlarged into "investigation" and prevention into "security".

There are secondary functions, which may often assume great importance, viz -

1. to obtain intelligence about the enemy's Secret Services and about other secret matters and -
2. to initiate or co-operate with the armed forces in action intended to deceive or mislead the enemy.

The employment of secret means to obtain intelligence about the enemy's secret services often leads to intelligence being obtained about other secrets of the enemy, e.g. intelligence about his strategical or tactical plans or his political or economic aims. This arises from the fact that the enemy may employ secret agents to obtain intelligence which will be of use to him in furtherance of his political, economic, strategical or tactical fields. Intelligence obtained by the Security Service in this way is, or should be, communicated to any Departments of the British, Dominions or Colonial Governments which may be concerned.

The primary functions - detection and prevention of espionage and sabotage on British territory or directed against British political or military secrets - are governed by the law of the land, the Laws most directly applicable being the Official Secrets Act, the Treachery Act and the Defence Acts. Espionage and sabotage being criminal acts are countered by action taken under the law to bring the persons guilty of them before a Court of Law or to neutralise or prevent their activities by measures taken in accordance with the law or regulations framed under the law. The crimes of spies and saboteurs are not of the same kind as crimes committed by individuals out of personal, human motives. Enemy agents act in collusion with other agents or with officers of the enemy Secret Services and their acts are therefore done in pursuance of a criminal conspiracy. War is a legal state, but espionage and sabotage are not legal acts of war. They are illegal acts even if they are committed under the instructions of officers of the enemy's armed forces; and they are acts which are liable to entail the death penalty.

It is customary to indict the spy or saboteur but not the enemy officer who employs him even if, by an accident of war, he happens to be captured as a prisoner of war. (If he is captured in territory under British occupation he would be liable to be treated as a spy and not as a prisoner of war if concealing his presence). Nevertheless the fact that the enemy officer is a party to a criminal conspiracy in itself justifies the counter espionage service in making as full an investigation as may be feasible regarding the officer and the organisation to which he belongs. A knowledge of this organisation is also desirable as a means to more important ends.

This knowledge constitutes the Intelligence which the counter espionage organisations sets itself to obtain in order to facilitate further measures to counter the activities of the enemy Secret Service. These activities are a part of the enemy's military operations and may have an important influence on the course or even the outcome of the war; and in countering them the Security Service performs functions which pass beyond the realm of law into that of military operations. When the counter espionage service uses the Intelligence thus obtained to deceive the enemy it has passed completely into the latter field.

The functions of the counter espionage organisation are thus twofold: legal, which bring them within the province of the Home Secretary and the Law Officers of the Crown; and operational which bring them under the direction of the authorities responsible for the conduct of a war.

An estimate of the importance of the part played by secret intelligence and counter espionage in deciding a war - and consequently in some wars the fate of a nation - may be a matter of opinion and the practical achievements of these secret services may have varying degrees of value in different wars. No military authority is in doubt, however, about the vital importance of an adequate intelligence service, of which the secret intelligence or the organisation for obtaining information through spies is a part. (It may possibly be a diminishing part as a result of the development - and the immense advantages - of aerial reconnaissance). The great commanders of history, Napoleon among them, attached great importance and have in some degree owed their success to their secret agents. The success of the Germans in the Franco-Prussian War of 1870 has been attributed to the fact that the Germans had an elaborate spy system while the French were deficient in this respect and having no counter espionage organisation attempted to improvise one when it was too late. The circumstances of this campaign - the precursor of the modern wars of national effort - induced the widespread view among military authorities generally that a phenomenon such as the German Secret Service - it was partly based on the Police Force which is an essential part of the modern State and a representative development of the industrial age - made it necessary to provide for counter-measures in peacetime. A country threatened by military attack supported by such a system could not improvise an effective counter espionage service after war had started.

The organisation of the British counter espionage service, when it was originally formed in 1909, was therefore adapted to serve two aims: one legal and the other operational. This is a comparatively simple conception suited to the circumstances of the time and it proved adequate in August 1914. There was a straightforward - essentially military - problem and it has admitted of a clear-cut solution. By advising the Cabinet to form M.O.5. - later M.I.5. as a part of the Directorate of Military Operations - the Committee of Imperial Defence aimed at securing the assistance of the Civil authorities, chiefly the Home Office, the police, the Post Office and the Customs to deal with a situation in which German interest in the East Coast of England recalled a similar inquisitiveness before the Franco-Prussian war. The counter espionage service was therefore constituted as a part of the military machine with the function of co-ordinating the relevant acts of these Civil authorities and directing them towards measures for the prevention and detection of espionage and sabotage.

Purely military ends are subject to the supreme directing authority of the State which may subordinate its strategical planning to political (or politico-economic) ends. In theory therefore - and sometimes in practice - the counter espionage service may be subject to the direction of the authorities responsible for the political direction of affairs, i.e. especially in times of peace to the Foreign Office. It is, of course, ultimately subject to the direction of the Cabinet, and it is perhaps for this reason, and also because no single Department can take the whole responsibility for it, that the appointment of the Head of the Service is made by the Prime Minister.

As the war of 1914-1918 developed, certain new factors came to play a great part, which had not been anticipated, in the political and economic fields. This was, to some extent at least, a consequence of the conditions brought about by the industrial revolution and the social changes and technical developments which accompanied it. The most prominent of these factors were the Allied propaganda services and the naval blockade of Germany and other parts of Europe under German occupation under the systematical controls of modern economic warfare.

These factors and the part which they played in conjunction with the military defeat of Germany in 1918, combined with the inability of the German General Staff and its Secret Service under Colonel Nicolai to counteract - as they attempted to do - the forces leading to a breakdown of German morale, appear to have been among the causes which led Ludendorf and other military minds in Germany to develop a new outlook on war. There is a considerable literature on this subject, but for our immediate purpose it may be summarised by saying that reversing Clausewitz they held that it was no longer sound to regard war as policy carried on by other means. They taught that policy, i.e. foreign policy, should subserve the strategical interests and objectives of the German Reich, and hence they went on to the doctrine of total war from which was developed that of "Krieg in Permanenz". All of this fell into place in the general conception of a German hegemony as a national aim, and the Nazi racial ideas of the "continuing community" and of the German State as embracing the whole German people, past, present and future whether in Germany or beyond its boundaries.

Again, Ludendorf's "sealed train" which had taken Lenin into Russia gave rise to new ideas on the subject of disintegration behind the enemy front and this was further developed by the Nazis in their use of another factor which is not new in warfare although it was given a new name, i.e. the so-called "Fifth Column", and to some extent a new form.

It is not new, but very old and it was common, for instance, in the wars between the Greek oligarchies and democracies. It was unknown to the M.I.5. which was responsible for counter espionage in the war of 1914-1918; and it has assumed a new form in the war of between the modern democracies and the highly organised totalitarian States of today.

The term "Fifth Column" is subject to very loose usage in the Press and in public discussion and we have no exact description of its scope as conceived by the German Secret Services; by the Abwehr, the military Secret Service, or by Himmler's organisation, the Sipo und SD, both of which have resorted to methods of a "Fifth Column" type; or by the pre-war organisations which employed various forms of propaganda which aimed at influencing the attitude of English people towards Germany's aggressive policies. We can only judge by the results in this country or in Norway whose Quisling typifies certain forms of such action, or in France before the war, or in Poland in the autumn of 1939. The evidence about the German theory and practice in relation to the subject of the "Fifth Column" will be discussed more fully in the course of succeeding chapters with a view to arriving at a better assessment of their significance; so also will the cognate question of the extent to which the Communist Parties may fulfil a similar role. The crucial point to be considered here is the effect of the problem created by the "Fifth Column" on the shape which the organisation of the counter-espionage service should take and this will be dealt with in the final chapter.

"Fifth Column" activities may be illegal as in many instances in the Polish campaign of 1939 as described by the Polish General Staff. They may be outwardly and probably wholly legal as in the case of the pre-war Anglo-German Fellowship which owed its existence to German initiative but was largely financed - for purely business not for political reasons - by prominent English business houses; or of the pre-war British Union of Fascists when it was subsidised from German and Italian government funds.

In illegal matters the Security Service is responsible for obtaining intelligence about individual agents and about organisations; and for initiating preventive action by internment or otherwise. The case of "Fifth Column" activities co-ordinated with the enemy's military operations has not occurred on British soil and no evidence of an active conspiracy for this purpose is known to exist. If such a case occurred on a scale sufficient to affect military operations it would call for military action supplemented by action by the Security Service; and the question of the failure of the Security Service to acquire adequate intelligence and provide for preventive action beforehand would arise. This involves a serious responsibility - perhaps the most serious one which falls on the Service.

In the case of the "Fifth Column" activities which are not illegal - and cannot be declared illegal under a free democratic system - the responsibility of the Security Service is necessarily restricted to the acquisition of intelligence.

The functions of the Security Service, therefore, have never been defined but in practice they have covered the following fields:-

1. the detection in peace and in war of espionage and sabotage by the enemy or a potential enemy; and of any active conspiracy or organisation of a "Fifth Column" type;
2. the prevention in peace and in war of espionage and sabotage by the enemy or a potential enemy and of illegal "Fifth Column" activities;
3. the acquisition of intelligence about the Secret Services of the enemy; about their methods of espionage, sabotage and "Fifth Column" activities; and about their measures for carrying them out;
4. the initiation and furtherance of measures to deceive or mislead the enemy.
5. the communication of intelligence, if incidentally obtained, concerning the political, economic, strategical or tactical secrets of an enemy or potential enemy to the British authorities concerned.

Those under 1, 2 and 3 are executive functions in the sense that detection and prevention of crime are executive functions of the police; and in the more important sense that they are measures for combating or countering the instruments of an enemy General Staff. Those under 3 are functions which are complementary to those under 1 and 2 in the same way as the police obtain intelligence about other forms of organised crime. Those under 4 cannot be dissociated from military operations or from the duties of military intelligence and operational staffs. The part which Security Service officers play in them is sometimes of a purely intelligence and sometimes of an operational nature. The nature of the preventive function should be clearly understood. It is to impose such restrictions as are reasonable and practicable in order to make it as difficult as possible for secret agents to maintain themselves in British territory without detection, to move about to acquire secret intelligence or to communicate it to a foreign Power.

These are the essential responsibilities of the Security Service which is not, obviously, the ultimate executive authority in these matters. Its powers are limited in some respects while in others it has no powers and can only act in an advisory capacity.

(iii) General nature of the organisational structure.

At this stage it will be convenient to examine very briefly the general nature of the structure of the Security Service, i.e. of the machinery which has been devised to deal with the problems presented.

This machinery has two aspects: the internal organisation of the Security Service and its place in the machinery of government. In both of these aspects it has undergone important changes. In the early stages, from the beginning in 1909 and throughout the first World War, it was organically a part of the War Office but the nature of its functions, as described above, necessarily often brought them, even if they were exercised mainly or entirely in an advisory capacity, within the scope of other Government Departments and authorities, particularly of the Home Office and the Law Officers of the Crown. The position changed gradually after 1918 and there were two important reasons for this. One was that the change from a state of war to one of peace had the natural and obvious effect that while the War Office ceased to play an active role in the conduct of the nation's affairs and M.I.5., as it was still called, could no longer perform its operational function of assisting to mislead the enemy for the purpose of military operations, its responsibilities in the field of law and order for the detection and prevention of the crime of espionage were not in abeyance.

From 1909 until 1917 or 1918 M.I.5. devoted its attention almost exclusively to counteraction against the German Secret Service. No other Secret Service constituted a threat in the immediate, or even in the distant, future to this country; and in view of the necessity of economising resources and concentrating on the only danger of importance no serious attempt was made to uncover espionage by any other power if it existed. After the Russian Revolution, however, a section of M.I.5. was formed to deal with Russian espionage. It did not deal with the problems created by the Communist International and its secret agents which remained the care of the Special Branch of the Metropolitan

Police, except in so far as Communist measures for disintegration work within our Armed Forces were concerned.

After 1931, however, the staff which had been dealing with the secret agents of the Communist International at New Scotland Yard was transferred to M.I.5. and the functions of dealing with the related subjects of Communism in Great Britain, Comintern secret agents and Russian military espionage became the functions of M.I.5. This was the second reason for a gradual change because this much wider function brought its daily activities more definitely and constantly within the scope of the Home Secretary, and led to closer relations not only with the Metropolitan but also with the Police Forces of the United Kingdom as well as with the Police Forces of the Dominions and Colonies and India, all of which were concerned with the intelligence problems bearing on this threefold subject. This, in turn, affected the relations of M.I.5. with other Departments including the Dominions Office, the Colonial Office, the Foreign Office and the Services, which latter were directly affected by the existence of Communism among the personnel and Communist propaganda directed at the Armed Forces.

After 1934 a further step in this gradual process of change took place when M.I.5. was entrusted with enquiries regarding the British Union of Fascists and other Fascist organisations in the United Kingdom. The reason for this change was that there was ground for believing that the B.U.F. was not a purely British political party but that it had associations with foreign political organisations of a similar character and was largely financed by Mussolini. The relationship between the B.U.F. and German Nazis led to further enquiries regarding the NSDAP which, in turn, resulted in intelligence being obtained regarding the first stages of German "Fifth Column" activity (although it was not called by this name at that time). This took the form of propaganda by numerous German agencies which aimed at influencing British public opinion in matters connected with the forward policy which was being pursued by Hitler in Europe. Intelligence regarding such matters obtained by M.I.5. was a matter of interest to the Foreign Office.

The Foreign Office is the Department which is nominally concerned with the financing of the Security Service and the grants appear before the House of Commons under that heading, but for practical purposes direct relations with the Treasury are maintained. The complicated nature of the relationship with the Foreign Office, the Treasury, the Home Office and the Service Departments induced in Major-General Sir Vernon Kell and other members of his staff the feeling that some more centralised control was desirable. It was felt that no one of the various Departments had a full sense of responsibility for the functions of security in the conditions which arose between the wars and accentuated an anomaly which might have been less insistent at any other time. One proposal was that the Service should be placed under the direction of some centrally placed Minister without departmental responsibility, the ground being advanced that if it submitted advice to a Department on a security question and if that advice were rejected it had no redress; and that if the matter should ever get as far as the Cabinet there was no one to represent the security point of view. It was urged that it was inappropriate that it should be placed under the Home Office or any one Department. In his report on the Security Service in May 1940, Lord Hankey remarked that for twenty-five years he had been aware of a desire on General Kell's part that the Security Service should be attached to the Committee of Imperial Defence so that it would fall within the sphere of the Prime Minister. Lord Hankey added that, as Secretary to the Committee of Imperial Defence, he had always felt that it would be inappropriate to saddle the small Secretariat of an Advisory Committee with so large a Sub-Department.

In June 1940 the Security Executive was created under Lord Swinton as Minister without Portfolio and the Security Service came under his direction through the new machinery known as the Security Executive, details regarding which will be found in Chapter IV.

Such have been the changes in the nature of the Security Service in so far as its position in relation to the more important parts of the machinery of Government is concerned.

Later developments will be discussed in the Chapters dealing with the present war.

As regards the internal organisation of the Security Service, the "historical report on the work of the preventive branch" prepared at the end of the first World War remarked that -

> "the work and consequently the organisation........................is naturally divided into two main branches -
>
> (1) investigation of cases involving a definite suspicion of espionage and -
>
> (2) the construction of legal and administrative machinery calculated to embarrass and, if possible, frustrate such attempts in general and for the future.
>
> The first branch deals with the cure of hostile espionage and the second with its prevention."

This report goes on to describe the formation of a third branch which included the Secretariat and "that very important organ the Central Registry of all counter espionage information possessed by the British Government".

This third branch eventually developed into one dealing with all matters of internal administration and finance. During the course of the first World War the preventive branch developed two subsidiary branches, one of which dealt with Port Control and the other with liaison with the Dominions and Colonies on the preventive side of the work. During that war and afterwards there were numerous slight changes, especially changes of nomenclature. For instance the administrative branch was in turn known as "C", "H", "O" and "A", with corresponding changes in the others, and this fact makes it difficult to detail the history of the three main branches and their subsidiaries without becoming involved in a confusing mass of detail. This presents all the greater difficulty as after the war, when the Organisation shrank to very small proportions, the outlines of the preventive branch and that for internal administration became blurred until, eventually, the preventive branch almost disappeared except for the work on wartime legislation, under the Deputy-Director, and arrangements for vetting persons applying for various positions in the Services or in Government Departments, applicants for naturalisation and applicants for commissions with foreign parentage. (It should be noted that vetting here and elsewhere in this report refers to the purely negative test against Security Service records; and not to any positive examination or enquiry).

Apart from this legislative and vetting work the preventive branch has, with one exception, virtually disappeared in peacetime, because its chief functions such as those relating to the internment of enemy aliens and Port Control as exercised through M.I.5. staff had naturally lapsed. The exception was D Branch which was developed during the thirties and consisted of officers who may be described as being projected into the Security Service from the War Office, Admiralty and Air Ministry. Their functions are concerned with security in munitions and aircraft factories, arsenals, dockyards, railways, utility undertakings generally including gas, water and the electric power system as possible targets for spies and saboteurs. The responsibility for dealing with both the preventive and detective aspects of matters relating to Communism when it was transferred from Special Branch in 1931 therefore fell on the investigation branch, which had previously had a more limited outlook as a purely military organ for counter-espionage. As this branch became increasingly concerned with enquiries into matters relating to the Communist Party, the British Union of Fascists, the NSDAP and the Italian Fascio, the dividing line between the preventive, detective and intelligence aspects of this work came to be non-existent and both preventive and detective work came to be solely the concern of one branch, which simultaneously developed a predominating interest in obtaining and utilising intelligence. Thus it happened that when war broke out in 1939 B Branch, as the investigation branch was then called, had assumed responsibilities for some aspects of the preventive work, but not for vetting, that relating to port and travel control, "military security" or the D Branch duties mentioned in this paragraph.

There are two important auxiliaries of the investigation branch. One is the section which deals with the employment of secret agents for counter espionage purposes and for obtaining information about organisations such as the Communist Party, the British Union of Fascists, and other similar bodies. Other agents have also been employed directly by some of the investigation sections. The second auxiliary is the shadowing staff. This actually came into existence under the War Office prior to the appointment of Captain Kell. A detective named W. Melville, M.V.O., M.B.E., was employed with effect from the 1st December, 1903. Before and during the first World War the section was actively engaged in watching and reporting on German agents but from that time onwards it has been largely concerned with shadowing Russian agents and Communists with occasional cases of Japanese, German and other suspects. The circumstances of the present war have given little opportunity for this type of investigation as enemy agents have, generally speaking, been captured very soon after arrival, or have operated under control.

Developments after the outbreak of the war will be discussed more fully in a later Chapter.

(iv) Powers

The powers of the Security Service and of members of its staff naturally vary greatly in peace and in war, and the position has been very different in the second as compared with the first World War. In the earlier case the interrogation of spies and persons suspected of espionage was conducted as a rule by the police, Sir Basil Thomson, the Assistant Commissioner of Special Branch, being personally concerned in a large number of cases. Between the wars spies were few and far between and in such cases it was the rule that the handling of the case was entrusted to the police at the earliest possible stage, M.I.5. officers acting in an advisory capacity in the light of their special information and knowledge.

In the second war the position was entirely changed by the establishment of Camp 020 at which the interrogation of spies was done by Security Service officers under circumstances which will be described more fully later. It may be mentioned here that this arrangement gave important added facilities for obtaining intelligence by listening in to the conversations of known spies or suspects and by the fact that they were in the custody of an officer of the Service and not in police custody. A similar radical change was created by the institution of the London Reception Centre where travellers arriving in this country who were in any way suspect were detained for a limited period and interrogated. These two institutions gave the Security Service powers of a very different nature from anything which it had previously possessed to discharge its responsibilities. They gave it powers which enabled it to catch individual enemy agents through an immense documentation at the L.R.C. known as the Information Index and through interrogation based on that Index; and through intelligence amassed by more comprehensive and detailed interrogation at Camp 020. All this intelligence in turn made it possible, when taken in conjunction with interception of enemy communications and the control of captured enemy agents, to form an adequate view of the enemy organisations on which to base further plans for counter-action and measures, co-ordinated with military operations, to deceive the enemy. Thus the power to play a positive part both in defence and in attack was conferred on the Service.

As regards specific powers given to officers of the Service, the most important were those under Warrants from the Secretary of State giving powers under the Defence Regulations. The warrants authorised a number of senior officers, including the officer in charge of the L.R.C., to exercise the following powers on behalf of the Secretary of State:-

<u>Under Regulation No. 5</u> relating to the control of photography, etc. - as a person acting on my behalf for the purposes of that Regulation.

<u>Under Regulation No. 11</u> relating to the carriage into or out of the United Kingdom of certain prohibited articles by travellers:- as an Appropriate Officer under paragraph (9) (c) for the purposes of that Regulation.

<u>Under Regulation No. 12</u> relating to Protected Places:- as a person acting on my behalf for the purposes of that Regulation.

Under Regulation No. 19 relating to the departure of ships and aircraft:- as a person authorised by a Secretary of State to act for the purpose of that Regulation.

Under Regulation No. 25 relating to dangerous premises:- as a person authorised by a Secretary of State to act for the purposes of that Regulation.

Under Regulation No. 80A relating to requests for specified information or articles:- as a person acting on my behalf for the purposes of that Regulation.

Under Regulation No. 88A relating to entry and search of premises:- as a person authorised by the Secretary of State to act under paragraph (3) of that Regulation.

Limited Warrants under 80A and 88A, as above, were issued to a number of officers including the Regional Security Liaison Officers. Other powers given to a few officers are under Article 7(4) of Aliens Order; Arrival from British or Foreign Territory Order 1943; and Article 15A of Aliens Order 1920. Two officers of the Service are authorised to exercise the powers of a Superintendent of Police under the Official Secrets Act.

(v) Action in an Advisory capacity.

While the powers to act under various provisions, as described in the last paragraph, have been conferred on a number of officers, the view has generally been taken that, as far as possible, Security Service officers should refrain from using these powers except in an emergency and that, wherever circumstances allow, the police or other authorities should be advised to take the required action. The reason for this is that it is desirable that officers of the Security Service should come into the open as seldom as may be and that there are advantages in securing the co-operation of the police wherever executive action such as searching or arresting is required. In the case of persons detained at Camp 020 or the L.R.C., the advantages accruing from the exercise of executive functions cannot be over-estimated, and the procedure adopted has resulted in the accumulation of a vast and highly documented corpus of intelligence material which certainly would not have ensued if the methods adopted in the last war had been followed.

In regard to the more important preventive measures such as the internment of aliens and the arrest and detention of British subjects under the Defence Regulations, the Security Service has no executive but only advisory powers. If the initial action has been taken on the advice of the Security Service the Home Secretary has availed himself of the services of Advisory Committees appointed to examine each individual case.

In the relations with other Government departments the functions of the Security Service have been almost entirely restricted to giving advice or furnishing intelligence.

In matters relating to measures for deceiving the enemy, the action of the Security Service during the earlier war was of a very limited kind. In the last one this action has been developed on far bigger lines based on a large conception of control and co-ordination exercised by the Allied Staffs, the Home Defence Executive and the Security Service through the XX Committee and the W Board. The latter, which consisted mainly of the Directors of Intelligence and of the Home Defence Executive, was responsible for the policy of the XX Committee. This Committee's functions have not been clearly defined, but its chairman, an officer of the Security Service, has directed its activities with a view to fulfilling its primary purpose - that of acquiring counter espionage intelligence - through securing the co-operation and goodwill of the Services in the matter of supplying Service information to enemy agents under control. Out of this limited purpose has arisen the secondary but larger one of assisting actively to deceive the enemy in regard to our own strategical plans in addition to the more passive role of using our counter espionage machinery to prevent him from obtaining political, economic, strategical and tactical intelligence.

A detailed description of the elaborate machinery which was gradually built up in order to serve these purposes will be given in a later Chapter. The facts are briefly mentioned here to illustrate the point that the organisation of the counter espionage service must be adapted to serve operational as well as legal ends. Experience has shown that the machinery for these operational purposes could not be worked efficiently if it were not closely integrated with that concerned with the detection of enemy espionage and with the accumulation of general intelligence on the subject of the enemy's Secret Service organisation.

(vi) Liaison with other Departments and Authorities in the United Kingdom; with Dominions and Colonies; and with Allies.

We have seen above that in its main functions the Security Service necessarily has a very close liaison with the Home Office and the Operational Staffs. There is also liaison with the Home Office and with the Service Departments on the subject of undesirable elements in the Armed Forces and on matters connected with propaganda and other activities aimed at subversion. If these are the most important contacts, liaison is also necessary on various counts with the Foreign Office, Dominions Office, Colonial Office, the Ministry of Economic Warfare, Censorship and the police, to mention those next in importance.

During the earlier war the Censorship played an important part in detecting German agents, many of whom used the postal and telegraph services to transmit information from the United Kingdom to the continent and a number were detected by this means. In the present war Censorship has been responsible for the detection of messages sent by microphotography, mainly between the Western and Eastern hemispheres, and for a series of letters concealing secret writing emanating from parts of the Comintern organisation or from the Russian Secret Police in the Western hemisphere. Censorship has also produced very voluminous information of a general intelligence nature. It has only led to the detection of a single spy in the United Kingdom but its operations have been of value to the Security Service in a negative sense.

Relations with the police have always been regarded as involving one of the most important aspects of the work of the Security Service. As has been mentioned above, the police have responsibilities in connection with espionage and sabotage; and executive action in such cases is frequently taken by them. They are also important sources of information on almost all aspects of the work. Previous to the second World War relations with them were maintained through direct correspondence, but in 1940, under the threat of invasion, R.S.L.O.s were appointed to the twelve Regions into which the United Kingdom was divided and these officers acted as a filter between Head Office sections and the police and were responsible for maintaining good relations in which noticeable success was achieved. They also played a useful part in maintaining good relations with the local military authorities and, almost more important, as interpreters in security matters between those authorities and the police.

In all these connections liaison may affect both the detective and preventive sides of the work and details will be found in the description of the general history of the Service which follows as well as in the sectional records which have been prepared separately.

Liaison with the Dominions and Colonies is arranged through machinery, which includes the section known as Overseas Control, through Defence Security Officers at a number of important points - which number, however, has varied from time to time - and through the military, the police or other authorities in all five Dominions and nearly all Colonies, Protectorates and Mandated Territories, including some of the smallest such as Mauritius or the Falkland Islands. Of special interest are the relations with Intelligence Centres such as S.I.M.E. and C.I.C.I.; and the remarkable but in the circumstances generally satisfactory terms with the security authorities in Eire.

Many of these contacts were arranged during the first war and were maintained throughout the inter-war period although in the case of most of the smaller islands correspondence was intermittent and at times almost non-existent. Important information such as papers prepared on the NSDAP and on the opportunities of espionage presented by the position of German business houses and organisations and information in the shape of an overseas bulletin (discontinued after July 1944) was circulated to all but the smallest Colonies. In 1930 the Deputy Director visited India, Colombo, Singapore, Hong Kong, Shanghai and Ottawa in the course of a tour in connection with the establishment and development of liaison with the Dominions and Colonies, but no systematic arrangements for maintaining contact by visits of this kind have been made.

Relations with the Allies have normally been a function of S.I.S. but in the first World War M.I.5. established "Military Control Officers" and "Military Permit Officers" in Paris, Rome, New York and at certain ports (in the case of neutral countries this was done through M.I.1.C. as S.I.S. was then called).

Between the wars, by agreement with S.I.S., special contacts were maintained with the Deuxieme Bureau in Paris and the American Embassy in London. The former was concerned mainly with German espionage and the latter with enquiries and information about Communists, but towards the end of the period the investigation branch exchanged information with the American Embassy regarding suspected Germans. These arrangements continued after the outbreak of war until the F.B.I. attached its own officers to the American Embassy for the purpose of liaison with the Security Service. This liaison covered Communism as well as matters relating to counter espionage against the enemy.

As the various Allied Governments established themselves in London after their countries had been overrun by the German armies, liaison on security matters was established by B Branch (and afterwards carried on by E. Division). This liaison covered cases of their own nationals who came under their or our suspicion in this country. Liaison with the Allied counter espionage services in London was also effected in connection with interrogations at the London Reception Centre in which they were sometimes interested or were in a position to render assistance where their nationals were concerned. S.I.S. also maintained relations with the Allied Intelligence Services in London in connection with matters of mutual interest outside this country.

(vii) Functional relations with S.I.S.

To understand the functional relations between the Security Service and S.I.S. it is necessary to refer to the functions and structure of the former as outlined in (ii) and (iii) above and to describe in outline the organisation of the latter. Very briefly, it consists of "circulating sections" each of which has the function of communicating the appropriate intelligence to one of the Services or Departments including the Foreign Office, the War Office, Admiralty and Air Ministry. Among these circulating sections Section V communicates intelligence of the Security Service and it is the sole channel of communication in normal circumstances between S.I.S. and the Security Service. S.I.S. obtains its intelligence through representatives abroad, some of whom have the functions of Passport Control Officers. The Passport Control Officer is also part of the preventive machinery on which the Security Service depends, both in peace and in war. He is part of the preventive machinery in the sense that by applying intelligence about suspect individuals he may move the authorities concerned to prevent spies, enemy agents or Comintern agents from entering British territories or, during military operations, the zones of British Armies operating abroad. His normal duties bring him in touch with the police or the military security authorities of the country to which he is appointed. Their functions being analogous with those of the Security Service he inevitably obtains information from them in matters of common interest; but this common interest involves a certain delicacy because it implies some degree of alignment between the foreign policies of the two countries. The Passport Control Officer's functions are naturally associated with those of obtaining intelligence either by obtaining information from applicants for visas or by the employment of secret agents. Reports from S.I.S. representatives abroad are communicated to Section V as a circulating section and under the arrangement by which the M.I.5. Registry contained the records of all counter espionage information available to the British Government all this intelligence should be communicated to M.I.5. (the Security Service) whenever it has a bearing on counter espionage matters of sufficient importance for it to be kept on record for future use.

The main function of Section V is to provide and develop means to obtain secret intelligence from abroad about enemy or potential enemy Secret Services and their agents, and similarly about the Comintern as an international organisation and an instrument of the Soviet Government employing secret agents and conspiratorial methods.

S.I.S. also has other functions which relate to the collection of counter espionage intelligence in that it is responsible for the organisation and control of the Services known as R.S.S. (Radio Security Section), R.I.S. (Radio Intelligence Section) and G.C. & C.S. (the Government Code and Cypher School) which deal with the interception of enemy or potential enemy communications by wireless or telegraph including communications of a diplomatic and military as well as of a Secret Service nature.

By all these means it obtains a mass of intelligence, some of which is communicated to the Security Service as subserving its purposes.

Some of this information is recorded by Section V in the S.I.S. Registry, but that Registry has always been a very small body and the acknowledged practice in the past was that as full carding could not be done by it the Security Service Registry should undertake that responsibility as far as its much larger - but still limited - means allowed. The staff employed in the S.I.S. Registry numbered from about twenty before the war and was increased to about forty between 1939 and 1944. The Security Service Registry staff varied between about eighty before the war and nearly four hundred in 1941.

In 1941, however, it was decided that the overall responsibility for carding names and addresses in foreign countries should fall on S.I.S. and that the Security Service Registry should not card them except when they were of special and more than local importance; and this decision caused a fundamental change in the functional relations between the two Services. As the staff of S.I.S. Registry was not proportionately increased it was unable to provide for full carding or for systematic arrangements for filing by which all the intelligence obtained could be rendered readily accessible. A separate card index of the intercepted wireless communications of the German Security Service (the Abwehr, the Sipo und SD) was, however, set up by Section V, i.e. entirely separate from their Registry.

As a result of this change the M.I.5. claim at the end of the last war that their Central Registry was the repository of all counter espionage information available to the British Government was no longer fully valid. At the same time, and on this basis, Section V claimed more definitely than they had previously done that counter espionage matters outside the three-mile limit of British territory were no concern of the Security Service but were solely to be dealt with and recorded by themselves. This would seem to imply that Section V should be responsible for the collation of all counter espionage intelligence relating to matters outside British territory and for action to be taken in that connection. This they claimed to do in theory, but they were unable to achieve collation in practice for lack of suitable and adequate staff. The only action which can be taken by S.I.S. on this intelligence - under the limitations imposed by circumstances - is the collection of further intelligence and, to a limited extent, communication -

(1) to the Security Service when a spy or suspect enters British territory or when the intelligence is directly connected with any matter inside British territory in which the Security Service is actively interested and -

(2) to the Foreign Office whenever it is of sufficient importance as having a bearing on questions of foreign policy.

Post hoc, if not entirely propter hoc, the relations between B Division and Section V deteriorated and went through a period of considerable difficulty which was aggravated by the incompleteness of the S.I.S. records. Even if they had been complete, difficulties would necessarily arise from the need for obtaining traces from both Registries in a very large proportion of cases where a "look-up" was desired in either organisation. If the "look-up" produces a trace in the other Registry or in both Registries collaboration between the sections concerned in both organisations becomes necessary in order to make available all the relevant information about the individual or the subject in question.

Briefly, the position is that Section V in the course of the developments of recent years has come to occupy a position entirely different from that of all other S.I.S. circulating sections. It claims the duty of collating and carding intelligence outside the three-mile limit and the right to withhold information from the Security Service whereas in the other cases the function of the circulating section is to supply secret intelligence to the Department which collates it with intelligence received from other sources. The result is that the material derived from secret sources dealing with counter espionage matters, including individual spies or Communist agents, has been split in two parts rendering co-ordination and collation more difficult and more liable to errors and omissions that would be the case if complete carding and all collation were done in one Office.

The Security Service has, however, received intelligence material direct from R.S.S., R.I.S. and G.C. & C.S. and committees dealing with their material, under the chairmanship of Security Service officers, have provided for co-ordination and made available to the Security Service the valuable results derived from the intercepted wireless communications of the Abwehr and the Sipo und SD. R.S.S., R.I.S. and G.C. & C.S. have combined to produce important papers based on an analytical study of the internal evidence in the texts of these intercepted communications. This work, combined with information obtained by the Security Service from its interrogations, its double agents and other sources, has helped to expose a very full and detailed picture of the German organisations, their methods of work and their agents, all of which has been recorded in a number of reports prepared by the various organisations interested and circulated to those concerned. This mass of information has, in turn, been made available, wherever desirable, to the Supreme Headquarters of the Allied Expeditionary Force for counter espionage purposes.

Further details regarding the functional relations between S.I.S. and the Security Service will be found in later Chapters and in some of the sectional reports. These relations have been discussed here at length - but only in outline - on account of their intimate connection with the functions of the Security Service and because they present a difficult problem which is the subject of controversy and is not yet solved.

(viii) Functional relations with Service Intelligence Staffs in London and in Operational Zones.

The secret intelligence derived from the interception of enemy Security Service communications, i.e. counter espionage intelligence, is furnished direct by G.C. & C.S. and other parts of S.I.S. to the Directors of Intelligence of the three Services where there is an operational interest. In the same way any intelligence obtained from Security Service sources which may have an operational interest is also communicated to them. In connection with these matters direct liaison is maintained with several sections in the directorates of intelligence such as those receiving intercepted wireless material (M.I.14) and those dealing with prisoners of war (M.I.19) from whom Security Service intelligence as well as operational intelligence is sometimes obtained.

When British and Allied Forces are conducting military operations abroad there is inevitably a close connection between the activities of the enemy Secret Service against those forces and those against their bases in British territory. The operations of enemy agents and the machinery for controlling them are under centralised direction even when they cover different fields of operations. In this sense, just as the strategical direction of the war has been described as indivisible, so counter espionage may be described as indivisible, whether it is dealt with by the Security Service or Section V or by the I.B. Staffs in the zones of operations. To meet the conditions imposed by the above facts and serve the needs of the staff in the field an organisation known as the War Room was formed in March 1945. It consisted of staff from OSS (the American Office of Strategic Services), Section V of S.I.S. and the Security Service, was based on the records and on the information available to these three Services, and co-ordinated their work with that of the I.B. (G-2 CI) Staffs under SHAEF. Counter espionage during the Mediterranean operations in the second World War was handled by S.I.M.E in collaboration with Section V and the Security Service, but in the campaign in Burma the Security Service has played little part except in an advisory capacity and by assisting with trained personnel, counter espionage being handled from the headquarters of that theatre of war and by the Indian authorities.

This whole subject will be treated more fully in the Chapter dealing with the second World War.

(ix) The scope of the Security Service

The scope of the Security Service includes the countering of espionage directed against British territory and British military and political secrets in the broadest sense by any Power in the world. It has also been expanded to cover revolutionary movements such as international Communism and Fascist movements with international ramifications. Both of these extreme movements are frequently described as subversive, a term which presents some difficulty and sometimes tends to confuse the issues. Their real significance and their relevance arise from the fact that Communist and Fascist organisations have been the instruments of foreign Powers and have been, or are, potential nuclei of a "Fifth Column".

It has not been definitely laid down in any charter whether the Security Service has been entrusted with duties in connection with these revolutionary movements because they are, or have been, the instruments or potential instruments of Germany, Italy or Russia, whether in pursuance of "power politics" or as an ancillary to military operations and for the purpose of disintegration work; or because, as revolutionary movements inside this country they are, or tend to be, directed against the Constitution. It has not been decided, in any definite or authoritative sense, whether it is the function of the Security Service to deal with such movements qua revolutionary movements in this country. It was, however, only when there was good reason to believe that Sir Oswald Mosley's visit to Italy was connected with arrangements by which he was being financed on a considerable scale by Mussolini that the Government decided that the Security Service should undertake an intensive investigation of the activities of the British Unions of Fascists. This was started early in 1934.

Since it was formed as M.O.5. under the War Office in 1909 the Security Service has only devoted serious attention to counter-action against the German Secret Service, the Nazi and Fascist (British and Italian) organisations, the Russian Secret Service and the Comintern - which as suggested above, is to be viewed not merely as an international organisation as it is in theory but as an instrument of the Government of the U.S.S.R. as it is in fact. To a far smaller extent active work has been undertaken to deal with the Japanese and the Italian Secret Services. Since 1909 no other Power has made or threatened to make war against this country except the satellites of Germany in the two wars. No serious or organised espionage directed by any of these satellites or any other Power has come to notice and there has therefore been no occasion to develop an organisation for the purpose of combating them.

Since 1931, however, when the Security Service became responsible for detailed enquiries into the Communist movements in the United Kingdom, for liaison on this subject with other British countries and for a general study of the bearing of international Communism on these affairs, it has in fact, sometimes without any definite mandate, kept itself informed of the development of other movements and organisations which might develop tendencies likely to affect the British war effort or to bring them into conflict with the Constitution. They are often matters of "Intelligence" rather than counter espionage. Thus the Security Service has kept itself informed, sometimes rather superficially, of such movements as those of the Trotskyites, the Anarchists, the Scottish and Welsh Nationalist movements, Jehovah's Witnesses, Pacifist movements, Polish intrigues, the Palestinian terrorists, the Greek nationalists in Cyprus and others. The guiding principle is that while a serious attempt to penetrate such movements may not always be necessary, the Security Service ought to be informed at least in a general way in case such a movement may develop more serious aspects. For instance, the Trotskyites may become involved in strikes in wartime, and in such cases the Home Office may at any time desire to have an assessment of the importance of such movements. The Security Service is in a better position to examine them whether in relation to international movements or otherwise than are Special Branch and, eo fortiori, the various other police forces. Again, Polish or other 'Right Wing' Europeans may attempt to involve this country in international complications.

These - generally minor - matters are dealt with by the Security Service as a matter of convenience but they often do not come strictly within the four corners of the purpose for which it was originally established unless the function of acquiring 'straight' intelligence within the United Kingdom is accepted as a positive and permanent commitment. There have been, however, on rare occasions more important matters, the investigation of which has been entrusted to the Security Service as a special measure. For example certain delicate enquiries were made under the Prime Minister's directions in connection with the abdication of King Edward VIII. These were matters touching on the Constitution and ultimate issues of sovereignty and were very far removed from any question of guarding the King's Realm from penetration by external enemies or of rebellion by a section of the King's subjects. They involved its innermost integrity; and the enquiries were entrusted to the Security Service because no other suitable machinery existed for the purpose while its head, Sir Vernon Kell, had during a long period of service earned the respect and confidence of the highest authorities. So long as the Security Service occupies this position it is likely to be used on these rare and special occasions; and this fact is a powerful argument for requiring that its personnel should always be selected with special care and should be free from any political involvement or other ground which might cause doubt of their integrity. If the Security Service did not exist some special ad hoc body would have to be created under the Prime Minister or the Home Office, as the case might be, as was done, for instance, at the time of the Cato Street conspiracy.

To recapitulate, the functions of the Security Service are naturally divided into -

1. detection or investigation
2. prevention or security
3. intelligence including records, and -
4. active deception of the enemy.

The first three are closely inter-related and from the beginning the organisation was adapted to deal with them being divided into three branches known as the preventive, investigation and administrative branches, the records being placed under the last-mentioned. The different conditions which govern the practical working of the Security Service in peace and in war and the complications caused by the development of Communism on the one hand and Nazism and Fascism on the other, as potential component elements of the so-called "Fifth Column", helped to induce a blurring of these functions internally in the period between the wars. Further confusion arose through the developments connected with the functional relations between the Security Service and Section V of S.I.S. and the failure of the latter before the war to obtain good inside information about the German Secret Service - a very difficult task and one in which exceptional luck as well as skill may be necessary for success.

In consequence of the development of international anarchy and of the revolutionary movements of the 'Right' and 'Left' during the last forty years the main effort of the Service has been concentrated on measures for dealing with the two real threats to British security; that of Germany and her allies and that of Russia as a powerful military State controlling the Comintern organisation and utilising the National Communist Parties all over the world as an instrument of policy.

The action taken towards countering the German and Soviet Secret Service organisations - including those of the associated political parties, Nazi, Fascist or Comintern - furnishes, therefore, the two main themes of this report.

CHAPTER II: REACTIONS TO FOREIGN DEVELOPMENTS IN PEACE AND WAR

NOTE

Chapters II to V contain a description of the problems presented to the Security Service during the period 1909-1945 and include references to the machinery devised to deal with those problems from time to time. Counter espionage and security being essentially a reaction to the actions of others can only be appreciated in terms of those actions. This report is not intended to be a mere statement of the framework of the organisation of the Security Service, but an account of its responses to its environment, inside this country in relation to other parts of the machinery of government and externally in its reactions to developments especially in hostile or potentially hostile countries and to the actions of their Secret Services or of secret agencies such as those of the Comintern.

Part 1: The German Threat 1908-1914

(i) The origins of M.I.5. - in the War Office and the Admiralty in 1908.

During the long period of peace after Waterloo there was no British Secret Service (except for a small ad hoc organisation during the Boer War) and no counter espionage or security service. There was, however, a section of the General Staff employed under the Director of Military Operations which dealt with secret service and in 1908 the officer-in-charge of this section was Colonel J.E. Edmonds (later the official historian of the Great War of 1914-1918). He had studied the German army from the time when he was in France during the German occupation after the war of 1870, and in 1891 was able to acquire an insight into the methods adopted by the German General Staff as a result of the situation at that time when there was an exchange of information in regard to Russia between them and the British General Staff. On returning from a visit to Russia, made on behalf of the Intelligence Division of the British General Staff, Colonel Edmonds was ordered to report at the Ministry of War in Berlin and thus got into touch with a number of officers including Major Dame, head of the German Secret Service or Nachrichten Bureau in the Herwathstrasse. The Nachrichten Bureau then had two branches, one of which conducted investigations in France and the other in Germany. Colonel Edmonds and Major Dame maintained a personal friendship and contact until 1900 when the latter was removed from his post on account of his pro-English attitude. He was replaced by a Major Brose who was known for his anti-English views. Shortly after this Colonel Edmonds learned from several sources that a third branch of the German Secret Service had been formed to deal with England. Among the sources from which confirmation of this information was received were reports from a British officer serving with the International Contingents in Pekin and from French officers connected with their own Secret Service.

Detailed information was received about the German methods of collecting intelligence in peacetime including, inter alia, a study of maps and points of military importance (such as docks, bridges, magazines, railways and other objects which it was intended to damage on or before the outbreak of war). Intelligence of this kind was obtained from German official sources including those of attachés, diplomatic and consular officials, or officers and officials making official visits, as well as from officers and scientists sent on secret missions. All this was supplemented by the purchase of secret information and espionage.

These peacetime methods gave place in time of war to a system under which secret agents were employed in the midst of the enemy forces or in their rear. Thus in 1870 there was a German collecting agent at Lyons who forwarded all despatches to Geneva whence they were telegraphed to Germany. Other agents were employed to effect demolitions and a third class were instructed to travel to the enemy frontier where they were distributed to act as guides to the invading German army. These three classes of agents were apparently employed by the Germans with success in the campaign of 1870 and played an important part in the initial successes of the German army.

In 1908 it was reported that information had been received from a number of private individuals which indicated that a German espionage system on the lines which had been successful in France was being developed in England. It was emphasised that the War Office had received no reports from the police but that some Chief Constables had made enquiries when asked to do so; they had, however, made the General Staff understand that it was not their business. Late in 1908 the War Office had learned that the section of the Nachrichten Bureau which had been set up to act against England had established a branch in Brussels for this purpose and that the head of the Brussels branch was coming to England via Ostend. They therefore asked the head of the Criminal Investigation Department to allow his men at Dover to watch for the man among the arrivals by the boat, but that officer felt compelled to refuse on the ground that the man was not a criminal and that if the matter leaked out there might be awkward questions in Parliament. The Director of Military Operations who was informed of this considered that as the information which they had received indicated that the man was coming to interview certain new agents who were British subjects it would have been useful to learn the names of the persons with whom he got into touch.

The subject was discussed between the Director of Military Operations, the Chief of the General Staff and the Secretary of State for War. The Admiralty were also interested because on the one hand they found it difficult to obtain the intelligence which they desired from Germany on account of the restrictions imposed by German police and security methods; and on the other hand, they had received offers from persons who wished to sell information about Germany to them and they felt it was undesirable that the Admiralty should be in direct contact with such persons. At the same time, they had fewer facilities for making enquiries, regarding suspected cases of German espionage, than had the War Office and they had accordingly communicated with Colonel Edmonds in regard to certain cases of this description.

Following on these discussions a paper was prepared by Colonel Edmonds dealing with the German and French systems of espionage in time of peace.

(ii) The origins of M.I.5. - proceedings of the Committee of Imperial Defence 1909.

As a result of these and other comings and goings the Prime Minister decided in March 1909 that a Sub-Committee of the Committee of Imperial Defence should consider the subject of foreign espionage and, inter alia, the above facts were laid before it. The members of the Sub-Committee included Mr. Haldane, Mr. McKenna, Sir Charles Hardinge, three Service representatives and Sir Edward Henry, the Commissioner of Police. Its terms of reference were briefly to review the nature and extent of foreign espionage taking place in the country and to report whether if was desirable that the Admiralty and the War Office should be brought into official relations with the police, Postal and Customs authorities with a view to the movements of aliens suspected of being spies or secret agents being properly supervised; to make proposals regarding measures which might be desirable including those for increasing powers for dealing with persons suspected of espionage; and to report whether any alteration was desirable in the system then in force in the Admiralty and the War Office for obtaining information from abroad.

Evidence was placed before the Committee regarding a large number of cases during 1908 and the first three months of 1909 in which Germans had been suspected of some form of espionage in this country. It was reported that certain German officers had betrayed the fact that parts of England were allotted to them for intelligence purposes and that individual Germans had been noticed making sketches and taking topographical notes. In one case it was reported that over a period of eighteen months a series of Germans of soldierly appearance had been living at a house in Hythe, two or three individuals remaining for about two months at a time after which their places were taken by others so that about twenty had been seen in the course of eighteen months. They used the house as a centre for motoring and their interest in Lydd and the ranges had been noticeable. The general impression created by the facts observed in a number of cases and by the general circumstances of the time was that the position was similar to that in France before the German invasion of 1870. The view was put forward that the French failure in 1870 was largely due to the lack of a Secret Service and it was maintained as axiomatic that the great Generals of history including Frederick the Great, Napoleon and Wellington had owed their successes largely to carefully elaborated spy systems. Immediately after the outbreak of the war of 1870 the French had attempted to improvise a counter espionage service, but it was too late because such a service cannot be improvised but must be built up in the leisure of peacetime.

Among the evidence put before the Sub-Committee on Foreign Espionage was that of Captain Temple of the Admiralty who stated that there was no machinery at the Admiralty for carrying out investigation into espionage but certain cases had been followed up by the Admiralty from which it transpired that Brussels was the headquarters of a forwarding agency which had been inserting advertisements in the "Daily Mail" during the year 1908 asking for retired officers, engineers or clerks, who wished to increase their income by contributing articles to an American Naval Review, to apply to a poste restante address in Brussels. Correspondence with this address had led to an offer of £50 in payment for a report on a gunnery report which, according to the Press, was missing at Portsmouth. There was no evidence to connect the poste restante address at Brussels with the German Government but contact had been made with an individual using the address and he had supplied a list of points on which information was required and this list proved that the individual compiling it had a thorough knowledge of gunnery and a good acquaintance with reports and returns issued by the Admiralty. The same individual gave to his intended agent, who answered the advertisement in the "Daily Mail", cover addresses in Basle and Ostend. It was from beginnings such as these that the Special Intelligence Bureau - the forerunner of M.I.5. - got to work.

The Sub-Committee on Foreign Espionage had before it a number of papers going back to precedents at the time of the Spanish Armada and the Napoleonic threat of invasion, including statements of the position under the Common Law and with the Prerogative powers of the Crown. Among them was a memorandum by the Home Office making suggestions for the amendment of the Official Secrets Act, 1889, in which it was pointed out that the principal provisions dealing with espionage and like offences were contained in Section 1 of the Act; but the Section was extremely complicated and its drafting had been severely criticised in Stephen's "Digest of the Criminal Law" where it was pointed out that it created about eighty misdemeanours all of which were made felonies only if a certain condition were proved; and that that condition was almost certain never to be really absent but was one which it would be rarely possible to prove. There was no power to search under the Act; and it was held that it was clearly desirable that such power should be given.

Under the conditions prevailing in 1908 and 1909 it was held that no action could be taken to prevent the German investigations which were being conducted almost openly in England and an amendment to the Official Secrets Act of 1889 was therefore considered and recommended by the Sub-Committee. Other recommendations were that a Secret Service Bureau should be formed to deal with espionage and to act as a screen between foreign spies and Government officials; that a Bill for the control of the Press should be proceeded with having for its object the prevention of the publication of certain documents or information; that communications on the subject of secret service between the Admiralty, War Office and Secret Service Bureau on the one hand and the Post Office and the Customs on the other should not be through the ordinary official channels but through particular members of the two latter Departments with whom correspondence should be carried on direct; and - in view of the attention said to be given by the German General Staff to the question of demolition work on the outbreak of war - that an enquiry should be held by the Home Ports Defence Committee into the manner in which vulnerable points including dockyards, wireless stations, private ship-building yards, railway bridges and others were guarded with a view to assigning the responsibility.

At the same time it was suggested that one officer should be appointed to be free from other work and to devote his whole attention to Secret Service problems; that the registration of aliens which had been enforced by Act of Parliament in 1798 and 1804 should be revived and that there should be an informal conference between officials of the Home Office, the Post Office, the War Office and the Admiralty.

In August 1909 a meeting in Sir Edward Henry's room at Scotland Yard developed further proposals for starting the Secret Service Bureau and it is worth while to note that the scale of ideas and the outlook prevalent at the time were such that the proposals were limited to the appointment of a retired Chief Inspector of the Criminal Investigation Department as a suitable private detective under cover of whose name the Secret Service Bureau should be conducted, while the War Office proposed to appoint Captain V.G.W. Kell, South Staffordshire Regiment, (who was to retire from the regular Service for the purpose), and the Admiralty nominated Commander Cumming. These two officers actually shared an office leased by the retired Chief Inspector, but after a few months' experience it was decided that it was impracticable to conduct Secret Service and counter Secret Service work from the same headquarters.

(iii) The creation of the Special Intelligence Bureau in 1909

In this way the Security Service, as it is now called, first came into existence under the title of the Special Intelligence Bureau which was started in October 1909, when it consisted of one officer, Captain (afterwards Major-General) Sir Vernon Kell. The historical report (F Branch Report, Bibliography No. 28) on the work of the preventive branch which was written after the war 1914-1918 opens by saying "the work and consequently the organisation of such a Bureau was naturally divided into two main branches - (1) the investigation of particular cases involving definite suspicion of espionage and - (2) the construction of legal and administrative machinery calculated to embarrass and, if possible, to frustrate such attempts in general and for the future".

(iv) Developments from 1910-1914

In March 1910 Captain Kell received the assistance of a clerk. In January 1911 a second officer was added to the staff as well as a secretary but it was not till December 1912 that Captain Holt-Wilson joined. He afterwards became the head of the preventive branch as well as those concerned with Port Control and liaison with the Dominions and Colonies.

One of the most important early achievements of the Special Intelligence Bureau was the production of a report in 1911 which was drawn up at the request of Lord Haldane, then Secretary of State for War, to assist him in placing the new Official Secrets Act before Parliament. This dealt with some twenty-two cases of suspected espionage which could not be satisfactorily followed up because of the defects in the Act of 1889.

The passing of the Act of 1911 made it possible to establish the work of the Special Intelligence Bureau on a satisfactory legal basis and to develop it into an effective counter espionage and security service.

Very briefly, and in simplified non-legal language, the effect of the new Act was to make it a felony if it were done for any purpose prejudicial to the safety of the State, to enter or approach any "Prohibited Place" as defined in the Act or make any sketch, plan, model or note calculated or intended to be useful to the enemy or obtain or communicate to any other person any document or information calculated or intended to be useful to an enemy. In order to prove the existence of a purpose prejudicial to the safety of the State and so secure a conviction, it was sufficient that the purpose of the accused person should appear to be a purpose of that kind "from the circumstances of the case or his conduct or his known character as proved". The onus of satisfying a jury that his purpose was a right one was, as Lord Haldane explained in introducing the Bill before Parliament, on the person performing the act or found in the prohibited place. Thus effective action, which had been impossible under the old Official Secrets Act and the Common Law, could now be taken against German spies.

Another vital element in the development of the Special Intelligence Bureau was the arrangement by which the correspondence of suspected German spies was opened and examined under the authority of a warrant issued by a Secretary of State. A strong view had always been held that the power of interfering with correspondence in this way would be used as sparingly as possible and the Post Office had always held that it was very undesirable to shake public confidence in the security of the post. The Secretary to the Post Office had even argued in a paper submitted to the above-mentioned Sub-Committee on Foreign Espionage in 1909 that it appeared very doubtful whether any useful results would follow from the examination of correspondence in the case of spies as it was improbable that any letters of importance would be received or despatched by a spy without the use of devices for concealment. In spite of this attitude the Home Secretary's warrants were issued and played an important part in enabling the Bureau to detect an active network of German spies in the United Kingdom. In his book "The Crisis" Mr. Winston Churchill refers to his part in this matter when he became Home Secretary in 1910. Parenthetically, it may be remembered that the original purpose underlying the institution of the Post Office for the purpose of carrying mails was to enable the Executive to control and supervise undesirable communications. Mr. Churchill also refers to the action taken by him to safeguard the Navy's magazines against possible sabotage on the outbreak of war.

The policy of the Special Intelligence Bureau was not to disturb the network of German agents which had been established in this country in peacetime but to obtain all possible information about their organisation with a view to striking and disrupting it on the outbreak of war.

The adoption of this policy did not mean that no overt action would be taken in cases caught flagrante delicto. For instance in February 1914 a German officer was arrested in the act of taking some plans of a British cruiser and other documents out of the country.

The methods by which the general policy was pursued entailed the development of close co-operation with the police - as a remedy for the state of affairs disclosed before the Sub-Committee on Foreign Espionage - and the use of Home Office Warrants to intercept the correspondence of German spies who, contrary to the above-mentioned views of the Secretary to the Post Office, were found to use the post for correspondence which made it possible to discover and lay bare their network in this country.

At the same time progress was made with the registration of aliens but this had to be done on an unofficial basis because the authorities at that time were not prepared to come into the open with measures for official registration. They appear to have been influenced by apprehension of possible questions in Parliament on the point of the freedom of the individual. This unofficial registration was undertaken by the police at the instance of the Special Intelligence Bureau in 1910. No attempt was made to deal with the Metropolitan Police Area or any part of the United Kingdom except the east coast of England and Scotland. The census of 1911 showed that there were some 42,000 adult male Germans and Austro-Hungarians in England and Wales and it was therefore roughly calculated that as a result of unofficially registering 11,000 such persons in the coastal areas up to July 1913 the records were "tolerably complete". Even this rough and ready work was carried on under somewhat difficult conditions because the Home Office laid down that all the information was to be collected confidentially and no alien was to be asked a question "of an inquisitorial nature". Moreover, the Registrar-General considered that the information in census returns had been obtained confidentially and that the police must not let it be known that they were being used for the purpose of registration. In support of this very sensitive regard for the freedom of the individual alien in our midst it was even argued that it was an advantage to conduct enquiries confidentially as it was important to prevent potential enemies from realising the fact that they were being registered. On the basis of the information obtained by this partial registration the aliens concerned were classified under various headings, the most important being known spies, possible suspects, and Germans and Austrians who were to be watched because they were known to have been army officers or for similar reasons.

Part 2: The German Espionage System in War 1914-1918

(i) The Special Intelligence Bureau becomes M.O.5. under the Directorate of Military Operations.

The essential facts to be remembered about the Special Intelligence Bureau are that it was instituted as a military measure to defend the Services and the country against the attempts which were obviously being made by the German Secret Service to obtain intelligence; and that active attempts were being made against both the Army and the Navy during the years prior to its formation. The organisation under Captain Kell worked as a secret organisation but it was responsible to a section of the Directorate of Military Operations at the War Office and it will therefore be convenient at this stage to trace the development of the machinery in the War Office of which it formed a part.

Prior to August 1914 there was no Directorate of Military Intelligence, the functions of intelligence being included under the Directorate of Military Operations which was divided into six sections. Of these M.O.5. was responsible for policy in connection with a variety of matters including censorship, aliens and the civilian population in war, and legislation affecting the General Staff.

On the outbreak of war in August 1914 there was a rapid expansion in the Directorate of Military Operations the most important being in M.O.5. on account of the wide variety of its duties which included responsibility for all Secret Service work. On the 17th August 1914 M.O.5. was divided into eight sub-sections of which M.O.5. (g) now came under Major Kell who was responsible for counter espionage, aliens, and control of civilian traffic overseas. In April 1915 there was a further reorganisation when a plan for an I. (A) (Intelligence) and an I. (B) (Security) staff was partly put into operation, by the creation of a Directorate of Special Intelligence under Brigadier-General Cockerill who was put in charge of M.O.5., M.O.6. and M.O.7. - M.O.5. being under Lt.-Colonel Kell. M.O.5. was again reorganised in November 1915 when military Port Control officers were included in the section.

(ii) Creation of the Directorate of Military Intelligence - M.O.5. becomes M.I.5.

In December 1915 a Military Intelligence Directorate in addition to the Military Operations Directorate was formed under the Chief of the Imperial General Staff, and M.O.5. became M.I.5. as part of a similar change including all the M.O. sections from M.O.2. to M.O.9.

The account of M.I.5. as given in "The Historical Sketch of the Directorate of Military Intelligence during the Great War, 1914-1919" is as follows:-

> The history of what is now known as M.I.5. dates from October 1909 when, following on a decision of the Committee of Imperial Defence, Captain V.G.W. Kell was appointed under M.O.5. to conduct enquiries into German espionage in the United Kingdom. Later he had the help of three regular officers, who were transferred to the Reserve of Officers on undertaking this work, and a very small clerical staff.
>
> It worked as a secret organisation, and was responsible to M.O.5., Colonel, who acted as its paymaster, military chief and director.
>
> The staff on 4th August 1914 was:- 9 officers, 3 civilians, 4 women clerks, 3 police.
>
> In August 1914, it was put under M.O.5., Colonel, as a sub-section, M.O.5. (g) Its duties were defined as:- military policy in connection with civil population including aliens. Administration of Defence of the Realm Regulations in so far as they concern the M.O. Directorate.
>
> Before the war a register had been compiled of all aliens in the United Kingdom, outside the East End of London, and lists had been prepared and handed to Chief Constables concerned of those persons who were

known or were suspected of being German agents. The moment war was declared these persons were arrested, and in this way it is probable that the German Intelligence Service in the United Kingdom was thrown completely out of gear.

On the outbreak of war the regulations which had been worked out chiefly by sub-committees of the C.I.D., of which M.0.5. Colonel was a member, and as far as possible in the form of draft Bills and Orders in Council, became executive and necessitated a very largely increased staff. The section was housed outside the War Office, retaining only one room in the main building as a post office.

On 1st October 1914, M.0.5. (g) was divided into three sub-divisions:

> M.0.5(g) A. Investigation of espionage and cases of suspected persons.
>
> M.0.5(g) B. Co-ordination of general policy of Government Departments in dealing with aliens. Questions arising out of the Defence of the Realm Regulations and the Aliens Restrictions Act.
>
> M.0.5(g) C. Records, personnel, administration and port control.

On 11th August 1915, owing to the formation of a new sub-division to deal with Port Control, it was decided to reorganise M.0.5 (g) into four sub-sections as follows :-

One new sub-section was called M.0.5 (e) and dealt with military policy connected with the control of civilian passenger traffic to and from the United Kingdom, port intelligence and military permits. M.0.5.(g)A became M.0.5(g), M.0.5(g)B became M.0.5(f) and M.0.5(g)C became M.0.5(h).

With the formation of M.0.5(e) the system of military control of passenger traffic at home ports, which had steadily been growing in importance, was put on a new footing. The whole of this, as well as the subsequently formed Military Permit Offices in London, Paris, Rome and New York being directly controlled by M.0.5(e) and administered by M.0.5(h).

On 3rd January 1916, when the General Staff was reorganised the sub-sections M.0.5(a) to (d) became M.I.6 and M.0.5(e) to (h) became M.I.5(e) to (h).

On 21st September, M.I.5 [...] from M.I.5 (g) to co-ordinate counter espionage measures throughout the British Empire.

On 15th January 1917, M.I.5(b) was formed from M.I.5(g) to deal with questions affecting natives of India and other Oriental races.

On 23rd April 1917, P.M.S.2., a section of the Ministry of Munitions, formed originally from a nucleus supplied by M.I.5(f) on the 19th February 1916, to deal with aliens and others employed on munitions and auxiliary war services, was reabsorbed as M.I.5(a).

On 1st September 1917, M.I.5(b) was absorbed by M.I.5(d).

On 1st August 1919, Military control at home ports ceased and missions abroad were taken over by M.I.1(c).

On 1st September 1919, M.I.5(a) was absorbed by M.I.5(f).

On 31st March 1920, M.I.5 was reorganised as follows :-

M.I.5(f) became M.I.5(a)
M.I.5(g) became M.I.5(b)
M.I.5(h) became M.I.5(d) and was renumbered M.I.5(o).

Colonel Sir V.G.W. Kell, K.B.E., C.B., was head of M.0.5(g) in August 1914, became head of M.0.5 in March 1915, and is still in charge of M.I.5.

M.I.5 has throughout its existence acted on behalf of the Admiralty and, since its creation, of the Air Ministry, in all questions relative to counter espionage and preventive measures connected therewith."

(iii) The History of M.I.5. as compiled after the War of 1914-1918.

The internal history of M.I.5. was recorded after the end of the war in the form of the reports of A., D., E., F., G. and H. Branches. These reports are available for purposes of reference. The intention of compiling a consolidated report was never implemented and the following are very brief outlines of what took place during the war of 1914-1918.

The three main branches were F (Preventive), G (Investigation) and H (Secretariat, Administration and Records). The head of F Branch was Lt.-Colonel Holt-Wilson and he was also in charge of A (Alien War Service), D (Imperial overseas special intelligence including Irish, Oriental and Near-Eastern affairs) and E (Control of ports and frontiers). The various changes and developments in connection with these branches are described in the above-quoted historical sketch of the Directorate of Military Intelligence.

The principle underlying the organisation of the preventive side of the work was to establish controls which would facilitate the work of detection and in this and other ways frustrate the enemy secret intelligence service. These controls were established by the Defence of the Realm Act and the regulations framed under it; by the complete registration of aliens at the beginning of the war and the control of aliens by the Aliens Restriction Order; by the control of traffic by means of passports and visas and examination at ports; by the examination of credentials or 'vetting'; and by the control of communication through the postal and telegraph censorship.

In accordance with a decision of the Committee of Imperial Defence the Home Office became responsible for the administration of the Aliens' Restriction Order while the Defence of the Realm Regulations were administered by officers known as Competent Military Authorities nominated by the Army Council for the purpose. These officers exercised jurisdiction within a defined district under the instructions of the Army Council transmitted through the Horse Guards as the General Headquarters, Great Britain. The powers of the Competent Military Authorities, who were usually officers commanding troops in the various districts into which Great Britain was divided, were in practice subject to considerable qualifications and the control of the Army Council was in effect dependent on the advice of the Preventive Branch of the Special Intelligence Bureau or M.I.5(f) as it was eventually called. The Competent Military Authorities depended for their information to a greater or less extent on the Intelligence Officers of Headquarters Staff in the different Commands. M.I.5. was responsible for framing special intelligence measures in general and was therefore interested from the point of view of policy in a number of regulations with the administration of which it had no concern. It was more directly concerned with three classes of the Regulations, namely those concerned with espionage, with local restrictions for special intelligence purposes. These included such matters as the power of preventing embarkation of persons suspected of communicating with the enemy and powers under D.R.R.14 and D.R.R.14B for placing under personal restriction disaffected and dangerous individuals who, not being enemy subjects, could not be interned under the Royal Prerogative. A Competent Military (or Naval) Authority was empowered to prohibit by Order persons from entering or residing in specified areas under certain conditions. Competent Military Authorities were alone empowered to make orders under D.R.R.14 but orders under 14B were made by the Home Secretary acting on the recommendation of, in the words of the F Branch report, "the Competent Military Authority commanding M.I.5." It was found that local Competent Military Authorities were not in a position to deal satisfactorily with these questions and the Home Secretary declined to act on their recommendations.

In virtue of the position of M.O.5. under the Directorate of Military Operations (later M.I.5. under that of Military Intelligence) the records of the last war throughout put the emphasis on the military nature of all the controls discussed above.

The effective work done on the preventive side included the placing under control under the Defence of the Realm Act of some hundreds of individuals considered dangerous; the initiation from time to time of legislation; the maintenance of relations with the Censorship and other Government Departments; the investigation of personnel employed on confidential work; the investigation of persons entering or leaving the United Kingdom or visiting British military zones abroad; the preparation of lists of known suspects; and general supervision over seamen and the internment of enemy aliens.

On the outbreak of war a small number of enemy aliens on the M.I.5. lists were interned, the peak figure of internment being over 32,000 in October 1915.

The G Branch Report fills nine volumes and is very diffusely written. There is no succinct account of the cases investigated before and during the war and no indication as to how far M.I.5. obtained a general picture of the German Secret Intelligence organisation with which it had to deal. The enquiries made in the years immediately before the war showed that the German organisation was active in this country and was particularly interested in obtaining naval information. As a result of numerous enquiries a certain number of cases had been brought to light but in accordance with the policy mentioned above the main German organisation here was kept under observation and on the outbreak of war twenty-one out of twenty-two known spies in this country were arrested. It was reported during the war and confirmed after the Armistice that the capture of these spies completely broke up the German Intelligence organisation which was not able to act effectively again until some time in 1915. One result was that the Germans were without any information from this country and had no definite knowledge of the departure of the British Expeditionary Force.

In November 1914 a case, which attracted more attention than most, was that of Karl Hans Lody, a German officer who contrived to travel in England, Scotland and Ireland without betraying his presence, and to obtain military information; he ended in his trial by court-martial, he was shot at the Tower.

In 1915 three groups of spies and a few individual cases were dealt with. Altogether ten persons were shot, one was hanged and five were sentenced to penal servitude while four were interned under the Defence Regulations. Half-a-dozen of these spies were Germans, including British or American citizens of German birth. Others were of various nationalities including five Dutch, a Russian, a Brazilian, a Uruguayan and a Peruvian. In 1916 four groups of spies were dealt with. In the first, four persons were concerned, of whom one was interned and the other three were deported. In the second, a Swedish woman was sentenced to death, the sentence being commuted; and a Dane and a Dutchman were deported. In the third, a Spaniard and a Dutchman were sentenced to death, the sentence being commuted; and a German was sentenced to ten years' imprisonment. In the fourth, an American was sentenced to death but was subsequently released and sent to America at the request of the American authorities who desired to obtain evidence from him; while a Dutchman and a Frenchman were deported and interned respectively. In this fourth group the spies concerned had connections with America and the enquiries resulted in action being taken against some of their accomplices there.

In 1917 five spies were arrested. Of these a Spaniard was released for want of evidence, a Norwegian journalist was sentenced to death, the sentence being commuted. A Brazilian journalist was interned and a woman, a British subject of German origin, was sentenced to penal servitude.

A point of some interest is that the Germans at first depended on their own nationals to a considerable extent but after 1915 tended to give up the practice and employed an increasing proportion of foreigners of various nationalities.

There is no very clear account to explain how contact was first obtained with the German Secret Service and its agents, but it appears that one of the early sources of information was a British subject who was approached by the Germans and reported the fact. Another early clue is said to have been obtained through an officer overhearing a conversation in a railway carriage. Important clues were obtained as the result of the search of a suspect.

These early beginnings were supplemented by the use of the H.O.W. as a means of secret censorship which led to the uncovering of the whole German network at the beginning of the war.

It is stated that during the course of the war the most important sources of information about German espionage were obtained from M.I.1.C. (or S.I.S.) and as a result of censorship. One of the most important sources of S.I.S. information was the [...] and by this means a considerable amount of information regarding German agents passing through Holland - obviously an important centre of the German Nachrichtendienst - came into British hands.

In some cases information was obtained from agents abroad, as a result of which censorship was applied to addresses in neutral countries with the result that agents writing or telegraphing to these addresses were detected.

In one case an individual who is described as the best agent sent over by the Germans during the war reached this country from Hamburg via America and France in 1915. He came under the cover of being a representative of two well-known American firms and on the way here did some genuine business in France and procured introductions to English firms from the American head of a good French firm.

In another case a German agent in Holland represented a Dutch firm of tea merchants and sent young Dutchmen to England to travel in tea with instructions to obtain details about shipping movements. He was also concerned in the despatch of sailors from Holland for similar purposes and with the representatives of a Dutch firm of cigar merchants, some of whose representatives were his agents.

In 1917 information was received which gave details of instructions to the German Intelligence Service in Scandinavia. These instructions referred to the importance of obtaining information from business men arriving from enemy, i.e. Allied, countries, as well as from the officers and crews of merchant ships. Instructions also dealt with the proposals for arranging for suitable neutral firms to engage German commercial representatives to be employed on genuine business in Allied countries, and they mentioned that experience showed that where men were suspected a woman would arouse little suspicion. The chief danger of all such agents was recognised as lying in the means of communication but it was claimed that German chemical science had reduced that danger to a minimum. The experience of M.I.5. showed that secret writing and skilfully designed plain letter codes and telegraph codes were used by the German Intelligence Service. There is no reference to the use of wireless.

As the German Intelligence Service found that their agents were detected they changed their methods, and as they changed their methods M.I.5. secured changes in the regulations designed to facilitate measures for dealing with enemy agents. As a result of this duel the Germans were said to be relying towards the end of the war to a considerable extent on information obtained by word of mouth from persons travelling between England and neutral countries.

The scope of M.I.5. gradually broadened from the detection of espionage to the impersonation of hostile agents for the purpose of feeding the enemy with misleading information. In one case a German agent was impersonated after he had suffered the death penalty without the enemy's knowledge. Considerable sums were received by way of remuneration from the Germans in payment of these simulated services.

Double-cross agents were also used for the purpose of misleading the enemy in regard to sabotage. Minor acts of sabotage were arranged which did no harm but were sufficient to satisfy the enemy that his agents were active. The object was to prevent him from opening up new changes or infiltrating new agents which might have been dangerous or difficult to detect.

As a result of these preventive and detective measures and of what now appears in the light of the experience of the second war to have been a very small-scale attempt to mislead the enemy, the reputation of M.I.5. reached a high level before the end of 1918.

It was emphasised that the functions of M.I.5. were advisory and this fact governed its relations with all Government Departments and the Services. One consequence of this was that the police, acting on information obtained from M.I.5., were responsible for the conduct of cases against all enemy agents who were detected in espionage. Many enemy agents were examined by Sir Basil Thomson in his room at Scotland Yard. M.I.5. officers were present, but the responsibility for the proceedings appears to have rested with the police officers. Nevertheless, in a number of cases M.I.5. officers interrogated considerable numbers of suspects at the Cannon Row Police Station.

The result of this divided responsibility was to produce a certain rivalry, if not jealousy, between Sir Basil Thomson and M.I.5., and the system may therefore be said to have had marked disadvantages in this respect.

M.I.5.A. dealt with all questions regarding the employment of aliens in munition factories and in auxiliary war services of all kinds and with the importation of labour from abroad for employment on munition work.

M.I.5.D. was responsible for the co-ordination of Special Intelligence with the authorities in the Dominions, India and the Colonies and for the co-ordination of the work of Special

Intelligence Missions in Allied countries. It also dealt with correspondence connected with Near Eastern and Asiatic countries in matters of espionage, sedition and treachery.

M.I.5.E. was responsible for "military policy connected with the control of civilian passenger traffic to and from the United Kingdom"; for the control of Military Permit Offices in London and Paris; and for the control of Military Control Officers abroad. In the case of neutral countries communications with Military Control Officers were carried on through M.I.1.C.

M.I.5.H. constituted the Secretariat and the administrative branch of M.I.5. and included the Registry. The Registry was the repository of all counter espionage intelligence available to the British Government. Names of persons and places in different parts of the world were carded and as the war proceeded the volume of information received from all sources and on relevant subjects made the Registry a formidable weapon in the intelligence armoury. As branches on the investigation and preventive sides of the Office were progressively sub-divided it was found necessary to specialise in different parts of the world, and a number of women secretaries and Registry clerks belonging to or working in the different sections in A., D., E., F., or G. Branches grew up into a body of specialists with a thorough knowledge of their subject and able to contribute to the success of the organisation as a whole in virtue of this specialised knowledge.

The head of H Branch was responsible for the recruitment of staff including officers, secretaries and Registry personnel, and the records contained tributes by the heads of other branches to the success with which this important function was performed. A supplement to the H Branch report containing a report on women's work in M.I.5. emphasises the importance of the part they played both at home and abroad, and emphasises that the work in the Registry based on specialised knowledge was an important part of the intelligence process.

In regard to enquiries about suspects arriving at British ports from neutral countries, M.I.5. does not appear to have been in a strong position. In some instances a suspect traveller was examined by a number of officers representing the Home Office, the War Office, Admiralty, Customs as well as M.I.5. who in one case - at Harwich - sat round a horse-shoe table with the suspect in the centre. The object was to secure speed in the disposal of incoming travellers, but the result cannot always have been satisfactory, especially when time was pressing and the balance had to be found between the conflicting interests of different Departments. (These methods of control may be compared with the very different arrangements made for interrogation at the L.R.C. and Camp 020 in the second war.)

(iv) The dawning recognition of the concept of 'total war' under modern conditions.

After the end of the war of 1914-1918 two books especially germane to our subject were written on the German Secret Service. The first of these was published in 1920 entitled "Nachrichtendienst Presse, und Volkstimmung in Weltreig" and it was published in English in 1924 under the title "The German Secret Service" by Colonel W. Nicolai who had been Chief of that Service. The second was compiled in 1921 by the General Staff, War Office, i.e. by M.I.5. officers. It was not published but was confidential and for official use only. It was entitled "The German Police System as applied to Military Security in War" (Bibliography No. 36).

The M.I.5. Book was based on evidence obtained from all available sources including the examination of documents and German agents and prisoners of war and, apparently, as a result of enquiries made in Germany after the war. It drew freely on Nicolai's work which it described as a defence of the activities of the German General Staff and its Intelligence Bureau in regard to national security. One object underlying the M.I.5. compilation was to emphasise the all-embracing nature of national security intelligence in modern war and thus to point the moral that any security organisation should be maintained at a sufficiently high level even in peacetime. It maintained that a modern nation fighting for existence would attack its enemy with every conceivable weapon, moral or intellectual as well as commercial or physical, and by means of propaganda, espionage, or sabotage. It suggested that security functions were fourfold, i.e. political, defence, public security and economic. Of these, the first three covered the field of foreign affairs, naval, military, air and munitions security and security against the political warfare of the enemy including responsibility for measures against revolutionary propaganda, leakage of information and pacifist propaganda.

In adopting this attitude the M.I.5. book based itself on Nicolai's view that the world war had provided proof that a struggle between nations had grown out of the narrow limits of a decision by arms and had become a test in which the nation's whole strength was engaged in the political, economic and military fields and, "not least, in the very soul of the people"; and that in the place of a purely military Intelligence Service an all-embracing State Secret Service had developed which concerned itself with all that might give the State an advantage over its enemies in all these fields.

The authors of the M.I.5. book declared that the need for a study of the German police system necessarily followed from the fact of its being intimately linked with German methods of security in war, and they also showed the close relationship between the German Military Security Service or Abwehr and the Intelligence or Nachrichten organisations. The close relationship between Intelligence and the German Secret Police had dated back to the Franco-Prussian war in 1870, and it was pointed out that it was not unnatural that the Geheime Feld Polizei (Secret Field Police) in 1914 should have continued the methods of the Feld Polizei of 1870. In 1914 German Defence Security Intelligence was dealt with by special sections in the German Admiralty (Admiralstab der Marine, Abteilung "G", i.e. Geheim or Secret Section) and by the Generalstab Abteilung III.B. of the German General Staff. Abteilung III.B. worked in close co-operation with the seven Central Police Offices in the States or Provinces of Imperial Germany while the Admiralty section was almost exclusively concerned with the Central Police Office at Hamburg. During the course of the war the Secret Police organisation was enlarged and developed both in Germany and in occupied territories where the term "Sicherheits Polizei" (Security Police) came into prominence. Apparently in the absence of definite information the writers of the M.I.5. book were compelled to a conjectural description of the German organisation in certain respects, but one fact which stands out is that there was some degree of co-ordination between the Nachrichten or Intelligence organisations on the one hand and the Abwehr or Security branches on the other, and again between the Abwehr branches and the Geheime Feld Polizei and the other branches of the German Police; and that these organisations and the measures for their co-ordination were enlarged and developed as the war went on. This is of interest in view of developments, similar in principle but not analogous in detail, under the very different internal conditions in the Nazi State of the second War.

The reason for examining the part played by the German police and the German Security Services is ascribed in the M.I.5. report at that time to the fact that the German General Staff and German military and other writers were almost unanimous in declaring that the German defeat had not originated from any failure of the German army. On the contrary they had urged that it was due to Allied propaganda in Germany, to the acceptance of specious promises and to the growth of Allied influences and that the nation, not the army, the civilian, not the soldier, was to blame. It was therefore the object of German military thinkers to study measures for the control of the civil population in war. In future political, economic and financial security were to receive as much attention as had formerly been accorded to the purely military problem.

This is a point of first importance in view of the answer given to such problems by the establishment of the Nazi Party with its methods of control over the Home front in Germany through the Party organisation and the Gestapo and the whole apparatus of the Reichsicherheitshauptamt in the second World War. It is also worth noting that it was stated at this time, i.e. in 1921, that the German General Staff held the view during the war that the morale of the nation was being undermined by the Social Democratic Party supported by Jewish free-thinking elements; that there were many traitors among the people and the Reichstag; and that the great resources of the Allied Powers were concentrated against the political and social weaknesses of Germany which were played upon by Allied propaganda. This propaganda, it was maintained, was conducted regardless of expense and stopped at nothing to corrupt German national feeling. It was therefore felt that the German General Staff must take action to counteract such tendencies as a measure of security, and responsibility for this was undertaken by Ludendorf who utilised the services of Colonel Nicolai and Abwehrabteilung III by making him responsible for censorship and other internal security measures.

In their general conclusions, at the end of their report, the M.I.5. officers quoted Nicolai at length in his own defence. Among other things he said "the General Staff is not free from blame that the tasks which fell to the lot of Abteilung III.B. caught the latter unprepared and were then taken in hand with insufficient knowledge. The General Staff had studied war from the military standpoint alone. The kindred spheres, more especially war economics and the direction of public opinion had obtained no attention; no provision had consequently been made to set up the necessary machinery...........There was but one authority from which action was expected (by public opinion and the authorities alike) and that was the Chief of the General Staff of the Field Army." In this connection Ludendorf is quoted as saying that it was the deep feeling of responsibility which impelled the General Staff to constructive labours.

Both the German General Staff and the M.I.5. officers reporting on the situation appear to have come to the conclusion that the employment by the General Staff of their security and police machinery was associated with the collapse of German morale. While the German General Staff attributed the failure to insufficient organisation and inadequate co-ordination of the resources of the nation as a whole, the M.I.5. officers appear to have formed the opinion that failure was, in part, to be attributed to the over-centralisation and over-militarised control and to draconian methods which provoked opposition and resentment among the German people. They mentioned that Ludendorf endorsed all Abteilung III.B.'s efforts.

For a detailed description of the work of Abteilung III.B., whose duties included those of obtaining secret intelligence as well as preventive or security work and relations with the "Foreign Armies" (Fremde Heere) and the political sections of the German General Staff, reference should be made to the M.I.5. report in question (The German Police System as applied to Military Security in War). The whole subject is of great intrinsic interest in view of its bearing on the subsequent developments in Nazi Germany and the reactions to those developments in this country. Among those reactions is the attitude of mind towards our own security problems as created by Nazi Germany both before and after the outbreak of war in 1939. This question will be the main subject in later chapters dealing with the work of M.I.5. or the Security Service, but attention may be drawn here to the fact that outstanding aspects of the Nazi regime have been, internally, its measures for stiffening German resistance and strengthening German morale through secret police methods; and externally, the use of propaganda in peace and in war to influence the morale and public opinion of this and other countries; and the development of pro-German feeling and the support of parties on the Nazi model such as Mosley's Fascists. These parties eventually formed an important element in the German Fifth Column in countries subjected to military attack, and their leaders became the notorious Quislings of occupied Europe.

These two books, therefore, furnish evidence of a dawning recognition on both sides of the concept of "total" war under modern conditions; and of very different reactions to it in England and Germany. In both countries the Intelligence Services realised that it affected them but in England the lessons learned were quickly forgotten.

Part 3: Developments in Germany 1918-1931

The M.I.5. Report discussed in the last Chapter failed to have the intended effect, and during the years following the war the Security Service in this country was reduced to a minimum. Sir Vernon Kell remained in charge, but his staff consisted of only a handful of officers.

In the years immediately following the war contact was maintained with the Intelligence Staff of the British Army of Occupation in the Rhineland. Information was received regarding the German General Staff's measures to maintain an Intelligence Service under the cover of commercial intelligence in which assistance was given by some of the leading German industrialists including Hugenberg, Thyssen, Stinnes and Voegler, who undertook to furnish part of the required funds. The fact that German heavy industry was under less direct Allied control than German official services offered favourable opportunities for this type of subterfuge; but a more important fact is that as the basis of Germany's war potential their heavy industry also offered the most suitable field for obtaining commercial intelligence bearing on the war potential of Germany's past and future enemies. It was reported that officers of Abteilung III.B., the Intelligence Section of the High command, mentioned above, were employed in an industrial intelligence service of this type known as the Deutsche Uberseedienst which was an officially recognised organisation with the ostensible purpose of acquiring commercial information to facilitate the German export trade. For some time the Uberseedienst carried on legitimate work, but by the end of 1921, according to reports received, this had given place to illicit activities organised by members of the German General Staff. The agents of the Uberseedienst were in many cases said to be unconscious that they were engaged in other than bona fide commercial intelligence, the type of information required from them being of an industrial nature; but it included those aspects of industry, a study of which facilitated an appreciation of the capacity and readiness of other countries to make war. The Uberseedienst was particularly interested in factories connected with the aircraft industry and those capable of tank production. Other similar organisations were known as the Ostdienst and the Wirtschaftsdienst. Allied to the latter was an organisation known as the Wirtschaftspolitische Gesellschaft which was conducted by a woman named Margarete Gaertner as an information office financed by Krupps. She carried on correspondence with various people in the United Kingdom and collected information for propaganda purposes, e.g. for propaganda against the Treaty of Versailles. Among the individuals connected with the Uberseedienst were Goering as their Air Representative and Freiherr Freytag von Loeringhoven who was later known as the head of Abwehrabteilung II., the Sabotage Department, in the Second World War. An office affiliated to the Uberseedienst was known as the Nuntia Bureau and it has been suggested that this afterwards formed the nucleus of the Secret Intelligence Department or Abwehrabteilung I.

Other related enquiries by M.I.5. dealt with the employment of German Consuls in this country for intelligence purposes and with the submissions of secret reports by German journalists which often dealt with matters of a political or strategical nature.

The problems as they presented themselves at this time were not easy because the field of commercial intelligence was a large one and the dividing line between open and legitimate work on the one hand and secret intelligence on the other was not always easy to distinguish especially where the same individuals were concerned in both. This is especially the case where officials such as consuls are concerned; and diplomatic privileges are a serious obstacle in the way of counter espionage enquiries.

Part 4: Communism and the USSR 1917-1931

(i) **General Introduction (1917-1945).**

From the time of the Russian Revolution in 1917 onwards it has been recognised that the fact that the Communist Party seized power in Russia in October of that year posed a problem for M.I.5. Since the establishment of the Comintern or Third (Communist) International in March 1919 in Moscow and of the Communist Party as a section of the Comintern in August 1920, the nature of this problem has varied and the extent to which it has been appreciated as a problem has varied even more widely. It is safe to say that the machinery in M.I.5. - or the Security Service - has never been adequate to cope with this problem in the sense of formulating a comprehensive appreciation of developments as they occurred; and that during the greater part of the time the material for an adequate understanding of it has been lacking.

Attempts have been made, however, to present the available material in regard to parts of the problem, if there has been no attempt to present it as a whole. The most important of these attempts are to be found in the following documents:-

> *Communism in Great Britain Today*, prepared by the Security Service in June 1932
>
> - vide Bibliography No.11.
>
> Communism - (General aspects)
>
> - vide Bibliography No.12.
>
> *Communism - (Organisation and working)*, prepared by Section V (Major Vivian) in April 1934 and December 1934, respectively, by collating material available in Section V and the Security Service
>
> - vide Bibliography No.13.
>
> Paper prepared in F Division early in 1943 for the Home Secretary to submit to the Cabinet
>
> - vide Bibliography No.16.
>
> *The Communist Party - its aims and organisation*, prepared in April 1945
> - vide Bibliography No.14.

There are also numerous papers dealing with detailed enquiries into specific cases or developments in regard to the organisational machinery of the Comintern, the National Communist Parties, their auxiliaries or subsidiaries and their agents.

From the Security Service point of view an essential fact about the Comintern and its subsidiary organisations is that the Communist Parties admittedly aimed at seizing power in their own countries by revolutionary methods. They professed to believe that the possessing classes would not yield power to the 'proletariat' without a violent struggle.

This position was, however, to some extent modified by Stalin in 1924 when he wrote in the *Foundations of Leninism*:-

> "Of course, in the remote future, if the proletariat is victorious in the most important Capitalist countries, and if the present Capitalist encirclement is replaced by a Socialist encirclement, a 'peaceful' path of development is quite possible for certain Capitalist countries, whose Capitalists, in view of the 'unfavourable' international situation, will consider it expedient 'voluntarily' to make substantial concessions to the proletariat. But this supposition applies only to a remote and possible future. With regard to the immediate future, there is no ground whatsoever for this supposition."

While this does not appear to exclude the use of violent revolution, it would seem to imply that the Communist Party might, in certain circumstances, accede to power by other means. Another fact which directly affects the Security Service and cannot be altogether disassociated from revolutionary aims is the employment by the Communist Party of conspiratorial methods for conducting their affairs. These methods include the use of codes, cyphers, secret inks, cover addresses, secret agents and the secret subsidising and secret direction by the Comintern of the national Communist Parties which are its sections in all or nearly all countries. These national Parties are the potential source of an almost unlimited supply of agents for the purposes of the Comintern or the Soviet Government.

There have been considerable differences of opinion in the offices directly concerned - the Foreign Office, S.I.S. and the Security Service - as to the significance of the Comintern and its secret conduct of affairs; and of the relations between the policy of the Comintern and the policy of the Government of the U.S.S.R. Thus, divergent views are, or have been, held on the question whether the Government of the U.S.S.R. did or did not abandon the policy of promoting world revolution either at the time of the dissolution of the Comintern or even before that date; whether the Comintern, being dependent financially on the Government of the U.S.S.R. was the latter's instrument; and whether the national Communist Parties in various countries are to be regarded as instruments of Russian policy or as instruments for the promotion of revolution in accordance with a policy centrally directed from Moscow by the Executive Committee of the Comintern.

In a paper prepared in the Foreign Office and considered by the J.I.C. in 1944, (J.I.C. (44) 105 (0) (FINAL) dated 20th March, 1944) dealing with the probable impact on British strategic needs of Russian policy after the war, it was suggested that after Stalin's victory over Trotsky the doctrine of world revolution was dropped and Soviet interference in the affairs of other countries was directed to subserving the Soviet Union's own national ends by weakening the internal position in potentially hostile countries. A paper prepared in Section IX of S.I.S. by way of comment on this thesis suggested caution in accepting the statement that the aim of spreading Bolshevism or of fomenting world revolution for its own sake had been abandoned and in accepting the implication that this view could form a basis of British policy. It maintained that Russian policy could not entirely cut itself off from the roots of its recent past; that these roots were embedded in a twofold policy - the open policy of Stalin, Litvinov or Molotov in their conduct of foreign affairs and the second or underground policy which in the past had been associated with the machinery of the Comintern. It also maintained that there were reasons for thinking that machinery for giving direction to the activities of the national Communist Parties of other countries was still in existence after the dissolution of the Comintern; and that it would be an advantage in formulating policy to have the fullest possible information about the implications of this second Russian policy, its motives and the realities behind it.

These suggestions by Section IX were based on an examination of material available in the Security Service and in S.I.S. in regard to the secret workings of the Comintern and of the C.P.G.B.; in particular on the evidence relating to the adopting of the policy of "revolutionary defeatism" by the C.P.G.B. in the early stages of the second World War (prior to the German attack on Russia); the Communist agitation for the premature development of a "Second Front"; and the general background of information obtained by secret means regarding the manner in which the attitude of the C.P.G.B. in these matters had been directed from Russia. These representations led to a modification of the J.I.C. paper quoted above in the direction of stating that future relations between the Soviet authorities and Communist organisations in other countries required attention; that such organisations were potential instruments of Soviet policy and felt a loyalty to the Soviet Government often over-riding that owed to their own country: a dangerous tendency which had been demonstrated by the Communist Parties in Great Britain and France in the early stages of the war. It was also stated that there was no reason to suppose that the dissolution of the Comintern had destroyed the links between the Soviet authorities and Communist Parties abroad, but the view was maintained that these Parties would be used by the Soviet as a means of supporting its policy at any given moment and not as a means of bringing about world revolution as an end desirable in itself.

It is therefore an unresolved question whether British policy is to be based on the view expressed in the last sentence or whether there is evidence to determine the exact nature of the long-term policy of the Government of the U.S.S.R. in regard to the question of world revolution or the sovietisation of other countries. The evidence available to the Security Service from secret sources does not provide a clear and conclusive answer, but there is evidence which places it beyond doubt that the C.P.G.B. has not abandoned its policy of bringing about a social revolution in this country on Marxist lines and by the methods employed by the Communist Party, for instance, in Russia.

It is important - even if there is no reason to believe that the C.P.G.B. is in a position to bring about a revolutionary situation and to take advantage of difficulties and unrest which may arise so as to create such a situation in the foreseeable future - to understand the aims and policy of that Party and the methods employed in Russia and other countries; and to provide for adequate appreciations of the situation as it develops from time to time.

To facilitate a proper understanding of this matter it is desirable to provide for the collation of the material available - from open and secret sources - but adequate material is not on record for the purpose and collation has not been done on a suitable scale. The study of the subject has been altogether inadequate from the beginning and on account of the paucity of the collated material the history of the manner in which the Security Service has dealt with the problem cannot be written on comprehensive lines on the basis of the largely uncollated material in an immense number of files spreading over a quarter of a century. Apart from the larger questions of policy there are important matters of detail in regard to which some information has been received, but no satisfactory account has been put on record. Instances are the story of the International Brigade which fought in the Civil War in Spain and the subsequent activities of its members, many of whom are known to have played an active part in Communist intrigues; the schools in Russia at which British, among other Communists, have been trained in "illegal" activities; and the financing of foreign Communist Parties by secret means as disclosed by the interception of Comintern wireless messages in the middle of the nineteen-thirties.

Failure to collate the information in such cases and failure to follow it up often go hand in hand; and the reason for this failure is to be found in insufficient staff and in difficulties created by lack of funds. Responsibility for the subject as a whole was divided between three Organisations until 1931 and after that it was divided between two. The absence of centralised control inevitably tends towards divided efforts and incompleteness in results. A staff of two officers in Section V of S.I.S. and a number varying between two and six in the Security Service to cover the whole ground over a long period of years (between 1920 and 1940) was obviously insufficient. Moreover, the Section V officers were also responsible for dealing with every other aspect of counter espionage vis-a-vis Germany and all other countries. In the light of these facts both the quantity and quality of the work done can only be regarded as remarkable.

Some of the major difficulties must be borne in mind. In the first place it is always difficult to form an appreciation of the events of current affairs before they can be seen in historical perspective and in the light of the records and reports of the principal actors. It would have been unusually difficult for S.I.S. to supply an account of the inner history of the Russian Revolution at the time or shortly after it happened. In the second place there is the difficulty of collating the open material about such a large subject as the Comintern and its relations with the Government of the U.S.S.R. with information obtained from secret sources; and framing an appreciation of the bearing of both types of intelligence on the security of this country. In the early stages none of the three Offices dealing with the subject - S.I.S., M.I.5. or the special staff in Scotland Yard - had any clear comprehensive mandates. Moreover, the Foreign Office was only indirectly interested, if at all, in developments in the C.P.G.B. and the Home Office had no concern with the ramifications of the Comintern throughout the world; yet it is only by putting the whole in the perspective furnished by an appreciation of Russian policy that it is possible to arrive at an understanding of all the issues involved.

It is because it is a matter which concerns the interference in the internal affairs of this country by agents of an international organisation under the influence and domination of the ruling class - the Communist Party in Russia - that it transcends the scope of any one Government Department. It is a matter touching on sovereignty and therefore one which concerns the Prime Minister when viewed in broad perspective; but in the main it comes before the Security Service in the course of day-to-day working as a matter of minor detail. The detail is often dull and must be expected to remain so as long as the C.P.G.B. remains the small and almost insignificant force which it has hitherto represented in the political arena; but even so it is impossible to ignore its potential importance as a factor making for disintegration in the life of this country.

(ii) The Russian Revolution of 1917.

The Russian Revolution in 1917 had an almost immediate impact on M.I.5. A section of G Branch was given the duty of undertaking enquiries regarding Russian, Finnish, Polish and Czechoslovakian officers and the investigation of "activities in connection with Bolshevism, strikes and Pacifism in the U.K." It also investigated the bona fides of persons of the above nationalities entering or leaving the country and of all persons travelling to or from Russia. There does not, however, appear to have been any attempt to assess the significance of the Revolution or to provide for an appreciation of its probable reactions in this and other countries.

Without an adequate understanding of the Revolution and the Communist Party which made it in order to seize power, of the reactions in other countries and of the machinery of the Party in Russia (the Comintern or Third International) which was employed with the deliberate intention of utilising the circumstances of those reactions to promote revolution in other countries, it is impossible to form an appreciation of the development of the C.P.G.B. and the events and personalities connected with it. This is not the place to attempt a full and comprehensive account and it is not possible to do more than suggest some of the outstanding features of this whole subject which will serve to illustrate the problem presented to the Security Service by the C.P.G.B. and its relations with the Comintern and the Government of the U.S.S.R. under the dictatorship of the Communist Party of Russia.

The Revolution of February-March 1917 which led to the overthrow of the Czarist regime was followed in October of the same year by a more decisive revolutionary struggle which brought the Communist Party to power.

There are three important accounts of the events of the Revolution written by, or authorised by, three of the principal participants, Kerensky, Trotsky and the Communist Party of the Soviet Union. No critical analysis of these different accounts is available and each of them is necessarily written from a more or less biased point of view. *The History of the Communist Party of the Soviet Union (Bolsheviks)* printed in Moscow in 1941, edited by a Commission of the C.P.S.U.(B) and authorised by the Central Committee of the Party in 1938, may be presumed to have Stalin's general approval.

The system of Soviets (one account of this system is given in Chapters II to V of *Soviet Communism* by Sydney and Beatrice Webb) i.e. councils, was developed after the February Revolution. At that time the Soviets consisted of members of various Left

Wing Parties including the Socialists and Communists, the latter often being in a minority. The second, or October Revolution, gave the Communist Party control of the Soviets and by means of an armed insurrection of soldiers and workers brought the Soviets to power throughout Russia. A point deserving attention in this connection is that before the Revolution of 1917 the Marxists of all countries assumed that the parliamentary democratic republic was the most suitable form of political organisation for their purposes but, as a result of the Russian Revolution of 1905 and more especially the Revolution of February 1917, Lenin arrived at the conclusion that the best political form for the dictatorship of the proletariat was not a parliamentary democratic republic but a republic of soviets. The question is discussed at length in the conclusion of *The History of the Communist Party of the Soviet Union (Bolsheviks)* where it is emphasised that Lenin did not blindly follow Marxist theories or accept them as dogmas, but developed the Marxist theory in the light of experience so as to shape policy and action in accordance with the facts of a given situation. (This point was also made by Lenin when he wrote:-

"Let us try to replace sophistry (i.e. the method of clinging to the outward similarity of cases without a connection between the events) by dialectics (i.e. the method of studying all the concrete circumstances of an event, and its development)."

quoted on Page 115, Chapter IV of *The Betrayal of the Left* (vide Bibliography No. 7).

From the various accounts it is clear that the Russian Communists attached great importance to the fact that in 1916 and 1917 they, in opposition to the "Menshevik and Social Revolutionary policy of defending the bourgeois fatherland" advanced the policy of "the defeat of one's own Government in the imperialist war". This meant in effect open and underground activity which aimed at disintegrating the governmental machine of Russia. It was intended or assumed that the workers of other countries should simultaneously adopt the same policy and the Communists attacked the members of the Second or Socialist International because so far from doing so they had supported their own Governments, e.g. in the cases of Great Britain, France and Germany. (vide *Theory and tactics of the Bolshevik Party on the questions of War, Peace and Revolution* - Page 167 of *The History of the Communist Party of the Soviet Union (Bolsheviks)* - Bibliography No. 15).

These two points - the substitution of governmental forms based on Councils or Soviets for parliamentary institutions and the adoption of measures aimed at the disintegration of the governmental machinery of their own country in the event of an "imperialist" war, i.e. in effect a war conducted by any State under a non-Communist regime - are worth bearing in mind as throwing light on more recent developments.

According to Trotsky the Revolution of February 1917 came about "spontaneously" as the result of developments in a revolutionary situation. The stresses and strains on the Russian administrative machinery created by the war had brought to a head a crisis arising from the development in Russia of conditions which were part of the economic changes associated with the "Industrial Revolution" in the West. Trotsky shows, however, that the Second or October Revolution was the result of a plan deliberately worked out by the Bolsheviks to enable them to seize power and to replace Kerensky's Government. This was done in accordance with a general theory of revolution which may be roughly explained by saying that when a revolutionary situation arises it can be brought to a head by an armed insurrection; the armed insurrection being planned as a result of conspiracy. The conspiracy in this case was worked out by the leaders of the Communist Party of Russia who had to judge the decisive moment for insurrection. According to Trotsky the insurrection would have failed if it had been launched a few months earlier or later; the decisive moment probably fell within a period of three or four months. Lenin's leitmotiv in those days was: "The success of the Russian and world revolution depends on a two or three days' struggle". Effect was given to the conspiracy by winning over a sufficient proportion of the Russian regiments and the Russian Navy, influenced as they then were by the disastrous conditions of the Russian campaigns of 1916-1917; and a large proportion of the workers in factories in St. Petersburg, a number of the latter being armed and trained under the direction of the Communist Party and formed into the Red Guard.

His theory of revolution is explained by Trotsky in his *History of the Russian Revolution* - especially in the Chapters dealing with the Military Revolutionary Committee; Lenin's Summons to Insurrection; the Art of Insurrection; the Conquest of the Capital; the Capture of the Winter Palace; and the October Insurrection - where he also shows how it was put into practice so as to secure decisive results. According to him the Central Committee of the Communist Party decided on beginning the insurrection on or about the 10th October and a turning point was Lenin's resolution summoning "all organisations and all workers and soldiers to an all-sided and most vigorous preparation of armed insurrection", i.e. against Kerensky's Government, which was itself the product of the February Revolution. Trotsky maintained that the means by which the proletariat could overthrow the old power and replace it was the Soviets, the Soviets being organs to prepare the masses for insurrection, to implement the insurrection and, after victory, to be the organs of Government. The overthrow of the Government could only be brought about if the proletariat felt above it a farsighted, firm and confident leadership. This leadership was supplied by the tightly welded Communist Party as a vanguard of the class. In order to achieve success it was necessary - as in a military campaign - to have at the decisive moment, at the decisive point, an overwhelming superiority of force. This decisive political force in the October Revolution was found in the workers of Petrograd; and Trotsky, who organised the military side of the Revolution and afterwards organised the Red Army, argued that those who maintained that the Bolshevist Revolution was a "soldiers movement" were wrong. He held that "at the decisive moment the leadership of the soldiers was in the hands of the workers". At the same time, the first task of every insurrection was to bring the troops over to its side. The chief means of accomplishing this was the general strike, mass processions, street encounters and battles at the barricades. It was, he said, impossible to understand the mechanics of the October Revolution without realising that the most important task of the insurrection, that of winning over the garrison of the capital, had been accomplished in Petrograd before the beginning of the armed struggle. In the final stage the Bolshevik Party led the way in a military situation which was decided by rifles, bayonets and machine-guns.

The decisive force, the workers' army of Petrograd (the Red Guard) numbered less than 40,000 bayonets but they carried with them the troops and the sailors of the Russian fleet.

After the success of the insurrection Lenin outlined the programme of the Revolution: to break up the old Government apparatus; to create a system of administration through the soviets; to take measures for the immediate cessation of war relying upon revolutionary movements in other countries; to abolish landlords' property rights and thus win the confidence of the peasants; to establish workers' control over production. "The Third Russian Revolution" he said "must in the end lead to the victory of socialism."

Before Trotsky's quarrel with Stalin and the dominant clique in the ruling Communist Party - in which quarrel personal rivalry and doctrinal differences both probably played a part - Stalin had said that Trotsky, the President of the Petrograd Soviet, had conducted all the work of practical organisation of the insurrection; and that the Party owed to him principally and first of all the swift passing of the garrison to the side of the Soviet and the bold execution of the work of the Military Revolutionary Committee.

The account authorised by the Central Committee of the C.P.S.U. (B) of the events of the October insurrection - which cannot but have had Stalin's general approval - states that Lenin arrived secretly in Petrograd from Finland on October 7th (Kerensky's account implies that Lenin's arrival was due to the failure of his police to detect his disguise at the frontier and to arrest him as a measure designed to check the insurrection which the Government knew was being planned). The Central Committee goes on to describe its own decisive meeting on October 10th when Lenin in a resolution announced that the time for an armed insurrection was fully ripe. It minimised the part played by Trotsky and says that although he did not vote against the resolution, he moved an amendment which would have reduced the chances of the uprising to naught. The Bolsheviks, however, defeated the attempts of Trotsky and other capitulators within the Party to deflect it from the path of socialist revolution. The account concludes:-

> "Headed by the Bolshevik Party, the working class, in alliance with the poor peasants and with the support of the soldiers and sailors, overthrew the power of the bourgeoisie, established the power of the Soviets, set up a new type of State - a Socialist Soviet State - abolished the landlords' ownership of land, turned over the land to the peasants for their use, nationalised all the land in the country, expropriated the capitalists, achieved the withdrawal of Russia from the war and obtained peace, that is, obtained a much-needed respite, and thus created the conditions for the development of Socialist construction.
>
> The October Socialist Revolution smashed capitalism, deprived the bourgeoisie of the means of production and converted the mills, factories, land, railways and banks into the property of the whole people, into public property.

It established the dictatorship of the proletariat and turned over the government of the vast country to the working class, thus making it the ruling class.

The October Socialist Revolution thereby ushered in a new era in the history of mankind - the era of proletarian revolutions."

It will be obvious that if obscurity is to be avoided two points must be clarified as a means to understanding what lies behind this Communist phraseology. These points are the significance of the Soviet and the part it plays in the Socialist Soviet State; and the facts underlying the so-called dictatorship of the proletariat and the position of the "Bolshevik Party as the vanguard of the working-class".

In October 1917 Lenin referred to the Soviet as a step forward in the development of democracy. For this reason and because the same principle still holds good it may be worth while to examine the system, an account of which is given in chapters II to V of "Soviet Communism" by Sidney and Beatrice Webb. (vide Bibliography No. 53). Very briefly the system is based on village councils and similar bodies in the smallest administrative areas in the cities and towns. These Soviets appoint their delegates to the Soviets of larger areas, thus forming the base of a pyramid at the apex of which is the supreme Soviet of the U.S.S.R. Intermediate bodies are the district municipal and provincial Soviets and those of the constituent republics. This system is described as democratic, but it is obvious that it has not led to any alternative to the Communist Party at the top; and the dictatorship of the proletariat in effect means the dictatorship of the leaders of the Communist or Bolshevik Party. One aspect of the system which is relevant to this position is that described as "democratic centralism" by which the members of any Soviet body have the right to express their opinions on any subject within the competence of the body in question and to submit their proposals to higher authority. Once higher authority has decided the question, Party discipline requires that it shall be unquestionably accepted by those below. The local Soviets are only competent to deal with local affairs; and matters affecting foreign policy, peace or war, or internal sovereignty must necessarily be the preserve of those in supreme control of the Union of Socialist Soviet Republics.

(iii) The foundation of the Comintern and its early stages.

When the Revolution had been successfully accomplished in Russia, Communists generally expected that similar proletarian revolutions would occur in a number of other countries and that eventually - within a very short period - the whole world would be similarly affected. It was a cardinal doctrine that capitalism involving "the division of labour" on a world-wide basis would be replaced by a socialist system also involving "the division of labour" on a world-wide and international basis. It was held that the world could not be partly capitalist and partly socialist and that the socialist system must spread until it became universal.

As a corollary Russia could not arrive at socialism independently, but once having opened an era of social transformation she could supply the impetus to a socialist development in the more advanced countries of Europe and thus arrive at a more complete stage of socialism in their wake. This is the substance of the theory of "permanent revolution" which Trotsky claimed to have evolved even before the Revolution of 1905, as an original theory, according to which the Revolution which brought the "bourgeoisie", i.e. the middle classes into power would go directly over into a socialist revolution and prove the first of a series of national revolutions (vide Page 1259, Appendix III of Trotsky's "History of the Russian Revolution"). It was also held that the "bourgeoisie" in general would put up a fierce resistance to the proletarian revolution which could only succeed through the use of force, that is to say the existing possessors of property and power would resist the attempt of the working-class led by the Communist Party to seize power on the lines of the Russian Revolution.

In order to promote the development of revolution in other countries the Comintern or Third Communist International was established in Moscow in March 1919 as a "General Staff of World Revolution" (vide Page 409 of the Webbs' "Communism") and its first Congress was held in that month. The Second Congress held in Moscow in July - August 1920 was of greater importance as laying the foundations of subsequent developments and Lenin himself expounded to this Congress the indispensable conditions on which alone membership could be allowed. These were embodied in the statutes of the Communist International which laid down, inter alia, that the World Congress should elect an Executive Committee (The E.C.C.I.) to serve as the leading organ of the Communist International in the interval between World Congresses; that the bulk of the work and the greatest responsibility should lie with the Party in that country where the E.C.C.I. finds its residence; that the Party of the country in question should send to the E.C.C.I. not less than five members with a decisive vote and that ten or twelve of the largest other Communist Parties should send one each while the remaining Communist Parties and Organisations should enjoy the right of sending only one representative each with a consultative but not a decisive vote. The Communist International was to be constituted by the Communist Parties of all countries, each of which was a "section" of the Comintern. Thus the C.P.G.B., when formed in August 1920, constituted one "section". All the decisions of the Communist International as well as those of its Executive Committee were made binding upon all Parties belonging to it and every Party's programme was to be sanctioned by the Comintern or the E.C.C.I. It was also laid down that the general state of things in Europe and America made it necessary for the Communists of the whole world to form "illegal" organisations along with those existing "legally"; and that these should be under the control of the E.C.C.I. (The word "illegal" as used by the Communist does not necessarily always mean something contrary to the law of the country in question but it always implies the use of secret and conspiratorial methods). The general object in view was to bring about socialism and the "classless society" and to employ the method of a general strike conjointly with armed insurrection against the State power of the "bourgeoisie". An essential condition was intensified revolutionary work in the army and navy. This condition was afterwards expressly constituted or restated at the Sixth World Congress in 1928 but was implicit throughout in the light of what happened in Petrograd in 1917.

These briefly, are the facts underlying the problem with which Communism and the U.S.S.R. confronted the Security Service in this country after the Revolution and after the foundation of the Comintern. (The sources used here were, of course, not then available and many of the facts disclosed by the protagonists could not have been known at the time; but it is possible that a better general understanding of the nature of the Russian Revolution and of subsequent developments, including the project for sponsoring an early development of revolutionary situations in other countries through the Comintern would have furnished grounds for developing counter-measures on a more adequate basis.)

(iv) Counter Measures

Counter-measures to obtain intelligence to meet the situation indicated above could not but suffer to some extent in view of the fact that responsibility was divided between M.I.1.C. or S.I.S., M.I.5. or the Security Service, and Scotland House. In 1919 there was even a proposal to transfer the Bolshevist Section from M.I.5. to Scotland House, but effect was not given to this; and in the subsequent years M.I.5. was responsible for matters connected with Communism in the Armed Forces as well as for counter-espionage measures, while the Communist movement outside the Armed Forces was the responsibility of Scotland House until 1931.

As the staff in Scotland House which dealt with Communism in this country was afterwards (in 1931) incorporated in the Security Service and its records were simultaneously amalgamated with those in this office, a short reference to some of the outstanding matters dealt with by them will serve to explain the antecedents of the Security Service as it developed after 1931 with enlarged functions.

The restricted scope of M.I.5. while Communism in the Armed Forces was separated from a study of the subject as a whole was an obvious mistake, especially as the events of the Russian Revolution, if properly understood, had demonstrated the important part played by agitators who subverted the troops.

In May 1919 Sir Basil Thomson established a "Directorate of Intelligence" at Scotland Yard, apparently with the intention that it should form a combined military, naval, air and civil intelligence organisation. This obviously would have encroached on the functions of M.I.5. and it did not develop on these larger lines; but under his personal direction settled down to obtain intelligence about Communism, both at home and abroad. It received reports from S.I.S., and by arrangement with them occasionally sent agents abroad. One important agent travelled between New York, Paris and Amsterdam and made contact with revolutionaries in those cities and with the embryonic revolutionary movements which crystallised in 1920 in the form of the Communist Party of Great Britain. Another agent visited Hungary and reported to Sir Basil Thomson on the Hungarian revolution.

In the years immediately after the war, the Russian Communist leaders continued to expect with apparent confidence the development of a revolutionary situation in other countries; and it was not until about 1923-1924 that this idea appears to have lost ground in the dominant circles in the U.S.S.R. It was doubtless in this connection that Leo Kamaneff, one of the inner circle of the Bolshevist Party who played a leading part in the Russian Revolution, visited this country and in conjunction with Alexander Purcell attempted to establish Councils of Action. The nature of his activities was disclosed by B.J.s and he was subsequently expelled. Leonid Krassin also arrived in 1920 as the official Soviet Envoy at the head of the Russian Trade Delegation. About the same time the Finnish Comintern agent Eriski Weltheim arrived here clandestinely and attempted to form a Red Army in collaboration with Cecil Lestrange Malone. The latter was prosecuted and convicted. Russian B.J.s also disclosed that Soviet money was furnished to start the "Daily Herald" in the early 1920s. This subject was dealt with by the Government in the form of a White Paper.

Again in the early 1920s J.T. Walton Newbold, the first British Communist M.P., established the Minority Trade Union Movement with which "Chinese" Borodin was also concerned.

The general election of 1924 is famous for the affair of the Zinoviev letter which, though possibly a forgery, contained nothing that had not been seen in intercepted correspondence as going from the Berlin Bureau of the Comintern to the C.P.G.B. or the National Minority Movement. The evidence showed that the Communist Party was devoting a considerable part of its effort to propaganda in H.M. Forces. Party members were instructed to pay particular attention to serving soldiers and sailors and make the most of any grievances. Communist pamphlets were to be distributed by every available means.

The premises of the C.P.G.B. were searched on 14.10.25. and twelve of its most prominent members were prosecuted. During the miners' strike in the same year, the sum of over £2,000,000 was presented to the British miners under the guise of a spontaneous gift from the Russian miners, but evidence from B.J.s disclosed that the transfer of the money was effected by the Soviet Government. About this time Lord Curzon started his famous series of notes making disclosures about Soviet intrigues all over the world. An instance was a report of a transfer of notes found on a Sikh agitator on the Indian frontier which were subsequently traced to a joint account in the names of Krassin and Nickoli Klishko, Secretary of the Russian Trade Delegation in London.

The General Strike occurred in 1926. Although it had an economic basis, an important part in its development was played by penetration from below through the Minority Movement, and from above through the Anglo-Russian Trade Union Unity Committee.

In the meanwhile, early repercussions of the Russian Revolution had been the Spartacus struggles in Germany and of the short-lived Bela Kun regime in Hungary in 1919. Revolt in Italy had followed in 1920, and in 1923 Borodin was sent to China to reorganise the Kuo Min Tang on a revolutionary basis. The British Government recognised the Soviet Government in February 1924. The diplomatic and trade organisations subsequently set up in this country by the U.S.S.R. were used for conveying to the British Communist Party funds and instructions for subversive activities.

In June 1926 the British Government's protest at the subsidy sent from Russia to British strikers was met by the retort that the Soviet Government could not prevent the Trade Unions of the U.S.S.R. from aiding Trade Unionists in other countries.

In May 1927 the premises of the Russian Trade Delegation were searched (the Arcos raid) under the following circumstances.

An employee of the Trade Delegation who had been dismissed produced before our authorities a copy of a photostat of a pamphlet entitled "Signal Training, Volume 3, Pamphlet No.11" which, he alleged, had been made in January of that year under the direction of a Mr. Dudkin, one of the Russian managers of Arcos. The informant stated that he had been able to make and obtain possession of an extra copy of the photostat which he retained. The document was a military document which had been improperly obtained. It therefore furnished prima facie evidence that Mr. Dudkin, a manager of Arcos, was engaged in espionage and was using the premises and staff for the purpose. The results were not as conclusive as had been hoped owing to the decision of the authorities not to allow the search of other addresses of possibly greater significance. It was established, however, that a regular courier from the Soviet Embassy to the Trade Delegation brought correspondence which was subsequently distributed through the agency of the cypher clerks, and that the Trade Delegation was being used for the furtherance of Communism. Evidence was also obtained prior to the General Strike that there had been an active Communist Party cell which was comprised of Party members of all Soviet institutions in this country. This cell was in liaison with the C.P.G.B. and it was intended that it should take charge of events if a revolutionary situation developed in this country. These isolated cases are to be regarded as slight indications of the general plan to engineer revolution in this and other countries.

As mentioned above, revolutionary work in the Army and Navy was regarded as an essential condition for development of such plans. From 1919 onwards the Security Service received information which showed that attempts to cause disaffection in the Armed Forces in this country were being made. The circumstances left no room for doubt that these efforts were being instigated and directed from Moscow. A section was accordingly created in B. Division to deal with the problem and during the next twenty years it was responsible for countering this aspect of the work of the C.P.G.B. By 1926 suitable evidence had been accumulated to show that a special underground organisation of the Party was charged with the duty of making contact with members of the Forces in order to effect this type of disintegration work. One of the methods adopted was a campaign for the distribution of seditious leaflets which were secretly printed and distributed to members of the Armed Forces.

In order to meet this situation a system was developed under which the Security Service operated in close collaboration with the Staff of the three Services. Steps were taken to remove from the Forces soldiers, sailors and airmen who had come under the influence of Communist propaganda, when it was considered by the authorities that they were engaging in activities which were a danger to morale and discipline. In future cases prosecutions were launched under the Incitement to Mutiny Act of 1797.

(v) Developments in Russia: a change of policy.

After the General Strike in 1926, or perhaps earlier, the fact that Western Europe was not ripe for an early revolution must have been recognised by the Communist leaders in Russia, but it is not easy to trace the developments or to say exactly when this fact was recognised. The point appears to be obscured by the disagreements among these leaders on the subject of practical measures for meeting the economic difficulties of the U.S.S.R. at this period. These disagreements concerned economic policy within the U.S.S.R., questions of industrialisation and of the collectivisation of agriculture as well as the major question whether socialism could, or should be, developed in one country. This last question of doctrine centred round Trotsky's views on the subject of permanent or continuous revolution, according to which, the victory of socialism could not come through the development of socialism in one country - the U.S.S.R. According to the "History of the Communist Party of the Soviet Union", the Fourteenth Party Conference in April 1925 condemned the Trotsky theory and affirmed the Party line of working for the victory of socialism in the U.S.S.R. The opposition continued, however, and it was not until the Fifteenth Congress in October 1927 that over 700,000 Party members voted for the policy of the Central Committee, i.e. Stalin, and 4,000 for those of Trotsky and Zinoviev. The two oppositionist leaders were then expelled from the Party and Stalin and the Central Committee were left free to adopt their policy which involved the establishment of relations, both economic and political, with the outside world and - apparently - the abandonment of the hope of an early revolution in other countries. Again, according to the "History" (vide Chapter 10, Page 275, ibid) the victory of the proletarian revolution in the capitalist countries was still in the Party programme as a matter of vital concern to the working people of the U.S.S.R. One reason for this appears to have been the 'realist' view that there was a continued danger of intervention so long as the "capitalist encirclement continued to exist". This was the official Stalinist view as opposed to theory regarding the economic difficulties in the way of the establishment of socialism unless it was on a universal basis.

While the open policy of the Government of the U.S.S.R. changed course accordingly - the acceptance of the Kellogg Pact which condemned war as an instrument for settling international disputes is a landmark - the second or underground policy - conducted through the medium of the Comintern - continued to pursue the same general objective. The Comintern continued to be for its sections in other countries the symbol of the professed intention to work for an ultimate revolution. At the same time it was an instrument of policy used in the interests of Russian security against the apprehended intervention of capitalist Powers.

(vi) The development of the Comintern machinery.

The machinery of the Comintern was developed gradually during this period. An important development was the establishment of the Western European Bureau in 1925; and Balkan, Far Eastern, and South and Caribbean American Bureaux were also established. These Bureaux acted as relay stations and transmitted instructions received from the praesidium of the E.C.C.I. and other parts of the Comintern organisation to the national sections or other groups. The official reason for this was to provide for closer connection with the individual sections and for better guidance of their work, but in Colonel Vivian's "Communism" (Bibliography No. 13) on Page 16 it is suggested that it was mainly dictated by diplomatic expediency in that it served to conceal the responsibility of bodies situated in Moscow and organically connected with the Soviet Government for activities involving interference with the domestic affairs of countries with which the Government of the U.S.S.R. might be on terms of bon voisinage. Other developments in connection with the Trades Unions, the Profintern, the 'United Front' organisations and Comintern finances are described in detail in Colonel Vivian's book.

(vii) Soviet Espionage.

From an early date it became apparent that the C.P.G.B. and other Communist organisations in this country, in addition to the general objective of promoting the development of a situation favourable to revolution and such still-born and even fantastic projects as the establishment of Councils of Action and a Red Army, furnished the Soviets with opportunities for developing espionage organisations. This was a new phenomenon and something entirely different from the espionage systems of countries like Imperial Germany or Czarist Russia. At the same time, Soviet espionage organisations were established which had no connection with the Communist Party and it is reported to have been a rule that any Communist who engaged in espionage on behalf of the Soviet authorities took steps to dissociate himself openly from all the open activities of the Party.

From 1921 to 1929 there was a secret organisation under the direction of Jakob Kirchenstein, an American citizen of Lettish origin who worked in close association with Peter and Tom Miller, two of the cypher clerks at the Russian Trade Delegation in London. He was, however, also in close touch with certain members of the old Shop Stewards' Movement including J.T. Murphy, Jack Tanner - later head of the A.E.U. - and Dick and Charles Beech of the Seamen's Union. He was in charge of a clandestine courier service for the purpose of transmitting secret correspondence, documents and funds dealing with both political and espionage matters.

William Norman Ewer, a British subject, at one time diplomatic correspondent of the "Daily Herald", was employed in espionage on behalf of the Soviets from 1919-1929. It was not until 1924 that he came to the notice of the Security Service through an advertisement in the "Daily Herald" which read "A Labour Group carrying out investigations would be glad to receive information and details from anyone who has ever had any association with or been brought into touch with any Secret Service Departments or operation". An agent of the Security Service was instructed to answer the advertisement and eventually established contact which was of short duration as Ewer became suspicious, but not before the main object had been achieved and many of the people involved had been identified.

The success in securing this identification was due to the skilful combination of shadowing by the outside staff of the Office and prompt application to the problem of the content of intelligence by the section concerned. When the M.I.5. agent made contact with persons connected with the advertisement it was expected that the M.I.5. agent would be shadowed and arrangements were made for the shadower to be followed. Eventually, as a result of this following of the shadowers, the individuals connected with the advertisement, a man and a woman, were observed to enter the Soviet Headquarters in London at Chesham House. One of them was subsequently followed from Chesham House to a post office in the Strand where she was seen to transact some business over the counter. A description of the post office girl concerned and the exact time of the transaction were telephoned to M.I.5. by the shadower who followed the woman to the address of the Federated Press of America where she disappeared. The post office girl was questioned before she had time to forget the details and it was found that the woman who had been followed from Chesham House to the Federated Press of America had paid a telephone account on behalf of the F.P.A. The fact gave sufficient ground for the imposition of a Home Office Warrant and led to the uncovering of Ewer's espionage organisation.

Under cover of the Offices of the Federated Press of America, copies of confidential despatches from French Ministers in various capitals addressed to the French Foreign Office were sent to Ewer by George Slocombe, at that time foreign correspondent of the "Daily Herald" in Paris. Enquiries showed that Rakovsky of the Soviet Legation in London financed Ewer's organisation. It was also disclosed - in 1929 after five years' enquiry and observation - that Ewer and his associates were in receipt of information from two officials in Scotland Yard which included up-to-date lists of persons on whose correspondence Home Office Warrants had been imposed, or in regard to whom instructions had been issued to Aliens' Officers at the ports. Ewer was also forewarned by them of any impending action by the authorities against Communists or Communist organisations in this country. Ewer's organisation included a man named Walter Dale who was employed by him to maintain observation on the Offices of the British Intelligence Services and upon Russians resident in this country who were regarded with suspicion by the Soviet Government. He was also responsible for seeing that Ewer and other persons engaged on secret activities on behalf of the Soviet Government were not shadowed by agents of the Security Service or the Police. The two police officials were identified and later dismissed and shortly after this Ewer left for abroad. He returned in September 1929 but the view was held that his organisation did not function again.

This case is important because it illustrates both the potentialities and the limitations of the Security Service in peacetime. It shows how it could obtain great success in penetrating an espionage organisation and also how it was difficult to take action to bring such an organisation to an end. Against the argument that there were advantages in allowing it to run on for several years because it offered opportunities of obtaining further intelligence about it and the Soviet authorities behind it, is the counter argument that Ewer's organisation was obviously important enough to be dangerous, and that all its activities would not necessarily be disclosed by the methods available to the Security Service. Prima facie, the advertisement inserted in the "Daily Herald" was to enable Ewer to obtain agents who would be useful to him. Equally obviously, it was likely that the Security Service would attempt to put someone in touch with the persons behind the advertisement; and he may, therefore, have hoped that this would give him opportunities to penetrate our organisation and obtain information about it either by method of observation or double-cross, or both.

In January 1928 Wilfred Francis Remington McCartney, a British subject, and Georg Hansen, a German, were convicted for espionage on behalf of the U.S.S.R. and sentenced to ten years' penal servitude. McCartney had approached a friend of his, a member of Lloyds, to ask him to obtain some information about cargoes of munitions destined for countries bordering on Russia. McCartney's friend reported the matter to the authorities, and thereafter acted under instructions. Georg Hansen had been sent from Berlin by the Soviet authorities to assist McCartney. Both these men were members of their respective Communist Parties, but in McCartney's case the motive appears to have been to earn easy money rather that to serve the cause of Communism.

Early in 1930 information was received from S.I.S. that students from various countries were to attend a course due to commence in March 1930 at a school in Russia. Subsequent information proved that this was the Lenin School which had apparently been started in 1927 for the purpose of giving instruction to Communists of all countries in "legal" and "illegal" activities which it was its aim to promote. The syllabus included instruction in the history of espionage; espionage in theory and practice; the forging of documents; Communist, capitalist and political economy; practical world politics; and the methods of forming workers' committees in factories. Practical instruction was also given by attaching the students to Red Army units, and by making them familiar with the latest types of guns, tanks, aeroplanes and other weapons of war.

Those of the students who were selected to act as espionage agents underwent a further special course of training under the general auspices of the Razvedupr (the Russian Military Intelligence Service) and the G.P.U. (the Secret Police). (Subsequent enquiries showed that a considerable number of members of the Communist Party from this country attended the school during the period 1931-1935. It appears to have been closed down early in 1936.)

Part 5: Internal Organisation and Staff of the Security Service

The Staff on 4th August, 1914, was - 9 officers, 3 civilians, 4 women clerks, 3 police.

At the Armistice, the numbers were - at Headquarters - 84 officers and civilian officials, 15 men clerks, 291 women clerks, 23 police, 77 subordinate staff.

At controlled home ports, permit offices and missions in Allied countries - 49 officers and civilian officials, 7 men clerks, 34 women clerks, 255 police, 9 subordinate staff.

Total - 844

THE DOCUMENTS – II: REACTIONS TO FOREIGN DEVELOPMENTS IN PEACE AND WAR

By 1929 M.I.5. had received the title of the "Defence Security Service", the "Chief" being Colonel Sir Vernon Kell, and the "Deputy Chief" being Lt.-Colonel Holt-Wilson. At this time there were two branches - A and B. A Branch under Major Philips contained only three officers and dealt with administrative and preventive measures while B Branch under Mr Harker was responsible for investigation and consisted of five officers and one woman officer. There was also a staff of three in the 'Observation' section, for shadowing suspects and making confidential 'outside' enquiries.

This very small staff was responsible for all aspects of counter espionage work against German, Russian and other organisations. It was obviously precluded, if only by its size, from making any extensive enquiries and the machinery in S.I.S. on which it had to depend for information from abroad was also too small to cope with any volume of work. The methods available to the 'Defence Security Service', viz. the H.O.W. and agents employed in this country had obvious limitations. A factor which could not but have a very definitely limiting effect was the general atmosphere - both internationally and in Whitehall - in which the work had to be done. The pay was small and the prospects such as to make no appeal except to a certain number of officers with private incomes. The work itself was light and no one in authority in the War Office or elsewhere was closely interested. It is a tribute to Sir Vernon Kell's personality that the organisation was kept in being under such conditions and at least provided something to build on when the need arose. There were occasions when there was some danger of its being abolished.

CHAPTER III: REACTIONS TO DEVELOPMENTS ON THE 'RIGHT' AND 'LEFT' IN INTERNATIONAL AFFAIRS 1931-1939

Part 1: Communism and the U.S.S.R. 1931-1939

(i) Changes of function as the result of reorganisation affecting the Security Service, S.I.S. and Scotland Yard.

In 1931 the functions of M.I.5. were changed as a result of an enquiry presided over by Sir Warren Fisher (Treasury), with whom were associated Sir Robert Vansittart, (Foreign Office) and Sir John Anderson (then Permanent Under Secretary of State at the Home Office) and Sir Maurice Henksy.

This enquiry arose from the fact that S.I.S. had employed an agency for enquiries in this country and, as the information obtained was of value to M.I.5., had communicated it to them without disclosing the nature of its source. When this became apparent, the whole question of the functional relations between S.I.S. and M.I.5. was raised. At this meeting Sir John Anderson took the line that he could not agree to secret agents being employed inside this country by S.I.S. as an organisation which was not ultimately responsible to the Home Secretary. Sir Robert Vansittart felt that the converse held good, i.e. that M.I.5. should not employ agents abroad.

The result of the enquiry was that Section V was established in S.I.S. as a circulating section to serve as a channel for all communications between S.I.S. and M.I.5., in the same way as other circulating sections served as channels to the Foreign Office, the War Office and so on. Prior to the establishment of Section V individual officers in S.I.S. and M.I.5. had corresponded and dealt with one another indiscriminately, and it was held, in S.I.S., that the creation of Section V with expert knowledge of the requirements of this Office would conduce to greater efficiency in the despatch of the business of the two sister Services.

At the same time, it was decided that the staff which had been employed at Scotland Yard to deal with what were described as "intelligence duties connected with civil security" should be transferred to M.I.5., while Irish and anarchist matters were to remain with Special Branch.

This transfer of staff involved the transfer of the responsibility for the work previously done in Scotland Yard in connection with Communism. The functions of M.I.5. were thus expanded to an important extent. They became responsible for all intelligence dealing with the activities of the C.P.G.B. and therefore of the Comintern in this country.

The three organisations which had been responsible for intelligence work in this field were reduced to two, and the respective functions of the latter were more closely defined as a result of the creation of Section V.

The functional division as between Section V and B Branch of the Security Service was unofficially defined as being on the basis of the "three-mile limit" of all British countries. This definition served very well as a working rule under the conditions prevailing in the period 1931-1939; but it failed later in wartime. An essential factor during the period of its success was the goodwill and readiness for give and take between the officers concerned at all levels.

No contemporary document embodying these far-reaching decisions is now forthcoming, but in 1933 Lt.-Colonel Holt-Wilson drew attention to the fact that while the change had been communicated to the police all over the country, the Directorate of Military Intelligence was only aware in a vague way that the Security Service had taken over "certain civil duties from the Metropolitan Police on behalf of the Home Office" and there was no document relating to the transfer on record in the War Office; and that there were no accurate records in this Office on the point. A memorandum was then prepared by him so as to place the facts on record (vide SF.50-15-24). The memorandum mentions that "Sir John Anderson pointed out that the Intelligence Committee considered that M.I.5., in its position as the Combined Defence Security Service, was the most appropriate organisation to take over and centralise these national and imperial Security Services". It also mentioned that "it was agreed that the designation 'M.I.5.' should be retained for such official convenience as it could afford, without prejudice to the appropriate internal organisation of the Security Service to perform the duties required respectively by the Intelligence Committee and the heads of the Defence Services".

The object underlying this memorandum by Lt.-Colonel Holt-Wilson evidently was to make it clear that the Security Service was no longer in any sense a part of the Directorate of Military Intelligence, and that its functions included the duty of supplying intelligence to the Home Office and Foreign Office as well as to the Defence Services. There does not, however, appear to be any authority prior to this memorandum for the use of the terms "Combined Defence Security Service" or "Civil security", and they were evidently used as a means of facilitating the change in status.

Sir John Anderson had pressed that the change should be made from 1st October 1931, and Sir Vernon Kell had agreed to do so subject to the approval of the Chief of the Imperial General Staff and the heads of the Defence Services. This approval was obtained verbally.† The fact of the change was communicated to all British police officers and other authorities concerned, including overseas contacts. Even then no detailed reasons for the change were placed on record in the Security Service or, so far as can be learnt, in any other office, and no statement of its implications appears to be available.

---

† This is based on the statement of Brigadier Harker and the fact that there is nothing on record on our files to show that any written communication took place on the point.

(ii) Results of the changes: collaboration between the Security Service and S.I.S.

These changes inaugurated a period of close and fruitful collaboration between the Security Service and S.I.S. through the medium of Section V which, under the direction of Major Vivian, became expert in the wide range of subjects covered by the activities of the Comintern. In the course of the next few years he was able to develop the resources of S.I.S. for the purpose of obtaining intelligence by means of penetrative agents inside various Comintern or allied organisations in several countries. Intelligence thus obtained was augmented and amplified by the interception of Comintern wireless messages and by following up some remarkable enquiries in China and Brazil. These last-named enquiries arose from information supplied by one very valuable agent, [...] Other important agents were cultivated in France, Holland and Scandinavia.

These various enquiries made it possible - in combination with the results of enquiries made by the Security Service into the affairs of the C.P.G.B., the Western Europe Bureau and other Comintern organisations - to obtain a very detailed picture covering a very large part of the whole subject. This was embodied by Major Vivian in his "Communism (General Aspects)" April 1934, and "Communism (Organisation and working)" December 1934, an important part of the material for which was obtained from Security Service sources, while some part of the description of the framework of the Comintern was derived from papers prepared by the T.U.C. which has generally been well-informed on the subject of Communism.

This material is too voluminous to be summarised here. Some of the outstanding points have already been mentioned. Other points of cardinal importance are Major Vivian's analysis of the relations between the Comintern and the Soviet Government; his facts about the Comintern organisations, including the Central System, the National Sections, the Trade Unionists and Occupational Organisations, the "United Front" organisations and Communist finance. "United Front" organisations are mentioned as being, according to Stalin, the result of tactics set up by Lenin to make it easier for the millions of workers in capitalist countries..... to come over to Communism. In plain language, the "United Front" was a tactical manoeuvre devised for the purpose of bringing liberal-minded persons and "advanced thinkers", especially members of the Second International, into touch with Communists, and ultimately under their leadership. The "United Front" organisations included:-

> Workers' International Relief
> International Class War Prisoners' Aid
> League against Imperialism and for National Independence
> Society for Cultural Relations with Soviet Russia
> Friends of the Soviet Union
> International Union of the Revolutionary Theatre
> International Union of Revolutionary Writers
> International Juridical Association
> World Committee against War and Fascism

Major Vivian described them as a system of practically planned organisations driven by the momentum of a central force exerting pressure or inducement at every weak point in the political and social structure of every country in the world with a view to bringing about every kind of disintegration of the existing civilisation. He reached the conclusion that Communism was an international criminal conspiracy; and maintained that it was as such, rather than as a political movement, that the Security authorities of every country must treat it.

(iii) Light thrown on the C.P.G.B. as a Section of the Comintern by information obtained by S.I.S. in other countries.

The investigation of numerous individual cases and the collation of all the information available from abroad and at home illustrated the need for the closest possible collaboration between Section V and B Branch of the Security Service. The relations between the C.P.G.B. and the Comintern, of which it was a Section, appeared in a very different light when seen in conjunction with the intelligence obtained by Section V from Europe, Asia and America. Certain facts which emphasised this are therefore worth mentioning briefly.

In the early nineteen-thirties a joint mission of the Secret Military Section of the Comintern and the Intelligence Service of the Red Army was responsible for reporting on and furthering certain measures which aimed at developing the Chinese Communist forces as a potential counter to the Japanese forward moves in Manchuria and their threat to the position of the U.S.S.R. in the Far East. As a result of information obtained by the S.I.S. representative in [...] in connection with this joint mission one Hilaire Noulens was arrested on the 15th June, 1931, in [...] and the archives of two Communist organisations were seized. These were the Far Eastern Bureau of the Comintern and the Secretariat of the Pan-Pacific Trades Union Secretariat. These archives afforded a unique opportunity of seeing from the inside and on unimpeachable documentary evidence the working of a highly-developed Communist organisation of the illegal type. The documents of the Far Eastern Bureau were in German and in cypher. Those of the P.P.T.U.S. were in English and less guarded in phraseology. The personnel of the two offices was entirely distinct; their budgets and accounts separate; their controlling bodies were different; but the conspiratorial machinery for the secret receipt of correspondence was common to both. The Far Eastern Bureau was in constant communication with Communist Parties all over the Far East and with the Comintern via Berlin. Under close Comintern control it developed, in co-operation with the P.P.T.U.S., every phase of Communist activity including the selection and despatch to Moscow of students from all those countries for training in the Lenin school and in the Communist University for Workers of the East. The conspiratorial methods of both organisations included concealment of financial transactions by recourse to a number of Chinese banks and safe deposits; the use of cyphers, pseudonyms, "borrowed" or forged passports of many nationalities and the maintenance of an elaborate system of accommodation addresses. Noulens and his wife were sentenced to a term of life imprisonment by a Chinese Court.

Part of the Comintern apparatus which had been concerned in the joint Comintern-Red Army Mission in China was transferred to Brazil in accordance with a plan worked out in Moscow by Manuilski, the head of the War Section of the Political Commission of the

Comintern. Comintern opinion held that a favourable situation existed for the development of a revolution in Brazil between 1934 and 1935. Shortly before this time its chiefs had found in Luis Carlos Prestes an ideal leader for a Brazilian revolution which they intended should be fomented on a purely nationalist basis, the Communist nature of its background being most carefully concealed until the position had been consolidated. The disguise was then to be shed and Brazil was to be sovietised. S.I.S. obtained detailed and reliable information of the plans which were prepared in Moscow in October-November 1934 and subsequent evidence proved its complete reliability. Prestes secretly returned to Brazil in the spring of 1935 having been preceded by members of the Comintern apparatus from China. Early in 1935 these agents devised and brought into existence in Brazil the "National Liberationist Alliance" which by a clever campaign of publicity kept Prestes' name in the public mind as a coming liberator, but the members of the Alliance were unaware of Prestes' conversion to Communism and did not envisage the establishment of a Soviet regime in Brazil. While the Comintern experts made preparations for a revolt of the civil population, Prestes was working to obtain support in the Armed Forces for a military revolution with the ultimate intention of sovietisation. When certain difficulties arose, the question whether or not the civil population was to be considered ripe to participate in the military revolt was referred to the Comintern in Moscow. The Comintern procrastinated but Prestes' supporters in the army could not be restrained and unauthorised outbreaks occurred in certain regiments in the North of Brazil. This led Prestes to make a bid for power in Rio de Janeiro.

S.I.S. had arranged for a representative to keep in touch with developments. The Brazilian Government was forewarned and was enabled to take timely action to forestall the revolutionary attempt in the capital. Prestes and two of the principal Comintern agents were arrested and tried but others escaped.

An important aspect of this Brazilian Revolution was that events proved that the original information about the plans made in Moscow was correct. It is therefore a reasonable assumption that statements from the same source and forming part of the same information were also correct when they described the ultimate intention in the minds of the Commission of the Comintern that this Revolution should eventually lead to the Sovietisation of other American countries.

(iv) Comintern communications with the Communist Parties in Great Britain and other countries: information regarding Comintern finance and subsidies to its 'Sections'

In January 1935 information received from S.I.S. - it was based on the interception and decyphering of wireless messages - led to the discovery that the C.P.G.B. was communicating with Moscow through a wireless set which had been installed in January 1934. The location of the set was not at first known but it was eventually traced to an address in Wimbledon which was that of a member of the Communist Party named Stephen James Wheeton. The address was kept under observation with the result that it was learned that Wheeton was in the habit of meeting one Alice Holland, a well-known member of the Communist Party. Wheeton operated the set until April 1935 when his place was taken by another Communist named William Morrison. The set was operated until October 1937 after which date no further messages have been picked up. While it was operating the transmissions took place almost every night. Transmissions to and from Moscow were in code and the messages dealt with a variety of subjects. Those from Moscow included directions and instructions regarding the line to be taken in propaganda and in Party policy generally. They gave, among other things, details regarding subsidies paid by Moscow, a large part being allocated to the "Daily Worker". They were also concerned with details regarding the despatch of students from this country to the Lenin School in Russia and with the movements of couriers.

The London/Moscow transmissions were part of a large network with a number of stations in different parts of the world and the material dealt with a variety of the affairs of the Comintern and its Sections in different countries. As is usual with material of this kind the messages were often obscure and difficult to understand in the absence of a detailed knowledge of their context. These difficulties, together with the shortage of staff in Section V, had the unfortunate effect that a complete study and analysis of the messages was never made. Major Vivian was, however, able to extract useful intelligence from a number of messages and, in particular, obtained a certain picture of some of the details of Comintern finance and its measures for subsidising its Sections in other countries. Information about the names of couriers and active Communists, including certain British crypto-Communists, was obtained from this source.

An issue which cannot be evaded arises from the question whether more could not have been made of this material if it had been thoroughly worked up in such a way as to produce collated material of permanent value. To achieve this satisfactorily more detailed information about a number of foreign Communist Parties would have been necessary, but much of this could have been obtained from open sources such as the Press. Alternatively, better results might have been obtained if the S.I.S. Registry had been a much larger and effective machine than it was. Some details of the results of enquiries made by Section V into the subsidising of national Communist Parties by the Comintern are given in Major Vivian's "Communism (Organisation and working)" (vide Bibliography No. 13). Subsequent information has not been fully analysed.

The nature of the relationship between the Comintern organisation and the World Congresses was referred to in Chapter II, Part 4, (iii), where it was mentioned that the Sixth World Congress was held in 1928. The Seventh World Congress was not held until 1935; and this delay is to be attributed to the direction taken by Soviet foreign policy. In September 1934 the Soviet Union had joined the League of Nations and coincidentally the Comintern adopted "United Front" tactics as the policy of its Sections. The Seventh and last World Congress was held in Moscow from July 25th to August 21st, 1935, and George Dimitrov was appointed General Secretary of the Comintern. He had been living in the U.S.S.R. since his acquittal at the Reichstag Fire Trial when the Soviet Government had bestowed on him Soviet nationality and had demanded his extradition from Germany. The Congress dealt with the issues of war and Fascism and is famous for the reports by Dimitrov on "The offensive of Fascism and the tasks of the Communist International in the struggle for the Unity of the Working-class against Fascism", and by Ercoli, alias

Togliatti, an Italian member of the Comintern, on the "Tasks of the Comintern International in connection with the Imperialist preparation for a new World War". Summing up the results of the Congress, Dimitrov said they had been "the complete triumph of the unity between the proletariat of the country of victorious Socialism - the Soviet Union - and the proletariat of the capitalist countries which is still fighting for its liberation". Various reasons have been assumed for the failure to summon another Congress but there can be no doubt that it is not unconnected with the line taken in Soviet foreign policy in the face of the developing threat of Nazi aggressiveness and the view taken in Moscow of the world situation.

Throughout this period 1931-1939 - and indeed until the German attack on Russia in 1941 - the underground Party organisation responsible for disintegration work in the Armed Forces continued its activities. In 1931 the "incident" at Invergordon, for which the Communist Party was not responsible, was exploited by them and every effort was made to promote future disaffection and trouble in the Navy. In 1932 it was represented to the Government that the Law relating to this subject was cumbersome and out-of-date. As a result of continuous representations by the Security Service the Government eventually introduced and secured the passage through Parliament of the measure known as the Incitement to Disaffection Act. This measure only became law at the end of 1934 in a form which did not include all the provisions originally suggested when it was first promoted. In 1937 a successful prosecution under this Act was launched against a civilian who was sentenced to twelve months' imprisonment.

The underground Communist organisation which was responsible for this work was also concerned in a number of cases of sabotage in Government establishments and on H.M.Ships between 1928 and 1934.

(v) Soviet Espionage 1931-1939

The importance of the change in 1931 described above in regard to its bearing on counter espionage work soon became apparent. The wider scope given to the Security Service, in that it was concerned with the enquiry into the internal affairs of the C.P.G.B., led directly, not only to increased knowledge about the C.P.G.B. as a Section of the Comintern, but also threw light on the employment of individual members of the Communist Party as agents of the Soviet Military Intelligence Service.

A direct consequence of the re-organisation of functions in 1931 was that the agency which had been employed by S.I.S. and had furnished them with information about Communist matters inside this country came under the control of the Security Service, where it was later known as the M Section. The functions of the M Section were to specialise in the training and employment of agents for counter espionage purposes, i.e. to penetrate organisations such as the C.P.G.B., known enemy Secret Service organisations, and after 1933, the British Union of Fascists.

Percy Glading, who had for many years been one of the leading members of the C.P.G.B. and a paid official of the League Against Imperialism, resigned these positions and apparently severed all connection with them in March 1937. From that time onwards he was employed first under one Paul Hardt, an Austrian, and later under one Willy Brandes who posed as a French-Canadian, both being important agents of the Soviet Military Intelligence. Glading had formerly been employed in Woolwich Arsenal and through his contacts there he arranged to obtain a number of blueprints and other secret documents. Glading, as a rule, had them photographed and returned the same evening so that they could be replaced the next day without being missed. The photography was done by Soviet agents at a flat [...]

In due course, the officers of the Security Service came to the conclusion that Glading could not be allowed to continue to obtain documents in this manner, and steps were taken to arrange for the simultaneous arrest and search of various individuals who were party to the transactions for obtaining and photographing the documents. Glading was eventually sentenced to six years' imprisonment for espionage on behalf of the U.S.S.R.

Paul Hardt visited this country as the representative of a firm of textile merchants named Gada if Amsterdam which, though it was engaged in legitimate business, was evidently established in order to serve as a cover for espionage. The real nationality of Willy Brandes was not discovered. He had obtained a false Canadian naturalisation certificate with the assistance of an agent of the Soviet Intelligence in the U.S.A. He visited this country as the agent of a furniture company in New York and as a traveller for an American firm specialising in face powder. Glading was financed entirely by these two men.

There have been numerous instances in which investigations have shown that the Soviet Military Intelligence Service established business firms or companies to engage in legitimate trade and also to serve as a cover for espionage. One of the most important of these was the Far Eastern Trading Co. Ltd., of Upper Thames Street, London. In other cases the Soviet Trade Delegation has been used as a cover for espionage.

The events of this period, 1931-1939, made it abundantly clear that the study of the C.P.G.B., of the Comintern and of the Soviet Military Intelligence and their agents could not be separated or dealt with by separate British organisations without grave loss of efficiency and without causing an inability to plan action constructively and follow it up intelligently. They also proved that the closest co-operation was necessary between Section V and B Branch for similar reasons; and that given the necessary goodwill, satisfactory results could be achieved; that neither organisation could afford to be left in the dark about the important results obtained by investigations made by the other; and that the work of the two was complementary in the fullest sense of the word. If due allowance is made for the shortage of funds and of staff, the degree of success obtained as a result of good collaboration can fairly be claimed as being on a high level.

Part 2: The Nazi Threat 1933-1939

(i) The problems presented by Germany

The problems presented to the Security Service by Germany during this period fall under the headings:-

(a) the NSDAP (Nazi Party) and its Auslands Organisation;
(b) the Nazi Party and its relations with the Fascist Movement in England;
(c) general intelligence regarding Hitler's policy and preparations for war;
(d) German espionage 1933-1939.

(a) The NSDAP (Nazi Party) and its Auslands Organisation.

The Nazi threat attracted practically no attention in the Security Service between 1931 and 1933 and very little when Hitler and the Nazi Party came into power in Germany. About a year later, however, B Division, then B Branch, of the Office, reported to the Director of the Security Service that the activities of the Nazi Party organisation established in this country deserved special attention. At the same time, although there was no knowledge of any direct connection between the two for subversive purposes, the growth of the British Union of Fascists under Mosley gave grounds for increasing interest in his movement on the part of the Home Office; and it was decided early in 1934 that the Security Service should be entrusted with the duty of watching and reporting on Fascist movements. There appear to have been two reasons for this. Firstly the various Police Forces were not in a position to report on these movements from such a broad point of view as the Security Service, and secondly - and this was perhaps the decisive reason - there were good grounds for believing that the British Union of Fascists was being financed to a substantial extent by the Italian Dictator at the same time that it was observed to have certain contacts - apparently arising out of "ideological" sympathies - with the Nazis.

Some months elapsed before it was finally decided to institute active enquiries into the development of the B.U.F. and they were only started in April 1934. These enquiries very soon showed that there was close sympathy and some personal contact between the members of the Auslands Organisation in London and some of the principal personalities at Mosley's headquarters. They also showed that while the B.U.F. was being financed by Mussolini, there were elements in it, of which the leaders were W.E.D. Allen, William Joyce, Raven Thomson and a German Australian named Pfister, who had closer sympathy and contact with the Nazis. It was significant, however, that when these contacts showed signs of getting out of control Mosley issued orders forbidding any contact with foreign organisations except under the direct control of his own headquarters.

These developments, and the general political situation on the Continent with special reference to the general process of "Gleichschaltung" in Germany; the assumption of the chief military as well as civil offices by Hitler after the death of Hindenburg - and thus the unification in his own person of the offices of State which gave him dictatorial powers; and such incidents as "the night of the long knives" combined to focus attention on the potential significance from our point of view of all aspects of the development of the Nazi Party. The almost simultaneous occurrence of "the night of the long knives" and the ruthless beating up of their opponents by Mosley's Fascists at Olympia had the double effect of discrediting Mosley's movement in the eyes of many people who had tended to sympathise with it, and of drawing attention to its close affinities with the Nazis. In spite of attention in this Office being accordingly concentrated on both the German and the British organisations considerable difficulty was experienced in obtaining permission to investigate the activities of either movement in this country in the only way in which this Office could at that time obtain inside information other than by placing its own agents inside the organisations with a view to penetrating them. That is to say, the permission to intercept correspondence under a Home Office Warrant was refused for some time in both cases.

By an accident a German was reported to have been arrested in Switzerland in January 1934 with the London address of the Nazi Party Auslands Organisation in his possession in circumstances that appeared to indicate that the address was connected with the Gestapo. Whereupon Sir Vernon Kell saw Sir Russell Scott, the Permanent-under-Secretary of the Home Office, and asked him whether he expected the Security Service to take any special steps about Nazis in this country. Sir Russell Scott replied that unless we discovered in the ordinary course of our work any case of subversive propaganda or other inimical steps against the interests of this country we were to leave them alone and therefore no H.O.W. should be applied at any rate for the time being. Captain Liddell thereupon made further enquiries, and in June 1934, judging that a H.O.W. on addresses in Germany would be more readily obtained than one on the address in London, applied for and obtained permission to intercept the correspondence going to two addresses in Hamburg with which he knew that the branch of the Auslands Organisation in London was corresponding. The ground for this was given as being that the headquarters of the Nazi Party in this country was acting as an agency of the German Secret Police. Thus the accidental arrest in Switzerland eventually furnished a ground for getting over the Home Office reluctance to allow us to obtain intelligence about the Nazi organisations on British soil and led to the amassing of very voluminous and illuminating intelligence on the nature of the Nazi State and its aggressive tendencies (As explained below, Home Office Warrants were applied to a few unimportant members of the British Union of Fascists, but the Home Office consistently refused to do so in the case of Mosley himself.)

Looked at in retrospect, it is obvious that not only in official but in wider circles there was a general failure to appreciate the character of the Nazi Party and the part it played in developments in Germany during the years following its accession to power. In the light of after events it is easy to see how Hitler sought English friendship in pursuance of a general plan to secure German hegemony. The information which flowed into this Office as a result of the watch which was kept on the Nazi Party Organisation, gradually began to show how the whole power of the machinery at Hitler's disposal was used to promote goodwill in this country towards Germany, and even to encourage where possible the spirit of pacifism, while Germany was being rearmed and its people toughened in preparation for the war which he afterwards started.

It was not until 1935 that a full enquiry commenced into the subsidiary consequences of the general Nazi policy in the shape of the Auslands Organisation as established all over the world (except, as far as the evidence went, in Russia).

A report on this subject was prepared in B Branch in 1935 (vide Bibliography No. 3), in the course of which it was pointed out that the objects of the Auslands Organisation were "the welding together of all Germans abroad, and all seafaring Party members, into one great block", and that emphasis should be laid on the potentialities of the all-embracing organisation of a Party which has absorbed the whole apparatus of the State. Among the results in countries outside Germany was to be counted the fact that, since the Nazi machine had unprecedented power over the individual, it could direct the energies of every member of the Party in any desired direction. It was pointed out that because at that time the Führer desired English friendship, every German was adjured to act and speak with that end in view, but we could not lose sight of the fact that in certain eventualities the whole energy of the machine could be utilised in the reverse direction. The machine was a ready-made instrument for intelligence, espionage and ultimately for sabotage purposes. The idea of the claim to the allegiance of all Germans who had settled abroad was older than Hitler, and was not likely to be lightly abandoned. Still less was that expressed by Baldur von Shirach of the Hitler Jugend of "building in the hearts of Youth a great altar on which Germany stands". Hitler and his friends had placed before all the Germanic peoples the question whether this larger patriotism was to be a more powerful material and emotional influence than their older religions.

This report formed the subject of discussion with the Foreign Office, the Home Office and other Government Departments. Numerous supplementary reports outlining the development of the Nazi Party Organisation were submitted. The question was ultimately referred to the Cabinet, but it was not held that any action could be taken to curtail the activities of the Auslands Organisation on British soil. When, however, the German Government proposed to appoint Otto Bene, the Landesgruppenleiter or head of the Organisation in the United Kingdom, to be Consul-General for Germany in London, the Foreign Office raised objections and the German Government recalled him.

At the beginning of 1935 the Nazi Government reintroduced conscription and promulgated the new law under which "every German and every German woman was bound in time of war to serve the Fatherland". The law was made applicable to Germans who had British or other nationality in addition to their own. It even made provision for the punishment of dual nationals living in foreign countries who failed to report and register for service in Germany. (There was evidence that the Nazi Party machinery was used to enforce it.) The introduction of this law had a considerable psychological effect on Germans resident in this country. It was regarded as emphasising the nature of the total war of the future. At the same time information was received from S.I.S. regarding the large-scale rearmament which was going on in Germany.

In March 1936 Hitler, against the advice of the German General Staff, ordered the re-occupation of the Rhineland. From indications which reached M.I.5., and particularly the intercepted correspondence of the Nazi Party in the United Kingdom, it appeared that he was influenced by reports received from the Nazi Organisation in London, including those of the head of the German Chamber of Commerce, which forecast that the British Government would not take military action as the result of the German move.

Under the influence of this atmosphere officers in B Branch of this Office felt that recent developments in the general situation made it incumbent on the Security Service to examine the problems with which it was directly concerned with greater care than had been necessary at any time since 1918. They prepared a memorandum in the middle of 1936 (vide Bibliography No. 52) on the possibilities of sabotage by the organisations set up in British countries by the totalitarian Governments of Germany and Italy.

This memorandum was sent by the D.S.S. to the Joint Intelligence Sub-Committee of the Committee of Imperial Defence.

The memorandum suggested that the possibilities of sabotage by the Auslands Organisation or the Fasci all' Estero were of sufficient importance to be brought to the notice of the Minister for the Co-ordination of Defence, and that information which had accumulated regarding these organisations made it desirable to review certain questions relating to the employment of individuals of German or Italian origin or descent, in the Armed Forces, Government establishments, and firms concerned in the production of ships, aircraft and munitions. It was also suggested that measures to enable M.I.5. to watch these organisations satisfactorily would involve a considerable expense and an increase of staff.

After referring to the official Nazi view of the constitution of the Nazi State in which the State, the Party, and the Armed Forces, were all under the personal control and command of the Führer, it went on to mention the views put forward under the aegis of von Blomberg, the Reichskriegs-minister and Oberbefehlshaber der Wehrmacht, regarding the relations between National Socialism, the Wehrmacht, and what was described as Wehrpolitik. Wehrpolitik was explained as meaning "in the sense of National Socialism", the co-ordination of the fighting forces of the nation, and their direction and their steeling towards the will for self-assertion and the development of all their inherent political possibilities. As head of the State, leader of the Party, and Supreme Commander of the Armed Forces, Adolf Hitler was the lord of Germany, with a power almost unexampled in history. There was no longer any separation in the supreme direction of foreign policy and military strategy and the organisation of the whole people for military purposes was centralised. The new army was the creation of Adolf Hitler, and with other organisations of the Party and the State was to work, in accordance with his will to "educate" the "new" German people.

The memorandum went on to suggest that Hitler's intentions were indicated in his *Mein Kampf* and that his acts spoke more decisively than his words. All his acts showed that his constant aim was to secure power to promote and increase the strength of Germany until none could stand against her; that he had no conception of law as understood in British countries; and that he would shrink from no violence and no crime in order to have his way.

It was in the light of these circumstances that consideration should be given to the significance for Great Britain, the Dominions and Colonies of the Auslands Organisation of the National Sozialistische Deutsche Arbeiter Partei.

The memorandum also suggested that in the light of the conduct of the Abyssinian War, it was superfluous to say that Mussolini's principle in international affairs was the use of force without restriction and without restraint. It mentioned that there was reliable information that the heads of the Partito Nationale Fascista intended to use their organisation to sabotage British aerodromes and aircraft in the Mediterranean area, when it was expected that war between Britain and Italy might break out in 1935. The nature of the official British attitude and the complete failure to recognise the real position were demonstrated by the fact that a considerable number of Italians were at that time employed in the civilian establishment of British aerodromes in the Middle East. It was believed that some of these men were members of the Italian organisation for sabotage.

This memorandum was reviewed by the Joint Intelligence Sub-Committee, who recommended that attention should again be directed to the potential danger of Nazi and Fascist Party Organisations in this country and throughout the British Empire; that the Security Service should be directed to continue to study these problems; that detailed plans should be worked out for dealing with members of the Party Organisations in an emergency; that the Service Departments should take certain protective measures in regard to the Armed Forces, establishments and firms engaged in secret and general munition work; and that the Dominions and Colonies should be warned of these special dangers and advised by the Security Service regarding special measures for their own protection.

No important increase in the staff of the Security Service for dealing with these matters or with espionage was sanctioned as a result of these representations.

In 1937 B Branch prepared additional notes on the Auslands Organisation (Vide Bibliography No. 4) and sent them to the Home Office, the Foreign Office, and the Directors of Intelligence of the three Services. Copies were also sent to the Dominions, India and the principal Colonies; later copies were sent to the State Department in Washington and the Deuxieme Bureau in Paris.

These notes dealt with the Auslands Organisation on more comprehensive lines than previously and emphasised the question of principle as affecting sovereignty, which arose from the fact that it was an extension on British territory of the machinery of the Party-State; and pointed out that its branches functioned as subsidiary organs of the German Police system. They mentioned that E.W. Bohle, the Gauleiter of the Auslands Organisation had been appointed to be chief of that Organisation as now incorporated in the German Foreign Office. They enlarged upon previous references to the part which it was expected that the Party Organisation abroad might play in time of war; and the part which it was apparently intended to play in the furtherance of the general policies of the Nazi leaders.

Evidence was supplied of the manner in which Germans were allowed to acquire other nationalities while retaining their German nationality, when it was considered to be in the interests of Germany that they should do so, the implications being that the loyalty to Germany was regarded as binding, while the supposed allegiance to the foreign State was an empty form. For this and other reasons it was suggested that the whole question was one of special interest to the Dominions.

At the beginning of 1938 a report on the Auslands Organisation in Canada was received from the Royal Canadian Mounted Police. It followed the lines taken in our reports and added important details regarding the Canadian Society for German Culture or the Deutscher Bund (composed wholly or mainly of Canadian British subjects of German origin or extraction), which it was explained was intended to serve as an auxiliary of the NSDAP. The control exercised by the Auslands Organisation over the Canadian Society for German Culture was described as of a positive nature, and a confidential circular to district leaders in Canada was quoted to the effect that "the recognition of the Bund had been granted by the Auslands Organisation for certain reasons it is impossible openly to documentise this or even make it known to the members". There was also evidence of a report having been called for, asking which of the local leaders were still German citizens; and there were indications of the same attitude towards dual nationality which had been observed in Great Britain. The importance of this question in Canada was associated with the fact that there were nearly one hundred thousand German immigrants between April 1925 and March 1936. Evidence of the part which members of the Nazi Party thought that the Germans in America ought to play as a medium between Nazi Germany and the American people, had come to our notice and there was also evidence that in spite of the American objections to the establishment of the Nazi Party Organisation in the U.S.A., the Organisation did in fact function as an entity separate from the German American Bund.

B Branch exchanged information with the authorities in Australia, New Zealand, South Africa and some of the Colonial administrations in regard to local developments of the Nazi Party and supplied them with copies of memoranda compiled here and other general information on the subject. Not unnaturally the problem assumed special importance in the two former German Colonies in Africa, i.e. Tanganyika and the South West, both of which are referred to in the Additional Note on the Auslands Organisation - 1937 (Bibliography No. 4). Subsequent to that date the police authorities in Pretoria and East Africa informed us of local developments.

Their close contact with the development of the Auslands Organisation machine convinced officers of B Branch that these developments must ultimately involve a conflict of interests between the "Deutschtum" of the Nazis and the established order both in the U.S.A. and in the British Empire. It therefore seemed desirable to arrange for an exchange of information with the U.S.A. authorities, and in the beginning of 1938 steps were taken to provide for this. The underlying idea was that an exchange of information - even on these restricted and relatively unimportant lines - would have a tendency to lead in the direction of closer collaboration, perhaps on more important issues, between the Governments of Great Britain and the U.S.A.

(b) The Nazi Party and its relations with the Fascist Movement in England.

The enquiries by B Branch into the British Fascist Movements, including the British Union of Fascists, began in April 1934 and for the next two years frequent periodical reports on the subject were forwarded to the Home Office and the Foreign Office. Information contained in these reports has been summarised - and amplified on the basis of later evidence - in a booklet prepared in this Office in July 1941 (vide Bibliography No. 6). All the information contained in this booklet was not available in the early years of the enquiry and, in particular, the use of such an organisation as machinery for internal disruption as a part of German military strategy was not in the circumstances of the time clearly envisaged, although the general nature of the danger was perhaps rather dimly perceived, but as a political rather than a military one. Experience in other European countries has thrown more light on this subject but the full facts regarding the German plans to use such organisations as the "Fifth Column" are not fully known even now (in 1945). There would seem to be no ground to doubt that when the German army invaded Holland some of the NSB Party played the part designed for them by the Germans; and similar events occurred in Norway and elsewhere. It is to be noted, however, that wherever the "Fifth Column" was used it was only an auxiliary in a military situation in which the preponderance of German power was already decisive. On the other hand, when the Germans retreated from the Western European countries they attempted to use members of the native National Socialist Parties as stay-behind agents, with little success, for obvious reasons, as the individuals in question were almost invariably well-known as collaborators. This, however, is to anticipate but the point is made here in order to emphasise that from the purely military point of view the enquiries into the activities of the British Union of Fascists were fully justified by after events.

Enquiries were, however, made under considerable difficulty as, especially in the early stages, the Home Office were unwilling to allow Home Office Warrants to be applied to leading members of Mosley's Party and only consented to this procedure in the case of some of his less prominent adherents. When Mosley's close contact with Mussolini and Hitler was known, as well as the fact that he had been subsidised by the former to the extent of about £100,000 and when it was probable but not established that he was being subsidised by the Nazi Party, B Branch pressed for a carefully restricted examination of his correspondence, but the Home Office consistently refused.

In particular, a B Division memorandum was sent to the Home Office on 27.1.37 stressing these points and emphasising that we were reliably informed that many members of the B.U.F. would support Italy or Germany against their own Government in the event of war. At a meeting in February 1937, information about Mussolini's subsidising of Mosley was communicated by us to Sir Robert Vansittart who handed the papers to Sir Russell Scott, Permanent Under-Secretary to the Home Office, in an attempt to strengthen his hand and secure the application of H.O.W.s. The whole subject was raised again by B Branch in a letter of 9.6.37 when it was recommended that a Warrant restricted to Mosley's foreign correspondence should be approved and that others should be applied to his principal lieutenants, Robert Gordon-Canning, Ian Hope Dundas and Archibald Garrioch Findlay, all of whom had contacts in Germany or Italy, were connected with the negotiations for, or payments of, German and Italian subsidies and were suspected of being intermediaries for the communication of secret information. The report that such information was being conveyed was from a source which had been tested over and over again and always found to be extremely reliable in several other connections.

No Warrant was sanctioned until 31.3.38 when one was imposed on Robert Gordon-Canning. Another on Findlay was dated 13.4.39, but in the case of Dundas approval was never obtained.

After Mosley's arrest it was evident that some of his banking accounts had been manipulated in such a way as to disguise the nature of some of the transactions by which B.U.F. funds were received. As mentioned in the booklet on the British Union of Fascists, Sir Oswald Mosley seems to have aimed at making any investigation into the finances of the B.U.F. impossible and the investigators had to content themselves with the observation that the funds were derived for the greater part from "unknown sources", only a very small proportion being received from members' subscriptions.

It is therefore obvious that, should it become possible, the question of the financing of the British Union of Fascists and the possibility of funds being received from Nazi sources deserves further examination.

(c) General intelligence regarding Hitler's policy and preparation for war.

Political Intelligence. Thus the enquiries about the British Union of Fascists and about German espionage, which were normal functions of this Office, led to an enquiry into the activities of the Nazi Party Organisation. All these various enquiries combined to build up a corpus of general intelligence which centred on the organisation of the totalitarian state in Germany as a threat to British security. The following is a very brief summary of some of the more important ingredients of this general intelligence as obtained from sources in or in touch with the German Embassy in London. It is given here in order to sketch in outline the problems with which the Security Service was confronted in the formative period between the wars; and to indicate how, with a very inadequate staff, attempts were made to deal with them.

Towards the end of 1935, with a view to obtaining information about the German Intelligence system and the activities of the Nazi Party in London, the Director placed B Branch in touch with a representative who had a number of contacts in German official and diplomatic circles.

Early in 1936 this representative informed us that he had cultivated friendly relations with [...] of the German Embassy in London. He was not in the ordinary sense an "agent", but he believed that by giving certain information regarding Nazi tendencies to our representative [...] he might to a certain extent influence the British Government in the right direction. He was encouraged in this idea by the fact that when he gave information in this way regarding the German intention to appoint Otto Bene, the Landesgruppenleiter in London, to be Consul-General for Germany in Great Britain certain action was taken. This appointment appeared to be very undesirable to this Office from a security point of view. It would have involved official recognition of the Party and therefore probably have made it impossible to take action against the Party Organisation without embarrassment, especially in a time of crisis. It also seemed likely that it would help to increase the Party's power over German nationals in this country. The Foreign Office took the same view and made it known to the German authorities that they would not be willing to grant an exequatur. [...] thus had reason to think that his information had been responsible for a result which appeared to him to be very desirable in that it involved a rebuff to the Nazi Party on a matter which they regarded far more seriously than it appeared in English eyes.

Towards the end of 1936, [...] urged the view that the British Government ought to show the greatest energy in insisting that the German troops should leave Spain. He said that such a demand would come at the right psychological moment as the Reichswehr had been urging that these troops should be recalled.

At about this time he also furnished some illuminating facts regarding Ribbentrop's attitude towards the abdication of King Edward. He said that Ribbentrop had given orders to the German Press in London to refrain from mentioning the subject. The motive was not, as was wrongly supposed, due to a desire to be tactful towards the British people, but to a desire to be in the good books of King Edward, whom he "regarded as a certain winner". Ribbentrop had even attempted to have a message conveyed to the King that the "German people stood behind him in his struggle". When the King abdicated, Ribbentrop's report to Berlin contained the following; "The abdication of King Edward is the result of the machinations of dark Bolshevist powers against the Führer-will of the young King. I shall report all further details orally to my Führer". He issued strict instructions that no one in the Embassy was to make any report to the German Foreign Office on this subject. [...] reaction was "We are absolutely powerless in the face of this nonsense.

In September 1936 [...] had told us that a war with Russia was regarded as being "as certain as the Amen in church", and that it was felt that developments were getting beyond the stage where the Wilhelmstrasse or the more intelligent sections of the Reichswehr could influence their course. The view in Nazi circles was that a point would be reached in the not distant future when Germany's relative superiority in armaments would begin to decline and that the optimum date for war against Russia should not be missed. These circles were convinced that England would not move a finger if Hitler launched an attack against Russia. It may be noted here the general indications were that Ribbentrop hoped, when he came as Ambassador to London, to ensure that Nazi Germany would have English sympathy on an anti-Comintern basis. It appears that when his mission did not meet with the success he expected, his whole attitude towards this country changed.

At about the same time as the abdication [...] learnt that Berlin was financing the anti-Blumites in France on a large scale. He mentioned a single payment in one week of Ff.8,500,000. - which went into French pockets.

When Ribbentrop arrived in London he was accompanied by a huge staff including members of his Dienststelle, A.D.C.s, secretaries and "detectives from the Schutz Staffel" (the SD?). [...] found that members of the Embassy staff noticed that their desks were searched at night; and he felt that he was working in what he called "a complete madhouse".

Ribbentrop returned to the Embassy from his interview with the Prime Minister and announced "the old fool does not know what he is talking about". Ribbentrop declared to his staff that his mission in England was to keep this country neutral during the coming conflict with "the Red Pest". [...] mentioned that the Reichswehr had had useful experience in Spain, and had found that some of their arms (incendiary bombs were mentioned) which had been tested there, had not proved satisfactory. Hitler was setting the pace and giving orders to a reluctant Reichswehr and Foreign Office.

[...] was encouraged to give our representative information regarding the activities of the Nazi Party as seen from the Embassy; and regarding any matters connected with improper contact with underground activities on the part of attachés and other members of the Embassy staff, in regard to which there appeared to be increasing tendencies during 1936 and 1937. During this period numerous reports obtained from [...] on matters connected with German foreign policy were communicated by us to the Foreign Office.

By November 1937 he told us that Ribbentrop was more anti-English than ever, and was anxious to leave his post in London. Hitler, however, said "he always wanted to go to London, let him stay there". At the same time Hitler had referred to Ribbentrop as "ein aussenpolitischer Genie" (a wizard in foreign affairs).

Early in 1938 we learnt from [...] that in consequence of a decision by Hitler which was thought to have been prompted by Ribbentrop, the policy of seeking English friendship had been abandoned; and Ribbentrop had issued orders to this effect to his subordinates and commented that this meant that their objective should be to work for the weakening and ultimate downfall of the British Empire.

At the same time the Italian Government had decided that the Non-Intervention Committee in connection with Spain had created an impossible situation for them and that it must be brought to an end. This view was placed before the German Government and the Party leaders acquiesced in it. The Italian Government had accordingly decided to despatch fresh Italian troops to Spain; and openly to adopt the attitude that they were taking part in the war in Spain, thus abandoning the "farce" of the Non-Intervention Committee. It was believed that this decision was not acceptable in army circles in Germany, and that this fact had been one of the underlying factors in the recent crisis in that country. This information was communicated to the Foreign Office; and we were informed that it agreed with information received from other sources and that the Secretary of State was impressed by it.

At the same time, i.e. early in 1938, [...] told us that orders had been issued to intensify arrangements for espionage against this country. The Abwehrabteilung had issued instructions to this effect to the Military Attaché in London; and the German consuls in this country had been asked to furnish reports and to supply the names of agents suitable for obtaining military secrets.

In the middle of February 1938 we sent to the Foreign Office a summary of views expressed by [...]. They were to the effect that the Army would in future be an obedient instrument of Nazi foreign policy; and that the recent purge had left the Nazis in complete control of the Army. Ribbentrop's foreign policy would be an aggressive forward policy. Its first aim - Austria - had been partly achieved. Austria "falls to Hitler like a ripe fruit". After consolidating the position in Austria the next step would be against Czechoslovakia. The view in German official circles was that in the immediate future a block of a hundred and thirty millions of well-organised people with armies prepared to march to order (Germany, Austria, Italy and Hungary) would face the two great Western Democracies whose people did not want to fight. It was quite clear that a bargain had been struck between Hitler and Mussolini. This involved German support in the Mediterranean and a free hand for Germany in Central Europe.

[...] felt that Britain was letting the trump cards fall out of her hands. If she had adopted or even now adopted, a firm attitude and threatened war, Hitler would not succeed in this kind of bluff, i.e. in bluffing his way into a stronger position than German strength at the time could support. The German Army was not yet ready for a major war. He emphasised again and again that the English failed to understand the crudity of people like Ribbentrop and made the mistake of applying their standards of thought and diplomacy in their dealings with them. He said that, in his opinion, in view of the weakness of the British attitude war had now become inevitable, i.e. as soon as Hitler felt himself strong enough to undertake it. It was considered in Nazi circles that we were now at the beginning of a Napoleonic period; there would be big events and things would move with extreme rapidity. Ribbentrop had said in the German Embassy in London "there will be no war before we are on the Bosphorus". It was also mentioned that it was hoped that Jugoslavia would come under German and Italian influence. During the summer of 1938, we continued to receive and to send on to the Foreign Office reports from [...] and other sources, regarding Hitler's aggressive policy and German preparations for war. In the middle of August, [...] sent us a cryptic message to the effect that drastic action was contemplated. By arrangement with S.I.S. we sent a representative to get in touch with him, and he informed us that a paper had been circulated to German Embassies and Legations abroad, dated the 3rd of August, and signed by Ribbentrop. It was described as an "Erlass", covered four pages and was drafted in typical Ribbentrop style. The scope and nature of the document showed that it had been issued with Hitler's authority. The sense was as follows: the Czech question must be settled in accordance with our views before the autumn and, though we prefer peaceful methods, war must be envisaged. I do not agree with those who maintain that France and Great Britain will interfere. The lightening speed of our action will make any such effort on their part in vain. If they should decide to be involved in a quarrel, I would point out that the German army is far stronger and better prepared than in 1914 and we shall emerge victorious from this war.

There followed detailed instructions regarding German mobilisation. The date of action against Czechoslovakia was mentioned as "before the 20th of September". [...] added that Schulenburg, the German Ambassador in Moscow, had reported that Russia was not in a position to come to the aid of Czechoslovakia. His report stiffened Hitler's attitude.

There was reason to believe that opinion in the Reichswehr, and particularly in the Intelligence Branch of the German General Staff, was to the effect that war was inevitable; and that in this connection Hitler was now on the same side as Ribbentrop, Himmler and Goebbels. There had been a serious difference of opinion between Goering and Ribbentrop. The Reichswehr believed that they would lose the war, but they realised that it was impossible to oppose the Führer's decisions. Those who had advanced cautious counsels had been told that the Reichswehr did so on previous occasions (the Rhineland and the march into Austria) and each time they were wrong.

The German Secret Service (Abwehr) under Canaris was posting a number of representatives to Embassies and Legations abroad; and a base for Abwehr action against France and Britain was established in Holland. They were already very active in that country.

Two German Intelligence officers name Piepenbrock and Maurer had informed [...] that they had agents everywhere in Holland. They added that hotels and restaurants were honeycombed with them; and boasted that they could get any documents that they wanted in Holland. (Oberst Hans Piepenbrock was known to us later as Admiral Canaris' principal assistant.) All this information about plans regarding Czechoslovakia and preparations for war was communicated to the Foreign Office, Home Office, S.I.S. and the Director of Military Intelligence.

On the 13th September 1938, we reported that there had been changes in the German dispositions; and the second stage of the German plan, the secret mobilisation, would accordingly have been developed by Monday the 25th of September to a stage at which it could only be necessary to press the button at any time after that date when it was desired to set the forces in motion for the invasion of Czechoslovakia. The invasion was regarded as inevitable; and it was considered that Great Britain would not be able to prevent it. This and supplementary information from the same and other sources gave us a clear forecast of the line which Hitler subsequently developed during the Munich Crisis of September 1938.

It seemed to B Branch officers that the nature and the far-reaching implications of this information of August and September and the subsequent crisis in September, furnished very strong grounds, among other things, for a substantial increase in the strength of the staff responsible for counter espionage. When the crisis had passed and there were no signs of any large-scale reorganisation of this Office to meet the obvious danger of Hitler's aggressive policy being further developed in future, B Branch prepared a further report summarising all their information derived from [...] and from various other sources (vide Bibliography No. 19). (Great care had naturally to be taken to conceal the identity of […] and other Germans, official or unofficial, from whom most of this information had been derived). This summary included a character sketch of Hitler as derived indirectly from some of his intimate friends in the Nazi Party. It described how he was pursuing, in high politics, tactics which he had previously followed in smaller matters:-

> "He caused his opponents to be confused with a feint here and a serious blow there, and simultaneous offers of peace, and when having given them no rest, he had got them where he wanted them, he made an energetic attack, falling upon them like lightning".

Goebbels was quoted as saying that this was a very good description of Hitler's character as he now was. The only man who would make any impression on Hitler, said Goebbels, was one who should firmly say "no" and answer his threats with effective counter-threats. Any other attitude only egged him on to attempt to destroy his opponent. His associates thought it was comical that other countries did not recognise these methods.

According to a report from the same source the Führer was very fond of making jokes about the "umbrella pacifism" of the once-imposing British World Empire and referred to Mr. Chamberlain in terms of school-boyish obscenity.

One of these reports, which Sir Alexander Cadogan remarked had proved to be true, was to the effect that the Nazis considered that Mr. Neville Chamberlain had become too popular in Germany and that the continuous hymns of praise about him were not desirable. The Propaganda Ministry therefore proposed to do everything possible to pour ridicule on him; at the same time they were to emphasise that the Opposition in England was a war Party which would break the Munich Agreement. The Germans, according to this Nazi view, had never taken the Munich Agreement seriously but they intended to direct their future action in such a way as to make it appear that the first breach of the Munich Agreement came from the other side.

It was suggested that if these indications were reliable, it must be anticipated that Hitler would make increasingly drastic demands. This was extremely probable if, as seemed beyond doubt, he lacked the will and power to defend the British Empire.

We concluded by saying that this information raised the question whether, apart from the paramount need for rapid re-armament, further measures should not be taken to develop our Intelligence system and provide for a comprehensive review of all steps necessary to ensure security.

This report was read by Lord Halifax at the end of 1938 and we were told that parts of it had been read by him to the Prime Minister (Mr. Chamberlain). Adequate measures to improve the organisation of this Office were therefore expected, but nothing substantial eventuated before the war broke out.

We were informed, however, that the obscenity of Hitler's reference to him made a considerable impression on the Prime Minister (we had in fact included it in the hope that it would make some impression) and that it, read with our report as a whole, had contributed materially - if only as a minor factor - towards Mr. Chamberlain's reformulation of policy including the introduction of conscription early in 1939.

Propaganda. Colonel Nicolai, in his book quoted in Chapter II above, referred to the ideas about propaganda which he had conceived as a result of his experience in the last war, and suggested that the Intelligence Service had to play an active part in this field.

Hitler has shown in "Mein Kampf" and in his speeches that he has attached the greatest importance to the question of propaganda. He was greatly impressed by the effectiveness of British propaganda during the war of 1914-1918. In the course of the campaign which brought him to power in Germany, his propaganda machine played a very significant part and subsequently it continued to play an equally important part in his conduct of affairs on a larger canvas.

This is a very wide subject and, regarded as a whole, has always been treated as a matter beyond the scope of this Office; but certain aspects of it have from time to time compelled out attention.

In Nazi Germany propaganda was controlled by the Propaganda Ministerium under Goebbels, and it naturally followed that German journalists in the United Kingdom had a part to play.

As mentioned above, the Auslands Organisation was concerned with propaganda to promote goodwill towards Germany in this country. The conduct of this propaganda was, however, on a larger scale than was covered by the Organisation under Bohle. The whole machinery of the Party in Germany lent a hand. Not merely Goebbels' Propaganda Ministry but also, among others, Ribbentrop's Deinststelle in Berlin and London, Rosenberg's Bureau, the Hitler Jugend and other subsidiary organisations combined to put forth a considerable volume of propaganda inspired and controlled with the same end in view.

Information regarding all these activities reached M.I.5. in a steady stream as a by-product of enquiries, the immediate aim of which was to investigate espionage, possible plans for sabotage in the event of war and other activities likely to concern the security of the State.

At the end of 1937 a summary of information relating to German propaganda in the United Kingdom was prepared by B Branch (vide Bibliography No. 38) and distributed to the principal Government Departments in this country and our own correspondents in the Dominions.

When forwarding it to the Dominions we pointed out that it was not part of our business to investigate the activities of English people who were consciously or unconsciously furthering the aims of German propaganda, but that the propaganda itself was of interest to us as there was evidence to show that his attempt at influencing public opinion here in such a manner as to affect foreign policy was all inspired from one group of sources - the leading offices of the NSDAP in Germany. We knew that Goebbels and Bohle of the Auslands Organisation claimed credit for having influenced British public opinion by methods which included those outlined in this summary. Attention was drawn to the possibility that an over-optimistic view of the results of their work might lead the activists of the NSDAP - and Hitler - into a mistaken policy based on false premises.

It was pointed out that as no direct enquiry had been made into these propagandist activities, the view which we had obtained of them was not necessarily complete and comprehensive, but that it seemed worth while to bring all this material together in one summary because of the manner in which the whole Nazi machine was working with a common object; and in order to understand that object it was necessary to bear in mind that great, possibly exaggerated, importance was attached to propaganda and its effects by Hitler and other leaders of the Nazi Party. The object of all this propaganda was to promote sympathy for the New Germany among English people who were to be taught to understand the German point of view, but there was no question of teaching the Germans to see the English point of view. It was impossible to resist the inference that - partly under the guise of anti-Bolshevism - the object was to carry out the ideas outlined by Hitler in "Mein Kampf" in regard to German foreign policy, i.e. to bring about an alliance or understanding with England, which would give Germany a free hand in other directions.

When Ribbentrop came to London to take up his appointment as Ambassador, he made it clear that he hoped actively to promote Anglo-German friendship on lines and by methods somewhat different from those of traditional diplomacy, including the utilisation of a Bureau or Dienststelle maintained by him in Berlin as an organ which had enabled him to play the part he did in German foreign policy. Ribbentrop's Bureau was in direct touch with Hitler's Bureau, the Reichskanzlei, and it had played an important part in the negotiations conducted by Ribbentrop and leading up to the German-Japanese Anti-Comintern Agreement (with its secret clauses), and the subsequent German-Italo-Japanese Anti-Comintern Agreement (without secret clauses).

Ribbentrop maintained a considerable section of his Dienststelle in London; and important members of it were constantly coming and going between London and Berlin. The activities of these individuals were aimed at influencing English opinion in very wide circles in a sense favourable to Germany. For this purpose the Dienststelle included persons with contacts ranging from the Royal Family to diplomatic, political and industrial circles; and religious and political institutions were included in its scope. It supported and in some cases actively promoted such societies as:- the Anglo-German Fellowship; the Angle-German Circle; the Anglo-German Kameradschaft; the Link; the Angle-German Brotherhood. Similar objects were pursued by the Auslands Organisation through the Anglo-German Academic Bureau, and the Anglo-German Information Service. The Anglo-German Academic Bureau was responsible, subject to the ultimate control of the Landesgruppe and the Party Organisation, for matters connected with teachers and students. There was evidence that German teachers and students were encouraged to deliver lectures of a political and semi-political nature in this country. The lectures had to be approved by the Nazi Party officials before delivery. The Anglo-German Information Service distributed large numbers of pamphlets and other propaganda. It was entirely controlled by the Auslands Organisation. Mosley's Movement, the British Union of Fascists, and the small national socialist organisation which had recently broken away from it, were known - but clear and direct evidence was not available - to have been subsidised from German sources; and it was believed that one of the objects of this subsidy was for purposes of propaganda likely to be favourable to German policy. The Germans, presumably impressed by the results which they thought they had achieved in the United Kingdom, planned to set up similar organisations in the Dominions. Although Goebbels would be primarily concerned as being in charge of propaganda, there was reason to state that these Dominion and Colonial organisations would be subject to the general supervision of Bohle's Auslands Organisation.

If the ultimate object of all this propaganda conducted under the direction of Hitler, Rosenberg, Goebbels and Ribbentrop, was the aggrandisement of Germany on the Continent, it was suggested that they must view with satisfaction the fact that sums running into hundreds of pounds were obtained for this purpose from English sources (including the contributions of firms like Unilever, Dunlop Rubber Company, Imperial Chemical Industries Ltd., etc.) by working on the prevalent desire for peace and the business interests of English people.

It should be emphasised that propaganda of this type in many forms was addressed directly and indirectly to individuals in various walks of life after Ribbentrop had announced in his Embassy that their aims were to work for the downfall of the British Empire.

(d) German Espionage 1933-1939.

The great difference between our knowledge of the German espionage system in the second World War and our previous knowledge of it is to be found in the fact that prior to the outbreak of war in 1939 communications between the German organisation and its agents were carried on by letter through the post or through couriers and wireless was not used. The first concrete evidence of the intention to use wireless was found when the German Abwehrstelle at Hamburg supplied a wireless set to the agent [...] in January 1939 for use in the event of war.

Previous Chapters have shown how the H.O.W. and the Postal Censorship were most important sources of information by making it possible to intercept the communications of German agents in this country before and during the first World War. In the period under review the H.O.W. continued to give useful results, but it only led to the agents in this country and their employers in Germany or other neighbouring countries. It did not furnish any clear or comprehensive detail from which a general picture of the German organisation could be built up.

It was noticeable that during the war of 1914-1918 very little was learned about the German organisation and the M.I.5. book on the German Police system already mentioned (Bibliography No. 36, vide Chapters 7 and 8 ibid), shows how this information was only acquired after the partial occupation of Germany at the end of the war and then only to a limited extent. The information then obtained showed that there was a distinction between the Intelligence or Nachrichtenstelle and the Counter-Espionage or Abwehrstelle. It also showed that the German Secret Intelligence Service was closely associated with the German police.

After 1933 the same general conditions held good. We now know that in consequence of conditions imposed at the end of the war of 1914-1918 the Intelligence Branch (Nachrichtenabteilung) ceased to function, and espionage was eventually included in the duties of what was nominally and ostensibly the Counter Espionage (Abwehr) Branch.

Prior to and during the war of 1914-1918 the German Admiralty was closely associated for intelligence purposes with the Central Police Offices at Hamburg and Berlin and it is probable that this explains the fact that the Abwehrstelle at Hamburg was chiefly concerned with espionage against the British Empire and the U.S.A. in the earlier period and again in 1933-1939. The enquiries made into cases which occurred during this later period failed to furnish us with any detailed information about the organisation at Hamburg beyond the fact that it appeared to have a branch in Cologne, which was also concerned with operations against England. The information obtained about the German personnel in Hamburg and Cologne was confined to a knowledge of the pseudonyms used in correspondence and the accounts given to us by individuals who interviewed some of them when they were recruited as agents. The German methods and our counter-measures therefore resulted in our being in the dark about the organisation in Germany and its personnel and only obtaining information about actual agents who came to our notice in this country. We had to depend on S.I.S. to penetrate the German organisation and to obtain inside information about its scope, its methods and its personnel, but they did not achieve any results in this direction.

During the period in question thirty agents who either worked or were asked to work for the Germans, came to our notice. Of these twenty-one were British subjects, many of whom made no attempt to collect information of value to the Germans but supplied them with details of no importance in order to extract the maximum of reward for the minimum of effort. Most of these British subjects were given virtually no training and all the circumstances of their employment indicated that the Abwehr was run on a very crude basis. Quantity, not quality, in agents seemed to be the aim; but it was and is impossible to say whether a cloud of agents of low quality served to hide a few good ones. In half of the British cases the persons concerned were of low mentality with no capacity for obtaining secret information of any importance. Among the more suitable persons whom the Germans recruited, or attempted to recruit, were four unemployed ex-officers, four business men and four serving officers or men, most of whom reported the fact to the authorities immediately or soon after they were approached by the Germans. One German method of approach was by answering advertisements in the Press, especially the advertisements of ex-officers, business men and technical workers. The Germans also themselves inserted advertisements in the English papers offering employment to commercial or technical experts.

From 1936 onwards the Hamburg Abwehrstelle increased its activities considerably and twenty-six of the thirty known cases occurred between that year and the beginning of the war.

During the period there were three known cases of Germans visiting or residing temporarily in this country or Eire to act as recruiters of agents and three cases of German women - one each in England, Scotland and Eire - who acted as post-boxes for communications received by the German Secret Service from their agents in the U.S.A. and France. All three were employed by the Hamburg Abwehrstelle, which, however, never wrote to its agents via these post-boxes, apparently because, although they knew that incoming post was liable to be opened, they did not realise that letters posted by their agents were equally dangerous. (They often used couriers on German ships.)

Of the thirty agents eleven reported the fact of the German approach to us; nine were discovered through H.O.W.s on addresses already known; five were reported by private people whose suspicions had been aroused; one was reported by an Immigration Officer; one by an anonymous informant and the remaining two came to notice adventitiously. The general circumstances showed that, while the H.O.W. on correspondence produced some results, it was far from giving satisfactory reason to believe that it could bring all the fish into the nets - the meshes were too large. The evidence regarding the known recruiters indicated that agents were obtained in England by means of personal contact, but only one agent recruited in this way was discovered otherwise than by pure chance. Of the agents who reported to us, and who but for that would probably never have come to light, six cases out of eleven were recruited by personal contact; there must therefore be considerable uncertainty regarding the number who never reported the approach, and whom our facilities for detection were inadequate to discover. In spite of this there are good reasons for believing that at the beginning of the war the number of active agents reporting intelligence to the Germans and left behind by them in the United Kingdom was limited to a handful of individuals. In the circumstances of the case, however, conclusions of this kind cannot be final.

The three women post-boxes provided the more interesting evidence regarding the German system although they were not directly concerned with espionage in this country. Of the three Mrs. Duncombe in London was receiving intelligence obtained in France; Mrs. Jordan was the post-box in the U.S.A. case which was widely advertised in the Press, the leading character being an individual named Rumrich. Rumrich's brother was simultaneously arrested in Prague and the address of Mrs. Brandy - the third post-box - who lived in Dublin was found on him. A H.O.W. on her correspondence showed that she was receiving accurate, and therefore dangerous, espionage reports from an officer in the French Navy. The means by which they were forwarded by her were never discovered but they were probably carried by couriers on boats travelling between Eire and Hamburg. As a result of these enquiries we gave information to the French and a French Naval officer named Aubert was found to be the author of the reports in question. He was arrested in November 1938 and shot. These three cases also suggested that the German methods included the use of correspondence or post-boxes in countries other than those against which they were operating and that the intelligence reports about

British countries might be received by them in a similar way, but no evidence of this was forthcoming although they gave addresses in neutral countries to some of their "agents" who reported to us.

Of the agents who reported to us either at the beginning or shortly afterwards a certain number were instructed to work for the Germans under our direction and did so for periods varying from a month to three years. The problem of running double-cross agents in peacetime presented serious difficulties, mainly because it was almost impossible to supply them with information that was both innocuous and at the same time satisfactory to the Germans. A great deal of elementary information and even some of the highest importance was to be had in England for the asking, and the Germans were not content for long to receive handbooks which could be bought at any bookstall. The important information bearing on our heavy industries, scientific research and our war potential in general which was readily available to the German Intelligence Service, included not only such things as maps and plans of railways, public utilities, docks and bridges, but masses of detailed information of an industrial nature which was available to numerous Germans engaged in business in this country. All this was focussed in the German Chamber of Commerce which was established in London by the Nazis and described by them as a "bulwark" of their Party. Although there was no evidence of a secret nature relevant to this point the facilities were so great that it is impossible to believe that information, much of which came under the heading of commercial intelligence but also threw an important light on industries capable of expansion for war purposes, was not regularly and systematically collected and forwarded to the proper quarters in Germany. There were even cases of Germans in close touch with our aircraft industry; and the German command of the Machine Tool industry provided them with almost endless facilities for obtaining a wide variety of information regarding the capacity of particular plants and the output in general of aeroplanes, tanks, lorries and munitions of all kinds.

The extent of the German organisation for dealing with matters relating to war industry and industrial mobilisation is described in Appendix A to the Report on the German Secret Service, prepared in this Office in August 1942 (vide Bibliography No. 33). This note mentions the relations between the Wehrwirtschaftsstab of the Oberkommando der Wehrmacht and the Abteilung Wirtschaft of the Abwehr and indicates the comprehensive nature of their functions under the general conception according to which the leading German industrialists - with their special relations with international cartels - were charged by the Führer with the duty of co-ordinating all matters involving the relations between the German military machine and German industry. In view of the fact that the modern war machine of great Powers is largely based on their heavy industries and general technical development, the facilities at the disposal of the Wehrwirtschaftsstab for obtaining information of vital importance were obviously of a far-reaching nature. In this respect the position in the Western democracies is very different from that in a country like Russia in which security measures of an extreme nature can be and have been imposed. The German system also made it possible to enforce a much greater degree of security than was possible here. Even if our Security Service before the war had been very much larger than it was, it would have been impossible to provide any reasonable degree of security against the inquisitiveness of the Wehrwirtschaftsstab with all the open and secret sources of information available to them in this country. The most that could have been done would have been to detect any secret agents employed by the Party organisation or the Abwehr including the Wirtschaft Abteilung. As it was, we had no practical working knowledge of the Abwehr before 1941 and we were thrown back on the necessity of making enquiries regarding individual Germans who appeared to be well-placed to obtain information of a particularly secret nature. As mentioned in the concluding paragraph of Appendix A to the note referred to above, instructions were given to the Abwehr in 1938 to intensify its activities in the United Kingdom. This information was, in fact, derived from [...] and in view of the circumstances described above was regarded as unimpeachable. The specific mention of the cement industry led to enquiries regarding Germans connected with that industry and in particular the Concrete Pump Co Ltd., owned by a German father and British-born son (liable to be called up for service in the German Army) whose work gave them access to and a detailed knowledge of the measurements, purposes and location of a number of aerodromes and secret naval installations as well as numerous other defence works all over the country. Similar enquiries gave reasons for apprehension in numerous other trades and industries.

Other information from an unconscious informant who was a prominent member of the German Foreign Office, and who had given us important early information regarding the negotiations between Germany and Russia in 1939, also told us, without his being aware of the fact, that the office equipment trades had been a source of valuable intelligence to the Germans.

The effect of all the information available to us up to the beginning of the war was to suggest that while the Abwehr employed a number of agents of very low quality and of little or no value they were able to score major successes as in the cases in U.S.A. and France which had come to light through the post-boxes in the United Kingdom. There could be no guarantee that there were no similarly well-placed agents in this country having contact with Germany through other countries who had escaped detection. The open field for obtaining intelligence of vital importance regarding our war potential and our aircraft and munition factories was so vast that security enquiries could not cover more than a fraction of it. Nevertheless we were driven to undertaking security enquiries into numerous cases of suspects which presented themselves and to making enquiries having special reference to important secrets such as new aeroplane inventions, radiolocation and a number of other similar secrets of special importance.

In this way the enquiries made by B Branch were not confined strictly to the investigation of espionage but covered a much larger field of a generally preventive nature. Many of these enquiries involved co-operation between B Branch and D Sections, who were responsible for security in factories and resarch stations, especially in connection with air matters. In fact, many of the more alarming cases of apparent insecurity were brought to notice by D Branch officers.

(ii) Preventive action suggested by the Security Service.

In addition to the reports and memoranda mentioned in Chapter III, Part 2, (i), numerous reports on the subject of the Nazi Party organisation were forwarded to the Foreign Office and the Home Office during 1936 and subsequent years.

In April 1936 B Branch prepared a paper which was handed by the Director to a Permanent Under-Secretary to the Home Office in which it was argued that the development in the direction of the form of the one-Party Nation-State in Germany and Italy - without precedent in the ancient or modern world - compelled a more clearly defined attitude towards the question of British sovereignty and British nationality as raised by the existence and activities of the Auslands Organisation and the Fasci all'Estero. Reference was made to the German conception of total war involving an attack without warning to be made by the air forces not only against the armed forces of the enemy but also against the civilian population. It was argued that the two organisations mentioned were part of the machinery available to their Governments for the waging of total war and pointed out the possibility of their being used for sabotage purposes. Attention was also drawn to their attempts to bring dual nationals of German and Italian origin or extraction under their influence. This paper was prepared with a view to the consideration of legislation aiming at the prohibition of these Party organisations on British soil.

It proved impossible, however, to take preventive action on the basis of an agreed policy. When the general question was raised in the Cabinet in July 1936 the Prime Minister asked the Home Secretary and the Secretary of State for Foreign Affairs to bring it up on some later occasion when the moment was more opportune for taking action. We suggested that with the growth of German rearmament it would probably become more difficult to take action as time went on. The Secretary of State for Foreign Affairs reverted to the question in October 1936 when the Cabinet again deferred a decision on the question.

As a result of our representations, the Permanent Under-Secretaries of the Foreign Office and the Home Office and the Director of the Security Service prepared a joint memorandum in April 1937 for submission to the Cabinet proposing that informal and friendly suggestions should be made to the German and Italian Governments through their Embassies in London that they should take steps to secure the closing down of branches of the National Socialist and Fascist Parties' organisations established in the United Kingdom. The question was again considered by the Cabinet in July 1937 when they came to the conclusion that it should not be allowed to drift indefinitely and must be kept under continuous observation, but that in view of the existing difficulties in securing agreement over questions relating to Spain no drastic action should be taken at the moment. In September 1937 the question was again raised by Sir Robert Vansittart in view of further developments including those connected with the Congress of Germans abroad held at Stuttgart in August of that year and in July 1938, in consultation with the Director of the Security Service, he again raised the question in a note addressed to Lord Halifax and Sir Samuel Hoare as a result of a request from the Ministry of Foreign Affairs in Paris to be informed "of the practical steps which His Majesty's

Government intend to take to circumscribe the activity in Great Britain of the Nazi organisation".

In the meanwhile, as a result of information obtained by intercepting the correspondence of the Nazi Party, we continued to submit reports on various aspects of the subject such as the "Gleichschaltung" of members of the German Embassy staff in London by their being induced to join the Nazi Party organisation for German officials; and numerous other similar matters. In view of the attitude of the German Government to Germans who acquired British nationality and retained their German nationality when it was considered to the advantage of Germany that they should do so, steps were taken to restrict the admission of such persons to the armed forces in this country.

In the absence of an agreed policy preventive action could only be taken as a result of enquiries into individual cases as they occurred either by preventing Germans from entering the country or doubtful characters, whether Germans or dual nationals, from working in factories connected with the manufacture of aircraft and munitions.

One of the more important cases of a German being refused permission to stay in this country was that of Otto Karl Ludwig who arrived in this country on 10.4.37. and attracted the suspicion of the Immigration Officer. As a result of enquiries he was deported after being arrested under the Official Secrets Act. It was clear from the examination of his papers that he had come here to set up a Political Intelligence Bureau and that three German journalists in London, Nidda, Crome and Edenhofer, as they admitted, had been supplying him with political intelligence reports of a semi-secret kind. This case led to more careful enquiry into the position with regard to German journalists in this country. Their number attracted the attention of British journalists and our enquiries showed that sometimes quite small German papers with very limited circulations had more than one nominal correspondent in London.

The question was brought to the notice of the Foreign Office and on 4th May 1937, a meeting (attended among others by Sir Vernon Kell and Captain Liddell) was held by Sir Robert Vansittart, who opened the discussion by saying that he felt that this question was closely bound up with the much bigger question of the German and Italian organisations on British territory. The Foreign Secretary thought that the matter was one of internal security and therefore one for Sir John Simon, the Home Secretary, to put to the Cabinet. Sir John Simon had said that if the Foreign Office were prepared to make it a "cardinal facet" of their foreign policy towards Germany, he would be ready to implement it. The position therefore was that the Foreign Secretary would support the Home Secretary and the Home Secretary would support the Foreign Secretary, but neither was anxious to put the matter before the Cabinet.

With regard to the German journalists, Sir Robert Vansittart thought that, pending some action regarding the general question of Nazi and Fascist organisations, steps should be taken to deal with them as opportunity occurred. He had been through the documents of the Ludwig case and he thought that Nidda, Crome and Edenhofer should be asked to leave the country.

It was decided that other German journalists who had come to notice as being engaged in undesirable activities should also be asked to leave; but that steps to do this should be taken gradually.

Another meeting (also attended by Sir Vernon Kell and Captain Liddell) on the subject of German journalists was held by the Home Secretary on 21.6.37. The Home Secretary said that a distinction should be drawn between journalists who had been connected with the Ludwig case and others selected as undesirable; the general question of the reduction of the large numbers of German journalists was a matter for the Foreign Office; and he did not wish to take action which would produce violent headlines in the papers at the moment when von Neurath was coming to London. As regards the general question of Nazi and Fascist organisations, he would like time to give the whole matter further consideration.

At the end of August 1937 we submitted a report on the question of the German journalists for the consideration of the Foreign Office. We referred to a list of seventy such persons which we had prepared in the previous April and said that the number had by then risen to about ninety, although some few of these might not be working under the various organs of the Nazi Government. The Nazi head of the German journalists in the United Kingdom had stated as a result of a reference to the matter in the Press that the number did not exceed thirty. It appeared that various German Nazi organisations were interested in obtaining political information from this country and it was possible that their work was not completely co-ordinated. The offices interested in obtaining information about the affairs of this country appeared to include the following:-

> The Auslands Pressestelle of the NSDAP;
> The Propagandaministerium in Berlin with which is linked-
>   Johannsen's Bureau in Hamburg;
> The Auslands Organisation;
> The Ribbentrop Bureau;
> The Auswärtiges Amt;
> The Aussenpolitisches Amt with which is linked-
>   The Anti-Comintern Organisation;
>   The Reichswehrministerium;
>   The Luftfahrtministerium.

One fact which might to some extent explain what was happening was that at the time of the occupation of the Rhineland in March 1936 the German Army was opposed to this step whereas the Party organisations reported to the effect that it would not produce any serious reactions here. Hitler acted on the advice of the Party and against that of the Army. He was right; and it seemed reasonable to infer that the Army, and possibly other German offices and Departments, consequently desired to obtain more accurate and detailed information regarding the state of public opinion over here.

Again, we knew that von Ribbentrop in addition to being Ambassador in London had at his disposal a Bureau for the collection of information on which he based the advice he gave to Hitler. After referring to his part in the German-Japanese treaty and his special interest in Austria and South-Eastern Europe, we pointed out that he required reports from very varied and well-informed sources in connection with the campaign of propaganda which he was at that time conducting among English people with a view to promoting good feeling towards Germany. There had been indications that Ribbentrop was personally interested in the Information Bureau which Ludwig had intended to establish in London.

With regard to the Reichswehrministerium we believed that there was some division of opinion on political matters and that there were two prominent groups. It was probable that both had agents among the journalists. Two who were known to us had been proposed for removal from this country. Another journalist whose removal had been proposed had been obtaining information about air matters in an improper manner.

We represented that, apart from the questions of high policy the position from our more restricted point of view was a difficult one. With an Ambassador engaging in extra ambassadorial activities (in the way of intrigues in both countries and propaganda in that to which he was accredited) and with so many agencies employing such a variety of agents, the work of detecting those concerned with espionage and at the same time keeping touch with the political background was reaching proportions which were proving overwhelming to our small organisation. The activities of these numerous journalists diverted some of our attention and since it was found impossible to keep in touch with all of them, it became increasingly difficult to know which of them was concerned with really objectionable activities.

Consideration of the question of the removal of more of these journalists remained before the Home Office and the Foreign Office during 1937 and 1938. In the first place six were asked to leave on account of objectionable activities, but it was decided that nothing was to be gained by more wholesale action. While the German Government claimed that only thirty-one German journalists were officially recognised by them, it was felt that so long as various German Government and Party offices maintained their foreign affairs bureaux, they would obviously seek information from representatives abroad. If we turned out their present agents, our Foreign Office considered that we would merely annoy those Departments and Offices to little or no purpose, as they would find means of sending other agents. It was also suggested that many of these journalists had furnished objective reports to Germany which probably did a considerable amount of good in removing any false impressions held in Germany of British decadence or weakness.

From a report which we received from a reliable source we learned that the action taken in removing the six journalists caused some dispute between Goering and Himmler and that Himmler decided to employ agents under other guises in consequence. (In the light of our more recent knowledge this would go some way towards confirming the impression that Ludwig was an agent of the Sicherheitsdienst).

In April 1939, as a result of our representations, Lord Halifax saw the German Charge d'Affaires and told him that a decision had been taken that three of the leading members of the Nazi organisation in this country should be asked to leave in the near future. They were:-

    Herr Karlowa — Landesgruppenleiter of the Nazi Party in this country;
    Herr Himmelmann — "Organisationsleiter" of the Nazi Party in this country;
    Frau Johanna Wolf — the leader of the Women's Section of the German Labour Front in this country.

We received very reliable information that the action taken against Karlowa as the Nazi Party leader in Great Britain made a deep impression on the Nazi leaders and made them realise that we understood the significance of his position here and realised the point of disrupting the Party organisation.[†]

Again in April 1939 - after keeping a close watch on correspondence going to certain addresses in Germany - we prepared a report on German propaganda and forwarded it to the Deputy-Director of Military Intelligence. We pointed out that the Germans had been attempted in various ways to form direct personal communications between His Majesty's Forces and their propagandist organisations, and we suggested that it was a matter for consideration whether men in the Services should not have it impressed upon them how ill-advised and dangerous correspondence with these organisations was. Inevitably their correspondents in Germany would be selected for their ardent support of the Nazi regime, and any hints as to public opinion in England and any information about the Services which might inadvertently be put into their correspondence, would certainly be passed on to those responsible for directing Nazi foreign policy. The D.D.M.I. had agreed that it was desirable to issue instructions to officers in the Forces.

As a result of a consideration of all the evidence regarding the Nazi Party (Auslands) Organisation in London and the part it was playing in the furtherance of Hitler's aims, B Branch suggested to the Director that arrangements should be made to arrest all members of the Party in this country in the event of war. With the threatening situation which led to the Munich Crisis in September 1938, the Director obtained the approval of the Home Office to arrangements by which the names of all members of the Party and its subsidiary organisations were communicated to the police; and telegrams ordering their arrest as well as those in the case of individuals suspected of espionage on behalf of Germany were kept in readiness for despatch at a moment's notice. These telegrams (known as the "Ansabona telegrams") were ultimately despatched on the outbreak of war in September 1939.

[†] According to a report dated 23.5.39. the Foreign Office received information to the following effect:- 'In Munich Party circles it was now particularly feared that England's example might give other and smaller States the courage to destroy the Nazi organisations in their area. "It is clear" said Boettiger "that in the case of war the Nazi organisations abroad would have highly important and also very dangerous tasks to fulfil. The Nazi groups in the so-called neutral States would have the most to do. It is astonishing how slow these democracies are to realise the importance of such compact political organisations in their midst". Boettiger concluded by saying that Dr. Kordt was of the opinion that the expulsions from England were not yet at an end and that there might be many further surprises in the future. (Vide 102x of SF.66/U.K./63).

(iii) Liaison with the Eire Authorities.

In April 1938 the Agreement had been signed between the British and Eire Governments which provided, inter alia, for the withdrawal of British garrisons from Eire ports. On the 31st August 1938 - at a time when the German aggressiveness which led up to Munich was coming to a head - Mr. Walshe of the Department of External Affairs in Eire raised with the Dominions Office the question of liaison on counter espionage matters and said that he was anxious to see a representative of our counter espionage organisation. His approach arose out of discussions which followed on certain information regarding Defence Plans being communicated by His Majesty's Government to the Eire authorities, a mark of confidence which apparently touched Mr. de Valer. He immediately made arrangements for Mr. Walshe to get into touch with the authorities here. Thereupon, under the Director's instruction, Captain Liddell saw Mr. Walshe and Mr. Dulanty and the former explained that the Eire Government was anxious about the NSDAP Group in Dublin and that they felt that it virtually infringed their sovereign rights. As a result of this meeting Captain Liddell again saw Mr. Dulanty at his office in London on the 10th September 1938, and handed to him a copy of our memorandum on the NSDAP (vide Bibliography No.4) and a memorandum drawn up by B.Branch to meet Mr. Walshe's request to the Dominions Office. This latter memorandum opened by emphasising that it contained suggestions based on our experience here - Captain Liddell had already mentioned that his experience had resulted in a typically English organisation which had grown up gradually and had had pieces grafted on to it at different stages of its existence. The memorandum suggested that a counter espionage organisation would probably be most suitably controlled by the Ministry of Defence and that the officer-in-charge should, when necessary, have direct access to the Minister. Upon the personality of the officer-in-charge would depend to a very large extent its success or failure; the highest degree of tact was necessary in order to obtain collaboration and assistance from the police and other Departments of State. Experience had shown that it was essential for such an organisation to be adequately provided with measures for the control of -

(a) the entry and exit of aliens
(b) their supervision while in the country
(c) the interception of correspondence, telegraphic and telephonic communications.

It also offered to place at the disposal of the Eire organisation information about suspect aliens obtained by the Security Service. It mentioned that it was understood that the powers of the Eire organisation would be based on our Official Secrets Act (1911-1920) and our Aliens Act (1914-1919).

Colonel Liam Archer was appointed by the Eire Department of Defence to take charge of their Counter Espionage Organisation and during October 1938 meetings took place between him and the Security Service officers. His Organisation had to be built up from scratch under conditions of great secrecy without experience, personnel or funds; and subject to an internal political situation in which a factor was divergence of views on the subject within the Eire Government itself. From the time of its formation until the outbreak of war it was in fairly regular correspondence, carried on through the Eire High Commissioner's Bag, with the Security Service. The correspondence was for the most part confined to matters relating go Germans. The value of this liaison arose from and depended on the good personal relationships which were cultivated between the counter espionage officers on both sides.

There had always been a small number of Germans or persons of German origin in Ireland, but after 1921 the policy of independence from Great Britain - particularly industrial, cultural and linguistic independence - led to a steady increase in their numbers. The Shannon Hydro-Electric scheme, the contract for which was given to the German firm Siemen Schukert, was one of the most important symptons of the move towards industrial independence and led to an influx of German technicians. The Germans also took an interest in the revival of the Gaelic language and culture, which had been a fundamental part of the nationalist development and among the leading German archaeologists and Celtic scholars who interested themselves in this was Dr. Adolf Mahr. He was appointed Curator of the Dublin Museum. He also held the appointment of Ortsgruppenleiter of the NSDAP in Dublin and in this dual capacity played a part in developing cultural relations between the two countries, which were also furthered by the exchange of students and lecturers under the auspices of the Nazi Party organisation and by the establishment of a branch of the German News Agency, the DNB, under one Carl Petersen.

In June 1939 there were grounds for thinking that Carl Petersen had made approaches to the I.R.A. with a view to the possibility of co-operation in the event of war between Germany and England and early in July 1939 S.I.S. reported that a conference had taken place in Berlin between Admiral Canaris, head of the Abwehr, a representative of the German War Office and a responsible member of the I.R.A., who was said to have reported on the bombing campaign which was then being conducted in Britain. Canaris was reported to have undertaken to supply him with arms and funds.

The branch of the Nazi Party organisation which supervised German seamen was known to arrange for German Intelligence Service reports to be transmitted by hand through officers of German steamers plying between Dublin and Germany. In August 1937 a German named Kurt Wheeler Hill arranged for one [...] to visit Hamburg where he was introduced to leading Abwehr officials and asked to establish wireless communications with Hamburg and to recruit agents in the Royal Tank Corps, the R.A.F. and the Royal Artillery. In 1938 Campbell came to London and reported on his dealings with the Germans at the War Office. An attempt was made to play [...] as a double agent but only a limited amount of information was obtained as Kurt Wheeler Hill left Dublin hurriedly, possibly as a result of being alarmed. There were other indications of attempts by the Abwehr to recruit Irishmen, but nothing substantial was known to have been achieved by them.

(iv) Liaison with the American authorities.

In Chapter III, Part 2, (ii), (d), above, reference was made to the U.S.A. case in which a leading character was one Gunther Gustav Rumrich, a member of a "spy ring" in the

U.S.A. In 1937, in the course of his general enquiries into German espionage in this country, Lt-Colonel Hinchley Cooke was intercepting correspondence going to an address in Hamburg used by the Hamburg Abwehrstelle and, among other things, this disclosed that Mrs. Jessie Jordan, who was being used as a post-box in Scotland by that Abwehrstelle, was receiving reports from America and forwarding them to Hamburg. One of these reports described a plot to overpower an American officer and obtain important documents from his possession. As soon as this fact was known to us it was communicated to Colonel Lee, the American Military Attache in London, who cabled the essential facts to the authorities in the U.S.A. This led to an enquiry which ultimately resulted in an indictment by a Federal Grand Jury against certain German officers in the Abwehr in Germany, who organised the 'spy ring', and the conviction of a number of individuals in the U.S.A. The case was widely publicised at the time.

In March 1938 Captain Liddell visited the U.S.A. and saw a number of officials in the War Department, the Political Relations Department of the State Department, Mr. Hoover and the F.B.I. officers concerned with the enquiry in connection with which Rumrich had been arrested. Mr. Dunn of the State Department expressed himself as anxious to have an exchange of information on the subject of the activities of the German and Italian (Nazi and Fascist) Parties abroad. He explained that the U.S.A. Government had made it clear to the German and Italian Ambassadors that they would not tolerate the existence of organised Party groups which they felt constituted a virtual infringement of sovereignty. Captain Liddell was able to inform Mr. Dunn that although the German Ambassador had given an assurance that no such organisation existed in the U.S.A. he could take it as a certainty that Nazi Party groups did exist, although not openly.

In the course of these conversations with various officials it became clear to Captain Liddell that the scope of the F.B.I.'s activities was gradually widening and that it covered espionage and that, although it had no "Charter" to do so, it had on the quiet been going thoroughly into Soviet activities.

Captain Liddell also visited Ottawa where he discussed the same general subjects with the Commissioner of the Royal Canadian Mounted Police, who was in close touch with Mr. Hoover in connection with their common interests in such matters as German and Italian activities; but, as the Commissioner explained, by agreement between them their correspondence was based on criminal rather than political lines.

From further discussion in the U.S.A. with a Staff Officer G-2, and Mr. Turrou of the F.B.I., Captain Liddell learned that Rumrich had admitted that the establishment of post-boxes in England was intended to throw the onus on the British in the event of unpleasant revelations. Arrangements for a full exchange of information in detail in connection with the case both in the U.S.A. and this country, where Mrs. Jessie Jordan had been arrested, were made. Among other details Mr. Turrou informed Captain Liddell that Eric Pfeiffer of the German Intelligence Service was in the habit of selling a large percentage of the information obtained by the Germans in the U.S. at a very high figure to the Japanese.

On his return to London in April 1938 Captain Liddell discussed the circumstances fully with Colonel Lee, the American Military Attache, and Mr. Herschel Johnson, the American Chargé d'Affaires. It was apparent that the State Department were anxious to keep matters regarding a liaison under their own control. It was agreed, however, that liaison in the espionage case, then current, should continue to be conducted with Colonel Lee. Captain Liddell handed to Mr. Herschel Johnson a copy of our memorandum on the N.S.D.A.P. of 1937 (vide Bibliography No. 4) and impressed on him the fact that the German espionage case in America had disclosed that the whole machinery of Party and State had been brought to bear in order to facilitate the operations of the agents whose object was to acquire information regarding military secrets and the U.S.A. war potential over a wide field.

Underlying this exchange of information about the Nazi organisations was the intention not only of promoting co-operation with the Americans on the basis of common interest but also of helping to ensure against the possibility that Nazi aggressiveness would lead to war, i.e. to a war in which American goodwill would be in the national interest.

In October 1938 Colonel Lee, the American Attache in London, informed the Security Service that he was more than ever convinced in the light of recent developments that our two countries would have to work very closely together as regards German espionage activities. He asked for a general sketch of a plan for a new Counter Espionage Service in the United States, and a general statement of our own organisation was conveyed to him on lines similar to those given to the Eire authorities as mentioned above. In addition, the importance of good relations between the Fighting Services and industry with a view to safeguarding the design of equipment manufactured at Government arsenals and by private firms as well as new inventions was stressed. The necessity for a staff to visit factories in the interests of security was also mentioned. Colonel Lee made a thorough examination of the whole problem but it is understood that at the time no action on his note on the subject was taken by the War Department at Washington. He stressed the importance of keeping the Counter Espionage Service free from political flavour and mentioned that certain reasons had given ground for enlisting public sympathy in the U.S.A. by publicity about the Federal Bureau of Investigation. He suggested that a successful counter espionage service did not require this publicity and that on the contrary its work should be confidential. In a characteristically American way, however, an important part in counter espionage work in the U.S.A. was played by the F.B.I. with whom our liaison was further developed when America came into the war.

As the work of the Security Service was intimately affected by the internal organisation of the American Services, the following facts extracted from "Travel Control Guide, Part II (Travel Control) of the Office of the Chief of Naval Operations, Division of Naval Intelligence (1st May 1943)" should be mentioned.

In a memorandum of June 26th, 1939, the President of the U.S.A. instructed all heads of Government Departments and Agencies that the investigation of all matters pertaining to or involving espionage, counter espionage, sabotage and subversion, actual or potential, should be the sole responsibility of three agencies; namely the Military Intelligence Service, the Office of Naval Intelligence and the Federal Bureau of

Investigation; and he further directed that any such matter which came to the notice of any of the Government Departments or agencies should be immediately referred by them to the Federal Bureau of Investigation. In order to clarify the respective responsibilities of the three agencies a Delimitation Agreement was drawn up and adopted. This Agreement attempted to define those matters in which the interest was essentially naval, military or civilian and the extent to which each of the three Intelligence agencies would participate in investigations.

The exact terms of the Delimitation Agreement are not known to us, but uncertainty regarding the responsibilities of these three agencies continued to have constant repercussions on the relations of different parts of the Security Service and their American opposite numbers. The investigations of B Division and the security work of S.C.O.s at the ports and of A.D.D.4. were most nearly affected.

The difficulties of this situation were accentuated by the difficult relations between the Security Service and S.I.S. on the one hand and S.I.S. and Security Co-ordination, New York, on the other; but these difficulties only developed during the subsequent war period.

Part 3: Italian and Japanese Aggressiveness

(i) The Italian Secret Intelligence Service and the Italian Partito Nazionale Fascista.

Prior to the outbreak of the Italian war against Abyssinia in 1935 the Security Service had had no reason to study the question of either the Italian Fascist Secret Intelligence Service or the Italian Fascist Party's organisation in British territory. The question of the application of sanctions by the League of Nations and the consequent tension, resulting in the despatch of the main British Fleet to the Eastern Mediterranean, produced a demand for measures to make good these deficiencies. The only information on record was a general summary which had been prepared a few years previously by Section V of S.I.S. which dealt with the Italian Intelligence system on broad lines, but no up-to-date information was available. We accordingly pressed Section V for a detailed account of the Italian Secret Intelligence Service and of its position in the Italian military machine, but they were unable to supply us with any information of value.

Simultaneously enquiries were commenced in this country regarding the local branches of the Fasci all'Estero and information was exchanged with our correspondents in the Dominions and Colonies and the Middle East. A report from Egypt at an early stage of the period of tension disclosed that the headquarters of the Royal Air Force in the Middle East had removed a number of Italians from employment on the civilian establishment of British aerodromes. Information which was believed to be completely reliable was received to the effect that the heads of the Partito Nazionale Fascista intended at this time to use the Party organisation to sabotage British aerodromes and aircraft in the Mediterranean area in the event of war. Information from independent sources was also received by S.I.S. to the effect that definite plans had been made to employ the

Italian Fascist militia in Greece to hinder the mobilisation of the Greek army in the event of war between Greece and Italy resulting from the proposed closure of the Suez Canal to Italian ships. The plan was reported to embrace the sabotage of railways and bridges in Greece and the Fasci were alleged to have been told that war was likely to occur without a diplomatic rupture.

All the enquiries possible in view of the scanty resources of the Security Service at this time failed to disclose any evidence of serious Italian espionage in this country. Such indications as there were showed that intelligence reports of a crude kind regarding the despatch of troops and material from the United Kingdom to the Middle East were being collected through the agency of the Italian Consulates and the Italian Fascist organisations. In fact the general conclusion was drawn that Italian intelligence was in the main obtained through official channels aided by the Party organisation. The latter were therefore kept under close observation and the results of these enquiries were embodied in a note of 1936 on "The Organisation and Activities of the Italian Fascist Party in the United Kingdom, the Dominions and Colonies" (vide Bibliography No. 44). Again in 1936 the question of the potentialities of these Italian organisations for sabotage purposes was discussed in the "Memorandum on the possibilities of sabotage by the organisation set up in British countries by the totalitarian Governments of Germany and Italy - 1936" (vide Bibliography No. 52). The subsequent directions from the Sub-Committee of the J.I.C. to the effect that M.I.5. should continue to keep the question under observation also applied to the Fasci all'Estero (vide Bibliography No. 10). One of the salient features was the Italian Youth organisation abroad (Giovani Italiani all'Estero) Many of the Italian children in British countries were British subjects by birth but all the influence of the Italian organisation was brought to bear to maintain their "Italianita", and among the measures to this end was a summer camp in Italy at which children from Italian Colonies all over the world were assembled in considerable numbers in order to be subjected to intensive patriotic propaganda and to be drilled and to have the spirit of militarism inculcated in them.

While it was felt that all this indoctrination necessitated our attention in view of the possibility that in the event of war some harmful results might follow, it was always realised - as Mussolini himself was known to have recognised - that there was little prospect of the Italian people being imbued with a military spirit in any sense comparable with that of the Germans.

Additional notes on the Italian Fascist organisation were prepared in 1937 (vide Bibliography No.45).

Enquiries made up to the outbreak of war in September 1939 failed to elicit any serious information about Italian espionage in the United Kingdom. There had been a few cases of minor importance in Middle Eastern countries and various indications of Italian intrigue and Italian propaganda which aimed at promoting Italian and diminishing British prestige among the peoples of the Middle East. In brief it may be said that the problem presented by the Italian Secret Intelligence Service and the Fasci all'Estero was an unsatisfactory one in the sense that we failed to obtain reliable inside information which would enable us to see the purely espionage aspects in clear perspective. At the same time, while it was necessary to devote some of our scanty resources to an examination of the whole problem, there was a natural tendency not to take the military (or espionage) threat to British security from Italy very seriously. It was recognised that its most important aspects in the event of war would probably be found in the Middle East and the Defence Security Officer in Cairo was accordingly encouraged to develop his resources for obtaining information and for taking other counter espionage measures.

(ii) Japanese

After the termination of the Anglo-Japanese Alliance we received indications that the Japanese were concentrating on obtaining intelligence on naval matters in this country. In the years immediately preceding the second war the Japanes Naval Intelligence undoubtedly acquired a great deal of intelligence by visiting British war factories which they were permitted to do officially, and they availed themselves of the opportunities on numerous occasions. In 1926 an ex-naval officer named Colin Mayers retired from the Service at his own request and subsequently took up work at Vickers. He was found to be in touch with the Japanese Naval Attache in London who was paying him for information. He was sent for trial under Section II of the Official Secrets Act in April 1927 and was bound over after admitting minor offences (retaining documents).

In 1923 the Japanese Government employed the Master of Sempill (as he then was) as a technical adviser with special reference to aviation. During the years 1923-1926 there is little doubt that Sempill technically, at any rate, infringed the provisions of the Official Secrets Act and while the Director of Public Prosecutions did not feel that a prosecution was expedient, he took a very low view of the part Sempill was playing. From then onwards Sempill was constantly the subject of enquiry and while there is no evidence that he committed any further offence, his conduct generally gave cause for disquiet over a long period.

In 1923 they similarly employed an ex-Air Force officer named Frederick Joseph Rutland as a technical adviser to their Fleet Air Arm. He was kept under observation by the Security Service over a considerable period. This observation was often carried on under difficulties and on one occasion he challenged the shadowing staff who were following him, but was persuaded by the attitude they adopted to agree that he had made a mistake. His case was a good illustration of Japanese methods as from 1933 onwards he was being employed by them in espionage not against this country but against the U.S.A. The Japanese intention was to use an organisation which he established in America and the Pacific in the event of war between Japan and America. The arrangements for this organisation were made by Oka, the Japanese Naval Attache in London and the facts were disclosed as a result of the interception of the Naval Attache's messages from London to Tokyo and H.O.W.s on Rutland's correspondence. In addition to the use of diplomatic cypher Oka attempted to conceal his meaning by the use of a plain language code in which Japan was referred to as Denmark, and other details were similarly disguised before encyphering. The messages and correspondence showed that Oka was reporting to Tokyo on the arrangements which he was making for

Rutland to set up his organisation under cover of a business agency in the West End of London with a head office in California and branches in Vancouver and various ports in the Pacific. The object was for Rutland to obtain information of military importance on the West Coast of America and in the Pacific with a view to developing the organisation in the event of war. The case was handled in the first place by S.I.S., who, however, failed to make a satisfactory analysis of the evidence. This was done by the Security Service in the light of the fuller information at their disposal. In the summer of 1941 the Americans arrested a Japanese officer on a charge of espionage and there is no doubt that for some time previous to this Rutland had aroused their suspicions. Rutland approached the Americans with an offer of his services which was declined, and subsequently approached the British authorities. At the same time the F.B.I. represented that they were in a position to prefer serious charges against Rutland and that they contemplated doing so. In view of the scandal that might ensue arrangements were made to get Rutland out of America. On the outbreak of war with Japan, Rutland was arrested and interned as a person of hostile associations. The case is of value as furnishing a good instance of the employment by the Japanese of a national of one Western country to establish an organisation for the purpose of espionage against another.

Numerous reports were received from time to time to the effect that the Japanese Espionage Service was active throughout the Western Pacific, especially in Singapore and the Dutch East Indies. but few authenticated details were received beyond allegations such as that Japanese officers disguised as fishermen were habitually taking soundings and generally making enquiries throughout the area. In order to cope with this menace D.S.O.s were established at Singapore in 1936, and Hong-Kong in 1937, but few concrete results were obtained and no very satisfactory counter organisation to Japanese espionage was established either from these centres or in collaboration with the Australians.

General security measures were taken and the Overseas Defence Committee considered measures to secure the fortress of Singapore. In March 1938 an interdepartmental meeting was held at the Foreign Office in London to examine the position of foreign entry into and residence in Malaya with special reference to the defence of Singapore. It was agreed that everything should be done to reduce the size of the Japanese colony in Malaya and that the aim should be to get rid of all persons known or suspected to be dangerous and the Governor was addressed on the subject. It was pointed out that it was particularly important to secure the expulsion of all persons who might be likely to be or to become key-men in the local Japanese Intelligence Service. Dormant deportation warrants were to be held against suspects to be used well in advance of an emergency.

Part 4: Internal Organisation and Staff of the Security Service

As mentioned in Chapter III, Part 1, the position regarding the staff and work was fundamentally changed in 1931 when Captain Liddell, Captain Miller and other staff were transferred from Scotland House to the Security Service. Captain Liddell became

Deputy to Mr. Harker, who was head of B Branch, and until about 1935 the staff of this branch was primarily concerned with matters relating to Communism and the U.S.S.R. From 1934 onwards certain increases in staff took place. D Branch was formed to deal with the security of factories, railways and public utility undertakings of military importance. At the same time B Branch was gradually strengthened. It commenced to deal with British Fascist Movements and the Nazi Party in 1934 and with the Italian Fascist Party organisations in 1935. It also received slight additions of strength to deal with German espionage and Communism during the years 1935-1937. There was no marked increase until about half-a-dozen new officers joined in the summer of 1939.

The Admiralty and the War Office made arrangements for a small number of officers to receive training by being initiated into the work of the Security Service with a view to their being employed on liaison or intelligence duties connected with security in the event of war. The War Office scheme was a complete failure as unsuitable candidates were selected by Commanding Officers who, as was to be expected, did not desire to lose their best officers for duty in a sphere which in any case made little appeal to the regular regimental or staff officer. None of the War Office nominees, after finishing the course, was employed on duties connected with the Security Service. The Admiralty arrangements proved more satisfactory as they decided to appoint for this purpose naval reserve officers who proved suitable and useful. No financial provision was made for arrangements to train officers with a view to the expansion of the Security Service itself.

At the end of 1938 the Security Service was divided into four Branches A, B, C, D, under the Director Colonel Sir Vernon Kell and the Deputy-Director Lt.-Colonel Sir Eric Holt-Wilson. The latter had no normal functions as a Deputy and was not in charge of any of the Branches. He was employed in connection with the preparation of regulations and other measures to be adopted in the event of war.

A Branch was under Captain Butler and included the Registry and sections dealing with finance and internal administrative matters.

B Branch was under Mr. Harker with Capt. Liddell as his Deputy and was divided into a number of sections dealing with internal security in the Forces, Communism and Soviet espionage, German espionage, the Nazi Party, the Italian and British Fascist Parties and Italian and Japanese espionage.

C Branch consisted of Captain Bacon who was in charge of "vetting" and D Branch of three officers Lt-Colonel Norman, Commander Monie and Wing/Commander Archer, who were responsible for the security of factories working in the interests of the War Office, the Admiralty and the Air Ministry respectively with a somewhat vague responsibility for railways and electricity undertakings.

The total strength employed at this time was 30 officers and 103 secretaries and Registry Staff.

The principles of internal organisation were designed so as to enable this staff to discharge its functions as described in Chapter I. The principal means by which secret as opposed to open intelligence was obtained - in so far as the United Kingdom was concerned - were by the use of Home Office Warrants to intercept correspondence and to listen into telephone conversations, the employment of penetrative agents, most but not all of whom were controlled by the M Section and the shadowing staff. In so far as secret information from abroad was concerned the Security Service was dependent upon Section V of S.I.S. and on its correspondents in the Dominions and Colonies. These latter were usually the chief Officers of Police or in some cases Colonial Secretaries.

For the interception of letters as authorised by the Home Office Warrants the Security Service was dependent upon a small special staff at the G.P.O. connected with which there was a single officer who specialised in technical work connected with secret inks and the chemistry of this subject. Apart from this the organisation was conspicuously lacking in officers with any technical or scientific knowledge or training. In cryptographic matters it was entirely dependent on S.I.S. who had developed an efficient instrument for the purpose in the shape of the G.C. & C.S.

As early as 1928 the Committee of Imperial Defence had approved the setting up of an organisation for the detection of illicit wireless transmission under War Office control with technical staff and instruments to be provided and financed by the Post Office. The interception of Comintern wireless in 1935 (vide Chapter III, Part 1, (iv) above) had brought prominently to notice the importance of keeping under review the bearing of progress in wireless technique as well as the necessity of developing improved methods for intercepting the wireless communications of organisations such as the Comintern and those of potential enemy Secret Service organisations. Up to the middle of 1938 no effective action had been taken however and the War Office - possibly because it had less direct responsibility than formerly for the Security Service - had tended to concentrate on the question of providing mobile units to accompany an expeditionary force. The Post Office, on the other hand, was directly concerned with the detection of illicit transmitters not from the counter espionage point of view but from that of the revenue to be derived from licences.

The developing threat of Nazi aggressiveness led to the question being taken up more seriously in 1938 when Lt-Colonel Simpson was appointed to advise the Security Service in all matters connected with wireless. Crucial decisions were taken at a meeting at the War Office on December 7th 1938 after an attempt had been made to induce the Security Service to take over the responsibility for establishing R.S.S. or the Radio Security Section. The responsibility was not accepted on account of the large administrative expansion and the financial commitments which would have been involved. It was therefore decided that the organisation for detecting illicit wireless should be under M.I.19., later M.I.8., at the War Office and it was laid down that "M.I.5." was only to be interested in results while the Post Office was to provide equipment and assistance. Financial provision for the establishment of R.S.S. under the War Office acting in collaboration with the Post Office was received in March 1939 (eleven years after the proposals of the Committee of Imperial Defence had first been made).

This refusal to accept the responsibility for the administration and finance of R.S.S. had very far-reaching consequences. The fact of the refusal points inescapably to a fundamental weakness in internal organisation. This weakness in turn is attributable to external as opposed to internal causes. The same causes allowed the Security Service - three months after Munich and its own urgent representations raising "the question of measures to develop our intelligence system and provide for a comprehensive review" - to carry all its responsibilities with a staff of thirty officers and no trained reserves for expansion in the event of war; and left the responsibility for controlling and developing R.S.S. as a vital source of intelligence for counter espionage purposes uneasily suspended between M.I.8., M.I.5., and the Post Office.

Ultimately these causes are to be found in the circumstances of the failure inside and outside the Security Service to face the fact that it is part of the executive machinery of Government with positive functions and responsibilities of its own - to combat the operations of an enemy Secret Service - which it cannot unload on to other Departments. In this sense they are mainly external causes but they have produced internal weakness in the shape of failure to accept essential responsibilities. The attitude which has given rise to this avoidance of responsibilities is closely associated with the plea of being a purely advisory body; and this attitude of mind has produced failures in organisation and planning and an absence of thinking on sufficiently big lines. One of the conspicuous illustrations of these tendencies has been the refusal in December 1938 to grapple with the problem of wireless and the consequent establishment of R.S.S. under M.I.8. with results recalling the principles of Greek tragedy.

The question is much more than one of internal organisation and finance. It is necessarily a controversial one and the theme, which runs through the record of the war years, has not yet worked itself out. Its circumstances and its implications are too complex for discussion at this stage and an attempt to assess its part in the whole story must, therefore, be left over for separate consideration.

CHAPTER IV: REACTIONS IN THE SECOND WORLD WAR - FIRST PHASE

INTRODUCTORY NOTE

Part I of this Chapter deals with the period from the outbreak of war to the fall of France and Part 2 deals with the following period up to the time of the German attack on the U.S.S.R. and the reorganisation of the Security Service which roughly coincided with this date (being spread over the summer months of 1941). They are difficult periods to describe adequately, as our organisation was in a state of confusion which at times amounted to chaos.

The original cause of the confusion is to be found in the fact that no adequate preparations had been made in 1938-1939 to foresee and face the conditions of the war as it developed and this, in turn, was due to lack of sufficient funds. The question how far the lack of funds was due to the policy of the Government or to insufficient pressure to enable the Security Service to make adequate preparations is one which cannot be answered. It is among the imponderables.

The record of these periods (from the beginning of the war to the summer of 1941) does not fit into a clear design or pattern. The position will perhaps be clearer if the following "leit-motiv" is kept in mind:-

During the first few months of the war while the Security Service was attempting to expand rapidly and to improvise machinery to deal with the war situation, a breakdown occurred in B Division and in the Registry. In addition to and as a consequence of the inadequate financial provision, sufficient staff had not been trained and in spite of the lessons of the last war steps had not been taken to deal with the inevitable rush of work. B Division and the Registry were overwhelmed by the flood of denunciations and reports about suspects received from the police, the public and other sources and by the volume of vetting enquiries for numerous purposes, including travel permits and visas. The position was greatly aggravated by the unexpected change of policy on the part of the Home Office in regard to the internment of enemy aliens; and this presented a serious problem in view of the fact that the Security Service had virtually no knowledge of the machinery of the German Secret Service which it was its function to combat. This in turn had far-reaching consequences because of a new factor which had not been partly foreseen in the period after 1933 -i.e. that of the so-called "Fifth Column" which, in the absence of definite information regarding the German organisation behind it, intensified the apparent need for a policy of preventive action against enemy aliens in general and Nazis in particular, as well as against their British sympathisers in Mosley's and similar organisations.

When Lord Swinton became responsible for the Security Service in the summer of 1940 he sought to remedy the confusion by improvising machinery of his own in the shape of the Security Intelligence Centre outside the Security Service through which he attempted to deal with the "Fifth Column" problem; and W. Branch which was established inside the Security Service and was intended to deal with the interception of enemy communications for the purpose of detecting their agents. Both these improvisations duplicated the work of B Division and both eventually proved a failure. In addition to these measures Lord Swinton appointed a lawyer (Mr. Crocker) with no previous experience to be joint head of B Division and this step had disastrous consequences. These three measures combined to damage the morale and effectiveness of the organisation as a whole.

In December 1940 Lord Swinton proposed by dividing B Division into three, to separate the sections dealing with the component parts of the "Fifth Column". While keeping B.I.C. (the Sabotage Section) in B Division he put the sections dealing with the internment of enemy aliens (German and Italian) in E and that dealing with the B.U.F. in F Division. This proposal was opposed by B Division officers and a decision on the question was postponed pending an examination of the whole problem. This examination was made by Sir David Petrie should took charge of the Security Service as Director-General at the beginning of March 1941 and decided to adopt the proposal to divide B Division into B., E and F.

Chapter IV, therefore, deals with the difficult situation which arose in the early stages of the war and led to a partial breakdown of the central organisation of the Security Service and the Divisions; and the next Chapter will deal with the new growth which took place in the sections of the various Divisions and the subsequent developments after the reorganisation of 1941.

It is not possible within the limited scope of this record to make a full and satisfactory analysis of the causes of the breakdown; or to give an adequate answer to the charge that Sir Vernon Kell and the other senior officers of the Security Service failed to improvise an adequate organisation to cope with the situation in 1940. Briefly, to recapitulate the above mentioned points, it may be said that their chief difficulties arose from the absence during the preceding years of adequate financial provision and of arrangements for training the necessary staff for expansion. Among the most important causes of the subsequent difficulties it is obvious that the attitude of the Home Office was a contributing factor and that this attitude was due to the fact that they looked at the question of internment of enemy aliens from the political point of view rather than as a factor in the military situation. Again it is clear that Lord Swinton's attempts at dealing with the internal situation tended to aggravate rather than to alleviate it, whatever relief may have been afforded by his efforts in other directions. Perhaps the most important factor in the situation was that until the spies started to arrive in the autumn of 1940 the Security Service was not in touch with the enemy so that it had no concrete problem to grapple with until the interrogation of the spies and the interception of the enemy communications began to provide it with substantial material in the spring of 1941. As the next Chapter will show, the organisation began to take shape as soon as the problem was presented in this concrete form.

Prior to these developments it was difficult - once the organisation had fallen into confusion - to give it a compact form, to arrange for a clear allocation of functions or to visualise the objectives and the means of reaching them. Moreover, since the Security Service had been divorced from the War Office in 1931, there was no appropriate authority to which it could readily turn to present its case and to obtain crucial decisions in a crisis such as that created by the Home Office attitude to internment. In the meanwhile modern developments had made it clear that the War Office could not in itself be regarded as the appropriate authority for this purpose. Circumstances had shown the need for the co-ordination of the three fighting Services and for joint planning under the Chiefs of Staff and the Defence Minister. The responsibilities of the Security Service in regard to the enemy espionage organisation, the "Fifth Column" and the planning of deception were not unaffected by these changes, but no one who dealt with the problems of the Security Service in 1940 was in a position to lift them to this level.

Part 1: The 'Phoney' War before the Fall of France

(i) Developments immediately before the outbreak of war.

After Munich, and especially after the German occupation of Czechoslovakia, the British Government's decision to introduce conscription and the guarantees to Poland and Rumania it became clear, even to those most unwilling to accept the fact, that an early outbreak of war was almost inevitable. Information from sources developed by B Branch - which had led up to this conclusion during 1937 and 1938 - continued to indicate the aggressive nature of Nazi policy. Reports from a variety of sources including [...]. German journalists in London and intercepted communications all pointed in the same direction. In spite of them all the organisation was not strengthened on a scale which would obviously be desirable on the basis of what was found to be necessary in the last war; and there was no room for doubt that the conditions of the coming war would involve the Security Service in a much more complicated situation and in more serious difficulties. The main grounds for this argument were the development of the theories of total war in Germany and the existence of a certain sympathy for Nazi Germany in this country as embodied in the British Union of Fascists. While the British Union of Fascists and its sympathisers represented a relatively small and unimportant part of the population they had to be regarded as a symptom of a widespread disease which, when viewed over the larger field of Europe as a whole, evidently involved us in a more serious problem with important military as well as purely political aspects. In this field the two extremes, commonly known as the Right and Left Wing, combined to establish a situation of instability very different in kind from that in which the dominant factor was the compact highly developed nationalism of the leading states which fought the first World War. B Branch information about the German Trade Agreement with Russia in the spring of 1939, which confirmed more important Foreign Office intelligence to the same effect, suggested that the two extremes might come together in order to destroy what they described as capitalism and imperialism or pluto-democracy but in other eyes appeared to be the embodiment of Western civilisation based on ideals of humanism and individual liberty, or what remained of that civilisation after the schism created by the totalitarian developments in Germany, Italy and Russia. France, Belgium, Holland and other Western countries were obviously weakened to some extent by the reactions from this schism inside their own borders; in other words by the development of their Communist and their pro-Nazi Parties. Perhaps the most serious aspect of this situation was presented by France where extremist politics appeared to have had a more generally disintegrating effect, not unconnected with the failure to rearm on any adequate scale in the face of the series of German aggressions in the Rhineland, against the Sudetenland and against Czechoslovakia. The German theory - as was obvious from even a casual study of their military and Party literature - required the concentration of all available forces at the critical point in time and place; and these forces included the use of organised Parties favourable to the process of disintegration in their enemies' countries. As has been mentioned in Chapter III, Part 1, above, the bare outlines of this problem had been put before the J.I.C. in 1936 but no definite results had followed. The problem appeared to be one which no single Department in Whitehall could deal with, and to deal with which no combination of Departments could be effected. It was, in part, the problem which afterwards became known as that of the "Fifth Column" and as this country was not invaded it is improbable that any satisfactory evaluation of its significance will ever be possible unless clear and definite evidence about the German theory and the existence or otherwise of concrete plans for putting it into effect on an organised basis come to light as a result of the occupation of Germany.

In 1939 we had no adequate knowledge of the German organisations which it was the function of the Security Service to guard against either in this wider field of the "Fifth Column" or in the narrower one of military espionage and purely material sabotage. We had in fact no definite knowledge whether there was any organised connection between the German Secret Service and Nazi sympathisers in this country, whether of British or alien nationality (The information acquired during subsequent years had led the Director of B Division to form the opinion that there was in fact no organised "Fifth Column" in 1939 or 1940 in this country. This view is based on negative evidence, including evidence from a case which has been under investigation for a long period in B.1.C. This case shows that there are a certain number of Nazi sympathisers of various nationalities or origin, who would have been willing to assist the enemy if there had been any organisation to get in touch with them. There is also the fact that such evidence as has come to hand concerning the organisations of a similar type in other countries - as derived from the intercepted wireless communications of the Abwehr and Sipo und SD - has no counterpart in the ISOS material relating to this country. Although the Brandenburger Units with British speaking personnel were assembled on the Channel coast in 1940, with a view to their forming part of the invading forces, there is no evidence that they had any plans for collusion or collaboration with any organised body in this country). With regard to the narrower field of military espionage and purely material sabotage, some slight indication of the German intentions had been received from [...] when he gave us such details as he could obtain at the time of Munich about the establishment of Abwehr branches in Holland and Belgium which were intended to operate against this country. The few cases of espionage which came to light, while of a minor nature, confirmed the impression that the German Secret Service was active, that operations were mainly directed from

Hamburg, and that its activities were largely unknown to us. These few cases gave us no general picture of the enemy organisation. All the circumstances, therefore, appeared to justify the view that it was better to overestimate rather than underestimate that part of the enemy's military machine which was our particular concern. In order to enable the Security Service point of view to be represented in the highest quarters and to counteract the above-mentioned tendencies under which security came to be no Department's business, B Branch officers - on various occasions before the outbreak of war - put forward the view, which had long been held by Sir Vernon Kell, that there should be a Minister with responsibility for security and in a position to represent security problems not only to the Chiefs of Staff, but, if necessary, to the Cabinet. This question has been discussed in Lord Hankey's report of May 1940 (vide Bibliography No. 42).

(ii) The outbreak of war.

An inter-departmental committee to consider, in consultation with the Service Departments, the terms of the Emergency Powers (Defence) Bill and Defence Regulations under the chairmanship of Sir Claud Schuster (often referred to as the Schuster Committee) had been set up towards the end of 1935. It was later asked to revise all the draft regulations previously assembled by the War Emergency Legislation Sub-Committee of the Committee of Imperial Defence, with a view to the preparation of a comprehensive code containing all the Defence Regulations which would be required in the opening stages of a major war. The War Emergency Legislation Committee then reviewed the whole field of War Legislation and submitted a list of Bills which would be required in order to make available the special emergency powers which would be needed in the first few months of war. This list was based mainly on the Government War Book. The Government War Book was prepared by the Committee of Imperial Defence and finally issued in 1936. (No copy of the Government War Book is available in the Security Service records). The War Office War Emergency Legislation Sub-Committee, on which the Security Service were represented by Lt. Colonel Holt-Wilson, had discussed from time to time the points raised by the War Emergency Legislation Committee. By 1939 the latter had submitted to the Committee of Imperial Defence a draft of the Bill and a code of Defence Regulations which would give all the Emergency Powers required in the opening stages of a major war. Cabinet approval was obtained in July 1939, and on the outbreak of war this Legislation, the Defence Regulations and the War Office War Book came into effect. Lt. Colonel Holt-Wilson had been closely concerned with the drafting, amendment and preparation of the provisions which affected the Security Service and were framed on the basis of the experience gained in the last war (vide Bibliography No. 56).

From the Security Service point of view the most important security measures were the introduction of the measures mentioned in the last paragraph; the internment of enemy aliens; the establishment of travel control; and the establishment of postal and telegraph censorship.

The question of internment of enemy aliens is an extremely complicated one and has been discussed at length in "The Enemy Alien Population in the U.K." (vide Bibliography No. 24). Outstanding points in this clear and dispassionate account of the facts are that although no definite decision had been taken about internment, the position regarding Government policy a week before war broke out was that it was assumed that in fact a large proportion of the male Germans and Austrians in this country would be interned, and that two days before the outbreak of war Sir Alexander Maxwell wrote to the Security Service to the effect that the Home Secretary had decided after due consideration that there would be no policy of general internment, but that tribunals would be set up which would review all cases of male enemy aliens over the age of sixteen. Again on the 8th September 1939, the Security Service sent a circular to the S.C.O.s at ports directing that all enemy aliens leaving the country should be closely interrogated and searched, and that if there was any suspicion that the alien might have information of value to the enemy, he should not be allowed to leave. After midnight on Saturday, the 9th September, no enemy alien was to be allowed to leave without being in possession of an Exit Permit. The Home Office announcement on this subject was not made until the 12th September 1939 and read as follows:-

> "Germans wishing to leave the country now require an Exit Permit, a requirement which also applies to British subjects. In the absence, however, of special reasons, they will receive this Permit without difficulty."

This decision was taken by the Home Office without consulting the Security Service. The report brings out very clearly the fact that the Home Office was not primarily influenced by considerations of security, but was induced to swing from one decision to another by a variety of influences. The general effect of this state of affairs on the Security Service was to involve it in a position where there was no consistent policy in regard to security against espionage by enemy aliens, or subversive activities of a "Fifth Column" type. The Security Service was left to fall back on the impossible task of obtaining concrete evidence against individual enemy aliens, and this process contributed to overwhelm it in a mass of detailed enquiries. This is a position which could hardly have arisen if the Home Office had felt any real responsibility for the Security Service and its problems, or had regarded the enemy alien at large as a potential factor, however, small, in the military situation.

For the purposes of travel control a new section D.4. under Colonel Adam, was formed in D Branch on the basis of plans which he had been preparing during the previous twelve months. The staff at Head Office and at the ports came into full operation on the outbreak of war.

Judging by the experiences of the last war B Branch expected to be able to rely to an important extent on Censorship for the detection of enemy spies, but it was also realised that wireless was lidely to form an important means of communication between the Abwehr and its agents.

The only concrete evidence of this still was the wireless set produced by [...] as having been given to him by officers of the Hamburg Abwehrstelle (vide Chapter III, Part 2, (i), (d) above.) Further developments are described in Part 2 of this Chapter.

THE DOCUMENTS – IV: REACTIONS IN THE SECOND WORLD WAR – FIRST PHASE   151

(iii) Preventive or security investigations by B Branch.

As described in Chapter II, Lt.-Colonel Holt-Wilson had been in charge of all the preventive branches of the Office during the last war, but when the new one opened his duties were confined to those concerned with legislative measures. He had also drawn up plans for the detention and internment of enemy aliens which, however, had not been adopted by the Home Office (vide "The Enemy Population in the U.K. - Bibliography No. 24).

In regard to the remaining security or preventive functions B Branch as a whole, in the absence of any adequate knowledge of the Abwehr or SD organisation or of any important cases of espionage, was led to concern itself to a very large extent with enquiries of a preventive nature. In view of the little that was known and the large scope for suspicion among the uninterned enemy population and of the expected "Fifth Column" technique, this field was a very large one, and a very wide variety of enquiries were made by B Branch on their own initiative. These enquiries, although they disclosed no concrete proof to connect individuals with the enemy Secret Services frequently provided very strong circumstantial evidence to support the Security Service view that enemy nationals should be interned, at least as a preventive measure.

To mention only a few, a leading German named Kuchenmeister in the machine tool industry went over to Ireland at the beginning of the war and from there, sponsored by influential British interests, made attempts to return. Although no direct evidence of espionage was available he was known to have consorted with German Staff officers, taken some of them to British factories, to have been supported and consulted by a German Consul, and to have visited Germany frequently. He was eventually interned, but in order to keep him in internment B Branch was compelled by the requirements of the Birkett Committee to spend many hours in preparing an elaborate case to prove that this German was likely to be loyal to his own country and therefore disloyal to this; and the same work had to be done in numerous similar cases to an extent which by itself was sufficient to overwhelm the small staff available and to throw the Registry out of gear, thus diverting the Office as a whole from its proper function of combating the enemy Secret Services as a part of their military machine engaged in active operations which aimed at the destruction of the British Empire. Again, the affairs of the Concrete Pump Co., Ltd., mentioned in Chapter III, Part 2, (i), (d), above, involved prolonged investigations before arrangements could be made for the affairs of the Company to be managed by a firm of Chartered Accountants appointed by the Board of Trade, while the British-born German, Markmann, who was now the owner, was interned. Again, the trade in optical instruments required for precision work in gunnery and for other purposes was found shortly before the war to be largely in the hands of Germans some of whom were nationalised British subjects and, according to [...], had been closely associated with the German Military and Naval Attaches before the war. Information from another source had given grounds for enquiries regarding a number of equipment companies which had connections with a company at Zella Mehlis in Thuringia. "Zella Mehlis code-typewriters" had been mentioned rather cryptically as connected with an extremely important source of German intelligence by an "unconscious agent" in the person of

Rüter, a highly-placed official of the Auswärtiges Amt who had simultaneously - and without knowing - given us information about the German-Soviet negotiations to which he was a party. Numerous cases came to light as the result of a flood of information from the public and sometimes from other Government Departments about suspicious enemy aliens (the H Branch report compiled at the end of the last war had placed on record a warning that a flood of information of this kind was likely to reduce the Office to a state of chaos at the beginning of a war, but unfortunately no attention had been paid to this warning and the staff - in B.10 and other sections - to cope with the flood was over a period of months recruited at a rate which could not prevent it from being perpetually engulfed by the incoming tide. A typical case was that of a worthy old German, for many years resident in this country and with no claim to be a refugee from Nazi oppression, who suddenly specialised in selling ice cream, not so much to the general public as to nearly every aerodrome and anti-aircraft battery over a large sector of the defences of London. There was no direct evidence against him and nothing to connect him with any German organisations but the circumstantial evidence raised strong grounds for thinking that he might be communicating to the enemy some of the very comprehensive information about the defences which he could not help but obtain as a result of his daily tours by car to numerous sites. There were many cases of a somewhat similar kind, but it seemed useless to move the Home Office for their internment at a time when the Birkett Committee was showing itself anxious to release Germans against whom there were equally strong suspicions; and the Birkett Committee appeared to be persuaded by irrelevant evidence in cases where Germans made a good impression on them as being straight-forward and honest men, overlooking the fact that such persons might be loyal to their own country.

One case which illustrated the difficulties caused by the Advisory Committee - in this case presided over by Sir Walter Monckton - was that of Dr. Otto Bernhard Bode. He was physician to the German Embassy for many years before the war and on the staff of the German Hospital in London. He was granted British naturalisation on the 5th May 1933, for which purpose he gave guarantees that he had no connection with any foreign political organisation and did not intend to apply for the retention of his German citizenship. He subsequently broke both these guarantees retaining his German citizenship in November 1933 and became a member of the NSDAP in 1934, thus swearing on oath of absolute allegiance to Adolf Hitler which was incompatible with his oath of allegiance to H.M. the King. He was interned as a member of the NSDAP. When the grounds for this were questioned by the Advisory Committee on the ground, inter alia, that he had told the Committee that he had joined the Nazi Party for sentimental rather than political reasons, B Branch urged that if he were free they could have no confidence that the same sentimental feelings would not lead him to attempt to act in the interests of Germany. These interests, according to the former leader of the NSDAP in London, had led him to take British nationality as well as German, thereby, in our eyes, breaking his guarantee and committing a breach of faith. This was represented to the Home Office, but the Home Office on the advice of the Advisory Committee released him. A storm of indignation from several quarters followed and B Branch was then compelled to prepare an elaborate case, some thirty pages long, which involved setting out in full all the evidence available on our files. This finally resulted in Bode's re-internment, but B Branch protested that the elaboration of evidence against enemy aliens and members of the Nazi Party in this and numerous other cases in order to satisfy a quasi-judicial body that there was positive evidence of their loyalty to Hitler rather than to this country involved unjustifiable pressure to the detriment of their work and duty to make fresh enquiries with a view to further preventive action and the detection of enemy agents. In some of these cases the enemy alien in question had not even assumed a false allegiance to this country in the interests of Germany.

Some of the cases which engaged a great deal of the energies of the small cadre of B Branch officers had a substantial basis such as those of members of the NSDAP who had moved over to Ireland on the outbreak of war. One of these, Werner Unland, carried on correspondence with Germany through neutral countries by a plain language code; but of the letters which came into our hands none appeared in virtue of the nature of the text to indicate that he was sending important information to Germany, but rather that he was attempting to make preparations to do so. Another group of enquiries was based on information given by [...] regarding the Abwehrstelle in Holland and its relations with two closely connected firms - the Todan Maatschappij in Holland and the Thor Corporation in London. One of the representatives of these firms named Hans Arnheim had been convicted of espionage by the French in North Africa after prolonged visits, before the war, to London and India where he had skilfully made contacts with a number of British Military and Naval officers.

Besides the numerous cases in which B Branch attempted to make 'preventive' enquires on their own initiative, some of the D. sections, particularly D. 3 - the Air Section under Group-Captain Archer - brought to notice numerous matters which appeared to require close investigation from a security point of view. As a result of these circumstances an attempt was made to induce the Home Office to feel a greater sense of responsibility for security, but without success; in fact the Home Office showed no sign of appreciating the security point of view, and it was clear that they had no feeling of responsibility in this respect but that their main object was to protect their Minister from having to answer awkward questions in the House. The Home Secretary at this time was not very successful in commanding the confidence of the House and was unable to give it a lead which would doubtless have secured the support of the great majority of Members if the security issue had been clearly and firmly presented. As he was unable to lead the House he wavered from one position to another in a manner which has been set out in detail in "The Enemy Alien Population in the U.K."

The D Branch sections dealing with security in munition and aircraft factories not only brought to notice a large number of cases which appeared to require investigation, but their small staff was occupied in an attempt to cover an immense field as the war industries expanded and their function of ensuring that adequate security measures were adopted in factories and public utility undertakings became widely extended in consequence. In many cases they found themselves compelled to concentrate almost exclusively on bottleneck industries or factories.

Early in the war D.2, the Naval Section, brought to notice the fact that while security arrangements had been initiated in regard to British shipping throughout the world there were no arrangements for investigating certain incidents which had occurred such as fires believed to be due to incendiary bombs in a ship's officer's cabin or a cargo of coal. D.3, the Air Section, also emphasised the importance of high-grade octane fuel which was of vital importance to Fighter Command and was brought across the Atlantic in tankers. These circumstances led Mr. Curry to propose the formation of a special section, B. 18, later B.1.C., to deal with the investigation of enemy sabotage throughout the world. He was supported by the D.N.I. who made it clear that this type of investigation could not be conducted by the Admiralty and thus overcame reluctance in the Security Service to the undertaking of an added, but inescapable responsibility. In the circumstances at that time Mr. Curry was convinced that the difficulties of the Security Service were largely due to the fact that the responsibility of the Service as a whole and its parts had not been clearly defined. He therefore decided that it was desirable to frame instructions defining the responsibilities of the new section for whose creation he was responsible. The main points of this instruction, which was dated 16th March 1940 were as follows:-

> The new section B.18 had been formed to assist the Director of the Security Service to discharge his functions and responsibilities in relation to sabotage and this included action to counter the activities of enemy sabotage agents as directed by the enemy Intelligence Services. In the light of the information then available, it was assumed that those of the German Intelligence Service might be supplemented by those of the Russians; and that their agents might be recruited either from among enemy aliens, other aliens or those elements of the British people who had been influenced by subversive ideas either of the extreme Right or of the extreme Left. After six months of war no large-scale sabotage had been directed by the enemy, but our knowledge of German military theory suggested that such action would be reserved to make it synchronise with the general requirements of their military strategy. They would aim at combining sabotage behind their enemy's lines with a military campaign as in the case of Poland. Preparations had, therefore, to be made to deal with intensive sabotage in a critical military situation.

The Director of the Security Service was responsible for the functions of B and D Divisions, i.e. for investigation and security and the responsibilities of B. 18 must conform. They were charged with the collection, collation, dissemination and utilisation by all practical means of all information relating to sabotage from whatever source whether within the United Kingdom, the Dominions or Colonies or in foreign countries (the last-named through S.I.S.). It was, therefore, necessary for B. 18 to assist the police in investigations of cases of sabotage and to establish liaison with all the Departments concerned, especially the Service Departments through D Division, in regard to munition and armament factories; the Government establishments of the three Services; railways; electric supplies and distribution; and other public utilities - in short everything covered by the term "Home Front" which offered a target to the saboteur. In addition to this, liaison was to be maintained with the Ministry of Shipping with regard to sabotage of the Mercantile Marine and neutral vessels in British charter.

The section was also made responsible for obtaining advice from experts (scientific and engineering) in regard to possible methods of chemical, bacteriological and technical sabotage.

When the responsibilities of the section were thus defined, Camp 020 had not yet been formed and the Security Service was not in a position to control the interrogation of arrested agents in the manner made possible by that institution. All the precedents of the previous war and of the peacetime work of the Security Service implied that all action connected with the interrogation of persons under arrest and the preparation of prosecutions should be arranged through the police. Moreover, the police would in the normal course investigate any case of sabotage which involved a felony. After Camp 020 had been established this position was entirely changed and the responsibility for dealing with the cases of arrested enemy sabotage and other agents rested with the Security Service.

In view of the importance of establishing good relations with the police the section was placed in the charge of Sir Francis Griffith, who had recently retired from the Metropolitan Police and undertook the duty of initiating this work for six months. The section was, however, handicapped by the fact that no officer was available in the Security Service with the necessary scientific knowledge and training to cope with all the technical problems involved. To meet these needs Lord Rothschild was appointed to the section and shortly afterwards took over charge of it from Sir Francis Griffith. With his knowledge and training and with the advantages of contact with a wide range of experts in all the relevant fields of scientific enquiry Lord Rothschild was able to raise the work of the section to a higher level and to deal energetically with the wide range of problems involved.

When the section was formed it had been realised that while material or physical sabotage would constitute the problem in regard to which its functions could be closely defined, it must also be concerned with the other activities of the enemy organisation in the field of moral sabotage or the "Fifth Column" problem. In regard to this latter, its function could not be so closely defined because the subject was a large one which directly or indirectly concerned the whole of B Division and particularly the sections dealing with the NSDAP and the British Union of Fascists. At this time the Security Service was almost entirely ignorant of the enemy organisation which it had to combat and although there was no direct evidence regarding the relation between the German General Staff and their organisations for moral and material sabotage, it was assumed on the basis of a general knowledge of their methods that these relations would be close. It was, therefore, considered necessary that B. 18 as the section dealing with sabotage should be responsible for obtaining intelligence - in whatever way might be possible - over this whole field. It was known that before the war the wide ramifications of German industry in this and other countries had been utilised by them for the purpose of obtaining intelligence of a varied and comprehensive nature about our war potential; but it was not known how far the enemy organisation had arranged to avail itself of the numerous opportunities open to it for establishing by these means a wartime espionage network. A considerable part of the energies of B Division had been devoted to the Herculean task of attempting to throw light on this question but without any positive results (it is now known that the Germans had not left any such network behind and the Security Service was, therefore, in the position of searching in the dark for something which did not exist). Partly because in the absence of any cases of sabotage the work of the section was not sufficient to occupy Lord Rothschild's energies, partly on account of his special qualifications and contacts and partly in order to enable him to assist in attempting to solve this general problem, Mr. Curry handed over to Lord Rothschild a number of enquiries connected with various aspects of German industry including the machine tool industry, the affairs of the German firm of Siemens Schuckert (Great Britain) Ltd and several others. The majority of the more important German members of Siemens Schuckert had left for Germany shortly before the war and in the spring and summer of 1940 most of the Germans and dual nationals who remained were interned, but Lord Rothschild conceived and executed a successful plan for arranging for an agent to get into touch with one of the known pro-Nazis connected with the firm. This was the beginning of the elaborate enterprise which aimed at penetrating the German "Fifth Column" organisation in this country and would undoubtedly have done so if the five hundred or so pro-Nazis with whom direct or indirect contact was established by our agent had also been in touch with the enemy organisation. The result of this most carefully manipulated case which was kept running throughout the whole period of the war was to establish - as far as it is possible to make reliable inferences in such a matter - that in fact the enemy had no such organisation among the individuals concerned and, therefore - with a possible exception in the unanswered question in the case of the British Union of Fascists - had no organisation prepared to render assistance at the time of the German invasion. These inferences however could not be drawn in 1940 or 1941 and it was only after 1942 and 1943 that they could be accepted with any degree of confidence. This case, therefore, played an important part in the attempt to probe the question of the "Fifth Column".

(iv) The establishment of travel control.

The establishment of travel and port control on the outbreak of war was based on the experiences of the previous war when these measures were first introduced in this country as part of a plan for preventive action in the general scheme for counter espionage. In working out the plans before the war Colonel Adam availed himself of the E Division report of the last war, the responsibility of the Security Service in this respect having been outlined in the Government War Book prepared by the Committee of Imperial Defence and finally issued in 1936 (vide Appendix to SF.50-24-44(56). These responsibilities are further defined in the War Office War Book (vide idem). Briefly, the effect of the security measures introduced as a result of the work of the War Emergency Legislation Committee, of which Lt.-Colonel Holt-Wilson was a member was to control the entry and exit to and from the United Kingdom under the Aliens' Order 1920, as amended, by preventing travel except through an "approved port" (of which there were twenty-three including air stations), subject to leave being given by an Immigration Officer and other conditions such as the possession of a valid passport or documents of identity and any information reasonable required by an Immigration Officer being produced. The regulations enabled the Secretary of State to declare any premises to be a protected place in order to keep places where passengers or seamen arrived or embarked free from undesirable and would-be illicit travellers and also in order to facilitate precautions against sabotage. All docks and airports were declared protected places shortly after the outbreak of war by the Secretary of State for War.

Before the war the provisions of the Aliens Order 1920 had been enforced by Immigration Officers in accordance with the requirements of peacetime conditions, but to fulfil the requirements of security in wartime a staff of Field Security personnel were appointed under Security Control Officers who were established at approved ports.

Other regulations which were ancillary to the above prohibited the possession of a camera or photographing or sketching in a prohibited place and provided that the Secretary of State might make orders prohibiting the despatch of postal packets or documents or articles recording information from being sent out of the United Kingdom except by post, and enabled the appropriate officer (which term included Customs Officers, Immigration Officers, a Constable or, under Warrants from the Secretary of State for War, Security Control Officers) to request travellers to declare whether they had any such documents or articles and to produce them; and also gave the appropriate officer the right to search the traveller if he had reasonable ground for suspecting that he had such an article. (For full details of the security measures reference must be made to the Defence Regulations and other relevant official papers including the D Division Report SF.50-24-44(56).

At the same time the Exit Permit system was established and the Permit Office referred certain categories of cases to the Security Service for advice before granting a permit to British or neutral subjects. In the early stages of the war, before the German army had commenced to attack neighbouring countries, travel to neutral and allied countries in Europe and the Western Hemisphere was permitted with considerable freedom.

(v) The breakdown in the Registry.

The large number of references to the Security Service in connection with travel permits was an important factor in overwhelming the Registry and contributed greatly to the chaos which resulted from other causes. One of these was that before the war, in order to enable the small Registry staff to cope with the rapidly increasing volume of work from 1936 onwards, a very large number of "omnibus" files had been made in preference to a far larger number of subject files or personal files for individuals. It became apparent within the first three months of the war that, as a result of the enormous flood of new papers, the requirements of vetting, the references for Exit Permits and the demands of the Advisory Committee, the Registry was heading for an early breakdown.

It was frequently found that the same files were required simultaneously by several officers for several different purposes. For instance investigations or representations to the Birkett Committee were frequently interrupted by the need for transferring the files to other sections to enable the question of Exit Permits to be decided. Moreover, in the early stages of the war when there were only about half-a-dozen officers in B Division with any knowledge of the work or of the "traces" on the files, the sectional officers were frequently unable to decided these questions themselves without reference to the handful of pre-war officers.

As a result of these conditions large bundles of files frequently accumulated in many of the sections and the work of all sections was slowed down by demands for files in these accumulated bundles constantly received from other sections. A further effect of this congestion was that the Registry staff were unable to obtain the files in order to put papers away in them and consequently masses of unfiled papers accumulated in the Registry.

By Christmas time it was obvious that a serious breakdown had occurred. No action to remedy this was taken because of the difficulty of obtaining financial provision for sufficient additional staff, and the whole question of the organisation of the Service was left over for an examination by Lord Hankey which took place in March 1940. So far from reporting on the breakdown he referred in eulogistic terms to the efficiency of the Registry which he said he had visited. Miss Paton-Smith, the head of the Registry, had made timely representations about the need to expand the staff, but the difficulty was to obtain Treasury sanction with sufficient rapidity to keep pace with the constantly mounting flood.

(vi) Lord Hankey's Report.

The position of the Security Service as in March 1940 was reviewed at length in Lord Hankey's Report, a copy of which was received at the end of May of that year. This report not only failed to disclose the serious condition of the Registry and the urgent need for further strengthening it, but, while fairly exhaustive in certain respects, was somewhat superficial in others. In particular he made no reference to the fact that the Security Service had received no information from S.I.S. of any practical value about the organisation of the German Secret Service which Section V and the Security Service had jointly to combat; and this in spite of the fact that some eighteen months previously the latter had informed Section V that the Abwehr had established bases in Holland and Belgium to operate against this country and that S.I.S. had established counter organisations in those countries which had, however, been unable to obtain any information of substantial value about their adversaries or the main organisation behind them.

To say this does not imply criticism of Colonel Vivian of Section V (who had achieved marked success in penetrating Comintern organisations before the war). The penetration of an organisation protected (as we now know in more detail) by Abwehrabteilung III and the Sicherheitsdienst was no easy problem and required good luck as well as skill and organisation. The point is that Lord Hankey ignored the dependence of the Security Service on Section V in this respect; failed to make an adequate examination of the vital nature of their functional relations and failed to bring out the fact that both organisations had not been adequately staffed in peacetime to enable them to prepare for the conditions of modern war - and as a corollary to insist on the urgent need for giving them a chance to develop on efficient lines.

In his reference to the function of the Security Service Lord Hankey described it as being "to provide a centre where all intelligence concerning espionage, sabotage and other subversive and illicit activities is pooled" and as being to "supply the utmost possible information, advice and assistance to the Government Departments concerned in the prevention and detection of all such activities whether directed against the State in general or the fighting Services and the Home Office and the Scottish Office in the investigation of alleged breaches of the law in the matters referred to above".

Lord Hankey failed to understand the responsibilities of the Security Service for executive action in combating the German Secret Intelligence under the Oberkommando der Wehrmacht by denying intelligence to the enemy, by the detection and prevention of espionage and sabotage and by helping the fighting Services in active deception as a vital part of our military operations. He overlooked the distinction between executive action for the detection of espionage and sabotage and executive action against the persons detected. His wording in his definition of the functions of the Security Service must be attributed to confused thinking in regard to the action against persons.

While it is difficult to account for his failure to penetrate to the essential principles involved in the above distinction it may be accounted for, in part, by the fact that in the previous war and throughout the period between the wars open executive action in espionage cases had invariably been taken by the police on the initiative or under the guidance of M.I.5. officers who remained in the background. At the time his report was written the machinery by which the Security Service subsequently developed its methods of detection by the action of the S.C.O.s at the ports, by interrogation of persons detained at the L.R.C. and at Camp 020, and the machinery by which it assisted in deception through the double-agents of B.1.A. had not yet come into existence. The Home Secretary had not yet delegated to B Division of the Security Service the authority to decide - on the basis of their information from intercepted enemy wireless and other sources - that Immigration Officers should in individual cases exercise their powers - without option or discretion and without knowing the relevant facts - of refusing leave to land. Nevertheless, even before those developments occurred, the Security Service had the same responsibilities for combating the enemy by denying intelligence and assisting in deception, and Lord Hankey, in fact, mentioned that the latter had taken place - although on a very small scale - in the previous war. The essential principles involved were the same in both wars and in the intervening period even when the action against persons was taken by the police and Immigration Officers as the executive machinery under the Home Office and in virtue of the executive authority of the Home Secretary. This is what Lord Hankey failed to perceive when he referred to "information, advice and assistance to the Government Departments concerned in the prevention and detection of all such activities."

Lord Hankey did not mention the splitting up of the preventive functions between B and D Branches and the Deputy-Director, although he described in some detail those functions as performed by the Deputy-Director Lt.- Colonel Holt-Wilson and the Assistant Director (General Staff Branch) Colonel Allen, but he made no reference to the essentially preventive nature of the enquiries which at that time so fully occupied almost the whole of B Branch. He mentioned the immense burden thrown on the Security Service by the necessity of dealing with the Advisory Committee's attitude to the release of enemy aliens and said that among other things two hundred and fifty enemy aliens had been interrogated at length and that full reports had been sent to the Advisory Committee on over six hundred cases. He referred to the view taken by the Security Service of German espionage as differing entirely from that of August 1914 and as involving us in an attempt to cope with the plans for total war in which all the resources, not only of the State but of every individual, were bent to the use of the State; to the Wehrgesetz which applied to every Reich German including those who had British nationality; and to the work of the German intelligence - as it had been observed by the Security Service before the war - when all the resources of German industry, German railways and steamship lines and all the information collected in the ordinary way of business by the German import and export trade had to be counted into the equation. (He did not mention the part played by the German heavy industries and their connection with international cartels). He referred to the preventive action taken by the arrest of members of the SNDAP and other suspects at the beginning of the war and defended the Security Service against the attacks of Mr. Birkett for having arrested Germans "for no better reason" than that "under pressure" they had joined the NSDAP or the Deutche Arbeitsfront by saying that at the outset of the war the Security Service were bound to play for safety in their advice and the Home Office were bound to accept it; and quoting the maxim "salus populi suprema lex" he maintained that some cases of hardship to enemy aliens were inevitable and that "hard cases made bad law".

(vii) The breakdown in the Security Service.

Lord Hankey's report would have been of more immediate assistance to the Security Service in preventing the 'rot' from developing if he had emphasised the inadequacy of staff in B and D Branches and in the Registry at that time, and the urgent need for measures for recruiting competent personnel. The real position was that not only had the Registry broken down through inadequate staff before the war and inadequate expansion after it, combined with a failure to heed the warning of H Branch in the previous war to the effect that a flood of paper was inevitable, but that there was no one under the Director who was responsible for all preventive action and preventive or security policy; and that B Branch was overwhelmed with an immense volume of investigation work of a mainly preventive nature, as already described.

A contributory factor both to the breakdown of the Registry and the breakdown in the Security Service as a whole, was the volume of vetting, including vetting for Exit Permits. Early in the war this work reached unforseen proportions - the peak figure being nearly 8,200 cases per week in the quarter ending June 1940. This included vetting for numerous Departments, many of which suddenly became security-minded as a result of the "Fifth Column" scare after the fall of France. Sometimes almost Gilbertian proposals were made, such as a demand for the vetting of enemy aliens who were to be allowed to send parcels abroad. The mere weight of this work was a serious burden on the Registry, but it also had the effect of creating a situation in which officers were unable to pursue enquiries. The demands of the Advisory Committees added to the chaos, and their demands were sometimes couched in peremptory terms with a suggestion that if the relevant facts were not produced the internee would be released. The time of the head of B Branch was, during the first six months or more, largely taken up with rendering personal assistance to the Director, Sir Vernon-Kell, and the duty of controlling and expanding the Branch fell to Captain Liddell, the Deputy-Assistant-Director of the Branch. It must be emphasised that B Branch as the one which initiated all action aiming at detection and a large part of the action of a preventive nature, was the crucial part on which the efficiency of the whole depended. In the early stages of the war there were only about half-a-dozen officers with any experience of the work, and having worked at high pressure for a long period before the war they were compelled to work for impossible long hours for the first twelve months and more of the war, when nine to twelve hours a day for thirteen days a fortnight was not uncommon for a large number of officers, secretaries and Registry staff. These long hours - all limitations of regular hours were forgotten - were done on the initiative of individuals and as a result of a recognition of the urgent need of the situation, both in the Office and outside it, at a time when the Government and the country as a whole was indulging in the complacency which arose from the conditions of the "phoney war".

(viii) Attempts to develop B Branch.

Thus in the early months of 1940 it fell to Captain Liddell to attempt to develop and expand B Branch, to co-ordinate the work of B Branch with the security controls under D Branch and to cope with the problems of the enemy alien as presented to us by the Tribunals and the Birkett Committee. The Branch was expanding rapidly during these months and this expansion was marked by an absence of co-ordinating machinery within the Branch. The section under Lt.-Colonel Hinchley Cooke which had always dealt with German espionage continued to be in the same isolated position which it had held for some years. Certain other of the more experienced officers had been set apart to deal with special cases at the beginning of the war but as no special cases materialised they had drifted to other fields of activity much as the general preventive enquiries mentioned above. One of them, Mrs. Archer, became involved in a long enquiry into Russian espionage which resulted from General Krivitsky's visit to London and the information which he was willing to give us as a result of his break with Stalin. Major Sinclair was attempting to develop machinery to work on "double-agent" lines for the purpose of deceiving the enemy and in conjunction with the Inter-Services Liaison Board. Captain Robertson was dealing with the case of the double-agent [...] and was attempting to find a key to the Abwehr system of wireless communications as a result of the clues furnished by [...]. He was also in charge of the section responsible for the investigation of all reports of illicit wireless transmissions and for co-ordinating the work in this connection of the police, the Radio Security Service and the G.P.O. Mr. White was supervising the work connected with the Communist Party and the Comintern and the arrangements for liquidating the Nazi Party and those for dealing with the repercussions of the work of the Enemy Aliens Tribunals and the Birkett Committee.

---

† For details see "Notes and lessons" at the end of the "Summary" volume, H Branch Report (1914-1918) [Note not attributed to text in Curry's original.]

It was obvious to everyone that arrangements for the better integration of these various activities were desirable, and at the suggestion of Captain Robertson a weekly meeting known as the "Lower Deck" meeting was organised under Mr. Curry. The purpose of this meeting was to exchange information on B Branch matters, i.e. on the results of the numerous current enquiries made by the B Branch sections, the number of which had increased from the pre-war half dozen to over twenty (some of which had several officers in them) in the early months of 1940. The meeting served a useful purpose in giving all the officers concerned a wider outlook and frequently made it possible to co-ordinate enquiries which were being pursued in isolation and would otherwise have remained isolated although they were concerned with closely related subjects or individuals. They also produced an even more acute realisation than had previously existed of the need for developing the machinery specifically to deal with the Abwehr, a detailed report on which was obtained from the Czechs early in April 1940 as the result of a special liaison established with them by an outside representative under the instructions of Mr. White and Mr. Curry.

The Czech information was important as it gave us our first real knowledge of the organisation of the Abwehr and it helped to further developments at which Captain Liddell had been aiming. During the previous two or three months he had attempted to develop a plan to divide the work of B Branch into two parts, one under Mr. White to be primarily concerned with an active enquiry into the nature, organisation and methods of the German Intelligence System, and the other under Mr. Curry was to be concerned with the security or preventive investigations in which the greater part of B Branch was then involved. Full effect, however, was never given to this plan. At the same time, attempts were made to set up nationality sections especially Dutch, Swiss and Swedish, the main object of which was to examine the possibilities of German agents coming to the United Kingdom from the countries concerned. The reason for this was the fact that it was known that the Germans had set up organisations in their Embassies in neutral countries for such purposes and that they had allies in the shape of sympathisers such as members of the Dutch Mussert Party. These sections were not intended to deal with the nationals of the country in question as such. After the invasion of Norway on the 9th April and Belgium and Holland on the 10th May, the work of these sections was radically altered as they had to deal with swarms of refugees including British subjects and the subjects of other countries including, for instance, Spanish Left-Wing Groups from France. The invasion and the fall of France inevitably had large repercussions on the work of the Security Service. It had to meet a situation for which it was unprepared. As far as the refugees were concerned it was mainly met by obtaining the assistance of some personnel from S.I.S. with local knowledge (e.g. Passport Control Personnel) and by establishing liaison with the émigré Governments as they established themselves in London as well as with General de Gaulle's organisation as representing the France which had not surrendered.

The liaison with the Polish authorities led them to provide us with a comprehensive statement of the use made by the Germans of their so-called "Fifth Column" in the course of the invasion of Poland in September 1939. According to this report the German minorities in Poland were extensively used to create alarm behind the Polish front. They had helped to create a feeling of insecurity in the Polish Forces by armed action, in some cases by men wearing Polish uniforms in order to seize strategical points or to signal to and otherwise assist the German Forces either by sabotage or by spreading alarming rumours. The Polish General Staff suggested that these methods had played an important part in causing demoralisation in combination with the rapid advance of the highly mechanised German forces.

In brief, by the time of the fall of France the organisation of the Security Service as a whole was in a state which can only be described as chaotic. Some of the reasons for this have been suggested but they cannot be disassociated from the fact that B Branch had no real knowledge of the German Secret Service organisations, that it was therefore compelled to assume that the Germans were in a position to run an efficient organisation for espionage, sabotage and, above all, for disintegration or "Fifth Column" purposes, which it was unable to detect and against which it was unable to provide adequate preventive measures. Moreover, the policy of the Home Office in dealing with the problem of the enemy alien was governed by considerations other than those of security as the Security Service saw them. There was no machinery inside the Home Office for the study and appreciation of intelligence dealing with the unprecedented phenomena of the totalitarian Nazi State; and the Home Office, which had always dealt with individual cases on a purely ad hoc basis, was influenced in formulating a policy by the questions of M.P.s in the House. The M.P.s who asked questions on such matters were frequently those who were least representative of the opinion of the House and the officials of the Home Office were governed very largely by a desire to protect the Home Secretary from difficulties arising out of questions, however unrepresentative they might be. The problems of security over the whole field of espionage, sabotage and the "Fifth Column" fell on B Branch which was simultaneously attempting to evolve means of detecting German agents without any inside knowledge of the German organisation. At the same time the Registry system had broken down and the Service as a whole had found itself overwhelmed by the problems of expansion necessitated by the outbreak of war for which no adequate preparation had been made beforehand.

Part 2: The Crisis from the Fall of France to the German Attack on the U.S.S.R

(i) The retirement of Major-General Sir Vernon Kell and Lt.- Colonel Holt-Wilson.

Very shortly after taking office on the 11th May 1940, as Prime Minister, Mr. Churchill retired Major-General Sir Vernon Kell and Lt.-Colonel Holt-Wilson and appointed Brigadier Harker to be Director of the Security Service. For some time previous to his retirement Sir Vernon Kell had felt that the onerous nature of his duties weighed heavily on him, but his actual retirement took the Service by surprise and had a profound effect in view of the fact that it came at a time of crisis. The Security Service had been initiated by him and had acquired a high reputation by reason of its successes in the war of 1914-1918 under his direction. His character had always commanded the trust and respect of his staff. He performed an important national service by keeping it together in the difficult times between the wars when it had been necessary to carry on the work with machinery which was obviously inadequate. It was always a peculiarly personal affair in the sense that this Office was built round his personality. As such it received the confidence of a succession of Governments and Departmental officials in virtue of the quality of his reliability and discretion.

(ii) Preventive measures taken by the internment of enemy aliens and British subjects.

The military situation shortly before and after the fall of France, when invasion seemed to be an imminent possibility, led to preventive action being taken by the internment of enemy aliens and British subjects who were likely to assist the enemy. The Home Office, succumbing to pressure from the War Office and supported by public opinion which became vocal under the pressure of events, decided on the general internment of enemy aliens. Almost immediately afterwards, influenced by the voices of another side of public opinion - partly roused by the inadequacy of the measures for the proper care of the internees - they swung round and proceeded to release them nominally by categories, but without binding themselves by these categories. (One result which was unsatisfactory from a security point of view was that it was possible for individuals whom the Security Service considered ought to be interned to be released on a medical certificate). One of the principal reasons for the inadequacy of the arrangements for internees was that the camps, which had been prepared for them by the military authorities in the light of the policy laid down before the war, had been utilised for other purposes in the interval. They could not, therefore, be made available when the general internment took place.

The same causes - arising out of the military situation - led to the internment at the end of May 1940 of Sir Oswald Mosley and other leaders of the B.U.F. The circumstances which led up to this and its consequences have been described at some length in Mr. Aiken Sneath's "The British Union of Fascists" (vide Bibliography No. 6). Briefly, the facts are that during the period of international crises from the German invasion of Austria in March 1938 onwards B.U.F. propaganda had been conducted on behalf of Germany. This propaganda included slavish adulation of the German Government and completely uncritical approval of every act of the German Fuehrer. After the outbreak of war anti-war propaganda was continued and it emphasised such slogans as "stop this Jews' war". Mosley was more outspoken to his immediate followers; on one occasion he said that a revolutionary situation would develop within six months and the British Union must do all in its power to expedite this so that they would be in power within eight months. He continued to emphasise that it was purely a Jewish war. Many Fascists expressed a desire for a German victory and when the Germans invaded Norway the British Union supported the German claim that Norway's neutrality had been violated by this country. No voice in the British Union was raised to criticise the German invasion of the Low Countries. Considerable agitation was started in the Press regarding "Fifth Columnists" and British pro-Nazis, and the Government was urged on all sides to take drastic action against possible traitors. There were a certain number of cases of acts of treachery by members of the British Union and there was some evidence that members of this organisation were so indoctrinated by ideas based on anti-semitism and anti-

Communism that they were likely to assist the enemy in the event of invasion (similar acts of treachery also occurred after the internment.)

The entry of Italy into the war. Shortly before the declaration of war by Italy on the 10th June 1940 there were some 19,000 Italians in Great Britain registered with the police of whom about half were in London and the rest in the provinces, Scotland and Northern Ireland.

Arrangements which had already been made to intern members of the Fascio were carried out, some 1,200 Italian and British-Italian dual nationals being involved; in addition some 4,400 Italians who had not resided in this country previously to 1920 were interned in accordance with Home Office instructions under the general internment plan (for details vide "The Enemy Population in the U.K." - Bibliography No. 24).

Shortly afterwards when members of the Nazi Party were deported to Canada and Australia members of the Partito Nazionale Fascista were treated in the same way. A number of them were on the "Arandora Star" which was torpedoed by a German submarine on the way to Canada and this incident caused a reaction of opinion in some circles in London, largely owing to the fact that a number of well-known London hoteliers were among the members of the Fascio. Opinion in governmental and other circles in London was inclined to be favourably disposed towards them and argued that well-known and amiable Italians of this kind could not entertain any sinister intentions against this country.

The Security Service found itself somewhat isolated in putting forward another view of the implications of membership of the Fascio on the ground that people who had joined it, either under pressure or for business advantages would be likely, in the event of invasion to be subject to the same influences and would be led to play a part in any schemes for "Fifth Column" purposes which the Fascio might have planned. Their enquires into this organisation and its branches in British countries had shown that the branches were under strict centralised control from Rome exercised through the Italian Consular officials. The Security Service had also been impressed by the extent of the influence of the Fascio on young Italians in this country including dual nationals (British-Italian). Members of the Fascio as well as those of the youth organisation were required to swear the Fascist oath to obey the orders of the Duce without discussion "and if necessary with my blood". It had come to notice that a camp for training and indoctrinating large numbers of the members of youth organisations from different parts of the world was held in Italy every year and was attended by a certain number of youths from this country. Moreover the Fascist Secret Police or O.V.R.A. (Organizazzione de Vigilanza par la Repressione Anti-Fascista) was known to look to the Fascii as a useful source of information. In all these circumstances it was felt that there were good grounds for believing that membership of the Fascii involved a serious security issue from our point of view. Our experience suggested that some of the Italian Fascists were fanatical in their support of Mussolini's doctrine and policy and in their opposition to this country. (This suggestion was confirmed by later experience when the cases of internees were examined; and the proposition that some of the Italians were fanatical held good up to the end of the war, as was shown by enquiries made in internment camps).

There can be no doubt, although there is little direct evidence, that when she went to war Italy possessed a useful Intelligence Service which was fairly well informed about opinion in this country and its war potential. Investigation into the affairs of the Partito Nazionale Fascista disclosed that it was the duty of all members to report incidents or give information to the Secretaries of the Fascio upon any matters likely to be of use to Italy. In 1936 evidence had been obtained from the Middle East that Fascists were to be organised for acts of sabotage on British airfields and oil plants in the event of war. In 1937 it was learnt that the overseas Fascist organisation had plans for sabotage in other parts of the British Dominions, and in 1940 similar evidence was obtained of preparations for sabotage in Canada in the event of war with Italy. There were branches of the Fascio in most of the large towns in this country and in many of the Dominions and Colonies. They were important sources of intelligence much of which was derived through Italian business interests, especially shipping and tourist companies, and others such as Pirelli's which had British War Office and Admiralty contracts. The Italian military and naval attachés were also known to employ secret agents in this country. One of these came to light in the person of Anna Wolkoff who obtained important information from Tyler Kent an employee of the American Embassy in London shortly before Italy came into the war.

The Foreign Office, however, did not take a favourable view of the internment of Italians on the ground that not to intern them might be of assistance in virtue of the fact that, as they suggested, the Italian people were not behind the Fascist Government in their war against this country. At the same time, the Home Office was anxious to revise the policy of general internment very soon after it had taken place by providing for release by categories in accordance with the White Paper. The Loraine Committee, which dealt with Italians, had not considered that membership of the Fascio was in itself sufficient ground for keeping an Italian in internment, and our Italian section formed the opinion that Sir Percy Loraine was working on lines which appeared wrong to us and that there was a probability of a number of dangerous Italians and duels being released. The Security Service officers felt that the Loraine Committee, like the Hurst and Birkett Committees, had not a sufficiently developed sense of responsibility for security in view of what they considered to be the possibilities of disruptive work in the event of invasion.

During the summer and autumn of 1940 we learnt that the Home Office were releasing Italians under the various White Paper categories without making any reference to us on the erroneous assumption that if we had not recorded any concrete fact against an Italian on a Home Office file we did not consider that he should be interned as a preventive measure. As a result of this there were releases to which, had we been consulted, we should have raised objections. In addition to this, Italians whom we had regarded as dangerous on account of connection with Italian Intelligence - for instance an Italian in the shipping world - had been released on a medical certificate. Representations were made to the Home Office and the worse cases were re-interned. The Home Office, however, were often very inconsistent. For instance they proposed to release one Italian who had made a declaration of alienage in 1939, but they refused to release another merely on the ground that he had not led a moral life and was given to gambling on horse-racing (incidentally, he was one of a large number whom Lord Beaverbrook wanted released for work in aircraft factories).

In November 1940 we learnt that Mr. Morrison, the new Home Secretary, was more favourably disposed to the Security Service point of view than his predecessor in matters connected with the internment of Italians and the Fascio.

The position in regard to preventive measures and the "Fifth Column" in 1940-1941. In 1940 and the first half of 1941 when the threat of a German invasion hung over this country and our rearmament had made relatively little progress, it seemed to officers of the Security Service that it was an essential part of their duty to attempt to provide for preventive measures against the possibility that the Fascio might join the Germans and the British Union of Fascists in disruptive action at the critical point of an attempted invasion; and that, even if the Italians did not appear as a rule to be very dangerous, it was always possible that in combination with the other elements they might by acts of sabotage and by spreading panic create a temporary effect at a crucial point and thus bring about consequences out of all proportion to their intrinsic importance.

The position therefore was that in the early summer of 1940 action had been taken by the breaking up of the NSDAP organisations in this country at the beginning of the war; by the general internment of enemy aliens (never fully completed) and by the internment of members of the B.U.F. and other individuals including purely British subjects and British subjects of enemy origin or extraction. This action - although it may have required to be supplemented by further action against a certain number of individuals based on further enquiries - was in itself sufficient to render any "Fifth Column" organisation which may have existed largely, if not wholly, innocuous. These "Right-Wing" Movements, German, Italian and British, were the obvious foci of any "Fifth Column" and by analogy with what had happened on the continent might be expected as organisations to co-operate with the enemy. Although some parts of these organisations might have been left in being, their centres had been destroyed and, by arrest and internment if there were a number of individual "Fifth Columnists", their capacity for harm must have been greatly diminished by the elimination of the organisations. Nevertheless, as a subsequent enquiry by B.1.C. showed, there was at all times a considerable number of individuals, both German and British, at large who were so imbued with Fascist doctrines that they believed that a victory for Germany was preferable to a victory for the "Jewish controlled pluto-democracy" which they were deluded enough to think was in control in this country. Many of these individuals sincerely held this opinion and regarded themselves not as traitors but as patriotic people who saw the interests of their country in their true light. The effect of the internments was, however, gradually diminished by the releases of Germans, Italians and British subjects, but the immediate danger of invasion receded after the summer of 1941.

This, in brief, was the "Fifth Column" problem with which the Security Service had to deal; and it was closely allied to the purely counter-espionage problem because, in view of the inadequate state of our information at the time, it seemed probable that the German Intelligence Service might be receiving important military information from such sources. Subsequent enquiries established - but this was only two or three years later - that while such persons were willing to supply information to the enemy, the enemy had no organisation in being through which they could avail themselves of their opportunities.

While the real potentialities of a "Fifth Column" had been met as far as was possible in the face of the difficulties created by Home Office and Foreign Office policy, the Security Service was distracted by reports - largely of an imaginary nature - received, as a result of a not unnatural scare, from the public. There was less excuse for high officials who insisted on enquiries by the Security Service or the police into numerous supposedly suspicious incidents. These enquiries included an elaborate analysis of marks on telegraph poles, a memorandum on which was sent to the Home Office in July 1940 with the result that advice was sent to the police and the R.S.L.O.s to the effect that the marks were innocuous and were attributed in some cases to Scouts and Girl Guides. The organisation responsible having readily agreed to refrain from the practice, the marks were gradually obliterated. There were numerous enquiries regarding allegedly suspicious lights, some being due to reports from the military, naval or other authorities. One report sponsored from a very high quarter was a story that trees had been felled in a wood so as to make an arrow pointing to a neighbouring aerodrome. None of these numerous reports (some further details of which will be found in the B.3.C. report in Chapter V) had any substance, and none led to any positive results, to the uncovering of any real "Fifth Column" activities or even to the detection of a single enemy agent. The very great volume of paper involved had an overwhelming effect on the working of the machinery of the Security Service. Another phenomenon of this type which was never satisfactorily sifted was the frequency of reports in the summer of 1940 to the effect that "Lord Haw-Haw" had given precise details about some local event. These stories purported to show that the enemy had informants from whom they obtained prompt reports about local affairs in towns and villages. Enquiries made into numerous reports of this kind led to no positive result, but the possibility that in some cases such stories had been deliberately put about in order to provoke a scare could not be completely ruled out.

All these points served to emphasise the necessity for the Security Service being prepared in similar circumstances to deal with a flood of reports of all kinds at the beginning of a war. The establishment of the R.S.L.O.s went a long way to meet these difficulties and would have been more effective if it could have been achieved when the war began.

(iii) The appointment of Lord Swinton and the Security Executive.

On the 28th May 1940 the Security Executive was formed with the title of Home Defence Security Executive, under the chairmanship of Lord Swinton who also became the ministerial head of the Security Service. The purposes underlying the creation of the Security Executive were described by Lord Swinton as being due to the need to avoid duplication and hiatus resulting from the fact that in Great Britain the authorities mainly responsible for security were the Home Office (and under their general direction the Police Forces), the War Office and the Commander-in-Chief Home Forces, while many other Departments and Services had security functions within their own sphere. The Security Executive was therefore set up by the Prime Minister and charged with the duty of co-ordinating all security activities, preventing overlapping and omissions, affording opportunity for the sharing of experience and maintaining a proper balance between security and other national interests. It was explained that in practice security meant defence of the national interests against espionage, sabotage and attempts to procure defeat by subversive political activity. Security in this sense was not confined to the United Kingdom but extended to British Colonies, to the Dominions and India with whom liaison was maintained, and it covered such British interests abroad as the security of British ships and cargoes in foreign ports. The Chairman of the Security Executive was made responsible to the Prime Minister and in regard to internal security to the Lord President of the Council who acted for Prime Minister in this sphere.

The Chairman was assisted by two independent members without departmental association or responsibilities and by representatives of the Prime Minister and the Lord President of the Council. An important method of conducting the business of the Security Executive was that by which the Chairman held regular meetings at which various Departments of the Government including the Intelligence Directorates of the three Fighting Services were represented as and when desirable. The Security Executive was a co-ordinating body and did not take operative action to give effect to its recommendations. Its function was to see that responsibility for action was assigned to the appropriate Departments. The Admiralty, War Office, Air Ministry, Home Office, G.H.Q. (Home Forces), the Ministry of Information, Postal and Telegraph Censorship, S.I.S., Security Service and the Metropolitan Police had regular liaison officers attached to the Executive, which was served by a small full-time staff of Civil Servants.

By the creation of the Security Executive, under Lord Swinton who also described himself as Executive Head of the Security Service,[†] many of the difficulties which had previously affected the Security Service were solved; but further difficulties were created by Lord Swinton's assumption of the position of "Executive Head of the Security Service" which appeared to imply that he held a position not analogous to that of the ministerial head of a Government Department but one involving the direction of the internal working of the machinery and direct control of the staff.

(iv) Developments during the summer of 1940.

<u>The internal affairs of the Security Service</u>. In pursuance of this assumption Lord Swinton introduced three new members to the staff of the Security Service and appointed Mr. Crocker, a solicitor, to be joint head of B Branch, Mr. Horrocks to deal with reorganisation including the Registry, and Mr Frost to be in charge of a new Branch known as W Branch. Mr. Crocker's appointment placed the Director and Captain Liddell, who had succeeded Brigadier Harker as head of B. Branch in a difficult position. Lord Swinton did not define the respective functions of Mr Crocker and Captain Liddell as joint heads of B Branch and this unprecedented administrative anomaly created a situation which by August 1940 induced Captain Liddell and a number of the senior

---

[†] In a letter dated the 5th March 1941 (vide 18a in SF.51/30/36(I)) to Sir James Grigg, Permanent Under Secretary for War, he said "under the Cabinet decisions the operational control of the Security Service and of S.I.S., so far as it operates in this country, is vested in me working to the Lord President as Minister". In the same letter he refers to the Secretary of State for Foreign Affairs as the Minister responsible for expenditure incurred both by S.I.S. and the Security Service and remarks that "this need not involve him in the control of administration and operation".

officers of B Branch to consider the desirability of resigning, but they decided that this course could not be adopted in view of the critical war situation.

Mr. Horrocks proceeded to take immediate steps to remedy the situation in the Registry for which purpose he was able to obtain Treasury sanction to an immediate increase of Registry staff bringing the total up to nearly four hundred. With this large increase of untrained staff he decided that it was necessary to change the system which had been in force since the last war and to adopt a system which simplified the processes in the Registry. Under the old system importance was attached to specialised knowledge in Registry sections and especially on the part of the heads of those sections, each of whom was expected to acquire a thorough knowledge of the subject dealt with in her section. The change of system which abolished these heads of sections dealing with separate subjects necessitated a further change by which responsibility for decisions in regard to carding and extracting was transferred from the heads of registry sections to the sectional officers in B and other Divisions who were concerned with the action taken on the files.

The position when Mr. Horrocks took over was one of serious difficulty. He brought about a great improvement in the mechanics of the Office and gradually introduced order where there had been disorder and confusion.

This change involving the abandoning of specialised knowledge of the subject of the files on the part of the Registry staff was opposed by B Branch officers and was not well received by some of the able heads of Registry sections who had acquired knowledge as a result of application and industry, had worked the old system efficiently until they were overwhelmed by an immense increase of work without the staff to deal with it; and had maintained their morale for months in the face of this disaster. B Branch officers were unwilling to see such a drastic change of system in the middle of a crisis and were afraid that the more mechanical alternative adopted by Mr. Horrocks would deprive them of the assistance which they had previously enjoyed as a result of co-operation based on specialised knowledge. Mr. Horrocks, however, held that it was necessary to make the change and to adopt a more mechanical system which divided the work in the Registry into a number of simple processes. In addition to the large increase in staff a great effort extending over several months was required before the eventual high standard of efficiency was reached and this period of preparation and gradual improvement involved a considerable and unavoidable strain on the whole staff.

It is not possible to discuss all the arguments for and against the change. It may be mentioned, however, that it was felt that on the one hand the old system had the advantage of sustaining the morale of the Registry staff by developing a sense of responsibility based on knowledge of a subject and pride of workmanship. On the other hand it was decided that it was necessary to solve the immediate problem arising from the existing breakdown and that there was no practical alternative to a more mechanical system. The whole problem was one of considerable complexity both intrinsically and on account of the difference of opinion to which it gave rise.

The long duration of the controversy on the subject - it lasted from the summer of 1940 until March 1941 - had an unfortunate effect on morale. This was only brought to an end by Sir David Petrie's decision in favour of Mr. Horrocks' scheme. Mr. Horrocks' account of developments in the Registry will be found in Chapter V, Part 4.

Mr. Frost was appointed on the 24th July, 1940 to start the new W. Branch, the chief object being the location of enemy agents by the detection of their channels of communication. Captain Robertson was appointed as his Chief Assistant and took with him his work in connection with double-agents. In addition to taking over existing work in connection with censorship, wireless and broadcasting, lights and signals, pigeons, leaflets and signs, for all of which sections in W Branch were created, another section was formed to report on communications between the enemy and their agents or prospective agents by means of advertisements in the British or Foreign Press. Arrangements were made to obtain the necessary information from the Service Departments about operations likely to be of interest to enemy agents. In view of the extremely secret nature of the information available in the last named section it was proposed that only a limited number of officers of the Security Service should have access to the information in what was described as "the Operations Room".

As one of the main functions of B Branch - the detection of enemy agents - involved and to a great extent depended on the detection of their communications, it soon became obvious that the formation of W Branch involved reduplication as between W and B and the desirability of deciding on the legitimate and proper functions of W became increasingly pressing. This reduplication of machinery to exercise the same functions and to deal with the same problems could not but lead to friction between B and W Branches; and an atmosphere of intrigue which had previously been entirely unknown in the Security Service, began to develop.

On the 10th June 1940, at a meeting of the Home Defence Security Executive, Lord Swinton explained proposals for establishing the Security Intelligence Centre, and on the 17th July, 1940, he briefly reviewed the work done since its establishment. He said that, broadly speaking, the information which should be communicated to the Centre was any information which could throw light on any suspected "Fifth Column" activities in this country. Such information might be conveniently classified under the headings:-

1. Information pointing to an organised body or group, and individual agents.
2. Information pointing to means of communication to or from the enemy.
3. Instances of "Fifth Column" activity, including propaganda by wireless, leaflet, poster or speeches; leakages or information; sabotage; improper endeavours to obtain official information; attempts to slow down production; trading with the enemy; and suspicious activities by refugees.

There were several other minor headings. This comprehensive charter duplicated all the work of the Security Service in relation to "Fifth Column" activities; and, to a great extent, to sabotage and the detection of espionage. On the 10th March, 1941, Lord

Swinton laid down that Mr. Abbot of the Secretariat should be the channel for enquiries from himself or the Centre directed to the Security Service. On the 19th March 1941, he informed the Director-General that the presence of a member of the Secretariat, as the Security Executive's liaison with the Security Service, would facilitate the transaction of this kind of business. The Security Intelligence Centre in the meanwhile became involved in enquiries connected with peace feelers, in which a direct approach was made to the police by utilising the Home Office Special Branch Summary instead of addressing the Security Service. The position of the Centre as duplicating our functions thus became extremely complicated and it ceased to function after April 1941.

During the summer of 1941 the position therefore was that Lord Swinton was attempting to duplicate the work of B Branch:-

1. In connection with the detection of espionage by setting up W Branch to deal with all problems relating to the interception of communications; and
2. in connection with "Fifth Column" work through the Security Intelligence Centre.

At the same time he had helped to reduce B Branch to a state of chaos and had seriously damaged the morale of its officers by appointing Mr. Crocker virtually to be joint head of it with undefined functions. None of these moves achieved any success. He was also regarded as changing horses in mid-stream by raising controversy at a time of crisis, without finding satisfactory solutions, especially in that he was responsible for the re-organisation of the Registry on new lines and for discarding the system based on the specialised knowledge of the Registry staff which had been recognised as a factor contributing towards the success of the whole organisation in the war of 1914-1918 and had afterwards been maintained to the general advantage in spite of inadequate numbers. The result of all these measures was that Captain Liddell, as head of B Branch, was in the position all through the critical months from the fall of France to the reorganisation in April 1941 of having almost unlimited responsibilities without the necessary powers to discharge them, while Lord Swinton was attempting to supersede the B Branch organisation by improvisations of his own.

The reasons which led Lord Swinton to adopt this policy or to abandon it are not known. The most obvious explanation would seem to be that he formed the opinion when first taking over his duties that the whole of B Branch was inefficient, but was unable to make up his mind to abolish it; that he failed to understand the nature of the work and the extent to which it is necessarily based on the Registry, i.e. the files and card index; and that eventually circumstances forced him to see that his improvisations in the Security Intelligence Centre and W Branch could not supersede B Branch.

When Captain Liddell took over from Brigadier Harker as head of B Branch it was decided that Mr. Curry should become Deputy-Director of B Branch, but in view of the anomalous position created by Mr. Crocker's appointment effect was not given to this until the beginning of September when Mr. Crocker left. As soon as the position was cleared up by Mr. Crocker's departure, Captain Liddell made arrangements to reorganise

B Branch which at this time consisted of ninety officers. The problem of effecting a reorganisation was complicated by the fact that the three senior officers in B Branch were overwhelmed with work and discussion frequently had to be carried on until late at night. The greatest practical difficulty in the way of reorganisation was the absence of concrete knowledge of the German organisation and the complexity involved in dealing with preventive or security enquiries with special reference to a "Fifth Column" problem of uncertain incidence. It was therefore decided by Captain Liddell and his senior assistants that until the position could be clarified by concrete evidence regarding the German organisation - possibilities in this direction were beginning to appear in September 1940 in view of the earliest attempts then being made to read the Abwehr wireless - it would be better not to attempt a drastic reorganisation but to group the twenty-five B sections which then existed under seven controlling officers as an interim measure. Each of the controlling officers was made to be responsible for a subject or group of subjects, i.e.

1. The internal security system in the Forces.
2. Co-ordination of counter-espionage measures against Germany.
3. Co-ordination of counter-espionage measures against the Soviets and collation of intelligence regarding Communist activities.
4. Collation of intelligence regarding the British Union of Fascists and other similar movements.
5. Co-ordination of counter-espionage measures against Italy.
6. Co-ordination of counter-espionage measures.
7. Enquiries into cases of suspected espionage.

In addition to the above-mentioned seven groups there were organisations for the control of Regional Security Liaison Officers, and W Branch (which came under B now elevated from a Branch to a Division). The organisations for dealing with agents, the shadowing staff and other outside enquires were also part of B Division, as well as certain officers retained for special enquires.

The ideal at which B Division officers aimed was to secure the closest possible co-ordination in day-to-day working on the well-known lines associated with the name of Nelson. Each officer controlling a group was intended to have close touch with his staff and to control all their actions in detail in relation to other branches of the office or other Departments of Government. The ten senior officers were to form a compact body each of whom knew the mind of the head of B Division so well that he could whenever necessary act without instructions in accordance with general principles which had been thrashed out in discussion. The head of the Division was to be in a position to control the co-ordination of detection, prevention and intelligence, and all important contacts with the outside world, while his deputy was made responsible for internal organisation and co-ordination.

Lord Swinton effectively put a stop to all this. Before this re-organisation could be brought into force, and within a month of the initiation of discussions after Mr. Crocker's departure, Lord Swinton intervened and gave instructions to the Director that no further re-organisation of B Division should be attempted as he proposed to arrange for a re-organisation on other lines.

The Regional Security Liaison Officers. Early in the summer of 1940, on the suggestion of Captain Liddell and other B Branch officers, it was decided that Regional Security Liaison Officers, should be appointed to the twelve regions into which the United Kingdom had been divided for purposes connected with an attempted invasion, and Mrs. Archer was placed in charge of a section known as B.R. to develop this scheme. The object was, in the first place, to provide an officer of the Security Service in each region to be in touch with the Regional Commissioner, the local military authorities and the Chief Constables of the cities, boroughs and counties to deal with all questions which might arise in the event of an invasion. They were also intended to relieve Head Office of a great deal of miscellaneous correspondence about minor details with the police and to establish a close personal liaison with police officers in order to obviate the difficulties which were arising from the lack of personal contact and from the fact that the circumstances had made it inevitable that a large number of untrained and inexperienced officers in different sections were carrying on correspondence with Chief Constables about the numerous cases of persons suspected of espionage or other dangerous activities as a result of information received from the public or other sources.

The R.S.L.O. scheme proved to be very satisfactory from the beginning. It involved a high degree of organisation and close contact by telephone between B.R. and the Regional Officers. The effectiveness of the scheme was also improved by a series of conferences for Regional Officers usually held at Blenheim after the move. When Mrs. Archer left in the autumn of 1941 Lt.-Colonel MacIver took charge of B.R.

Owing to the confusion and difficulties of the time when R.S.L.O.s were first appointed in the summer on 1940 their charter and terms of reference were deliberately left in a vague form and no attempt was made to express them in concise terms. The position was explained to Chief Constables in a letter which made it clear that all future correspondence between the police and Head Office sections was to take place through the R.S.L.O. except in the case of Fascist or Communist matters. In regard to these two subjects the police were asked to correspond direct with Head Office, but to send a copy of each letter to the R.S.L.O. While no difficulty arose in regard to Communism the R.S.L.O.s soon became involved in a number of matters connected with the British Union of Fascists which, inevitably, entered into the general nexus of the "Fifth Column" problem. B.7., the section which dealt with the B.U.F. and other cognate matters had been inadequately manned to cope with the mass of enquiries which arose when Fascists were detained under D.R. 18(b). After the fall of France the section had been swamped and unable to deal with correspondence with the police and others without great delay and the R.S.L.O.s to a great extent stepped into the breach. Partly as a result of this assistance and partly as a result of the staff of B.7. at Headquarters being strengthened this position was gradually improved. By the end of the year the officers in B.7. felt that it was necessary that they, rather than R.S.L.O.s should be in control of the investigations regarding Fascists which were their responsibility. The question was discussed at a conference of R.S.L.O.s held at country headquarters on 6th January 1941 when the question was discussed with B.7., other B. sections similarly affected and the deputy-Director of B Division. As a result instructions were issued with the approval of Director, B Division, which provided that an R.S.L.O. should not arrange for an arrest or for a search except in agreement with the section of Head Office (unless in a case of great emergency). It was made clear that the section at Head Office must be a repository of all important information and that it only was in a position to initiate or develop policy in regard to subjects within the scope of its duties.

One of the principal functions of B.R. was to provide for smooth running in the relations between R.S.L.O.s and other parts of the Security Service. In addition to this it dealt with all administrative and personnel questions under the guidance of the head of A Division.

German invasion plans and the arrival of agents in Eire. During the summer of 1940 while a German attempt at invasion was expected and indications of their preparations were reported, the Security Service was still without definite information about their Secret Service or its agents and it was left with the very uncomfortable feeling that there must be agents in this country whom it was unable to discover. It was not until a long time afterwards that it was possible to arrive at the conclusion that the Abwehr had, in fact, failed to establish an efficient network. In May, June and July six of their agents arrived in Eire by parachute or by sea. Captain Liddell's arrangements for an exchange of information with the Eire authorities - when advising before the war on measures to meet their request for co-operation - now bore fruit and valuable results were obtained in the way of prompt details. This was important because these cases reflecting, as they did, preliminary moves by the Abwehr appeared to be an indication of German strategical plans for the invasion of the British Isles (vide "The German Secret Service, August 1942" Bibliography No. 33).

The Irish Section of the Security Service, known as B.9., consisted of one officer, Mr. Cecil Liddell and a secretary. Like all the other sections of B Division it was overwhelmed with a mass of correspondence and reports of suspected cases which inundated it and after a time tended to render effective action difficult. In spite of these difficulties Captain Liddell and Mr. Cecil Liddell were able, through their contact with Colonel Liam Archer of the Eire Intelligence and with the Dominions Office and other authorities in London, to lift the main problems on to a level of high policy and to arrange for security measures on a sufficiently comprehensive scale to cover what might otherwise have been a very dangerous gap.. The manner in which these various problems were solved will be described in Chapter V below.

The effect of German air-raids: the records damaged by enemy action. During the summer and autumn of 1940, however, German air-raids, which appeared to be a precursor of invasion, seriously interfered with the work at Head Office. The structure at Wormwood Scrubs in which the office was accommodated was regarded as unsafe except on the ground floor and three-quarters or more of the staff were ordered to leave their rooms on the upper floors during air-raids. This sometimes resulted in many hours of the day being virtually lost and thus added to the other difficulties under which we were labouring.

In September an oil-bomb fell on the Registry and destroyed nearly all the card index and some files. This would have been even more disastrous than it was but for the action taken (as a result of Lord Rothschild's suggestions) to have the cards photographed when serious danger from air-raids threatened. It was decided in consequence of the fire that the records and the greater part of the staff should be moved from London to Blenheim Palace.

The move to Blenheim. The removal of the greater part of the Office to Blenheim in October 1940 inevitably dislocated the work in numerous ways. The Director, Colonel Allen as head of C and D Divisions and Captain Liddell with the staff in B Division most actively engaged in counter-espionage work remained in London, while numerically the greater part of B,C and D Divisions together with the Registry and an important part of A Division under Colonel Butler moved to the country. In spite of special facilities for communication by telephone, and transport by car supplemented by Despatch Riders carrying lighter papers over the seventy miles separating the two parts of the Office, difficulties were naturally experienced in matters of direction and co-ordination.

(v) Developments from October 1940 to June 1941.

Arrival of enemy agents in the United Kingdom. In the beginning of September 1940 as they intensified their air attacks, the Germans began to despatch agents by sea or by air as part of their projected invasion operation. These men were captured almost immediately and the evidence showed that arrangements to send them here had been hastily made. They had instructions to act as operational agents to supply information for the use of the invading troops.

In September, October and November 1940 over twenty-five German agents are known to have arrived in the United Kingdom, mostly by parachute or small boats in connection with the preparations for an invasion to which the Battle of Britain was a preliminary (for details vide "The German Secret Service, August 1942" - Bibliography No. 33).

The establishment of Camp 020. As these agents were captured they were sent to Camp 020 for interrogation. Camp 020 had been established early in the summer of 1940 on the initiative of Mr. White and Major Stephens who had previously been engaged in interrogating members of the NSDAP arrested in the United Kingdom. The suggestion was taken up and carried through by Lord Swinton, and in the first place Camp 020, when established, was used for the examination of members of the British Union of Fascists as a component of the potential "Fifth Column". Partly as a result of questions in Parliament, the examination of B.U.F. members presented difficulties and no great success was achieved. As soon as the German agents started to arrive the institution proved its usefulness, and the Security Service is indebted to Lord Swinton for carrying through a project which would probably have been impossible but for his energetic support. It soon became evident that the institution of Camp 020 radically changed the status of the Security Service by enabling them to deal directly with the Security Service by enabling them to deal directly with the interrogation of German agents - instead of having to act through the police as was done in the last war - and materially added to the efficiency with which they were able to take counter measures against German spies and saboteurs.

Illicit Wireless Interception and the development of R.S.S. In the early stages of the war numerous reports were received from the public and other sources regarding the suspected use of wireless for the purpose of communicating with the enemy and, as in other similar matters, the great majority of these were without any substantial foundation. None of them led to the detection or discovery of a spy. Many cases, for instance, arose through individuals accidentally picking up Morse signals on their wireless receivers thus leading to their neighbours or passers-by reporting "the suspicious circumstances" to the authorities. The large number of these and similar cases contributed to swamping the police and the Security Service with a vast volume of enquiries which, however fruitless they might appear, involved a great deal of care and labour.

A section known as B.3., under Lt.-Colonel Simpson, C.M.G., R.E., had been established at the beginning of the war to deal with these enquiries. The result of the decision of 7th December 1938 (mentioned in the last Chapter) to establish R.S.S. under the War Office, had the effect of virtually confining B.3. to two duties apart from liaison with R.S.S. These two duties were -

(a) to receive reports from informants and the police about suspected illicit transmissions in the United Kingdom and take appropriate action in each case, and -
(b) to arrange for intelligence officers to accompany and direct mobile units attempting to locate illicit wireless sets with a view to arranging for the necessary executive action in conjunction with the police if the search proved successful.

In the meantime the R.S.S. organisation had been set up on the lines suggested by Lt.-Colonel Simpson in his report of the 10th October 1938 (vide SF.51/30/36). Lt.-Colonel Simpson , who had been Deputy Managing Director of Marconi's Wireless Telegraph Company, Ltd., Director, Wireless Telegraphs, of the Government of India, and had had experience in this subject in the last war, reported that the position had entirely changed owing to developments since 1918 and that the existing arrangements for Security Service purposes at the end of 1938 were totally inadequate, while the interception and D/F stations belonging to other branches of the Services were fully occupied in attending to their own requirements. He had recommended that R.S.S. should consist of three fixed D/F stations, six portable D/F stations, one fixed interception station and one portable interception station, all to be connected by the necessary land lines for communication purposes and to be supported by an Observer Corps of voluntary interceptors. He emphasised that these voluntary interceptors, to the number of some fifty or sixty picked amateurs, would have to be very carefully selected as the work required a very high degree of keenness, initiative, coolness and power of concentration and that to become a first-class interception operator was a life study. Experience had shown that first-class operators knew what was going on in the air almost as it were by instinct and were often able to make valuable suggestions as to the nature of a message even if the actual contents were not known. The question of selection and training was, therefore, of the highest importance. He also emphasised the difference in the objectives of the Post Office and the Security Service and urged that the real solution was to be found "in centralising all work of this nature (as part from the requirements of the Fighting Services) in a separate section <u>having its own permanent establishment of equipment and personnel</u>.

The headquarters of R.S.S. had been located in the same building as the Security Service at the beginning of the war and the closest liaison was, therefore, possible and was effected; but on February 2nd 1940 Lt.-Colonel Simpson reported that the state of affairs concerning the detection of illicit wireless was extremely unsatisfactory and that this was largely due to the failure of the Post Office to provide the right type of personnel. On the 20th March 1940, however, at a conference at which the Security Service, R.S.S. and G.C. & C.S. were represented, it was revealed that R.S.S. had realised that in their search for illicit wireless transmission in this country they had intercepted transmissions of the German Intelligence Service which had no direct connection with the operation of agents in this country, some of these messages having been deciphered by the combined efforts of officers of the Security Service and R.S.S. Arrangements were made at this meeting for G.C. & C.S. to form a separate section to study this traffic. This was the beginning of the I.S.O.S. section of the G.C & C.S. and of the material known as ISOS.

As these developments progressed it became obvious that the joint control by M.I.8., the Post Office and the Security Service was breaking down. In November 1940, however, Major E.W.B. Gill of R.S.S. prepared a paper which described the work done since the beginning of the war and brought certain new facts to notice. This paper constituted a turning-point in the history of the interception of German Secret Service wireless messages because it showed that while no enemy agents using wireless had been detected in this country it was possible to develop a system which could produce, and had already produced, important information about the organisation behind the agents. He mentioned that the Security Service had supplied R.S.S. with two facts at the beginning of the war. The first was the type of message which agents would probably send and the second the station to which they might work in Germany. (This information had been derived from the agent Owens who had instructions from the Abwehr station in Hamburg regarding the use of the wireless set which he had handed over in London before the war). A special watch was therefore kept on wireless traffic to and from this station and messages of the type expected were picked up. In the first place - in the spring of 1940 - these messages were found to be communications with a ship which was evidently moving round the coast of Norway. As a result of the combined efforts of Captain Trevor Roper and other officers of R.S.S. and the Security Service the cyphers were "cracked" and it appeared that this ship was the "Theseus" and was sending in reports on neutral shipping. The next step taken by R.S.S. had been, instead of confining attention to Hamburg, to investigate traffic from any station which appeared to be of the same or of a closely approximate type. This revealed - again in the spring of 1940 - an organisation working from Germany to agents in Holland, Belgium, Luxembourg and later in Paris. The agents were supplying information about defences, road-blocks, troop movements and similar matters and the main enquiries from Germany had been directed to the region over which the German advance had shortly afterwards been made. After the fall of France other ships similar to the "Theseus" moved down channel and shortly before the projected invasion of England a group of stations had been detected as working between Cherbourg, Brussels, Paris and Germany and using the same type of message as the "Theseus". These messages were read and it became apparent that the stations were intended to communicate with agents whom it was hoped to land in England by various methods. Enough information had been gained to make it possible to identify most of the agents who had been landed and arrested almost immediately. Further enquiries along the same lines had led to the discovery of agents in widely separated parts of the world including the U.S.A., Eire, Greece and Spanish Morocco. Another similar group of traffic was identified as probably based on Vienna and as working to agents in the Balkans. On this group a number of questions had been asked about the whereabouts of Rumanian and Russian Divisions when the German troops entered Rumania.

All the messages mentioned above had been deciphered, mainly by G.C. & C.S., after the establishment of the ISOS section mentioned above, but R.S.S. had picked up a very large and important group whose messages had not proved readable. They had first attracted attention because inaccurate bearings had suggested that some of the stations were in England. The difficulty of the cyphers, the magnitude of the traffic and the fact that the centre of the group was at Berlin with stations all over Europe indicated that the group was more important than those of which cyphers had been read.

Major Gill pointed out that these facts indicated the great potentialities of the information to be obtained as a result of R.S.S. working on these lines. He also drew attention to the problem of providing for the necessary expansion: in R.S.S. for the purpose of interception and in G.C. & C.S. for that of deciphering.

Major Gill's document was an effective answer to the doubts which had been expressed about the efficiency and usefulness of R.S.S. and about the desirability of its being transferred from M.I.8. to "M.I.5." as had been strongly recommended by the M.I.8. Colonel.

Discussions regarding this proposed transfer had been going on since it was first made by M.I.8. on the 9th October 1940. In the middle of December Major Frost put up a memorandum suggesting that R.S.S. should be transferred to his control as Director of the "W Division". Lord Swinton referred the matter in January to Sir David Petrie who was then examining the organisation of the Security Service and asked for his opinion. He suggested on the 30th January that R.S.S. should be transferred completely to S.I.S. to be equipped, staffed and run purely as an intelligence instrument and he referred to it as "so potentially valuable an auxiliary of the Security and Secret Service".

On the 7th March 1941 the Secretary of State for War formally authorised the transfer of R.S.S. from the War Office to M.I.6. (S.I.S.) with the agreement of the Foreign Secretary and other interested parties. This decision was of crucial importance in more respects than one. If R.S.S. had been transferred to W Branch it would to all appearance have involved a serious dislocation in the relations between W Branch and B Division and the virtual supersession of the latter by the former in so far as the direction of work connected with the German Secret Services was concerned. For this reason apart from the fact S.I.S. had - and the Security Service had not - the technical and administrative equipment to enable it to cope with R.S.S. problems, it was preferable from the point of view of B Division officers that the control should rest with S.I.S. By this time they had lost the services of Lt.-Colonel Simpson, their only officer who could have developed and administered the necessary technical organisation on their behalf. They did not and could not foresee the subsequent attitude of Lt.-Colonel Cowgill of Section V and the developments which will find their place in the next Chapter.

The beginning of effective counter-espionage work. During the period September 1940 to June 1941 the organisation, under Mr. White as controlling officer for the co-ordination of counter espionage measures against German agents, began to take shape as planned by 'B' and 'Dy.B' and in an embryonic form some of its important components began to fit into place. These were: Camp 020 for the interrogation of agents under Major Stephens; a special Registry section for the card-indexing of ISOS (the Abwehr w/t) working directly to Mr. White (this subsequently grew into a B.1. section and the B.1. Registry, a group of Registry staff with a specialised knowledge of the German Intelligence Services which was essential in order to make readily accessible the results of intercepting their wireless, or the ISOS material, and to marry it to the information obtained by interrogation at Camp 020 or from other Security Service sources); and the manipulation of double-agents under Major Robertson. One very weak spot at this time was the section known as B.24, which subsequently was transmogrified into the "R.P.S." and later known as the L.R.C. (London Reception Centre). B.24 was responsible for interrogating refugees who arrived from the continent but the staff - provided mainly from S.I.S.- was not very competent and it failed to evolve any systematic method of dealing with its problems. The heads of B Division at this time were conscious of the urgent need for reorganising this staff but were prevented from doing so by Lord Swinton's embargo on any further reorganisation until he had evolved his own scheme. For a time the difficulty in finding suitable staff proved insurmountable; it was even difficult to find an experienced officer to take charge of B.24.

Further arrivals of German agents. In the meanwhile, the arrival of other German agents in 1940 and early 1941 proved the need for a careful examination of arrivals from enemy-occupied territory among whom it was now evident the Abwehr was contriving to insert its secret agents (for details vide Part 2 of "The German Secret Service, August 1942" - Bibliography No. 33). In particular arrivals by small boat from Norway with the object of securing naval information or penetrating Allied organisation in this country; a few agents with long term missions; and some seamen provided B Division with reasons for improving the arrangements for interrogation at the L.R.C. When agents were uncovered among the arrivals at the L.R.C. they were transferred to Camp 020 where a series of more intensified interrogations laid the foundation of much of the subsequent knowledge of the German organisation, its methods and its agents, which enabled the Security Service gradually to arrive at a feeling of confidence that they had the measure of their opponents. This took time, however, and the manner in which the organisation was built up will be described in detail in the next Chapter. The first results of these early beginnings of effective counter espionage work were summarised in a report prepared by Mr. White entitled "The German Secret Service" in December 1940 (vide Bibliography No. 39).

<u>Lord Swinton's re-organisation.</u> Lord Swinton had vetoed further reorganisation of B Division by its own officers in the first week of October but it was not until the 17th December that he put forward his own proposals in a final form. He professed himself as entirely satisfied with the organisation of C and D Divisions and addressed himself to the problem of B which he proposed should be divided into three new Divisions to deal with -

1. active espionage
2. subversive movements
3. aliens control

This plan was based on a remark made by Mr. White in a lecture to new officers in which he had said that each of these three elements came into the work of every section; and in his first tentative scheme Lord Swinton attempted - a very different conception - to devise a plan to divide most of the existing sections into three elements on these scholastic lines. At a meeting held by Lord Swinton on the 17th December Captain Liddell, on being asked for his opinion, gave reasons for opposing the scheme for dividing B Division as it aimed at carving into three parts a unit, most of whose members were conscious of the strongest possible grounds for closer co-ordination rather than separation. One of the objections to the scheme was that it proposed that the section dealing with the internment of Germans and Italians should be in one Division, that dealing with members of the British Union of Fascists and other British extreme pro-Nazis in another Division, while the section dealing with the German organisation for prompting subversive activities remained in the third, i.e. B Division. It was therefore considered that in the event of invasion, if the pattern which had been followed elsewhere were repeated here, preventive measures against the different components of the so-called "Fifth Column" seemed likely to be rendered unnecessarily cumbersome as a result of this divided direction. Again, the B section in question, i.e. the sabotage section, was concerned with active enquiries in pro-German circles in this country which included that of the British Union of Fascists and its sympathisers. At the same time the M Section which was responsible for controlling agents to penetrate German, Italian, British, Fascist and Communist organisations in this country was placed in B Division while its work was chiefly connected with that of the other two new Divisions as proposed.

At this meeting Captain Liddell put forward a suggestion by Mr. Curry that the major Departments of Government should be moved to accept a more positive responsibility for security measures. In particular the intention was that the Secretary of State for War and the Home Secretary should be moved to look at the question of the internment of enemy aliens as a preventive measure with a view to dealing with espionage and to the possibilities of invasion. It was hoped that if Lord Swinton agreed to take this up it would tend to relieve B Division from the pressure imposed on it by concentration on security problems and leave it more free to develop machinery for getting to grips with the Abwehr. Lord Swinton, however, refused to discuss the suggestion. He insisted on the division of B Division into three "blocks", but finally appeared to agree that these should all be controlled by one officer.

Sir David Petrie's arrival. Lord Swinton, however, made it clear that he was determined to carry through his scheme to divide B Division in spite of all opposition, but he delayed putting it into effect pending an examination by Sir David Petrie who had been called home from Egypt for the purpose. Sir David Petrie started his examination at the beginning of the New Year and reported towards the end of February. He accepted the appointment of the head of the Security Service with the title of Director-General and took up the appointment at the beginning of March.

When Sir David Petrie took charge of the Office as Director-General it was decided that Lord Swinton should occupy a position analogous to that of a ministerial head of a Department and that the control of the staff and internal direction of the Office should be in the hands of the Director-General. The instructions defining the functions of the Security Executive were subsequently altered accordingly; the phrase "the Chairman of the Executive happens also to be the Executive Head of the Security Services; this, although convenient is not essential to his functions" being altered to "The Chairman of the Executive has certain personal responsibilities with regard to the Security Service and M.I.6.; this, although convenient, is not essential to his functions."

Part 3: Communism and the U.S.S.R 1939 - 1941

(i) The outbreak of war and Comintern policy.

In 1938 the C.P.G.B. had received instructions from the Comintern that it was to oppose the Chamberlain Government in the event of war, but the actual outbreak in 1939 faced it with a dilemma. It had been conducting a campaign of strong opposition to Fascism in Europe and, in particular, against Nazi Germany; and it attempted to seize both horns of this dilemma by proclaiming that it had to wage a war on two fronts, against Fascism abroad in the person of Hitler and against Fascism at home in the person of Mr. Chamberlain.

Within a month, this policy was thrown into confusion by the Soviet attitude to Germany, the Soviet advance into Poland and by the receipt of instructions from the Comintern in the shape of a "short thesis of the Third International" news of which was brought from Moscow by D.F. Springhall. This, when received immediately afterwards (vide Bibliography No. 17 and No. 18) contained categorical instructions to the C.P.G.B. that it was to regard the war as an "imperialist and unjust war". The effect of this Communist phraseology was to imply that the war was a struggle for supremacy between two imperialist powers and was one which the working classes should not support. Springhall attended a meeting of the Central Committee of the C.P.G.B. on the 25th September and explained the views of the Comintern as stated to him by Georg Dimitrov, the Secretary of that organisation and Andre Marty, a veteran French Communist Party representative at Comintern Headquarters. Further discussion was postponed until the 2nd and 3rd October on account of the existence of opposition to the Comintern line and the Political Bureau appointed a Secretariat consisting of D.F. Springhall, W. Rust and R.P. Dutt to deal with the question. At the renewed discussions Dutt read the text of the short thesis as received from the Comintern and said that its whole substance should be literally incorporated in a resolution by the Central Committee of the C.P.G.B. for communication to District Committees and other Party organisations.

R.P. Dutt, as one of the Party's leading interpreters of Communist theory, made it evident that he was prepared to accept the line afterwards known as "revolutionary defeatism" with all its implications. It implied, as the discussion at these meetings showed, that the Communist Party should work for the military defeat of their own country on the lines laid down for the Russian Communist Party by Lenin in the last war. Dutt made it clear that on this issue of the attitude to the war "we must have absolute identity and (? in) the international line of all Parties" and that "Every section of the International needs equally to understand this new situation and be capable of adopting its tactics in relation to it". He showed that they did not want a mechanical acceptance of the Comintern line but that everyone must willingly recognise the necessity of conforming to the line. Underlying his argument was the theme that the existence of the Soviet Union was a powerful factor making for the advance of world revolution and that the sections of the Comintern must therefore support and follow Soviet policy. The result of the discussion was that the Central Committee was prepared to accept the policy laid down by the Comintern, except for Harry Pollitt and J.R. Campbell.

Copies of the Minutes of this meeting came into the hands of F Division, as did those of the letters of recantation mentioned below, and they afforded a good illustration of the working of the Communist Party.

The extremely lengthy Minutes of these discussions are very instructive as showing the means by which the C.P.G.B. was induce to follow the International line against the judgment of two of its most important and experienced leaders. These two, Pollitt and Campbell together with Gallacher, were referred to by Dutt as being three of the four members of the Executive Committee of the Communist International on the Central Committee of the C.P.G.B. The fourth was Dutt himself, and he made it clear that their open opposition to the decision of the E.C.C.I. was a tremendously serious matter for the Party. It was, he said, a thing which went beyond the competence of "our Party" and a matter for the concern of the International. Pollitt and Campbell maintained their opposition until the middle of November 1939 when they sent in letters of recantation to the Central Committee. Pollitt admitted his mistake, explaining how he had fallen into error and recognised that he had been wrong in opposing the line of the Comintern, and had thereby done harm to the Party and played into the hands of the class enemy, especially into the hands of the reactionary labour leaders.

(ii) The C.P.G.B. adopts the Comintern policy; "revolutionary defeatism".

On the 7th October 1939 the change of line by the C.P.G.B. was proclaimed in a manifesto which introduced the policy of "revolutionary defeatism" - a policy which was maintained until the attack on Russia in June 1941. Having thus adopted the Comintern line, the Party proceeded to attempt to hinder war-production by promoting strikes. As one

Party leader put it, the position was that there was no factory in which there was no grievance, and there was no grievance which could not be utilised to promote a strike. Thus the Communists took a leading part in pressing for strike action, but it cannot be said that the strikes themselves had no industrial basis. Industrial unrest of this kind was fermented by the 'New Propellor' the new periodical of the Communist auxiliary, the Engineer and Allied Trades Shop Stewards National Council, while the 'Daily Worker' persistently attempted to obstruct the prosecution of the war.

The activities of the French Communist Party had also been directed mainly against its own Government and the effect on the morale of the French Army was reported as being serious. The French Government declared the French Communist Party illegal, and some of its leaders were arrested and tried. The C.P.G.B. feared that the British Government might take similar measures, and for a time the Communist Party headquarters in London was almost deserted while Party leaders sought refuge in industrial employment.

In August 1940 the Communist Party began to form local "Peoples' Vigilance Committees" under the direction of a "Peoples' Convention" with the slogan "for a peoples' Government and a peoples' peace". The effects of these movements were not always what the Party desired, but this propaganda was not entirely without effect on public morale. Its chief vehicle, the 'Daily Worker', was banned under DR.2D by the Home Secretary on January 21st 1941. (This ban lasted until September 7th 1942).

(iii) The German attack on the U.S.S.R.

The attack by Germany on the Soviet Union on 22nd June 1941 took the Communist leaders by surprise. The Political Bureau of the Party met hurriedly and issued a statement which described the attack as the sequel to secret movements which had been taking place "behind the curtain of the Hess mission" and declared that the Communist Party should have no confidence in the present Government. D.F. Springhall, the national organiser of the Party was asked in the late afternoon of the 22nd June whether it would not have been better to await the Prime Minister's speech before publishing this statement, but he replied "We can make up our minds without waiting to listen to that enemy of the workers".

(iv) Alien Communists in the United Kingdom 1939 - 1941.

During the period 1939 - 1941 alien Communists in this country, like the C.P.G.B., took part in the campaign against the Allied war effort after receipt of the Comintern instructions in September 1939, although prior to this a number of alien refugee Communists had offered their services to the British Government to fight against "Hitler and Fascism". At the beginning of 1940 an open letter by a German Communist Party Leader in the U.S.S.R. was circulated in this country. It stated that the German Government had declared its willingness to maintain peaceful relations with the U.S.S.R. while the Anglo-French bloc was aiming at war with the Soviet Union and with the Russian people, and that German workers had a common interest in frustrating the English war plan which was contrary to the interests of all workers. It laid down that it was impossible to fight for democratic freedom by means of an alliance with the "reactionary forces of British imperialism".

In May 1940 a large proportion of the German and Austrian Communists in this country were interned as a consequence of the general internment order. Inside the internment camps, as well as outside, alien Communists led a campaign against enlistment in the Auxiliary Military Pioneer Corps. Many of the internees were released as a result of the Home Office policy in favour of release by categories as announced in August 1940, and many of the alien Communists who were released were absorbed into agriculture, forestry and industry. From June 1940 until June 1941 Communist agitation was prominent among Greek seamen whose legitimate grievances were exploited through the Greek Seamen's Union (N.E.E.) which owed its origin to the Greek Section of the Communist International of Seamen and Harbour Workers which operated for a time from New York City where it was linked to the Communist Party of the U.S.A. The headquarters of the Union were later transferred to this country and were a constant source of trouble among Greek seamen. In the meanwhile, Communists of countries occupied by the enemy came to this country to serve in the Allied Forces or as merchant seamen attached to their respective national shipping pools.

(v) B Branch policy in regard to Communism.

All these phases of Communist policy as formulated and translated into action were kept under observation by the section of B Branch which dealt with this subject. They formed the subject of reports to the Government Departments concerned. They had also to be taken into consideration in connection with vetting for employment.

The general effect of the Communist attitude and of the relations between the Governments of Germany and the U.S.S.R. were to add to the difficulties of B Branch in dealing with the problems relating to counter-espionage. There were occasions when the possibility of individual Communists or the Russian Secret Service assisting the enemy could not be ruled out, as described under the sub-heading "Soviet Espionage" below.

Apart from this question of counter-espionage the essential function of B.4.A. and B.4.B., the sections dealing with British and foreign Communists respectively during the period prior to the German attack on Russia, was to obtain the widest possible range of intelligence on their subjects. The main impact of the policy of "revolutionary defeatism" fell in the industrial sphere and it became clear that it was here that the Communist Party could do the most immediate harm to the war effort. The change from peace to war conditions inevitably created a number of grievances which could be exploited by the Party; and it was natural in the circumstances that there should have been pressure from various quarters for drastic action either against individual Communists or against the Party as a whole. The Security Service always resisted this pressure and in this course found itself in alignment with the policy of the Ministry of Labour. The Security Service also supported the view of the Ministry of Labour that a positive policy to deal with grievances was preferable to any attempt to take repressive action. A distinction was, at the same time, drawn between agitation which fomented industrial unrest and the physical sabotage of industrial plant. Industrial unrest was necessarily a matter which involved the position of the Trade Unions; and when the Security Service obtained information regarding Communists' attempts to undermine this position, information on the subject was communicated to the Ministry of Labour on the understanding that it might, when considered suitable, be communicated to the Union leaders. It was not considered desirable that the Security Service should have any direct contact with the Union leaders, although occasional contact with the T.U.C. had been established and Sir Walter Citrine had given assistance in certain enquiries into minor cases of sabotage which, it was thought, might be attributable either to enemy inspiration or to the results of Communist agitation; but the results failed to establish direct or definite evidence on both points. The Security Service further took the view that action should never be taken against members of the Communist Party because they were Communists but that if they infringed the law they should be dealt with for that infringement and not on account of their political views. In view of the fact that the Communist Party was a highly centralised organisation pursuing a single policy throughout the whole country under a central control it was held that it was desirable that counter action should be similarly centralised and that the Police Forces throughout the country should be advised to act on the above lines.

The result was that while in many cases action was taken against Communists at the request of other workmen it was done through the ordinary channels of industrial negotiation and not as the result of police action.

An important consequence of this general policy was that DR.18B was not generally applied to members of the Communist Party. The only instance of a member of the Party being detained was that of one, John Mason, in whose action case was taken by the Home Secretary at the suggestion of the Security Service and with the agreement of the Ministry of Labour. Mason was detained on 15.7.40 and in the following September appeared before the Home Office Advisory Committee which recommended his continued detention on the grounds of his "having been concerned in acts prejudicial............". The evidence against his was partly based on letters seen as the result of a H.O.W. which proved that he had been actively concerned in organising meetings and action inside factories to interfere with production in the English Steel Corporation of Sheffield where he had started work in December 1938. There were numerous protests against his internment from Communists and Communist-controlled organisations and one from the Executive Council of the A.E.U. of which Mason was a member. A meeting was arranged between five members of the A.E.U. councils and officials of the Home Office on 20.9.40. at which a member of the Security Service was present. As the A.E.U. were not satisfied the detailed evidence was communicated to them at a further interview and one of them then expressed the view that Mason ought not to have been detained but should have been shot. In spite of the attitude of the Trade Union, Mason was subsequently released on 7.6.41. by the Home Secretary after an interview between Sir Alexander Maxwell and Mr. Gallacher, the Communist M.P. Whereupon, Mason renewed his activities but he and the other parties concerned were saved from the embarrassment which might have been expected to ensue by the fact that the Party changed its policy shortly afterwards as a result of the German attack on Russia.

An important factor in the impact of Comintern policy on the industrial situation in this country arises from the development of the unofficial Shop Stewards' Movement. In order to explain what lay behind this movement Mr. Clarke of B.4.A prepared a paper on the subject (vide Bibliography No. 54). Although this paper was prepared in this period it was not issued until November 1941, but it will be convenient to refer to some of the main points made in it as it dealt almost entirely with developments prior to the German attack on Russia. The paper explained that the Shop Steward first came into existence some years before the last war and originally as an official of his union in the shop where he was employed. This was recognised by agreement between the engineering employers and certain unions in 1917 and, in the meanwhile, unofficial Shop Stewards had also obtained practical recognition in other industries. From these circumstances the unofficial Shop Stewards' Movement eventually arose and during the remainder of the war of 1914-1918 was engaged in fighting industrial conscription which it defined as a control of labour by the Government for the benefit of the employers. In 1919 when the Profintern, the Trade Union section of the Communist International, was established the Shop Stewards' Movement was affiliated to it. Some years later conditions in the aircraft industry became similar to those which gave rise to the Shop Stewards' Movement in the last war. The industry was a new and growing one and the unions had been slow to adjust their machinery to fit the new circumstances. In 1933 a newly formed body called The Aircraft Workers Movement declared in its statement of policy: "We want the union back to the position of the days of the Shop Stewards' Movement". The movement grew until in 1936 the Aircraft Shop Stewards' National Council which had developed from the Shop Stewards' Movement challenged Trade Union leadership; and after the outbreak of war in 1939 it followed the Communist Party line very closely, adopted the policy of "revolutionary defeatism" and served as one of the main channels for the Communist Party's approach to industry. For the first twenty-two months of the war these Councils consistently followed a policy of obstruction to the war effort. In 1940 the Shop Stewards' Movement extended to other sections of the engineering industry, but it did not succeed in obtaining a secure foothold in the heavy engineering industry. It attracted many members of the Electrical Trades Union and the Shop Stewards of certain Ordnance factories became affiliated to the National Engineering and Allied Trade Shop Stewards' National Council.

This National council is described in the F Division paper as a parasite within the Trade Union structure. Not only were the ranks of the Shop Stewards penetrated by the Communist Party, but the leadership of the Movement was entirely in the hands of Party members. The paper went on to explain the methods by which the Communist Party controlled the Shop Stewards' Movement and the place which the Movement occupied in the Party's programme by saying that the office of Shop Steward was not one to appeal to the ordinary member of a Trade Union and that the Communist Party instructed its members to put themselves forward for this office and saw that they were trained to fulfil its duties. Apathy towards the election of Shop Stewards often played into the hands of the Communist Party, but penetration by the Party into the ranks of Shop

Stewards had also meant penetration into the governing machinery of the Trade Unions. The degree of penetration varied greatly from place to place.

The political implications of this situation were important. Whether the Shop Stewards' Movement was giving practical expression to a policy of "revolutionary defeatism" or to a "united front" policy; and whatever tactics the Communist Party might adopt from time to time, its long-term aims remained the same. These revolutionary aims were clearly visible in the activities of the Shop Stewards' National Council and the Communist Party was seeking to draw away the rank and file members of Trade Unions and to create a split which would ultimately shatter the whole Trade Union structure and enable the Communist Party to achieve its aims - an essential part of its revolutionary programme - of securing the leadership of the industrial masses. It was along these lines that the C.P.G.B. was carrying out the policy of the Comintern.

It should be added, however, that subsequent events proved that the Communist Party's aims were often greater than its achievements and their position was not so strong as might appear from their success in securing the election of their members as Shop Stewards. It often happened that because the Communist Shop Steward had few Party supporters in his shop his disappearance, for any reason, destroyed the whole position which had been built up in that particular shop. (Later developments are described in Mr. Clarke's book on the Communist Party - Its Aims and Organisation in the chapter on Industrial Organisation - vide Bibliography No. 14).

Early in 1940 when it became apparent that the Communist Party might under certain circumstances present a serious menace in view of the relations existing between Germany and the U.S.S.R., a memorandum was sent to the Home Office (on April 12th) making recommendations regarding the following measures:-

(a) the refusal of facilities to British Communists for foreign travel;
(b) the prohibition of export of Communist publications;
(c) the internment of Communist leaders in the event of hostilities with the Soviet Union.

The Home Office policy at this time was to allow exit permits to France to be issued to Communists but to warn the French authorities. Measures banning the export of their publications were brought into force in May-June 1940.

In May 1940, the Security Service prepared a plan for dealing with the C.P.G.B. in the event of an attempt to organise widespread resistance to greater production. Thirty-nine officials of the Party were listed for detention on lines calculated to paralyse the Party and these detentions were intended to coincide with the search of selected Party premises. The scheme was submitted to the Home Office who authorised arrangements to communicate it to the Chief Constables concerned. It was arranged that on receipt of a telegram "Put Complan into effect" the necessary action would be taken by the police. It was held that the existing powers under DR.18B would not cover the detention of Communists in the circumstances contemplated and the Home Office undertook to ask for further powers should the intended action become necessary.

As the Communist Party is a political Party it can be fought with political weapons and the question of a White Paper, which - by the publication of inside information - would expose the realities behind it was also under consideration and was an integral part of the Security Service proposals for dealing with the Communist Party as put forward during 1940 and 1941.

The principle underlying these plans - the arrest of a sufficient number of leaders to paralyse the Party and the exposure of its secrets - was based on the view that the Party consisted of a revolutionary core and a large number of sympathisers, many of whom were attracted by the surface ideals of Communism, by the economic and industrial policy of the Party, or by its agitation for improved conditions; but did not realise either the immediate or the long-term implications of "revolutionary defeatism" or "the class war". The proposed action was therefore designed to split the outer covering of sympathisers from the hard revolutionary core. For this purpose a powerful weapon had been placed in the hands of the authorities when the Guildford police discovered in the course of a search the Minutes of the meetings of the Central Committee of the Party and the short thesis of the Comintern already mentioned (vide Bibliography No. 17 and No. 18). The crisis never developed and the proposed action was therefore never taken.

(vi) Soviet Espionage.

A case of Soviet espionage which was under enquiry towards the end of 1939 led to the conviction of John Hubert King, a British subject employed in the Foreign Office as a cypher clerk, who was sentenced to ten years' penal servitude. He had been supplying to a Soviet agent named Hans Christian Pieck copies of telegrams and reports from British Embassies and Legations abroad which were received in the Foreign Office between the middle of 1935 and some time in 1936 when Pieck's place was taken by Paul Hardt already mentioned in connection with the case of Percy Glading.

The special interest of this case lies in the fact that it reveals a thorough and resourceful technique, the employment of lavish financial resources and painstaking and successful preparation over a long period on the part of the Soviet intelligence organ responsible for penetrating the official secrets of this country.

Hans Christian Pieck, a Dutchman of good family and an artist by profession, came to the notice of S.I.S. in 1930 and again in 1935 as a Communist. He had visited Moscow in 1929 when he became a member of the Soviet Intelligence Service and was charged with the special duty of penetrating the British Foreign Office. For this purpose he was established in Geneva as an artist, and for two and a half years he carefully cultivated the British official community there. His expenses in this connection are believed to have been approximately £20,000 spread over a period of two and a half years. In the course of this cultivation of the British Community he secured King as an agent inside the Foreign Office, and then in 1935 transferred his residence and activities to London where he entered into a business partnership with a British subject. In 1939 this partner made a statement that he had been in business with Pieck and had discovered the existence of a photographic dark room, and that Pieck's wife had said that he was obtaining documents from the British Foreign Office through a cypher officer whose name was not known.

An S.I.S. agent had been in touch with Pieck in Holland and had obtained an address in London from some of Pieck's private papers. The significance of this address was not understood at the time, but after the disclosures in 1939, it was connected with the address of Helen Wilkie, King's mistress who was also implicated. About the same time Krivitsky, the author of the book "I was Stalin's Agent" informed H.M. Ambassador in Washington that one King employed in the Communications Department of the Foreign Office was a Soviet agent. The result of the bringing together of these independent pieces of information was that certain notes and documents were found in Helen Wilkie's safe deposit. The notes were traced to Pieck's personal account, and a credit of just under £2,000 was discovered at another bank in King's name. Certain of these monies were traced to Paul Hardt, and King eventually made a statement to the effect that between 1935 and 1937 he took money amounting to £2,000 in payment for copies of secret telegrams decoded in the Foreign Office. This case illustrated the complementary nature of the work of Section V and B Branch,

Shortly after the disclosure by Krivitsky in the King case as mentioned above, Section V and B Branch combined to arrange for Krivitsky to be brought from the U.S.A. to the United Kingdom. He had been an important member of the Fourth Department of the Soviet Military Intelligence Service and had fled to America because he was recalled to Russia for the purpose of an enquiry connected with one of the "purges".

Krivitsky was interviewed by Colonel Vivian, Captain Liddell and Mrs. Archer. The main burden of the enquiry fell on Mrs. Archer who conducted a series of interviews during which Krivitsky talked at great length about the affairs of the Russian Secret Military Intelligence Service or the "Fourth Department". The results are contained in PF.R.4342 - YB.837. Those voluminous details gave the Security Service, for the first time, an insight into the machinery of the Russian Secret Intelligence Service and their Security Service; their methods; and substantial information about their operations in Europe and against this country. In all these activities Krivitsky had played an active part, but he repudiated any suggestion that he was directly responsible for Soviet activities directed against us.

He explained that while the Fourth Department was concerned with obtaining secret military intelligence as part of the Soviet Military Intelligence Service (Razvedupr), the Russian Security Service was known as the G.U.G.B. which was the headquarters organisation of the Security Service of the Soviet Home Office or N.K.V.D. The staff of the G.U.G.B. was known as the O.G.P.U. The operational staff of the O.G.P.U. was divided into three sections:

  (a) the I.N.O. or foreign sections responsible for O.G.P.U. agents abroad;
  (b) the Osobietodel, dealing with counter espionage within the Soviet Union, and -
  (c) Spetsodel, dealing with espionage by and disciplinary action against Soviet

officials and Party members. He added that at the time that he was last in Moscow in May 1937, it was proposed to amalgamate the Security Service sections under one head as a general service to be known as the K.R.O. (Kontre Razvedupr or counter-espionage) and subsequent information indicates that this reorganisation took place.

The detailed information given by Krivitsky can best be studied in the relevant files and is too long to be summarised here. Some of it is now out of date, but the most important points mentioned by him are to be regarded as constant factors. Among its outstanding features are the thoroughness with which Russian Secret Intelligence Services have been organised and the power wielded by the Secret Services. According to Krivitsky, Stalin expressed his long rooted conviction that on them depended the safety of the Soviet State. They maintain a close watch on everything that may be considered likely to threaten the regime, and it would seem that nothing in Russia or in its Embassies abroad is free from their ubiquitous supervision. The all powerful O.G.P.U. was in a far stronger position abroad than the officers of the Razvedupr and were in a position to maintain a tighter hold over their agents. They were able to demand unpaid services, both from Soviet officials in foreign countries, and from the members of the local Communist Party. There was jealousy between the two organisations, and both maintained an elaborate system of "legal" and "illegal" resident agents abroad, the former being individuals holding official positions, and the latter those acting under cover of business or other occupations.

Krivitsky was of the opinion that Stalin no longer thought in terms of world revolution or Socialist theory, but nevertheless supported Communist Parties abroad as instruments of his policy. For such purposes two Comintern organisations had been of special importance; the Lenin School for training Communist agents, and the O.M.S. (Otdyel Mezhdinarodnoi Svyazi). The O.M.S. was the organisation through which the Comintern financed, maintained contact with and disciplined Communist Parties abroad; it was the instrument through which Stalin would make preparations for a state of war. Krivitsky was emphatic that in the Soviet Union the Communist Parties in British countries would constitute a very real danger. The Comintern no longer had any genuine concern in the interests of the British working-class, but in his opinion the C.P.G.B. organisation was a Russian agency to be used as an instrument of military policy in the event of war when steps would be taken to organise active and passive sabotage on a large scale. Disintegration work among the Armed Forces which was conducted by the C.P.G.B. was, in spite of its ideological character, directed by the Soviet Military Intelligence Service and not by the O.G.P.U. or the Comintern.

Important British Communists such as Pollitt and Gallacher had been interviewed when visiting Moscow by officers of the Military Intelligence Service and their views had been obtained on such subjects as the political situation in Britain, the British General Staff, conditions in the British Army and other matters of military interest. Stalin was determined on the destruction of the British Empire and would go to any lengths in collaboration with Hitler to attain this object. Krivitsky believed that Bolshevism, Leninism and Socialism in the Soviet Union were dead. The Soviet Union was a rigid dictatorship maintained by wholesale purges and Stalin was attempting to maintain his unstable position by a policy of military aggression.

While Krivitsky's views were coloured by his enmity against Stalin and the circumstances of the time - the end of 1939 - his statements were accepted as factually correct, honest and reliable. Many of his facts in connection with intelligence matters were corroborated by information received from other sources and many of them served to explain obscurities in regard to cases which had been under investigation by B Branch. His knowledge of the ultimate aims of Stalin's policy was not regarded as being necessarily complete.

Krivitsky confirmed and elaborated some previous rather sketchy information concerning collaboration between certain officers of the German and Russian Secret Intelligence Services. There was not sufficient evidence to justify the statement that they were in fate collaborating against ourselves at the end of 1939 although Krivitsky was definitely of opinion that after the pact between Stalin and Hitler there could be no doubt that the two organisations would be working together in this country and that it could be taken as certain that the Soviet diplomatic bag, which was always used for Soviet espionage material, was being used for the despatch to Berlin and elsewhere of the fruits of German espionage. This last statement was undoubtedly intended to be an honest and friendly warning by it was coloured by his anti-Stalin bias, was never substantiated and seems improbable in the light of later information. The Security Service, however, could not be certain of the true position at that time and there was reason to believe that some collaboration between the Germans and Russians was based on personal friendships of long standing. Krivitsky said that there had been a special relationship of this kind ever since the Treaty of Versailles and he mentioned General von Seckt as having counted on Soviet assistance towards the eventual liquidation of the position created by this Treaty. He also stated that prior to the Hitler regime the Soviet Military Attaché in Berlin directed Soviet espionage against England with the knowledge of the German authorities and exchanged the results with them. He gave certain specific details of collaboration of this kind in the pre-Nazi period.

The general result was that during the crisis of 1940 the Security Service had serious reasons for apprehension regarding the effects of Russian espionage directed against this country and the possible repercussions on the war with Germany. At the same time, the staff of B Branch was overwhelmed with the effort of expanding itself to cope with the situation created by the war and by the general inadequacy of its information about both the German and the Russian Secret Services. The few officers who had experience of cases of Soviet espionage - Brigadier Harker, Captain Liddell and Mrs. Archer - were fully occupied with work directly bearing on measures for the investigation or prevention of espionage by the enemy.

END OF VOLUME I

TOP SECRET

THE SECURITY SERVICE

ITS PROBLEMS AND ORGANISATIONAL ADJUSTMENTS
1908-1945

VOL. II. (CHAPTER V, PART 1)

MARCH 1946

VOLUME II

	Page
CHAPTER V: REACTIONS IN THE SECOND WORLD WAR - SECOND PHASE	199
INTRODUCTORY NOTE	199

PART 1: THE GERMAN SECRET SERVICES UNDER THE NAZIS
1941-1945   201

(i)   The German attack on Russia   201
(ii)   Abwehr agents sent to British territory 1941-1945   201
(iii)   The re-organisation of the Security Service 1941   201
(iv)   B Division 1941-1945   203

     (A) A group of Sections under centralised control   203

     1. ISOS or the intercepted wireless system of the Abwehr and the Sipo und SD   206
     2. The examination by S.C.O.s of persons arriving at sea or air ports   215
     3. Interrogation at the L.R.C. of British and alien subjects and all persons arriving from enemy-occupied territory or from neutral countries   221
     4. The interrogation of suspected or known spies at Camp 020 (in close association with B.1.B.)   228
     5. Investigation of sabotage   233
     6. Employment of captured enemy agents who had been turned round with a view to using them to supply the enemy with false information or to carry through deception plans   245
     7. The co-ordination by the Director of B. Division of the Intelligence and security work leading to the successful countering of the enemy Secret Services   257

     (B) Auxiliary Sections of B Division   259

     1. Subject Sections   259
        - Neutral and Allied diplomatic representatives   259
        - Finance and currency enquiries   261
        - Seamen and personnel of air-lines   262
        - Industry and commerce   263

     2. Neutral Territories' Sections   270
        - Middle East   270
        - Spain, Portugal and South America   274
        - Ireland   277

	3.	Liaison Security Sections	286
		- Liaison with Censorship	286
		- Liaison with R.S.S.	287
		- Liaison with the B.B.C.	292
	4.	Security Sections	292
		- Lights and Pigeons	292
		- Signals Security	295
	5.	Research Section	297
		- Information Section	297
	6.	Shadowing Staff	302

(v) E Division 1941-1945   303
(vi) Section F.3. 1940-1945. Fascist, Right-Wing, Pacifist and Nationalist Movements; pro-Germans and defeatists   308
(vii) C and D Divisions   313
(viii) A Division (Regional Control)   328
(ix) War Room   332

END OF VOLUME II

CHAPTER V: REACTIONS IN THE SECOND WORLD WAR - SECOND PHASE

INTRODUCTORY NOTE

The 'leit-motiv' in this phase (from the summer of 1941 to the end of the SHAEF period in the summer of 1945) is to be found in the establishment and the working of orderly administrative and executive machinery under the control of Sir David Petrie. The prime factor in the re-establishment of order out of chaos was his insistence on his position as head of the Office, responsible to the Chairman of the Security Executive for its efficient working, but not liable to interference in matters relating to his staff or the day-to-day work. Lord Swinton as Chairman of the Security Executive remained responsible for policy and for the general co-ordination of security problems over the whole field of the machinery of government.

Sir David Petrie restored confidence - almost immediately internally and more gradually among the officers and Departments with whom the Office was in external relation - and helped to secure recognition of the Security Service as an efficient instrument adapted to the discharge of its duties and responsibilities. He accepted Lord Swinton's scheme for the divisions of the former B Division into B, E and F Divisions. The senior officers of B Division who had opposed Lord Swinton's attempt to impose this re-organisation so long as it was an open question naturally accepted it as a decision of their new head made on taking over most onerous and delicate duties, under circumstances which required that he should have the loyal support of the whole staff. Within three months of Sir David Petrie's taking charge the German attack on Russia went far to remove some of the more immediate reasons for opposing the division into B, E and F. An important effect of this division was to remove from the head of B the duty of combining action and collating information for dealing with the problem of the "Fifth Column" and the hidden British Quislings and to lift these duties to the level of the head of the whole office. The objections to this originally had their strongest motive in the fact that it meant - before Sir David Petrie's assumption of office - a concentration of detailed control in the hands of Lord Swinton and the Security Executive. This threatened not only to produce a concomitant lack of cohesion within the Security Service itself, but even to involve the supersession of B Division in respect to its more vital functions by the Security Executive. These objections now had no force.

The attack on Russia removed the immediate danger of invasion and relegated to the background the question of possible active assistance to the invaders. From this point onwards - within the framework of the newly established order of the reorganised machinery - a new motif became increasingly insistent. By good fortune and good work B Division had at last come to grips with its particular enemy, the German Secret Service or "Abwehr"; and in place of the almost complete ignorance on the whole subject which had been the dominating fact of the position in 1939 and 1940 it began to take the measure - uncertainly at first - of its opponents, the agents of the "Abwehr" and the organisation behind them. This improvement in knowledge - and consequently in confidence - arose from the capture of agents parachuted or landed in the British Isles, from the extraction of information from them by interrogation, or by using them as double-agents and above all by the comprehensive knowledge of the organisation under the Oberkommando der Wehrmacht secured by an intensive, skilful and scholarly study of their secret wireless communications. The most effective part of this study was done by R.S.S., G.C.& C.S. and by a committee consisting of representatives of those bodies and of the Security Service and Section V of S.I.S. under the chairmanship of Mr. White.

As the Security Service by these various means developed its power to combat the enemy Secret Services (including the Abwehr and the SD - which latter became increasingly important) a fresh cause of discord was introduced. It arose from the claim of the head of Section V to be responsible for the security of ISOS (the intercepted wireless material) and for controlling its use; and at the same time to have the right to limit the functions or the freedom of action of the Security Service in various ways and especially by confining them to action and to the recording of intelligence within the three-mile limit of the United Kingdom and other British countries. This attitude gave rise to a long drawn-out controversy which was also marked by the failure of S.I.S. - in the Security Service view - to maintain adequate records for the purposes of the collation of information as a basis for counter-espionage action outside the three-mile limit, with consequent reactions within it.

This controversy was unresolved throughout the war and at the close of the SHAEF period was the subject of an independent enquiry. In the meanwhile, the centre of interest shifted after D Day from the British Isles to the Continent where the backbone of the counter-intelligence staff of SHAEF was formed by the deputation of some eighty Security Service officers under Mr. White who was appointed to be a temporary Brigadier on the staff of SHAEF for the purpose. On the Continent, as in the British Isles and on the high seas, the efforts of the Abwehr and SD were successfully combated by the Security Service in the whole field covered by its responsibilities for counter-espionage, counter-sabotage and deception.

NOTE

The arrangement of the material in Chapters IV and V of this record is, in some respects, anachronistic. This is necessary because, while the summer of 1941 provides a dividing line in the story of the Organisation as a whole - and of the main subjects with which if had to deal, the Russian and the German, it is not so in the case of individual sections and divisions. In A, B, C & D Divisions certain new growths had a beginning in 1939, 1940 or 1941 and developed continuously during the period 1939 - 1945. It is therefore logical to describe these developments in one place. Any attempt, in these circumstances, to make an artificial separation of the material and to place some of it in Chapter IV and some in chapter V would break an essential unity.

Part 1: The German Secret Services under the Nazis 1941-1945

(i) **The German attack on Russia**

The German attack on Russia which completely altered the military situation also had important indirect effects on the working of the Security Service. It removed the immediate apprehension of an attempted invasion of the British Isles and therefore reduced the urgency of the question of the organisation of a "Fifth Column" by the Abwehr and other parts of the Nazi machine. As the months went on and it became apparent that the German army would not have the success in overrunning Russia which it had expected, the dangers of invasion receded further into the background. The problems which presented themselves thus became gradually simplified and it was possible to concentrate, with more freedom from distraction, on developing a knowledge of the German organisations directing espionage and sabotage. The increase in this concrete knowledge also helped to diminish the need for the indefinite search for the "Fifth Column". The invasion of Russia further affected the work of the Security Service in that there was no longer any reason to apprehend collusion between the German Secret Service on the one hand and the Russians or the Communists of various nationalities on the other. All these factors combined to produce favourable psychological reactions.

(ii) **Abwehr agents sent to British territory 1941-1945.**

In the period from July 1941 to September 1941 German agents continued to arrive in this country. (vide Part 2, pages 20 and 21 of "The German Secret Services, August 1942 - Bibliography No. 33). They fell under the three categories of those arriving by small boats from Norway, long-term agents and seamen, but it is a remarkable fact that between September 1941 and the end of March 1942 no fresh cases of the kind came to notice. This period coincides with that in which the Germans were preparing for their attack on Russia. As mentioned in "The German Secret Services, 1944" (vide Bibliography No. 34) the attention of the Abwehr had been mainly directed towards Russia, the Middle East, Africa, Italy and the Americas, and when in the second half of 1942 the despatch of agents to the British Isles recommenced they were, for the most part, of an uninteresting and unimportant type. The details are given in "The German Secret Services, 1944" which deals with the information available to the Secret Service up to November 1943.

(iii) **The reorganisation of the Security Service 1941.**

Sir David Petrie adopted Lord Swinton's proposals for dividing B Division into three parts to be known as B, E and F, but it was not until the 1st August that this scheme was finally brought into effect. Reorganisation instructions issued on 22nd April, 1941, announced the decision of the Lord President to alter the title of Director to that of Director-General. Consequential changes were that the heads of the three existing Divisions A, B and C & D, became Directors, while certain B sections were placed under a Deputy-Director E Division and others under a Deputy-Director F Division. Further instructions announcing the Office reorganisation and renaming and renumbering the sections in B, E and F Divisions came into effect on 1st August 1941.

The question of the organisation of the Registry was also finally settled by the Director-General's approval of the scheme which changed the system in force since it had grown up in the last war (by which sections of the Registry specialised in a knowledge of the work of the sections in the various Divisions) and substituted a more mechanical one. It was simplified in the sense that the whole process was split up into a number of acts each of which was performed by a member of the staff while the responsibility for carding and extracting was placed on sectional officers; and after the agreement with Section V officers in April 1941, the overall responsibility for carding names abroad was allocated to Section V while, subject to certain reservations, the Security Service retained the practice of carding only important names of more that local importance in foreign countries.

Special sections in the Registry continued to subserve the purposes of the B sections dealing with German espionage and of the section dealing with the Communist Party of Great Britain, as will be described in greater detail below. They provided for fuller carding including, in the case of the German Intelligence Service and its agents, the carding of names abroad.

The fact of a decision on these two questions which had been the subject of divided opinion inside the Office for a long period - since about July 1940 in the case of the Registry and since December 1940 in the case of B Division - had a good psychological effect on the staff as a whole. During the period in which Lord Swinton had directly interfered in the internal working of the Office, but had delayed for so long in giving effect to the ideas which he had adopted, morale was inevitably adversely affected; and this was aggravated by the consequences of the fire in the Registry and the move to Blenheim.

The Director-General's decision removed the organisational question from the arena of discussion and the staff settled down to work on the lines prescribed for it and on the basis of the new internal division of functions. Briefly, there was no important change in the functions and working of A Division (Director Lt.-Colonel Butler) or C & D Divisions (Director Brigadier Allen). B Division (Director Captain Liddell, Assistant Directors Mr. White and Major Frost) remained responsible for the investigation of enemy espionage and was relieved of the work described as "Aliens Control" which was transferred to the newly created E Division (Deputy-Director Mr. Turner, Assistant Director Major Younger), and that for "Subversive Activities" which was transferred to the new F Division (Deputy-Director Mr. Curry, Assistant Directors Mr. Hollis and Mr. Aiken-Sneath). In effect the responsibilities of E Division were for dealing with cases of internment and release of enemy aliens (except the Japanese whose cases remained with B Division) and for liaison with the Allied Governments and for questions connected with all Allied and neutral aliens in the United Kingdom. The functions of the section dealing with Aliens War Service (Lt.-Colonel Ryder) also came under the Deputy-Director of E Division. F Division's responsibilities covered all the so-called "Left" and "Right" subversive movements and included Pacifism. They were also responsible for all investigation work connected with Russian espionage.

At the same time the Director-General's staff was created and consisted of a Deputy-Director-General (Brigadier Harker), the Secretariat, Legal Advisers, Operations Section and Room 055. The Secretariat (under Mr. Abbot) was responsible for the preparation of papers dealing with all policy questions and other major problems, especially those concerning more than one Division, which required the Director-General's decision, and for matters connected with the Security Executive; the Legal Advisers under Mr. Pilcher were available to give advice to the Director-General or any officer of the Security Service on matters connected with his duties; the Operations Section under Major Lennox was responsible for obtaining and co-ordinating information from the Fighting Services and other Departments regarding military operations and certain matters of special importance which it was desirable to protect by security and other measures from the attentions of the enemy Intelligence Services. Room 055 at the War Office, under Mr. Orr, performed certain special functions based on the former relationship between M.I.5. and the War Office, serving as a means of contact with the public where it was desired to screen the identity of the Security Service and also facilitating contacts between sections in the Security Service and different parts of the War Office. In October 1941 an addition was made to the Director-General's staff in the shape of "Research" to which Mr. Curry was appointed. Mr. R. Butler was the Personal Secretary to the Director-General.

The most outstanding activities of the Security Service in connection with the war were now centred in B Division as being responsible for the investigation of all cases of known or suspected agents directly connected with the German, Italian and Japanese Secret Services, while the preventive and security functions were divided between C, D, E and F Divisions, of which E and F continued to be responsible for investigation of a preventive nature and in cases not directly connected with the enemy Secret Service.

Thus an important effect of the separation of B Division into B, E and F was to centralise the control of the whole Office in the hands of the Director-General assisted by his staff, and to remove the control of the sections which now constituted the new E and F Divisions and the co-ordination of their work with that of other parts of the Office from the head of B Division.

(iv) B Division 1941-1945.

The sections of B Division may be roughly divided into two groups; (A) a group of sections under centralised direction, and (B) the auxiliary sections of B Division.

(A) A Group of Sections under centralised control.

During 1940-1941 a group of sections in B Division directly in touch with the German Secret Service, either through their communications or their agents, gradually grew up to form, as it were, a central organ under the direction of Mr. White as Assistant Director B Division (later D.D.B.).

The early stages of this growth were referred to in Chapter IV above under the heading "The beginning of effective counter-espionage work". As indicated there this development arose from the combination under Mr. White of a system for absorbing the intelligence derived from ISOS and using it to supplement the information obtained by interrogation at Camp 020 and from other sources including the results of Major Robertson's manipulation of double agents. During 1941 steps were taken to deal with the situation created by the influx of refugees from German-occupied Europe and this brought the intelligence work at the Royal Patriotic Schools (later London Reception Centre) and then the S.C.O.s at the ports into the orbit of this centralised direction. B.1.C., as the section responsible for the investigation of enemy sabotage, was also in direct touch, through ISOS and the investigation of sabotage cases, with enemy agents and the organisation behind them.

Mr. White's view was that as B Division was organised on a subject basis (in contrast to Section V, which was on a territorial basis), it followed that the principle sections of the Division were organised by sources, among which he included the products of Section V. He explained that in order to focus the sources upon the subject - the German Secret Services - it was necessary "to create a central mart, or exchange of information, which was the daily 12 o'clock meetings" held in his room. At these meetings he co-ordinated the study of the enemy Secret Services as organisations. The individual officers of the B.1. sections described current developments in regard to individual cases and the accumulation of intelligence regarding enemy organisations. While it normally fell to these officers to take action within their own province on their own material, there was a considerable amount of overlapping and this made it necessary for a daily allocation of work to be made at these 12 o'clock meetings.

Mr. White further described these meetings as the B Division "committee of action" and said that out of its daily discussions emerged a consciousness of counter espionage methods which had been lacking prior to their inauguration. They became training grounds for counter-espionage specialists and he formed the opinion that it was hardly too much to say that they resulted in placing the Security Service in a predominant position in the counter espionage field at a time when the control of ISOS might have placed Section V in that position. Out of the discussions at the 12 o'clock meetings a definite sense of direction was developed and, in consequence, it fell to Mr. White, with the approval of the Director of B Division, to take the lead in formulating Security Service plans and procedure in counter espionage work.

These 12 o'clock meetings were at first confined to the small group of specialists in the B.1. sections, but they gradually developed during 1942 into a medium for keeping all officers of B Division in touch with the central action against the Abwehr and the Sipo und SD. They thus became too large to fulfil their original function and they were, therefore, contracted to their original size while the secondary purpose of keeping the whole of B Division informed was fulfilled by a weekly meeting under the chairmanship of Captain Liddell.

A detailed description of the working of these principal sections follows under the headings:-

1. the study of ISOS or the intercepted wireless system of the Abwehr and the Sipo und SD (B.1.B.);
2. the examination of persons (including refugees from enemy-occupied Europe, whether arriving by regular means, by sea or by air, or by an 'escape' boat or 'escape' plane) by the S.C.O.s at the ports working under the direction of A.D.D.4;
3. the interrogation at the L.R.C. of British and alien subjects and all persons arriving from enemy-occupied territory or neutral countries otherwise than on fully authenticated business (B.1.D.);
4. the interrogation of suspected or known spies at Camp 020 (in close association with B.1.B.);
5. the investigation of cases of enemy sabotage (B.1.C.);
6. the employment of captured enemy agents who had been "turned round" with a view to using them to supply the enemy with false information or to carry through deception plans (B.1.A.).

From this account it will appear that ISOS and interrogation at the ports, at the L.R.C. and at Camp 020 were primary sources of intelligence and that under the centralised direction of Captain Liddell and Mr. White the officers at the ports - under the supervision of Lt.-Colonel Adam, A.D.D.4. - and at the two interrogating centres became, in effect, the principal part of the executive machinery for countering the enemy organisations as an instrument of the German General Staff. In the same sense an important part was played by the machinery of B.1.A. under Major Robertson, which contributed through its double agents towards the execution of the plans formulated by the machinery under the Allied Chiefs of Staff for the deception of the enemy.

While Mr. White co-ordinated the counter-measures against the Abwehr and SD and their agents, Captain Liddell supervised and directed this work and, in addition, co-ordinated the working of B Division with the general security or preventive work of B and other Divisions and gave shape to the work of the whole office in its relations with military operations in the most extended field of counter espionage, security and deception under the general control of the Director-General. This work culminated in the successful measures which ensured the security of the landings in North Africa, Sicily and Normandy, but before this successful culmination was reached B Division went through a long and sometimes difficult period of development during the years from 1941 onwards. In order to understand this period it seems desirable to refer in some detail to the developments in some of the principal sections.

As mentioned in Chapter IV above, the first results of the integration of information received by the interrogation of German agents arriving in this country and that derived from the intercepted wireless of the Abwehr and the SD was contained in Mr. White's report on the German Secret Service dated December 1940 (vide Bibliography No. 39).

The second compilation of the same kind was prepared by Mr. Curry in 1942 in two editions; one known as the esoteric edition for very limited circulation (vide Bibliography No. 32) was produced in June of that year, and the other for wider circulation was printed in August (vide Bibliography No. 33). These two editions summarised the information available up to the end of March 1942. A further report on the German Secret Service was prepared to include the information available up to November 1943 (vide Bibliography No. 34) by which time the detailed knowledge of the Reichssicherheitshauptamt (R.S.H.A.) had been greatly improved as a result of further interception of their communications and the capture of some of their agents. Several other papers were prepared on different aspects of the subject, notably a paper on the R.S.H.A. prepared in Section V, a technical note entitled "Amt Auslandsnachrichten und Abwehr" (vide Bibliography No. 5) on the intercepted material prepared by Mr. Palmer of G.C. & C.S., and several papers by Major Trevor Roper's section. (At the time of writing no final and comprehensive report for the last period of the war has been prepared).

Of all the sources of information from which these compilations were prepared and from which the day to day work was done in the shape of collating evidence against individual agents and in building up the compilations about the different parts of the enemy organisations prepared in B.1. Information, one of the most important was ISOS or the intercepted wireless. Its importance lay in the fact that it not only led directly to the detection of enemy agents, but it also connected the agents directly with the Abwehr organisation behind them as an instrument of the Oberkommando der Wehrmacht (the German General Staff); and it illuminated in a positive if often incomplete manner the whole structure of that organisation in a way which could not be done by the unaided interrogation of captured agents, if only for the reason that few, if any, of those captured had any detailed knowledge of the organisation as a whole. It was not only positive evidence, but, in so far as it could be correctly interpreted, irrefutable. Many agents had only a slight knowledge of certain parts of the organisation and even individual Abwehr officers were very far from being acquainted with the whole machine of which they formed a part. At the same time the interrogation of known agents at Camp 020 or the L.R.C. and the work of B.1.A. in dealing with the traffic of agents who were turned round, all combined to furnish complementary pieces of evidence without which the ISOS material by itself could not be fully understood or explained, and had a very limited practical value.

1. ISOS or the intercepted wireless system of the Abwehr and the Sipo und SD.

ISOS was the generic name (for security reasons it was officially changed subsequently) given to a wide range of Abwehr and SD wireless communications as intercepted by R.S.S. and deciphered by G.C. & C.S. This important and fruitful source of information about the enemy became available to us as a direct result of the manipulation by the Security Service of the double agent [...] as already mentioned. While wireless traffic was being monitored one of our wireless operators noticed that the Hamburg Control Station was carrying on wireless traffic with a number of other points which subsequently proved to be other Abwehr Stations in regular wireless contact with Hamburg. At first the suggestion that the series of messages thus noticed as passing to and from the

Hamburg Control were of counter espionage importance was greeted with scepticism,[†] but after an amateur had succeeded in deciphering one of them there was no room for doubt on the point and G.C. & C.S. then developed a section to deal with the network which R.S.S. had disclosed with Hamburg as a centre.

From the autumn of 1940 onwards R.S.S., starting from this small beginning, developed their organisation for the interception, identification and "discrimination" of Abwehr and SD traffic until it, eventually, uncovered the almost world-wide Abwehr network and led to the identification of German agents in many countries, and furnished authentic evidence or the working of the R.S.H.A. and the Sipo und SD. The intercepted messages were deciphered and translated and distributed by G.C. & C.S. to representatives of the D.M.I., D.N.I., A.C.A.S.(I), the Security Service and various sections in S.I.S. The Ds of I were included as from the first it was obvious that this material was of operational importance, but it was only at a later date that this operational importance was properly appreciated and exploited.

All through 1941 and well into 1942 the study and exploitation of this material was dealt with in separate compartments by the different recipients largely as a result of the attitude of Colonel Cowgill who was constituted the guardian of the security of the material in consequence of instructions emanating from the Prime Minister himself to the effect that material of this kind should be kept strictly secret and only communicated to those directly concerned in the work arising out of it. Colonel Cowgill's interpretation of his position was the cause of acute controversy between himself and the Security Service over a long period, but whatever the merits of his attitude may have been, the fact remains that great benefits accrued when, without his knowledge or contrary to his intentions, different recipients got into touch with one another and exchanged views on the nature of the material and the possibilities of exploiting it. The necessary study of the material before it could be exploited was in the nature of textual criticism and the expert skill in such work of the trained minds of classical scholars and others (such as Mr. Palmer, Major Trevor-Roper and his assistants) was appropriately applied to its elucidation.

[handwritten: Palmer an analyst like H.T.R]

A partial synthesis of the structure of the German organisation sending or receiving messages or referred to in them was constructed from inferences based on the results of the gradual collection and collation of a large number of details compiled from many series of messages. These messages were very largely administrative in character and they sometimes only gave a clue to the identity of an Abwehr agent or prospective agent as a result of oblique references. The analogy to textual criticism was enhanced by the fact that when the messages had been deciphered they were often found to contain codes and code names within the ciphers, and these in turn had to be subjected to a process of induction - or of trial and error - from a number of known facts

---

[†] As an instance of the difficulty of this work the following may be quoted:- On 26.9.39. the Security Service sent a copy of a message believed to be from the station that worked to [...] which, it was thought, might be in the Stuttgart area. S.I.S. replied that G.C. & C.S. could not break the messages and suggested that they were Russian telegrams and orginated from Shanghai; it was not thought that they were German. They were, however, subsequently identified as Abwehr traffic in Europe.

[handwritten: another SIS blunder or lie]

before their full meaning could be determined and the resultant intelligence could be exploited.

It is necessary at this stage to go somewhat fully into the question of Colonel Cowgill's attitude to the whole scale of problems arising out of ISOS, because this attitude dominated the use of ISOS for counter espionage and operational purpose and, incidentally, had far-reaching effects on the relations between Section V and B Division. In the first place it is necessary to understand the factors which went to make up the situation. Chief among them were the facts that ISOS material was of practical value in the following directions:-

(a) It led to the identification and arrest of spies.
(b) It filled in - in the course of time - a large detailed background picture of the Abwehr and SD organisations, their methods of working, their technique of espionage, their cover addresses, their secret inks, the identity of their officers and their relations with other parts of the German military machine.
(c) It supplied information regarding the technique of sabotage, especially against British shipping, and thereby assisted in the development of counter-measures by the Security Service.
(d) It provided a valuable means of checking the elaborate and complicated working of an extensive ring of double agents manipulated by the Security Service.
(e) It provided information of operational value, e.g. the formation or assembly of Abwehr Commandos before and in the neighbourhood of a projected German advance.
(f) It provided political information, e.g. the nature and extent of Spanish collaboration with the Germans.
(g) It provided valuable material concerning the German organisation and its detailed working which was used with good effect in order to obtain information during the course of interrogation.

A second point was that, broadly speaking, action on the information obtained from this material could be taken by the Security Service in the way of arrest of enemy agents in British territory, or on the high seas, or for the purposes of interrogating captured agents. On the other hand there was little or no action, except to make enquiries in neutral countries, which could be taken by Section V except, perhaps, in the later stages of the war through S.C.I. units employed by them in the field, i.e. in the operational zones in Africa, Italy and after the Normandy landing. The enquiries in neutral countries took the form of supplementing intelligence obtained from ISOS by the employment of agents to obtain information about the German organisation in such countries and in some cases they were able to obtain information officially or otherwise from the local police and other authorities about the names of travellers and numerous other details. This type of information was often useful in identifying Abwehr officers or agents or in helping to explain the meaning of ISOS references. It thus played a part in building up the general body of intelligence, but unless it concerned an agent who arrived in or was intended for British territory the normal attitude of Section V was that it did not concern the Security Service.

Again, as the result of the practice of maintaining separate compartments, i.e. as between G.C. & C.S., the Security Service, Section V and the Fighting Services, there was over a long period, as a result of a failure to compare notes, not only a lack of understanding of each other's problems, but often the failure to interpret correctly the information available in the various isolated compartments.

This "compartmentalisation", to use the ugly current work, also occurred within Section V, where the geographical sub-sections suffered similarly in kind, if not in degree.

The Security Service view was that this excess of security by isolation not only served no useful purpose, but should not have occurred, because, in fact, all the different parts of the organisation, R.S.S., G.C. & C.S., V.W. (afterwards R.I.S.), Section V and the Security Service all existed in order to achieve a single objective, namely, the arrest of enemy agents and the compilation and use for that purpose of all relevant intelligence. It involved the risk of failure to act in matters involving operational or Security Service responsibilities, such as the prevention of sabotage, for the sake of the mistaken aim of ensuring an impossible degree of security - impossible because the essential fact, i.e. that Security Service action was often based on wireless interception, necessarily became known to many hundreds of people in the Security Service, in S.I.S. and in the intelligence and operational staffs of the armies in the field.

Thus the practical value and use of ISOS material was marred by a failure to co-ordinate the machinery dealing with it and this lack of co-ordination was accentuated by - and in a sense the cause of - the fact that a number of independent indices were maintained, some of which were too incomplete to serve as a basis for adequate exploitation of the intelligence available from it.

The enormity of this mistaken point of view in handling this very valuable source of information can only be fully appreciated in the light of a knowledge of the geographical area covered by the Abwehr wireless system and its relationship with the military operations directed by the Oberkommando der Wehrmacht under Feld Marshal Keitel to whom the Abwehr under Admiral Canaris was subordinated. This has been partly set out in the various reports on the German Secret Service already mentioned; and the fact that the Abwehr was in many ways ineffective and incompetent did not in any real sense diminish its usefulness if properly interpreted by the British Services or mitigate the errors involved in the obstruction of their smooth functioning which was due to Colonel Cowgill's attitude. These errors would have been mitigated if he had appreciated the intrinsic importance of the material at its real value and established an adequate machine to cope with it based on an efficiently organised ISOS index, but he only did so in 1943 as the result of pressure from B Division. These are the main facts of the situation in which his attitude dominated the use of ISOS for counter espionage and operational purposes.

The direct effect of all this on certain Security Service problems is illustrated by the following instances in which Colonel Cowgill attempted to prevent the Security Service from obtaining information which was essential to the proper discharge of their responsibilities:-

(a) A small fraction of the wireless of the R.S.H.A Intelligence Service, i.e. the Sicherheitsdienst, was intercepted in 1940 and 1941, but at the instance of Colonel Cowgill this was suddenly stopped, and in June 1941, after it had been withheld for some time, the Security Service came to hear unofficially that there were references on it to an attempt by the SD to arrange for London telephone directories to be smuggled out to them through Japanese diplomatic channels. Copies of these messages were only obtained after considerable delay and as a result of a request to Section V for information. When a general request for the whole series was made, Section V replied that it was of no counter espionage interest and that they had adequate and efficient machinery for communicating any material of a counter espionage nature which might appear in it. In fact it was of the greatest interest and importance as is shown by the references to the R.S.H.A. in "The German Secret Service, August 1942 and August 1944" (vide Bibliography Nos. 33 and 34) and subsequent developments. The event proved that the machinery in Section V was not adequate at that time, and for a long time afterwards, to formulate a proper appreciation of this (SD) material, which as a result of inadequate general knowledge about Nazi Germany they did not understand, and in regard to which their first duty and their principal function was to keep the Security Service informed so as to enable it to take necessary counter-measures. B Division were themselves at the time (i.e. 1940-41) ignorant of the important facts that this group of traffic represented SD communications and even that the letters SD in ISOS stood for Sicherheitsdienst. At the instance of Section V they had interpreted them as representing an unexplained "Sonderdienst". It was only when the facts came to the notice of "Research" in the Security Service that the identification of the SD and ISOS with the Sicherheitsdienst and its real significance were recognised early in 1942.

(b) In pursuance of his policy for safeguarding ISOS Colonel Cowgill decided that the interrogators at Camp 020 should not be allowed the undisguised text of intercepted messages relating to agents or suspects whom they were interrogating and that blanketed versions only should be supplied to them, and he obtained the unwilling consent of B Division to this course. The inevitable happened and experience soon showed the danger of this arrangement, but it was only after a great deal of argument and subject to the restriction that the Director of B Division should personally decide on the appropriate arrangements in each case that Colonel Cowgill waived his objection. From September 1941 onwards - subject to restrictions which were only eliminated by slow degrees - the examiners at Camp 020 were allowed to see the material on the ground that it was only in this way that they could appreciated the nature and delicacy of the source and avoid putting questions to persons under examination in such a way as to avoid the risk of giving it away.

(c) As a result of a slip on the part of someone in Section V it was discovered in April 1942 that G.C. & C.S. had been instructed to withhold certain ISOS messages which were believed, very often mistakenly, to refer to British agents. By the time these facts were disclosed it came out that more than a hundred messages had been withheld from the Security Service, some of which directly concerned double agents who were operating under Security Service control. In many cases these arrangements had a direct bearing on the control which had been exercised, and the fact that they were withheld involved a serious risk of avoidable contretemps. In spite of the obvious importance of these facts it was only after protracted negotiations that it was agreed that this type of message (known as ISBA) should be supplied to B Division, and then only with the unreasonable and useless proviso that they should be received and kept personally by the Director.

(d) In May 1941 arrangements were made for a fortnightly meeting of a joint Committee composed of officers of Section V and the Security Service to consider the technical aspects of the work of radio interception by R.S.S. in so far as these two departments were considered. Colonel Cowgill aimed at confining discussions to these technical aspects and to the question of regulating the priority of the various ISOS services. As was inevitable, however, the intelligence content of the messages of these services formed the basis of discussion, and many members of the Committee were persuaded by the facts before them that the representatives of the Intelligence Directorates of the Services who received the ISOS material as well as representatives of G.C & C.S. ought to attend the meetings of the Committee. They were also convinced that the terms of reference should be extended to deal with any aspect of the problems arising from the interception including questions of their intelligence content. These proposals met with the strongest opposition from S.I.S., who attempted to have the Committee closed down on the ground that it had outlived its usefulness, in spite of the fact that all members, with the exception of Colonel Cowgill, were agreed that the terms of reference and the membership should be extended. With the assistance of Mr. Reilly of the Foreign Office, at that time personal assistant to C.S.S., a decision was obtained on the lines desired by the Security Service and from that time onwards, i.e. the beginning of 1943, the reformed Committee attained greater importance and efficiency and played a useful part in a much more successful exploitation of the intelligence content of the intercepted material.

(e) The evidence of the intercepted messages showed that the enemy claimed to have a number of agents in the Middle East, including Egypt, in 1941, but it became evident that the S.I.S. representative in the Middle East, who was responsible for communicating this type of information to S.I.M.E. had no adequate means of doing so. Some of this intelligence was derived from a particularly delicate type of material (because the cryptographical solution which had been achieved by G.C. & C.S. was one involving such unusual skill that the enemy could be assumed to regard it as insoluble). It was therefore treated with special care and was only communicated to the S.I.S representative in the Middle East in a scrambled form with the result that the information supplied to S.I.M.E. was insufficient in quantity as well as inaccurate. From the point of view of the Security Service officers here who understood the problem of applying this type of information to the practical question of identifying a spy and obtaining the requisite evidence against him, it appeared that the officers in Section V had no conception of what the Security organisation in the Middle East required. To meet this difficulty an officer from the Security Service in London was deputed to S.I.M.E. to receive and deal with the ISOS material. (Further details are given below in dealing with the Middle East).

(f) In the light of experience the Security Service officers concerned formed the opinion that the ISOS material could only be properly exploited as the result of analysis by experts who were in a position to make a complete study of the whole material including a large quantity of undeciphered material which, again, in the hands of these experts, was capable of producing intelligence of great value. A body of qualified experts existed in Section V.W. (later R.I.S.) under Major Trevor-Roper, assisted by Mr. Palmer of the intelligence section of G.C. & C.S. Colonel Cowgill, however, had a different opinion and regarded these experts as unreliable on the ground that they made mistakes by basing themselves on the internal evidence of the texts without access to other sources of information. His view on this point was contested on the ground that what was required was to integrate the evidence obtained by an analysis of the texts with information available from other sources. Colonel Cowgill also claimed that the personnel of Section V were the experts in the interpretation of this material and the proper staff to decide questions of making use of it in conjunction with other information. Section V, however, were handicapped by the fact that they were divided into sub-sections on a geographical basis and studied the material after dividing it into corresponding geographical groupings with the result that their inexpert and more or less isolated sub-sections were not able to understand much of the material or to see it as a whole as could be done by the experts in V.W. The Security Service pressed for an extension of the charter of V.W. because they were convinced of the value of their analyses. As a result the sub-section was ultimately separated from Section V and in 1943 became a separate department of S.I.S. directly responsible to C.S.S. with the title of R.I.S. With the extended charter then granted to it R.I.S. made contributions of great value to all recipients of the material.

It must be emphasised that as a means of detecting enemy agents ISOS, by itself, had in a sense a limited usefulness. Full value could only be extracted from it in combination with the records of the Security Service as a repository of information received from other sources. These sources included records which were obtained for the purpose such as crew lists and passenger lists which helped to identify agents when travelling, even if they were only known to us as code names in ISOS. Other most important sources were names and information derived from interrogations at the L.R.C. and Camp 020 or from such mundane and routine papers as a list of clerks at the Portuguese Embassy in London. In some cases Section V was able to obtain evidence of movements which made it possible to identify an agent otherwise only know to us under an Abwehr cover name. In effect ISOS did not supplant other records but was complementary to them and in combination with them made it possible to take action leading to arrest either in this country or in other British countries, especially in Trinidad and the African Colonies, as the result of the control by British authorities of the movements of vessels on which they were travelling. During the period 1940-1944 inclusive, out of a total of 102 German spies known to have been sent to the United Kingdom 18 were caught as a result of information derived from ISOS and 9 who were caught in other ways or surrendered themselves could have been arrested on ISOS information. Some corroboration was furnished by subsequent references on ISOS in the cases of 53 of those who were arrested either on ISOS information or in other ways. During the same period the number arrested at Trinidad and brought to the United Kingdom for a more thorough interrogation than was possible abroad was 21, while 3 were arrested in Africa, 2 in Iceland and 3 in Gibraltar.

The following table indicates the proportion of spies who were caught as a result of the ISOS information to the total detained in the United Kingdom or brought here for interrogation and detention as well as that of those who were referred to in the ISOS messages:-

	Total of spies detained in the U.K. or brought to the U.K. for detention	Numbers caught on ISOS information	Number subsequently reflected on ISOS
1941	28	7 (25%)	9 (32.1%)
1942	43	15 (35%)	24 (55.8%)
1943	54	21 (40%)	39 (72.2%)
1944	41	9 (22%)	21 (51.1%)

It is possible that some of the German agents who were arrested here as a result of ISOS information would have been detected without it, but it is virtually certain that very few of those who were captured overseas and brought here would have been caught but for the fact of this interception of Abwehr communications. It would have been virtually impossible for interrogating officers at various points such as Trinidad or the African ports to have detected the enemy agents among the large numbers of travellers whom they had to scutinise. Their capture, which can therefore be attributed solely to ISOS, had in many cases important consequences apart from the fact that they were prevented from carrying out their particular missions. For instance, the case of Osmar Helmuth who was arrested at Trinidad and examined at Camp 020 was one which was largely responsible for the rupture of relations between the Argentine and Germany and, even more important, for exacerbating the deteriorating relations between the Abwehr and the SD. The capture of numerous Spaniards who were acting as German agents led the Foreign Office, in accordance with our views and advice, to adopt a stiffer attitude towards Spanish collaboration with the Germans. In some of these cases this was substantiated by a signed confession which Camp 020 was able to produce for the benefit of the Spanish Ambassador when he made a complaint to the Foreign Office. Moreover the widespread nature of the action which it was possible to take on the basis of the intercepted messages as a centralised source of information - as opposed to the very different position which would have obtained if local officers had been dependent on local sources of information in isolated British territories or foreign countries such as those in South America - resulted in the assembling of a large amount of information covering every field of German espionage in different parts of the world through the interrogation of this wide range of spies after they had been roped in and brought to this country. This information derived from interrogation eventually - after being compiled and assembled - began to rival in importance and comprehensiveness the ISOS information itself; and this had the advantage that it was possible to utilise it for the instruction of outlying branches of the Security Service with far greater freedom than was possible in the case of ISOS information which could therefore be held in reserve without exposing it to undue risks.

The delicacy of ISOS as a source of the information made it difficult at first to provide for the arrest of German agents discovered through this widespread interception in the case of those passing through overseas British territories en route to other countries. With this in view, the Security Service took steps in 1942 and was able to induce the Colonial Office to advise the various Colonial Governments to pass legislation enabling them to remove an alien from vessels or aircraft by an administrative act not subject to appeal to a court or an advisory committee. This legislation made it possible to effect arrests under conditions which did not compromise the source of information and the usual practice was to obtain an order under D.R.18BA from the Home Secretary to provide for the transferring of the individual agents from the Colonial territory for detention in the United Kingdom. There was no appeal against detention under D.R.18BA; and ISOS as a source was protected accordingly in this country. This important preventive action was taken as the result of advice tendered by B Division.

An extraordinary, and from our point of view troublesome, feature of the Abwehr was the number of fictitious reports which came to notice through being communicated from Abwehr posts to Berlin. Vast numbers of these fictitious reports, which were invented by unreliable enemy agents and sometimes condoned by corrupt Abwehr officers, had to be carefully checked by the Security Service because many of them had a sub-stratum of fact and some appeared to contain dangerous information. Among this mass of fraudulent fiction there was at the end of the war in Europe a hard core of three cases in which it had not been possible to establish definitely whether the ISOS evidence represented real spies who had escaped our controls or imaginary characters. There were also half a dozen cases of agents mentioned as being destined for British territory without any express reference to their arrival or agents destined for an unspecified destination which might be British territory.

Apart from this use for detecting and dealing with enemy agents in British territories and for preventing or countering the work of the Abwehr and SD on the lines sketched above, the operational significance of the corpus of intelligence which was mainly based on the intercepted wireless material was of considerable importance. This question was raised in Part 4, Paras. 210-221 of the German Secret Service, August 1942 (vide Bibliography No. 33). Para. 215 in particular raised the question of how far the existing machinery was suitable for the purpose; and subsequent to this arrangements were made whereby intelligence arising directly out of the analysis of the material by Mr. Palmer of the Intelligence Section of the G.C. & C.S. was passed directly and immediately to the officers concerned in the Directorates of Intelligence in the War Office, Admiralty or Air Ministry. This direct communication was necessary because of the delay involved in passing it through the sub-sections of Section V and the impossibility of a complete integration by its geographical sub-sections, inexpert and restricted as they were. This development was due in part at least to the emphasis laid on the operational significance of this material in "The German Secret Service" of August 1942. In March of that year in the course of preparing this document "Research" was led to get into touch with Major Melland in the Directorate of Military Intelligence with a view to including in it more comprehensive details concerning the German military machine. This contact led directly to a liaison with Mr. Palmer in G.C & C.S. who was introduced to various officers in the Security Service on a basis which had to be unofficial in view of Section V's attitude to G.C & C.S. and - incredible though it may appear - their objection to direct relations between them and the Security Service. The liaison was immediately fruitful and enabled Mr. Palmer to interpret certain important texts which had previously defied him. The first of these was one dealing with the technical arrangements for sabotaging British ships in Spanish ports. The resultant interpretation of the message enabled him to give warning of the enemy's plans so that they could be forestalled. It also led to preventive action by Lord Rothschild of B.1.C. which greatly minimised the possibility of losses to British shipping through enemy sabotage. The liaison with Mr. Palmer and the emphasis placed by "Research" on the operational significance of ISOS also led to Major Melland being introduced to the fortnightly meetings of the Technical Committee and to a general exchange of information which enabled various parts of the whole machine to arrive at a better appreciation of the operational significance of the material. There are further references to the general question of the operational significance of ISOS in "The German Secret Service, August 1944" (vide Bibliography No. 34).

Lt.-Colonel Melland, after leaving M.I.14(D), gave it as his opinion that ISOS contained material of operational value in various ways. Its potential value was recognised from the beginning and it was for this reason that it was supplied to M.I.14(D). Subsequent experience had shown that the material was often of negative value in that it showed what the Abwehr did not know; and again, it showed in many instances that the information obtained from their agents was of little value or very doubtful accuracy. ISOS was of negative value in one important instance when it showed that the Abwehr had no previous information about the landings in North Africa. There had been indications that the Germans were preparing to withdraw from Greece and there had been important indications regarding their plans in connection with their offensive in South Russia. Just as, when the German armies were advancing, the assembling of Einsatz Kommandos had indicated preparations for an advance, in the same way when they were preparing for a withdrawal in Western Europe the fact was indicated by the decrease or disappearance of fixed Abwehr posts and the formation of mobile units. ISOS, he added, had been of special importance in connection with the landings in Normandy and had shown that the Abwehr attached great importance to and relied on the information they obtained from double-cross agents under the control of B.1.A. In this respect there was of course the unknown factor: that we did not then know how far the German General Staff relied on Abwehr reports. The fact that the Abwehr was relying on this double-cross information which we planted on them and had no other important sources of information was a factor in building up our General Staff's appreciation of the whole position. (The very great importance and significance of this question of Abwehr reliance on double-cross information is dealt with under the account of B.1.A. below).

A number of papers based on ISOS and containing appreciations of its operational value were prepared by M.I.14(D).

2. The examination by S.C.O.s of persons arriving at sea or air ports.

The work of D.4 and S.C.O.s at sea and air ports in connection with the arrival of aliens or British subjects illustrates the complementary nature of the preventive functions of D and the investigation work of B Divisions. This has been brought out in the "Manual on the German Secret Service and British Counter Measures", pages 1 and 2 (vide Bibliography No. 31), in which the part played by the different sections is clearly, if briefly, explained. It is more fully set out in the L.R.C. History (S.F.50/24/44(32)), and the D.4.History (S.F.50/24/44/(56)).

The functions of D.4 and the S.C.O.s were preventive in the sense that by examining the canalised traffic into and out of the United Kingdom they prevented the incoming and outgoing, without the knowledge of B Division, of suspects, known agents, or those elements which might be expected to include such suspects or agents; and they arranged through the Immigration Officers to divert them to the L.R.C. or supplied intelligence about them to other divisions of the Security Service for use as might be desirable. Their functions also included the preliminary stages of detection whenever by search or interrogation they obtained intelligence relevant to counter espionage problems. It should be added, however, that the position of the S.C.O. at a port is not an easy one as there is usually neither time nor suitable facilities for detailed interrogation.

The conditions under which S.C.O.s worked varied during the course of the war as a result of changes in travel conditions. At the beginning of the war, as a result of the Home Office decision, aliens were encourage to leave, and Germans, except those notified for detention, were allowed to go. Thereafter all Exit Permits were referred to the Security Service, while travel into the United Kingdom was only permitted, and visas were only granted, when it was in the national interest.

There were passenger services between neutral countries calling at United Kingdom ports and those required attention from the S.C.O.s A number of enemy aliens, particularly seamen, were taken off and interned. Early in 1940 France demanded relaxation in the restriction of travel in the national interest in order to maintain tourist travel to the Riviera.

After the collapse of France and the occupation of Western Europe in May and June 1940, Spanish, Portuguese and U.S.A. vessels were not allowed by their Governments to enter the United Kingdom, and passenger traffic was consequently severely restricted. A little later U.S.A. ships were registered in Panama and arrived here under the Panamanian flag bringing supplies and munitions. In 1941 about a thousand Norwegians escaped to the Shetlands in fishing vessels, but this traffic was practically stopped by the Germans in 1942, although a certain number, sometimes including German agents, continued to trickle through. From 1941 until the landing in Normandy large numbers of refugees and persons escaping from enemy territory were allowed to come to this country in response to the call to join the Allied Forces. Others came for the same purpose from North and South America. After France was liberated in 1945 a limited amount of passenger traffic across the Channel was allowed.

The work of S.C.O.s at the ports was based on W.S.18 and their legal powers were set out in W.S.18(A).

At the beginning of the war passenger travel was heavy and S.C.O.s were guided by the Central Security War Black List, and in the absence of more authentic information could only rely on impressions formed while interrogating individuals. Aliens arriving at United Kingdom ports could be sent to Cannon Row Police Station for examination (subject to the Immigration Officer agreeing to refuse leave to land under the Aliens Order 1920). This procedure was in accordance with that followed in the last war when aliens were sent to Cannon Row from the ports to be examined by Special Branch under the direction of Sir Basil Thomson, but in June 1940 Sir Norman Kendal, in a letter to Captain Liddell, suggested that the Security Service should deal with all such cases and carry them through to the end.

Just before the fall of France it was proposed that large numbers of refugees should come to the United Kingdom. It was decided that these should all be examined, aliens being sent to camps in London and British subjects detained if necessary under special powers. The Defence Regulations were amended by the addition of D.R.18 (3) to give the necessary authority.

On the fall of France the flood of refugees from occupied territories was dealt with from the security point of view by a section of B Division (B.24), which was formed mainly from staff previously working under S.I.S. This section interrogated the refugees in a somewhat haphazard and very unsatisfactory manner until better arrangements could be improvised. The first flood having been disposed of, it became clear that numbers of aliens would continue to arrive and would require more detailed examination. It was decided that these aliens must be diverted to a central point, to which they could be brought under escort from the ports, or from authorised landing places. It was not until the 10th January 1941 that the Royal Patriotic Schools were opened for this purpose, with a view to facilitating arrangements for a more thorough examination than was possible at the ports.

It is worth noting that this change from examination by Special Branch at Cannon Row to the establishment of an intelligence organisation (later known as the L.R.C. or London Reception Centre) had an important effect in altering the status of the Security Service and in rendering possible systematic intelligence work based on an appropriate type of intelligence records. (This will be described in the next sub-section). The fact that the authority to refuse leave to land or refuse leave to embark rested in the early stages with the Immigration Officer on the advice of the S.C.O. led to difficulties as there were frequent disagreements. When the coast of Western Europe was occupied from Norway to Bordeaux, it was essential to have a clear understanding about their respective responsibilities in view of the increased likelihood of the arrival of enemy agents. For example, information received from S.I.S. showed that the Germans were seizing the clothing of Breton fishermen. It was clear that this might mean an attempt to introduce agents in this guise. While individuals could be checked at the ports there was also the possibility of an attempt to send fishing boats to the United Kingdom. Similarly the Ministry of Labour were recruiting certain classes of technicians from among refugees in Spain, Portugal and elsewhere. While this was necessary from the point of view of the supply of munitions, it offered an opportunity to the Germans to arrange to include agents among them. It was agreed that they should be subjected to security examination on arrival.

The question was taken up and as a result the Immigration Branch agreed to an instruction being issued to Immigration Officers and S.C.O.s. On 9.1.41. A.D.D.4. issued a circular to S.C.O.s explaining this agreement, which was to the effect that certain categories of aliens should be refused leave to land and sent to the L.R.C. The categories were mainly aliens without a visa, those wishing to join any of the Allied Forces, those who in the opinion of the Immigration Officer or the S.C.O. gave any ground for suspicion of being connected with any hostile or subversive or otherwise undesirable organisation, refugees, or the crews of foreign fishing vessels arriving from enemy occupied territory, alien technicians from Spain, Portugal or Northern Africa. A secret memorandum explaining the reasons for these instructions was furnished to Security Control Officers, who were instructed to communicate its contents to Immigration Officers on request. This secret memorandum was based on the information which had been accumulated by the Security Service regarding the activities of the German Secret Service up to that point. It was to the effect that the German Secret Service was very active in recruiting and despatching a large number of agents to this country, presumably in the hope that some at least would get through and obtain useful information. The agents in question were mainly unimportant people with no previous contact with the German Security Service and no experience as agents. They were to be looked for among people who would have no difficulty in entering this country legally and included applicants for enlistment in the Allied Forces; seamen signing for service on British or Allied ships; women of Allied nationality joining their husbands serving with the Allied Forces and neutral journalists. Certain details were given regarding the German questionnaires, the use of [...] for secret writing purposes and other similar points.

This action proved to be timely as shortly after the issue of this circular two foreign fishing vessels arrived from occupied territory, both of which, it subsequently transpired as a result of further examination, had been sent by the Germans for the purpose of committing sabotage. In one case the Immigration Officer was satisfied with the crew and wished to land them, but was prevented from doing so on the authority of the above-mentioned instructions. Another case was that of Joseph August LAUREYSSENS, who had arrived on 5.12.40. The S.C.O. wished to refuse leave to land, but the Immigration Officer disagreed and granted leave. It was proved that he was an enemy agent when the Censorship detected his reports in secret ink to the Abwehr.

The general question was referred to Lord Swinton, and on the 21st March 1941, as a result of an agreement between him and the Home Office, the latter issued instructions to Immigration Officers to the effect that the Security Control Officer was the representative at the port of the Security Service, and would often be in possession of information which was not available to the Immigration Officer. The Immigration Officer should, therefore, refuse to any alien leave to land or to embark if the Security Control Officer advised him that it was not in the interest of national security that the alien should be granted such leave. The instructions went on to say that the S.C.O. would give his reasons to the Immigration Officer whenever possible, but if he were unable to do so (e.g. because he was acting on instructions from headquarters) he would notify the Immigration Officer accordingly and the latter would refuse leave, a report being forwarded to the Home Office by the Security Service in such cases.

The effect of this, one of the most important results achieved by Lord Swinton, was to give the power of decision as to the landing and subsequent interrogation to the Security Service. It thus gave - in effect - executive powers to enable the Security Service to discharge its responsibilities, and incidentally lifted that responsibility from the shoulders of the Home Office. (It should be noted that in law the powers remained with the Immigration Officers not with Security Service officers).

These arrangements, however, did not always work smoothly as the Immigration Department are reported by A.D.D.4. to have collaborated fairly well on the whole, but to have taken every opportunity to raise objections. As a result, at the instance of B. Division, an attempt was made to restrict or eliminate the S.C.O.'s discretion by a list of categories exactly defining which aliens should be sent to the L.R.C. Protracted discussions on a draft agreed at a meeting with the Home Office on 27.10.42. resulted in a final decision which they did not issue until the 3rd December 1943. It specifically mentioned that S.C.O.s should use their discretion and furnished a list of categories to be used as a guide. It laid down that the S.C.O. should give one of the following reasons to the Immigration Officer in making a request for a male or female alien, other than a volunteer for the British or Allied Forces, to be refused leave to land:-

(a) Security Service Headquarters have information which makes it advisable for the individual to be sent there for further examination.
(b) From impressions formed during the examination, as to his manner or statements, the S.C.O. considers further examination is necessary.
(c) The individual has been in circumstances or in an area where he may have been subject to enemy influences.

It also pointed out that the procedure of sending people to the L.R.C. was not a punitive measure, but was intended to ensure that aliens who might be dangerous to the national interest should not be landed without full examination. It was further laid down that members of Allied Forces or those coming to join the Allied forces should be examined at the L.R.C. prior to their becoming entitled to the legal privileges accorded to members of the Allied Forces enlisted in the United Kingdom.

Immediately before the fall of France in 1940 it was proposed that some eight hundred thousand refugees from France, Belgium and Holland should be conducted to this country and the Home Office finally agreed to accepted three hundred thousand; but, as a result of the rapidity of the collapse, only about thirty-five thousand arrived. Among the aliens were a certain number of British subjects, many of whom had scarcely any other connection with England beyond the technical fact of nationality, e.g. as a result of birth on British territory. In view of the possibility that some of them might be suspect the "Arrival from Enemy or Foreign Territory Order" was issued as an amendment to D.R.18 under the heading of D.R.18(3). The object in view was to make it possible to detain British subjects in these circumstances, but defects in the Order came to light, and it was not until the 22nd December 1943 that the Home Office decided on its final form. The essential provision in the Order of 1943 was to enable the Secretary of State to make orders for securing that, if there was reasonable cause to believe that a person had recently been assisting, or associating with persons assisting, the enemy, he might be detained pending enquiries.

In the meanwhile, in the summer of 1942, B Division had realised that a number of individuals having British nationality were arriving in this country under circumstances similar to those of the aliens who were being sent to the L.R.C., and early in 1943 arrangements were made to deal with them on similar lines and in the light of the L.R.C. records. On the 16th April 1943 the Home Office issued an instruction enjoining the same principles of co-operation as in the case of aliens between Immigration Officers and S.C.O.s in respect of refusal of leave to embark on the part of British subjects under Article 2 of the Passenger Traffic Order 1939.

A case occurred in December 1942 which illustrated the possible danger of British subjects arriving here in the employ of the enemy as well as the impossibility of binding S.C.O.s strictly to categories and the desirability of trusting to their discretion and of keeping them as fully informed as possible of current intelligence relevant to this subject. This was the case of Johannes de GRAAF, who arrived in this country from Spain having been employed since the previous April on the staff of the British Embassy in Madrid in the section dealing with individuals escaping from occupied Europe. The S.C.O. formed the opinion that he was a suspect and arranged for him to be sent to Brixton prison under the "Arrival from Enemy or Foreign Territory Order" 1751/1940 under D.R.18(3). After two interrogations by the L.R.C. examiner, the view was taken that there was nothing against him, but later, on his story being checked with details in the Information Index, it became apparent that part of de GRAAF's escape from Belgium early in 1942 had been arranged by a suspect enemy agent. This led to further interrogation and to his eventual confession that he was an enemy agent with instructions to commit sabotage. This confession could not have been obtained but for the initiative of the S.C.O., which was thus responsible for results having an important bearing on the preventive and intelligence work of the Security Service.

The point is emphasised because the question of categories and discretion was the subject of some divergence of views between B and D Divisions. It is also to be noted that in the case of aliens arriving from Western Europe under enemy occupation the S.C.O. had no option but to send persons from those countries to the L.R.C. In the case of British subjects, in the absence of a satisfactory regulation and of arrangements for dealing with them, the matter depended entirely on the S.C.O.'s discretion and on his having the knowledge or insight which might enable him to detect a suspect.†

---

† The S.C.O. was also in a position to take action on the basis of information received from other parts of the Security Service so as to disclose the presence of an enemy agent in the traffic flowing through the ports. An instance of this is the case of John Oswald JOB. The only clue to his identity received from a B.1.A. double agent was that he would be carrying a bracelet and a tie pin (exact details were not available). Six weeks later he was picked out. He proved to be a British subject of German extraction and subsequent enquiries produced evidence on which he was hanged.

Thus the S.C.O., stationed as he was at the point of entry into the United Kingdom, played an important part - under the general guidance of A.D.D.4. and backed by the general intelligence and records of the Security Service. He was in fact, if not in name, the executive officer by whose action the body of a suspect of a spy came into the hands of the L.R.C. or the custody of Camp 020 under the authority of the Home Secretary.

The question whether adequate steps were taken to keep the S.C.O. well enough informed and to make him feel himself a full member of the team was the subject of the divergence of views between B and D Divisions. It can only be said here that, prima facie, the mere fact that D Division felt that they were not sufficiently well informed is an indication of an unsound tendency to keep knowledge about the enemy too exclusively to B Division. The reason for this is to be sought in the importance of maintaining the secrecy of ISOS and other sources of intelligence; but in retrospect, at least, it may be suggested that via media satisfactory to both parties should have been found.

3. Interrogation at the L.R.C. of British and alien subjects and all persons arriving from enemy-occupied territory or from neutral countries.

The means by which the L.R.C. (London Reception Centre - earlier known as the R.P.S. or Royal Patriotic School) was made to play its part in the machinery for counter-measures described in the "Manual on the German Secret Service and British Counter-Measures" (vide Bibliography No.31) were developed gradually and in the light of experience of the difficult conditions of 1940-41. The solution was found in a combination of interrogation and elaborately developed records of a special kind known as the Information Index of the L.R.C., which differed in scope and purpose from any other index used by the Security Service.

The elaborate system which was eventually developed at the L.R.C. has been fully explained in the L.R.C. History (S.F.50/24/44(32) and this cannot be readily abridged so as adequately to explain the extremely competent manner in which this part of the machinery was developed.

It has been mentioned in the last sub-section that the Royal Patriotic School was opened on the 10th January 1941 for the purpose of dealing with the circumstances arising from the arrival of refugees from occupied Europe; and that at the same time, i.e. in the first week of January, a circular was issued to S.C.O.s based on the information which had been accumulated by the Security Service up to that point. This information showed that the German Secret Service had been despatching a number of agents to this country and that they were relying on quantity rather than quality and employing indifferent types in the hope that some at least would get through our controls and prove useful. Details about the agents who were detected are given in Part II of the Report on the German Secret Service dated August 1942, on page 19 of which it is mentioned that the preparations seemed to have been hastily made and the men had been led to expect that they were to play a part in an imminent invasion. These agents mostly arrived by parachute or small boats. During 1940 the Germans were evidently not prepared to take advantage of the flood of refugees for the purpose of inserting agents among them.

As mentioned above in Chapter IV, Part 2 (v), the hastily improvised section, B.24, was unable to evolve any systematic method of dealing with the problems connected with these refugees; but the urgency of these problems impressed itself on the heads of B. Division, to whom the possibility of agents arriving among the refugees was an obvious danger. It was decided that the best course was to arrange for examination at a central point, and the Royal Patriotic Schools were made available for the purpose by the Home Office. It was not, however, until the autumn of 1941 that satisfactory arrangements were made to deal with the problem, and in the meanwhile the examiners made the best of a bad job in the face of insuperable difficulties. The Security Service at this time had no records with which to check an alien's story when he arrived, and an individual's bona fides, or otherwise, could only be based on interrogation and the examiner's personal impression. The examinations were often cursory, reports on each case were very brief and no attempt was made to build up systematic records which could form the basis of intelligence for dealing with future arrivals.

As mentioned in the report on the German Secret Service dated August 1942 in Part II (page 20) - (see also the cases of the M.V. "Taanevik", M.V. "Hernie" and M.V. "Hornfjell" pages 103-109 idem) - the Abwehr began to insert their agents among refugees and persons escaping from occupied Europe.

These cases emphasised the danger and steps were accordingly devised by Mr. White to reorganise the staff at the L.R.C. and to establish a system of records which would help the examiners in their interrogation by making it easier to distinguish between the "sheep" and the "goats", i.e. between genuine refugees and would-be recruits to the forces on the one hand and suspects or enemy agents on the other.

All through the years 1941-1944 refugees were being allowed to land in this country, having got away clandestinely by 'escape' boat or 'escape' plane, or by escape routes into Vichy France and the Iberian Peninsula. Many of them were encouraged to come to join the Allied Forces which were being recruited and developed in this country by the Allied Governments established here. The escape routes in question were organised by the Allied Governments or their intelligence services. Some were used or organised by S.I.S. or S.O.E. for the purpose of facilitating the journey to this country of their agents or of Allied officers and other personages whose presence was desired for purposes of the war effort. These circumstances led to the gradual development of the solution already mentioned, i.e. of the combination of interrogation and elaborate records devised specifically for this purpose. The new system was started in October 1941 and some time between January 1942 and June 1942 the L.R.C. began to be an effective instrument for counter espionage purposes. From about the middle of 1942 onwards it achieved positive results by its success in throwing up suspect enemy agents for further and more elaborate interrogation at Camp 020.

In 1942 - as indeed in 1940 and 1941 - the German Intelligence Service obviously required information about British, and later Allied, plans and the Allied war potential, and apart from Russia the three areas from which they could obtain information directly concerned with our war effort were the British Isles, the Middle East and the Americas. Some time during 1941 it began to be apparent - contrary to our previous and justified over-estimate of their efficiency - that the Germans had no previously established espionage network of any appreciable size or effectiveness. The obvious conclusion, therefore, was that if they had no established network and could not land or parachute agents clandestinely with any success, the only means open to them was to use the channel offered by the refugees and other Allied subjects coming to join the Allied Forces from occupied territory, or -a much smaller category - the neutrals coming to fight on the Allied side.

In the circumstances of that time when Western Europe was occupied by the enemy from Norway to Bordeaux it was possible to provide for a system of travel control round the whole coast of the United Kingdom which effectively intercepted all arrivals and diverted virtually the whole stream (that is of those from occupied Europe and those otherwise suspected) to the L.R.C. in accordance with the control exercised at the discretion of the S.C.O.s at the ports. This fact created an entirely new situation, which made it possible to develop the L.R.C. on the specialised lines which it assumed from the autumn of 1941 until the landing in Normandy in 1944.

At first the separation of the "sheep" from the "goats" was of necessity based largely on guesswork, but, as has been explained, the Germans were fortunately as unprepared to utilise their opportunities as we were to meet the situation prior to the reoganisation of the L.R.C.

By card-indexing details regarding methods and routes used by enemy agents or bona fide members of the Allied resistance movements, together with a great variety of other relevant details obtained from hundreds of incoming travellers, a body of valuable information was gradually built up in an accessible form for the use of the officers examining the new arrivals; and at the same time a sound system of interrogation was developed.

The underlying idea of this system - the first object of which was to detect all enemy agents attempting to enter the United Kingdom - was that it was not a hostile cross-examination, but was conducted on a friendly, if formal, basis. The reason for his temporary detention and the examination at the L.R.C. was made clear to each individual, and the result, in the vast majority of cases, was a readiness to supply any information which would be valuable to the British Intelligence officers. In all cases the first statement was checked against records of all available information, and if, for instance, a man was found to have travelled on a suspect escape route known to have been penetrated by the Abwehr and used to despatch their agents among bona fide refugees, the individual was naturally the subject of a more intensive interrogation.

An illustration of the comprehensiveness and competency with which the L.R.C. was organised is the "Analysis Book" filled in by the Information Section at the time of carding each alien's report. The object of this was to make it possible to re-examine past L.R.C. cases whenever a new class of agent (as regards background) or a new cover story came to light, in order to see whether a similar agent might not have slipped through previously.

The Information Index facilitated the uncovering of suspects in virtue of its comprehensive nature. An outstanding feature of it was that - unlike the Central Registry or other counter espionage registries - it carded the "sheep" as well as the "goats", the object being to compile information about individuals and organisations on the Allied side, because this information was necessary to enable the interrogating officer to recognise a friendly arrival and distinguish him from a suspect or an enemy. In other words it was necessary to have a large background of real general knowledge about each country in addition to secret intelligence narrowly restricted to the enemy organisation. The Information Index eventually contained some hundred thousand cards, and was composed of two distinct parts: a Name Index gave all the available details about an individual's description, addresses, occupation and history; the Geographical Index was sub-divided for addresses, town cards and subjects. The subjects carded included an immense number of details under headings including pro-Allied organisations or resistance movements, escape routes, pro-German organisations, youth organisations, political parties, enemy, or other intelligence services, the police and other authorities, "including Mayors, Prefects, etc.", welfare organisations, regulations and controls in different countries and areas, prisons and concentration camps, the press including the secret press, boats used by the enemy Intelligence, firms, if used as cover by the enemy Intelligence, labour conditions, Government Departments, Embassies and Consulates in all occupied territories. In addition the Information Section collected a number of intelligence files giving general information for each country in regard to living conditions, suspect organisations and resistance movements, national minorities, political parties and photographs and originals of documents used for travel control and other purposes in occupied territory. Information was collected from a great variety of sources, including such reference books as the P.W.E. Basic and Zone Handbooks, Chatham House reports, S.I.S. and S.O.E. reports and summaries, French Black Lists, Belgian Sureté reports and reports from all sections of the Security Service, including Camp 020 material, D.S.O. reports on travellers and Imperial Censorship reports.

The vital part of L.R.C. work lay in the examiner's selection, interpretation and assessment of facts supplied by incoming aliens. In order to enable him to perform this function effectively it was necessary to ensure that each examiner should have at his disposal a large background of available information. This information was obtained from two sources: the examiner's own personal local knowledge, including that acquired by his experience in the L.R.C., and from records. The records included not only the information immediately accessible to him in the Information Section with its index, and the L.R.C. monthly summary of cases and other matters of current intelligence interest, but also three other registries (i) the Central Registry of the Security Service; (ii) the R.B. Registry; and (iii) the S.I.S. Registry. Of these (i) was of negligible value because after April 1941 it did not card names abroad and prior to that it had only done so to a limited extent; (ii) was of great value because it contained a fairly comprehensive record of Abwehr and SD personnel and of their agents carded from ISOS material; and (iii) was of great use as apart from the Information Index of the L.R.C. it was the only one which carded names and addresses on the Continent. It also contained information about S.I.S. agents and organisations which was essential for the purposes of dealing with certain classes of L.R.C. cases. Unfortunately owing to the inadequacies of its staff and methods, it was found to function very erratically. All these registries produced information only on specific names and addresses. The Information Index of the L.R.C. went further in that it made it profitable to look up such vague indications as christian names or an unnumbered address in a particular street. It also provided on cards or in intelligence files information of all kinds of specific areas: countries, districts, towns and so on; and it contained information specifically suited to L.R.C. purposes, such as, for instance, plans and routine details about prison camps, from which a suspect under interrogation might pretend to have escaped, or about which he might give details which would make it possible for the interrogator to discover that he was not telling the truth. The outstanding importance of the Information Index arose from the fact that it made all this information readily accessible; and the skill, care and thought with which it was compiled was a remarkable achievement. Numerous officers contributed to this, but the idea was originally conceived by Mr. White, and this conception was given shape and developed by Major Haylor, Colonel Baxter and Miss Wadeson, who was in charge of it from the time it was started at the end of 1941 until the end of 1944, initiated many of its important features and was mainly responsible for its outstanding success.

As has been mentioned above in connection with the S.C.O.s, B Division realised in the summer of 1942 that a number of individuals having British nationality were arriving in this country under circumstances similar to those of the aliens who were being sent to the L.R.C. On the 12th February 1943 a section known as B.1.D/U.K. was formally constituted under the orders of the Director General with a view to dealing with these British subjects. As a large proportion of them were persons escaping from enemy-occupied territory, investigations regarding them were necessarily based on the L.R.C. and its Information Index. Between February 1943 and the end of the war some 600 individuals were interrogated by the officers of B.1.D/U.K. at Devonshire House, where space was obtained for the purpose.

The procedure was that the circumstances of British subjects arriving in this country from enemy-occupied territory and of every other British arrival, against whom something was known or suspected, were scrutinised. Whenever it was thought desirable that he or she should be interrogated they were invited to call at Devonshire House with the intimation that their presence was considered desirable as it was thought likely that they might have information useful to the war effort. This form of invitation obviously involved a rather less intensive interrogation than was possible at the L.R.C., but in practice no difficulty was found in obtaining an individual's story and no invitation was ever refused.

As a British subject could not be refused leave to land and could only be detained if there were positive grounds for doing so, B.1.D/U.K. devoted its attention to obtaining information about British subjects who were liable to return to this country. This was done in a variety of ways, e.g. from persons who had already returned; by the appointment of a representative in Lisbon and later in Paris, whose function it was to forward reports, before they arrived, of individuals intending to return to this country; by the introduction on "repatriation" ships of a Security Officer as part of the administrative staff; and by the use of records, especially the Information Index of the L.R.C. and a card index kept in the section. This sectional card index incidentally produced a useful by-product. It became the main basis of the information available against the category of persons subsequently described as renegades.

The British subjects returning to this country fell into two main categories: those escaping from enemy or occupied territory and those brought home under official repatriation schemes.

In addition to interrogating persons on arrival the section made enquiries with a view to keeping track of individuals whose bona fides were not fully established. This was effected by means of a Home Office Warrant on the subject's correspondence; by collateral enquiries from other Government departments; by interrogation by the R.S.L.O.; and other routing methods.

An outstanding aspect of the functions of the L.R.C. arises from its inescapable connection with S.I.S. and S.O.E. organisations in enemy or enemy-occupied territory. L.R.C. examiners necessarily had to obtain from S.I.S. or S.O.E. agents vetted by them as much information as possible about the organisation for which they were working with the double purpose of keeping the Information Index up to date, and of discovering whether the organisation had been penetrated at any point. This information was vital for the purpose of checking any subsequent agents who might arrive and for the security of future operations in the field. This question was always a course of overt or covert friction between the L.R.C. and the department running the organisations. S.I.S. insisted - on the plausible pretext of limiting the circulation of such information - that as little as possible should be asked as was consistent with security requirements. Section V even went to the length of setting up a staff of three or four examiners at the L.R.C. for the sole purpose of establishing their claim that the Security Service was not concerned with names and addresses and organisations abroad, but this claim, as will be obvious from the facts given above, could not be sustained. Nevertheless the small staff was maintained by them although, as they did not avail themselves of the Information Index or any other comparable records, their interrogations, based on a fixed questionnaire, were of no practical value, whereas if they had known how to use it the Information Index would have been of great value to S.I.S. S.O.E. on the other hand, by means of a liaison with the Information Index, both supplied information to be put on the Index and obtained information from it relevant to cases under enquiry of agents who fell under suspicion. (It should be borne in mind that accredited agents of both S.I.S. and S.O.E. were not passed through the L.R.C., but only those who arrived in the United Kingdom for the first time after being recruited in the field).

There were several major disasters, some of which might have been avoided if S.I.S. and S.O.E. had arranged from the beginning for all the information about their organisations to be centered at one point in the L.R.C. S.I.S. consistently refused to do this, but S.O.E. were anxious to do it as soon as they realised the nature of the dangers and the protection which the L.R.C. could afford. As it was, the L.R.C. charter was never recognised as including responsibility for the security of these Allied organisations. On the other hand it included responsibility for the security examination of a limited category of their agents, i.e. those recruited in the field. As the L.R.C. report points out, such a dichotomy was patently absurd and proved to be so in practice. This whole question is an important illustration of the advantages to be secured either by the central direction of or close co-operation between the Security Service and the other two Services; and of the grave disadvantages which follow from fragmentation or a lack of co-operation.

It is not feasible to set out an estimate in any very concrete form of the part played by the L.R.C. in detecting spies and bringing their guilt home to them. The part it played was undoubtedly very valuable, but in practical working it interlocked so closely with other parts of the machine - and especially with those responsible for ISOS information and Camp 020 - that in many cases there is no dividing line on the basis of which it could be said that success was to be attributed to one or the other section. In numerous cases all played their parts in the co-ordinated machinery.

A few instances may, however, be quoted:

There were some cases in which the L.R.C. "broke" a spy unaided, for instance, †Joseph Van HOVE. There were others in which the result was mainly achieved by the L.R.C. substantially assisted by ISOS, of which the case of †Johannes DRONKERS is an illustration. A third category is illustrated by the case of †Lucien RAMBAUR, whose identification as a spy is to be attributed wholly to ISOS. There were cases in which the L.R.C., after interrogation, were not satisfied and sent the individual to Camp 020, where a confession was obtained. [...] the Icelander, was one of these. Again there were cases in which an admission or a partial confession was made to the L.R.C. interrogator, but the full story was only obtained after a more intensive interrogation at Camp 020, as in the case of †Gabriel PRY. Finally there were cases in which the L.R.C. Information Index furnished details which led to the realisation that an individual, otherwise unsuspected, was an enemy agent. The outstanding case is that of †Johannes de GRAAF (already mentioned on account of the important implications arising from it).

Altogether something over 50 individuals who eventually confessed were sent on to Camp 020 from the L.R.C.

The detection of enemy agents was not the sole function of the L.R.C. and a large part of their work was concerned with some 200 individuals who were sent to the Oratory Schools or were the subject of an Order under Article 12(5A) of the Aliens Order 1920, as amended, i.e. for deportation and, under war conditions, for detention pending deportation. These 200 individuals were dealt with in this way on the ground of being collaborators or generally having hostile associations without there being ground to regard them as agents of the enemy secret services.

Altogether some thirty-three thousand aliens were passed through the L.R.C. and examined, and so far as is know only three enemy agents with missions in this country got through without being detected.

---

† Reference to all these cases will be found in Chapter 3 of the L.R.C. Report.

The interrogators or examining officers of the staff were divided into six sections, each of which dealt with a specific nationality or group of nationalities: (i) French; (ii) Belgian and Dutch; (iii) Polish; (iv) Scandinavian; (v) Spanish and South American; (vi) South Eastern Europe and miscellaneous. It was found that this system of allocating officers to a nationality - and consequently a geographical area - made for efficiency; it enabled the officer to become thoroughly acquainted with all the vital background information to assist him in interrogation and the assessment of each case. The officers were selected on the bases of high language qualifications and as far as possible residence in the countries concerned. A senior officer was appointed to each nationality section, and he was responsible for its internal administration. Generally speaking the Allied Security Services were not invited or encouraged to assist in interrogation. Experience showed that the disadvantages which their permanent presence in a British establishment of this kind entailed outweighed any occasional advantage which might be obtained from their knowledge of their own countries. Exceptions had to be made in connection with Polish and Czechoslovak cases owing to the difficulty of obtaining British officers with a knowledge of the language. Among the disadvantages of introducing Allied interrogators were that the greatest secrecy had to be observed in regard to many matters, including the use of information obtained from intercepted enemy wireless. It was also found that central control of the L.R.C. staff was necessary and the presence of officers owing allegiance to their own national security services tended to lead to difficulties. It was found, on the other hand, that aliens coming to this country in time of war expected to be interrogated by British officers and were somewhat more willing to impart information to British officers in uniform than to civilians. For this reason it was advantageous to recruit the staff from a military establishment.

4. The interrogation of suspected or known spies at Camp 020 (in close association with B.1.B.).

Camp 020, which was opened on the 10th July 1940 at Latchmere House, Ham Common, eventually became one of the most important sources of information as a result of successful interrogation of enemy spies, but when it was first opened no spies had arrived and until they did so it could not develop its true functions.

For a few weeks it was primarily concerned with the interrogation of members of the British Union of Fascists as well as a number of suspect aliens, some of whom had been arrested in England and others brought over from Dunkirk in June 1940. None of these cases proved important from the espionage point of view. In the beginning of September the first Abwehr spies arrived in England and the real work began. They consisted of two groups of two each, who landed in small boats on the South Coast with English money, wireless sets and codes, and instructions to report military information and to join up with the German forces which were expected to invade this country almost immediately. Other spies followed in rapid succession.

In case of invasion or serious damage from air raids (a direct hit which only killed one German prisoner had been received in November 1940) a reserve camp was prepared at Huntercombe Place near Henley-on-Thames.

Up to the end of the war in Europe (9th May 1945) 440 internees were admitted to Camp 020, the yearly figures being as follows:-

1940:	107
1941:	55
1942:	67
1943:	65
1944:	119
1945:	27

Thirty-four nationalities were represented, namely: Belgian, German, French, Norwegian, Dutch, British, Spanish, Icelandic, Italian, Portuguese, Polish, Danish, South and Central American, Swiss, Swedish, Austrian, Hungarian, Russian, Roumanian, Czechoslovak, Greek, Irish, Canadian, Yugoslav, Lithuanian, Egyptian and stateless persons.

In addition a considerable number of women have been brought daily to Camp 020 for interrogation or examined by officers sent to Holloway Gaol as there were no facilities at the former place for the detention of women.

Of the 440 men examined, 50 were released as innocent. 14 spies were executed in England during the course of the war. Of the remaining cases about 180 had had some contact with the Abwehr in circumstances which precluded their release and about 200 were spies of whom one half had been sent on missions to the United Kingdom and the other to other countries. The reasons for not placing this considerable number before the courts are to be found in the policy which was adopted to the effect that it was undesirable that any spy should be tried where there was a risk of failure to secure a conviction and the death penalty. The proposal that it was undesirable to obtain a conviction on a minor charge which would result in imprisonment and thus lead the public and the enemy to believe that espionage could be punished otherwise than by the death penalty was put forward by Mr. Milmo of B.1.B. and approved by higher authority.

Cases in which there was no material evidence, such as the possession of a wireless transmitter or secret ink, were not sent for trial, nor were those arrested at British ports in Africa or America on account of missions in those continents or elsewhere abroad; nor the small number who were used as double agents by B.1.A. The view was also held that many of the spies were valuable to us as human reference libraries to assist in detecting other cases of espionage, and from this point of view were better alive than dead.

All enemy agents or other suspected persons received into Camp 020 were held under the following powers: for short periods under a "refusal of leave to land" by an Immigration Officer or by a detention order by an Immigration Officer or other authorised officer under the "Arrival from British and Foreign Territory Order"; and for long term cases under the Royal Prerogative in the case of enemy aliens; an order under Article 12(5a) of the Aliens Order or under D.R.18B in the rare cases of British subjects and D.R.18BA in the case of foreign nationals.

Colonel Stephens as Commandant was in charge of the military guard under the D.P.W., War Office, who were responsible for the physical security of the camp. He was also in charge of the Intelligence Officers as personnel of the Security Service. The relations with the Home Office were governed by the fact that prisoners were held under the authority of the Home Secretary who was responsible for the administration of all matters concerning their persons.

The cases handled at Camp 020 have varied greatly in importance and have illustrated the constant change in Abwehr espionage methods. Officers of Camp 020 have made an analysis of the trends of a series of 'waves' of espionage arising out of these changes directed against this country and our Allies.

The first of these waves began on the 3rd September 1940 when, as already mentioned, spies began to arrive either by boat or by parachute as a prelude to the planned invasion of England.

A number of German agents were captured in the autumn of 1940 on expeditions which had been sent to Greenland and Jan Meyen Island for the purpose of obtaining weather reports from that area. These were presumably required in connection with the proposed invasion and for the use of the Luftwaffe.

These were followed in the spring of 1940 by those who were inserted among genuine refugees arriving from Norway in small boats. There were also German agents among Norwegians who came via Stockholm. Two who were landed from a sea-plane in the north of Scotland in April 1941 immediately gave themselves up and professed to give full information about their mission and their German contacts. They arrived at Camp 20 on April 9th and were transferred to B.1.A. on the same day with a view to their employment as double agents.

The employment of seamen as agents, as might be expected, came to notice at an early date and continued to recur at intervals. There were also cases of Spanish trawlers, equipped with wireless, employed for transmitting shipping information and weather reports from the Eastern Atlantic, which came to notice through ISOS messages. The case of a Portuguese cod-fishing vessel with a wireless operator who was arrested on the 6th August 1942, on the basis of two intercepted messages giving details of Allied war vessels and shipping at St. Johns, Newfoundland, assumed importance as the boat returned to Lisbon at the time that the Allied fleets were massing for the invasion of North Africa in November 1942.

As already mentioned in connection with the S.C.O.s at the ports and the L.R.C., the Abwehr realised that the influx into the United Kingdom of persons escaping from occupied territory gave them opportunities for inserting agents among them; and this continued sporadically until the early months of 1944. In most of these cases they came via Spain and Portugal, but some came direct from France and Holland.

Another category consisted of a large number of agents who were sent to the American continent from the Iberian Peninsula and were detained at Trinidad and other ports; arrangements being made for their eventual interrogation at Camp 020.

From the end of 1941 onwards numbers of Belgians were sent through Spain and Portugal with the intention of reaching the Congo. Other agents were found to be operating in the Union of South Africa from a base in Laurenco Marques and the crews of vessels plying between Portugal, Portuguese East Africa and intermediate ports were found to be acting as couriers. Many of these agents destined for Africa were intercepted at various places and brought to Camp 020.

Shortly before the invasion of the continent the Abwehr sent a number of agents to Iceland to obtain military information, evidently on the assumption that that country would serve as a base for the purpose.

After D Day, 6th June 1944, large numbers of operational agents were brought from the Allied military zones and liberated territories in Europe.

Among the miscellaneous interrogations undertaken at Camp 020 were those of a certain number of Italian spies, and some cases examined on behalf of the French authorities. One of the most interesting of the miscellaneous cases was that of Edward Arnold CHAPMAN, an Englishman with a long record of crime in this country, who was in prison in Jersey when the German occupation began and after his release was taken to Paris in November 1941. He was trained as an agent by then and was the subject of a large number of ISOS messages which supplied numerous details about the German plans for using him and their intention to drop him by parachute. On his arrival in this country in December 1942 his first step was to approach the police and ask for an interview with the intelligence authorities. After an intensive interrogation lasting for a week it was decided to use him as a double agent. Messages were transmitted, replies were received and after a notionally successful act of sabotage at the De Havilland works he was sent back to Germany via Lisbon. The Germans then employed him in Norway for a year where he occasionally acted as an instructor for the W/T and sabotage schools. Early in 1944 he was prepared for a further mission to England in order to obtain information about British anti-submarine devices, American bombers, details of radio location apparatus fitted to night fighters, the effect of V weapons and other details. After numerous delays he was eventually dropped on the night of June 27th, again reported to the police and again, after detailed interrogation at Camp 020, was transferred to B.1.A.

Numerous other cases of varying interest are described in detail in the Camp 020 report. An outstanding point is that the great majority of the agents were not German nationals and very few of the other nationalities were influenced by ideological sympathies. Many of them were half-trained, ill-equipped for their missions and "small fry" in every sense of the word; but even so their interrogation helped to build up information about the Abwehr and SD organisations. Many were recruited by pressure being put on them in some form and the Germans hoped to maintain a hold over them in the same way. For instance in the case of CHAPMAN, mentioned above, they hoped that as a convicted prisoner he would avoid the British authorities. Some were influenced by hope of gain. The Intelligence Officers at Camp 020 sometimes received the impression that 'waves' of these agents were sent out hurriedly and without proper preparation in order to meet the demands of higher authorities.

The outstanding success of Camp 020 was one of the most important contributory factors in the general success of B Division in countering the Abwehr and Sipo und SD. This success is attributed to the personality of Colonel Stephens and his flair for this work; to the skill developed by the staff; and to a number of other factors, among the most effective of which was the psychological reaction produced by the atmosphere of efficiency deliberately created for the purpose. A prisoner on arrival was treated with a display of military precision and efficiency. Arriving in handcuffs he was stripped, given prison clothes, allowed no contact with other prisoners, photographed, put through a personal catechism, brought in for interrogation, faced by an array of four or five officers and treated with apparent severity (but no physical violence and no curtailment of rations was ever allowed). In almost all cases guilty agents signed confessions within a few days of their arrival. The number who were known to be guilty and did not confess is insignificant, while the number of doubtful cases is scarcely greater.

The success is also to be attributed to three important sources of information. By far the most valuable of these was ISOS, because it was completely reliable and gave concrete facts and circumstantial evidence regarding the agents and the actual messages concerning them transmitted between the various Abwehr officers. Every precaution had to be taken not to jeopardise this source, and it could therefore not be used directly in interrogation. The ISOS messages obviously required careful examination in order to ensure a correct interpretation, especially, as often happened, when all the relevant messages were not intercepted. The second source of information consisted of 'traces' from Security Service records including those based on S.I.S. agents' reports; though important these were less valuable because less circumstantial, and it was often difficult to assess their accuracy. A third source to which the officers of Camp 020 attached great importance was their own index of the records of statements obtained from interrogation. This information was recorded on index cards which eventually reached a total of over 100,000. It should be remarked, however, that some officers held a different view and considered that it was a mistake to maintain records at Camp 020 and a separate index. This view presupposes that the necessary information could have been made readily accessible to the interrogating officers through the sub-section of B.1.B. under Mr. Milmo, which gradually developed an unexpected relationship with Camp 020. The original intention was that Mr. Milmo's sub-section should serve for liaison purposes between Camp 020 and the sections at headquarters, but it developed wider functions. This development arose mainly from the fact that Camp 020 was necessarily outside the centre of London and therefore affected by the factor of distance; and also that its own function was limited in that it was solely an interrogating centre. Mr. Milmo's section therefore had in one sense the functions of a research section in obtaining all traces from the records and information from all other sources which might be of use to interrogators, but it also dealt with all questions arising out of Camp 020 cases on behalf of the Director and Assistant Director of B Division. This resulted in all questions relating to the disposal of spies being dealt with by Mr. Milmo in accordance with precedents and on lines laid down by decisions on the early cases. For instance as soon as a case appeared to be likely to be one that would go to the Director of Public Prosecutions, Mr. Milmo got in touch with the legal advisers (S.L.) After the D.P.P.'s views had been obtained in a certain number of cases, subsequent cases were dealt with on the same lines; reference being made to the Director B or higher authority, only when a release was recommended or in certain cases where a vitally important source of information or of paramount security interest might be jeopardised by disclosures at a trial. In cases which did not go to the Director of Public Prosecutions, e.g. because the evidence was not sufficient to secure a conviction involving the death penalty, Mr. Milmo referred to the Home Office direct in regard to disposal by internment. A ruling made by the Director B had laid down that the final decision in Camp 020 cases should be by the section at headquarters and not by the officers at the Camp who would necessarily be influenced by the personality of the individual. The B.1.B. sub-section also dealt with all correspondence with any other department in relation to matters arising out of Camp 020 cases.

The joint establishment at Camp 020 and Camp 020 R (at Huntercombe) consisted of one Commandant, one Assistant Commandant and twenty-five intelligence officers, including the administrative officers. There were two part-time medical officers and at each camp a large guard, under five officers at Camp 020 and seven at Camp 020 R.

The selection of suitable intelligence officers presented considerable difficulties, especially at first. It was essential to have a combination of a thorough knowledge of certain languages and experience of conditions abroad with the general qualifications of a good education and the other qualities required in an intelligence officer. The English, French, German, Dutch, Flemish, Norwegian, Swedish, Danish, Spanish, Portuguese and Italian languages have been employed in interrogation. The staff included about forty women secretaries who were sometimes employed on work of a research nature as well as on secretarial duties.

5. Investigation of sabotage.

The formation of B.1.C. (originally B.18) was described in Chapter IV, Part 1 (iii) above, in which an account of the functions allotted to it was outlined. Broadly speaking there was no great change in the section's terms of reference, but they were set out more fully, as they had developed in the light of experience, by Lord Rothschild in July 1942 (vide S.F.50-52-1(5)). Briefly experience showed that it was necessary for the Security Service to have a section which could make an expert study of all intelligence relating to enemy sabotage; supervise the investigation of suspect or actual cases of sabotage; make available all the specialised knowledge acquired by these means; and initiate, prepare and recommend counter-measures to Government Departments and undertakings concerned in the war effort both in the United Kingdom and abroad. As it was not possible for the Security Service to have on its permanent staff all the necessary technical experts to deal with all the sabotage problems which might arise in the innumerable types of installation or establishment concerned with the war effort, it was necessary to have a small staff with the necessary scientific knowledge, training and contacts to enable it to obtain this expert advice and to understand how to use it to the best advantage when obtained. For these purposes liaison was established with some thirty distinguished experts ranging from professors at universities to steel consultants in industry, all of whom made their services available in an unpaid capacity. To illustrate the wide range of problems involved reference may be made to instances such as that of obtaining authoritative information on all the aspects of the problem suggested by the possibility of agents bringing the Colorado beetle into the United Kingdom as a means of attacking the potato crop.

In order to initiate counter-measures it was necessary for B.1.C. to obtain and collate all the available information about the enemy organisations for sabotage, Abwehrabteilung II and later Amt VIS of the RSHA, as a part of the enemy Secret Service as a whole, the Amt Auslandsnachrichten und Abwehr under the Ober-kommando der Wehrmacht and later the RSHA under Himmler.

There were three main sources from which this intelligence was obtained: ISOS or the intercepted wireless communications of the Abwehr; the investigation of cases of sabotage including interrogation of arrested saboteurs and the examination of enemy sabotage equipment; and the employment of agents and double agents, the latter being controlled by B.1.A.

This intelligence picture was built up from nothing in the beginning of 1940 to a very comprehensive and detailed corpus of intelligence. As the information became available, it was distributed in the appropriate quarters in the Admiralty, the Air Ministry, the War Office and among the intelligence staffs of the armies in the field as well as among all the parts of the Security Service and its contacts at home and abroad. This work of distribution reached very large proportions in the latter years of the war and was carried out with due regard to the fact that much of the information was of a high grade of secrecy.

The information regarding the German Secret Services as a whole, including the sabotage branches, was first summarised in the report on the German Secret Service of August 1942 and later supplemented by that of 1944 and the War Room report of April 1945 (vide Bibliography Nos. 33, 34 and 35). The voluminous documents prepared by B.1.C. will be found in S.F. 50-24-44(31) and Supplementary Files.

The intelligence eventually received about the Abwehr confirmed the inference that the sabotage division (Abwehrabteilung II) would be closely integrated with the German military machine so that it might be used in subordination to military operations and that it would combine the direction of material and moral sabotage. Abwehrabteilung II was in fact responsible for sabotage in its broadest sense. This included straightforward material sabotage (S-Arbeit); disintegration work within the enemy countries (Zersetzung or Z-Arbeit); the subsidising and inciting of nationalist elements, racial minorities or peoples under foreign rule (Insurgierung or I- or J-Arbeit). There was a headquarters organisation at Berlin with branches under the several Wehrkreis in Germany. There were sabotage training schools - the most important of which was at Quenz near Brandenburg - and a technical laboratory for developments. Abwehrabteilung II was represented in the Abwehr stations outside Germany; in the more important cases by independent 'II' units.

A special para-military formation variously known as the Lehrregiment Brandenburg z.b.V.800, the Sonderverband Brandenburg and the Brandenburg Division, was used as a pool for agents for all the divisions of the Abwehr, but mainly for Abwehrabteilung II, in addition to being engaged in guerrilla warfare, Commando raids in German uniform, operations in enemy uniform behind the enemy lines or operations by small groups and even by individual saboteurs in civilian clothes. This formation originally consisted of Germans from abroad (Auslandsdeutsche) and it was assembled on the Channel coast at the time of the preparations for the invasion of England. Later, foreign nationals were recruited, including men from prisoner of war camps, Arabs and Indians. It was attached to and under the administrative control of the head of Abwehrabteilung II but for operational purposes units were sometimes attached to military formations in the field.

In July 1942, under Himmler's orders, a section for sabotage and political subversion was formed as part of Amt VI, the Foreign Intelligence Service of the Nazi Party under the RSHA. In August 1943 this section was disbanded by Himmler who was dissatisfied with its achievements and a new department, known as Amt VIS, was formed. After the Abwehr as an independent organisation was dissolved in June 1944, it was re-created as a subordinate office (the Militaerisches Amt) of the RSHA. By the end of the summer of 1944 all German sabotage and political subversion was under the control of Otto Skorzeny, head of Amt VIS, who also became head of the Militaerisches Amt D, the new name for Abwehrabteilung II. The functions of Skorzeny's services were:-

(i) to threaten Allied lines of communication by sabotage and by fomenting political trouble in Germany and the former occupied countries, using for these purposes German nationals or Fascist and anti-Allied elements of the countries concerned;
(ii) to mount military operations of a special type which the regular army would not normally undertake.

The close integration of the sabotage organisations, Abwehrabteilung II and Amt VIS, with the para-military formations was the cause of a difficulty in distinguishing between German military or naval operations and Secret Service operations and, therefore, in drawing a line to show where the interests of B.1.C. came to an end. For instance, to carry out his functions Skorzeny had at his disposal a number of units whose headquarters and training camps were widely dispersed throughout Germany. These included an unknown number of SS jaegerbataillone, later known as SS Jagdverbaende and the Frontsaufklaerungskommandos und Truppe of Mil.Amt D. Other associated formations were the 150 Panzer Brigade, the Eins Kampfgeschwader (the Luftwaffe formation responsible for parachuting agents and for supplying them by air) and the Marine Einsatz Abteilung, afterwards known as the Kommando der Kleinkampfverbaende. The last-named was a purely naval operational service, not a Secret Service, but using secret tactics and devices and controlling the Xth M.A.S. Flotilla, an Italian naval organisation which operated from a neutral country (Spain) as well as from Italian military bases and employed naval personnel - not always in uniform - and scored successes by attaching bombs to the hulls of British battleships and other operations of a secret type. Abwehrabteilung II established liaison with the Xth Flotilla M.A.S. in July 1943 and after the capitulation of Italy not only the Abwehr but also the German Navy and Amt VIS were anxious to obtain control over this unit of whose exploits the Germans had a high opinion. One of its Italian experts was sent to Turkey in 1943 in order to sabotage Allied shipping and succeeded in attaching mines to the bilgekeels of four ships, but all except one were found before they exploded.

The main German sabotage efforts were directed against (1) the British Isles; (2) British shipping in Spanish ports and Gibraltar; (3) the Middle East; and (4) the U.S.A.; but the elaborate organisation set up for the purpose achieved surprisingly small successes. Of these efforts that against (2) was by far the most important.

Not a single case of sabotage occurred in the United Kingdom during the whole course of the war although Abwehrabteilung II made attempts from time to time to introduce sabotage agents, but all these attempts failed. Some of those arrested were used by the Security Service as double agents to obtain useful information about the enemy's plans and sabotage targets. The first of the sabotage agents was [...] already mentioned as having been recruited before the war. After the war started no agent arrived from Germany until three were landed in Eire in July 1940 and six others in the United Kingdom towards the end of the same year. Two Norwegians who arrived in April 1941 were turned into double-cross agents. All the above arrived either in small boats or by seaplane. After April 1941 there were no arrivals until June 1942 by which time the method of introduction had changed and the agents appeared in the guise of refugees. Two of these arrived in 1942, one in 1943 and one in 1944. They were French, Canadian and Belgian by nationality and either confessed their mission at once or were discovered through interrogation at the L.R.C. In December 1942 a British subject was dropped by parachute as a sabotage agent and immediately reported his mission.

The main effort of the Abwehrabteilung II in the West before the invasion of the Continent was directed against Gibraltar and Allied shipping in Spanish ports. The headquarters was in Madrid with representatives in Huelva, Seville, Cadiz, Algeciras, Cartagena, Tangiers, Melilla, Las Palmas. In the most active period about twenty German officials organised networks of Spanish agents, extensive use being made of German ships interned in Spanish ports. Sabotage equipment was manufactured in Spain or sent from Germany as diplomatic luggage and the fullest co-operation of a number of Spanish officials facilitated the German enterprises. The un-neutral attitude of the Spanish Government hampered counter-measures while the only restrictive effect on German sabotage was their insistence that the workings of the German organisation must be so camouflaged that the Spanish authorities would not be too openly embarrassed. This meant that sabotage directed from Spanish soil must not be attributed to German nationals. As a consequence Spanish agents were employed and they tended to be both inefficient and venal - characteristics which were largely responsible for the poor results achieved. In January 1944 Abwehrabteilung II headquarters in Berlin sent orders to Madrid forbidding all sabotage in the Peninsula until further notice. This was a direct result of British protests about explosives in cargoes of oranges and the evidence which was produced to fix the responsibility on the Germans.

As was the case in Great Britain, Abwehrabteilung II had made no adequate preparations for sabotage in the U.S.A. on the outbreak of war and it was, therefore, necessary to attempt to introduce agents into America and to attempt to recruit and organise a large number of potential agents among the population of German origin in the U.S.A. Ambitious attempts were made in June 1942 when parties were landed in the U.S.A. from two submarines. In order to establish direct contact with the American authorities responsible for the enquiry Lord Rothschild visited the U.S.A. and obtained detailed information regarding the equipment supplied to these agents, some of which was new. In return he was able to supply the F.B.I. with information for the purposes of interrogation and an assessment of the equipment.

Some months prior to the Allied landings in Italy and France information was accumulated, from ISOS, through double agents and by interrogation - about German plans for sabotage in both theatres of operations. It became known that a large sabotage stay-behind organisation with a network of agents and buried sabotage dumps had been arranged. B.1.C. compiled a note on Abwehrabteilung II's plans for France and the Low Countries on the basis of information from the above-mentioned sources combined with the results of enquiries about the German sabotage preparations in North Africa and Italy. This was circulated to G-2 CI counter-sabotage specialists and members of the S.C.I. units organised by S.I.S. In the event both the Abwehrabteilung II and Amt VIS sabotage networks failed to operate. Their agents were arrested and their dumps were discovered. The Germans thereupon made attempts to re-activate these networks after the occupations of France and Belgium by the infiltration of other agents, some being sent through the lines and others being dropped by parachute. These new agents were given specific missions of sabotage or assassination, but all the undertakings failed because the agents were either known collaborationists and were arrested on that ground or they had no incentive to carry out work for the defeated side. Many of the agents had accepted their missions as a chance of returning to their own countries and had been recruited by the Germans without having any intention of working for them. Moreover, the German security arrangements during training were defective and the recruitment of a number of agents from the same collaborationist organisation meant that many agents knew of each other's activities and the arrest of one led to the arrest of others.

In regard to the question of German sabotage technique and equipment, the Security Service started the war with no information. There were two early reports - one in February and the second in March 1940 - of bombs being placed on board British ships. The first of these was investigated by the Greek police because the steamer was in one of their harbours and the second by the Ceylon police at Colombo as being the first port of call. In spite of attempts to obtain full reports and detailed descriptions in these two cases the Security Service failed to obtain any satisfactory material. The first clear and useful evidence of the existence of a German sabotage service resulted from a report from Cairo in April 1940 when Francis ARKOSSY was arrested in Alexandria with thirty time-clocks and thirty incendiary bombs which had been given to him at the German

Consulate in Genoa. Here again great difficulty was experienced in obtaining details and in spite of repeated requests samples of the equipment did not reach London until May 1941. In the next case which occurred when, as mentioned above, the saboteur Obed and his party arrived in Eire, although descriptions were received immediately, the equipment was retained by reason of the neutrality of Eire. The first equipment actually received in London was that brought from Lisbon by the agent [...] in March 1941 and consisted of time-clocks and detonators concealed in articles such as soap, torches and a delay-mechanism, a micro-incendiary disguised as a fountain pen spinal in a leather case. In September 1941 information was received from S.I.M.E. concerning the attempted assassination of the British Ambassador at Istanbul and Turkish diagrams of the delay-mechanism used showed it to be identical with that of ARKOSSY and [...] thus proving that the German Secret Service was concerned in the attempt. From time to time further samples of German equipment came to hand and in July 1942 B.1.C. considered that they had sufficient information to justify the publication of a booklet "Enemy Sabotage Equipment (Technical)" (vide Bibliography No. 25).

The technical details of the various types of equipment are too voluminous to be summarised here and will be found in the numerous papers on the subject distributed by B.1.C. during the war (vide S.F.50-24-44 (31) and Supplementary Files). An important feature was the series of clockwork fuses labelled by Lord Rothschild Mark I, II, III, IV, V and VI.

Until the landing on the Continent gave access to a number of sabotage dumps the largest sources of new types of German sabotage equipment were double-cross organisations in Gibraltar and Turkey, the latter being under Turkish control but operated in close liaison with our organisation in the Middle East. The Mark V and Mark VI clockwork delays were obtained from Gibraltar and Turkey respectively and from nowhere else. These types were all expensive to manufacture and were only used by the Germans for important operations. This fact by itself is, therefore, evidence of the value of the two double-cross networks. Incidentally they furnished useful information of errors made by the Germans in points of detail. For instance, in one case some camouflaged equipment had a printed label with an address in the German style "57-56 Chancery Lane" instead of "56-57 Chancery Lane".

At the beginning of the North African campaign it was learnt that German saboteurs were supplied almost exclusively with captured S.O.E. equipment and from 1942 onwards this fact was a source of constant trouble. Attempts were made to persuade S.O.E. to give B.1.C. full details as soon as there was reason to believe that any particular item had been compromised, but it was some time before arrangements with this end in view worked satisfactorily. It sometimes happened that the first intimation that an item had been compromised was received as the result of the interrogation of a captured saboteur. On one occasion a certain item of equipment had only been used in one undertaking which was believed to have been successful until the equipment in question was dropped by the Germans for delivery to the two Norwegian saboteurs in Scotland, who were under control as double agents working for us. This incident thus illustrated not only the value of the Security Service intelligence as a means of furnishing the necessary information to guide the operations of S.O.E., but also the short-sightedness of the

Germans in making use of this equipment in such circumstances. The reason for doing so was that the S.O.E. equipment was simpler and more reliable than the German equipment and large quantities of it fell into German hands through misadventure. One marked disadvantage from our point of view was that if any act of sabotage were committed with S.O.E. equipment by an unknown saboteur, it would be impossible to prove that the perpetrators were German. Liaison between S.O.E. and B.1.C. was fruitful of good results on a number of occasions; for instance it was of assistance in elucidating the facts connected with the alleged attempt to assassinate General Sikorski. S.O.E.'s assistance was of value to B.1.C. because their experts were able to assist B.1.C. with technical advice as well as the supply of dummy equipment for demonstration purposes. They gave the greatest help in analysing incendiary or explosive mixtures found in enemy equipment and in identifying articles suspected or known to be connected with sabotage. They also assisted in delicate minor operations such as emptying, rendering harmless and examining the lump of explosive coal supplied by the Germans to one of the double-cross agents.

By 1941 B.1.C. had become the recognised centre of information about enemy sabotage equipment and when in February 1944 a bomb was found in a case of onions which had arrived from Gibraltar Lord Rothschild was sent for by the Chief Constable through the R.S.L.O. to dismantle it. The bomb consisted of blocks of TNT and plastic explosive, the initiating mechanism being two Mark II delays and primers. Lord Rothschild considered that it was important to secure this bomb intact as several others had previously exploded in cases of oranges and that if secured it would furnish valuable evidence of the operations of the German Secret Service based on Spanish soil. While dismantling the bomb Lord Rothschild dictated details of its structure over a field-telephone to a secretary some distance away so that a record might be preserved in case of accident.

As a consequence of this incident B.1.C. established closer liaison with the bomb disposal department of the War Office and the Admiralty. As a result expert knowledge of methods of neutralising and disposal was obtained; and this made it possible to include disposal instructions in information circulated to security counter-intelligence personnel, a course which seemed advisable even though they were not technically responsible for neutralising equipment. After D Day the chief function of B.1.C. was to act as a central body for the co-ordination and distribution of all information about enemy sabotage. Any equipment found in the field and not recognised was sent back to London for examination. By the end of 1944 the Germans, having run out of S.O.E. equipment, were manufacturing their own, for the most part copying British models such as the Flare, the Clam and the Tyre Burster.

The most important innovation made by the Germans was the use of the high explosive, nipolit. The first actual sample was not obtained until September 1944 when it came to hand through the Turkish double-cross network, camouflaged as a leather belt, but its existence had been known since the winter of 1942 when it had been mentioned by captured enemy saboteurs. During the last stages of the campaign in Western Europe it was found in many different forms including a raincoat, a walking-stick, "Clams", hand-grenades and underwater bombs twenty feet long and six feet in diameter.

Only one important item of Italian sabotage equipment (excluding under-water sabotage equipment) was found during the North African campaign. It was known as the P-Delay, was used by the Germans as well as by the Italians and was said by M.I.10 to be similar to Italian army equipment. Italian incendiary and explosive mixtures normally contained a higher proportion of aluminium than the German or British equivalents.

The interrogation of enemy agents and the employment of double-cross agents were subjects which - as sources of intelligence - received constant attention from B.1.C. while they were necessarily in the hands of other sections, namely B.1.B., Camp 020 and B.1.A. In the case of the Middle East, interrogations under the control of S.I.M.E. were an important source of intelligence about sabotage. M.I.19, the section under the D.M.I., which interrogated enemy prisoners of war was similarly useful. B.1.C. prepared questionnaires for use at these centres with good results. Interrogation reports received from these various sources were analysed and extracted for special files under headings dealing with incendiary mixtures, explosive mixtures, home-made fuses, camouflage and targets as used or designated by the enemy. Case histories of all sabotage agents were also maintained by the section under headings dealing with the life history of the agent, details of recruitment, training, equipment, target, the staff of the enemy organisation and arrangements for despatch of the agent to his destination. These special files and case histories proved useful during the training of counter sabotage personnel as they gave in a concise form information not otherwise available in office files.

Double-cross agents were a profitable source of intelligence. They were employed to obtain information on the types of target of interest to the enemy, methods of attack and samples of new sabotage equipment. During the course of the war three important double-cross sabotage cases were run in this country by B.1.A.; a number in Spain through the D.S.O. Gibraltar under directions from London and the important case already mentioned as run by the Turks while the German effort was directed against Syria. The part of B.1.C. was to collaborate with B.1.A. by supplying technical information and advice in interrogations and in measures to carry out faked acts of sabotage. The double agents were also used to communicate false information to the enemy. From the counter sabotage point of view the use of double-cross agents was most successfully exploited in Spain. The long and detailed story can only be studied satisfactorily in the sectional report, but it may be mentioned that apart from providing samples of new equipment these cases led to the acquisition of considerable information about the organisation and personalities of Abwehrabteilung II and on the possibility of neutralising enemy sabotage attacks on British shipping and targets in Gibraltar harbour. A questionnaire also came into our hands which made it possible to send advice to Gibraltar on possible counter-measures to meet German sabotage activities planned as part of the military operation for an attack on Gibraltar. B.1.C. was responsible for dealing with the London end of the Gibraltar double-cross sabotage cases and because of certain complications which arose, owing to the inter-relations of sabotage and other intelligence, it was decided in December 1943 that B.1.C. should be the focal point for all B Division information from Gibraltar and should be responsible for its distribution to the relevant sections. The Gibraltar double-cross cases were extremely complicated in themselves, as many as fifteen to twenty agents being employed and difficulties also occurred in the relations with Section V of S.I.S. A number of faked acts of sabotage were carried out, including the detonation of 1,000 lbs. of TNT in Gibraltar Bay for which a German saboteur is believed to have been decorated.

The Turkish double-cross case already mentioned was successfully run from the autumn of 1942 to the autumn of 1944 and from the Turkish and our Middle East point of view was a complete success. It was responsible for saturating the sabotage field and preventing a large amount of sabotage material from being used there. In spite of the difficulties arising from Turkish neutrality a considerable amount of new and useful equipment was obtained from the Turks and the British security authorities were able to assist them by supplying accounts of accidental fires and explosions which could be passed off as acts of sabotage by the notional organisation in Syria. In February 1944 a faked act of sabotage was staged near Beirut.

The successful carrying out of faked sabotage in the United Kingdom presents almost insuperable difficulties arising from the risk of injury to innocent persons in the vicinity, with which is connected the difficulty of deciding on the number of people who must be informed of the plan in order to strike a happy medium between allowing the facts to become general knowledge and causing unnecessary enquiries and action by uniformed authorities. Relations with the police through R.S.L.O.s necessitated their being informed; and the question of publicity in the Press was a major difficulty especially in view of the Government ruling that the Press must not be used in deception plans. In spite of all the difficulties faked acts of sabotage were effectively staged on four occasions during the course of the war.

As in other spheres ISOS was an important source of counter sabotage intelligence and covered the whole field including enemy plans both general and specific, the agents and organisation connected with acts of sabotage, information about the equipment used and the enemy organisation in general. It also furnished a valuable cross-check on double-cross work and furnished us with advance information about the despatch of enemy agents.

Shortly after the material was made available it became obvious that it must be studied by an officer with specialist knowledge from the sabotage point of view, in addition to the study from that of general intelligence. It often contained words in plain language code which could only be interpreted in the light of a knowledge of sabotage equipment. For this purpose B.1.C. maintained a card-index of German code names and terms and compiled a glossary of the correct translations of German technical terms and the interpretations of plain language code names which was supplied to G.C. & C.S. and Section V without which it would not have been possible for G.C. & C.S. to interpret much of the material relating to sabotage (vide S.F.50-24-44(31) in Appendix I).

The traffic of Abwehrabteilung II in the Peninsula was the most important from this point of view and was closely studied, but all parts of the Abwehr network contributed to fill in the picture of German sabotage intentions. Miss Clay of B.1.C. was acknowledged (by S.I.S. and G.C. & C.S.) as the expert on the sabotage aspects of ISOS and by her knowledge of the technicalities played an important part in elucidating the texts. As a result of the study devoted to it this traffic helped to disclose the Abwehr plans in Persia and the Middle East generally, in the Balkans, in Italy and in France and in the Low Countries where preparations were made to organise stay-behind networks for sabotage with a view to the Allied landing on the Continent. All this was concerned with material sabotage or, as the Germans phrased it, S-Arbeit. ISOS also furnished information regarding the plans and operations of Abwehrabteilung II in connection with disintegration work and the subsidising and inciting of nationalist elements and minorities - Zersetzung und Insurgierung. Instances of the latter were observed, at the time of the invasion of Jugoslavia, in Southern Russia, the Middle East and in North Africa. Special formations of White Russian, Caucasian, Arab and Indian elements were organised in the Balkans and Southern Russia in preparation for the advance through Egypt and the Caucasus which was checked at Stalingrad and El Alamein. After the serious danger of an invasion of England had passed this aspect of the German organisation was of little more tha academic interest in this country, but it would have been a problem of great importance in the East if the tide had not turned at the end of 1942.

The staff of B.1.C., having been trained in the methods of scientific research, realised perhaps more acutely than others the defects which arose from the fact that, until the formation of the War Room in the spring of 1945, there was no one body which had access to all the fields of intelligence about the German sabotage organisations as part of the general problem of the Abwehr and the Sipo und SD. There was, therefore, no one in a position to utilise material from all these sources in order to compile comprehensive records and maintain them in a form which would serve the purposes of all the workers in these various fields. The staff of Section V, R.I.S., G.C. & C.S. and within the Security Service of B.1 Information, B.1.B., B.1.C., Camp 020 and the L.R.C. could all have contributed, and the special needs of each would have been met more satisfactorily than was the case if this centralised and comprehensive study could have been arranged. This was eventually done in March 1945 by the War Room and especially by WR-E; and the B.1.C. history suggests that if this had been formed earlier in the war, it would have resulted in a considerable saving in manpower, paper and energy and produced results which would have benefited all the Services concerned and especially the G-2 CI Staff in the field during the invasion of Western Europe.

In the early stages of the war our general lack of information about the enemy's organisation made it necessary to examine all possible fields for enemy action and to plan security measures on as thorough a scale as possible in conformity with the requirements of production and other major war interests. As intelligence increased the elaborate nature of the enemy's organisation had a similar effect and counter-measures were planned or attempted accordingly. In retrospect the position may be summed up by saying that the enemy achieved very slight results in his efforts to organise sabotage against the Western Allies where the conditions were generally difficult. Their only substantial successes were scored in Spain where the special local conditions offered certain advantages, but even in Spain British counter-measures, to a great extent, succeeded effectively in reducing the results of their work.

Counter-measures fell under the following headings: (1) physical counter-measures of a security nature; (2) moral counter-measures; (3) the collation and distribution of information; (4) general and special enquiries.

Physical counter-measures included arrangements for guards on British ships in Spanish waters which were initiated by B.1.C. and the elaboration of instructions for security measures for the benefit of everyone concerned with the movement of shipping across the seas. Details of the enemy's sabotage successes and his attempts against British shipping will be found in Appendix II of the sectional history. There can be no doubt that but for the counter-measures initiated by B.1.C. the losses would have been much heavier.

In the United Kingdom the Security Service had been concerned in the general discussions concerning the security of electricity and gas undertakings, while certain sources of water supply of Service interest were declared protected places on the outbreak of war. In the middle of 1941 one of the double-cross agents was asked by the Germans to supply information about the layout and protection of water supplies in this country. At the same time the Bacteriological Warfare Committee of the Cabinet was interested in the subject. In August 1941 Lord Rothschild was instructed to prepare a paper on the general subject for the Home Defence Executive. After some discussion regarding the respective responsibilities of B and D Divisions in the matter, it was decided that B.1.C. should deal with it from the point of view of protection against sabotage. Protracted discussion ensued with all the interests involved, for details of which reference must be made to the sectional history. Among outstanding points which emerged was the fact that if some twenty generating stations in Great Britain could be put out of action simultaneously, the whole war production of England would be completely stopped and consideration was, therefore, given to this and other priority and super-priority undertakings. The question of which parts of an electric generating station were most vulnerable to attack by the small amount of high explosive which a saboteur could carry was the subject of much difference of opinion among the experts. The whole subject was investigated in great detail by B.1.C. with assistance of the R.S.L.O.s. Special precautions were taken in the period before D Day as it was thought the enemy might make more intensive attempts at sabotage with a view to its possible effect on the operation.

Other subjects dealt with in a similar way were the security of explosives, the control of chemicals and the examination of objects dropped from aircraft.

Moral counter-measures took the form of protests and prosecutions in the Gibraltar area. In spite of the penetration of the enemy network by agents and double agents and in spite of elaborate security measures, it was impossible to stop all sabotage directed against Gibraltar and Allied ships in Spanish ports. These measures had the effect of compelling Abwehrabteilung II to alter its methods by placing high explosive bombs in the cargo before loading. This method, although less efficient than the others, was often impossible to prevent and the next counter-measure was to attempt to force the Spanish authorities to take action against the German sabotage organisations in Spain.

This took the form of direct protests by the British Minister in Madrid, direct protests by the Governor of Gibraltar to the Military Governor in Algeciras, protests in Madrid accompanied by memoranda compiled in London and interviews between the Foreign Secretary and the Spanish Ambassador. A number of facts were furnished regarding the sabotage committed and lists of names of agents were given against whom it was considered that the Spanish authorities could take action.

In June 1943 two Spaniards were arrested in Gibraltar and after protracted proceedings were executed in January 1944. Both of them had been working for Abwehrabteilung II. One of the men was employed in H.M. Dockyard in Gibraltar and succeeded in placing a "Clam" underneath a fuel tank. The explosion was successful and considerable damage was done. The other was a Spaniard who was working for a group consisting mainly of young Spanish army officers who, in turn, were working under the directions of Abwehrabteilung II. He was persuaded to accumulate a store of sabotage equipment which was smuggled into Gibraltar in a car.

In connection with counter-measures Lord Rothschild made a number of journeys abroad visiting, besides the U.S.A. as already mentioned, Gibraltar (three times), Cairo, Persia and Italy. The purpose of these journeys was to institute and develop counter-measures in connection with enemy attempts against shipping and to look into the arrangements for running double agents in the Gibraltar area. In the Middle East he dealt with the problems of setting up a counter sabotage network with particular reference to Syria and Iraq and with the establishment of counter measures at the Abadan railway. In Italy he supervised the digging up of stay-behind sabotage dumps and co-operated with S.I.S. in investigation and in running double agents.

After the landing in Normandy he was in charge of counter sabotage for SHAEF, including all work connected with sabotage double-cross cases and the supervision of measures for digging up, clearing and examining the enemy's dumps of material. He was also responsible for the re-organisation of counter sabotage for the 21st Army Group in Belgium and in Germany was in charge of counter sabotage, the interrogation of saboteurs and the control of sabotage cases for the 12th U.S. Army Group.

In addition to the large number of papers for which B.1.C. was responsible (vide S.F.50-24-44(31) and Supplementary Files) numerous lectures were given by Lord Rothschild. The general object in view was to ensure that as much information as possible regarding the methods of the enemy should be given not only to Security Service officers, but to police, military and other officials who might be concerned in taking the necessary counter-measures. Among the many detailed arrangements made B.1.C. was in close touch with the L.R.C. and took steps to provide for the examination of luggage of refugees arriving there. Special arrangements were made for X-raying. Suitable apparatus was installed at the L.R.C. and where necessary articles to be examined were sent to technical laboratories for the purpose. All the numerous types of enemy equipment which came into our hands were photographed and the photographs were given a wide distribution in this country.

Although no case of sabotage by the enemy occurred in the United Kingdom, there were a large number of cases in which sabotage was suspected and enquiries had to be made. Some of these cases were due to malicious damage either by 'disgruntled workmen' or otherwise and some as the result of accident or misadventure. In the conditions of wartime it was necessary that all such matters should be thoroughly sifted because if this was not done such cases were liable to leave in the mind of the public or of the authorities concerned the impression that sabotage was being committed by the enemy without being detected. This effect would obviously be bad for morale and, moreover, it was apt to leave the impression outside the Security Service that sufficient attention was not being paid to the matter. It might also raise doubts in the minds of Security Service officers as to the extent of the activities of the enemy and the efficiency of his sabotage organisation. A further point of some importance which affected all these issues was the natural tendency of insurance companies to attribute all such cases to war damage, i.e. enemy sabotage, unless an enquiry was held to prove the contrary. For all these reasons an important part was played by the competent staff of police officers under Chief Inspector Burt of Scotland Yard which was attached to B.18 (B.1.C.) for the purpose of visiting the scenes of such occurrences and maintaining contact with a large number of enquiries relative to this aspect of the problem.

B.1.C. was also responsible for counter sabotage instruction in preparation for the "Second Front". Between December 1943 and August 1945 thirty-seven officers passed through the section from the armies and navies of Great Britain, the U.S.A. and France. These men were given various periods of instruction and in some cases a week was spent in this office to hear lectures by officers of B.1.C., B.1.B., B.1.A. and B.5. The men also received a week's practical training at S.O.E. and later two or three days' revision and examination in Paris by Lord Rothschild.

In addition to covering the wide field of sabotage, including the investigation of the mechanical and other sabotage equipment of the enemy, in regard to which their technical knowledge in matters of general science and engineering was indispensable, the officers of this section made a study of the German sabotage organisation on the basis of the material available from all sources. They supplemented this by enquiries into possible component elements in a "Fifth Column" here. Finally they filled an important gap in that, but for them, the Security Service had no contact with the general field of scientific enquiry and no means of getting into touch with the right persons or acquiring essential knowledge. In a world dominated by scientific achievement this is a gap which has to be filled.

6. Employment of captured enemy agents who had been turned round with a view to using them to supply the enemy with false information or to carry through deception plans.

The question of running double-agents was first considered in 1938 as a result of consultation with the French Deuxième Bureau, who were using this method. At that time the work was entrusted to Major Sinclair, but few details are now available and it appears that very little progress was made. Early in the war Major Sinclair collaborated in this matter with Major Cowgill of Section V, and one of his cases, that of †RAINBOW, continued to run for several years afterwards.

It may be noted that the system of giving pseudonyms to this type of agent, which was also followed by the Germans, was adopted for obvious security reasons, and the pseudonyms appeared on all ordinary papers connected with such cases.

The first case which led to any really valuable development of the use of double agents was that of †SNOW (the [...] already mentioned), an agent who had been working for S.I.S. In 1938 we had reason to believe that he was working for the Germans, and we learned that he was to received a wireless transmitting set from them. Arrangements were made by which we were able to examine it without his knowledge before he obtained possession of it. After he obtained it he showed the set to us, and it was arranged that he should keep it. Being a British subject he was interned under D.R.18(B) at the beginning of the war, but a little later, after obtaining considerable and important information from him with regard to the Abwehr system of codes employed by them for agents' wireless traffic, Major Robertson decided to attempt to exploit him as a double agent. Incidentally this information about his codes was one of the most important factors which led to the unravelling of their wireless system and the subsequent developments described above under the heading of "ISOS".

During the first year of the war, the fact - as already mentioned - that we had very little knowledge of the German Secret Service and were completely in the dark as to the extent of their espionage network in this country made the business of running a double agent an extremely difficult one, based as it necessarily was on a number of unknown factors which obtruded themselves at every turn. In actual fact - although we did not know it - and were therefore bound to overestimate the enemy's efficiency - no effective German network existed in this country at that time.

---

† RAINBOW - a commercial agent, son of a Portuguese father and German mother, who lived in Germany until 1938 when he came to England to marry a Rumanian girl. In this country he made friends with a certain Gunther SCHUTZ, a commercial spy for Germany. In January 1940 an approach was made through SCHUTZ to recruit him for the German Secret Service. He became afraid and reported the matter to the police with the result that the British Secret Service recruited him instead, and he was duly despatched to Antwerp to make contact with SCHUTZ. His meeting was successful and he was established as a double agent.
† SNOW - a Welsh electrical engineer employed before the war by S.I.S. to supply information obtained during his business visits to Germany. SNOW independently made contact with the German Secret Service and, to all intents and purposes, acted henceforth as a straight German agent in England. Some months afterwards he admitted this association, but no action was taken and he continued his career unmolested until the outbreak of war when he was taken into custody on 4.9.39. In the previous January he had received a radio transmitter from the Germans and had handed this over to the British authorities. By means of this radio SNOW was now induced to contact the German Secret Service and a personal meeting was arranged for him in Holland. This meeting, which duly took place, resulted in the supply to G.C & C.S. of information of the greatest possible value to the future history of the war. SNOW's subsequent career continued to be one of drama and double-crossing in the period in which his services were used.

The obverse of these facts presented a problem for the Germans, as after the fall of France they were as entirely cut off from England as we were from the Continent. They had no satisfactory means of obtaining intelligence and the problem of introducing their agents into this country presented serious difficulties. In the autumn of 1940 they made various attempts to introduce agents by small boats or submarines and by parachuting them, as has been described above and in "The German Secret Service, August 1942" (vide Bibliography No. 33). Their object at this time was to obtain intelligence for purposes directly connected with the invasion of this country. Under the circumstances two courses were open to us: one was to treat it as a simple security problem and to have every agent we could lay hands on apprehended and executed; the other was to employ some at least of those caught as double agents and to let the Germans think that they were still at large and working for them.

The second course was adopted because by that time some of the many advantages of the double agent system had become apparent.

It will be convenient not to attempt to describe the system as it gradually developed - that is a very long story and is described in detail in the sectional report of B.1.A. - but to indicate in brief outline the eventual developments in B.1.A., the objects aimed at and achieved by the section and the methods by which its success was obtained.

The section was under a Directorate composed of Major (afterwards Lt.-Colonel) Robertson, Major Masterman and Mr. Marriott, which decided all matters of policy and dealt with relations with the operational and intelligence staffs of the fighting services and with other departments. An important part in these relations and the conduct of the whole double agent system was played by the Twenty Committee, of which Major Masterman was Chairman, Mr. Marriott Secretary and Major Robertson the Security Service representative. The Committee also included representatives of D.M.I., D.N.I., A.C.A.S.(I), S.I.S., Home Forces, C.C.O. (Lord Louis Mountbatten), SHAEF, L.C.S. (Colonel Bevan, responsible for working out cover plans in conjunction with operational planning) and the Home Defence Executive (Sir Findlater Stewart).

In the early stages two major problems presented themselves. One arose out of the case of the agent SNOW and was due to the fact that the Germans expected him to produce two daily weather reports. The problem was solved by obtaining the consent of the Air Ministry through Air Commodore Boyle, then Director of Intelligence, Air Ministry, with whom Major Robertson had been in touch for some time for the purpose of exchanging information about questions asked of this agent by the enemy. The other difficulty was a more serious one and arose out of the question whether accurate information should be transmitted to the Germans through their agents under our control about the bombing of British cities. The responsibility for deciding that attempts should be made to mislead them by giving false information about the bombing of British cities which might have the consequence of diverting their bombers to other cities or places was taken by Sir Findlater Stewart of the Home Defence Executive. These two cases will serve as an illustration of the type of problem with which the Twenty Committee had to deal.

The scope of B.1.A. and the Twenty Committee was, however, much wider than this implies and as the double agent system developed it became clear that it could be used for the following specific purposes:-

(1) <u>To control the German Intelligence system in this country</u>. This was an end in itself because we felt that if we provided a reasonably satisfactory reporting system from this country the Germans would be satisfied and would not make excessive efforts to establish other agents. Naturally it was better for us to know what was being reported from this country than not to know. Even if a good deal of true information had to be given, we did at least know what information the Germans had and what they had not. Furthermore, we could not enjoy the other benefits on the deception side unless we had a fairly complete control of the German Intelligence system.

(2) <u>For the apprehending of other spies.</u> This was a primary object of the system, but it became less and less important because, while ISOS, the S.C.O.s, the L.R.C. and Camp 020 were uncovering new agents as they arrived, the Abwehr showed signs of being satisfied with the intelligence they were receiving from those agents working under our control.

(3) <u>Code and cipher work</u>. Apart form the original 'break' through the use of SNOW's traffic already mentioned, the traffic of some of our later agents was found to be of great assistance to G.C. & C.S. in reading messages over an important part of the widespread Abwehr network. G.C. & C.S. said on one occasion that †GARBO's new cipher had saved them nearly six months' work, and some agents were kept going, e.g. †TREASURE, merely to act as a crib to G.C. & C.S., after their value as agents had otherwise ceased.

(4) <u>Assistance to Censorship</u>. Information provided by letter-writing double agents in the form of cover addresses in neutral countries and types of secret ink used by enemy agents were communicated to Censorship, thus enabling them to keep in touch with German secret ink technique and developments, to discover the best re-agents and to put on the Watch Lists all over the world the addresses thus obtained. One important indirect consequence of this was to enable the U.S.A. authorities to obtain an insight into and watch over the activities of enemy agents in the Western Hemisphere.

(5) <u>To gain evidence of enemy intentions</u>. The questionnaires and individual questions given to agents gradually built up a very complete picture of what

---

† GARBO - a Catalan industrialist, equally hostile to Communism and Fascism, who induced the German Secret Service in the Iberian Peninsula to accept him as an agent operating from England. His purpose in so doing was to enhance his value to the British Secret Service who had hitherto refused to employ him. In this objective he succeeded, and in April 1942 he was brought to England where his subsequent career as a double agent became a classic of brilliance and ingenuity.
† TREASURE - a French citizen of Russian origin, an intelligent but temperamental woman, taught by the German Secret Service to receive instructions by radio but to communicate with them by secret writing. Later she succeeded in obtaining a transmitter of her own.

the Germans wanted to know and therefore what their operational intentions were. For example, when their questions about this country shifted from anti-invasion defence in South-East England to the location of food dumps and kindred subjects, we were able to suggest to appropriate authorities that German strategy no longer envisaged an invasion but was busy with the thoughts of a more long drawn-out war of attrition based on a submarine warfare and an attack on our supply lines.

(6) To gain knowledge of the personalities and methods of the German Intelligence Services, particularly of the Abwehr. This is self-explanatory.

(7) To prevent enemy sabotage by controlling their saboteurs and thus securing knowledge of their methods and equipment. One of the most remarkable aspects of the generally low standard of efficiency in the Abwehr during the war was the ineffectiveness, broadly speaking, of their sabotage in this country (the work of Abwehrabteilung II). We were satisfied that apart from the sabotage carried out under our control the Abwehr achieved practically nothing, certainly nothing of any importance. The most important incidents were three which were effected through †MUTT and JEFF (which were duly publicised in the press) and a fourth by †ZIGZAG, which was important as it supplied us with knowledge which made it possible to take precautions against other attempts on the same lines, i.e. by placing explosives contained in a piece of coal on board a ship (in this case the s.s. "City of Lancaster"). The Germans dropped special sabotage equipment for the purposes of these incidents staged under our control and the fact that most of it proved to be captured S.O.E. material indicated that they regarded it as superior to their own at that time.

(8) To give misinformation to the enemy; in other words to take part in deception. Further details on this subject are given below.

These eight points cover the aims and objects of the work of B.1.A. as they gradually developed in the light of experience and the changing circumstances of the war. The

---

† MUTT and JEFF - MUTT, a ladies' hairdresser, son of a [...] father and British mother, born in London and consequently possessing British nationality. He spoke English, German and [...] fluently; was intelligent. unsubtle and impetuous. He arrived with JEFF.
[...] ostensibly to join the free[...] forces in this country, but covertly on a [...]. He and JEFF handed themselves over to the authorities upon arrival, and MUTT thereafter under supervision operated a radio transmitter, with which he had been equipped by the Germans, and was successfully established as a double agent. JEFF proved less tractable and was only used in support of MUTT, for most of the time being detained in the Isle of Man and at Stafford Gaol and Dartmoor.
† ZIGZAG - a British criminal with a long pre-war police record who was in prison in Jersey for safe-blowing and other activities. When the Germans took over the island in 1940 he offered his services with intent to escape. He was duly recruited for the German Secret Service and received instruction in sabotage and radio transmission. In December 1942 he was dropped by parachute in England, and immediately reported his story to the authorities. He agreed to act as a double agent and was successful in establishing radio contact with the enemy. He made several journeys abroad to meet members of the German Secret Service both on German and neutral territory, and was apparently much respected and trusted by them.

original - and fundamental - idea and the basic policy which throughout governed all the rest was to control the German Intelligence agents in this country in such a manner as to satisfy the Abwehr and thus to facilitate means of preventing them from establishing other agents not under our control both by making it appear to be unnecessary and by apprehending those who arrived. These two primary objectives were the complementary parts of a whole; and governed the policy of the Security Service in combating the efforts of the Abwehr as conceived by Captain Liddell and carried out by B Division under his direction.

In order to achieve these objectives B.1.A. controlled a team of agents - the number varied with circumstances - including some who were captured and others who presented themselves to us. This team was first built up at the end of 1940 and during 1941 consisted of about twenty-five members. These twenty-five agents were controlled by case officers, the number of whom ordinarily did not exceed five. Each case officer was responsible for not more than one or two important agents and others who were quiescent or of minor importance. The case officers were responsible for the preparation of the agent's wireless communication with the Abwehr and for the well-being and care of each agent and all matters connected with him.

This was not a simple matter; on the one hand agents' traffic had to be run not as that of individuals, but in accordance with plans and general conceptions co-ordinated by the directorate of the section. On the other hand extensive administrative arrangements were necessary; for instance a single wireless agent, if of enemy origin, e.g. a parachutist, needed a complete establishment of his own, a house or flat, a house-keeper to run the establishment, a wireless operator and at least two guards. His actual living conditions had to be very carefully arranged so that he should not attract attention and comment in the district where he lived. The administrative problem included all arrangements for the control of the agents and their establishment, negotiations with the police, with the Registrar-General, with Food Control Officers, and so forth. In the early days the situation was complicated by the fact that B.1.A. had no means of knowing whether there were other, and if so how many, uncontrolled agents whose reports to the Abwehr might contradict those arranged by us, or otherwise complicate the position of each individual agent under control. To meet these difficulties the principle laid down and followed was to instruct each case officer that he must, as far as possible, lead the life of each important agent; steep himself in the style and thoughts of the agent; make a careful psychological study of him and introduce into his messages every sort of confirmatory detail which might convince the Germans that the agent was free and working honestly for them. If, for instance, the Germans required a report on an aerodrome, the agent himself or an officer specially detailed for the purpose was sent to that aerodrome to make a report, and such visits were always made on the assumption that the visitor was in fact a spy who would risk his neck if he were caught asking questions or finding his way into any place or area to which admission was not open or in which his presence would attract the attention of the authorities concerned. Another important point which required close attention was the necessity of arranging for suitable answers to personal questions relating to the agents. When they were satisfactorily given they often proved to be a means of convincing the Germans that the agent was not under control. (An important instance of this is proved by the statement of Dr. Friedrich Karl PRAETORIUS (P.F.602299) on the subject of the double agent known to us as †TATE).

It is important to understand the methods followed by B.1.A. in achieving the general objects outlined in the eight sub-headings above. This question of methods had two aspects arising out of the fact that B.1.A. was dealing through these agents and their employers in the Abwehr with the German General Staff (Oberkommando der Wehrmacht) on the one hand, and with the authorities responsible for British operations on the other. The object of the Abwehr, acting under the general control of the Oberkommando der Wehrmacht, was to obtain intelligence through the secret agents. The more limited counter espionage - or Security Service - object was to prevent them from doing so and the British authorities in question were pursuing a wider objective, i.e. to use the B.1.A. agents for the purpose of deceiving the enemy - in conjunction with larger deception plans - about major military plans and operations.

An important point is that the agents in question were German agents and not agents employed by our own organisations, except in the case of S.I.S. and S.O.E. agents on the Continent who had become "blown". In this last case the main object was to give the agent a chance to get away, and they played a minor part in the general scheme. The essential part was played by four types of agent of whom the best was that which on being approached by the Germans immediately reported the fact to a British authority. One of the best examples of this was †TRICYCLE. Another type consisted of those who arrived in this country after being despatched on a mission by the Germans and gave themselves up immediately on arrival. A third consisted of those who were genuine German agents, and after being captured were induced to work for us. Important results were also achieved by grafting real or notional sub-agents on to another agent. There were cases where the Germans appeared to dangle an agent in front of us, but these were, for obvious reasons, regarded as unsuitable.

A serious difficulty which presented itself to the Germans, because of the fact that they had no adequate organisation in this country at the beginning of the war, was that involved in the problem of making payments to agents after they arrived here. Their difficulties in arranging for payments assisted us in detecting the agents and also enabled us to realise the inadequacy of their organisation here. Agents under our control obviously required considerable sums to enable them to carry on if they survived for any length of

---

† TATE - a Dane of German parentage who arrive in this country by parachute of 19.9.40. on an espionage mission. He confessed and agreed to act as a double agent, establishing contact by radio transmitter with the enemy in October 1940. He became a most successful and trusted agent and was instrumental in securing large sums of money from the German Secret Service. He held the long-distance record of all double agents for radio transmission, which he maintained from October 1940 until the fall of Hamburg in May 1945.
† TRICYCLE - a Yugoslav of good family, educated in France and Germany. Due to his social connections he became a figure of interest to the German Embassy in Belgrade, members of which considered that his entree to British social circles might prove of espionage value to them. TRICYCLE reported these developments to the British representative in Belgrade, and it was agreed that he would encourage the Germans in their aspirations. At the Germans' behest he came to England on 20.12.40., was established successfully as a double agent and thereafter organised an espionage network of his own on behalf of the Allies.

time, and an important point in dealing with an agent was to arrange for him to agitate for money at frequent intervals. One such agent, TATE, was paid by means of a plan evolved by B.1.A. known as plan "Midas", by which having invented a wealthy but chicken-hearted Jew who required money in his name in dollars in New York, for which purpose he was prepared to pay over sterling in this country, the Germans were persuaded to pay out the dollars in New York, while B.1.A. on behalf of the imaginary Jew went through the motions of handing over the sterling to TATE in this country. By a similar plan, known as plan "Dream", the Germans were persuaded to pay pesetas to nominees in Madrid, in return for which certain Spanish fruit merchants paid sterling to an important self-made double agent, GARBO, who had reported to the British authorities that he had successfully provoked the Germans into recruiting him and had been brought to this country by us to facilitate their designs - and ours. In all, between 1940 and the spring of 1945 the Germans paid about £85,000 to the B.1.A. for running their agents under our control. This fact alone is some indication of the quantity of the material which had to be prepared to satisfy the Abwehr that they were receiving value for their money. It was conveyed to them partly by wireless and partly by secret ink letters.

The obvious question suggest itself, whether the Germans swallowed whole everything produced by the B.1.A. team of agents? This question presented itself constantly in the early stages when it could not be answered, but the answer was found eventually in ISOS which provided evidence that the messages of all our controlled agents were transmitted over the Abwehr network, and also that many of the most important deception plans were successful in the sense that the Abwehr officers concerned attached importance to them and treated them as reliable intelligence. (This does not mean that all the messages of all our controlled agents were always reflected on ISOS. All of the agents appeared some time in some form or other and we could, therefore, be reasonable certain that because no others appeared as operating in the United Kingdom, none existed or would come into existence without being known to us). In a number of instances - some of them of the first importance - evidence has been obtained from captured German documents that this intelligence was accepted and acted on by the Oberkommando der Wehrmacht and its subordinate formations in the field and at sea. ISOS thus provided negative evidence in the sense that it was a legitimate inference that any agents not under our control would sooner or later be reflected on ISOS; and apart from the very small number of doubtful cases mentioned under sub-heading (1) ISOS above, no such case ever occurred. There was a further check in that R.S.S. watched receiving stations on the Continent and would have obtained indications if any had been receiving wireless messages in Abwehr or SD procedure from this country. This check again was double-banked by the co-operation between R.S.S. and voluntary interceptors watching for messages emanating from this country. (These checks, of course, would not apply when an agent was replying by methods other than wireless; but even in such cases it was to be expected that his reporting would be reflected in internal messages between Abwehr stations). Additional assurance that there was no German agent in the United Kingdom unknown to us was found in the fact that whenever a new agent came over here he was invariably given a life-line in case of a crisis in the shape of one of the existing agents already under control. Usually money was the difficulty, and there were frequent cases in which the Germans made use of controlled agents as a last resort for the provision of money to any new agent in the event of difficulties.

It must be emphasised that the claim that there were no uncontrolled agents in this country can only be made for the period between the fall of France in 1940 and its liberation in 1944, and it was only towards the end of 1941 that we could feel even a partial assurance that this was the case. Before and after this period there was considerable traffic between Great Britain and the Continent, and under those circumstances no security system, however elaborate, could claim to stop all the holes. During the period 1941-1944, however, when the S.C.O.s and the L.R.C. were functioning at their fullest effectiveness in the circumstances created by the German occupation of Western Europe, it was reasonable to assume that German agents were not getting through undetected; and, as already mentioned, there is the ISOS confirmation of this fact.

This being the position with regard the B.1.A.'s relations with the enemy, it remains to mention their relations with our own authorities, for which purpose the Twenty Committee was the channel.

The Twenty Committee was technically a sub-committee of the W Board, which originally consisted of the three Directors of Intelligence, C.S.S. and Captain Liddell as representative of the Security Service. To these were added Sir Findlater Stewart of the Home Defence Executive and Colonel Bevan of the London Controlling Section (operational cover plans). The W Board was created to co-ordinate the dissemination of false information, but in practice it undertook the responsibility for the control of double agents, exercising that responsibility through the Twenty Committee. The Twenty Committee in turn acted as a clearing ground for information about the agents, approved traffic for them, discussed the policy adopted by B.1.A. in individual cases, passed on intelligence information gained from double agents to the proper quarters and indicated how the agents could best be used for the benefit of the departments concerned.

A cardinal principle never lost sight of by the Security Service was that no information of any kind was ever passed to the Germans by wireless or by letter unless it had the written approval of a competent authority, i.e. of the Intelligence or Operational Staffs of the Services, of the Home Defence Executive or of the Foreign Office. At the same time B.1.A. always maintained the right to veto any information which the Services wished to put over if it was considered by B.1.A. that it might jeopardise the agent concerned.

The position in regard to the civil authorities was particularly difficult, as it was important that the work of the double agents should be known to as few persons as possible. Reference has already been made to Sir Findlater Stewart's acceptance of responsibility in such matters as the reports of the effects of enemy bombing. As early as February 1941 he arranged a meeting of the W Board with the Lord President of the Council, at which the difficulty was discussed. The outcome of this meeting was that the Lord President discussed the matter on the highest level and Sir Findlater Stewart became the authority to whom B.1.A. applied for approval in the same way as they did the Directors of Intelligence in questions affecting the fighting Services.

The crown of the work of B.1.A. in connection with operational planning is to be found in the part played in supporting the military cover plan (Plan Fortitude) which misled the Germans in connection with the operations in France in 1944. Over a considerable period the ISOS traffic had shown that the Abwehr attached the greatest importance to information received from the double agents, especially GARBO and BRUTUS, whose reports were designed to supplement the military deception plans intended to mislead the Germans.

BRUTUS was a Pole who had been head of a secret organisation in France, had been arrested by the Germans, converted by them - as they thought - and allowed to "escape" to England in July 1942. His case presented considerable difficulty on account of the fact that he was a Polish officer and also, among other reasons, because Russo-Polish tension was such that the Foreign Office could not allow us to develop the political side of BRUTUS' mission to this country for fear of awkward repercussions. His circumstances made it difficult to build up a network of sub-agents which the Germans wanted. As a Polish officer holding military appointments he was, however, admirably placed for the transmission of military information and eventually he played an important part in building up our imaginary Order of Battle as part of the grand deception plan for the "Overlord" operation.

An even larger part was played by GARBO, see footnote on page 248. After overcoming the preliminary difficulties, in the course of which he pretended to the Germans that he was in England when he was still in Lisbon, he succeeded in getting himself brought to this country in April 1942. After his arrival here his case was handled by Mr. Harris of B.1.G. under the direction of B.1.A. with whose general policy it had to conform. GARBO is described as working with passionate and quixotic zeal for many hours a day to produce voluminous reports from a network of imaginary or "notional" agents which was eventually composed of no less than twenty-eight members, covering a considerable part of the British Isles with out-stations in North Africa, Canada and Ceylon. The transmission of the numerous reports which resulted involved immense labour to GARBO himself and Mr. Harris. The case was worked out by both of them with extraordinary devotion and skill over a long period. GARBO's reports in his own peculiar style had to be approved by the deception staff, made to conform to the requirements of B.1.A., then rewritten by GARBO and often altered a second time by all three participants before the final form for transmission was agreed upon. Further complications arose from the fact that, because the Germans broke the fundamental rules of the game and put one agent in touch with another, there was always a risk that if they learnt that one of their agents was under our control they might realise that this was the case with all of them and thus the whole B.1.A. network would be lost. Major Masterman has said in the B.1.A. sectional history that the system which was designed to play a part in the grand deception plan for "Overlord" only went through by a narrow margin. In spite of the dangers that the betrayal of one agent would betray the rest, it held together long enough to play its part by contributing to the strategic deception of the enemy on a crucial issue.

In February 1943, acting on a general directive from L.C.S. (London Controlling Section), the staff responsible for deception plans, Home Forces, had begun to construct a false

Order of Battle. It was agreed that the deception plan must combine the reports of our double agents, the necessary W/T traffic purporting to emanate from and concern the bogus formations as well as camouflage and dummies which would deceive the enemy's aerial reconnaissance. By the winter of 1943-1944 this W/T cover was available and the creation of the false Order of Battle began to develop. In broad outline the plan was to create through the medium of the agents two Army Groups, one real (the 21st Army Group) and one notional (the 1st U.S. Army Group or FUSAG). When the 21st Army Group went overseas FUSAG would be left consisting of the U.S. 3rd Army (a real one) and the British 4th Army (a notional one). In the final stage when the U.S. 3rd Army had gone overseas on about D+3, FUSAG would be left with only notional formations, these being eventually the 14th U.S. Army and the 4th British Army. The object of this plan was to induce in the German General Staff the belief that the invasion of Normandy was a diversionary move and that the real attack was to come in the Pas de Calais area. A great mass of detailed information was built up to support this deception plan and it was transmitted to the Germans mainly through BRUTUS and GARBO. A German map of the British Order of Battle as on the 15th May 1944, which was later captured in Italy, showed how completely our imaginary Order of Battle had been accepted. It was largely based on the information supplied by these agents. A recognition booklet captured in France, which had been issued to German field commanders included drawings of our notional divisional signs.

There is an immense documentation to support this thesis in Major Masterman's B.1.A. report and that of Mr. Harries on the GARBO case (vide S.F.50-24-44(23A) and S.F.50-24-44(23B)). An important light was thrown on the whole situation by the Japanese diplomatic messages which came into our hands in great volume. One, dated 9th June, from the Japanese military attache in Berlin to Tokyo said "……..but because one separate Army Group is stationed on the South East coast of Britain, it is expected that plans will be made for this to land in the Calais and Dunkirk areas". The Japanese military attache was kept closely informed of the information available in the Oberkommando der Wehrmacht.

On D+3 GARBO, after a conference with all his agents, sent over a full report which, he requested, might be submitted urgently to the OKW. In this he set out in a concentrated form the Order of Battle in this country, claimed that seventy-five instead of about fifty divisions were in being on D Day and pointed out that no FUSAG formation was taking part in the attack which, he deduced, was a diversionary one to be followed by the real assault in the Pas de Calais area. ISOS messages showed that this, like all the rest of GARBO's reports, was regarded by the Abwehr as of the greatest importance.

Subsequent information, mainly based on captured German documents, has shown that GARBO's information unquestionably influenced the strategy of the German High Command at the time of the landing in Normandy. The evidence shows that Plan Fortitude, the cover operation for the invasion, owed the greater part of its success to the work of BRUTUS and GARBO. The verbatim messages of these two agents, who were "controlled" respectively from Paris and Madrid, were sent on immediately to the RSHA who, in turn, gave them a wide distribution, including the OKW, OKH (Oberkommando des Heeres) and the C. in C. West (Rundstedt). The information in these messages is reflected in the Daily Situation Report of the OKH, a complete set of which for the year 1944 has come into British hands. An examination of this material confirms the opinion that the success of the cover plan was due to the Germans' acceptance of the reports of the controlled agents rather than to the other means of deception which were the complementary part of the grand plan. For instance, the wireless traffic of FUSAG, which was built up alongside that of the 21st Army Group with the object of inducing the Germans to believe in the threat to the Pas de Calais, first came on the air on the 24th April 1944. The agents reported the identity and grouping of these imaginary formations over an extended period continuing well into June. Had the enemy Y Service been responsible for supplying the details about FUSAG, the information about them would normally be expected to follow soon after the opening of this wireless deception network on the 24th April. In fact in most cases reports of the notional divisions appeared in the German Daily Situation Report a few days after they were first mentioned in one of the agents' reports.

GARBO's report on D+3, i.e. the night of 8/9th June above mentioned, was seen and initialled by Jodl on the following morning. Certain passages were underlined by him and it was submitted to Hitler. Lt.-Colonel Fleetwood-Hesketh, who is examining the German material and has supplied the details here mentioned, has suggested that, in his opinion, these events may not be wholly unconnected with the fact that Rundstedt, who had ordered the movement of large and powerful formations from the north towards Normandy on the 8th morning, cancelled this order so as to retain them in the Pas de Calais area on the 10th as a result of "information received", i.e. after GARBO's message had been despatched. Direct evidence is not at present available to justify a statement that Rundstedt's cancellation was propter GARBO, as well as post GARBO, but there are strong grounds for this assumption in view of the circumstantial evidence as outlined above. (Rundstedt, in an interview on the 26th March 1946, placed the responsibility for the decision of the 10th June 1944 on the OKW and the part played by GARBO in influencing this decision has not been finally assessed).

Lt. Colonel Fleetwood Hesketh adds that by various means the notional threat to the Pas de Calais was maintained until about the 10th August and that the strength of the German 15th Army in the north was only diminished by two divisions between D Day and that date. He adds that under interrogation Jodl has stated that he believed in the threat to the Pas de Calais area until the 3rd American Army appeared in the bridgehead, but that the retention of the German 15th Army after that date was due to Hitler's decision. Jodl has described the German strategy which retained these forces in the Pas de Calais area as fatal, although he appears to have no suspicion of the means by which it was induced - the creation through BRUTUS and GARBO of direct and positive intelligence - which the OKH accepted as reliable - of a notional Army Group in the South East of England. It is understood that the Allied Chiefs of Staff also took a view that the German retention of these forces in the north was decisive. Keitel has virtually admitted that the retention in the Pas de Calais area was the result - after a difference of opinion - of the importance attached to Abwehr, i.e. GARBO's information.

After this important success contributing to the defeat of German strategy the B.1.A network of controlled agents played an important part by misleading the Germans in regard to the targets hit by V.1. and V.2. As in the case of the strategic deception B.1.A. were not responsible for the policy or details, but provided the channels through which the desired misinformation could be sent to the enemy. In a complicated situation great skill was employed to induce the enemy to alter the range of these missiles so as to minimise the damage done by them.

One further success was achieved mainly through the veteran agent, TATE, who reported to Hamburg and had been transmitting since October 1940. Towards the end of 1944 the U-boat menace had become more serious. A new invention, the "Schnorkel", enabled U-boats to recharge their batteries without coming to the surface and the only effective counterstroke was the laying of deep minefields. An old "minelaying friend" of TATE's was revived and became the source of information which led the Germans to close thirty-six thousand square miles of the Western Approaches to U-boats. The exact credit balance of this deception cannot be assessed, but on a modest estimate it must have ensured the safety of many of our vessels which would otherwise have run considerable risks in that area, and it is not impossible that it led U-boats into dangerous areas. The Admiralty attached importance to these results.

7. The co-ordination by the Director of B Division of the intelligence and security work leading to the successful countering of the enemy Secret Services.

As mentioned at the beginning of the above account of them, these six sections (part of B.1.B., D.4., B.1.E., Camp 020, B.1.C., and B.1.A.) came to constitute a central organ capable of countering the German Secret Service - as part of the executive machinery of the Crown - by detecting enemy spies and saboteurs, by obtaining intelligence about them and the organisation behind them and by deceiving the German General Staff in regard to strategical plans.

These six sections dealt with different aspects of the general subject, with the cases of individual agents and with the evidence linking the agents with the organisation - the Abwehr and behind it the Oberkommando der Wehrmacht. They were concerned with the investigation of a conspiracy in which the organisation and its agents played their parts; they performed their functions under the law and they subserved the purposes of the great operations of the Fighting Services.

The work of this central organ was supplemented by that of other sections of B Division which played an auxiliary part in obtaining intelligence and to some extent in deception, but mainly in general preventive measures as part of the grand design of denying intelligence to the enemy. The most important of those auxiliary sections were those which were concerned with neutral territories; B.1.B., the Middle East; B.1.G., Spain, Portugal and South America; and B.1.H., Ireland. (The other neutral countries, the most important of which were Switzerland and Sweden, attracted less attention. The sections concerned were in E Division). The remaining sections of B Division also played an important auxiliary part, mainly on the preventive side of the machinery.

C and D Divisions, E Division, the section of F Division which dealt with the Fascist movements and pro-Germans (F.3.), and the D.G.'s staff all played their part mainly on the preventive side (except in the case of the Operations Section, whose functions were connected with the co-ordination of intelligence, minor operations (including Secret Service operations) and deception plans). In view of his position as the head of B Division and its system of intelligence, it fell to Captain Liddell to co-ordinate the work of B Division with that of all the others, subject to the control of the Director General. The co-ordination of the intelligence work of B Division combined with the discharge of its executive responsibilities and the preventive work of the whole organisation led up to a culmination of effort at the critical point in the security arrangements made in connection with the Normandy landing. These arrangements covered the widest possible field and were carefully reviewed and considerably strengthened by Sir Findlater Stewart's Committee which worked out the details for a Cabinet Committee specially set up by the Prime Minister. The most important measure which resulted - the ban on diplomatic communications - is described under B.1.B. below.

All this work which was co-ordinated with the operations of the central organ in B Division was concerned with countering the enemy Secret Services with special reference to the United Kingdom as a potential field of enemy operations and the Allied military, naval and air operations based on it. It was also concerned, less directly, with the same kind of counter-measures in the Middle East, Africa, the Mediterranean, the Atlantic and the Americas; and still less directly with the Far East - mainly, as already mentioned, by furnishing advice and a small number of its trained staff. At the time of, and after, the landing in Normandy the Security Service was in a position to supply personnel - partly derived from B and partly from other divisions - for the staffs employed on counter intelligence and security duties at SHAEF and the headquarters of the Army Groups, and Armies under its control and direction. This became manifestly desirable because officers trained in the Security Service stood out as qualified for the I(B) (or counter intelligence) work in virtue of their thorough grounding and special knowledge. It was recognised as necessary because the I(B) staff could not function with anything like the same degree of efficiency without them. These facts demonstrated - as will appear more clearly from the account of the working of the "War Room" and the G-2 CI staff under SHAEF recorded below - that the work of counter espionage (or counter intelligence) is essentially indivisible and that the staff in the field and the staff at headquarters in London must work in the closest collaboration and that their work must depend - both in its joint and in its several aspects - on the records of the Security Service and on the joint use of intelligence derived from records based on the interrogation of captured agents and on the intercepted communications of the enemy Secret Services. These aspects of the organisational problem were brought to a head by the formation of the War Room and will be further discussed under that heading.

The low quality of the effort made by the Abwehr does not detract from the triumphant success with which B Division built up this system from the chaos of 1940 until it was completely master of the situation at the time of the Normandy landing.

(B) Auxiliary Sections of B Division.

The auxiliary sections of B Division included sections dealing with subjects, neutral territories, liaison security, research and shadowing.

1. Subject Sections
    Neutral and Allied diplomatic representatives (part of B.1.B. Major Blunt)
    Finance and currency enquiries (part of B.1.B. Sir Edward Reid)
    Seamen and the personnel of air lines (B.1.L. Mr. Stopford)
    Industry and Commerce (B.4.B. Mr. Craufurd)
    Special Cases (B.1.C. Lord Rothschild and Mr. Hill)

2. Neutral Territories' Sections
    Middle East (part of B.1.B. Mr Kellar)
    Spain, Portugal and South America (B.1.G. Lt. Colonel Brooman-White)
    Ireland (B.1.H. Mr. C. Liddell)

3. Liaison Security Sections
    Liaison with Censorship (B.3.A. Mr. Bird and B.3.D. Mr. Grogan)
    Liaison with R.S.S. and with the B.B.C. (B.3.B. Mr. Hughes)

4. Security Sections
    Lights and Pigeons (B.3.C. Fl. Lt. Walker)
    Signals Security (B.3.E. Lt. Colonel Sclater)

5. Research Section
    Information Section (B.1. Information Captain Gwyer and Mr. Bird)

6. Shadowing Staff (B.6. Mr. Hunter).

1. Subject Sections.

Neutral and Allied diplomatic representatives (part of B.1.B.). It had long been realised that some of the neutral and Allied diplomatic missions in London were possible sources of leakage to the enemy about important political and military matters and an even more serious danger arose from the possibility that a German agent might be employed in one of these missions; and the event proved that this apprehension was well founded in that the Germans employed agents in the Spanish and Portuguese Embassies during the war. In the early stages the responsibility for dealing with this problem had rested with each country section, but under the re-organisation scheme of 1941 most of the country sections were transferred from B to the newly created E Division. One of the more important country sections remained in B Division, i.e. that dealing with Spain and Portugal and South America. The Czechoslovak country section was in E, but B Division maintained special relations with the officers of the Czech Security Service in London. The Japanese section also remained in B Division and had a special problem to deal with prior to December 1941.

B Division officers felt that it was necessary that the problem of diplomatic missions should be studied as a whole and in March 1941a special section was established for the purpose. Under the re-organisation it became one of the B.1.B. sub-sections under Major Blunt.

The problem of the sub-section originally presented itself as being:-

(a) to collect material which was already available in other places, principally in S.I.S., but which was not reaching us;
(b) to study diplomatic communications to and from London;
(c) to evolve means of controlling neutral and Allied diplomats in this country so that they should be prevented from obtaining and transmitting information likely to be of value of the enemy;
(d) to obtain the fullest possible information about the activities of diplomats by the placing of agents and by other special means.

One of the first results of this under-taking was to emphasise what had long been known, i.e. that there was voluminous material in the possession of S.I.S. which was of great interest to the Security Service but was not being passed to us. The reasons for this were that our interests and responsibilities were not fully understood or appreciated in S.I.S., and that because of its highly secret nature it was wrapped in complicated prohibitions. This material was of three kinds:-

(i) B.J.s, i.e. deciphered diplomatic cables and telegrams;
(ii) Special Material, i.e. the recorded telephone conversations of diplomats in London;
[...]

All three of these sources involved complex and delicate problems which are discussed in the sectional report.

In addition to these various methods of intercepting diplomatic communications steps were taken to obtain agents of the Security Service inside various diplomatic missions. These agents fell under four classes: diplomats, the personal contacts of diplomats, secretaries in missions and servants. During the war certain neutral diplomats were found who were so strongly anti-Fascist and anti-German that they were prepared to work as far as it lay in their power to help the Allied cause. One of the useful functions served by diplomats and their contacts was to assist us in clearing up problems by obtaining information about individuals who for various reasons fell under suspicion.

[...] they were able to furnish not only filled in gaps in our information but served as a check on possible inaccurate information from other sources. The employment of servants was the work of a sub-section of M.S. which is described below.

Some months before D Day when restrictions of all kinds were being imposed on the British public and on foreigners in this country it was realised that the most serious danger of leakage about the intended invasion was through diplomatic channels. By this time B Division were virtually satisfied that the German Secret Service had no serious agents at large in this country, but it was thought quite possible that ambassadors or service attaches might obtain information of vital importance and sent it out of this country without our knowledge. Various suggestions were made to minimise these risks by delaying telegrams or holding up diplomatic bags. It was finally realised that none of these methods would cover more than a small part of the danger and finally on the representations of the Security Service, strongly supported by Sir Findlater Stewart, the Cabinet agreed to a total ban of diplomatic communications of all types from March 15th onwards. After this date no missions in this country, except the American and the Russian, were allowed to send cipher telegrams or uncensored diplomatic bags. These measures, which were effective, were justified not only on the principle that the use of diplomatic cipher was a concession and not a privilege, but from the security point of view by the information which had previously been obtained to show that some of the diplomatic missions constituted a real danger in this sense.

Finance and currency enquiries (part of B.1.B.) This section originated in 1940 as part of B.15, when its function was to provide information about financial and commercial matters generally, and in particular to examine and report on the papers of various suspect internees. When the office was reorganised in 1941 the section developed in a new direction and its functions were as follows:-

(a) the study of the methods by which enemy agents were paid and the carrying out of investigations arising out of such study;

[...]

(c) the provision to B.4.B. of information on banking and commercial matters.

The first of these functions developed as B.1.A. and other B sections obtained an insight into the work and methods of the Abwehr and its agents, particularly through the running of double agents which brought to light the German methods of financing them. The knowledge thus acquired has led to the conclusion that the Germans have used two methods -

(i) the making of remittances through neutral banks and -
(ii) the supply of currency to their agents.

Consequently two methods of routine investigation have been adopted.

Payments made to individuals in this country by order of neutral banks known or believed to be used by the enemy have been investigated. The result has shown that Portuguese banks have been used and arrangements were made to receive periodical lists of remittances after it had been ascertained which of the accounts were actively used by the enemy. Most of the remittances were, as might be expected, of an innocent character. Enquiries disclosed payments made by the Abwehr to B.1.A. double agents, and with possibly one exception (a case which has not been cleared up) the enquiries have in no case led to the detection of a hitherto unknown agent.

Bank of England notes brought into this country by enemy agents have been traced backwards with the result that certain series of notes issued before the war have been discovered to be suspect. For instance, notes drawn from a certain block of a thousand £5 notes at the time of the Munich crisis by a German controlled Dutch bank were traced with certainty to five known German agents, and possibly two others. With the help of the Bank of England a watch was therefore kept for the return to this country of other notes from this block in case other agents might have received them in payment. This process was repeated with numerous other groups of notes. Here again no hitherto unknown enemy agents were detected.

These investigations could have had more positive value of B.1.A. had not in fact controlled the German espionage system in this country. As it was, the negative effect of the evidence tends to confirm the inferences, examined above, as to the completeness of B.1.A. control.

The enquiries made by the section suggest that particulars of recent remittances of Bank of England notes to banks known to have acted for the German Secret Service should have been obtained at, or even before, the outbreak of war, and that a watch for the return of these notes to this country should have been kept.

Other activities of the section supplemented the work of other sections in a valuable way.

His knowledge of banking enabled Sir Edward Reid to render valuable service in the investigation of a variety of problems not only in the positive sense indicated above but also owing to the fact that his expert advice and understanding of the subject enabled the officers of other sections to grasp what could or could not be done in particular cases and to comprehend the size of problems which presented themselves for consideration over a wide and varied field.

Seamen and the personnel of air-lines (B.1.L.). The work of this section was largely of a security nature; its other function being to employ agents among seamen. Its history, which began in 1941 at the suggestion of the Security Executive, makes confusing reading on account of this duality of functions and the uncertainty of aim at different times. The section was never part of the machinery for investigating the activities of the German Secret Service in any concrete form, but it was intended that it should run double agents under the general direction of B.1.A. This was done, however, not by controlling agents of the enemy but by attempting to induce the enemy to recruit the section's own agents.

The section was first started by Lieutenant Jones of the Security Intelligence Centre who reported in April 1941 that at that time nine separate bodies in this country were recruiting seamen agents independently. Mr. Stopford, who took over the section in August 1942, was of opinion that the failure to take account of the implication of the differences between the two types of agent was the cause of many of the section's difficulties.

When Mr. Stopford took over the charter of the section was extended to deal with the personnel of air-lines. He disagreed with the policy followed by his predecessor, under which some three hundred and fifty seamen were at one time employed as agents, and decided to concentrate on a small number.

In so far as the section was responsible for passing deception material to the enemy it was obvious that this side of the work had to be co-ordinated by B.1.A.

In November 1942 the D.N.I. brought the question of the section's functions to a head on account of his misgivings as to the desirability of supplying traffic to the intended double agents who would be in indirect touch with the enemy. As a result three reasons were given for the maintenance of a system of seamen agents by the Security Service:-

(a) to watch other seamen who were exposed to German influence;
(b) to check special sources of information where it concerned the enemy's work among seamen;
(c) to provide a counter espionage network in case special sources, i.e. the interception of the Abwehr wireless, broke down.

It was pointed out that a B.1.L. agent at Lourenco Marques had unearthed an important enemy agent and had been responsible for his arrest. Further, letter smuggling to and from Eire had been largely suppressed as a result of the section's work and a probable enemy agent mentioned on the Abwehr wireless had been apprehended through a B.1.L. agent. The final result of the discussions was that the D.N.I. informed the Director General that he felt that in general the dangers of running seamen agents could be accepted in view of the advantages.

The section also attempted to deal with a variety of problems which included letter smuggling centring round the B.O.A.C. air-lines in Cairo and Lagos which led to improved arrangements for censoring legitimate correspondence; contact with the Japanese in Lisbon; the German use of Spaniards on their lines of communication between the Iberian Peninsula and the Argentine; and suspicious characters and haunts in the Irish Channel and on Irish ships which plied regularly between Eire and Lisbon and only passed through a somewhat perfunctory British control.

<u>Industry and Commerce (B.4.B).</u> Soon after the first world war the Security Service recognised the potentialities of industry and commerce as channels for intelligence under the conditions of a modern war in which the effort of the whole nation is engaged. This was brought out by the results of Lt. Colonel Holt-Wilson's visit to Germany as embodied in his book on the German Police System as applied to Military Security in War (vide Bibliography No. 36). It was further emphasised by the information already mentioned in Chapter III above regarding in employment of German Intelligence officers in the Deutsche Ueberseedienst and similar measures designed to overcome the disabilities imposed on German Intelligence officers by the Treaty of Versailles.

By the time when the outbreak of war occurred in 1939 enquiries had provided good ground for the belief that a mass of detailed information, much of it of military value, was reaching the German Government in Berlin as a result of the ramifications of German industry and commerce throughout the world.

This was effected in three ways:-

(a) Germany's big industrialists, their cartels and other combinations employed their own economic intelligence departments, conspicuous among them being the Reichsbank, the I.G. Farben Industrie A.G. and A.E.G. The wide field covered by these economic intelligence departments involved much that was of interest to the German General Staff which, under the Nazis, developed close co-ordination with the organs of the German Government concerned with trade and industry.

(b) The Abwehr and the RSHA developed the practice of securing the inclusion of their own confidential agents in the foreign organisations of German industrial companies. The companies were forced by the German Government to co-operate in this way, but they did so unwillingly because the exposure of an agent who might not be fully qualified commercially would be liable to prejudice the companies' business. From the point of view of obtaining secret military intelligence it also had a drawback in that foreign representatives of German business were in themselves the objects of some suspicion in other countries.

(c) Agents were recruited locally from the foreign branches of German industrial undertakings through the Foreign Organisation of the NSDAP or otherwise. An important organ of the NSDAP in London before the war was the German Chamber of Commerce which was established by the Party as part of the process of the nazification of Germans abroad and was regarded by them as " a bulwark of the Party".

Counter-measures in time of peace presented virtually insoluble problems in the absence of good information from inside the German organisations. Special difficulties arose from the fact that an agent might be unaware that he was obtaining intelligence for other than commercial purposes. Again, information was not necessarily acquired by German businesses directly from this country. It might be acquired by the German firm through an associated company in a neutral country.

For these reasons the Security Service had felt impelled to attempt to cover as much of the ground as possible before the war; and under the very different conditions of wartime it was necessary to keep the whole field under close and constant review.

B.4.B. (originally B.15) was charged with the duty of dealing with enemy espionage through industry and commerce. The section's duties were defined in Director General's Circular No. D.G.27/41 of 22.9.41. which ran as follows:-

> The function of B.4.B. is the detection and prevention of espionage through industry and commerce and it is particularly concerned with the possibility of espionage through firms who have access, for the purpose of supplying or servicing their goods, to Government Departments, Naval, Military or Air establishments and factories engaged on Government work.
>
> Any case where the possibility of espionage through industrial and commercial concerns is suspected should be referred to B.4.B.
>
> B.4.B. is also available for advice in cases where the commercial and industrial element may be only incidental, and also for purposes of liaison with M.E.W., T.E.D., the Board of Trade and other departments dealing with industrial and commercial matters.
>
> Certain cases where industry and commerce are concerned have been specifically assigned to B.1.C., who will continue to deal with them and matters arising out of them.

This section was in charge of Mr. Craufurd, who was assisted by Mr. Noble and Mr. Hill. By a peculiar but successful arrangement Mr. Hill was responsible in some cases to Mr. Craufurd and in others to Lord Rothschild, who eventually delegated to Mr. Hill the cases which had been assigned to him.

In view of the especial nature of the problems with which they had to cope, the activities of B.4.B. covered a large field and were very largely preventive. They acted on the possibility or suspicion of espionage and did not often obtain conclusive proof of it.

The outbreak of war severed the usual direct lines of communication between this country and Germany. The invasion and occupation of various countries by Germany and the declaration of war on Germany by others diminished the number of indirect lines of communication. It was, however, considered desirable throughout the war to maintain the activities of B.4.B. in view of the indirect lines of communication which remained.

B.4.B. maintained special contacts and exchanged information with the following departments:-

(a) Board of Trade, Companies Department (subsequently merged in the Trading with the Enemy Department). This department inspected companies under the Trading with the Enemy Act, a process whereby the connections of a company from the security point of view could be investigated, under the cover of an enquiry as to trading, more effectively than by the police. B.4.B. would suggest inspections and the Companies Department would usually comply with their request.

The Companies Department, where the controlling interest in the share capital of a company was vested in enemies, made orders vesting this interest in the

Custodian of Enemy Property, thus bringing the company under his control. This process extended over the first years of the war and, when necessary, B.4.B. would suggest that vesting orders should be made.

(b) The Custodian of Enemy Property. This liaison was used for obtaining information as to controlled companies and pointing out where the control should be strengthened.

(c) The Trading with the Enemy Branch, later Trading with the Enemy Department, which dealt with the administration of the Trading with the Enemy Act.

(d) The Ministry of Economic Warfare which dealt with the enforcement of the blockade of enemy countries.

(e) The Department of Overseas Trade, the liaison with which enabled B.4.B., apart from obtaining information, to discourage that department from supporting suspects and undesirables on commercial grounds.

There were two cases during the war in which B.4.B. made enquiries regarding known German agents. One was Hans ARNHEIM, a German Jew, who came to this country as a financial expert advising the subsidiaries of the Wodan Handel Maatschappij, a merchant banking house of Rotterdam. ARNHEIM made a number of contacts with British officers and sent reports to H.W.K.R. von GOERSCHEN, a member of the Abwehr organisation established in Holland in the autumn of 1938. He had been arrested by the French in Tunis and condemned to death in January 1940, but the circumstances necessitated elaborate enquiries into his connections in this country and enquiries about von GOERSCHEN and his contacts here.

The other was Ludwig WARSCHAUER, a German Jew who was interned in 1940 under the general internment order before the true facts about him had been discovered. He was trained by the Germans for economic espionage in Poland and was provided by them with an agency for a German company in London. He denied having worked against this country and there is no evidence to implicate him in doing so.

B.4.B. was concerned with the following:-

(i) Cases concerning the internment of aliens where the interest in the case arose from the individual's business position or connections.

(ii) Advice to D.1., D.2., and D.3. and other sections of the Security Service in questions arising out of the business interests of British firms.

(iii) Advice to C Division in connection with the vetting of candidates from industry and commerce for official posts.

(iv) Advice to D.4. in similar circumstances in connection with exit permits and visas on account of the obvious possibility of leakage from this country to the enemy.

Enquiries over this wide field involved a large volume of work. After they had attained considerable experience of the intricacies of this very large subject, the officers of this section were able to render useful advice to other sections in the Security Service.

Special Cases (B.1.C.). As mentioned in Chapter IV, Part 1 (iii), Mr. Curry arranged early in 1940 for a certain number of special cases to be undertaken by B.1.C. mainly, but not always, on account of Lord Rothschild's technical knowledge and his contacts in scientific circles. The most important of these was the enquiry into the Machine Tool Industry which arose from the initiative taken by Wing Commander Archer in bringing its significance to notice. The enquiries made before and after the outbreak of war into the case of C.W. KUCHENMEISTER, whose internment early in the war was only secured with the greatest difficulty, had made it clear that through him, and possibly others like him, the German authorities had access to a wide field of intelligence about our rearmament. The circumstances were such that KUCHENMEISTER was in a position to inform the German authorities in a great variety of detail of the progress made in rearmament in the period immediately preceding the war; and probably to forecast developments over almost the whole field - aeroplanes, ships, guns, tanks and other weapons and equipment - for the next twelve months or more. He was able to obtain this information not by the employment of secret agents but by the methods of more or less open commercial intelligence; and it was always possible that he might have used his position to suborn British subjects or by underground means to obtain details of secret processes. In any case it was necessary to deny all this open intelligence to the enemy and the need for this became acute when, after the outbreak of war, he attempted to establish a chain of communication by setting up a representative in Dublin as an intermediary for ordinary business correspondence in connection with machine tools between Dublin and this country on the one hand and Dublin and Copenhagen on the other. This attempt was nearly successful because, as already mentioned in Chapter III, he was supported by influential British interests - with an eye only on production - and the Advisory Committee was unwilling to keep him in internment. He was kept in internment and eventually sent to Australia on the basis of the circumstantial evidence of his connection with German authorities, including representatives of the Reichskriegsministerium, the Reichswirtschaftsministerium as well as the local German consul.

Some of Mr. Craufurd's enquiries had indicated that other firms connected with the machine tool industry offered similar opportunities to the enemy as they contained strong German elements. It was also apparent that an even more doubtful situation existed in the case of German interests in the U.S.A. in connection with the armament industry and firms which were supplying the British Services with munitions of war.

When Captain Liddell, Wing Commander Archer and Mr. Curry saw Lt. General Sir Maurice Taylor and Sir Harold Brown at the Ministry of Supply on this subject early in June, the latter adopted the attitude that the needs of production came before everything else and that if the Security Service could not arrange for the internment of Germans and ex-Germans in the industry whom they suspected, the Ministry of Supply would feel free to do business with them. On the 6th June 1940 Mr. Curry thereupon drew up instructions for B.1.C. to examine the whole position and to aim at -

 (a) getting the matter into proper perspective so that it might be dealt with on a high level;

(b) giving a concise and fairly comprehensive picture to the Americans so that they could put Mr. Hoover and the F.B.I. on to it.

An important question was whether the elimination of all the Germans and ex-Germans in the machine tool industry in this country would have the effect of seriously impeding our war effort, and it was argued that it was not a question of production versus security, but of production versus production, because of the risk that the German penetration of the industry might facilitate sabotage and aerial bombing.

The whole question was vigorously taken up and examined by Lord Rothschild and Mr. Hill in the course of a long drawn-out and detailed enquiry. In the first place the distinction has to be drawn between "general purpose" and "special purpose" tools, the former being of no interest from the security point of view. A "special purpose" tool is one constructed to do a particular job, e.g. to make a small component of a plane or a gun. These special purpose tools were very numerous and varied and it was possible by collating the information about a number of them to obtain very varied and comprehensive details about processes, quantities, plans and programmes in regard to an immense variety of instruments and weapons of war. The enquiries showed that members of the office staff of a machine tool firm, service engineers and demonstrators, representatives in contact with customers or with ministries and draughtsmen, provided they possessed technical qualifications, all fell into the category of potentially dangerous persons from the point of view of intelligence and espionage.

Prior to the outbreak of war a very high percentage of the machines needed for the progressive rearmament of that time had to be imported - very few of these from America and reputedly ninety per cent from Germany. The German machine tool industry was then being subsidised by its government with the effect that their prices bore no relation to costs, while this in turn prevented the development of the British machine tool industry by undercutting, prevented American competition and gave Germnay a stranglehold through which she had access to information of the greatest importance. (The fact that an important, perhaps the chief, German motive was to obtain foreign exchange is not to be overlooked).

After KUCHENMEISTER had been safely interned the question remained whether the Germans had any other similar channel for obtaining this type of information. The question presented difficulty and uncertainty in this country and even more so in the U.S.A. and Canada, both of which were playing an important part in supplying instruments of war. The outbreak of war had cut off the chief source of supply to the United Kingdom, i.e. that from Germany, and the production capacity of American manufacturers thereupon increased enormously. It was, therefore, not improbable that the German authorities would arrange to obtain intelligence about this country through the trade in the U.S.A. On the 4th July 1940 we sent a memorandum to the Americans embodying our conclusions on the subject. That these apprehensions were not groundless was shown by a letter written by a German representative of "Eildienst" in New York to a colleague in Lisbon, which gave information partly based on American trade journals but apparently supplemented by details about the machine tool industry, which could only have been obtained through inside contacts in the trade. "Eildienst" was directly connected with the Reichswirtschaftsministerium, but there was nothing to indicate any connection with the Abwehr or the Wehrwirtschaftsstab. Their representatives in Lisbon were, however, believed to be connected with the Abwehr, although this was not clearly established.

In the period between the summer of 1940 and the passing of the Lease Lend Act the following steps were taken by Mr. Hill's sub-section of B.1.C., in conjunction with the Controller of Machine Tools at the Ministry of Supply and with Censorship, to prevent information useful to the enemy reaching the U.S.A.:-

(i) A close scrutiny of letters and cables showed that the orders given by machine tool importers to their American manufacturers could furnish a fairly detailed and accurate picture of the manufacturing programme of this country as well as the chief centres of production. Action was, therefore, taken to prohibit orders from being placed direct by British importers and to provide that they should be placed through the British Purchasing Commission in New York and by an order of 21.12.40. British importers were prevented from disclosing the names and addresses of their customers in the United Kingdom, subject to sufficient detail being given to avoid unnecessary shipping diversions.

(ii) At the time of the severe bombing raids in the autumn and winter of 1940 the Machine Tool Control realised that arrangements made on the original basis for the repair of machine tools damaged by enemy action might involve a risk of the leakage of information of great interest to Germany and special censorship arrangements were made accordingly.

(iii) Arrangements were made to censor the correspondence of aliens in America who were acting as buying representatives of firms in this country. Several of these aliens were Germans and, while they were believed to be refugees, could not always be accepted as above suspicion.

(iv) The technical terms used in cables in connection with machine tools were tested in case they might contain plain language codes, but with negative results.

(v) Eight machine tool companies, in addition to that of KUCHENMEISTER, were placed under the control, under Defence Regulation 53(C), of the Machine Tool Companies' Direction Board and steps were taken to exclude undesirable aliens from the industry. An examination was made into the circumstances of most of the more important companies in this country with negative results.

After the passing of the Lease Lend Act machine tools were obtained through the British Purchasing Commission in New York. An enquiry made by S.I.S. in the U.S.A. showed that the industry in that country had suffered considerable German infiltration, which suggested that this was a possible source of some of the information obtained, as mentioned above, by "Eildienst". During the period between the passing of the Lease Lend Act and the entry of the U.S.A. into the war, it was noticed that machine tool firms in Switzerland were making enquiries for catalogues and descriptive matter from American manufacturers, much of which would be of value to the enemy. Enquiry by the Ministry of Economic Warfare showed that there was no legitimate trade in machine tools between the U.S.A. and Switzerland and very little trade of any kind. Arrangements were, therefore, made for all such letters to be stopped. According to information from British sources German infiltration into the Swiss industry had been effected to a large extent and German agents had been placed in firms whose principals were known to be pro-British.

As soon as America became a belligerent, the more rigid censorship which was enforced greatly diminished the risk of a leakage of information from these sources. Special arrangements were also made for the vetting of American machine tool experts who were then visiting this country on war work.

The result of these elaborate and varied enquiries into the whole of this large subject was to lead to the development of all possible measures to prevent leakage on the lines described above, and the general conclusion suggested by the results was that what had been an open book to the Germans before the war was, to a great extent, closed to them by the internment of KUCHENMEISTER and by the subsequent preventive measures, these measures being more effective after the American entry into the war. While no direct and positive evidence of espionage through these channels was obtained, the necessity for all preventive measures, which could be adopted without an adverse influence on other important interests, especially that of production, was self-evident; and so far as humanly possible that was achieved.

Numerous other enquiries of a miscellaneous nature were made by B.1.C., or by Mr. Hill acting in conjunction with B.1.C. and B.4.B., in a wide variety of cases, into some of which technical or scientific questions entered, while others were purely cases of firms, occupations or trades which appeared to offer facilities to the enemy for obtaining information. Many of them led to preventive measures after the pattern of the machine tool enquiry, but all were on a smaller scale.

Similar matters dealt with by Lord Rothschild included enquiries into circumstances connected with the security of important secrets such as Radar, and scientific investigations generally.

2. Neutral Territories' Sections.

Middle East (part of B.1.B.). Prior to the re-organisation of 1941 the Middle East had been primarily of interest to B Division in connection with Communist intrigues and it followed that Mr. Kellar, the officer dealing with this area, was in B.4.B., one of the Communist sections; and after the re-organisation he remained attached to the same section, which became F.2.B. Both the Director of B Division, Captain Liddell, and the Deputy Director of F Division, Mr. Curry, felt that this position was anomolous as our main Middle East interest arose out of the fact that it was an important centre of military operations and that in connection with those operations the Abwehr was concentrating its attention on the Eastern Mediterranean and the Middle East generally. In the first instance the Director General decided that the specialised section should be transferred from F to E Division where, still under Mr. Kellar, it became a sub-section of E.2.B. Later in the light of further experience he gave instructions that it should be moved to B Division. The reasons for this change were that important information regarding Axis intelligence and Axis intrigues in the Middle East continued to reach B Division and information in the same connection was coming in through the interception of their wireless, but as this was treated as "Most Secret Material" which E Division was not allowed to see, the section was seriously handicapped in its attempt at specialising in current intelligence about Middle Eastern affairs; and B Division continued to be handicapped in dealing with matters in this area and in its relations with the counter espionage and security organisations there by the lack of a section forming part of its own organisation to deal with its most important counter espionage material.

In the meanwhile the counter espionage and security organisations in the Middle East had naturally developed from the small pre-war organisation under which a Defence Security officer as the representative of the Security Service in Cairo sought to fulfil all the functions of the Security Service in Egypt; and maintained relations with the parent body in London and with the British Embassy in Cairo as well as with the various military, naval and air authorities. While the Security organisations in the Middle East had expanded enormously they had to a great extent lost touch with developments in London and during 1940 and 1941 had received little benefit from London's developing experience and knowledge of the Abwehr and its ramifications. There had been no direct personal contact. The general confusion in the Security Service in London during the early stages of the war in part accounts for the failure to provide for close co-ordination with Security Intelligence Middle East (S.I.M.E.) which had developed out of the position of D.S.O. when Brigadier Maunsell, the former D.S.O., had taken over the position of head of S.I.M.E. as a section of the Middle East Intelligence (M.E.I.C.) in the summer of 1939. Another reason for the failure to keep the security organisations in the Middle East and other important centres abreast of our increasing knowledge is to be found in the fact that no part of the organisation in B Division had been made specifically responsible for doing so.

It is not possible to describe here the numerous permutations which took place in the course of the development of S.I.M.E. and the other security organisation known as Combined Intelligence Centre Iraq and Persia (C.I.C.I.). The latter was organisationally a separate body and the definition of the relations between them has always presented difficulty. Their separate existence arose from the fact that during the greater part of the war there have been two commands in the Middle East: Middle East (M.E.F.) in Cairo and Persia and Iraq (P.A.I.C.) with headquarters at Baghdad. C.I.C.I. directed and controlled all the counter espionage and security work in the Persian and Iraq command.

The position inside the Security Service was further complicated by the fact that a section known as Overseas Control in A Division has exercised its normal functions in regard to all overseas security organisations with somewhat loosely defined responsibility mainly concerned with the functions of A Division and D Division, i.e. the organisational and preventive sides of the work.

Various attempts to arrange for Brigadier Maunsell to visit London with a view to associating S.I.M.E. more closely with the counter espionage work of B Division having failed, owing to the constant need for his presence in the Middle East in connection with developments in the military situation, Lt. Colonel Robertson of B.1.A. visited Cairo during March and April 1942. On his return he made a number of recommendations which closely agreed with similar recommendations made nearly a year later by Brigadier White after a visit to Cairo in the beginning of 1943. The difficulties in adopting the recommendations as put forward in 1942 arose largely from the complicated position of S.I.M.E. as part of the military staff of the command in the Middle East and its relations with naval security officers and with the Egyptian police. Brigadier White, in his report, pointed out that its work was considerably hampered by dependence upon military procedure and, in particular, by War Office establishment committees which prevented developments involving an increase of staff even though that increase appeared essential if certain badly needed improvements were to be made in the scope and quality of their work. For this reason Brigadier White recommended that S.I.M.E. should be amalgamated with the Security Service. The Director General, however, decided that in view of the difficulties the decision should be postponed until after the conclusion of hostilities. The difficulties which he foresaw arose out of the assumption of responsibilities outside the three mile limit and outside British territory which would involve adjustment with higher military authorities and with S.I.S.; and out of the fact that amalgamation would involve a substantial addition to the budget of the Security Service.

In spite of these difficulties Brigadier White's visit resulted in substantial improvement as a result of the development, inside the S.I.M.E. organisation, of machinery based on the experience of B Division in this country. Provision for this machinery was partly made by lending officers from B Division and secretarial and registry staff to work in S.I.M.E. In particular arrangements were made to set up a centre on the lines of the L.R.C. to deal with arrivals from enemy occupied territory by deputing Major Haylor, the head of the L.R.C., to Cairo to help in establishing what was known as the Travellers Examination Centre in Aleppo and at other points. Major Stephenson was appointed as a full-time officer to deal with the analysis, checking and use of the ISOS material, the importance of which had already been stressed by Lt. Colonel Robertson. An important reason for this appointment arose from the fact that Section V had been communicating the contents of the ISOS material to S.I.M.E. through their representative in the Middle East in a form in which it was so disguised that it could not be adequately understood. The circumstances were even considered by B Division officers to constitute a danger of misdirection as well as of causing S.I.M.E. to be badly informed about this important source of intelligence directly bearing on their responsibilities. Brigadier White also recommended that an establishment on the lines of Camp 020 should be set up and that all these developments should be centrally co-ordinated by a new group at S.I.M.E. headquarters to be known as B Division as its work was to follow the lines which experience had led B Division to develop in London.

As a result of these recommendations which were adopted S.I.M.E. and later C.I.C.I. were more closely associated with B Division to whom they henceforth looked for expert guidance and assistance.

At the same time, i.e. in March 1943, Mr. Kellar's section was transferred from E Division to B Division and, as part of B.1.B. with access to all the most secret sources of information, his section became qualified to perform the necessary functions of a "country" or "area" section dealing with all aspects of B Division work.

Subsequently visits to Cairo were paid by Lord Rothschild (to instruct S.I.M.E. and C.I.C.I. in counter sabotage technique and recent developments), by major Cayzer (to inspect and advise on port control), by Mr. Clayton (to report on Middle East controls and security measures) and by Mr. Kellar (three visits during the war to deal with B Division interests).

Mr. Kellar's sub-section of B.1.B., being now established on a suitable functional basis, proceeded to develop rapidly in several directions. It established liaison with various government departments, especially the Foreign Office and the Colonial Office; with Section V and Section IX of S.I.S.; arranged for liaison visits to this country by the officers on the staff of S.I.M.E. and C.I.C.I.; and dealt with the numerous internal security problems of the Middle East countries, especially Palestine and the problem created by Jewish-Arab relations. In regard to these internal problems the section did more than establish liaison with the Foreign and Colonial Offices. It came to be recognised not only as the channel for obtaining information from reliable sources but also of being capable of its significance.

An important consequence of Lt. Colonel Robertson's visit had been the development of arrangements for double-agent and deception work on the lines practised by B.1.A. in London. The scope and the extent of the major double-agent work in the Middle East has been governed largely by the operational situation in the Mediterranean theatre of war. This most important task, which has involved co-operation between Section V, Mr. Kellar's section and S.I.M.E., has meant developing and maintaining a number of channels for the purpose of deceiving the enemy in conformity with the plans of "A" Force which was responsible for operational planning to deceive the enemy by a variety of measures, including the notional movement of armoured divisions in the desert war. A number of secondary double-agent channels were also developed with the object of penetrating enemy intelligence organisations operating against the Middle East, including Iraq and Persia from Turkey.

The foundation for the work in Turkey had been laid in January 1941 when S.I.M.E posted an officer to Istanbul for liaison with the Turkish Secret Service, who received instructions to co-operate from the President of Turkey himself. Other representatives of S.I.M.E. were posted to Izmir, Adana and Iskenderum and similar co-operation was developed in Syria and with the French Intelligence Service in the Middle East. In December 1941 S.I.M.E. posted a representative as Defence Security Officer, Syria, who, by confining himself strictly to counter espionage against the enemy, was able to do much to allay French suspicions and to establish friendlier relations with the local Sureté. Since 1942 the Defence Security Officer, Aden, has come directly under S.I.M.E. control as did the D.S.O. Palestine and Transjordan. The geographical area of S.I.M.E.'s territorial expansion was completed by the appointment of D.S.O.s in Cyrenaica, Tripolitania and

Eritrea. As these territories were taken over from then enemy, Defence Security Officers, who had been trained in advance, took over as soon as active operations gave way to more settled conditions.

Information coming in from all the sources thus established was canalised through Mr. Kellar's section as an "area" section of B Division specialising in all intelligence relating to this important group of Allied and neutral territories.

At the time of writing this report no final summary of the work of the Abwehr and of the Sipo und SD has been prepared. The cases of a number of espionage and sabotage agents in this area have been described in the section dealing with the Abwehr in the Balkans, the Middle East and North Africa, and the SD in Turkey and the Middle East in Part 3.A and Part 3.B of the report on these organisations prepared in this office in 1944 (vide Bibliography No. 34). Briefly this information shows how the elaborate German network in Italy, North Africa, the Balkans and South Russia was responsible for despatching and controlling a number of agents and enterprises intended to penetrate our organisations in the Middle East or to commit sabotage. These enterprises included the Sonderverband Felmy which was intended to function as a large-scale independent fighting group capable of operating ahead of the main German armies and in collaboration with dissident minorities in the Middle East. Other important enterprises included the Franz MAYER mission which was established in Persia with a view to developing a fifth column in that country; and the Mammut expedition, a party of three Germans and an Iraqi who were dropped by parachute near Mosul in June 1943 with the object of inciting the Kurdish tribes to active rebellion as well as engaging in espionage and preparing for a second expedition, Mammut II, which was intended to engage in sabotage on a considerable scale. These and numerous individual agents were dealt with by S.I.M.E. and C.I.C.I.

Spain, Portugal and South America (B.1.G.). The section dealing with Spain, Portugal and South America known as B.1.G. first came into existence as a separate section when the Low Countries were overrun in 1940 and it became apparent that enemy intelligence operations against this country were canalised through the Iberian Peninsula to an important extent. The information available in the office on this subject was extremely limited and little had been done before the war apart from a number of enquiries about Spanish Falangists in this country as part of the general "Right Wing" problem. Some aspects of this had come to notice through contacts between B.U.F. officials and Spanish Falangists, but in 1940 the question became more acute in view of the possibility that Spain and Spanish officials would adopt a more or less hostile attitude even if Spain did not come into the war against us.

It was found that S.I.S. was not in a position to render any useful assistance as their knowledge of the Spanish situation and of the organs of the German intelligence which had been established in Spain and Portugal was deficient. One of the first activities of the section was to assist in obtaining particulars of escape routes through Spain and full details of the system of documentation and control in force in the Peninsula with a view to helping to check the stories of individuals escaping from enemy-occupied territory and Spanish seamen arriving here. Close attention was also devoted to the Falange organisation and other Spanish institutions in this country. The preparation of lists of Spaniards to be interned in the event of war with Spain which occupied a great deal of time in 1941 and early 1942 was both an end in itself and a means of developing intelligence.

The outstanding development in this section arose from the enquiry into the case of Miguel Piernavieja del Pozo, who proved to be a Spanish Secret Service agent working for the German Abwehr organisation in the Peninsula. He arrived on the 27th September 1940 and brought £3,500 in notes to be handed to a British subject who was acting as a double agent. This individual was a sub-agent of the agent [...] already mentioned. POZO gave this sub-agent, who was posing to the Germans as a Welsh nationalist, a number of questions covering a wide field and extending far beyond Wales. POZO was kept under observation by B.6., the shadowing staff; H.O.W.s and telephone checks were imposed; contact was established with him in the Athenaeum Court where he was living and in the night club world which he frequented; and events proved that this network covered him very thoroughly. In January 1941 one Alcazar de VELASCO arrived in London with the title of Press Attaché and he proved to be POZO's superior who was himself working for Serrano Suner, the Spanish Foreign Minister. The latter, as we knew from Japanese B.J.s, had promised to pass on to the Japanese Minister in Madrid reports received from Spanish diplomatic representatives abroad. Eventually it was proved that Alcazar was the source of intelligence reports sent by the Japanese Minister in Madrid to Tokyo and that much of it was invented while some of it was based on the reports of another member of the Spanish Embassy who was in fact a double agent controlled by us. These beginnings led to the development of an elaborate counter-espionage network which was very competently and successfully handled by Lt. Colonel Brooman White and the other officers of B.1.G. and afforded good grounds for assurance that the German efforts to obtain intelligence through officials of the Spanish Embassy in London were well covered. Among other consequences of the elaborate Spanish intrigues on behalf of the enemy was the arrest on the 12th February 1942 of a Spanish journalist named Luis CALVO on his arrival at Whitchurch aerodrome from Spain. He was immediately sent to Camp 020, but the delicacy of the sources (the double agent already mentioned, B.J.s, material [...] and our agents in the Embassy) made interrogation difficult. One outcome of this arrest was an incident at the Spanish Embassy when the Duke of Alba examined the contents of all letters received, and this in turn led to difficulties in communication between the German agents among the Spanish officials and Alcazar in Madrid, all the details of which reached B.1.G. through their network of agents.

B.1.G. learnt that the Germans recruited at least five journalists and a press attaché for espionage purposes through Alcazar.

B.1.G. also covered the Portuguese Embassy in London which proved of little interest except for two cases. One of these, de Menezes, came to our knowledge through the intercepted Abwehr wireless messages. He was eventually arrested and confessed, was tried under the Treachery Act and sentenced to death, but the sentence was commuted at the request of the Portuguese Government. At the same time Sir Alexander Cadogan presented to the Portuguese Ambassador a detailed account of the German espionage network operating against this country from Portugal. Faced with the scandal of a German agent employed in their own Embassy the Portuguese Government took action and arrested seventeen German agents, a result out of all proportion to the intrinsic importance of the case of Menezes, whose mission in this country was of a very low grade.

The other case, that of Ernesto Simoes, is an interesting example of the methods developed by the Security Service in the identification and apprehension of enemy agents. The first information about him was also received from the German wireless and he was deliberately allowed to pass through the controls as a test case without informing the S.C.O.s or the L.R.C. examiners. He was employed at an aircraft factory and kept under close observation by putting agents in touch with him. This proved instructive as it illustrated the fact that the routine machinery of the controls could not be a complete safeguard if not aided by inside information and could not be relied upon to disclose the presence of an enemy agent. It also showed, as the result of experiment, the limitations of our own agents when placed in touch with an enemy spy. Simoes was eventually arrested and examined at Camp 020 and supplied information about the German organisation which employed him.

The circumstances of the summer of 1940 had brought to notice the fact that among the staffs of the South American Embassies and Legations in London there were a certain number of individuals who were either Fascist-minded or were inclined to count on a German victory, but it was not until March 1941 that systematic work in enquiring into South Americans in this country was undertaken by B.1.G. as the section responsible for this area. One of the first results was to show that, while the number of South Americans living or carrying on business here was very small, most of these countries were furnished with lavish diplomatic and consular representation. The diplomatic and consular representatives accordingly provided the main interest for B.1.G. in South American affairs. It may be mentioned incidentally that the Foreign Office records of South American Consuls were found to be several years out of date and it was some time before the confusion was cleared up in correspondence with R.S.L.O.s.

Enquires were mainly concerned with individuals suspected of sympathies with the enemy and enemy nationals or suspects in different parts of the world. Other enquiries led to the discovery of irregular transactions in connection with Bank of England notes which received attention on account of the possibility of their being connected with payments to enemy agents. It was proved, however, that this was not the case. Members of the Chilean and Argentine Embassies who were chiefly involved were engaged in smuggling and black bourse transactions.

The strong position of the German industrial connections in many South American countries was one of the principal causes for our interest in that part of the world and, as has been shown in the reports on the Nazi Party in South America (1941) and on the Abwehr organisation (1942 and 1944) (vide Bibliography Nos. 33 and 34), branches of the Abwehr organisation were very active in those countries. The circumstances suggested the possibility that German firms in South America constituted a medium for the development of German industrial intelligence after the war and that this in turn might furnish opportunities for maintaining some part of the German Military Intelligence Service in a covert form.

The employment by the M.S. Section (first in B Division and later on the Director General's staff) of servants as agents in embassies is described under the heading "Director General's Staff" below. An important part of this work concerned the Spanish, Portuguese and South American Embassies and the results were achieved by close co-operation between B.1.G. and Mr. Dickson and Mrs. Gladstone of the M.S. Section. Between June 1941 and June 1944 twenty-six servants were employed as agents in this manner either in the embassies or in the private houses of diplomatic representatives. [...] Some of these were employed for a few weeks and some held their positions for a few months.

Ireland (B.1.H. Mr. C. Liddell). The work of the section was dominated by the political relationship between the British and Eire Governments and the geographical position with special reference to the problem of the border between Eire and Northern Ireland. This border was purely administrative and political. There were no physical barriers and as far as freedom of movement was concerned Ireland was in fact one country. Important factors of the political situation arose from the Agreement of 1938, which terminated the economic war and brought about the withdrawal of British garrisons from Eire ports and then, in virtue of the improved relations, led to an exchange of information on defence plans between the British Government and that of Mr. de Valera. These in turn led, inter alia, to the establishment of the Security Service contact with Colonel Liam Archer. Perhaps the most important political factor was the policy of neutrality qualified by Mr. de Valera's guarantee that his Government would not allow Eire to be used as a base for operations against this country. This guarantee was the only safeguard against a potentially dangerous consequence of the neutrality policy, namely that it might provide the enemy Intelligence Services with a very favourable situation for operating against us on ground which they had had many years to prepare with many facilities for doing do (vide Chapters III and IV above). At the time the guarantee was given it appeared to relate only to military operations, but in practice it was given a wider interpretation which included the possible activities of hostile Intelligence Services. The onus was thus placed on the Eire Government of satisfying the British Government that Eire was not being so used and provided the political justification for the development of the Dublin link (with Colonel Archer) and the putting into force by the Eireann authorities of various security measures which operated in favour of the British. These measures, however, always stopped short of endangering neutrality by the internment of enemy nationals. The Eireann civil and military authorities, hampered as they often were by their political superiors, lack of experience and inadequate means, did try, to the best of their ability, to watch and control the activities of enemy agents and their Eireann sympathisers.

In Northern Ireland the Royal Ulster Constabulary dealt with all enemy aliens without any reference to the Security Service apart from the fact that after 1938 they reported the presence and activities of certain Germans.

At the outbreak of war various controls were gradually established both here and in Eire. It was not until the early summer of 1940 that a trial scrutiny of Irish mail was authorised by the Cabinet Committee on leakage of information, although the Security Service had asked for censorship in September 1939. The Eireann coast-watching service and their service for the interception of illicit wireless, which had been discussed before the war, also did not come into full operation until the summer of 1940, the delay being largely due, as indicated above, to the Irish attitude of self-sufficiency, their desire to act independently and their lack of means, experienced personnel and equipment.

While most of the members of the NSDAP in Dublin, like those in England, left for Germany on the outbreak of war, a small number of Germans from England moved over to Eire a few days before that date. One of these, Werner UNLAND, carried on correspondence in plain language code with an address in Denmark. The Irish section and the Eire Intelligence therefore co-operated in keeping a watch on him until April 1941 when, as a result of his photograph being found in the possession of a German agent named Gunther SCHUTZ who arrived in Eire by parachute, he was interned. Early in 1940 a German, named Ernst Weber DROHL, came to the notice of the Eireann authorities. It transpired much later that his mission was to hand over a sum of money to the I.R.A. and he is believed to have accomplished it. At the time the Eireann authorities were suspicious of his story but could not convict him of anything more serious than "an illegal landing". These cases illustrate the general attitude in Irish political and official circles which rendered the task of the Eireann Military Intelligence and our liaison with Colonel Archer more difficult.

Two events led to a great change in this attitude. The invasion of the Low Countries and the fall of France induced a sudden realisation by the people and the Government of Eire that their country might be invaded; and in May 1940 a German agent named Hermann GOERTZ arrived by parachute with a mission to the I.R.A., a W/T set and 20,000 American dollars, which later were found in the house of an Irish accomplice, named Stephen Carol HELD. The most important single item of this discovery, made on the 23rd May, was that of the papers connected with GOERTZ's mission, which involved plans for a joint German-I.R.A. attack on Northern Ireland and arrangements for establishing secret wireless transmitters. HELD was tried and sentenced to five years' penal servitude, but GOERTZ remained in hiding until November 1941.

On the 15th May 1940 Captain Liddell and Mr. Liddell of the Irish section had a meeting with Colonel Archer, the original purpose being to effect an improvement in the arrangements for the interception of illicit wireless in Eire. Colonel Archer, however, at once stressed the danger of a German airborne landing in Eire to which, he said, very little resistance could be offered. He guaranteed that the "Fifth Column" in Eire would be dealt with, but could give no assurance that all enemy aliens would be interned. He urged that contracts for arms and equipment for Eire placed in this country should be fulfilled and the possibility of Staff talks was discussed. The Security Service officers returned to London and gave an account of this meeting to Lord Hankey, Lord President of the Council. At a further meeting the next day with the Secretary of State for the Dominions, Sir John Maffey, who was present, stated that Mr. de Valera had expressed the same views as had Colonel Archer and that he had brought with him a list of Eire's unfulfilled contracts.

All these circumstances showed the menace to the safety of this country of an Eire incapable of defending her own neutrality and obstinately refusing - until a German invasion should actually take place - to afford to the British forces the facilities necessary to ensure her defences. On the other hand they also showed the value of the good personal relations which had been established between Captain Liddell and Colonel Archer. At the most critical moment these relations provided a friendly and unofficial channel for co-operation between the two countries and were largely responsible for the subsequent despatch of a British Military Mission to Dublin, through which the G.O.C. British Troops in Northern Ireland was able to concert with the Eire Military Command joint plans for defence in the event of a German invasion.

The arrival of five other German agents, in addition to GOERTZ, which was mentioned in Chapter IV above, furnished indications of the Abwehr's pre-invasion plans for espionage, sabotage and for co-operation with the I.R.A. In the summer of 1939 the Eire Government had declared the I.R.A. to be "an unlawful organisation" and at that time and again later in June 1940 had introduced legislation to enable action to be taken against it. The Emergency Powers (Amendment) Act of June 1940 was due to the fear of "Fifth Column" activities and to the discovery of the GOERTZ and HELD (German-I.R.A.) conspiracy. Arrests and internments of I.R.A. leaders and members followed and led to a close and valuable understanding between the Eireann Civic Guard and the Royal Ulster Constabulary, which continued throughout the war and led to the breaking up of the I.R.A. organisation; and thus played an important part in removing the menace of German-I.R.A. collaboration.

During the late summer and autumn of 1940 indications were obtained through Censorship, particularly that of prisoners-of-war mail, that the Germans were attempting to form from prisoners of war an Irish Brigade which, as far as could be learnt, was to accompany the German forces invading Eire and to co-operate with the I.R.A. Collaboration was arranged with S.I.S., M.I.9. and the Censorship; and it was decided that as the information related to possible operations in Ireland its collection and collation was an S.I.S. responsibility in which, however, the Irish section was interested and was able to assist. It proved possible to piece together a fairly complete picture of the extent and development of the German plan.

In March 1941 Captain Liddell arranged for the appointment of an additional officer (Captain Caroe) of the Irish section to act as liaison between the Security Service and the G.O.C., B.T.N.I. in connection with the previously mentioned arrangements for the British Military Mission in Dublin and the Staff talks between the Eireann and British Commands. It was also arranged that he should represent S.I.S. at H.Q., B.T.N.I.

In July 1941 an Eins Luft agent, that is an agent employed to obtain intelligence for the German Air Force, was dropped by parachute in Eire with a mission to make weather reports by wireless and to report on troops and shipping in Northern Ireland. He was an

Irish agricultural labourer named Joseph LENIHAN who had escaped from the Channel Islands and after being captured by the Germans had agreed to work as an agent (as an ultimate means of escape). The aircraft which brought him was not detected either over Eire or Northern Ireland and as an Irishman with a simple story of having been at sea, he aroused no suspicion. After a short time he gave himself up. His case indicated the nature of the existing dangers and led the Irish section to arrange for a special watch by Censorship on the correspondence of all Irishmen on the Continent and in the Channel Islands. Detailed information thus obtained was passed to and circulated by the Eire Intelligence. As a result information was obtained about three Irishmen who were trained by the Germans as agents. This information could not have been obtained in any other way and the cases illustrated the advantages to be gained by the intelligent application of Censorship controls.

In December 1940 the J.I.C. had drawn attention to the dangers of a leakage through the German Legation in Dublin and a special watch was put on to D/F all the out-stations on the wireless network of the German Foreign Office. In May 1941 Mr. Liddell met Colonel Archer in Dublin and discussed the question of wireless transmission from the German Legation in view of the technical and other difficulties which prevented satisfactory solution of the problem of picking up and monitoring them. Mr. Liddell has suggested that there was a failure to visualise the problem as a whole. If so responsibility for it must be shared by everyone concerned, i.e. all those concerned with intelligence and the monitoring of enemy wireless transmissions. It was not until the beginning of 1942, when R.S.S. took over the problem from the Y Unit concerned that a satisfactory solution of the monitoring side of the problem was reached.

(An incidental result of great importance arose from the above-mentioned meeting of May 1941 when Colonel Archer expressed his anxiety about the proposal to apply conscription to Northern Ireland. Captain Liddell brought the facts to the notice of Sir John Anderson, Lord President of the Council, who discussed the matter at a meeting of the Cabinet, after which the proposal for conscription was dropped. Thus at a moment of great political tension the personal link between Captain Liddell and Colonel Archer again provided a friendly and unofficial channel for the transmission of information on a political matter which went far beyond the normal scope of an intelligence liaison).

The problem of the German Legation wireless was a constant source of anxiety and attempts to cope with it were proceeded with during 1941 and 1942. In February 1942 the German battle-ships "Gneisenau" and "Scharnhorst" and the cruiser "Prinz Eugen" escaped up the Channel. Advance weather information was vital to this enterprise and it was said in the Press and elsewhere that this had been transmitted by W/T from the German Legation in Dublin. It is probable that the German admiral acted on information given by aircraft but, as a result of the incident, the Eire Government warned the German Minister that it was known that messages had been sent by W/T from the Legation and that further transmissions would lead to the set being confiscated and might result in the breaking off of diplomatic relations. After this no message was sent by the legation W/T until the set was finally handed over on Christmas Eve 1943 at the request of the Eire Government. The German Foreign Office continued throughout the war to communicate with the Minister by wireless and, although he was most urgently requested to reply by wireless, he never did so. There was, however, always the danger that the German Minister would risk the consequences for the sake of passing on vital operational information in a crisis. The fact that the transmission had been made would be known to us, but it could neither be read nor stopped. This question assumed importance at the time of the Allied landing in Morocco in November 1942 and gave rise to the most anxious consideration of all the relevant problems created by the presence of German, Italian and Japanese diplomatic representatives in Eire, including the question of the effect of stopping and dealing with communications by cable from Eire. In point of fact the German Legation had obtained information about the movements of shipping from Belfast shortly before the landing in North Africa and the information was accurate as far as it went. It related to the Allied operations, but it had been obtained third hand and was not very clear. It was sent to Germany by cable and the German Foreign Office repeatedly asked for further particulars. The Minister, however, was apparently unable to supplement or amplify his original information.

From the beginning of 1943 onwards the contents of the German Foreign Office wireless messages to their Legation in Dublin became known to us and it was clear that so long as the W/T set remained in Dublin, it represented a grave threat to the security of future operations based on this country. The question was the subject of frequent consultation between the Irish section, Captain Liddell, S.I.S., the Foreign Office, the Dominions Office and Sir John Maffey. Early in May 1943 a note on the subject was handed by the Dominions Secretary to the Prime Minister, who directed that the situation should be kept under continuous review, but that a request should not be made to the Irish for the removal of the W/T set at that time. In October 1943, when the Security Executive was given the task of examining the whole security position in the light of "Overlord" - the plans for the invasion of the Continent - the Irish section put forward their view that steps should be taken to obtain its removal apart from any request for the expulsion of the Legation itself. Sir John Maffey thought it probable that the Irish would agree to the suggestion, but that it must be made with the full intention of carrying it through. A refusal by the Irish or by the German Minister might raise the question of Eire's neutrality which it had been British policy not to raise as a direct issue. In November 1943 Mr. Liddell visited Colonel Bryan who had succeeded Colonel Liam Archer in Dublin. During his visit he was invited to stay the night with Lt. General McKenna, the Eire Chief-of-Staff, who, during a long talk, elicited the fact that the W/T set in the German Legation was a source of grave anxiety, because it could give vital information about the generally expected landing on the Continent. General McKenna, who had established the most friendly relations with General Franklyn, G.O.C., B.T.N.I., also valued the good relations which had been established through Captain Liddell and Colonel Archer. Mr. Liddell considered that, though strictly loyal to the interests and policies of his political chiefs, General McKenna was sympathetic to the Allied cause. The General realised that if vital information reached the Germans through the Legation W/T set, it might mean the loss of thousands of lives and that if there should ever be a suspicion that a leakage of information had occurred in this way, the relations between Eire and Britain would, as he said, be put back a hundred years. From information subsequently obtained from the German Foreign Office communications it appeared that shortly after this interview

General McKenna must have suggested to Mr. de Valera that he should take action by demanding that all foreign representatives in Dublin should surrender their wireless transmitting sets and thus prevent the undesirable consequences which, he had learnt, the British authorities were anxious to forestall. In any case Mr. de Valera informed the German Minister that he contemplated making this demand. The whole question was again considered at a meeting at the Dominions Office on the 15th December 1943 when it was learnt that the situation had been complicated by the intervention of the American Minister in Dublin.

While the matter was under discussion in all the interested quarters, two German parachute agents were dropped in Eire on the 19th December and on the 21st Mr. Walshe, Secretary of External Affairs - again the fact was learnt from the German communications - sent for the German Minister, informed him that the British and Americans had learnt of the agents' arrival and that the British representative had seen Mr. de Valera and demanded that the German Legation W/T set should be removed. The two parachutists were Eireann nationals, John Francis O'REILLY and John KENNY, who had been trained by the Sicherheitsdienst of the RSHA. The German Minister complained bitterly to the German Foreign Office about this and begged that no further agents should be sent. The capture of the agents was materially assisted by the Eire Air Observer Corps and by an interesting arrangement, by which the British authorities, without being informed, were put in a position to learn the facts (it was tacitly accepted that they would read the Eire Air Observer Corps wireless); and this arrangement provided a convenient means for Mr. de Valera to implement his promise that he would not allow Eire to be used as a base for operations against the British and, at the same time, enabled him to deny that he was infringing Eireann neutrality by passing information to them.

The removal of the German Legation W/T set was of outstanding importance because it was the most dangerous channel of leakage and the circumstances in which it came about showed the very great value of the Security Service contact with the Eire authorities. There were other directions in which the Irish section took steps to improve security. Throughout the war large numbers of Irish labourers were employed in the United Kingdom in a variety of works connected with the war effort such as at aerodromes and war factories and sometimes in connection with projects of great secrecy. Among the latter were the component parts of "Mulberry" - the now well-known cover name for the artificial harbours intended for use on D Day - on which thousands of Irish workers were employed over a long period. Similarly large numbers of Eireann workers were employed in the dockyards of Londonderry and Belfast on the building and repair of men-of-war. Large numbers of these workers returned frequently and sometimes even daily to their homes in Eire. While it is known that leakages did occur in consequence of this situation, it is also known that for the most part the information obtained by the enemy was of little value and was more often than not incorrect. The situation obviously offered great opportunities to the enemy Intelligence Service had it been efficiently organised in Eire. If they had not found it worth while to collate the mass of casual information available through Irish workers, they could have made use of the opportunity to infiltrate trained agents.

Again Irish merchant ships trading with the Continent provided a potential source of leakage of information and one which it was extremely difficult to control. In March 1941 it was learnt that Irish merchant ships were trading direct to the Iberian Peninsula and Colonel Archer's attention was drawn to the security risk involved especially in view of the fact that Spain and Portugal were important centres of the German espionage organisation, and although he did not reply it was learnt that Irish controls of these ships had been tightened. Information from ISOS showed that in July 1941 the Abwehr were interested in this question and in the possibility of getting a passenger on board one of the ships and steps were taken accordingly. Another potential channel of leakage through Eire arose early in 1941 from the use of Foynes as a port of call for sea and land aircraft then operating between England and Lisbon. As far as possible security measures were taken by arranging for security controls of passengers and mail, and in spite of various complications arrangements for censorship were eventually worked out as well as arrangements for a British visa from the Passport Control Officer in Dublin who was thus able to refer applications to the Irish section of the Security Service. Arrangements were also made for a Security Control Officer to be appointed at Foynes under the immediate direction of the passport Control Officer at Dublin.

In February 1943 ISOS showed that the Abwehr in Lisbon had received a cypher message by the hand of a member of the crew of one of the Irish ships. Enquiries showed that the sender was an Irishman who had been associated with the German agent GOERTZ and wished to profit by his knowledge of the cypher to work for the Germans. S.I.S. succeeded in recruiting the Portuguese intermediary in Lisbon, but this was discovered by the Germans. The whole episode therefore came to nothing, but it illustrated the difficulties of controlling communications between Eire and Lisbon. It also furnished yet another instance of the co-operation of the Irish when Mr. Liddell went to Dublin with an officer of G.C. & C.S. Not only did the Irish render effective and indispensable assistance in reading the cypher, but they voluntarily agreed to allow the messages to run on to enable the British to read them without knowing what they might reveal or what Irish nationals might be compromised. As it turned out the messages did, in fact, indicate that the G.O.C. of the Second Division of the Eire Army, who was well-known to be anti-British and pro-German, had been in touch with GOERTZ before his arrest. It need hardly be said that no allusion was ever made to this by either side. There is no doubt that this co-operation was partly due to Colonel Bryan's enthusiasm as an Intelligence officer and to the Irish cryptographer's zeal; and little doubt that it would not have been countenanced by their political superiors.

The preparations for the landing on the Continent, i.e. the planning of the "Overlord" operation, naturally led to an intensification of all security measures. On the 2nd February 1944 the Prime Minister asked for the opinion of the Chiefs of Staff on the dangers of leakage of information about "Overlord" through the German and Japanese representatives in Dublin, and stated that in his view a demand should be made by the United States and the British separately that "the German and enemy Embassies should be sent away forthwith". He added that "we ought not to be behind when the United States themselves were pressing in a matter of this kind against the hostile gang in Dublin". It is believed that this minute by the Prime Minister was due to a letter from the

American Minister in Dublin to his Government, asking for permission to request the Eire Government to expel the German Legation, having been forwarded by Washington for consideration in London.

The J.I.C. submitted a report on the dangers of leakage through the Axis Legations in Eire and on the pros and cons for expulsion. This was entirely based on a note prepared by Captain Liddell setting out these pros and cons, but clearly indicating that in the view of the Security Service there would be very little, if any, security advantage in the removal of the German Legation whose communications we then controlled. If it were removed it might be replaced at the most critical period by enemy agents with means of communication which it would take time to discover, all the more so as our relations with Eire would be so strained that it was at least doubtful whether we should continue to enjoy the assistance we had hitherto received in matters of this kind. It was eventually decided that an American Note should be presented to the Eire Government and that Sir John Maffey was to inform Mr. de Valera verbally that the British Government had been consulted and concurred. The American Note was presented on the 21st February, and on the 7th March the Eire Minister in Washington replied that it was impossible for the Irish Government to comply with this request.

The presentation of the American Note was regarded with great misgivings by the Security Service, who feared that at a most critical period the intelligence co-operation with the Irish might be seriously prejudiced. Fortunately this did not occur. It is believed that the Irish realised that the move was inspired by the Americans, although it had British support.

On the 9th February 1944, the War Cabinet called for a report on the measures to be adopted to prevent any information about the preparations for "Overlord" passing out of the British Isles. As far as the interests of the Irish section were concerned, this involved measures for the more stringent surveillance of ships and aircraft leaving Great Britain and Ireland and the complete prevention of all Irish contacts with neutral countries. The necessary preparations for the suspension of travel between Great Britain and Ireland were also made. The suspension of travel came into effect on the 15th March 1944, but the effectiveness of this measure was largely stultified by the Service Departments at whose request it had been imposed. They continued to send men on leave to Eire, even when they belonged to well-known units of the Eighth Army which had been brought home to take part in the "Overlord" operation. In view of this the Home Office refused to cancel compassionate leave for civilians to Ireland, with the result that large numbers of persons, some of whom were well-informed, were able to avoid the travel ban. An attempt was made by the Irish section to have this situation reviewed by the Home Defence Executive, but with no success owing to the lack of support by the Service Departments.

On the 15th March the Prime Minister called for proposals for action in connection with the answer he had given in Parliament on the previous day about isolating Southern Ireland from the outer world. Sir Findlater Stewart of the Home Defence Executive was asked to prepare a report on the isolation of Eire, and at his request the Security Service prepared a note in which they pointed out their concern lest drastic measures might antagonise the Irish and terminate their co-operation on intelligence matters at the very time when it was most needed. The report was submitted to the Chiefs of Staff on the 18th March and instructions were given to the Dominions Office to implement the recommendations which included arrangements to charter the nine Irish ships plying between Eire and the Iberian Peninsula, the suspension of the Irish civil air service between Speke and Dublin and the suspension of the right of the Eire Government to send official bags and passengers to Lisbon. After meetings with the representatives of the Eire Government it was agreed that further measures should be taken affecting Ireland. These included the suspension of all public telephone services between Great Britain and Ireland.

Mr. Walshe, Secretary of External Affairs, visited London in connection with these discussions on security measures, and suggested a conference of British, American and Eire security officers for further discussion and to suggest further action where necessary. This meeting took place in Dublin and the discussions covered the whole field, including the supervising of Axis Legations and Axis nationals and persons of pro-Axis sympathies in Eire; German airmen and seamen interned in Eire; neutral legations; watch at the Irish end of Eire/U.K. traffic; Eire censorship; the problem of the leakage of information from Northern Ireland and the intensification of the police watch on the Eire side of the border; the coast-watching service and the Eire Observer Corps; the detection of illicit wireless and the control of authorised Eire Government wireless services.

Close co-operation ensued between the Irish section and the representative of O.S.S. dealing with Irish intelligence. O.S.S. were, not unnaturally, almost entirely dependent on the Security Service for guidance and information about Ireland, and they very readily accepted this position. The British and American officers reported the results of the conference in Dublin to their superiors and to Sir Findlater Stewart of the Home Defence Executive. The result of all these efforts was the most effective and comprehensive series of security measures which could be attained. The details will be found in the section report (vide S.F.50-24-44(36)).

The problems of the Irish section were more self-contained than those of most other parts of the Security Service. They were not only concerned with liaison with the Eire authorities in matters relating to the investigation of the cases of enemy secret agents and therefore of the enemy organisation behind them, but also with enquiries into all kinds of circumstances which gave opportunity to the enemy for obtaining intelligence - through the position of Eire as a neutral country - either in Northern Ireland or in the United Kingdom. It fell to them to suggest, and as far as possible provide for, all the necessary preventive security arrangements. They enjoyed the closest possible collaboration with their opposite number in S.I.S., which enabled both parties to see the problem as a whole. Above all they were in direct contact with the whole machinery of government which was concerned with the questions arising from the fundamentals of the problem, that is to say the geographical position and the neutrality of Eire. This included contact with those responsible for decisions on the highest level of policy. All these factors offered great advantages to officers who were capable of rising to the occasion, of accepting responsibility and of dealing with their problems with imagination tempered by restraint, knowledge and a sense of what was practicable.

3. Liaison Security Sections.

Liaison with Censorship (B.3.A. and B.3.D.). When the Postal and Telegraph Censorship was instituted at the beginning of the war a section in B Division was created to act as a liaison section and to deal with all problems affecting the Security Service in relation to censorship on both the investigation and security sides. This arrangement did not prove satisfactory as the section had no direct contact with the Censorship but worked through M.I.12, and this faulty arrangement was not corrected until April 1941. As already mentioned, during the last war Censorship had proved a fruitful source in the detection of enemy agents by intercepting their communications, but no such case occurred in the second war except the insignificant cases of LAUREYSSENS, described below, and Werner UNLAND in Eire, mentioned elsewhere, and certain important cases of microphotography after America came into the war which will be dealt with later.

Censorship interceptions gave rise, however, to a considerable number of enquiries regarding persons who were brought under suspicion by this means and a certain number of cases of the use of secret ink, not by enemy agents but by persons who for various reasons wished to avoid censorship in their private correspondence. In the early stages, therefore, while censorship was of little direct help in the investigation of the enemy espionage organisation it was yet another factor in the overburdening of the investigation sections and the Registry as a result of the large number of look-ups and miscellaneous enquiries which it necessitated.

The only case of an enemy agent in the United Kingdom detected as a result of Censorship was that of Josef August LAUREYSSENS, a Belgian seaman who wrote letters about shipping to a cover address in Lisbon. The secret ink which he used was detected by Censorship and, according to his own account, he had succeeded in writing seventeen letters in secret ink during the two months he was at large in this country before he was captured.

The Censorship in the Caribbean area played an important part in the detection of German espionage by the Federal Bureau of Investigation in the U.S.A. during the period 1940-1943. The means of communication were by secret ink and by microphotography, the latter of which included a number of reports on economic matters and the American war potential obtained from open publications as well as other sources. Censorship was also successful in disclosing a number of spies in South America.

The Anglo-Soviet-Persian Censorship, which was established in the Middle East, offered facilities - advantage of which was taken by the local Defence Security Officer - to obtain information about couriers crossing the Persian frontier. These couriers were employed by the Abwehr in Turkey to maintain contact with the agents whom they employed in Persia for subversive purposes. The Anglo-Iraqi Censorship also played a part in the uncovering of Iraqi organisations which during 1942/1943 worked for the Germans.

Apart from the individual cases of this kind Censorship played a useful part in complementing the counter espionage work of B Division in that it had a negative value for the purpose of assessing the position as a whole. It also played a positive part by furnishing information about leakages. As in the case of all similar measures its preventive or deterrent effect was obviously of the greatest importance.

Liaison with R.S.S. (B.3.B.). This section, while primarily concerned with liaison with R.S.S., also had other important functions of a security nature. It derived from the section under Captain, later Lt. Colonel Robertson and Lt. Colonel Simpson which, before and soon after the beginning of the war, was concerned with the arrangements for developing the R.S.S. organisation and for maintaining liaison with it as described in Chapters III and IV.

After the decision of the 7th March 1941 by which R.S.S. was placed under the administrative and technical control of S.I.S., B.3.B. was responsible for liaison with R.S.S. in such matters as -

(i) the investigation of reports alleging the existence of illicit wireless transmitters in the United Kingdom whether received from R.S.S. or from other intelligence sources;
(ii) the investigation of cases in which a leakage of information had occurred and the channel of communication with the enemy appeared to be by wireless. These cases frequently arose from statements in B.J.s or the ISOS material and came from various sections of the office as well as from the three Services;
(iii) supplying information to R.S.S. resulting from a study based on information from all available sources of the corresponding German methods of performing the same functions as R.S.S.; and
(iv) furnishing R.S.S. with information obtained by building up a card index or wireless transmitting stations used by S.I.S., S.O.E., B.1.A. and the Allied Governments.

In addition to these the section performed general liaison duties between B Division, especially B.1.A., and R.S.S. as well as between R.S.S. and S.O.E.

The staff of B.3.B. included that of a technical sub-section with wide commitments covering all the directions in which electrical communications affected security work. Experience early in the war brought the realisation that certain cases, which, when dealt with by non-technical personnel, might involve long and expensive investigations, could be almost immediately resolved by officers with technical knowledge. Cases of this type comprised the greater part of the section's work in assisting to cope with the vast number of reports of suspected illicit wireless transmission.

In 1940 Lt. Colonel Simpson produced "Notes on the Detection of Illicit Wireless 1940" (vide Bibliography No. 58) with a view to assisting such enquiries. He explained the problems connected with Ionosphere or Reflected Ray communication and ground rays; and suggested that secret agents would be able to avoid bulky or intricate apparatus and that only low-power would be employed. He said that, assuming an efficient receiving station in Germany, it would be possible to select a suitable wave-length, having regard to range and seasonal conditions, which would give a regular, reliable service. If such a station were to be established in a carefully chosen locality in this country it would very likely not be heard at all at our permanent interception and D/F stations. Such a station could be situated in the centre of a densely populated area or alternatively installed in a small car. He set out detailed instructions for procedure in dealing with investigations in these circumstances.

The technical sub-section was started in 1941 by the appointment of one officer to assist in investigation and to act as a technical adviser to the section. The number of these advisers was eventually increased to four and as time went on the work of the sub-section became more varied and equipment and facilities were added until a great variety of technical work could be undertaken. A laboratory and workshop was set up which enabled a higher standard of technical service to be provided. Besides assisting in the investigation of suspect cases of illicit wireless transmission and assisting in the liaison with R.S.S. for the purpose of directing mobile D/F stations, the technical sub-section had the following duties -

(a) as advisers to other sections on technical matters arising out of their cases;
(b) as experts in the technical examination and testing of captured enemy equipment and -
(c) liaison with other government departments and organisations in security matters in which electrical communications were involved.

It also engaged in research on a limited scale in new types of apparatus and maintained a reserve of specialised equipment.

The function of liaison with R.S.S. impinged on questions of policy which transcended the work of B.3.B. and were the direct concern of the Director and Deputy Director of B Division as playing a vital part in the direction of all the work of the Division in -

(a) obtaining intelligence about the enemy organisation and its agents and -
(b) developing preventive measures.

B.3.B., as the section formally responsible for liaison with R.S.S. and as one of the instruments for the discharge of B Division functions, was concerned in every aspect of the work of R.S.S. and was thus placed in a functionally difficult position. To understand this it is necessary to examine the manner in which R.S.S. functioned.

Reference has been made in Part 1, (iv), A.1. of this chapter in connection with the sub-section of B.1.B. dealing with the ISOS material, to the committee which, after the beginning of 1943, met under the name of the Radio Security Intelligence Conference under the chairmanship of Mr. White, who has recorded the following remarks about it:-

> "The R.S.I.C. was brought into being for the purpose of co-ordinating the somewhat illogical organisation of radio intercept work. Owing to the fact that the Radio Security Section was administered by Section VIII of S.I.S. and that consumers of its product were Section V of S.I.S., B Division of M.I.5. and the Intelligence Section of the R.S.S. itself, the points of view of these three departments were apt to be divergent and it was therefore necessary to agree between them an order of traffic priorities. Besides this it was felt that some formal and regular meetings were required for the purpose of pooling expertise on the subject of the R.S.S. product, and the R.S.I.C. came to be in addition to a "fair-play" committee, a forum for discussion and for planning. For example, at the time of the operation HUSKY, plans were drawn up under the auspices of the R.S.I.C. for traffic priorities in connection with the campaign and movement of equipment etc.
>
> There can be no doubt that the R.S.I.C. proved a very useful safety valve, preventing friction between the technical administrators of the R.S.S. and the several consumer interests. The fact that M.I.5. furnished the Chairman (Mr. White and subsequently Lt. Colonel Robertson) somewhat restored their sense of loss over the fact that the R.S.S., which began the war under M.I.5.'s technical direction, was subsequently handed over to S.I.S. Moreover, the slight rivalry which had developed between the R.I.S. interpretations of the product and those of Section V were able to be ironed out."

From the point of view of B.3.B., which was also that of the Director of B Division, it was maintained that R.S.S. did not take adequate steps to provide security against the establishment of illicit transmitters in this country. Against this point of view R.S.S. maintained that, while they acknowledged the commitment of searching for illicit transmitters in this country, it was virtually impossible to ensure security by elaborating preventive measures in the shape of a watch for all possible transmitters. Their experience proved, however, that more positive results could be obtained by watching the known enemy transmitting stations and picking up any transmitters which answered their calls or communicated with them.

This subject was discussed in a paper prepared by Major Morton Evans of R.S.S. in April 1942 (vide 45a in S.F.50-30-36(I)) in which he explained the organisation of R.S.S. and the technique which enabled it to achieve the great success which made it possible to build up a very full picture of the organisation, firstly of the Abwehr and, secondly, of the Sipo und SD under the RSHA.

In the process of achieving this success R.S.S. had departed from its original charter which was confined to the detection of illicit wireless transmissions within Great Britain. At the time the paper was written R.S.S. had five intercept stations at Barnet, St. Erth, Gilnahirk, Thurso and Hanslope, which provided between them sixty-nine receiving positions. It also had two active overseas units, one at Gibraltar and one in the Middle

East. Gibraltar had six receiving positions and the Middle East fifteen, but some of the latter had to be diverted to local requirements involving investigation by mobile units. In addition to the full-time interceptors at these stations there were, in the United Kingdom, one thousand three hundred voluntary interceptors - in place of the fifty or sixty originally contemplated before the war - a large number of them being highly skilled. The voluntary interceptors were grouped in nine regions, each under a regional officer and about one thousand reports were received from them daily.

Seven Direction-Finding (D/F-ing) stations were available and were situated at St. Erth, Cupar, Thurso, Gilnahirk, Bridgewater, Sandridge and Wymondham and there was a mobile unit section with vans fitted with D/F-ing apparatus for locating more exactly suspect transmitters proved to be in this country by the fixed D/F-ing stations.

In the internal working of R.S.S. a most important part was played by the "Discrimination Section" which was responsible for "the allotment of tasks, the feed-back of general information about time-tables to interceptors and for the general direction of interception". In the case of overseas units directives were sent by the Discrimination Section by telegram to Gibraltar and the Middle East and there was also a liaison with the Royal Canadian Signals and with the U.S. Coastguards and the Federal Bureau of Investigation through an R.S.S. representative in Canada.

Without going into technical details it may be said that R.S.S was able to eliminate - for the purpose of watching for secret agents' transmitters and those of the enemy organisations - all but a certain range of frequencies, but within this range an enormous number of transmissions were taking place daily, the number being probably of the order of a hundred thousand or more. In order to prove that a transmitter was located in this country, the quickest way was to take bearings with radio D/F apparatus and, with the system available, the number of reliable sets of bearings which could be obtained throughout the twenty-four hours was of the order of a hundred. The purpose of the Discrimination Section was to provide for the necessary process of elimination. Having eliminated the unwanted transmitters (such as those of known and authorised or friendly undercover signals) the wanted transmitters were classified and the details were circulated in the form of R.S.S. schedules. These R.S.S. schedules contained the call signs, frequencies, times and other data useful to an interceptor of the transmissions of the enemy organisations.

Further assistance for these purposes was given by Section V.W., afterwards R.I.S. under Major Trevor Roper. This section had access to other sources of intelligence as well as to de-cyphers of R.S.S. traffic and one of its functions was to feed-back to the Discrimination Section all information which had any bearing on the problem of interception as well as being in daily touch with discriminators and receiving details about interception from them. The fusion of these two sources had often produced knowledge which could not have been obtained from either source alone.

R.S.S. had a dual function: firstly, to watch and record the traffic of the enemy organisations, and secondly, to search over a wide field for previously unidentified undercover transmissions with a view to identifying new systems of enemy communications if any such existed and also to uncovering his wireless agents in this country if any were transmitting. This latter was known as "General Search". In the exercise of this dual function they were subject to pressure from those who desired all available resources to be placed on the first objective and those who were interested in the detection of illicit wireless in Great Britain, i.e. those who looked at the matter from the preventive point of view. Major Morton Evans considered that the two functions were complementary and that in practice a fair balance between them was maintained. He based himself on the facts that if all the sets employed on watching the enemy traffic were transferred to "General Search" this would only provide an additional coverage of thirty percent at the cost of losing all the enemy traffic; and that on the other hand, if all the "General Search" receivers were transferred to the watch on traffic, the additional intake would not appreciably add to the efficiency of the services rendered.

He argued that the abandonment of "General Search" would mean that "new wanted transmissions and the many changes which take place daily in the known time-tables could no longer be observed" and in that case the watch on traffic would suffer as well as the interception for preventive purposes. He considered that the only possibility of increasing the preventive measures would be by an increase in the overall size of R.S.S.

It is obvious that this is a point of the highest importance from the point of view of the policy of the Security Service in its attempt at obtaining the fullest possible information about the organisations which it is its function to combat. The machinery however was not under its control and it was not responsible for the necessary financial arrangements for enlarging R.S.S. as these were in the hands of Section VIII of S.I.S. and subject to the general influence of Section V under the control of C.S.S. Ultimately the questions at issue are twofold:

(a) whether to enable it to discharge its responsibilities for counter espionage the Security Service ought to have financial and administrative control over the development of R.S.S. as a most important instrument for the purpose and -

(b) whether, at any given point of time, it is justifiable to develop the preventive side of this work.

Looked at in retrospect it is clear that the general picture of the Abwehr and Sipo und SD organisations obtained through the operations of R.S.S. was sufficiently complete to have rendered any large-scale increase in expenditure on "General Search" unnecessary, but in the earlier stages of the war and in the period before "Overlord" it would always have been difficult to maintain this position or to argue that it was unnecessary to provide for R.S.S. methods of search for unknown enemy wireless agents in this country on a scale more nearly complete than a coverage of a hundred in a hundred thousand.

Posed in this form this question may seem more acute than some others, but it is typical of all the problems of the preventive aspect of the work of the Security Service. Moreover, the difficulties of the subject do not end here as there are other issues than those which directly concerned B Division after 1941. These include, for instance, the coverage by R.S.S. of other than enemy organisations including clandestine Soviet Secret Service and Comintern transmissions. The latter were the concern of Section IX of S.I.S. and F Division and were not dealt with by B.3.B.

This is not the place to discuss possible lines of creative action to find a remedy for these functional maladjustments. It must suffice to record the fact of their existence.

Liaison with the B.B.C. A sub-section of B.3.B. was responsible for liaison with the B.B.C. for security purposes. This involved the vetting of personnel, contact with questions of censorship and with those relating to leakages of information and contact with the B.B.C. monitoring service in connection with the "Haw-Haw" broadcasts and the activities of British renegades. One reason for maintaining this close contact was that it was considered that, while the B.B.C. was not an ideal channel for espionage, it presented certain advantages as a cover for these purposes. It would provide status and a reasonable explanation for what might appear to be an unorthodox mode of life and exceptional opportunities for meeting people "in the know" and for contact with foreign embassies and other official bodies as a means of obtaining accurate and up-to-date information on current events.

The B.B.C., like the Press, accepted the principle of voluntary censorship and responsible members of the British staff were accepted by the Ministry of Information as delegate censors.

In June 1940 Lord Swinton set up a sub-committee of the Security Intelligence Committee to study possible methods of communication between the enemy and his agents in this country through broadcasting by the B.B.C. and the Reichsrundfunkgesellschaft. There was no positive indication that the B.B.C. was ever used in this way.

Verbatim reports and in some cases recordings were made by the B.B.C. monitoring service of broadcasts by persons believed to be British subjects from enemy controlled stations and these were made available for the purposes of investigation and prosecution in cases dealt with by section F.3. and section S.L.B.3.

4. Security Sections.

Lights and Pigeons (B.3.C.). After W Branch was included in the reorganised B Division in 1941 the functions of the former W sections continue to be discharged under Major Frost as A.D.B.3. Apart from the liaison with Censorship and with R.S.S. the other subjects were concentrated in B.3.C. under Flight Lt. Walker. His functions extended beyond "Lights and Pigeons", by which B.3.C. is described in the office organisation chart, and included measures of a preventive kind in connection with suspected codes, the landing of enemy agents by parachute or from the sea as well as a general survey of suspected fifth column activities in the shape of markings on the ground, suspicious pieces of paper and messages, marked maps and markings on telegraph poles.

The need for this work was most acute from the summer of 1940 until about the end of 1941; but much of it continued until the end of the war.

It was in fact developed in many respects and systematised by Flight Lt. Walker under the guidance of the Director of B Division. It was however essentially work of a preventive type and did not involve investigation into the cases of enemy agents or enemy organisations. In brief, B.3.C. inherited from W.7. the function of watching for all forms of communication between the enemy organisations abroad and their agents in this country other than wireless, as well as communications which might have been made between agents landed here for "fifth column" purposes and the invading German forces. This process of watching involved not only elaborate precautionary measures but also detailed enquiries into a large variety of facts and circumstances as they came to notice from time to time. For instance the facts, including data dealing with signs and signals, regarding the working of the "fifth column" were collected from high and responsible Dutch, Polish, Belgian and French officers. (Vide S.F.50-24-44(40C)).

The results of nearly all the work of B.3.C. were entirely negative, but it was none the less essential work and it was essential for two important reasons. Firstly, in the early stages of the war the Security Service had not sufficient positive knowledge of the Abwehr and its agents to be able to ignore numerous suspicious stories as they were reported. Secondly, it was necessary that these stories should be thoroughly tested and examined in order to satisfy not only the Security Service itself but the officers of the fighting services and members of the public who reported them. The volume of these reports was very large and, as Flight Lt. Walker has graphically put it, a certain portion of them (those concerning Lights only) filled files five feet high. The amount of labour involved in sifting this material was enormous and the work of this kind which fell on B.3.C. as well as on other sections of B Division in the early stages of the war played a large part in producing chaos in this Division and in the Registry. This was an inevitable effect of the circumstances when England was awaiting invasion. Something similar had occurred under the far less acute circumstances of the last war; and the second war therefore reinforced the lesson that steps ought always to be taken beforehand to provide machinery to cope with a flood of reports and other material of this kind.

Ultimately the problem became more manageable as the danger of invasion diminished and each aspect of the problem was systematically examined.

Although the Germans and Italians both used pigeons for the purposes of communication and the British services used them for espionage, there is no known case of a pigeon being used by an enemy secret agent in this country. The evidence points to the conclusion that none were in fact used. The possibilities of their use were however carefully examined. These included an examination of the possibility of smuggling birds in through neutral ships, of the possibility of their use in Eire and a study of all the technicalities of the subject, including the use of trained falcons for the interception of enemy pigeons. Reports were received from the Royal Observer Corps of pigeons seen flying out to sea and were examined in detail, a map of England marking each significant report of this kind being maintained.

Although they did not use them in this country the Germans used pigeons for secret intelligence work in France, Belgium, Holland, Norway, Spain, Jugoslavia, Albania, Greece, Bulgaria and in Germany itself. This included their use by stay-behind agents after the Allied landing on the Continent (vide S.F.50-24-44(40A)).

Of all the hundreds of reports about suspected signalling by lights which were examined, none led to any positive result in the shape of the detection of an enemy agent. Numerous cases of this kind were reported by the public to the police, who made enquiries and reported the result to us through the R.S.L.O. when its significance was estimated by B.3.C. Numerous other cases were reported direct to us and the reverse process took place. Some of the reports were very circumstantial, including those from responsible senior officers in the armed forces. Notable among these was the case of the Admiral at Yarmouth in 1941. Elaborate tests which were made by the Security Service gave convincing proof of the extreme fallibility of the judgement of observers when Verey lights and other lights were exhibited to test them. There was no known case of an enemy agent signalling by lights throughout the war (vide S.F.50-24-44(40B)).

Reports regarding the suspected use of codes which reached the Security Service filled six thick files. None of them had anything to do with the enemy Secret Service and most were attributed to cranks, lunatics or hoaxers (vide S.F.50-24-44(40D)).

B.3.C. was also responsible for systematic examination of the circumstances connected with the landing of enemy agents by parachute or from the sea and of all suspicious incidents which might indicate such landings.

In connection with airborne landings of parachute agents close liaison was maintained with Fighter Command and the Royal Observer Corps. This involved the study of any suspicious tracks which might suggest the landing of an enemy agent and the study of day and night "recce" flights which might suggest enemy observation over areas mentioned in deception material.

The duty officer at Fighter Command, on seeing what he considered a suspicious track, at once telephoned the officer of B.3.C., by day or by night, giving the facts and his views on the degree of suspicion. This officer in turn communicated with the R.S.L.O., who arranged for police action according to the circumstances. If the suspicion were red-hot, for instance if squadrons of the German Air Force known to have been connected with agent-dropping were reported, arrangements would be made to check identity cards for a few days, if necessary with the co-operation of the Home Guard and the military authorities.

In nearly every case in which enemy agents arrived by parachute they either gave themselves up on landing or were detected and arrested within a few hours (vide S.F.50-24-44(40E)).

In the same way that this section relied on the Royal Observer Corps in the case of the air they relied on the coastguards for reporting any indications of an agent having been landed by sea. Naval patrol vessels and military units and the Home Guard co-operated. In the months before D Day, when the arrival of enemy agents could be expected, liaison with all these became tighter and excellent co-operation was maintained, especially with the Chief Inspector of Coastguards.

The enemy only used seaborne agents against this country in the early days of the war. There were landings at Dymchurch, Kent on September 2nd 1940 from two French fishing smacks; at Buckie, Banffshire on September 30th 1940 from a German seaplane and a rubber dinghy; on the Nairnshire coast on September 25th 1940 from a seaplane and a rubber dinghy; and at Gardenstown, Banffshire on April 7th 1941 from a seaplane and a rubber dinghy. All aroused the suspicions of the public or the police and were caught almost at once, except the last two who gave themselves up. There is no known case of a landing from a submarine except in Eire and Iceland. Agents are known to have been landed in the U.S.A. from submarines (vide S.F.50-24-44(40F)).

The work of the section was essentially that of the preventive side of the Security Service. If its enquiries had brought an enemy agent to light, the case would have automatically come within the orbit of B.1.B., Camp 020 or B.1.A.

Signals Security (B.3.E.). After the re-organisation of 1941 Signals Security was handled by Major Frost, A.D.B.3., and when he left in January 1943 this part of his work was taken over by Lt. Colonel Sclater and B.3.E. was formed for the purpose.

Experience early in the war showed that important information could be obtained by listening to the enemy's radio communications, even if their cypher was unreadable, but this lesson was not applied to the security of signals organisations of our own services and of certain civil departments and organisations, many of which often carried information of value to the enemy. While R.S.S. and "Y" units had been established to intercept the enemy's naval, military and air communications, as well as those of interest to the Foreign Office, no steps had been taken in the early stages of the war to complete the watch on the air by setting up an organisation to monitor signals made by British stations or those of our Allies. General instructions and warnings of the danger that their signals might be overheard had no doubt been given, but it appears that the majority of army operators, for instance, having been informed that their sets were for limited communication over short distances, failed to realise and were not taught that reception of the sky-ware might be possible hundreds of miles away in enemy territory.

Early in 1942 a note on the subject was prepared in the Security Service as a result of which the question was taken up in the War Office.

It transpired that there were a number of British organisations using radio transmitters of which the Security Service had no official knowledge as, for example, experimental establishments of the Ministry of Supply, Ministry of Aircraft Production, Police, Fire Brigade, Railways, in addition to all the G.P.O. and Cable and Wireless stations. It was estimated that, excluding the Supply Ministries and the Services, there were about a thousand transmitters operating in this country.

The serious nature of the danger caused by the lack of wireless security is illustrated by an incident at an R.A.F. station on the South coast where it was reported that our fighter aircraft always found enemy fighters coming up to meet them over the Channel soon after they started an operation. The interest of the Security Service was emphasised by the fact that the R.A.F. reported that there must be an enemy agent with a radio transmitter near the airfield. An investigation by the mobile units of R.S.S. proved that there was no evidence of an enemy agent but that our fighter pilots gave the facts away by chatting to one another over the radio while they were forming up before taking off; and it was concluded that the enemy interception service listened in and was able to anticipate that a sortie was about to take place.

The Security Service made large-scale investigations into the whole subject and found that intelligence of value to the enemy was endangered by a deplorable lack of a sense of security. In particular, the wireless networks of the Home Office, Police, Railways, National Fire Service, the Home Guard, the Air Training Corps, the Merchant Navy and other civilian wireless operators, as well as the armed forces, were liable to give away military secrets, and steps were taken to provide for this by making it a responsibility of the Security Service assisted by R.S.S. for monitoring purposes.

The Security Service was brought to attach importance to the long-term value of much of this intelligence. With the approach of D Day, as a result of breaches of security revealed by monitoring and in conformity with decisions made by the Sir Findlater Stewart Committee, the Home Office found it necessary to restrict still further the matter transmitted by radio by the Police and National Fire Service. The growing realisation by the Ministries concerned that guidance in such matters could be obtained from the Security Service led to a large number of reports. The existence of unofficial radio communication systems sometimes involving complete networks operated by unauthorised personnel in a quasi-official capacity was disclosed. An important instance was a large network established by important firms in the Midlands under the aegis of the Air Minstry to communicate information of damage by bombing to essential war plant. The information thus broadcast could only be presumed to reach the enemy, thus frustrating the efforts by the Ministry of Home Security to conceal such damage. Numerous other cases included the unwitting betrayal of the exact course, time and height of a bomber raid on Germany through the indiscretions of a Searchlight Unit.

The Security Service received the most ready and willing assistance and co-operation from everyone concerned, the offenders being generally horrified to learn the risks they had taken through lack of knowledge.

The signals security of the Fighting Services is the direct responsibility of the Service concerned, but the Security Service is often directly affected. On numerous occasions reports from Service Departments have indicated that the enemy possessed information with the implication that it must have been obtained from an enemy agent. One such report concerned the Airborne Divisions which had operated in France on D Day and had returned to England in preparation for further operations. The Security Service were able to show that this information could easily have reached the enemy through their wireless interception services. Other similar instances concerned the embarkation of an important contingent of troops in Southern England on December 2nd 1944, when two ships of the convoy were sunk between Southampton and Cherbourg with heavy loss of life.

The whole question was examined by the J.I.C., which on the 20th March 1945 endorsed the following recommendations:-

(i) That the Services should remain responsible for their own security and monitoring their own traffic.
(ii) That R.S.S. should be asked to allocate six monitoring sets from existing resources to cover such Civil or Service traffic as shall appear to the Security Service desirable.
(iii) That since the Security Service have a special interest in the security of all radio channels in or from the United Kingdom an officer should be nominated from each Service to work with the Security Service. The officers so nominated by the Services should meet ad hoc with the Security Service when the occasion required.
(iv) That indiscretions on Service channels should be brought to the notice of the Service concerned while Civil indiscretions should be dealt with by the Security Service.
(v) That the J.I.C. should approach SHAEF to nominate an officer to represent them in connection with the scheme.
(vi) That the Services and SHAEF should make available such full information regarding all radio channels from the United Kingdom as the Security Service might require.

5. Research Section.

B.1. Information. Research work of various kinds and in different degrees was carried out from 1940 and 1941 onwards in B.1.A., B.1.B., B.1.C., B.1.D. and B.1. Registry separately for the purposes of each section. In June 1942 the B.1. Information Section with rather wider functions came into existence, although it was not officially recognised. It consisted of Captain Gwyer of B.1.A. and Miss Hall of B.1.B., who, while remaining in their sections, were instructed to devote as much time as possible to the following:-

(a) the general study of the German Intelligence in order to draw attention to any development or discoveries in its technique or organisation;
(b) the compilation of a Who's Who of those officials of the German Intelligence Service whose names occurred most frequently in cases handled by this office;
(c) the preparation of Intelligence Notes on various aspects of the German Service as these might be required.

By this time, i.e. in the middle of 1942, it had become apparent that a great deal of material about the Abwehr and the Sipo und SD had been accumulated, mainly through the interception of the enemy wireless; the interrogation of captured agents at Camp 020 and of persons passing through the L.R.C. with some knowledge of their operations in occupied territories; and through the operations of B.1.A. Some information, not comparable in bulk to that obtained from these main sources, was also available in the form of reports from Section V and Allied Intelligence Services. Section V.W. (later R.I.S.) and Mr. Palmer of the Intelligence branch of G.C. & C.S. had also done important research work and had produced useful papers based on it, but they were in the main confined to material derived from ISOS and other intercepted enemy communications. There was, however, no officer or section whose business it was to study the material, to collate it and to produce suitable reports and papers to enable B Division to obtain an accurate and detailed picture of the enemy services as a whole or of each of its parts. Comprehensive and detailed compilations of this kind were required in order to furnish a thorough knowledge of the objectives, methods and organisaton of the enemy service and thus to facilitate the investigation of captured agents and their precise mission and exact status in the enemy organisation. Without such a knowledge of the enemy service it was not possible to run a double agent system with any assurance. It is indeed obvious that the more comprehensive this knowledge is, the greater will be the margin of safety in the conduct of any individual double agent case and in the manipulation of the system as a whole with all its inherent dangers.

From the outset the position in this respect was complicated by the attitude and position of Section V and by their claim to be the only students or authorities on the subject of the enemy organisation and its operations outside the three-mile limit. By the middle of 1942 Section V had produced no full assembly of the known facts relevant to the organisation and methods of the Abwehr and still less of the Sipo und SD, the latter of which they had failed to recognise although they had been receiving their traffic for nearly two years. They were in fact not organised to perform research work of this kind, their only attempt in this direction having been to produce "purple primers", a type of compilation not generally adequate for the purposes of the Security Service and in any case never up-to-date nor available for all the territories in question.

The purpose of B.1. Information was to fill all the gaps and to collaborate with all the research workers - the compilers of facts - in the different organisations which were disjointedly dealing with different aspects of the same problem. In the process of serving these purposes the section grew in numbers - to eight in September 1942 until it reached its peak in the summer of 1943 with a total strength of twenty-one.

The method adopted was to assemble in an orderly and accessible form information already on the files but scattered over a large number of interrogation reports and otherwise unassembled. When this was done it was found that the total of information had increased because many of the facts which, by themselves, meant little or nothing and had at first been ignored, took on a new significance when fitted into a logical framework; and other facts, apparently unconnected with a subject under enquiry, were gradually brought, as the enquiry proceeded, into a proper relation with it. Before this work was undertaken the only means of tapping the resources of the Registry, where the bulk of the required information was in the files, was to "look-up" in each individual case the various names and addresses referred to in the papers. As the knowledge of the enemy service increased, this method became increasingly cumbersome. It was not uncommon for the look-up on a single interrogation report of a captured agent, even if restricted to the main registries (B.1. Registry, Central Registry, S.I.S. Registry, L.R.C. Index and later the Ryder Street ISOS Index) to produce traces of ten or fifteen addresses and twenty or thirty names. The case officer was, therefore, often faced with a mass of information, much of which was contradictory or undigested. Moreover Abwehr officers were often referred to by various aliases and in many cases no systematic attempt had been made to identify the individual behind the alias. The resultant difficulties were cumulative. They could only be remedied by research; and a purely mechanical registry process was proved to be inadequate and insufficient for this purpose. For instance, sometimes an Abwehr officer's name was not known, but research made identification possible through a personal description, an association or the general circumstances of the case.

The information about each part of the enemy services was being added to from day to day and it was, therefore, an advantage to keep the information up to date. For instance, if traces of an individual showed that he was connectd with I TL/W of Eins Paris, it was important to have accessible all the available information about this section which was responsible for the collection of technical information for Air Force (Luftwaffe) purposes, in order to understand the part which individuals connected with him were playing. This information was not available from the files but it was compiled by the Information Section in its study of the enemy organisation as a whole; in the shape of the Intelligence Notes on its various parts and of the "Who's Who" of its officials. The material, which was derived from all relevant sources, secret and open both inside and outside the Security Service, was analysed on a basis partly geographical and partly dictated by the structure of the German organisation.

At its maximum development the Information Section was divided into seven sub-sections, of which six were concerned with a geographical area and the seventh, consisting of Captain Gwyer and one or two asistants, co-ordinated the whole and made a special study of the more general aspects of the German organisations.

Eventually more than twenty volumes of the "Who's Who" were completed. They covered the greater part of Western Europe, Norway, Holland, Belgium, Spain and Portugal. The "Who's Who" for France was started in 1944, but only the volumes relating to Paris were completed. The "Who's Who" for Germany was projected but was never carried very far. Two volumes on a slightly modified plan dealt with the German organisation in South America which, by the end of 1943, had become of considerable interest on account of the active work of the German agents there and the number of them who were intercepted in the Caribbean or on the high seas and brought to this country.

Each volume of the "Who's Who" was in five parts: a general account of the organisation in the country concerned with particular reference to its work against England; a short classified list of known enemy officials; addresses and cover addresses connected with the German organisation; history sheets of the German officials; and history sheets of local agents, recruiters, hangers-on and other suspects, many of whom figured frequently in espionage cases.

The primary object of all this work was to assist case officers by presenting the facts; not to draw conclusions. The value of the presentment of the facts depended on a complete documentation, the source from which each item came being fully noted - a point of cardinal importance in this type of work.

This object was successfully achieved and the work of B Information was regarded by the Director, B Division, as being a valuable contribution both in this country and later in the field after D Day.

Similar or parallel work was done by R.I.S., G.C. & C.S., the sub-sections of Section V, M.I.14(D) as well as by B.1.B. and B.1.C. The ideal arrangement would have been for all these resources, in so far as they were available purely for research purposes, to have been concentrated in a single section and so designed as to meet the needs of all the departments concerned, i.e. of Section V for the purpose of enabling them to penetrate enemy organisations abroad; of G.C. & C.S. for the purpose of reading the material fully and accurately; and of R.S.S. to facilitate their measures for the comprehensive interception of the enemy Secret Service wireless communications; all of which subserved the general purpose of enabling the Security Service to discharge its responsibilities for denying intelligence to the enemy and misleading him.

Co-operation was satisfactory with all the British authorities concerned, including the Services, and with the Allied Intelligence representatives in London, in spite of the difficulties which might have been caused by the number of unco-ordinated pieces of machinery dealing with the same general subject. The only exception to this was Section V of S.I.S., who resented what they regarded as an intrusion by the Security Service into their own sphere but, even in this case, the difficulty arose only on a level of policy while day-to-day relations with the officers in the sub-sections of Section V were generally good. The difficulties in policy arose from the fact that Section V regarded themselves as the prime authorities on the German Secret Services. They did not realise that by the greatly retarded development of the ISOS Index they had failed in discharging the functions of research for the purpose of the Security Service, whose requirements they did not always fully understand and were inclined to regard as exaggerated and over-meticulous. On the contrary they held an entirely different view of their functions based on the idea that the relevant intelligence work could be divided into compartments, their sphere being abroad and that of the Security Service within the three-mile limit of British territory. Having no responsibility for dealing with the interrogation or prosecution of arrested enemy agents they seemed unable to appreciate the need for research work and the fact that - if such work is done at all - it must be done as comprehensively as possible. Moreover they tended to ignore the fact that one of the most important sources for obtaining information about the German organisation abroad was the interrogation of enemy agents and other persons arriving from occupied territory. In the case of the latter they had provided a small staff of three or four interrogators at the L.R.C. who were completely inadequate to deal with all the cases and were restricted to a limited questionnaire which left insufficient initiative to the interrogator and thus prevented him from taking a fully intelligent interest in his work and extracting the information required. Proof of their failure to realise the manner in which records must be compiled for research purposes was given by the fact that these interrogators had no access to the L.R.C. Information Index or any comparable records and their interrogations were, therefore, of very little, if any, value. Section V based themselves mainly on the ISOS material combined with reports from their representatives abroad, but these representatives were mostly ill-informed and never fully acquainted with the available information on the subject as a whole. Finally, while Lt. Colonel Cowgill of Section V never succeeded in discharging, to any great purpose, his primary function, that of penetrating the enemy organisations, he based himself largely on an incomplete study of ISOS because he failed to understand the need for comprehensive research and the nature of the work required of his section if his interpretation of its sphere and its functions held the field. He did not recognise this even after pressure by Mr. Hart and others had led him eventually to improve the standard of work on the ISOS Index. These were the most important of the facts relevant to the circumstances in which he objected to the preparation of the "Who's Who" by B.1. Information. Unfortunately he was able to obtain the approval of his superiors to the course he adopted.

It was obvious that the results of the research done by B.1. Information would be valuable not only for the purpose of dealing with agents sent by the enemy to this country but also for the purpose of guiding and assisting the I(B) staff of the armies after they had succeeded in invading the continent. Under a directive from the J.I.C., Section V was responsible for supplying the I(B) staffs with all the information necessary for their work which was available from sources in London. For the reasons outlined above the results were never wholly satisfactory. Moreover Section V normally confined itself to questions of counter espionage whereas the I(B) staff had wider responsibilities for every aspect of security. Again, Section V did not possess the trained personnel with the experience of Security Service officers. Eventually it was decided that the I(B) staff under SHAEF (or their American equivalent the G-2 CI Staff) should deal direct not only with Section V but with the other departments able to assist. These were listed as follows:- M.I.5., M.I.6(V), M.I.6(R.I.S.), M.I.9., M.I.14(D), S.O.E., P.W.E., T.I.S.[†], O.S.S. and later the Norwegian, French, Belgian and Dutch Security Services.

Captain (now Major) Gwyer was appointed at the end of August 1943 to assist the I(B) staffs in preparing their plans and in making arrangements for the provision of the requisite material and for this purpose he drew on the Information Section which also contributed by lending nine of its staff to assist Section V in the preparation of their own material.

On the 1st March 1945 Major Gwyer handed over the section to Mr. Bird. By this time the new War Room had come into effective existence and the section, whose numbers

---

[†] The Theatre Intelligence Section was SHAEF which undertook certain I(B) work, e.g. the production of target-lists.

had been greatly depleted, had a different role to play. It served as a liaison section between the Security Service and the War Room. In practice this meant that it received from the War Room any information which was of interest to the Security Service in so far as it was a matter of counter espionage inside the United Kingdom. The fact that no enemy agents had been sent to this country by Abwehr or SD officers for several months and that none was sent during the period of the War Room's existence had the effect that the Information Section, in its liaison capacity, had no material to pass to the War Room. All the relevant ISOS material was dealt with directly by the War Room and the enemy officers and agents, who were sent to Camp 020 for interrogation, were handled not by the Security Service but by the War Room section concerned, i.e. W.R.-C.

B.1. Information continued to prepare the "Who's Who" for Paris as part of the projected "Who's Who" for France, but it was not circulated in the field, the reason for this being that it had been decided by Brigadier White and Mr. [...] that the preparation of the "Who's Who" series should be discontinued and that they should not be circulated in the field; but that the SHAEF pink cards were to be the sole form in which relevant information about enemy Secret Service officers and agents was communicated to G-2 CI or the formations under SHAEF, including those of the Army Groups or Armies. The machinery which was eventually developed in the War Room for these purposes will be described under (ix) War Room, below.

6. Shadowing Staff.

Although the shadowing staff was included in the B sections after the re-organisation of 1941 it played little part in the detection of enemy agents during this war. This was due to the fact that these agents were not at any time at large in this country and there was, therefore, no occasion to shadow them. The shadowing staff was employed in connection with investigations about all kinds of suspects for B, E and F Divisions.

The history of the section refers to its origin in 1903, i.e. before the formation of M.I.5., and mentions a number of cases in which successful work was done as well as the various difficulties in obtaining, training and keeping suitable staff for this very difficult and usually very dull work. The numerous cases in which remarkable success has been obtained in the past prove the need for special steps to ensure that the right type of man is recruited and of measures to retain his services by offering sufficient inducement. The spectacular successes are few and far between, but especially in the conditions of peace-time the shadowing staff can play a very important part in securing results in combination with other methods, including the employment of agents and the interception of communications. Some of the most important cases in which the shadowing staff has played a crucial part have been mentioned in previous chapters, but it is not only in connection with the more outstanding cases that this staff has proved its worth. Throughout the history of the Security Service it has constantly helped by bridging gaps, by filling in details and by clearing up difficulties and obscurities encountered in the course of enquiries by other sections.

(v) E Division 1941-1945.

E Division was formed at the time of the re-organisation in the middle of 1941. It was entitled E Division (Aliens Control), but for future readers it should be made clear that the word "control" is here somewhat loosely used and does not imply any direct control by E Division. Control was exercised by the Home Secretary under the Aliens Order, 1920 and by orders for internment or various forms of restriction issued under the Defence Regulations. Aliens were also subject to restrictions under the Aliens Movement Restriction Order of May 28th 1940 and by a series of orders issued during 1940 and 1941 declaring certain areas of Great Britain and Northern Ireland to be aliens protected areas, i.e. areas from which enemy and non-enemy aliens were removed in the case of the more vital areas including coasts, and enemy aliens were removed in the case of certain other areas. When the immediate danger of invasion diminished these restrictions were gradually relaxed. By an authority conferred on him by the Home Secretary on the 12th August 1940 the Assistant Director of E Division was empowered to grant exemption from the Aliens Order, 1920 and from various other restrictions under subsidiary orders and regulations. Many of these exemptions were granted on grounds of employment in protected places by aliens working for British Government Departments and in war factories.

The Division dealt with a variety of matters concerning three classes of aliens, namely, enemy aliens, neutrals and Allied subjects, and its functions were therefore varied accordingly. It did not deal with aliens of Spanish, Portuguese, South American or Japanese nationality. These subjects remained with B Division at the time of the re-organisation.

The history of measures regarding the internment and release of enemy aliens is dealt with in Mr. Aiken-Sneath's Memorandum (Bibliography No. 24) and this has been elaborated in the E Division report (vide S.F.50-24-44(60)). Questions relating to the administration of internment camps from the intelligence point of view are dealt with in S.F.50-24-44(70). The actual adminstration of the camps was under the control of a Commandant responsible to the War Office in matters of discipline and to the Home Office in every other respect. The camps were situated in the Isle of Man, where a Chief Intelligence Officer was established with headquarters in Douglas, one or more Intelligence Officers being appointed to each camp. The work of these officers was supervised by the section E.5. of E Division.

A case of considerable importance illustrated the need for close supervision over arrangements for the internment of individuals who had been used as double agents. At one time it transpired that certain persons who had been connected with the working of B.1.A.'s double agents were confined in a camp in close proximity to one in which there were aliens who were being released. Clandestine communications took place between the two camps and as a result information about the fact that certain agents were operating under control leaked out and became known to the enemy. (For details see L.305/Gen/2).

In the case of neutral and Allied subjects in the United Kingdom E Division was responsible for dealing with all matters of a security interest; and in the case of suspects detained under Article 12(5A) of the Aliens Order for dealing with cases which came before the Home Office Advisory Committee known as the Lindley Committee, but this work was subsequently handed over to S.L.A. (on the D.G.'s staff).

Apart from its responsibility for investigating the cases of aliens suspected of subversive or "fifth column" activities, the most important function of the Division was liaison with the Allied Security Services after these were established in London in the case of the Norwegian, Dutch, Belgian, Free French, Polish and Czech.

The American section (E.1.A.) was naturally in a class by itself in view of the special relations with the Americans. There was never any serious security problem in the sense of "Alien Control". The relations between the various branches of the British and American intelligence organisations - the Federal Bureau of Investigation, the Office of Strategic Services, the Office of Naval Intelligence and G.2., the Intelligence Branch of the Army, on the one hand and the Security Service and S.I.S. on the other, with special reference to Security Co-ordination in New York - were extremely complicated. Some details are furnished in the sectional report, but in so far as these particular relations are concerned it is hardly possible that history will ever repeat itself or that the tangled record could have any value in the future. It illustrates the difficulty of maintaining relations with the counter espionage services of an Allied power through S.I.S. under conditions where co-operation between the various components of the British machinery is not on a satisfactory footing. The circumstances induced the Director of B Division to maintain that it was necessary for the Security Service to be in direct contact with its American counter-part. This direct contact was effected when the F.B.I. established its representatives in the American Embassy in London. The circumstances of this double liaison gave rise to considerable controversy and difference of opinion which, as is usual in such cases, were partly a matter of organisation and partly one of personalities, but fortunately the relations between the Security Service and the F.B.I. were maintained on a very satisfactory footing.

The Yugoslavs, Greeks and Danes had no Security Service in this country but liaison was established with official representatives.

The E Division enquiries and their liaison were mainly concerned with matters of preventive interest as all cases of actual espionage were dealt with by B Division. In 1943 parts of the section dealing with the Greeks and Middle East nationalities were transferred to B Division in view of the fact that Greece and the Middle East had become centres of interest from the point of view of espionage and closer co-operation with S.I.M.E. was considered necessary. E Division, however, continued to exercise its normal functions in regard to subjects of these countries in the United Kingdom.

In May 1942 - nearly a year after the first formation of E Division - Mr. Horrocks, the Deputy Director of Organisation, and Mr. Turner, the Deputy Director of E Division, came to the conclusion that in the interests of efficiency it was necessary to make extensive changes in the organisation of the Division. Mr. Turner pointed out that for two years the sections now included in E Division had been fighting a very necessary defensive action in connection with the internment of aliens in the United Kingdom; and that the enormous number of internments, searches and investigations had not brought to light any organisation of enemy aliens among the population settled here. They had found nothing which looked like a "fifth column" or a skeleton of a hostile organsation. (He might have added that the result of B Division enquiries into the cases of enemy agents who had arrived in this country during the war had the complementary tendency of showing that there was a high degree of probability that the enemy had not established any such organisation).

Mr. Turner also mentioned that whenever a case appeared to be becoming interesting it was liable to be taken from the E Division officer and transferred to B Division. He had found that the general result of these and other factors was a tendency on the part of the more efficient officers to feel frustrated and on the part of the less efficient, either consciously or unconsciously, to devote less interest and energy to the work; and that the work in E Division was rarely such as to entice a good man or to hold his interest. He accordingly recommended that Mr. Horrocks' proposal should be accepted that the sections dealing with Allied and neutral nationals should be transferred to B Division while E should be left to deal with enemy aliens in internment and at large and matters connected with Aliens War Service Permits.

The Director General did not accept these proposals and maintained that B Division was an extremely heavy and steadily growing charge and that it must on no account be further loaded with things that did not properly pertain to it. He held that it was necessary to keep up the general observation which E Division was designed to provide (vide S.F.50/50/Misc/2Y.B.2090).

Shortly afterwards Mr. Turner resigned his appointment in the Security Service and his place as the head of E Division as taken by Major Younger.

In the summer of 1942 the military situation led B Division officers to suggest that the "fifth column" problem should be examined anew and a paper was prepared in "Research" with the assistance of B Division.

In August 1942 the Director of B Division, when discussing this paper, expressed the view that the whole problem of the so-called "fifth column" should be considered on the basis of the worst disasters that could befall: a Russian defeat while we were driven out of the Middle East and faced with a concentration of anything up to two hundred German divisions in the West. What action, he asked, would we consider necessary to deal with the possible "fifth column" in this country? He pointed out that responsibility for a "fifth column" was split up between various sections. E.7. (Mr. Aiken-Sneath and Mr. Robson-Scott) were dealing with the various German, Austrian and Czechoslovak political groups in this country: E.5. were reviewing the cases of internees and former internees of German or Austrian origin: B.4.A. and B.4.B. were investigating the cases of all suspect Germans, Austrians and also British subjects; E.6. were dealing with the

Italian enemy alien and dual national problem. None of these sections, as far as he knew, were tackling the problem on the lines of a case which was being handled by B.1.C. which, to his mind, was the only method of approach (this method was the use of agents to get in touch with disloyal elements in the population). He also made the point that there was no co-ordinating policy with regard to internment on the basis of B Division's knowledge of the German Intelligence system. He did not mention the point which was made in the research paper that F.3. was dealing with cases of British Fascists and pro-Nazis. He concluded that an enquiry should be made as to how the work of all the sections concerned could be better co-ordinated and how they could receive such knowledge of the German Intelligence system as was necessary to promote a policy of more active investigation; as there appeared to be a divided responsibility so that each section was inclined to think that the pursuit of this subject was somebody else's business.

After the Allied victories at El Alamein and Stalingrad and the successful landings in North Africa the possibility of invasion again receded and the "fifth column" question therefore again lost its actuality. The question of a policy making for freer release of internees was even considered, but it was decided that the defensive attitude of E.6. and F.3. should be continued as a measure of security in view of future major operations and landings on the Continent.

A further factor which is reported to have influenced the morale of E Division officers is that after the formation of the Division and its separation from B its officers had less access to most secret sources of information and were largely kept in ignorance of the knowledge acquired by B Division regarding the working of the German Secret Services. The officers in the nationality sections who were in liaison with the security officers of Allied Governments also found that their official (Allied) contacts were more fully informed than they were on important cases. The Allied officers sometimes referred E Division officers to cases of which they had not even heard, leaving them with the choice of two alternatives: losing face through admitting ignorance or bluffing - either of which made it difficult for them to retain the confidence of our Allied Staff Officers with whom they were in contact (vide S.F.50-24-44(66)).

Major Younger left E Division in February 1943 and his place was taken by Captain Brooke-Booth who again left in December 1944 and was succeeded by Mr. Hale who carried on the duty of head of E Division in addition to his duties in S.L.A. In 1944 and 1945 the importance of the work of E Division continuously declined.

Nevertheless the enquires made by E Division sections were an essential part of the preventive machinery of the Security Service, although it may be questionable whether some of it could have been reduced if the Division as a whole had had a better comprehension of the real potentialities and methods of the enemy Secret Service. One of the sections (E.1.B.) was responsible for preventive work of this kind in connection with alien seamen and the necessity for care in this field was proved by the number of cases in which seamen were found to be acting as Abwehr agents. In one of these cases E.1.B. contributed to the identification of the seaman in question, J.A. LAUREYSSENS (vide page 81 Appendix G in Bibliography No. 33). Elaborate records were established for the purpose of tracing alien seamen, details of which are given in the sectional report (vide S.F. 50-24-44(65)). The index of alien seamen prepared by the section eventually included about seventy-two thousand names. It also built up a record of ships' movements from the daily list of shipping movements published by Lloyds and valuable series of crew lists and Allied ships provided by S.C.O.s at the ports. Experience showed that the seamen's section filled a gap in the structure of the Security Service. The work was mainly preventive, but the records also proved of assistance for the purpose of investigation.

E Division has been able to claim with reason that it established very satisfactory relations with the Allied Security Services; and this in spite of the difficulties created by the fact that the Allies were simultaneously in contact with the nationality sections at the L.R.C. and with those of Section V of S.I.S. The principal Allied officers concerned expressed a desire that liaison with E Division sections should continue after the war. The liaison covered the work of the Security Service except the L.R.C., and in the case of the Czechs a special direct liaison was maintained by the Director and the Assistant Director of B Division (one of the many anomalies in detail).

The Aliens War Service Department, E.4., although included in the Division worked as an independent unit with its own methods and its own problems. These are dealt with at length in the sectional report (S.F.50-24-44(69)). Lt. Colonel Ryder, who was in charge of the section throughout, draws attention to the more important points which arose in the course of the war in his minute in the front of volume 2. The basis of the work was the granting of permits for the employment of aliens in the principal categories of protected places according to a Schedule. Lt. Colonel Ryder raises the question (at page 108 of his report) whether the wide casting of the net may have given those responsible for the Schedule a comfortable feeling that security had been fully safeguarded while, in fact, it entailed on those engaged on its administration a dispersal of effort which in many directions was unnecessary. Mr. Osborne in a note after page 112 suggests that in a future war the Schedule might be abolished and an order might be made directing the Secretary of State or some other appropriate officer to make, and to revise from time to time, a list of employments, occupations, workshops, factories or other premises or places in which no alien might be employed without the permission of the Secretary of State. This would seem to merit consideration in connection with the preparation of legislation and orders for the future.

To sum up, the most important function of E Division was of a preventive nature: to secure the internment of, or other restrictions on, aliens within the United Kingdom - whether enemy, neutral or Allied - who were potentially dangerous as likely to assist the enemy in case of invasion or by acting as spies. It inherited this responsibility for countering the foreign elements in a possible "fifth column" from B Division which had dealt with it in the more critical and difficult phases in 1939 to 1941. (It was, in fact, mainly staffed by the same personnel as had composed the previous B sections). B Division in the earlier period and later E Division were in the position of fighting, as Mr. Turner puts it, "a defensive action" against a Home Office and its Advisory Committees with a strong inclination to release individual enemy aliens against whom nothing concrete was known while generally refusing to accept any a priori assumption that Germans and Italians would engage in subversive activities in the interests of their own country. E Division was therefore constrained in virtue of its responsibility for security to make painstaking enquiries into a very large number of cases, and in the course of doing so established and maintained good relations with the Home Office.

This responsibility for obtaining intelligence about and countering a "fifth column" was shared with B.1.C. and F.3., the former being directly concerned with the enemy and his communications and both with the potential British quislings.

While it is impossible to be certain on the basis of evidence which is partly negative, the grounds are now (in 1945) almost overwhelming in favour of the inference drawn from intercepted enemy wireless, the interrogation of his agents and the examination of his documents that - at any rate after the internment of the leading members of the NSDAP in 1939 and the Fascio and the British Union of Fascists in 1940 - there was no body with a plan or an organisation to assist the invader in conjunction with the Abwehr or the Sipo und SD or any other enemy organisation. In the summer of 1940, however, this was far from being established and even in 1942 there was serious room for doubt. The resources at the disposal of E Division and the type of enquiry they could make were not such as to induce full confidence that negative results would provide a working basis of assuming that no such organisation existed or that some of the released internees might not be concerned in promoting it.

The fact that the enemy obtained no information about major operations launched from this country in 1942-1944 proves, however, when read with the information relevant to the work of B.1.A., that they were unable to establish contact with such persons for this purpose.

The important function of maintaining a good liaison with the Allied representatives in this country was discharged with conspicuous success. This and all the other duties of E Division involved the disposal of a great volume of often dull routine correspondence.

(vi) Section F.3. 1940-1945. Fascist, Right Wing, Pacifist and Nationalist Movements; Pro-Germans and Defeatists.

The section which dealt with the British Union of Fascists was known as B.7. before the re-organisation of 1941 when it became F.3. and its charter was extended to cover Fascist, Right Wing, Pacifist and Nationalist Movements, Pro-Germans and Defeatists. The effect of this was to include within its scope enquiries about a variety of British subjects who were either definitely pro-Nazi or belonged to movements which it was thought might lend themselves to German penetration. Pro-Nazi or pro-German movements included besides the British Union of Fascists, the Imperial Fascist League, the National Socialist League, the Nordic League and the Right Club. There was good reason to expect that many of their members would be likely to assist the enemy in the event of invasion and subsequent enquiries have left no room for doubt that this danger was a real one. A considerable number of individuals of this kind were interned, one of the most important being Captain Ramsay, M.P. of the Right Club.

The detentions were followed in almost every case by an appeal on the part of the person interned to an Advisory Committee appointed by the Home office to review all such cases. From the second half of 1940 onwards the major task of the section was to examine the documents connected with the cases, including transcripts of long and patient hearings given to the detainees by the Committee. (Incidentally this work in connection with the detentions necessitated an important change in the records. Prior to the war, owing to shortage of staff, personal files had not as a rule been prepared for individual Fascists and such records of individuals as existed were distributed over a number of volumes connected with the organisation and cognate subjects. The necessity of dealing with individual cases for the purpose of the Home Office or Home Office Advisory Committee necessitated the preparation of a large number of personal files).

The Home Office Advisory Committee and the Security Service held views on the subject of the release of internees which were often irreconcilable and involved a fundamental difference of principle. The Committee maintained that its duty was to decide, firstly, whether a detainee had been an active member of the British Union and, secondly, whether it was necessary to exercise control over him by means of detention. The Security Service maintained that when active membership of the British Union was established it was automatically necessary to continue detention. Sir Norman Birkett, the Chairman of the Committee, expressed the opinion that members who had been active up to the time of their detention, save in exceptional cases, should be kept in internment, but those who had dissociated themselves before or after the outbreak of war should be judged on their merits. The Security Service urged that it was necessary to be cautious in making classifications because they had information that officials of the British Union had been supplied with faked resignations for this very contingency. This and ancillary differences of opinion involved lengthy three-cornered correspondence between the Home Office, the Advisory Committee and the Security Service, represented by Mr. Pilcher of S.L.A., and the section F.3. (then B.7.). The Security Service continued to maintain that because the action against British Union officials had been taken against them as such and not as individuals it was a reversal of Home Office policy for the Committee to judge individual cases on their merits. In brief, the Security Service regarded the whole question as a factor in the military situation. The Advisory Committee regarded each individual with a judicial eye as a matter of equity and the Home Office was influenced by considerations of the liberty of the subject and the political aspect in so far as it was or might be reflected in questions in the House. The Committee endeavoured to judge whether each individual who appeared before it was, on the evidence, the kind of person who was likely to be a danger to the State. If the appellant appeared to the Committee to be honest, reliable and patriotic they felt impelled to recommend his release, whether or not he had been an active Fascist up to the time of his arrest. The Security Service believed that it was impossible to attach much weight to the impression made on the Committee by the personality of an appellant; and they were induced to this belief by evidence of a general nature relating to the Fascist movement associated as it was with National Socialism in Germany and Fascism in Italy and other countries. British Fascists were, as a general rule, sincere idealists and regarded themselves as true patriots but, believing as they did that Britain was controlled by Jewish financiers who had plunged half the world into war for their private gain, many Fascists were profoundly convinced that the best interests of their country required its liberation by any means and at all costs from its Jew masters. If, they argued, collaboration with Nazi Germany was the quickest and best method of establishing National Socialism in Britain, then it was the duty of every patriot to collaborate with the Nazis who would free Britain from her alien chains (vide S.F.50-24-44(70) and S.F.91-2-6 volume 1).

By the end of September 1940 the Advisory Committee had recommended release in some hundred and ten cases and continued detention in fifty-three. The section (B.7.) had opposed the Committee's recommendations for release in fifty-nine cases. It became necessary to resolve the deadlock between the Security Service and the Committee because it was causing delay and mutual recriminations. The problem was discussed at a meeting of the Home Defence Security Executive in November 1940. As a result it was decided that cases in which it was established that there were reasons for detention other than office in, or membership of, the British Union, the Home Secretary was therefore compelled to abandon the principle which they had tried to maintain. Disagreement with the recommendations of the Advisory Committee continued to occur, but the Home Secretary, Mr. Morrison, not infrequently found himself on the side of the Security Service. He maintained the Order of Detention in about eight percent of cases in which the Committee recommended release.

The importance of these disagreements diminished as the danger of invasion receded, but in the early stages at the time of the invasion of Denmark and Norway and, later, of Belgium and Holland, Quisling of the National Socialist party in Norway and Mussert in Holland seemed to justify the words Hitler was alleged to have used in 1932 "we shall have friends who will help us in all the enemy countries". It seemed obvious that if there were any party designed to play this part in the United Kingdom it was Mosley's British Union. Urgent representations by the Security Service, therefore, led to the action already described against Mosley and his leading officials on the basis of a new regulation D.R.18B(1A) which came into force on the 22nd May 1940. Again, as already mentioned, the circumstances after the German attack on Russia diminished the importance of this question which came to the fore again, only temporarily, in the summer of 1942 when it seemed possible that the German armies might achieve outstanding success in Southern Russia and the Middle East.

In September 1940 the Home Office had empowered Regional Commissioners to detain certain classes of British subjects and non-enemy aliens in the event of invasion. For this purpose a suspect list was a prepared, and it fell to B.7. (F.3.) to prepare their part of it, i.e. that part dealing with British subjects who came within the scope of the charter of the section. The Suspect Lists were submitted by R.S.L.O.s to their respective Regional Commissioners and this work was substantially completed by the summer of 1941. These lists did not include the names of all persons released from detention. In many cases the information obtained about an individual during his detention and his replies to the questions of the Home Office Advisory Committee were sufficient to convince the section that there was no further danger of his rendering active assistance to the enemy. The Suspect List also included persons of German origin or associations, even if unconcerned with Fascist or Right Wing politics, as it was felt that in the event of invasion they were liable to be influenced by German national feeling to assist the invader. The whole question of the Suspect List formed the subject of consultation and correspondence between the section on the one hand and R.S.L.O.s and Special Branch on the other. Although this work was done in view of a contingency which never arose and therefore it never served its primaary purpose, it achieved the important secondary purpose of promoting a feeling of additional security against the event of invasion. It also had the effect of keeping a large number of doubtful cases constantly before the police and the Security Service. The Security Service was empowered by arrangements with the military authorities to exclude from call-up for H.M. Forces persons appearing on the Suspect List. The Suspect List was finally abolished in September 1944. In November 1943 F.3. took over from F.1. their duties in respect of Fascists, Anarchists and miscellaneous cases of cognate interest in H.M. Forces. (For fuller details regarding the change in functions of F.1. see Chapter V part 2.).

The banning of the British Union under D.R.18AA on the 10th July 1940 combined with the arrest of the leaders brought the Fascist organisation in this country to an end and attempts to revive it in an underground form proved abortive. Other organisations, some of them of a semi-Fascist kind, attracted people with this attitude of mind. These organisations, mostly unimportant in themselves, therefore became the subject of enquiry by F.3. They included the Liberty Restoration League (1940 onwards), the Constitutional Research Association (August 1941 onwards), the People's Common Law Parliament (1941 onwards), the British National Party (May 1942 to May 1943) and the English National Association (June 1943 until its virtual disappearance in the spring of 1944).

In the Research paper on the "fifth column" mentioned above, it had been suggested that a method of obtaining intelligence about elements of the "fifth column" was by a few good and carefully selected penetrative agents, and the Director of B Division had supported this view and had instanced the enquiry which B.1.C. was then making through a well-tried pre-war agent who had for many years given good inside information about the British Union and was in touch with a number of people of British and German origin who held Fascist views. The Director General had, however, decided at that time (in 1942) that he was unwilling to encourage the employment of agents for this purpose on any considerable scale. Experience proved, however, that good information could be obtained in this way and that it was necessary as a complementary measure to the interception of correspondence under Home Office Warrants. Section F.3. was successful in obtaining a small number of good agents who kept them informed of the developments in connection with the various small leagues and associations mentioned above. The most important of these proved to be the Constitutional Research Association in which the leading spirit was one Major Harry Edmonds (vide S.F.50-24-44(79) and S.F.91-1-5(4) Y.B. 4301). The enquiry into these cases proved the nebulous character of much of the Fascist mentality and the vagueness of the programmes which were designed to attract sympathy on the basis of such a wide variety of subjects as anti-semitism and a dislike of the "money-power" and even of opposition to an extension of bureaucracy.

The results of the B.1.C. case already mentioned were placed at the disposal of F.3. because they covered ground which was primarily F.3.'s concern. This case was originally started in 1940 when Mr. Curry, who had been kept in close touch with the M.S. agent for some years, arranged with Major Maxwell Knight for him to be placed at the disposal of Lord Rothschild in order to attempt to penetrate "fifth column" circles in this country as part of the counter-sabotage work of B.1.C. (then B.18). In the first place the penetration of a group of individuals connected with the German firm of Siemens as a potential field of this kind was attempted. During the next four or five years the enquiry gradually spread until the agent was directly or indirectly in contact with some five hundred Fascist-minded people - not all of British origin - through a number of unconscious sub-agents. The details of the case were very skilfully worked out and are too long to summarise here. The importance of the case arises from the fact that it showed that there was a considerable number of people in London alone - and no similar enquiries have been made to cover the whole of the country - who were ready and willing to help the enemy. Many of them supplied information of military value to our agent in the belief that he was in a position to communicate it to the German Secret Service. His contacts covered such a wide field that it was possible to argue with good reason that if the Germans had had any organisation in touch with such elements in this country they would inevitably have been in touch with some of the wide circle embraced by this enquiry. The argument that they had no such organisation was therefore held to be strongly supported by the circumstances of this enquiry. (vide P.F.64307 Y.B. 912 held B.1.C.).

The idea of developing the case on these lines was conceived by Lord Rothschild and it was put into effect by the combined efforts of himself, Miss Clay and the agent who proved that he had unusual ability in this direction. The object was to obtain information which should be used only in the crisis of an invasion and not for the purposes of a prosecution. All possible steps were taken to avoid provocation, but the circumstances under which pro-Germans were induced to believe that they were dealing with a secret German agent made it difficult to avoid the appearance of it. At any rate in the event of a prosecution the defence would almost certainly use the argument of the "agent provocateur". It was always intended, however, that no prosecution should ensue, but only preventive action in the event of the supreme crisis of invasion. The result was to furnish valuable information to enable the Security Service to assess the situation without admitting of action against individuals on the basis of this information.

The enquiries made by F.3. during the war, especially those concerned with the new Fascism as it developed during its later stages, showed that it cannot be regarded as a transient phenomenon. It goes back, for instance, to Hobbes and in its modern form it has not been killed by the circumstances of the war. At the end of the war there were still British people of Fascist - or National Socialist - mentality who looked upon Adolf Hitler as a great and inspiring leader. They looked on the defeat of Germany as the defeat of all their hopes.

The problem of Fascism is therefore one which, as far as can be foreseen, seems likely to engage the attention of the Security Service in the coming peace as it did in the inter-war period, but in very different circumstances. It must nevertheless be expected that the parties in various countries which were associated with National Socialism in Germany - such as the Quisling, Mussert or French Fascist Parties - will continue to exist and that, as happened before the war, there will be continued association between them and people of a similar mentality in this country.

(vii) C and D Divisions.

C and D Divisions were together responsible for the preventive work of the Security Service, except in so far as certain aspects of it were dealt with by B Division. They were nominally separate divisions, but they were under an Assistant Director from January 1939 and have had a common Director throughout the period 1941-1945 in the person of Brigadier Allen. C Division, which was responsible for the examination of credentials or vetting, had existed in the period between the wars as C Branch under Captain (afterwards Lt. Colonel) Bacon. D Division as constituted at the time of the re-organisation in 1941 had come into existence gradually as a result of the creation from time to time of sections to deal with specific subjects. Of these sections D.1, 2 and 3 came into existence during the period before the war when British rearmament was being started, their function being to offer advice regarding security measures in factories making equipment for the Armed Forces. D.4, which administered and directed the work of S.C.O.s at sea and airports, came into existence on the outbreak of war; but Colonel Adam, who was in charge of it throughout the period, had been engaged in preparatory work for about a year prior to the outbreak. D.5, which dealt with administrative questions connected with the employment of military personnel in the Security Service, also came into existence at the outbreak of war and D.6, dealing with protected places and areas, the control of photography, identity documents and permits and other matters concerning the War Office, inherited these functions from Lt. Colonel Holt Wilson, who had been engaged on them and on preparations to bring the necessary arrangements into force in the event of war while he held the appointment of Deputy to the Director of the Security Service during the period 1918-1940. Brigadier Allen joined the Security Service in November 1938 and became Assistant Director of C and D Divisions in January 1939 and finally Director of those Divisions in April 1941.

The process by which the preventive side of the Security Service was formed to meet the exigencies of the second world war makes it difficult to give a clear and coherent account of its development. It may be a little easier to understand if we refer back to the history of M.I.5. in the war of 1914-1918 when the preventive side was known as F Branch, a short reference to which is contained in Chapter III, Part 2 (iii). At that time the principle underlying the organisation of this side of the work was clearly recognised. It was to establish controls which would facilitate the work of detection and in this and other ways frustrate the enemy Secret Intelligence Service. The problem in that war was relatively simple. It was one of preventing first Germans and later persons of other natonalities employed by the Germans as spies from remaining at large in or securing entry to this country and from communicating with the German Secret Service by letter or telegram or by messages delivered personally through travel to neutral countries. As these various aspects of the problem became manifest as a result of M.I.5. investigations, steps were taken to improve the preventive arrangements. The problems created by the "total" organisation for war by the Nazi party and by the existence of ideological sympathisters in the shape of British Fascists and other pro-Nazis - people of similar mentality to Joyce, Amery or Mrs. Eckersley - did not exist in any comparable form.

In the period between the wars there was virtually no preventive machinery and over a very large field matters of military importance appeared to be an open book for any German to read, especially when their Service Attachés in London and the Nazi Party organisation were in close touch with Germans in a large variety of trades and industries with access to the Services and other Government Departments and a large range of factories engaged in making aircraft and many types of military equipment.

An outstanding case was that of a German, Dr. LACHMANN, who, as chief designer for Handley Page since 1934, was in a position to obtain detailed technical information over the whole field of the British aircraft industry, including military aircraft. He was admittedly loyal to Germany and visited his own country frequently in circumstances which can leave no doubt that he was willing to place his knowledge and ability at its disposal. Equally there was no doubt that the Nazi authorities were aware of the position. He was on very friendly terms with the German Air Attaché in London. Handley Page, with an eye to their own profits, resisted security objections to his employment, but in 1936 at the request of the Air Ministry arranged to keep him away from their main works where he would have unlimited access to the firm's secret work for the R.A.F. After Munich the Air Minister personally intervened and informed Handley Page that they must dispense with his services. None the less he was still employed by Handley Page at the outbreak of war and was interned. D.3. maintained that even if there were no evidence against him, information about our aircraft reached him legitimately in virtue of the position he held in our aircraft industry and that this position made counter espionage and security measures ineffective. There was no need for Germany to employ spies in the aircraft industry so long as he held this employment. LACHMANN has been released from internment and (in 1946) his future is still under discussion.

As a result of enquiries made during the period 1936-1939 by B Branch and D.1, 2 and 3 attempts were made to narrow the field open to the German Intelligence Services, but the effect was similar to an attempt to block half-a-dozen holes in a sieve containing hundreds.

The conflicting interests of production and security are one of the perennial difficulties of all aspects of security. These difficulties were accentuated before the war and after the beginning of the war by the fact that the major Government Departments had little appreciation of the problems of security and as a rule had no specialised staff of their own with any direct security responsibilities. The result was that in the Services and in other Government Departments responsibility for security was not felt in any real sense. Referring to the War Office, for instance, Brigadier Allen remarks that it was fairly safe to say that before the war broke out in 1939 general defensive security measures were not being considered except in M.I.5. (and in the "Control of Aliens in War" Committee) where Lt. Colonel Holt Wilson was engaged in the preliminary work connected with Defence Regulations, Passes, Permits, DR Forms and the control of entry to protected areas, but no one else in the War Office had any knowledge of what was being done, while M.I.5. had no executive authority to enable it to bring the necessary measures into force.

D.1, D.2 and D.3. The development of arrangements to control access to protected places - to places of military importance including war factories - by the construction of physical and the provision of human obstacles has been the subject of elaborate study and had produced a large volume of D Division literature on the subject which is contained in divisional reports (vide S.F.50-24-44 (50) to (59)).

"Notes on Munitions Security", of which the fourth revised edition appeared in August 1942, supplies detailed advice for the benefit of factory managements and staff on a great volume of details under headings dealing with enemy agents and methods of munitions espionage, methods of munitions security, passes, credentials, employment of aliens, secret documents and their custody, disposal of waste-paper, precautions against sabotage, various forms of sabotage and the control of photography among numerous other details. "The Notes for the Guidance of the Approved Authority in Charge of a Protected Place" is another example of detailed instructions which have been prepared and issued.

The subjects which are common to D.1, 2 and 3 include the detailed consideration of the layout of factories from the security point of view with special reference to problems of fencing, the layout of factory entrances, the "lane" system of entry for employees, problems concerning factory Home Guards, air-raid precautions, the employment of aliens and the assessment of risks in employing aliens. In fact there is almost no limit to the detail with which security problems relating to factories have been examined.

The employment of aliens has involved a close liaison between A.W.S. Department and the D sections, the latter, in view of local knowledge of individual factories, having been in a position to weigh up facts which could not be known to the A.W.S. Department. The nature and the variety of the problems is illustrated by the considerations involved in the employment of neutral aliens in view of the existence of channels of communication between England and neutral countries such as the transit of documents by diplomatic bag or by individual travellers.

A subject which received attention from D sections was the possibility of leakage through insurance policies taken out by factories. Enquiries into this subject were made by B Division. Insurance is essentially world-wide and international; and in connection with re-insurances information about the industry of one country is passed to insurance companies in another. Discussions were accordingly opened with the insurance market about the steps which could be taken to safeguard information in their possession. The problem was found to present considerable difficulties which led to the conclusion that a scheme to solve them should be considered in the event of another major war.

These few instances which have been selected almost at random will serve to illustrate the amount of specialised study which has been given to the subject and the extent to which security measures can be elaborated.

D.1 besides dealing with the Minstry of Supply was concerned with the Ministry of Food, the Ministry of Health, Railway Companies and Public Utility Companies.

D.2 was mainly concerned with the liaison with the Admiralty to cover the security of secret contracts and with security advice to civil engineering and contractors' firms handling Admiralty contracts. They were also concerned with special measures to cover Radar training, special measures preceding D Day and shipping security.

D. 3. was concerned with security problems affecting the Air Ministry, the Ministry of Aircraft Production, aircraft factories and the companies responsible for the storage and distribution of petroleum products.

While D.1 was limited in scope to the subjects mentioned above, D.2 and D.3 had wider functions. They were in a sense representatives of the Director of Naval Intelligence and of the Director of Intelligence, Air Ministry respectively; and they played an important part as liaison officers between sections of all Divisions in the Security Service and different parts of the Admiralty or Air Ministry. Various problems arose from time to time in which officers of B sections, for instance, found it necessary to make enquiries affecting various aspects of the administration of the Services. D.2 and D.3 were in a position to arrange the necessary contacts and furnish advice and guidance to the parties concerned. The move to Blenheim at the end of 1940 made it difficult for these sections to maintain satisfactory contact in many cases and after a time either the heads of sections or a representative was moved back to London.

<u>D.6, G.1 and G.2/C & D</u>. Similar functions in relation to the War Office were discharged by the Director C & D assisted by D.6 and by G.1 and G.2/C & D. The latter dealt with matters of interest to the War Office both in policy and in detail and also with other departments when the subject matter was of interest to them. Military security cases which necessitated a personal interview with officers at the War Office were handled in London by G.1 or G.2/C & D. D.1 and D.2 worked at country headquarters, D.3 partly in London and partly in the country after the move to Blenheim and subjects of common interest to these three sections were co-ordinated by D.6 in the country and by G.1 or G.2/C & D in London.

From the end of January 1941 onwards a weekly meeting of representatives of D.1, D.2 and D.3 was held under the chairmanship of Lt. Colonel Norman who was then Deputy D. When he retired in April 1944 D.6 supplied the chairman and the secretary for this meeting, the object of which was to exchange ideas and discuss points of mutual interest so that all the three sections should work on a common security plan and furnish their views as might be desirable to the Director C & D.

D.6 dealt with questions which affected the War Office in connection with -

    (a) the declaration of protected places;
    (b) "controlled areas";
    (c) general permits, passes and identity documents;

(d) military security and -
(e) control of photography and sketching.

The detailed work connected with the issue of individual permits in connection with the control of photography, protected places, protected and regulated areas and the declaration and cancellation of protected places was dealt with by D.6; while questions of policy which required consideration by the Security Executive or consultation with Services or other Departments were handled in London by G.1 or G.2/C & D who also dealt with a variety of subjects, including the use of Defence Regulations for the protection of secret trials and tests, measures to safeguard the security of operations, policy regarding the enlistment and employment of aliens in the Forces, travel to operational areas, security matters affecting Allied contingents in the United Kingdom, liaison with the United States Forces, security questions concerning prisoners of war, general policy and liaison with supply departments on matters of common interest to D.1, D.2 and D.3 and matters raised at the monthly D meetings.

Monthly D meetings were inaugurated by the Director C & D in May 1943. The object was to extend the purposes served by the weekly meeting to a larger membership including representatives of other Services or Departments closely associated with D Division in security matters. Among those attending were the Chief Security Officer, Ministry of Supply and representatives of the Ministry of Aircraft Production, of the Admiralty and of different branches of the War Office. The monthly meeting quickly became established as a recognised link in the security network. It served to focus the discussion of a very wide range of subjects with results profitable to the Security Service and the other Departments concerned.

D Division in relation to the War Office, the Admiralty and the Air Ministry. In spite of the separation of the Security Service from the War Office which in effect dates from 1931 - although the separation was never formally acknowledged - the War Office has continued to deal with D Division in some respects as though it were a part of the War Office. War Office files on security matters affecting all branches of the War Office are received in D Division, replies to questions raised therein being dealt with by G.1 and G.2/C & D or the Director C & D after consultation with other Divisions of the Security Service concerned; and Security Service advice is thus conveyed to the War Office through this channel. The Director C & D is frequently asked to brief the General Staff on subjects coming before the Chiefs of Staff, ministerial meetings and the Cabinet and by this means opportunity is afforded to express Security Service views on questions which would not have come to notice through any other channel. War Office telegrams, Army Council papers and inter-departmental correspondence are forwarded to the Director C & D for information if there is any security flavour in them. In short the War Office is the only major department through which the Security Service has been kept in touch with many matters on which its views are relevant and desirable. The Director C & D and G.1/C & D as his personal Staff Officer have served to co-ordinate matters affecting other Divisions of the Security Service and to furnish advice which during the war has often been sought and expected at very short notice. Officers of D Division have attended briefing meetings in the War Office to ensure that Security Service views were properly presented.

The Director C & D has been the Security Service representative on the J.I.C. His attendance, accompanied when necessary by a specialist officer from other Divisions, has enabled him to fulfil an essential function and to represent security interests at these meetings. The receipt of a large volume of J.I.C. papers has assisted him and through him the Security Service as a whole to keep in touch with a wide range of security problems and to know when to apply the necessary correctives or to ensure that security interests are properly covered.

From March 1940 to October 1944 Brigadier Allen held the position of D.D.M.I.(S) under the D.M.I. at the War Office in addition to his appointment as Director C & D in the Security Service. This dual appointment was made at the request of the D.M.I., War Office, primarily to ensure a closer co-ordination between the Security Service and the War Office and to assist the War Office in building up their own security procedure on a sound foundation. The effect was to weld the two systems more into one by preventing overlapping and filling in the gaps. It became a process of advice, education and co-ordination. The War Office gradually became aware that they were really dealing with the domestic security of the Army and they learned of the contribution which the Security Service could make from the wider background of national security.

Although the War Office learned these lessons the same process had to be adopted later to persuade COSSAC and SHAEF that the best method of organising an I(B) Staff in the field was to draw largely on the Security Service for personnel qualified in "civil security". The War Office Manual defines Civil Security as "Measures taken within a civil population to defeat any covert attack made either on the armed forces or on the national war effort as a whole by hostile influences working through the civil community". The fundamental fact is that until a military force enters a theatre of war overseas it has had no practical experience of how to handle "civil security" or counter espionage.

The position of D.2 vis-à-vis the Admiralty and that of D.3 vis-à-vis the Air Ministry were as follows:-

In the early stages of the war the head of D.2 was to a large extent involved in work other than that concerned with industrial security. This arose from the fact that the A.D.N.I. relied on him to collaborate with other sections of the Security Service in order to deal with purely Admiralty interests in -

- (a) the declaration of protected places to cover Admiralty interests;
- (b) the detailed organisation of the Fleet base security officers;
- (c) the employment of labour from Eire within the protected areas;
- (d) Contraband Control problems;
- (e) naval identity documents in general including the provision of passes for officers and ratings proceeding into protected areas;
- (f) questions arising from the declaration of Admiralty establishments as protected places;

(g) the control of enemy aliens and British merchant ships and anti-sabotage measures;
(h) war-time policy for the vetting of Admiralty employees.

He was also regarded as the channel through which sections of the Security Service directed almost all enquiries involving a naval interest, including port security control questions. The effect of this attitude of the A.D.N.I. was to render it difficult for the head of D.2 to devote sufficient time to security problems connected with important contracts and factories. At a later stage A.D.N.I.'s office widened its security field and became accustomed to deal with several individuals in the Security Service on various problems. This suited the Admiralty better and D.2 was able to devote the bulk of its time to munitions security.

D.3 in addition to acting as advisers and inspecting security arrangements in M.A.P. factories had duties which necessitated liaison with the following among others at the Air Ministry and M.A.P.: -

Liaison with Air Ministry

(i) D. of I.(S), D.D.I.(S) and sections under them;
(ii) Provost Marshal, who implements the security policy within the R.A.F. laid down by D. of I.(S);
(iii) Inspector of R.A.F. Accidents, whose investigations may bring to light suspicions of sabotage of aircraft;
(iv) Secretarial Branches who handle recruitment of civil staff.

Liaison with M.A.P.

(i) P.S.6. (Security);
(ii) Aeronautical Inspection Department H.Q., to whom their staff in factories report suspicious circumstances which come to light during their duties;
(iii) M.A.P. Regional Officers, who handle routine physical protection measures for factories;
(iv) Secretarial Branches who handle recruitment of staff.

The fact that the Security Service had grown out of M.I.5. which was originally a part of the War Office was responsible for a desire in the Air Ministry and M.A.P. to see vetting carried out by D.3 as being a staff with "Air" interests. A system has accordingly been evolved whereby D.3 do this work in co-operation with the Assistant Director, C Division, working to a general policy and under his guidance. For this purpose D.3 deals direct with several branches of the Air Ministry and of the M.A.P.

D Sections and Intelligence. The D Sections have direct relations with sections in all parts of the Security Service and among other important functions have been responsible for bringing a number of new problems to the notice of B Division. For instance, Group Captain Archer, as already mentioned, first emphasised the importance of the machine tool industry and long before the war assisted in obtaining information about the important part played in this industry by the representatives of German firms with consequent danger to security. Again D.3 was concerned in working out practical measures for the security of Radar. Captain Bardwell of D.2 early in the war brought to notice the absence of arrangements to deal with enquiries about sabotage to shipping in foreign ports or on the high seas.

Whenever any of the D sections came into touch with or discovered a new problem, steps were taken to have it investigated in co-operation with other Divisions. Owing to the secrecy surrounding the special intelligence dealt with in B Division, officers in D Division were apt to feel that they were left in the dark and that it would have been possible to take preventive measures more effectively if they had been more closely and constantly informed of the position in regard to what was known to B Division about enemy espionage.

D.4 and S.C.O.s at Ports. The work of D.4 and S.C.O.s at sea and airports and the establishment of travel and port control has been referred to in Chapter IV, Part 1 (iv) and Chapter V, Part 1 (iv). The former dealt briefly with the developments at the beginning of the war and the latter with the important positive part played by S.C.O.s in assisting B Division in detecting enemy agents arriving from enemy-occupied territory. It has been shown that the crucial importance of the S.C.O.s' part was the result of the Home Office decision that Immigration Officers should refuse to any alien leave to land or embark if the S.C.O. advised to that effect, the reason for this procedure being that the S.C.O.s, as instructed by B Division, would often be in possession of information (i.e. information about the German Secret Service derived from secret sources) which was not available to the Immigration Officer.

In addition to these important functions the S.C.O.s, under the guidance and control of A.D.D.4., had other important duties to fulfil. These have been described at great length in the sectional report (vide S.F.50-24-44(50)) which cannot be adequately summarised here.

Some essential points not dealt with above may be mentioned The S.C.O.s at sea and airports were the only part of the Security Service organisation which was in direct contact with the public and they were in this position as military officers and other ranks in uniform. Unlike a police officer who has a personal liability, a military officer is bound to obey the orders of his superior and, in the case of any complaint or action regarding irregularity, it is sufficient defence for him to say that he was carrying out an order; and responsibility for his action would then fall on the officer who gave the order, in this case A.D.D.4. The situation, therefore, was one of some delicacy because, in the event of serious complaint from the public, the War Office could hardly have accepted a position under which complaints were addressed to the Secretary of State for War in regard to personnel not under his direct control and carrying out policy for which he was not directly responsible. In practice no serious difficulty arose.

The work done by D.4 and the S.C.O.s has been classified as follows:-

(a) documentary control of travel into the United Kingdom;
(b) documentary control of travel out of the United Kingdom;
(c) control of travel through the military Permit Office;
(d) physical control of travel at ports;
(e) censorship;
(f) security of military embarkations and operations;
(g) security of shipping;
(h) collection of intelligence;
(i) liaison with Government Departments and Allied Services;
(j) maintenance and distribution of a Black List of suspects for use at ports in this country and abroad.

A.D.D.4. has emphasised the distinction between paper control and physical control. The former is concerned with all the details connected with passports, visas, exit permits and the vetting of such cases or reference to Security Service records. Vetting can only have a negative effect in that the Security Service records can never be complete and comprehensive. They cannot contain information about all individual agents of the enemy or even of all persons in regard to whom it may be undesirable to allow them to travel in wartime. Security Service objections were usually upheld by the Passport Control Department, but sometimes when a refusal was likely to lead to a question in Parliament the case was referred to the Home Office and the Security Service point of view was not always adopted.

The physical control at ports involved the whole of the Security Control Officers' work in connection with travellers, seamen, fishermen, the physical protection at ports, protection against sabotage and the control of air traffic. The S.C.O.'s personal knowledge and the general body of intelligence collected by him locally and derived by him from the Security Service as a whole were main factors in this.

The distribution of duties in D.4 at Head Office was as follows from the beginning of the war until 1942:-

D.4	(in control of section):	Lt. Col. J.H. Adam 3 secretaries.
D.4.a.	Exit Permits and Military Permits:	Capt. W.S. Mars Lt. T. Nesbitt 4 secretaries.
D.4.b.	Port Intelligence, General Correspondence and Telephone Communi- cations with ports:	Lt. Col. C.H. Burne Lt. T. Bardwell 2 civilian officers 2 secretaries.
D.4.c.	Inspection & Port Security Measures:	Cdr. Burton 2 secretaries.

D.4.d.	Circulars, Black Lists and Visas:	Cdr. Cazelet Lt. Prioleau 2 secretaries.
D.4.e.	Liaison with Home Office & Passport Office re files and records:	in charge of Head of Section 2 secretaries.

From March 1942 onwards D.4 was re-organised on the advice of D.D.O. on the following lines:-

D.4	Security control at sea and airports; Travel control; Liaison with V.P.A. re provision of police and guarding of vulnerable points:	Lt. Col. Adam in charge Major C.H. Burne deputy.
D.4.a.	Travel, Entry and Exit of Travellers at ports, vetting of applications for Visas and Exit Permits; Military Permits:	Major W.S. Mars in charge.
D.4.b.	Intelligence and seamen, receipt and distribution of port intelligence and allied matters; security of shipping and seamen etc:	Major M.B. Heywood in charge.
D.4.c.	Administration, administrative matters connected with S.C.O.s, issue of D.4 Daily Report and circulars to S.C.O.s, co-ordination of administrative information and instructions to S.C.O.s; military travel and embarkations; Black Lists:	Major A.P. Noble in charge.
D.4.d.	Inspection, visits to and inspection of S.C.O.s as directed by officer in charge of D.4:	Major J.G.F. Robb
D.4(L)	Liaison section in London:	Miss [...]

At the outbreak of hostilities S.C.O.s were posted with one section comprising one Warrant Officer and twelve other ranks except as otherwise stated as follows:-

Avonmouth:	Capt. G.L. Stratton, M.C.
Barry Docks:	Col. S. Mathews
Birkenhead:	Lt. Col. P.B. Kemble
Cardiff:	Col. Idwal Jones
Falmouth:	J.T.W. Filson, Esq.
Folkestone:	Sir Arthur Jelf, C.M.G.
Fishguard:	Capt. R.S. Kelway
Glasgow:	Major J.G. Ferrier Robb, M.C.
Heysham:	Major O.N. Wightman, T.D.
Holyhead:	Capt. O.B. Edwards
Hull:	B. K. Barton, Esq.
Leith:	Capt. V.M. Price
Liverpool:	Capt. A.J. Macphail
London:	W.H.A. Webster, Esq. C.I.E.
Newcastle:	Capt. F.C. Clayton, M.C.
Newhaven:	Major A.F. Mills
Newport:	Capt. T.H. Vile
Plymouth:	Capt. F.R. Floyd, M.C.
Stranraer:	W. Dyer, Esq.
Swansea:	Col. B.R. Benyon Winsor
Southampton:	J.C. Fairweather
Bristol Whitchurch:	Major E.S. Humphry
Liverpool Speke:	F.L. Taylor, Esq.
Pembroke Dock:	B.W. Allen, Esq.
Perth:	Major J.R. Couper
Poole:	Capt. C.C. Carter
Shoreham:	B.C. Gee, Esq.

This strength proved inadequate and early in 1940 representations were made that the strength should be made five officers per section. In July 1942 fifty additional officers were sanctioned. Further proposals for an increase were made in 1943, but these were not finally sanctioned until June 1944. In the meanwhile two Inspecting Officers had joined headquarters and there had been a constant demand to supply trained Port Security Officers for overseas stations in the Caribbean and Africa. In July 1942 two officers were sent to Canada to advise on the Port Security Establishment in that country. Four officers were supplied to North Africa in 1943. After the formation of SHAEF, Lt. Colonel Robb and twelve other officers together with a number of other ranks were lent for employment under the 21st Army Group. In October 1944 eleven officers and thirty N.C.O.s were supplied as the nucleus for the establishment of Port and Travel Control in India.

The actual strength of the Security Control personnel at ports grew from 29 officers and 328 other ranks in September 1939 to 117 officers and 825 other ranks in May 1943 and subsequently to 206 officers and 415 other ranks and 39 A.T.S. in April 1945. At the last-mentioned date an R.A.F. establishment was being set up at airports, to which 21 R.A.F. officers had been posted under D.4, the authorised establishment being 70 officers and 60 W.A.A.F.

Various problems and difficulties which arose during the war gave rise to proposals for future arrangements to avoid a recurrence of the difficulty caused by the absence of trained personnel prior to September 1939. These proposals were linked with other proposals regarding the establishment of an Intelligence Corps during peace-time as a reserve from which officers for a Security Service and other Intelligence duties could be drawn.

Brigadier Allen has made the following comments on the initial difficulties of creating the organisation at the ports:-

> "In creating this port organisation from absolutely nothing our resources at Head Office before war broke out were too slender. Some considerable effort had been made by a travelling officer who visited the major ports in the United Kingdom and began recruiting officers and other ranks on a gentleman's agreement to come forward in the event of war. Local Chief Constables were approached and the majority of names of officers were obtained with their co-operation. The officers themselves were responsible for collecting the names of suitable other ranks.
>
> We expected that if war did break out we should continue to recruit through our own resources; the growth of the organisation made this impossible and on grounds of manpower alone we became dependent on the 'I' Corps to provide us with personnel. The War Office did this handsomely.
>
> The chief lessons learned from those early days are:-
>
> (a) Head Office must know what an organisation of this kind is going to look like. In order to do this one must have a fairly detailed knowledge of the quantity and type of ship and air traffic and the capacity of ports.
> (b) Neither local authorities at ports nor departments in Whitehall were sufficiently aware of what we were going to do at the ports. Hence, port security personnel were regarded with grave suspicion, particularly by police in many places. Obviously our personnel had to learn their job from the very beginning and inevitably trod on the toes of certain local authorities such as the C.I.D. at Liverpool.
>
> This is only one more example of the general departmental ignorance as to the functions and methods of M.I.5. All these difficulties and disadvantages had to be overcome by a laborious process of liaison and education generally. Eventually, as the organisation grew in size and efficiency its value became generally recognised. If a Secret Service is

going to operate overtly in this way it is absolutely essential that all concerned should know what we are planning and why.

I would like to stress the value and importance of central control from Security Service Headquarters. Such work cannot be decentralised on a district basis.

It is essential that Headquarters should include at a pretty early stage officers who have already had experience at the ports, otherwise local problems and difficulties will not be properly appreciated.

Port Security overseas in maritime colonies and dominions had not been thought out on any proper basis. We soon learned this from reports obtained at United Kingdom ports, but we were unable to correct it until we had sufficient trained staff ourselves.

Problems which have to be handled are numerous and complex, and it is essential that the Security Service should be better prepared next time to create an organisation of this kind."

C Division. Before the war an attempt had been made to keep aliens of German and Italian nationalities out of the Armed Forces and to examine cases where persons of those nationalities applied for naturalisation as British subjects with a view to preventing undesirables from acquiring British nationality. The reasons in both cases arose out of B Branch enquiries regarding the organisation of the Nazi State. Certain cases had come to light which proved that the Nazi Government would consent to Germans acquiring British nationality while retaining their original nationality and membership of the Nazi Party if it was in the interests of Germany that they should do so. It was felt that from the security point of view this involved bad faith and constituted a danger. Up to April 1941 enemy aliens were ineligible for commissions, but after that date the door was opened, although commissions were generally limited to the Pioneer Corps. This limitation was slowly but progressively relaxed as a result of Army Council policy until eventually it became possible for an enemy alien to hold a commission in practically any corps or regiment of the army, even including the Intelligence Corps.

In consequence of the number of German and Austrian servants in this country before the war and the numbers of them employed in or near important military centres, steps were taken to prohibit the employment of a servant inside Service establishments without permission. This permission was not given without the approval of the Security Service, but there were no restrictions on the employment of aliens in the private households of members of H.M. Forces or Government officials. In May 1940 the J.I.C. recommended that all members of the Services and officials of Government Departments should be forbidden to employ enemy aliens and a month later instructions based on these recommendations were issued to all Commands at home. A circular was also issued with the approval of the Prime Minister to the heads of Government Departments drawing attention to their responsibility where aliens were employed in their households.

The main duty of C Division has been the examination of credentials of individuals, British and foreign, Service and civilian, wherever it was considered desirable to check them against Security Service records by reason of -

(a) the type of employment involving secrecy or reliability and -
(b) foreign nationality or connections.

The object of this check was the discovery and diversion from certain categories of employment of persons of undesirable foreign nationality or connections or persons sympathetic to Axis ideals or otherwise constituting a security danger.

This checking against Security Service records is of purely negative value; it does not mean that all undesirables are kept out of certain categories of employment, but merely that persons of whom the Security Service happen to have a record come to notice. The responsibility for deciding in each case whether an individual should be excluded from any category of employment is the responsibility of the Government Department concerned and the security records cannot be complete or comprehensive. They cannot include persons whose activities have not in some way or other brought them on to the records. Soon after the outbreak of war the numbers of names submitted for vetting was so large that it substantially contributed to the breakdown of the Security Service at that time. In the middle of 1940 it was agreed at the instance of Lord Swinton that the security vetting of many industrial grades of civilian state employment should be abandoned. Further reduction in "vettable" categories were later secured as a result of the Bridges Panel Report in June 1942. These categories were then virtually limited to employment involving duties of a Top Secret or Secret character or where complete integrity was essential in the national interests.

In April 1942 the Director General issued a circular on the duties of C Division, one of the main objects of which was to ensure that the Security Service should always speak with one voice in relation to vetting cases. In June 1942 a secret memorandum on the examination of credentials was issued for the guidance of officials in Government Departments and branches dealing with vetting cases in the light of the Bridges Report. This memorandum stressed the fact that a practice had grown up of telling applicants that they would be vetted by M.I.5. or informing applicants who had been classified by the Security Service as undesirable that they had been turned down by that Service. It was laid down that the fact that the Security Service was involved should never be mentioned in such cases.

During the period from September 1939 to December 1944 C Division gave adverse information and advice in the cases of 9,943 persons. It is claimed that this action cannot have failed to make an extensive contribution to defensive security and that the fact that serious complaints have arisen in but a very small proportion of this total suggests that our organisation and methods have been built up on sound principles. As far as can be judged, there has been no defect in vetting from the point of view of security against enemy penetration in connection with the war. The chapters in this report dealing with Communism make it clear that the vetting system is in no sense an effective protection against the infiltration of Communists into a wide range of important official posts, including those of commissioned officers in H.M. Forces. This is not due to any defect in vetting procedure.

The larger aspects of the security problem; the Cabinet Offices and the J.I.C. The account in Chapter II, Part 2 (iii) of the preventive machinery in 1914-1918 showed that branches under Lt. Colonel Holt Wilson included those dealing with preventive work generally, alien war service, overseas forces and control of ports and frontiers. During the period between the wars this organisation lapsed. Colonel Holt Wilson's duties were confined to those connected with the preparation of regulations, security chapters in Service manuals, lectures at Staff Colleges and arrangements for permits and passes and other preventive measures in the event of war. When war came he did not resume all the responsibilities which he had undertaken in the previous war. C & D Divisions, under Brigadier Allen, assumed some of them while those connected with Defence Security Officers in the Colonies and the organisation in the Middle East had become detached under the present A Division.

In the war of 1939-1945 C and D Divisions were not responsible over the whole field of preventive measures. They were not concerned with the internment of aliens or with action under Defence Regulation 18B. Again they were not concerned with the Postal and Telegraph Censorship and the B Division Censorship liaison, which covers a wide field of preventive security.

Apart from the question of security against espionage and of the measures necessary to prevent enemy agents from getting direct access to information, there is a wider risk, namely that of secrets becoming public property through carelessness or disregard of security instructions. Brigadier Allen has pointed out that in this sense defensive security cannot be the sole responsibility of the Security Service. The field is so wide and the channels of possible leakage so numerous that unless every Service and Government Department and every establishment concerned with important war secrets is fully alive to the dangers and is prepared to safeguard them on a carefully planned system, leakage on a dangerous and considerable scale is bound to occur. Real progress has been made in many directions and officers have been appointed to deal with security in most branches of the machinery of Government. Further developments are in progress. The Home Defence Security Executive with its original somewhat detached role has now become the Standing Inter-Departmental Committee on security under the wing of the Cabinet Offices. The (Bridges) Panel on security arrangements in Government Departments has made a useful contribution and it is expected that, in some form, it will continue to function and will be located in the Cabinet Offices. The Joint Intelligence Committee will continue as a sub-committee of the Chiefs of Staff Committee where inter-Services security problems can be discussed. Developments overseas point to the continuation of Joint Intelligence Committees in the main theatres, including occupied Europe and the Middle East, India and the Far East. Security interests will be represented on such committees and the Dominions will probably be invited to follow suit.

Brigadier Allen has emphasised the importance of the far-reaching security measures taken to protect the "Overlord" operation for the campaign in Normandy. These measures included a complete ban, with exceptions in the case of Russia and the U.S.A., on the movements and on uncensored communications of foreign diplomats. These security measures - combined with deception - gave the Allies the weapon they most needed - surprise, but with all these advantages and with the strategic initiative in Allied hands, the whole operation could have been jeopardised if the Germans had had one really first-class channel of information unknown to us, on which their High Command could have placed complete reliance.

(viii) A Division (Regional Control).

A Division Organisation. The organisation of A Division after the summer of 1941 is as given in the chart in Appendix II.

The main account of the work of A Division will be found under Part 4 (Internal Organisation and Staff of the Security Service), but one of its components, Regional Control, is described here because it originated from the circumstances of the war with Germany and its main functions were concerned with developments of the war situation. Correspondence between Head Office sections and Regional Security Liaison Officers in regard to Communism was conducted on different lines from that connected with the war: R.S.L.O.s only received copies of correspondence with Chief Constables. The ground for this differentiation was that the subject of Communism was handled on different lines as a matter of long-term policy.

Regional Control. This section was transferred from B Division to A Division in August 1941, but its main functions continued unchanged on lines already described in Chapter IV above. In May 1941, soon after his appointment as Director General, Sir David Petrie called a conference in connection with the regional organisation. He explained that the reasons for establishing the R.S.L.O.s had been:-

- (a) to bring the Security Service into closer touch with provincial Police Forces;
- (b) to reduce the accumulating amount of work at Head Office;
- (c) to expedite the treatment of reports and correspondence from Chief Constables;
- (d) to provide the basis of an organisation in case of invasion when Head Office might be cut off from provincial districts;

and that their principal functions were:-

- (a) to deal with Chief Constables and their staffs on all matters concerning the Security Service (with certain specified exceptions, e.g. Communism);
- (b) to assist and advise those concerned in dealing with problems of the arrest, search and interrogation of suspects of security interest;
- (c) to deal with individual cases locally where possible and to reduce the volume of enquiries sent to Head Office;

(d) to collaborate with the naval, military and air force intelligence officers in the regions on all matters of mutual interest;
(e) R.S.L.O.s should not normally make enquiries on their own, but should always act in this connection through the police.

Thus, by the summer of 1941 when the re-organisation of the Security Service was gradually put into effect the position of Regional Control and the R.S.L.O.s had crystalised and, after overcoming initial difficulties largely due to the flooding of the office with numerous denunciations and reports about suspected spies, the staff in the Regions had settled down to deal with its work on systematic lines. There were certain respects in which the position was not clearly established; although the functions of the R.S.L.O.s had been defined on such broad lines as to leave it open to them to deal in their regions with any aspect of the work of the Security Service, certain exceptions developed in practice. Sections D.1, D.2 and D.3, which dealt with security in factories and other establishments under the Ministry of Supply and the Ministry of Aircraft Production, did not delegate their work to the R.S.L.O.s. The reasons for this were that these D sections had close relations with and understood the problems of their own Services and their supply departments on the one hand and also had close personal relations with individuals at the factories and other establishments on the other.

There was none the less a tendency on the part of the regional organisation to claim that their functions should be understood as embracing this among all the other aspects of the work of the Security Service.

An exception was also made at first in the case of the section responsible for the internal security of the Forces and for War Office establishments and Ordnance Factories. This exception, however, disappeared when this section (B.1 afterwards F.1) was merged in the section dealing with Communists and Fascists (F.2 and F.3). The exception originally made in regard to Fascists had broken down from the beginning, but that in regard to Communists - whereby correspondence was conducted direct between the Communist section and the police - was maintained on the ground that it was a question of long-term policy and was not directly connected with the war effort.

The question of the relative spheres of the R.S.L.O.s and the S.C.O. at ports and airports under A.D.D.4. also gave rise to difficulties which were settled by the Director General in two circulars, one arising out of the Regional Officers Conferenceon the 13th and 14th May 1941 and the second in a circular issued on the 10th February 1942 which elaborated the instructions of May 1941.

The question came to a head because the section of B Division responsible for the investigation of sabotage had met with difficulties in dealing with the police in connection with enquiries in port areas. The Director General emphasised that the R.S.L.O.s and S.C.O.s were both parts of the same service and must speak with the same voice to the police and other local authorities. Each must keep the other closely informed of all matters of common interest and steps must be taken to ensure that both arranged for information to reach the sections concerned in Head Office through the appropriate channel. In practice it was found that close collaboration between the R.S.L.O. and the S.C.O. was of the utmost importance in connection with measures for detecting the arrival of enemy agents, and it was found that an intelligent and imaginative interpretation of the instructions on the subject of mutual co-operation removed the difficulties which had arisen in the early stages.

The R.S.L.O. played an important part not only as liaison officer with the Police, but also with numerous other local officials of different parts of the machinery of government. He was generally the security adviser to the Regional Commissioner for all purposes and he was in close contact with him in connection with the latter's powers for the detention of individuals under the Defence Regulations in the event of invasion. For this purpose the Regional Commissioner's Suspect List and the Enemy Aliens Invasion List were prepared. The process varied in different regions in accordance with the different roles played by the various legal advisers, Acting Inspectors of Constabulary, Principal Officers, Regional Police Staff Officers and the Regional Commissioners themselves. The R.S.L.O. had to establish satisfactory relations with all these officers and he had to prepare the Suspect Lists in consultation with the Police and with the various sections of the Security Service which were concerned with different nationalities and classes of persons. It was laid down that the R.S.L.O. should not agree to the deletion of a name from the lists without consulting the appropriate head office section, but that he could add a name on his own initiative. The cases were reviewed from time to time.

The Home Office had started to make releases of enemy aliens from internment in 1940 and this process continued throughout the war. Enemy aliens so released formed the bulk of the names on the Enemy Aliens Invasion List. Releases were not recommended by Head Office sections without consulting the R.S.L.O. and through him the Chief Constable concerned. This procedure removed grounds for complaint that in some cases aliens were released against the wishes of the Police and without their having any opportunity to protest in advance. When an alien was released the Head Office section supplied all available information to the Police through the R.S.L.O.

The R.S.L.O. was concerned with the detailed arrangements for restrictions on aliens under the Aliens (Movement Restriction) Order and with all measures connected with the restrictions placed on aliens to prevent them from entering areas adjoining the coast of Great Britain and certain other vulnerable areas.

The R.S.L.O. was responsible for liaison with the local representatives of the Ministry of Supply, the Ministry of Information, the Ministry of Labour, local Censorship units, the Radio Security Section, the Railway Police and certain semi-official organisations such as the British Council (which last undertook work among the alien communities in this country).

The contact with representatives of the Ministry of Supply was important because the R.S.L.O. was called upon to deal with questions where an individual was considered unsuitable for employment in a Royal Ordnance Factory or Ministry of Supply Depot on account of having been reported as doubtful or unreliable for reasons connected with any form of subversive activity.

Among the most important relations of the R.S.L.O. were those with the Military, Naval and Air authorities. Where the Army was concerned the R.S.L.O. was most directly concerned with the Security Officers at Command Headquarters who, in the early stages of the war, were under the Director of C and D Divisions and, after 1940, were officers on the General Staff and were known as G.S.O.2.I(B). The R.S.L.O.s had to overcome certain difficulties arising from the fact that the situation was new both to the Military authorities and the Police. They succeeded in obtaining the confidence of both. This was achieved in part by clarifying the position in regard to the functions of the G.S.O.2.I(B), the Police and themselves in connection with Security Service investigations regarding persons suspected of subversive activities. An important part in this was played by the Special Branches of local Police Forces which had been established throughout the country. R.S.L.O.s attended conferences of Police officers of Special Branches from their region and by arranging for G.S.O.2.I(B) officers to attend they were able to facilitate a mutual understanding of each other's problems.

It had been decided early in 1941 that in the event of invasion R.S.L.O.s should establish close liaison with the headquarters of Military and R.A.F. formations in their regions. For this purpose the R.S.L.O. was to be attached to Command Headquarters while his staff at the Regional Commissioner's headquarters was to be strengthened. Liaison was established on similar lines with the Provost Branch of the R.A.F. The R.S.L.O. was not in equally close touch with the Naval authorities as this function was discharged by the S.C.O. who was in day-to-day contact with them.

The arrival of German secret agents in connection with the projected invasion of this country in the summer and autumn of 1940 brought the R.S.L.O.s in coastal regions into touch with problems concerning the steps to be taken to render such landings difficult. Minefields and barbed wire provided physical obstacles, but the position was not satisfactory in lonely parts of the coast. As a result of representations made by the Admiralty and the Security Service the coastguard establishment was substantially increased early in 1942 and they were given the status of members of the Armed Forces; but the position continued to present difficulties. In January 1943 contact was made with R.A.F. Radar who undertook to report suspicious aircraft movements and the suspicious movements of vessels. An exercise staged eleven months later provided a 'rude shock' by showing that neither Radar nor the coastguards was infallible and all the six men who took part in the exercise landed without attracting attention. The arrangements were, therefore, further improved and steps were taken for information about suspicious movements of any unidentified vessels to be reported to the R.S.L.O. either direct or through the S.C.O.

As part of their general function of furnishing liaison between Head Office and the Police R.S.L.O.s were called on to play a part in enquiries connected with the arrest of enemy agents whenever these occurred in or concerned their regions.

Under the more settled conditions of 1942 and 1943, the pressure of work in connection with their earlier problems having diminished, R.S.L.O.s found themselves confronted with new duties such as rendering assistance to S.I.S., S.O.E. and later O.S.S. in connection with exercises - sometimes on a large scale - provided for students under training for despatch to enemy-occupied Europe.

After the arrival of the American forces in the United Kingdom R.S.L.O.s became responsible for liaison with the American security agencies under arrangements which worked satisfactorily and involved less difficulty than had been anticipated.

In connection with the preparations for the landing in Normandy or Operation "Overlord" R.S.L.O.s were directly concerned with the question of individuals suspected as enemy agents in operational areas, but they were not directly concerned with the security of the operation itself. This was entirely a Service responsibility. The preparations for "Overlord" proved the value of the good-will which had been built up during the previous years by R.S.L.O.s with all the Services, including the American Services and with the Police. Before the operation the security net was tightened throughout the country, more attention was paid to the danger of leakage of information and increased vigilance was exercised in regard to the possible arrival of enemy agents in this country. Steps were taken to prepare a list of suspects for exclusion or restriction orders to be issued by the Home Secretary in regard to persons in the coastal areas of the South of England between the Wash and the Severn. R.S.L.O.s were advised to endeavour to persuade Chief Constables to make the list as short as possible, but it was explained that Chief Constables should be satisfied that all necessary names had been included so as to avoid any possibility of their not being able to allay apprehensions about individuals in the minds of Military commanders. After full agreement had been reached between R.S.L.O.s and Chief Constables the total number of names included in the list did not amount to more than twenty-five. This was a striking proof of the entirely different atmosphere resulting from the change in the mentality of the public and of the Services as compared with the scare period of 1940.

After operation "Overlord" had been launched R.S.L.O.s generally found that their work began to subside. The number of R.S.L.O.s and their staff was simultaneously reduced, some of the officers concerned being made available for duty in the Counter Intelligence organisation under SHAEF on the Continent.

(ix) War Room.

When the plans for the invasion of Normandy were being prepared, first under COSSAC and later under SHAEF[†], Mr. (later Brigadier) White of B Division acted in the capacity of an adviser on counter espionage to the staff responsible for planning the organisation. Eventually, the American Army system being adopted, the organisation at SHAEF headquarters comprised the G-2 Operational Intelligence and G-2 Counter Intelligence (G-2 OI and G-2 CI) corresponding to the British formations G.S.I(A) and G.S.I(B); and G-2 CI under the direction of Brigadier White were responsible for discharging, within the zones of military operations, the same functions as were discharged by the Security

---

[†] In this section the American system of nomenclature and initials is followed as far as possible. This was, rightly, the War Room practice in the circumstances, i.e. under a joint British and American Staff.

Service inside the United Kingdom, that is to say, all the functions of security and counter espionage. In particular they were responsible for the arrest of enemy agents whether left behind by the Germans as they retreated or subsequently despatched by them to penetrate behind the Allied lines.

At the end of 1943 and at the beginning of 1944 a suggestion was put forward for the formation of a Central Counter Intelligence Bureau which was to be responsible for collecting and analysing, for the benefit of CI Staffs with Army Groups and Armies, all relevant intelligence about the German Intelligence Service and its agents. It was realised that O.S.S., the American Special Service, and the Security Service and S.I.S., the two British Services, between them possessed almost all the information which existed anywhere about the German Intelligence Services (the Abwehr and the Sipo und SD) and that they were the only organisations which had personnel properly trained to deal with this subject.

The problem, therefore, was to devise some means by which all information could be made available to the CI Staff in a satisfactory form. Difficulties arose because of objections raised by S.I.S. to the proposal for a Central Bureau drawing on the records and the expert knowledge of the three Services. These objections arose from the special position claimed by Lt. Colonel Cowgill, as the head of Section V, for his organisation. In order to understand this position it is necessary to go back to the spring of 1941 when two decisions were made. The first was that, under the circumstances referred to in Chapter IV above, R.S.S. should not come under the Security Service but under S.I.S. The second was that Section V of S.I.S. should be responsible for carding information about the German Intelligence Services and their agents outside the three-mile limit, while the Security Service should only card names abroad which were of more than local importance. This was subsequently modified in practice in that the special B Division Registry (the RB Registry) carded a considerable number of names of persons abroad, including names derived from the interception of enemy Secret Services' wireless. This position, again, was subsequently modified when full carding of this intercepted (ISOS) material was developed in the ISOS Registry of Section V.

These two decisions furnished the principal grounds on which Lt. Colonel Cowgill claimed that Intelligence concerning persons outside the three-mile limit was the concern of Section V but not of the Security Service; and that he was therefore entitled to withhold it at his discretion. His attitude obstructed the comprehensive study of the enemy organisations and the collation of intelligence about them at any point as a centre. It had the effect that when the Allies landed on the Continent there was no focal point through which G-2 CI could receive and transmit intelligence derived from ISOS, Camp 020, their own interrogations and other sources. The machinery was diffused instead of being centralised.

The difficulties created by the controversy between Lt. Colonel Cowgill and B Division officers had led to proposals in the summer of 1942 for the amalgamation of Section V and parts of B Division. These were known as the D.O.C.E. proposals. They were abandoned after lengthy discussions. They were, in fact, impracticable because by aiming at separating intelligence from the responsibility for preparing cases against individual agents they cut across all the responsibilities of the Security Service. They were, in fact, an abortive attempt at finding a focal point for intelligence in the counter espionage field by placing it in Section V; and the failure to find a solution dominated the relations between the two organisations during 1943 and 1944 with adverse effects on the efficiency of both of them. Arising out of this position an agreement was made to set up a joint organisation comprising the sub-sections of O.S.S. and S.I.S. dealing with France and the Low Countries to perform all the functions of the Security Service for the purposes of the G-2 CI formations. This new organisation was established under the name of the "War Room" and under the joint direction of the Western European sections of O.S.S. and Section V. A Security Service officer was attached as a liaison officer to whom all matters concerning the Security Service were referred and from whom information from Security Service records was received. French representatives were attached for a similar purpose.

It became apparent in the early autumn of 1944 that this organisation was not satisfactory. It did not furnish the necessary focal point for the centralisation of intelligence. On the contrary it represented a renewed attempt to place that point in Section V (instead of in the Security Service) with inadequate machinery and without the necessary staff of trained personnel. From October 1944 negotiations were carried on between the G-2 CI sub-division of SHAEF and O.S.S., the Security Service and S.I.S. (in the relevant SHAEF documents the latter are referred to as MI-5 and MI-6) for the purpose of setting up a new body of experts to inform and advise the CI Staffs in the SHAEF area about the organisation, operations and personalities of the Abwehr and the Sipo und SD (referred to in the SHAEF documents as the GIS), the former of which had now been absorbed (and purged) by the RSHA.

In February 1945 it was finally agreed that a new organisation to be known as the SHAEF G-2 Counter Intelligence War Room should be created under the direction of a British officer, Lt. Colonel T.A. Robertson, with an American Deputy, Mr. R. Blum, both of whom were to be carried on the strength of the SHAEF G-2 CI sub-division. O.S.S., S.I.S. and the Security Service (referred to as the Special Services) agreed to place at the disposal of SHAEF the personnel and records required for the purpose. It was not until the 1st March 1945 that this new machine came into effective operation. It lasted until the end of the SHAEF period in July 1945 when the "Director and the Deputy Director of the War Room became responsible to the heads of OSS, MI-5 and MI-6". The idea underlying this newly re-organised War Room was to create a single organ through which all the relevant and available information and advice from O.S.S., the Security Service and S.I.S. could be furnished to Counter Intelligence Staffs in the field. The War Room became the focal point of all information about the German Intelligence Services - the organisations under the RSHA and their agents - for use in the SHAEF area and for the purpose of co-ordinating the collation of intelligence and the action taken upon it both by the CI Staff in the SHAEF area and by O.S.S., the Security Service and Section V of S.I.S. outside that area. The work of the War Room now hinged on a combination of the records of the Security Service in the shape of subject and personnel files, records of the Western European sections of Section V ISOS Registry, the SHAEF pink cards and, as the Allied advance progressed, captured German documents and the interrogation reports from the field. (The SHAEF pink cards, which were specially prepared for the purpose, contained information about the known officers and agents of the RSHA. These cards were used not as information cards but as pointers to the personal and subject files in which the main information about the individual or the subject could be found). This combination of records was utilised by a combination of trained personnel from O.S.S., the Security Service and S.I.S. with special knowledge of different branches of the whole subject acting in close co-operation with the staff in the original sections of the three Services which had previously dealt with it. All the available material utilised with the expert knowledge of this trained personnel was made readily accessible to the CI Staff with the armies to assist them in dealing with the enemy personnel - when captured - and their agents operating behind the Allied lines.

The elaborate but efficient organisation thus created can only be described here in a highly condensed form. Fuller details are available in S.F.50-24-44(81).

In accordance with an agreement made on the 10th January 1945 between the SHAEF G-2 CI sub-division and the Direction des Services de Documentation (DSDoc) the French Service became one of the participating "Special Services" and French officers and secretaries were drafted into the War Room. Subsequently it was decided that the DSDoc office in Germany dealing with CI matters should deal direct with the War Room and that the War Room should be responsible for giving them advice and guidance, while DSDoc in Paris should be a collecting centre of information derived from the War Room and should reciprocate by communicating information obtained by the French in the course of their investigations. Eventually a similar arrangement was extended to cover the case of the French zone in Austria.

The War Room consisted of the following sections:-

Administrative Sections

  WR-A Supplies and internal administration.

  WR-B The handling and distribution of papers.

  WR-X The maintenance of liaison with the communications sections of the "Special Services" and of the military as well as ensuring that the War Room had all the channels of communication which it required.

  WR-H Based on the old RB Registry (in the Security Service) which was developed and set up as the central repository of all War Room files with the responsibility of indexing and maintaining the files and preparing the SHAEF pink cards.

Intelligence Sections

> WR-C Known as the Assessment Section, was concerned with the examination and appreciation of the papers dealing with interrogation reports and with briefing the CI Staffs and interrogators in the field. It dealt with individuals.
>
> WR-E Known as the Publications Section, was concerned with the study of the German organisations as a whole.
>
> WR-D The Documents Section, was responsible for studying, evaluating and distributing captured German documents dealing with the German Secret Service organisations.
>
> WR-F The Special Sources Section, was responsible for examining all intercepted wireless material with a view to its bearing on the work of the other sections and was responsible for controlling the transmission of this material to the field.
>
> WR/DSDoc Consisting entirely of French personnel, was responsible for all communications between the War Room and French stations abroad.

The following are a few of the outstanding points which deserve special mention in connection with the War Room. An example of the distribution given to liquidation reports prepared by the War Room indicates the extent to which information about its investigations was communicated to different parts of the machinery concerned with counter espionage in the field and among Allied organisations -

USFET	100
BAOR	100
AFHQ	2
US Forces Austria	20
Allied CC(BE) Vienna	20
OMG Germany (US)	6
G-2 Com. Z	2
OSS/X-2	10
MI-6(V)	30
MI-5	4
WR/DSDoc	4
G-2 War Dept.	2
ONI	1
MI-14(d)	2
MI-19 (for CSDIC/UK)	2

WR-X used O.S.S., S.I.S., SLU., SHAEF and army channels for its communications and while making use of their cyphers was thus responsible for the cryptographic security within the War Room of all telegrams concerned. The network of communications was, therefore, a large one.

The responsibilities of WR-H were as follows:-

> "to make index cards; to make new files; to put all papers into relevant files; to do the necessary look-ups on names; to extract information from reports into subject files; to be responsible for the custody and the transmitting of files to various sections and individuals within the War Room. In addition to this, they were called upon to provide trace summaries to assist the work of the Assessment officers. Finally they were responsible for preparing the pro-forma for the SHAEF Pink Cards of GIS (German Intelligence Service) personnel which were sent by them to EDS/CPI[†] for reproduction in thirty-four copies and distribution to the various recipients in the field and elsewhere."

WR-H was divided into four sub-sections on normal lines for processing purposes. Of these four, WR-H2, which was responsible for look-ups and the general direction of the index, was sub-divided into four sub-sections corresponding to the sub-sections of WR-C, which were in this way given considerable assistance through being in touch with registry personnel who were studying the same part of the GIS.

The maximum strength of WR-C was twenty-two officers supported by some twenty-five assistants and secretaries. It was divided into four sub-sections, each of which was responsible not for a geographical area but for a sub-division of the subject. Thus WR-C1 dealt with the officers and agents of "the old Abwehr I and III, except for IIIF and IIID, and for the KdMs and the Mil. Amt, except for Mil.Amt D, and the KOs in foreign countries", i.e. in the main with the espionage and counter espionage branches of the German Secret Services as they were finally organised with the exception of those which were connected with deception and with units in neutral countries. WR-C2 was responsible for all cases connected with sabotage and subversive activities. WR-C3 was responsible for the RSHA excluding certain details dealt with by WR-C1 and WR-C4 was concerned with the study of German counter espionage including those parts of the organisation which were concerned with deception and double agents.

WR-D, the Documents section, consisting of the head of the section and his deputy with twenty trained readers, was not only responsible for reading and distributing documents and making precis of their contents, but, in virtue of the experience of its staff, was able to make a positive contribution to the intelligence work of the War Room. For instance some documents captured by EDS/CPI early in April 1945 were subjected to examination by a reader who was studying materials connected with the Lower Rhineland who, as a result of a detailed analysis, made it clear that there was evidence of

---

[†] EDS/CPI was a SHAEF Intelligence formation which was responsible for collating, for use when the armies entered Germany, intelligence on the subject of Nazi Party, SS and Police formations. It formed a special card index for the purpose and also reproduced and distributed the cards prepared by the War Room for GIS personnel.

an intricate stay-behind network of Gestapo agents recruited mostly from the foreign worker population. The War Room at the time knew almost nothing about this particular sphere of RSHA activity, but action taken in consultation with the WR-C (Assessment section) officer led to arrests in the field and a more elaborate study of the whole operation.

WR-E consisted of three officers who had previously worked in the Radio Intelligence Section, had served as an intermediary between R.S.S., Section V and B Division of the Security Service and had produced a number of papers mainly based on ISOS material. Soon after its constitution WR-E produced a basic handbook on the German Intelligence Service as known to us in March/April 1945. This was given a wide distribution and was regarded as a standard work of reference for all CI formations in the field. It was translated into French. A number of other papers on important aspects of the German organisations were also produced (vide Appendix C in S.F.50-24-44(81)).

WR-F, the Special Sources section, was responsible for reading, interpreting and sending to the field all information obtained from the interception of GIS wireless. It was also responsible for extracting information from the same sources and sending it to the Registry for SHAEF pink cards. This section was extremely active up to the end of hostilities in passing information to SHAEF and the Army Groups, including AFHQ in Italy. The information from these sources was particularly useful in the interrogation of difficult cases with long records of work in the GIS.

The different sections of the War Room, working in combination with the Special Services and the field, combined to produce important results. Many of these were reflected in the various documents prepared and circulated by WR-E. WR-C dealt with a number of the most important members of the old Abwehr and of the RSHA, including well-known personages such as Kaltenbrunner, Chef der Sicherheitspolizei; Schellenberg, known as Amtschef VI (the head of the branch of the RSHA operating abroad); Skorzeny, who was head of the combined sabotage organisations of the RSHA and the old Abwehr; Korvetten Kapitaen Erich Pfeiffer, the head of I Marine, the naval espionage branch of the old Abwehr, who had played a prominent part in work against this country for many years; and Ohlendorff, Amtschef III, the head of the SD. Many of the more important cases, especially in the early stages, were brought over to England for interrogation at Camp 020.

The most important functions of the War Room were, therefore, to pass to the field the information obtained from ISOS and that available from the records of the Security Service dealing with enemy organisations, enemy personnel and their agents.

During the period of its existence and in the preceding months after the landing in Normandy, no enemy agents were arrested in this country, but considerable numbers were arrested in the field as the armies advanced. The majority of these were interrogated by the CI Staff at the headquarters of the Army Groups and Armies (only a few of the more important being dealt with, as mentioned above, at Camp 020) so that information based on these interrogations was flowing from the field back to the War Room and its Registry. The results of these interrogations involved an immense number of requests for traces from WR-H. The work of collating the results of these traces and passing them to the field interrogators fell to WR-C. At the same time the B Division records which, as mentioned above, were the basis of the War Room records were supplemented by material from OSS/X-2 and Section V(F) of S.I.S. In order to complete these records, the cards in the SHAEF pink index - about twenty-four thousand in number - were compared with the B Division records and, as a result, it was found that a further twelve thousand cards had to be prepared. During its existence the War Room made forty-two thousand SHAEF pink cards and over eight thousand amendments to existing cards. It was estimated that the making of these cards involved references to the index in respect of approximately a hundred thousand names. Some two thousand personal files were made and very nearly four hundred subject files.

These figures are some indication of the volume of work which passed through the War Room, and its importance arises from the fact that each card represented the available information about an official or agent of the Abwehr or SD and indicated an individual who was to be arrested. Unfortunately, as the War Room report states, arrangements for keeping statistical returns were not made and the number of arrests actually made is not known, but it was very large and probably exceeded fifty thousand.

In the War Room report it is suggested that the WR-H staff, which varied between fifty and seventy, was not adequate to cope with all the work required of it, because, in order to deal with the production of the pink cards, it was necessary to ignore to a very large extent the work of looking up and cross-extracting; and that this latter was of almost equal importance because all other services undertaken by the War Room for the field depended on this work being done. It is also pointed out that the position of WR-H at a distance of seventy miles from London increased the difficulties because of the lack of close personal contact.

Brigadier White has said that from the point of view of the field the War Room was a great improvement on its predecessor. It was responsible to the authority in whose interests it had been formed, namely the Intelligence Division of SHAEF, and it regarded itself as the servant of the CI Staffs. All its work was, therefore, related to the practical needs of the CI units in the field and it played a great part in the final liquidation of the GIS.

Once it was started it was efficiently organised and it achieved the purpose for which it had been created. It overcame the difficulties which had beset its predecessor - the Section V and O.S.S. War Room - which was unable to pass information sufficiently rapidly in both directions between London and the field.

An account of the War Room would be meaningless without some explanation of the organisation under SHAEF which it had to serve, that is the G-2 CI organisation mentioned above at the beginning of this section. The head of the G-2 CI and G-2 CI Staffs was Major General Strong, with an American officer as the head of G-2 CI and Brigadier White as the latter's deputy. The G-2 CI Staff consisted of three basic sections covering "Military Security", "Civil Security" and Port, Travel and Frontier control. Military

Security roughly corresponded to C and D Divisions, laid down preventive security policy and vetted personnel where necessary; Civil Security roughly, but only very roughly, covered the B Division field and laid down policy for the control of the civilian population in the occupied countries; Port, Travel and Frontier control was built up entirely on Security Service lines and staffed entirely by personnel seconded from the Security Service. The appointment of Brigadier White as deputy to the head of the G-2 CI Staff and the seconding of trained Security Service personnel - to the number of some 80 officers out of a total of 2,600 officers and men - gave the staff in the field the necessary "steel frame" with technical knowledge based on professional experience. The result was a much closer interlocking between the G-2 C1 Staff and the Services in London. Brigadier White's chief duties were to secure the necessary close collaboration. He left his position as Deputy Director of B Division to take up this new appointment towards the end of August 1944 and at once realised that the CI Staff in the field was handicapped by the fact that it had no records of the type upon which the Security Service relied. He therefore put up to Major General Strong proposals which the latter endorsed in letters addressed to the heads of O.S.S., S.I.S. and the Security Service on the 10th November 1944. These proposals eventually led to the creation of the new War Room, as described above, in March 1945.

The object in view when these proposals were framed was to cover two different situations. The first was that in which enemy agents - normally of French, Belgian or other non-German nationality - had to be detected behind our lines while operations were still in progress; the second was the very different one in which, after the occupation of Germany, steps had to be taken to "mop up" the GIS by arresting all their known officials as well as their agents.

The organisation at Supreme Headquarters in the shape of the three basic sections mentioned above was reduplicated in the CI Staff under the 21st Army Group (British), the 12th Army Group (American) on the Normandy front and the 6th Army Group (American), which advanced through France after the landing on the Riviera. Under the three Army Groups there were formations of Armies, Corps and Divisions; and at the headquarters of each were Field Security Police or CI Staff, to whom it fell to search for and arrest known enemy agents, whether of the stay-behind, line-crosser or parachutist variety. Many of these arrests were made on the basis of information obtained from ISOS, supplemented by interrogations and the results of references to the records of the three Services. The means by which this information was passed down to the lowest units who, in many cases, actually effected the arrest, was by a suitable distribution of the SHAEF pink cards which gave the necessary information to enable the Field Security Police to trace the individuals.

It was to facilitate this distribution of information that the pink cards were instituted in place of the information in the shape of a "Who's Who" as compiled by B.1 Information. The latter form, which was convenient for Security Service purposes in London, was not suitable for the purpose of effecting individual arrests in the field, i.e. in France or Belgium while the Armies were advancing or later, after the occupation of Germany. The cards could be broken up and distributed to the smaller units.

The War Room ceased to be subordinate to SHAEF at the end of the SHAEF period in July 1945. It had served as an intermediary between the records of the Security Service and the officers responsible for the executive action of making arrests and interrogating in the field. It thus acted as a research and analysis organisation on the grand scale; and as a centre of liaison between the Intelligence Staff in the field on the one hand and O.S.S., Section V of S.I.S. and the Security Service on the other. It achieved this purpose successfully because all the sources of counter espionage or counter intelligence information were concentrated in it instead of being separated by placing the results of ISOS (as representing the intercepted communications of the enemy) and the results of information obtained from other sources in two compartments, i.e. Section V and B Division. It thus demonstrated that if this unnatural separation had not been effected, the special arrangements to create the War Room would have been unnecessary. If all counter espionage had been concentrated in the Security Service, information would have flowed naturally between that Service and the G-2 CI Staff in the field. In other words the War Room showed that "counter espionage is indivisible", i.e. that when military operations are in progress the detection of enemy agents in the United Kingdom as a military base and in the military zone of operations are parts of an integral process. The staff in both places must depend on the same centralised records and must pool their information by contributing it to those same records. The necessity for this integration is not in any way affected by the fact that the staff in the field must be subordinate to Supreme Headquarters while that in London must continue to occupy the special position of the Security Service in the machinery of government. On the contrary these facts point more clearly and conclusively than any others, except those relevant to deception through double agents, to the conclusion that these closely related parts of a whole must both be ultimately subordinate to the Prime Minister as Minister of Defence and must be organically related to the machinery under the Chiefs of Staff.

This is the real position of the Security Service in the machinery of government. Viewed in this light its present position as nominally under the Foreign Secretary seems to be based on as complete a fallacy as are suggestions that the Home Office could control or direct its operations in spheres other than those - a very important reservation - where they touch on the province of the Home Secretary and affect the liberty of the subject, the Law and the keeping of the King's Peace.

END OF VOLUME II

TOP SECRET

THE SECURITY SERVICE

ITS PROBLEMS AND ORGANISATIONAL ADJUSTMENTS
1908-1945

VOL. III. (CHAPTER V, PARTS 2-4 AND APPENDICES)

MARCH 1946

VOLUME III

CHAPTER V

Page

PART 2 : COMMUNISM AND THE U.S.S.R. 1941-1945   349

   (i) The C.P.G.B.: reactions to the German attack on Russia   349
   (ii) The re-organisation of the Security Service 1941   349
   (iii) F Division: policy questions   350
   (iv) The Communist Party's Armed Forces Organisation   351
   (v) Penetration by the Communist Party and leakages   353
   (vi) The consequent attitude to the C.P.G.B.   357
   (vii) The formation of Section IX of S.I.S.   358
   (viii) The Comintern wireless system and developments after the dissolution   358
   (ix) Soviet espionage   361
   (x) The Fourth International and the Trotskyist Movement in Great Britain   364

PART 3: THE ITALIAN AND JAPANESE SECRET SERVICES   366

   (i) The Italian Secret Service   366
   (ii) The Japanese Secret Service   368

PART 4: INTERNATIONAL ORGANISATION AND STAFF OF THE SECURITY SERVICE   368
   (i) Administrative Services and Establishments   369
   (ii) Registry and Organisation   375
   (iii) Liaison with other Intelligence Services   381
   (iv) The Director General's Staff   384
      - The central administrative machinery   385
      - Prosecutions   385
      - Leakage of Information Section   386
      - Renegades   389
      - Operations Section   390
      - Research   392
      - Agents and the Press Section   392
      - Overseas Control   396
   (v) The Director General's review of the war period   400
   (vi) The lessons from the past   402

APPENDIX I: LIST OF DIVISIONAL AND SECTIONAL REPORTS.   409

APPENDIX II: ORGANISATIONAL CHARTS.   411

BIBLIOGRAPHY: NUMERICAL LIST OF PAPERS AND DOCUMENTS.   429

Part 2: Communism and the U.S.S.R. 1941-1945

(i) The C.P.G.B. reactions to the German attack on Russia.

The first reaction of the C.P.G.B. to the German attack on Russia was mentioned in the last chapter in connection with the statement issued by the Political Bureau of the Party before the Prime Minister made his speech on the evening of the 22nd June. For a few days afterwards there was a cleavage of opinion between those who desired to continue to attack the British Government and those who felt that the Prime Minister's promise of immediate aid to the Soviet Union forced the Party to support the Government and the war effort. On the 26th June 1941 Gallacher met representatives of the Press and said that the Party would support the Government in any steps towards collaboration between Britain and the Soviet Union. On July 4th the Central Committee declared that the war was a "just war" and issued a manifesto in which it said "the Communist Party in this grave crisis in which the fate of the whole of progressive mankind is at stake will work for and mobilise to win every citizen for the victory over Fascism". The confusion in the minds of the Communist Party leaders at this time was made evident by information which we obtained about the proceedings at a closed Party meeting, and the position was not clarified until Harry Pollitt addressed all branches of the Party on the 8th July. He declared in favour of a united national front of all those who were for Hitler's defeat; and stated that Comrade Stalin's reference to Churchill's declaration of support to the Soviet Union left no room for doubt what their attitude should be; that their fight was directed not against the Churchill Government, but against the secret friends of Hitler. One immediate effect of the changed situation was to restore Pollitt to the leadership of the Party.

The first characteristic of Party policy from now onwards was that their every effort was directed towards assistance for the Soviet Union and, incidentally, towards profiting by all efforts to promote Anglo-Soviet goodwill and to popularise the Soviet Union. The Communist Party asserted itself by staging displays on the occasion of Soviet anniversaries and other similar measures.

During the second half of 1941 the success of German military operations in Russia roused doubts whether that country would be able to resist the German military machine successfully. This had the effect of making the question of Soviet espionage and Comintern activity against this country a question of far less imminence from the Security Service point of view than that of combating the German Intelligence machine. Moreover, apart from the usual sources of information about the C.P.G.B., all other sources had largely dried up or disappeared. Section V had lost all their agents inside the Comintern and affiliated organisations and had no other good inside sources of information.

(ii) The re-organisation of the Security Service, 1941.

In the meanwhile, as part of the re-organisation of the Security Service, F Division had been constituted in April 1941 as a separate Division under Mr. Curry as Deputy Director with two Assistant Directors, Mr. Hollis and Mr. Aikin-Sneath, in charge of the Communist and Fascist sections respectively. (The work of the Fascist section, F.3., has already been dealt with in Part 1 (vi) of this chapter in view of the close association between the B.U.F. and the potential Nazi "Fifth Column"). The sections retained their lettering as B sections until the re-organisation was completed by the Director General's circular of the 15th July 1941 and the Division came fully into being with effect from the 1st August when the sections were renumbered as F sections. Lt. Colonel Alexander was in charge of B.1 which became F.1 (Internal Security in H.M. Forces and Government establishments belong to H.M. Forces) but the section maintained a partially separate existence and was not under the control or supervision of the head of the Division. Mr. Hollis, the Assistant Director, was in charge of F.2.a. (policy and activities of C.P.G.B.), F.2.b (Comintern activities generally; Communist refugees) and F.2.c. (Soviet espionage).

In July 1941 a new section, F.4 was formed to watch for and receive information about new politico-socialist or revolutionary movements, in addition to taking over the investigation of Pacifist and anti-war movements.

Mr. Curry left the Division to join a new appointment as "Research" in October 1941 when Mr. Hollis became the Assistant Director in charge of the whole Division.

F.1 was dissolved in 1943 and a new post, that of Military Adviser to F Division (F/MA) was created. The reason for this change arose from the fact that there had been criticism both outside and within the Security Service of a certain rigidity of working of F.1 and this became more prominent after the major change in the Communist Party line in the summer of 1941. It was found on various occasions that the Communist sections and the military section were interpreting events in different ways. Moreover [...] information which had become available to the Communist section allowed the Armed Forces Organisation of the Communist Party to be studied at the centre rather than at the circumference. It was decided that for reasons of security the detailed material could not be made available for purposes of action to F.1. Consequently for an uneasy period the Communist Party's Armed Forces Organisation was dealt with in F.2.a. while the cases in individual soldiers were handled in F.1. The eventual outcome of this unsatisfactory situation was that F.1 officers were transferred to F.2.a. and F.3 - the former dealing with Communists and the latter with Fascists in the Forces. This change resulted in an improvement in working and was welcomed by the Service links, i.e. the officers in the Armed Forces responsible for dealing with this aspect of security.

(iii) F Division; policy questions.

F.2.a., whose policy had to be interpreted in terms of concrete cases arising from the day-to-day work of the section, found it necessary very rapidly to adjust their policy to the major change resulting from the German attack. The evidence available to the section soon made it clear that in spite of the Communist Party's support of the war effort its long-term policy was unchanged and the long-term policy of the section had to be adapted accordingly. It was not always easy to put this view before Government Departments which were profiting from the cessation of Communist obstruction and were in receipt of offers of positive help. It fell to members of the section to convince their opposite numbers in Government Departments that their views were soundly based on knowledge and experience. They felt that they had to make it clear that their views were "not merely the reactionary outpourings of people who had stuck to one job so long that their opinions had become ossified". One means by which the section's aims in this respect were achieved was the circulation of papers including Mr. Clarke's paper on the Unofficial Shop Stewards' Movement in 1941 and on the Communist Party - its aims and organisation, in 1945. Both these books are reported to have been received as outstanding studies which added considerably to the Government's knowledge of the subjects and to the reputation of the Security Service. Mr. Hollis was responsible for the preparation of a paper for the Home Secretary to submit to the Cabinet (vide Bibliography No. 16) and others of more general application were circulated in the form of Red Books. The views adopted by the section were subsequently borne out by the cases of Springhall and Uren, which will be described below, as well as by the general circumstances of numerous leakages of important information.

F.2.b. was responsible for intelligence concerning the Comintern and its various ramifications, including that about alien Communists resident in or visiting this country. Its position in this respect was vitally affected by the failure of Section V to furnish it with any good inside information from abroad and by the change in policy regarding the carding of names abroad on the Central Index. Prior to the formation of Section IX of S.I.S., F.2.b. received from Section V a considerable volume of undigested papers. The effect of the situation thus created was to leave considerable doubt whether either the Security Service or S.I.S. accepted responsibility for maintaining adequate records about the Comintern after April 1941. The only palliative to this situation was that F.2.b. was in the hands of Miss Bagot whose expert knowledge of the whole subject enabled her to find and make available a large variety of detailed information based on the records of the past.

The work of F.2.c. has been discussed in detail under "Soviet Espionage". The only important success obtained during the war was Mr. Shillito's painstaking disclosure of Green's organisation as a result of interrogating him when in prison. Two other important cases, those of Springhall and Uren, were dealt with in F.2.a. on account of their close association with the British Communist Party.

(iv) The Communist Party's Armed Forces Organisation.

As already mentioned, the work of F.1 in connection with the Armed Forces was transferred to other sections and its place was taken by F/MA. After June 1941 the Communists in the Armed Forces concentrated on becoming efficient soldiers and F Division was therefore often in the position of warning the Army authorities about an aspect of security which had no immediate bearing on the discipline of regiments and other units and the natural reaction of a C.O. to representations on the subject of Communists under his command was that he was concerned with the present rather than the future. F Division, on the other hand, was unable to overlook the long-term problem which might arise if Communists attained high positions in the Armed Forces. They considered this question likely to be of special importance in the period after the occupation of Germany and represented the position as they saw it to the Secretary of State, the Adjutant General and the D.P.S. They also found it necessary to resist an attempt to cut down the internal security system under which "links" were maintained at Commands, and arrangements were made to vet the limited number of those holding temporary war-time commissions who were candidates for permanent commissions after the war.

This general question cannot be dissociated from the fact that the C.P.G.B. continued to maintain an organisation which concentrated its attention on the Armed Forces; and this organisation is to be viewed in the light of the way in which Communists look back to the pattern of the Russian revolution and the part played therein by the Russian Communist Party's success in winning over the Russian Army and especially the Petrograd Regiments as a part of their general plan for revolution. (Compare the line taken in the "History of the C.P.S.U.(Bolsheviks)", vide Bibliography No. 15).

From October 1939 until nearly the end of 1941 this organisation had been in the hands of D. F. Springhall and little was known about it except that he had a room near Party headquarters at which he interviewed soldiers. F Division also had information of the existence of a number of organised Party groups in the Forces. Towards the end of 1941 Springhall handed this work over to R.W. Robson of the Control Commission under whom the work was developed and systematised. Robson himself interviewed officers and two of his assistants dealt with other ranks and with civilian contacts. Robson partly inherited from Springhall and partly built up an organisation which was designed to cover all the major military areas in this country. In many Communist Party districts an individual was appointed to be responsible to Robson for this work. These individuals were often under-cover members of the Party and each of them had a number of local contacts. It was the duty of these contacts to be in touch with Party members in the Forces in their areas and to notify the district representative of the particulars. The machinery did not work very efficiently and the headquarters records were also found to be inadequate for such a widespread organisation. F Division, however, obtained information of the names of some twelve hundred members in the Forces which is said to be about a fifth of the known number. Arrangements to extend the organisation among the Forces overseas were also made, but here again it did not always function efficiently.

The Party in Great Britain attached great importance to keeping the secret of their Forces Organisation. Most of their communications were sent by hand and those which went through the post usually took the form of a simple introduction to a friend who happened to be stationed in the neighbourhood. The secrecy of the interviewing room in London was also jealously guarded and Robson was, on one occasion, 'trailed' by Springhall in order to make sure that he was not being shadowed. The Party realised that the existence of a Forces Organisation might be used as a powerful weapon against the Party and their view seems to have been that the authorities knew little, if anything, about it. An additional reason for secrecy was that the Organisation brought a steady flow of secret information about weapons and about operations to Party Headquarters.

The war-time problem presented to the Security Service under the conditions of conscription was very different from that of the pre-war period when individuals could be excluded or discharged from the Armed Forces. The various complications which arose are discussed at length in the sectional report and cannot be detailed here.

The most significant result of F Division's investigations into the Communist Party's Armed Forces Organisation under Robson's control was the extent and importance of the leakage of military information to the Communist Party. In certain cases action was taken and a few officers were dealt with by being excluded from positions in Intelligence or other posts. One officer was prosecuted and convicted under the Official Secrets Act. The general effect of F Division's enquiries, however, was to show that the Security Service was not in a position to prevent members of the Communist Party from having access to important secret work or from obtaining positions of trust and leadership. One factor in this difficult situation was that members of the Communist Party were frequently chosen for secret work on account of their technical ability and zeal.

(v) Penetration by the Communist Party and leakages.

One [...] important source of information about the Armed Forces Organisation, as about other parts of the Communist Party's machine, [...] materially helped in disclosing two main types of leakage. The first was the disclosure of operational and political information which would be primarily of value to the Communist Party for its political purposes. The second was the disclosure of information about military and other equipment which was of no direct or immediate value to the Communist Party, but might be of interest to the Soviet authorities.

Some of the more important cases of leakage - including those from the Armed Forces and Government Departments - were the following:-

> Disclosure in the Daily Worker of conversation between Mr. Lees Smith and Sir Alexander Maxwell about the Communist Party.
>
> Offer of figures relating to strength and disposition of the R.A.F.
>
> Information about the War Office estimate of the results of the Dieppe Raid.
>
> Advance information about North African landings.
>
> List of duties of Military Intelligence Sections of the War Office.
>
> Disclosure by [...] of particulars about S.O.E. work.
>
> Two disclosures of the Ministry of Information weekly report on public morale (probably through Louis Moss).
>
> Two disclosures of details of radio-location equipment, one and probably both by Samuel Cohen.

Disclosure of S.O.E. operations by [...].

Disclosure by [...] Secretary of A.Sc.W. of report relating to jet propulsion and other matters.

Disclosure of Cabinet document relating to the Communist Party through [...].

Two disclosures of political documents circulated to Ministers by Margot Heinemann.

Disclosure of information about aircraft by Kerrigan and a member of the Soviet Trade Delegation.

Disclosure of anti-submarine device by [...].

Disclosure of formation of 2nd Army Headquarters at Oxford.

Disclosure about "Squid" by a member of a film unit by a naval officer.

Disclosure of information about Greek political situation by a member of P.W.E.

Disclosure of another anti-submarine device.

Statement that Professor Blackett (Scientific Adviser to Admiralty on Operational Research) had given information to the Party before June 1943.

Disclosure of a new type of periscope through Idris Cox and James Shields to the Russians.

Disclosure about Pluto by [...] and [...] Union officials. Disclosure about Mulberry by [...].

Disclosure of P.I.D. Overseas directive.

In addition there were a number of trivial cases and there were several disclosures in connection with the operation of the "internal security" system - i.e. that for dealing with Communists and Fascists in the Armed Forces.

In many cases the name of the Party member was discovered by subsequent investigation or because they identified themselves at the time that they made the disclosure, but no prosecution was possible in such cases because it was more important to safeguard the source of information. Where possible arrangements were made to neutralise the danger.

After the arrest of Springhall and Uren F.2.a. prepared a memorandum to which was attached a list of fifty-seven members of the Communist Party known to be engaged in the Services or in Government Departments or in the aircraft or munitions industries on work of some secrecy. It was pointed out that while some of these had obtained their positions through the inevitable loop-holes in the vetting system the cause in most cases was the absence of a general policy in different Government Departments towards the problem created by the existence of the Communist Party. While the advice given by the Security Service in such cases was uniform, some Departments followed it while others appeared to treat the matter as one having little practical bearing on their own responsibilities. The Security Service, therefore, suggested the desirability of a uniform policy being adopted by the different Departments.

These proposals were submitted to Mr. Duff Cooper who sent a short memorandum to the Prime Minister in which he suggested the transfer of all the persons named on the list to other work. The Home Secretary supported this memorandum and stated that he was in favour of a general circular to all Departments describing the risks involved in the employment of Communists and Fascists on secret work. He also suggested that there should be a public statement by the Government about the leakages of information to the Communist Party.

The Prime Minister decided against making any public statement. He ruled that instead of the whole responsibility for Communists already in employment in Government Departments resting on the Security Service a secret panel consisting of three members of the Security Executive, a representative of the Prime Minister, and those of the Treasury and the Department concerned should be appointed to examine all such cases. The final decision whether action should be taken was to rest with the Department. The system, however, proved ineffective and the Security Service proposal that a uniform policy should be adopted by Government Departments remained inoperative.

By July 1942 the Political Bureau of the C.P.G.B. was advocating mass pressure on the Government to compel it to take action to establish a second front. It maintained that there could be no second front without a great mass movement, and no such mass movement without the Communist Party organising and heading it. In this way, by its propaganda, the C.P.G.B. continued to act as an instrument of Russian policy.

At the same time evidence was obtained by secret means which showed that the Communist Party's aim of promoting aid for the Soviet Union had not caused any fundamental change in its long-term revolutionary aims. In the first half of 1942 a series of instructional classes were held in various parts of the country to train new candidates for positions of trust. It was explained that the classes were held for industrial leaders because similar classes were held in Russia before the revolution and without such classes "our own revolution will be disorganised and fail". It was emphasised that the Party was a revolutionary one, and that the workers had to break up the power of the capitalist regime by disintegrating the army, seizing key points, factories, railways and docks, and by eliminating the police. Control must be obtained by armed workers and, according to at least one instructor, bloodshed would be necessary, although he did not want to advocate it.

F Division prepared a report (vide Bibliography No. 16) in December 1942 for the Home Secretary to submit to the Cabinet which outlined the policy followed by the Communist Party from the beginning of the war until the attack on Russia, and on subsequent developments as outlined above in Chapter IV and in the preceding paragraphs of this chapter. In submitting this report they suggested that while every member of the Communist Party was not aware of the Party's revolutionary programme, the Party itself believed that its leaders, properly instructed, would be able to carry the rank and file with them far down the road to revolution.

The paper was put to the War Cabinet together with another paper dealing with Fascists in this country and the Home Secretary proposed that both should be published. The Cabinet, however, decided against publication. This decision appeared to F Division officers to be the right one in the state of public opinion at that time. A White Paper would probably have failed to have its full effect and circumstances might arise when the object of providing a check to the Communist Party could be more successfully achieved.

The new phase of Communist Party policy was marked by a change of attitude towards the Labour Party. This phase was inaugurated in August 1942 with an attempt to appeal to the rank and file over the heads of the leaders with the ultimate aim of bringing about affiliation. The campaign for affiliation became one of the biggest the Party has ever conducted in this country. As part of this campaign a congress was held in June 1943 in connection with which a balance sheet of the Party's finances was published and new draft rules were produced to replace the existing rules which were not suitable to the new circumstances.

A few days before affiliation had been rejected by the Labour Party Conference the dissolution of the Comintern was announced. Although a major obstacle to affiliation was thus removed, it was too late to help the C.P.G.B. on this issue. An interesting indication that the C.P.G.B. was not in close wireless touch with the Comintern is that it had no prior warning of the impending dissolution, and first heard of it through the ordinary press channels.

By a dramatic accident D.F. Springhall, the national organiser of the Party, was arrested the day after the rejection of affiliation in the presence of the whole Political Bureau on charges of espionage for which he was subsequently convicted. There is no doubt that this arrest was a serious shock to the Party and affected their line of action at that time. They denied all knowledge of Springhall's activities and expelled him from membership.

Springhall's case, which is briefly described below under "Soviet Espionage", was important, not only as showing how British Communists could serve as agents of the Soviet Intelligence on a large scale, but also because it led to our receiving further indications of the extent to which Communists in the Services and Government Departments were in a position to obtain information which could not but be of value to the C.P.G.B. for the purposes of pursuing its general aim of revolution.

The enquiry into Springhall's case led to the disclosure of the fact that he was in touch with an organised group of Communists among the professional and intellectual classes. This and other enquiries showed that a considerable number of Communists in these classes held positions of trust under the Government and that many of them were in a position and willing to give away to the C.P.G.B. or the Soviet authorities information about important secrets connected with new inventions and military operations. Thus, one Communist each was discovered in the Security Service, S.I.S. and S.O.E. respectively, although there was no reason to think that any of them had been able to give away information of first class importance. They were all removed from the service, and in the S.O.E. case Captain Uren was convicted. Other enquiries again had shown that there were Communists in institutions engaged in scientific research and in industry with access to various parts of important and secret technical processes. Many of these were known to be actual, and all were potential, sources of leakage of information to the C.P.G.B. or the Soviet Government. Finally, among a number of Communists in Government Departments there was one in the Home Office who was, at one time, in a position to see some of the F Division reports on the C.P.G.B. and cognate matters; and one in another Department with access to Cabinet papers.

Thus, while the Communist Party remained a very small affair and failed to make any effective appeal, or to obtain any important increase in influence or membership, the situation created by the fact that so many of its members secured important positions gave it a potential importance far greater than that warranted by its numbers. The alliance with the Soviet Government and the common purpose in the war were obstacles in the way of a more drastic policy for excluding Communists from positions of trust. Cases occurred where Communists in the Services were excluded from positions, for instance, on the Intelligence staff, but, owing to the difficulty of keeping in touch with their movements, subsequently obtained similar positions with the armies in the field.

(vi) The consequent attitude to the C.P.G.B.

In the absence of any definite charter or instruction as to the scope of its responsibilities, F.2.a., the section of F Division dealing with the C.P.G.B., has aimed at keeping itself informed of important developments in policy and the maintenance and development of records of individual members of the C.P.G.B. and of the Trotskyists.

The extent to which Party members belonging to the intellectual and professional classes, including scientific and technical experts, secured positions both in Government and in industry gave grounds for urging that full records of individual Communists should be maintained as far as possible. Against this, considerations of economy and policy in regard to the maintenance of records influenced the Director General in the opposite direction. In August 1945 the position was that no solution satisfactory both to the Deputy Director of Organisation and F Division had been reached - for details see the F.2.a. report (S.F. 50-24-44(76) Y.B. 6382).

(vii) The formation of Section IX of S.I.S.

In May 1943 the relations of F Division with S.I.S. were changed by the creation of Section IX of S.I.S. This new section was created by C.S.S. and Colonel Vivian because it was thought that recent developments had shown that the subject of Communism required to be handled by an officer who was not trammelled by the urgent needs of the Section V staff in connection with the war. Mr. Curry was lent to S.I.S. by the Director General to form Section IX.

The immediate result was to show that Section V had been unable to cope with current information on Communism which had been coming into S.I.S. and that the S.I.S. Registry was inadequate for the purpose. There were large numbers of undigested papers, some of which disclosed that Censorship material supplied important evidence regarding instructions issued from the Comintern to Communist Parties in the Americas, while others laid bare the working of an organisation in North and South America which was interesting itself in the case of Trotsky's murderer at that time in prison in Mexico. Some of the individuals connected with this organisation had belonged to the International Brigade and the enquiry raised important questions regarding the use of members of the International Brigade for conspiratorial work as well as that of Stalin's attitude to, or concern in, the murder of Trotsky. These questions did not, however, admit of satisfactory answers in the light of the available evidence, but they had a bearing on enquiries into members of the International Brigade with which F Division was occupied. Numerous cases occurred in which information was required by the Foreign Office, or otherwise, about the records of important Communists and experience showed that the S.I.S. Registry was often unable to produce records of information obtained for S.I.S. sources but that the information could be obtained by F Division of the Security Service from its records. This was due to the inadequacy of the staff of the S.I.S. Registry on the one hand and on the other to Miss Bagot's exceptional knowledge of the subject and her ability to connect traces from our records even when names abroad had not been carded in the Central Registry.

(viii) The Comintern wireless system and development after the dissolution.

The formation of Section IX was the result of Mr. Hollis' action in urging the importance of the question of the use of wireless for the transmission of messages between London and Moscow as raised by certain circumstances which had recently come to the notice of F Division. In February 1943 James Shields of the Control Commission of the C.P.G.B. had arranged to recruit a girl named Jean Jefferson, a former student of the Wilson School in Moscow, as a radio operator to work a station at her home in Wimbledon, for which purpose she was to retire from ordinary Party activity. From the information it appeared that the Party had been in radio communication with Moscow until a short time previously, but that at this time they were receiving messages in a cipher which they could not read. It also appeared that they knew that certain parts of the messages should be sent on to America. Robert Stewart, a member of the Control Commission who had conducted much of the Party's underground work and had directed its radio organisation (as part of the Comintern network) some years before the war, was in charge of some part of this scheme for wireless communications. A close watch was placed on the activities of these three individuals and the whereabouts of all Wilson School students were ascertained. Arrangements were made to co-operate with S.I.S. and R.S.S. and it was learnt that the latter had records of what were described as considerable "bundles of Russian traffic".

The dissolution of the Comintern took place at the end of May, and on June 10th Stewart, who had just come out of hospital, announced at the C.P.G.B. headquarters that the station had been put out of commission; that he had stopped receiving and transmitting a long time before, but he thought that the Russians must have been trying to send a message at the time when the dissolution of the Comintern was announced.

Within a fortnight of the dissolution Stewart arranged to see one Samuel Cohen and his wife, both of whom were ex-students of the Wilson School. Later, in September 1943, Stewart referred to Cohen as having worked for him for some time, and from this F.2.a. drew the inference that Cohen had been operating the Comintern radio station in this country and had probably ceased operations at the end of 1942 or early in 1943; and that the dissolution brought the transmissions to an end.

In the meanwhile Colonel Vivian and Section IX had taken up the matter with R.S.S. and G.C. & C.S. and it transpired that there was a network, the centre of which appeared to be near Moscow, the traffic of which had certain similarities with the old Comintern network. The cipher was complex and appeared to be unreadable.

Section IX, however, had come to the conclusion that certain documents received from the American Censorship which had contained messages in secret ink on letters from New York to Mexico City were indications that the machinery of the Comintern was continuing to function in some form after its dissolution. One message in particular called for reports on the effects of the dissolution, but in the absence of full background information regarding the context of these messages it was necessary to treat with caution the inferences which they suggested.

Early in 1944 G.C. & C.S. officers succeeded in reading some of the material. It showed that messages were being exchanged between a station near Moscow and a number of other stations, including some in China, Poland, Yugoslavia, France and possibly others in Holland and Scandinavia. Even then there was great reluctance to divert any resources and any energy or manpower from radio interception directly connected with the war; and Section IX found it necessary to exert continuous pressure for several months in order to provide for the development of this work. By the middle of 1944 a certain amount of material connected with China, Poland, Yugoslavia and France became available; and it was discovered that messages to the first three of these countries had been issued at the time of the dissolution in terms identical with the messages in secret writing intercepted by Censorship when passing between New York and Mexico City as mentioned above. In the light of these facts obscure words in the text of one message in secret writing from New York were safely identified as meaning that that message was from Georg Dimitrov, formerly Secretary of the Comintern and now Chairman of the

Commission appointed to wind up its affairs, and that it was addressed to Earl Browder, formerly head of the Communist Party of the U.S.A. now supposedly converted into "the Communist Association". The inference was drawn from this that the machinery of the Comintern was still functioning after its dissolution; and subsequent messages showed that there had been no change in the nature of the communications issued from the Comintern to the various countries, but they had continued on the same lines after the dissolution. This evidence obviously had an important bearing on the position of the British Communist Party as a section of the ostensibly dissolved Comintern.

Before leaving Section IX in November 1944 Mr. Curry prepared a summary of the conclusions which could be drawn from this material up to November 1944. Some of the more important points were that the Polish evidence showed that the controlling station near Moscow was that of the Comintern and that this conclusion was supported by evidence from Yugoslavia, France and China. The Comintern or "post Comintern" organisation had been closely associated with the Polish Communist Party in the arrangements which led to the establishment of the Polish Committee of National Liberation. The latter was placed in control of the Polish Armed Forces in the U.S.S.R. and Poland; and an organ had been created consisting of village, district and regional "Rada" or Councils with the P.C.N.L. at the apex. Communications between Moscow-Slovenia, Moscow-Croatia and Moscow-Tito Headquarters showed that a similar system of government was being established in Yugoslavia. The messages Moscow-France included reports on the Comites Departementaux de Liberation and on the Milices Patriotiques. (The Milices Patriotiques had been debarred by the de Gaulle Government from exercising police functions in connection with épuration). The texts Moscow-China reflected a completely different social and political structure from that in the European countries. In China the Comintern was concerned with a region completely under Communist control and an administration based on the Communist armies of China. The Communist Party of China was sending long reports to the Comintern of their difficulties with the Kuo Min Tang, on their partisan warfare and on the "disintegration" work - assisted by Japanese Communists - directed against Japanese troops. The messages showed the Chinese Communist Party as receiving assistance from the Comintern and asking them to obtain the advice of the Red Army Staff in matters connected with partisan warfare in Inner Mongolia.

The summary drew attention to the resemblance between the Rada (Council) of Poland and the Odbor (Council) of Yugoslavia, each including members of Communist and other parties under its Committee of National Liberation on the one hand and the Soviets of Russia on the other; and mentioned that the Soviets had been composed of the members of the Menshevik and Social Revolutionary as well as the Communist Parties after the February and before the October Revolution of 1917. It quoted the history of the Communist Party of the Soviet Union (Bolsheviks) and Trotsky as showing that the Communist Party came to power mainly through two important moves; through securing control of the Armed Forces and of the Soviets. These considerations gave rise to a number of questions regarding the national Communist Parties and the Comintern as instruments of Russian policy. It was suggested that this interception of Comintern wireless might furnish useful evidence and that it seemed desirable to take all feasible measures to extend its scope. At the same time the security of this material was of special delicacy in view of the extent to which the Communist Party here had succeeded in obtaining information through a number of Government Departments.

There was no evidence, either of a technical kind derived from R.S.S. or otherwise, to show that a station in Great Britain was included in this Comintern network. On the contrary, the circumstances in which the British Communist Party received its first intimation about the dissolution of the Comintern from the Press and the information obtained by F Division relevant to the project of establishing a radio transmission station in 1943 appeared to negative any such suggestion. At the same time the facts relating to Robert Stewart's meeting with Samuel Cohen and his wife a fortnight after the dissolution of the Comintern; the fact that the Communist Party in London had been in radio communication with Moscow shortly before February 1943 and knew that certain parts of the messages should be sent on to America, taken together with the fact that messages relative to the dissolution were received in the middle of 1943 in the U.S.A., China and other countries, all combine to suggest that the exact position regarding transmissions Moscow-Great Britain and Moscow-U.S.A. has not been fully cleared up.

All the circumstances furnished yet another illustration of the importance of the Security Service being fully informed by S.I.S. regarding developments abroad because of the light they may throw on the development of the British Communist Party as a section of the Comintern. Without this illumination the course of events may easily be misunderstood and their significance may be wrongly interpreted. This point is emphasised because until recently the attitude of S.I.S. has been - it is understood to have been greatly modified - to suggest that events outside the three-mile limit are not necessarily the concern of the Security Service unless they have a direct bearing on events or organisations inside it, whereas the Security Service point of view is that much may be lost if the whole picture is not made available to them.

(ix) Soviet espionage.

The general nature of the information derived from enquiries into previous cases, especially those of Percy Glading and Krivitsky, furnished the general pattern of the methods employed by the Soviet Secret Military Intelligence. These cases indicated that the Russians tended to work along the same lines, and also emphasised the importance of the fact that they had at their disposal an almost unlimited number of co-operators in the shape of British Communists as well as an efficient and highly trained staff of experts to control and organise them from the shelter of positions of diplomatic privilege. Percy Glading and his assistants were all British subjects and were all members of the C.P.G.B. who dropped Party work as soon as they were recruited. The Party had no official knowledge of their activities, although certain Party officials were fully informed.

Glading was the organiser of a group of sub-agents, but was not allowed a free hand in controlling it, being under the orders of a foreign resident agent in this country who was in control of finances. The methods employed were simple and practical. Sub-agents in the various departments of Woolwich Arsenal brought out plans and specifications in the evenings when they left work and handed them to Glading, who immediately had them photographed. The originals were replaced by the sub-agent when he arrived at work the following morning.

This pattern conformed to that described in detail by Krivitsky. Krivitsky mentioned the diplomatic bag as the chief means of communication with the U.S.S.R. and stated that the material for transmission in it was always recorded by photograph. He believed in the extensive use of women "cut outs" and considered that the only effective means of combating Soviet espionage were to effect the "growing up" of an agent from without (as was so successfully done against Glading) and, secondly, the bribery of known Soviet agents who, in such cases, would have an effective guarantee against reprisals. In 1942 Mr. Shillito of F.2.c. interrogated a British subject named Oliver Charles Green who had been arrested on a charge of forging petrol coupons when a search of his house had led to the discovery of photographs of certain War Office secret documents. Green was skilfully induced to furnish information on the subject of espionage and admitted that after joining the International Brigade in Spain he had agreed to engage in espionage in England on behalf of the U.S.S.R. His statement showed that Green was in touch with two Russians believed to belong to the Russian Trade Delegation, but that everyone else connected with the organisation was a male British subject. Green said that he had recruited a number of such persons as agents and they included an informant in the army, a fitter in an aircraft factory, a sailor in the Mercantile Marine, a member of a Government Department, an individual having access to aircraft factory output figures and a member of the R.A.F.

His statement also showed that the greatest precautions were taken in the conduct of the operations of this organisation. Meetings were most carefully arranged so as to avoid suspicion and prevent shadowing, and care was taken to see that no one, whether a member of the C.P.G.B. or otherwise, who was thought likely to have a security record was employed on this work. Green stated that a number of wireless operators and transmitters were used, care being taken to avoid power-operated transmitters on the ground that if the signals were D/Fd in a certain area and the power then cut the disappearance of the signals would confirm the accuracy of the D/Fing. Transmissions were made about once a fortnight late at night or early in the morning when fewer wireless owners were likely to listen in, and alternative wave lengths and automatic transmissions were employed, the tapes being cut, most probably, by hand punchers. Automatic high speed transmission was used in order to save time and to increase the difficulty of radio direction finding, but his remarks in this connection have not been substantiated. The organisation, as described by Green, conformed generally to the Krivitsky pattern and importance was attached to the fact that it was another instance of the wide use by the Russians of members of the International Brigade for recruitment as intelligence agents employed against this and other countries. Green's statements regarding the use of wireless transmitters have never been satisfactorily cleared up. The case was also another instance of the rule that the C.P.G.B. as an organisation was not concerned and that the Russian organisation was run independently of the Party, although individual Party members of prominence were probably involved.

The case of D.F. Springhall, who was convicted of offences against the Official Secrets Act on July 28th 1943, showed an important divergence from previous experience. Most notably he was not only an active member of the Party, but was head of its Organisation Department, a member of the Political Bureau and of the Central Committee. In spite of this, his arrest came as a complete surprise to the majority of Party officials and to the rank and file, except those associated with him. He used members of the Party but not the actual apparatus of the Party for espionage purposes and he was in direct touch with the Soviet authorities. At the same time, the methods were less skilful than those of his predecessors. There was reason to think that he had been active for some years and had some excellently placed informants and might have escaped detection but for a piece of negligence on his part. He was in touch with a Mrs. Sheehan, who was employed in the Air Ministry and gave him particulars of a new and highly secret device, details of which she had obtained from a file which had passed through her hands. Springhall interviewed Mrs. Sheehan at her flat which she shared with another woman whose suspicions were aroused by overhearing a description of Air Ministry passes and of the secret device. This woman communicated with an R.A.F. officer who seized an opportunity to steam open a letter intended for Springhall which contained, among other things, references to the secret device mentioned above. The subsequent enquiry led to the examination of a diary in which Springhall had made a large number of cryptic entries and some of these entries led to further information being obtained about middle-class Communists with whom he was in touch. Among these were a secretary in S.I.S. and Captain Uren of S.O.E.

The character of the information gathered by Springhall appears to have been very varied and much of it was of such a nature that it might be of interest either to the C.P.G.B. or to the Soviet authorities. For instance, Springhall was asked whether he had any knowledge of future military operations or of the establishment of a second front in the near future. The Communist Party at that time was actively engaged in propaganda in connection with a second front.

A survey of the cases of Soviet espionage which have been briefly mentioned in this and the preceding chapters leads to two main conclusions. The first is that counter espionage measures are not easily taken with success in time of peace or against the Secret Intelligence Service of a country with which we are at peace or in alliance; and that this is particularly so in the case of Russia. The second conclusion is that the cases which have been detected can only represent a small part of the effective work done by the Soviet Military Intelligence against us in any one period. The Soviet Military Intelligence Service has a great advantage compared with any normal state in virtue of the fact that it has so many opportunities of exploiting the position created by the existence of numerous British Communists and Communist sympathisers. Many of these individuals are in positions of confidence and trust and feel a greater obligation of loyalty to the Union of Soviet Socialist Republics than to their own country, or even to oaths by which they have been bound. The characters and sympathies of such persons are well known at Party Headquarters; their suitability or otherwise for secret work can be guaranteed and means of making contact with them can be provided.

The Soviet system of employing a "legal" resident agent in an official position who works through an "illegal" resident agent working under cover through groups of sub-agents provides a difficult problem for solution by the ordinary means at the disposal of the Security Service, namely, the H.O.W., the shadowing staff and the penetrative agent.

Difficulties have been enhanced by the conditions existing after the establishment of our alliance with Russia which caused the Foreign Office to place rigid restrictions on action by the Security Service aiming at the detection of the secret agents of the Soviet. In order to avoid compromising ourselves it has been necessary to rule out any attempt to penetrate Russian official or Trade Delegation circles in this country, either by winning over any of the staff or by introducing an agent among them. For the same reason any attempt by the use of mechanical means to obtain inside information has been impossible, although this means has been used with effect at the other end of the chain, i.e. among British Communists. All attempts at intercepting Russian wireless communications have produced negative results and it is only to be expected that if the Soviet Embassy wireless has been used for Secret Service purposes precautions have been taken to use unreadable ciphers. The Russian diplomatic establishment in London consisted of over ninety individuals at the end of the German war, and this number is much larger than that of the American Embassy but is parallel with the size of Russian Embassies and Legations in many other countries. Soviet officials and members of the Trade Delegation have paid numerous visits to every sort of factory and establishment in this country and have frequently been found attempting to see more than they were intended to see and, as the references to leakages through British Communists have shown, they must have received from such sources many indications of where to look and what to look for.

Observation on members of the Embassy staff has been a matter of extreme difficulty on account of the numbers involved and the location of the building they occupied. Moreover, as might be expected, Soviet officials in London are not only under strict discipline but under the supervision of a detachment of the NKVD - which no doubt helps as an incentive to moral rectitude and also creates the difficulty caused by the possibility of our shadowers being counter shadowed.

(x) The Fourth International and the Trotskyist Movement in Great Britain.

After Trotsky's expulsion from the Communist Party, mentioned in Chapter II, Part 4 (v), he founded the Fourth International and continued to propagate his views. Whether his quarrel with Stalin was mainly a matter of principle or of a personal struggle for power, the doctrinal differences between them centred round the question of the possibility of the victory of "Socialism in a single state". The Trotskyists held that the Stalinist policy was both theoretically wrong and impracticable. The insignificant number of Trotsky's adherents throughout the world did not, however, prevent his death from being an object of conspiracy in which members of the International Brigade were prominent.

The Trotskyist Movement in Great Britain was probably more insignificant than most others. In 1939 it consisted of a few small and disorganised groups, the official section of the Fourth International being known as the Revolutionary Socialist League. Another group of some slight significance was the Workers' International League, founded in England in 1938 by two South Africans. Some of the leaders went to Eire soon after the outbreak of war, partly to make contact with Irish Trotskyists and partly to avoid military service and the repressive measures which they thought would be taken against their organisation.

The crisis of 1940 led the Workers' International League to change their policy and members of the Party joined the Armed Forces instead of trying to evade service. They continued, however, to attack the Government and to voice their opposition to the "Imperialist" war.

By the time of the German attack on the U.S.S.R. the W.I.L. had consolidated their position and were ready with a programme - "a fighting programme to mobilise the masses for the struggle against Fascism, whether of the German or the British variety and for the defence of the Soviet Union". At the same time a main plank in this programme was to assist in bringing a Labour Government to power in Great Britain with the object of eventually persuading the masses to turn towards Trotskyism as a result of the failures which they expected would attend on a Labour Government in power. The ultimate aim was the full Marxist programme with "labour to power" as the slogan of a transitional period.

In 1942 the first national conference of the movement was held; a constitution was adopted comprising a Central Committee, a Political Bureau and a District Organisation on classical Communist lines. The "basic documents of the Fourth International and the transitional programme" were formally adopted as the foundation of policy. As a means of preparing a revolutionary situation the W.I.L. resorted to the promotion of strikes in industry wherever opportunity offered and so far as their limited resources permitted. Instances were at the Rolls Royce factory, Glasgow; at the Dalmuir Ordnance Factory and the Betteshanger Colliery in 1941; Vickers Armstrong, Barrow in 1943; and the Tyneside Shipyard Apprentices strike in 1944. The last of these led to four of the leaders being prosecuted after searches under D.R.39(A) had been carried out at the Trotskyist Headquarters in London, the Militant Workers' Headquarters in Nottingham and some houses in Glasgow and Newcastle. Sentences of imprisonment resulted, but on appeal were quashed on a point of law.

The movement now called itself the Revolutionary Communist Party, but the summer of the Second Front proved unpropitious for industrial agitation and its somewhat remarkable programme came to a standstill. In January 1945 the Revolutionary Communist Party decided that its political position had sufficiently improved to justify its contesting a Parliamentary election and it put forward a candidate in South Wales. While it did not hope for success it expected to consolidate its position and to receive publicity, otherwise unobtainable. The candidate, Jock Haston, polled 1786 votes and forfeited his deposit. No accurate figures of the present membership are available, but in February 1943 full members of the Party in Great Britain numbered 800 with an outer circle of 2,000 active associates.

Although the Trotskyist Movement is not financed, controlled or directed by a foreign power, it has been the subject of casual observation by the Security Service for some years. If this is not strictly within the four corners of the purposes for which the present Security Service was created in its original form, as M.I.5., it is a matter of convenience to the Home Office to obtain information about it from the Security Service sources. There is, in fact, no other organisation in this country readily available for the purpose of making enquiries by secret means. The Home Secretary has occasionally issued warrants for the purpose, and the Trotskyist Movement has now come to be included among the accepted responsibilities of the Security Service.

In 1942 an agent was introduced by M.S. into Workers' International League circles with results which proved more valuable than was realised at the time. Security Service references to the Police have led to a certain number of Police Forces undertaking enquiries and at least five Police Forces had placed agents in the movement by the end of the war. Some of these produced information of some importance. In the autumn of 1944 the Revolutionary Communist Party made an interesting attempt to run a double-cross agent against the Special Branch of the Metropolitan Police. They instructed him to accept the proposals of the Special Branch officer and hoped as a result to estimate the amount of information which Special Branch possessed and also to distract them with false information. Their plan broke down as the result of an indiscretion.

Since the middle of 1943 the Party's activities have been found to deserve closer interest than the somewhat casual attention which had previously been paid to them. The Revolutionary Communist Party uses conspiratorial methods and takes the strictest security precautions in connection with letters, telephone conversations and especially in its courier service with the headquarters of the Fourth International. It followed that the simpler methods of investigation could only fail to discover the real activities of the Party and if used alone would convey a false impression. As a result, observation on this movement has required a larger proportion of time and energy than the smallness of the organisation seemed at first sight to warrant.

Part 3: The Italian and Japanese Secret Services

(i) The Italian Secret Service.

There is no evidence to show that secret agents of any of the various branches of the Italian Intelligence Services were operating in this country either before or during the war (except in the very limited sense indicated in Chapter IV above). They appear to have directed their attention almost entirely to the Mediterranean area and from the information available it is not easy to assess their importance or to gauge the efficiency either of the organisations or their agents.

The available information was summarised by Section V in "The Italian Intelligence Service", dated 15th July 1943 (vide Bibliography No.46). According to this there were separate Services for the Army, Navy and Air Force, the Foreign Office and the Fascist Party, while the duty of counter espionage was entrusted to the Carabinieri Reale. The Military Service, known as the "Servizio Informazioni Militare", is mentioned as covering a wide field, but it was believed not to have achieved any conspicuous success and to have been the cause of dissatisfaction. The Naval Service, "Servizio Informazioni Navale", was believed to be the most efficient, but very little was known of its work. Its connections with naval operations in the shape of under-water attacks on British warships in Alexandria and Gibraltar are mentioned in Part 1, (iv), (e) above, under the heading of B.1.C. The Air Service, "Servizio Informazioni Aeronautica", was reported to have been a small organisation, but to have taken over the task of sending agents to Egypt and the Levant owing to the lack of success on the part of S.I.M.

On the other hand, after the British Services in Italy co-operated with S.I.M. against the Germans during the campaign in that country, a more favourable opinion was formed of their efficiency.

In all the circumstances counter espionage against the Italians fell mainly on S.I.M.E. and on the representatives of Section V in the Mediterranean area. Very little in the way of exchanging information took place on this subject between these two branches of our Intelligence Services and the Security Service in London. In summing up the position S.I.M.E. have stated that the Italian espionage system was crippled by the departure of consular officials and the large-scale internment of Italian civilians when Italy entered the war. No evidence was obtained that the Italians had prepared any efficient underground network. It was not until late in 1941 that they developed any serious attempt at espionage. This was chiefly based on Athens and directed against the Levant coast and Egypt. Between October 1941 and December 1942 eleven low-grade agents were despatched by S.I.M. from Athens to the Middle East. The majority were Armenians and were distinguished by their low mentality, poor efficiency and insufficient training. Early in 1943 the Italians left a W/T network of post-occupational Arab agents behind them in Tripolitania. This network was easily broken up, one of the agents being used for double-cross purposes. Co-operation with the Germans was reported to have been neither very productive nor free from friction.

In a note dated 10th July 1942 (vide S.F.52/Italy/10) R.I.S. dealt at length with an analysis of Italian wireless transmissions, some of which were believed to be part of a communication system for Italian under-cover activities which were partially identifiable with the known characteristics of under-cover transmissions intended to be undertaken by Italian agents in British controlled territory. It is not known whether this interception of Italian Secret Service W/T was subsequently pursued as it related exclusively to the Mediterranean area, and there was no indication of any station or agents in or connected with the United Kingdom. It is possible that if any further information was received, it was not communicated to the Security Service. The ground for this suggestion is that in certain other cases Lt. Colonel Cowgill gave instructions that results obtained by R.S.S. in the interception of German and Russian W/T of an under-cover nature should not be communicated for this reason, i.e. because they referred to stations or agents outside the United Kingdom. It is also not known whether any information on the subject of

Italian wireless was communicated by Section V to their representatives in the Middle East or to S.I.M.E.

All the circumstances would seem to indicate that contact between London and Cairo was not as close at it might have been and that, in war-time as well as in peace-time, closer co-operation and more frequent visits by senior officers from both ends are desirable.

(ii) The Japanese Secret Service.

Information about the Japanese Secret Service after the Japanese attack in December 1941 which became available to our organisations in the Far East and in India has not been received in London in any collated form. The picture of the Japanese Intelligence Service is still far from complete and information relating to the subject is still being assessed and collated by the Counter Intelligence Central Bureau operating under S.E.A.C. So far indications are that the Japanese Secret Intelligence Service was a somewhat diffuse organisation whose operations have on the whole produced poor results. The history of the action taken to deal with the problems created by it and of the adjustments made in our organisation for the purpose has not yet been written.

Some information on the subject was received through the interception of the communications between Tokyo and the diplomatic representatives in Europe. Several of these officials were in touch with the German and Italian Secret Services as well as with their Foreign Offices and other principal organs of government. Japanese diplomats in some of the European capitals conveyed information, often of a doubtful kind, to Tokyo in the shape of agents' reports and many of these were a mixture of official diplomatic intelligence and information derived from more underground sources. As explained elsewhere many of these intercepted Japanese reports furnished us with useful indications for the purpose of assessing German intelligence, including, for instance, their appreciations of the information planted on them by our double agents.

Part 4: Internal Organisation and Staff of the Security Service

The internal organisation and staff of the Security Service were the concern of A Division under Colonel Butler throughout the war. There were the following sub-divisions: Administrative Services and Male Establishments, Accounts and Finance, Women's Establishment, Regional Control, Registry and Organisation. Of these sub-divisions Regional Control has been dealt with in Chapter V, Part 1 (viii) above. Administrative Services and Male Establishment were under the Assistant Director (Lt. Colonel Cumming); Accounts and Finance (Miss Constant) was under the direct supervision of Colonel Butler; Women's Establishment (Miss Dicker) was under the Deputy Director Organisation (Mr. Horrocks), who was also responsible for the Registry and Organisation.

(i) Administrative Services and Establishments.

The Assistant Director Administration was responsible for the following subjects:-

1. Relations with the Ministry of Labour
2. Transport
3. Supplies
4. Technical Equipment
5. Communications
6. Scientific work
7. Ciphers
8. Evacuation schemes and accommodation
9. Recruitment of male staff (Lists 183)
10. Civil Defence
11. Security and Guards
12. Photographic reproduction of records
13. Billeting
14. Printing, Duplication and Photography
15. Messengers, Cleaners and Industrial Staffs
16. Insurances - Life and Property
17. Passes
18. Recruitment and training of manpower in war
19. Security Service versus M.I.5. (Supply anomalies)
20. Reckonability of service
21. Air travel
22. Booking of rail tickets and hotel accommodation
23. Booking of long sea passages
24. Internal security at Country Office
25. Lectures to Police
26. Usage of A Division 'links' for B, E and F Division purposes
27. Relations with local Police (Country Office)
28. Medical arrangements
29. Exemption from Jury Service
30. Administrative Services for I.P.I.
31. Catering and Canteens.

These subjects did not occupy the whole of his time and, as mentioned in the section report, he found that in practice as much as seventy-five percent of it was taken up with a number of matters of a miscellaneous nature concerning discipline and domestic matters of delicacy which were dealt with by the Director General personally, the Deputy Director General or the Director A Division.

In addition A.D.A. was responsible for dealing with all the administrative aspects of the work of the other Divisions of the Service in matters concerning the machinery for technical means of investigation. This included the administrative details connected with arranging for Home Office Warrants for telephones, microphones and other similar matters. As a result of this familiarity with the machinery of the "technical" means of investigation he was responsible for providing information and assistance to those concerned with the planning of major operations, including COSSAC, SHAEF, the 21st Army Group, A.F.H.Q. and S.I.M.E. and for arranging for trained staff to assist them. From 1942 onwards he was concerned with the administrative arrangements of this nature for the I(B) Staff of the 21st Army Group and for the elements of the Control Commission which it was proposed to set up in Germany after the war. Broadly speaking the field covered -

(a) the provision of staff and equipment for Field Intelligence laboratories and -
(b) the "offensive" and "defensive" aspects of sound recording apparatus.

Most of the subjects dealt with by A.D.A. are normal administrative matters, but present problems which vary according to the circumstances of the case. There are, however, three which deserve special mention, i.e. Technical Equipment, Scientific work and the problems arising from the fact that the staff of the Security Service was composed of individuals some of whom were classed as civil and others as military.

Technical Equipment. Prior to 1936 the imposition of a telephone check under the Home Secretary's warrant had involved a laborious and uneconomic process by which the G.P.O. provided a group of reliable supervisors to listen to telephone conversations using headphones. There were obvious limits and difficulties arising from the language problem and otherwise and to meet them the G.P.O. research station developed suitable equipment for recording the conversations. Other difficulties arose as a result of air-raids during 1941 and 1942, an important limiting factor in urgent cases of suspected leakage being the engineering problem of making the necessary electrical connection at short notice, particular at night. Other problems again were connected with arrangements for imposing telephone checks in distant parts of the provinces for which purpose portable recording machines and the necessary staff were despatched to a convenient local centre, the records being sent to headquarters for transcription.

A constant problem arising from telephone checks and microphones concerned the staff employed to listen to the records and make the necessary transcriptions. The problem of the human element arises from the extreme importance of accuracy and the strain which this imposes on the listeners. Some records for instance are much clearer than others and in practice it is often found that a listener has to hear a record three or four times before being reasonably certain of the accuracy of the transcription. In important cases records have to be listened to by more than one person and even good records give a surprising scope for different interpretations. Staff employed constantly on this duty find it extremely trying and even under war conditions it is often distasteful to many. The need for accuracy and for reliable staff was illustrated by a case in which the Security Service was compelled to duplicate the work of S.I.S. in listening in to the Egyptian Embassy. This case arose out of the suspicion that the Egyptian Ambassador had undesirable relations with persons suspected of pro-enemy sympathies or associations. The Security Service check proved that an unreliable listener had produced some of the more sensational items out of his own imagination. His dismissal was no compensation for the immense amount of time and labour wasted.

Scientific Work (Secret Graphic Communications). From 1918 to the beginning of this war all technical work connected with secret graphic communications and other matters into which problems of chemistry entered was centred in the M.I.5. laboratory, at first under the direction of Mr. S.W. Collins and later under Mr. H.L. Smith assisted by Mr. Collins in a consultative capacity. At the beginning of this war Mr. Collins was made responsible for Censorship testing and various Censorship laboratories were established both at home and abroad. One of these overseas laboratories was that at Bermuda which, under Dr. C.E. Dent, was successful in detecting secret writing and microphotographs in numerous series of letters and thereby proved a major factor in enabling the F.B.I. to uncover enemy secret agents in America.

S.I.S., S.O.E. and M.I.9. all developed aspects of this type of work for their own purposes and by the beginning of 1942 at least five separate technical establishments were concerned in producing and detecting secret graphic messages with virtually no collaboration and no exchange of information on new developments between them. This situation involved certain dangers. It was possible for example that one laboratory might independently discover an ink already developed and used by another and then unwittingly exploit it in a way which would compromise its original use; or again Censorship in the legitimate exercise of its functions might discover and apply tests for secret writing which, when observed by the enemy, might suggest to him methods unknown to Censorship but actually in use by, say, S.I.S. or S.O.E. There was also a certain amount of duplication of effort and a certain degree of unnecessary risk of the leakage of information especially where reference to outside experts was involved.

It was decided that the best solution was to be found in the appointment of a senior scientist to act as co-ordinator in the work of all the laboratories and to be responsible to a committee consisting of the deputies to the heads of the participating departments. In May 1942 Professor H.V.A. Briscoe was appointed in this capacity and the results were generally regarded as extremely satisfactory.

One important development in the Security Service field was to demonstrate the necessity for the close integration of this type of scientific work with intelligence. After 1942 the principle was accepted that a scientist should personally visit places where the interrogation of suspects was taking place, should consult with the interrogating officer, examine the whole of the suspects' baggage, papers, books and other possessions and when he considered it necessary take any of them away for examination in the laboratory. In many cases a substantial part of the property was thus taken for investigation by X-ray, for more detailed inspection by ordinary or ultra-violet light or for chemical analysis. This procedure has been fully justified by results and in a number of cases the evidence thus found has led to the detection of spies and in others it has afforded useful improvement in our knowledge of enemy methods. The essential condition for success in such cases is the close and untrammelled contact of the trained and experienced scientist with all the known facts about the suspect.

Arrangements were made for collaboration with overseas laboratories. In the summer of 1943 S.I.S., anticipating the developments to be expected in the war against Japan, decided to establish a specialised laboratory in Calcutta. In August 1944 it was agreed that the three clandestine services most concerned in the Far Eastern theatre, i.e. S.I.S., S.O.E. and O.S.S. should exercise joint executive control over this laboratory, the technical control being in the hands of Dr. Higgins acting in close collaboration with Professor Briscoe in London. Dr. Higgins' services were also made available to Censorship and D.I.B. Delhi. Again in 1943 when plans for the invasion of the Continent were being made the need for a similar Intelligence laboratory was recognised and SHAEF agreed that one should be equipped to go overseas with the 21st Army Group.

In the autumn of 1944 the post-war needs of S.I.S. and the Security Service, as the only two departments concerned with long-term considerations, came up for discussion and it was decided that the Security Service laboratory should absorb the work done for S.I.S. Similarly S.I.S. photographic research work was handed over to the Security Service laboratory in April 1945. Before the war the combined needs of the two services were covered by one whole-time and one part-time chemist. In April 1945 the technical staff consisted of one senior qualified chemist, two junior qualified chemists, two senior and one junior laboratory and photographic assistants.

The above are the two most important directions in which A Division contributed directly to the development of technical measures in aid of the Intelligence work of B Division.

The third subject described as deserving special mention is the purely administrative one arising from the fact that among the officers of the Security Service some had had civil and others military status, the choice being based on the needs and advantages of the Service, often without reference to the personal interests of the individual. The result has been to give rise to a number of anomalies which have created difficult administrative problems, a solution to which has not been found at the time of writing (the end of 1945).

While the other administrative functions of A.D.A. and his staff do not require detailed description as they are of an incidental nature, they nevertheless involve an important and indispensable contribution to the general efficiency of the Service and many of them have necessitated a great deal of labour. As Lt. Colonel Cumming himself put it - "The work of the 'Administrative Services' branch of A Division in war was largely concerned with harnessing the staffs of 'servicing' departments to the Security Service cause. Without taking any account of the Registry, Overseas and Regional Control and Accounts, the number of staff shown (e.g.) on any Organisation chart as coming under 'Administrative Services' comprised only some half dozen officers and a score of staff. In practice, however, A.D.A. had, at the peak, 326 members of ancillary services (messengers, drivers, etc.) for whom he was directly or indirectly responsible and through whom the administrative functions of the Security Service were discharged." A study of the details must be relegated to the divisional history (vide S.F.50-24-44(15)).

Fluctuations in strength of officers, secretarial and Registry staff. The following figures show how the strength has fluctuated between January 1938 and July 1945:-

Officers:-

January 1938:	26
July 1938:	28
January 1939:	30
July 1939:	36
January 1940:	102
July 1940:	175
January 1941:	230
July 1941:	254
January 1942:	307
January 1943:	332
January 1944:	323
January 1945:	273
July 1945:	250

Secretaries and Registry Staff:-

January 1938:	86
January 1939:	103
July 1939:	133
January 1940:	334
July 1940:	516
January 1941:	617
July 1941:	822
January 1942:	934
January 1943:	939
January 1944:	852
January 1945:	748
July 1945:	647

These include the strength of D.S.O.s abroad and R.S.L.O.s but do not include the figures of S.C.O.s at ports, a note about which is given in Chapter V, Part 1 (vii). The figures for women include those at home and abroad but the latter are sometimes only approximate owing to some staff being recruited locally.

Officers Establishment. Between the wars officers were recruited entirely by personal recommendations and in view of the conditions of service few were attracted who were not in possession of private means or a pension from other Services. The position of the permanent staff was completely changed as a result of Sir David Petrie's initiative in 1944 which resulted in Treasury approval of a pension scheme on lines similar to those of the established Civil Service. This scheme was equally applicable to men and women.

The rapid recruitment of the large increase of staff necessitated by the expansion after the outbreak of war presented problems of considerable difficulty. In the first place it was entirely done as the result of personal recommendations, but in the later stages a certain number of officers were obtained from the Armed Forces on the ground of special qualifications such as linguistic knowledge for the purposes of interrogation. A large proportion of the temporary staff were drawn from the legal profession, members of the Bar predominating. There were Dons from the universities and the engineering profession, archaeology, industry, the arts and science were also represented.

Questions of grading of the temporary staff are too complex for discussion here and numerous anomalies arose on account of differences of pay and questions of military rank.

Women's Establishment. As in the case of men the permanent staff between the wars was recruited entirely by personal recommendation. To meet the difficulties created by the war it was extended to application to secretarial colleges and even to advertisement in the Press.

The figures given above show that the proportion of women to men was often in the neighbourhood of three to one. While a considerable proportion of the work done by women was of a routine nature both in the Registry and otherwise, a large number of both the secretarial and Registry staff sometimes had opportunities to do work requiring initiative, powers of organisation and administrative ability.

The work of the Defence Security Officers overseas called for both secretarial and Registry staff. Sixty-six women have been sent overseas at various times to offices in the following places:-

Bahamas	South Africa
Bermuda	West Africa
British Guiana	Malta
Leeward Islands	Gibraltar
Jamaica	Palestine
Trinidad	Egypt
U.S.A.	Ceylon
Canada	Rangoon
Newfoundland	Singapore
East Africa	Hong Kong

As in the case of other Services a number of women were employed on officers' duties with rank either as Administrative Assistants or in Grade I. A few of these positions were filled by direct appointment, but most of them by promotion from the Registry or secretarial sections. In the latter case their previous knowledge and experience of office procedure often gave them an advantage over the untrained male officer. In all fifty-nine women have held officers' posts.

A few cases where women held posts which offered scope for special initiative and originality have been mentioned in the course of this record, but there were many others in which women officers displayed similar qualities and undertook duties involving responsibility or requiring experience in the presentation of evidence as well as resource and initiative. Women officers were employed in the preparation of cases in S.L.B.; in the work of collation and research in the preparation of papers for use in interrogation; in research work of the type done in B.1 Information and in the War Room. They were employed as sectional officers in all Divisions, including those dealing with enemy aliens, British and foreign Communists and British Fascists, and as such sometimes represented the Security Service at meetings with officers of other departments; took part in the interrogation of women suspects or agents; and in some cases "ran" agents, including in one case controlled double-agents.

A most important function performed entirely by women was that of the Accounts Staff under Colonel Butler and Miss Constant. The same applies to the cipher work and the printing press. Women also held responsible positions in D.4, where they had to deal with and take responsibility for decisions in more or less delicate matters referred to Head Office by the S.C.O.s at the ports when dealing with aliens' arrivals. In addition to all this were the important duties performed by women in administrative positions in charge of the staff to whom it fell to smooth over difficulties and to help in maintaining morale in adverse conditions such as those created by the evacuation of the country office; and the important administrative posts in the Registry.

(ii) Registry and Organisation.

From 1940 onwards Mr. H.H. Potter was head of the Registry under the general direction of Mr. Horrocks as Deputy Director Organisation.

Mr. Horrocks has furnished the following account of the development of the Registry:-

> "1. In June 1940 the organisation of the Service had all but broken down. The rapid development of the war and consequent growth of the Service were the causes.
>
> 2. An examination of the situation showed at once that while a re-organisation and redistribution of the work of officers was necessary, the provision of an efficient Registry was the first and most urgent need if a complete breakdown were to be averted.
>
> 3. While it is axiomatic that efficient intelligence work depends primarily on good records, the Registry had been allowed to lapse into a most lamentable position. The causes were assessed as follows:-
>
>   (i) The absence of directives to, or interest in the work of, the Registry by the officers.

(ii) The arrangements of the work of the Registry on a sectional basis by which each section dealt with files pertaining to a selected subject or subjects. Each section did all Registry action on its own files hence wide differences in procedure developed. The arrangements gave an officer the opportunity to divest himself of all responsibility regarding records and to become increasingly dependent on his Registry section for information and even guidance.

(iii) Under this system the work of the Registry sections developed into a scramble to keep the officers supplied on most urgent matters. Arrears accumulated and were often concealed. Files were not made and there was no time to train new staff, many of whom were completely ineffective after six months or more service.

(iv) There was a shortage of staff, but as mentioned above no means of making them effective had they been available.

(v) The Central Index had been allowed to lapse into a lamentable state:-

(a) cards were misplaced;
(b) there were practically no guide cards;
(c) the cabinets were overfull;
(d) there was duplication of cards;
(e) unnecessary carding abounded;
(f) new cards were not filed at once.

(vi) The basic system of filing was inefficient and inelastic. While a diminishing number of individual files were made the records of those individuals on which interest centred (Aliens, Right and Left Wingers) were filed on a subject basis (i.e. Communists in Northumberland). The effect was that to obtain complete information regarding an individual several files were needed, many of which were required by other officers for other individuals. So few obtained the files they needed and officers' rooms were stacked with unanswered correspondence and with files all awaiting other files which could not be obtained. Personal files were classified in series, this being a quite unnecessary complication in the process of file making.

(vii) There was no control of the transit and movement of files. Officers held on to files thus depriving others of their use.

(viii) To relieve the situation labour was wasted in searchers or "snaggers" whose average production was two files per day!

(ix) Accommodation was lamentable.

(x) There was an absence of accord and harmonious working between the Registry and the remainder of the Office. Each tried to score off the other with the result that both lost.

(xi) It was impossible to obtain any accurate figures of the arrears on hand. Sections referred vaguely to "many papers" or confessed their utter inability to count what they had.

(xii) The head of the Registry had insufficient status.

4. In determining the steps to be taken due consideration had to be given to:-

   (a) the necessity for keeping the Service going;

   (b) the certainty that any improvement would unloose a wave of criticism good or uninformed which had been dammed up by utter hopelessness;

   (c) the necessity to weld the Service, officers and Registry alike, into a co-operative whole, helping each other for the common cause.

5. The re-organisation began in July 1940 with:-

   (a) Re-arrangement of the work of the Registry sections on a process basis. The processes were:-

A3A	-	look-up, custody of indexes;
A3B	-	connecting, custody of files;
A3C	-	review, i.e. the examination of papers for the purpose of giving precise directions for Registry action;
A3E	-	filing of papers;
A3G	-	carding of current files (a sub-section carded p.a. files);
A3H	-	extracting;
A3K	-	file-making;
A3L	-	'snag' section, i.e. searched for files wanted before other files and papers could be released.

   (b) Authority was obtained for more staff which, because of (a) above, could be made immediately effective. Increased and better accommodation was also prepared.

   (c) The subject files referred to at 3(vi) above were recalled to the Registry. Tags were cut and the files housed in boxes. This enabled papers relative to any one individual to be circulated without immobilising those of others. From this stage the knot began to untie. One numerical numbering series was adopted for personal files.

(d) The marking of individual files was stepped up to some 2,500 per week.

(e) All arrears were brought to light - sorted - and a beginning made to liquidate them.

(f) The carding of all vetting cases and generally of names of those against whom nothing was known was discontinued.

6. In August 1940 a new system of controlling the transit of files was introduced.

7. The changes described above brought about an immediate improvement in the situation. The speed of improvement was, however, greatly hampered by the enforced cessation of work during air raids.

8. On September 29th 1940 the Central Index and some of the records were destroyed by enemy action. In consequence the whole of the Registry and certain other sections of the Service were evacuated to the country.

9. The first task on reaching the new quarters was to create an Index which would serve temporarily while the Central Index was reconstructed. This was done in a few days by compiling an Index of the names of all file holders - some 100,000.

10. The Central Index had been microphotographed and immediate steps were taken to produce prints. The re-production was very poor and the work of reconstructing the Index was formidable and it was not completed until June 1941.

The experience of reconstruction showed, however, that the Index was still a very imperfect instrument and that the eye strain from looking at the photographs was too severe to be contemplated for a long period.

The Index was re-typed and the opportunity taken to:-

(i) eliminate unnecessary cards;
(ii) abolish duplicates and amalgamate files where necessary;
(iii) re-group on a phonetic basis;
(iv) separate out cards for impersonal matters.

The work was completed by March 1944. The cards in the Index still numbered about a million and a quarter, though three-quarters of a million had been eliminated for one reason or another.

11. By early 1941 arrears had disappeared and the "snagging" section was abolished. The training of Registry staff in all processes continued and it

was possible by stages to amalgamate the processes of carding, filing and filemaking.

12. In April 1941 it was possible to make a major change in procedure, which, while adding to the working efficiency, was the means of fostering that cooperative working between the Registry and other parts of the Service which contributed so much to the success of the later war years.

Up to April 1941 all incoming papers were passed in the first instance to the officer concerned who, after a preliminary review, passed them to the Registry for previous papers or other action. The change made was to pass all incoming papers to the Registry in the first instance, where steps were taken either to pass the paper to the officer with all relevant files, or to register the paper and add to the Index immediately, or to take steps to obtain the relevant file for the officer. At the same time the duty of directing Registry action in carding, making new files or extracts was laid squarely on the officers. The Registry were given the right to question incomplete or excessive requests or to raise matters of principle affecting Registry action.

When certain matters of principle had been determined the new system proved of inestimable benefit to all. Visits by officers and secretaries to the Registry were encouraged. Officers assisted by giving talks to the Registry on their subjects. In April 1941 the Registry Examiners were formed on whom the duty lay of examining all files returned to the Registry and of acting as the focal point of contact between the Registry and other sections.

The total effect was to bring about the accord and co-operation essential to efficient working of the Service.

13. Subject and Policy Files.

Up to 1941 one section of the Registry had handled all "SF" files whether dealing with impersonal subjects for investigation or the policy and administration of the Service. The policy and administrative files were left with the special section, the remainder passing to the main Registry.

The Index to policy matters was entirely re-made and the files overhauled and re-classified. This began in August 1942 and was completed by January 1944.

14. Destruction.

In 1940 a number of old files of no current interest were destroyed. In 1942 a properly constituted destruction section was formed whose duty it is to review in conjunction with officers individual or series of files for destruction.

Much remains to be done, the measure of progress being only the staff available.

15. B Division Files.

When B Division began, early in 1941, to come to grips with the German Espionage Service, it became vitally necessary to safeguard certain particularly delicate sources, and a small 'local' Registry (then termed B.1 Registry) was created for the primary purpose of restricting knowledge of the sources and their products to those to whom the files passed for registration. In course of time B.1 Registry became a repository not only for information derived from certain secret sources but also for all material of significance to the study and frustration of German espionage. The files containing both types of material circulated only among B.1 officers and B.1 Registry.

16. War Room Registry.

For some three years B.1 Registry remained in London apart from the main Registry. Its records of personalities connected with the German Intelligence Service expanded greatly as knowledge increased. Towards the end of 1943 the pressure was such that criticisms of the performance of B.1 Registry began to be heard and these, together with the renewal of air raids upon London, in early 1944, and the then unknown risks of the threatened V weapons, led to the transfer in February 1944 of B.1 Registry to the country to come, with the designation R.B., under the control of the main Registry.

Many adjustments were made to the methods practised by B.1 Registry in order that they should conform whenever possible to the now proven standards of the main Registry. Each card in the R.B. Index was compared with the Central Index, and a great many discrepancies and omissions so revealed were adjusted. Additional staff for R.B. was recruited from the Central Registry staff and the considerable arrears of work tackled and eventually overtaken just before D-Day of 1944.

The records and performance of R.B. and of the officers served by R.B. put M.I.5. in the position of being the only intelligence body in this country which could continue to function adequately and at a sufficient speed. Consequently when the War Room organisation - originally a joint affair of M.I.6. and the American O.S.S. - came under criticism for its unsatisfactory performance, the revised War Room included a number of M.I.5. officers and the entire staff and records of R.B. were put at its disposal.

R.B. thus became partially a SHAEF unit, bearing the designation WR-H (i.e. sub-section H of the SHAEF C.I. War Room). Its functions continued along the familiar lines, but certain new tasks fell to it. The principal new duty consisted of an obligation to furnish from records details of individuals of interest to the C.I. staffs. These details, in the form of draft index cards, reached the C.I. staffs through the SHAEF organisation EDS, which reproduced thirty-five copies of each index card for distribution to the various holders of the SHAEF index, which was intended to contain the names of all persons of whom the C.I. staffs should be advised during the fighting and afterwards.

WR-H had thus a double duty to discharge upon each paper - first, to index and maintain its files in the normal manner, and second, to select and transmit to ESD those names appropriate to the SHAEF index.

As the armies advanced, and finally when Germany was overrun, enormous numbers of official German documents were captured. Those which contained material of interest to the War Room - i.e. those relating to German Intelligence Services - provided large numbers of names suitable for the SHAEF index, and many of these names, in so far as they were of internal "office" personnel rather than agents or senior officials, were naturally hitherto unknown to the War Room Registry; and many new details of people already on record came to light in the captured documents.

The burden of handling this great volume of material, together with a heavily increased flow of interrogation reports of captured persons, threw a heavy strain upon WR-H, and various technical amendments to the normal working arrangements had to be made to maintain a high standard of service."

Copies of the Organisation Charts dated July 1941 and April 1943 are attached at Appendix II. Developments in the war situation necessitated frequent changes, many of which have been mentioned in the text.

(iii) Liaison with other Intelligence Services.

Section V of S.I.S. The closest liaison was, in the nature of things, that maintained with Section V of S.I.S. which has been described at some length in Chapter I and referred to throughout this history. The difficulties which arose during the war years and have been the subject of frequent mention may, to a certain extent, have given a distorted view of the position. In the day to day work close liaison existed at all levels and covered almost all the subjects dealt with by the Security Service. It should be emphasised that the relations were excellent before the war and that even during the war they were good at the sectional and sub-sectional level. The difficulties arose from the different views entertained in the two Services of the functions of Section V.

As explained in the first chapter a principal cause of these difficulties was the claim by the head of Section V to have the right to withhold information about counter espionage matters on the ground that they and not the Security Service were concerned with persons or events outside the three-mile limit. This was to claim a position entirely different from that of any other circulating section of S.I.S. These circulating sections exist in order to furnish information to the major departments and there can be no reasonable ground for argument that the true function of Section V is other than to furnish information from abroad about foreign Secret Services to the Security Service; even if they may sometimes and incidentally communicate the Foreign Office such aspects of it as have a bearing on foreign policy.

The fact remains, however, that the great success of B Division during the years 1941-1945 would not have been feasible if R.S.S., R.I.S. and G.C. & C.S., for the efficient organisation of which C.S.S. was responsible, had not provided it with the ISOS material. It must be remembered that the Security Service had not taken advantage of the opportunities offered to it - in 1938, throughout 1940 and finally in March 1941 - to incorporate R.S.S. and to develop to the full capacity a unit which could have been constituted as an inseparable part of its own organisation. S.I.S. had stepped into the breach and, through the highly efficient staff provided for the purpose in R.S.S., R.I.S. and G.C. & C.S., had made the vast network of Abwehr and Sipo und SD wireless accessible to B Division. Without this help B.1.A., Camp 020 and the L.R.C. would have been compelled to work largely in the dark. The degree of success achieved in interrogation and the confident planning of deception would have been impossible. Criticism of the narrow, selfish and incompetent handling of the ISOS problem by Lt. Colonel Cowgill as the head of Section V should not be allowed to detract from the supreme achievements in this field by the organisations under C.S.S.

S.O.E. Liaison with S.O.E. was developed after 1942, in the first place through Commander Senter and Miss Sample, both of whom had previously served in the Security Service and afterwards joined the S.O.E. Intelligence Directorate under Air Commodore Boyle. Commander Senter arranged for Miss Sample to maintain a close liaison with Miss Wadeson, the head of the L.R.C. Information Index, and to exchange information on lines discussed above in connection with the L.R.C. In March 1943 this liaison was further developed by the appointment of Major Wethered of the Security Service to act in liaison with the staff under Air Commodore Boyle in order to examine the cases of S.O.E. agents who arrived in this country after being in enemy hands or after falling under suspicion for other reasons. The position was further strengthened by the appointment of Mr. Hardy of the Security Service to a position in the S.O.E. Intelligence Directorate. The procedure was that when such an agent returned from the field, he was examined in the course of a formal enquiry at which Major Wethered usually presided and if necessary he was subjected to cross-examination. The country section of S.O.E., i.e. the section responsible for the agent usually adopted the attitude that they had full confidence in him but that the Security Service must be allowed to examine people coming into this country from the security point of view.

These enquiries assumed importance because, as was known from the records at the L.R.C. and from other sources, many of the S.O.E. organisations abroad - especially those in Belgium and Holland - were badly "blown" by the spring of 1943. In these circumstances there was an obvious danger that through some of these "blown" organisations the enemy might learn not only of impending S.O.E. operations but of major military operations as well. This naturally became a matter of increasing importance on account of the preliminaries to the "Overlord" operation. Under Security Service advice every possible precaution was taken, such as a personal search of outgoing agents by Customs experts and an examination of clothes and documents to prevent or minimise the risk of their betraying the agent.

While the Security Service was anxious to ensure security from their own point of view, i.e. to prevent the enemy from obtaining information from or about this country through the S.O.E. agents whom they might have turned round, the S.O.E. country sections were also anxious from their own and entirely different point of view to ensure the security of their operations. For this reason they were always unwilling to supply to the Security Service detailed operational information. Apart from this difficulty the exchange of information between the two Services was reasonably free and full. S.O.E. supplied detailed information about cases and organisations which had gone wrong and Major Wethered obtained from the Security Service records, and especially from the L.R.C. Index and traces, all kinds of details about an agent's associations and other matters bearing on his case. Similarly information was supplied to S.O.E. about enemy organisations in occupied territory and such details as might facilitate the agent's movements through enemy controls. Copies of all interrogations at the L.R.C. were also supplied to S.O.E. during the latter years of the war, but S.O.E. depended on the L.R.C. Index and on Security Service Registry traces for the co-ordination of intelligence. They had no systematically planned intelligence of their own to support their operational undertakings, although each of their country sections no doubt accumulated intelligence as it went along.

The liaison with S.O.E. in connection with sabotage has been described above in the section dealing with B.1.C.

The facts as a whole suggest the possibility that closer liaison could have been arranged with mutual advantage, but from the Security Service point of view the position was regarded as satisfactory and was contrasted very favourably with that under which the Security Service had no information about S.I.S. agents who were "blown" and no opportunity of making enquiries into such cases.

<u>Allied Intelligence Services</u>. Liaison with Allied Intelligence Services in London during the war was in the hands of E Division sections in respect of Allied nationals in this country and of the L.R.C. in so far as cases of incoming Allied nationals were concerned. Before the war direct liaison on the subject of German espionage was maintained by agreement with Section V with the Deuxieme Bureau in Paris and on the subject of Communism through the American Embassy in London. As a result of this contact Captain Liddell visited New York and Washington before and during the war and developed an exchange of information in connection with the NSDAP and German espionage. After America came into the war the F.B.I. sent representatives to be attached to the staff of their Embassy in London and Mr. Mills, who went to Canada as the Security Service representative, also established contact with the F.B.I. The general subject of liaison with the Americans was among the many causes of difficulty and disagreement with Section V who maintained that all liaison should be done through

their representatives in New York and Washington. A specially close personal liaison with the Czech Intelligence Service in London was maintained throughout the war by Captain Liddell and Mr. White.

Dominions and Colonies. This is discussed below under Overseas Control.

I.P.I. (Indian Political Intelligence). Liaison with I.P.I. has been extremely close and cordial over a long period extending back to the war of 1914-18. It covers the whole range of Security Service subjects from enemy espionage and Communism to general questions of security. For many years I.P.I. has been located in the same building as the Security Service and a free exchange of information has taken place. For instance, I.P.I. has at times, through its agents, obtained inside information of value to the Security Service about the British Union of Fascists or about British Communists. By arranging Home Office Warrants the Security Service has co-operated in regard to individuals of interest to I.P.I.

I.P.I. is in effect the section of the Security Service which deals with Indians, Burmese and Afghans and information on these subjects is recorded in I.P.I.'s Registry and not in that of the Security Service. Surveys of specific subjects prepared in the Security Service are normally supplied to I.P.I., who contribute to the general pool by providing information on such subjects drawn from Indian and Burmese sources.

Throughout the war the arrangement continued by which I.P.I. worked in the same premises as the Security Service and in close liaison with them.

In 1941 I.P.I. was given free access to the Security Service files, and the position of the two Services was more clearly defined. The recording and indexing of all activities of Indians, Burmese and Afghans in the United Kingdom was recognised as an I.P.I. responsibility and was discontinued by the Security Service.

To their mutual advantage the working of the two Services became even closer as the war progressed and developments made the interchange of information and the use of one another's facilities essential.

I.P.I. work under the general direction of the India Office and in close contact with the Director of the Intelligence Bureau under the Government of India, and the Security Wing of the Burma Police.

(iv) The Director General's Staff.

The Director General's staff consisted of two groups of officers, of whom the first formed part of the central administrative machinery of the Office and the other performed miscellaneous functions which were associated with the functions of the divisions.

Those forming part of the central administrative machinery were the Deputy Director General, the Legal Adviser, the Secretariat and the Private Secretary.

Those associated with the functions of the Divisions were those concerned with prosecutions, leakage of information, cases against renegades, operations, research, agents and the Press Section, Room 055 War Office and Overseas Control.

The central administrative machinery. The Deputy Director General had no separate functions and relieved the Director General of general supervisory work and miscellaneous administrative detail. The Legal Adviser, Mr. G. St. C. Pilcher - first assisted and later succeeded by Mr. J.L.S. Hale - was also Legal Adviser to divisions and sections. In the early stages of the war they were mainly occupied with questions relating to internment or detention and releases of enemy aliens and British subjects. The Secretariat came into existence early in 1941 at the instance of Lord Swinton who considered that it was necessary to have a focal point for decisions of policy affecting the Security Service as a whole. He used the Secretariat to enable him to deal with questions of policy which were of considerable complexity and variety at this time when the Home Defence Security Executive under his chairmanship was seeking to co-ordinate security work in and between a number of Government Departments and authorities. The position was changed after the re-organisation of 1941 when Lord Swinton's interference in the internal affairs of the Security Service came to an end. From then onwards the Secretariat continued to perform a useful function in dealing with all questions involving policy, especially where there were conflicting views within the Security Service. The Secretariat served to assemble the views of divisional officers and present them to the Director General for his decision.

Prosecutions (S.L.B.1.). From September 1939 onwards the Security Service in the course of its work was continually being brought into contact with cases which, although they had to be investigated primarily from the intelligence and security standpoint, were none the less likely, sooner or later, to find their way into the criminal courts. Colonel W.E. Hinchley-Cooke, who had unrivalled experience in this field, was at that time attached to B Division and, although a number of cases were referred to him in order that he might advise upon the prosecution aspect, there was no hard and fast rule in force.

When the Security Service was re-organised in 1941 the Director General set up an additional legal section, called S.L.B., under the direction of Colonel Hinchley-Cooke, who was assisted by Mr. (now Lt. Colonel) Cussen. This section was charged with the duty of ensuring that intelligence and security investigation marched hand in hand with preparation for prosecution.

All sections of the Security Service was instructed that whenever they were dealing with a matter which might lead to prosecution they should at an early stage acquaint S.L.B. with the facts and act upon their advice as to the safeguarding of the prosecution interest.

S.L.B. in the result became the liaison between the Director of Public Prosecutions and the Security Service and also, so far as Army and R.A.F. personnel were concerned, between the Office of the Judge Advocate General and the Security Service. Where necessary S.L.B. were in touch with the Naval Law Branch of the Admiralty on matters affecting Naval personnel.

It soon became apparent that the existence of this section was of considerable value, and its work increased so that in August 1942 Mr. Sinclair was posted to S.L.B. as an additional officer and for a short time thereafter the section also had the assistance of Mr. Redfern.

It would take too long to give any indication of the number and variety of cases dealt with and it will perhaps suffice to say that all of the following cases of espionage were prepared for submission to the Director of Public Prosecutions by S.L.B.:-

> Jose Waldberg
> Carl Heinrich Meier
> Charles Albert van den Kieboom
> George Armstrong
> Karl Theo Drueke
> Werner Heinrich Walti
> Karel Richard Richter
> Johannes Marinus Dronkers
> Jose Estella Key
> Alphons Louis Eugene Timmerman
> Duncan Alexander Croall Scott-Ford
> Franciscus Johannes Winter
> Rogerio de Magalhaes Peixoto de Menezes
> Oswald John Job
> Pierre Richard Charles Neukermans
> Joseph Jan van Hove

When S.L.B.2. was formed the prosecution section became known as S.L.B.1.

Leakage of Information Section. In all wars, but particularly in modern wars, it is essential to keep secret the plan of campaign, the numbers and purpose of the forces to be employed and the weapons and devices which will be made use of. If information about these matters ceases to be secret and obtains a general circulation, valuable raw material is furnished to the spy. Moreover, innocent persons, whether British or foreign, who may be travelling out of the country, may, by passing on something they have heard quite innocently, give valuable information to the enemy. Of the various agencies employed in keeping secret what should be kept secret the Security Service was prominent both in an advisory and in an executive capacity. Thus there was in existence in December 1939 a section dealing with leakage of information under Mr. Maude of S.L.2. In April 1940 this work was discharged by a section known as B.19, of which Mr. Maude was in charge, he being assisted by Major Phipps. After the removal of the bulk of the Office to Oxford in October 1940 the work of this section lapsed to a considerable extent, but in February 1942 it was found necessary to revive and stimulate its activity and the section was renamed B.1.K. and transferred to the London Office, the personnel consisting of Mr. Machell and Miss Small.

At this time the functions of the section were briefly as follows:-

(a) the investigation of cases where a leakage of information had come to notice;

(b) the dealing with miscellaneous enquiries which were based partly on leakage or suspected leakage of information;

(c) surveillance of persons in possession of secret information who were believed to be liable to disclose it;

(d) liaison with other agencies working in this field - e.g. Postal and Telegraph Censorship, Press Censorship and the Security Officers of the various Government Departments;

(e) preparation and distribution of the product of certain telephone checks which had been imposed on persons suspected of having acquired or endeavouring to acquire secret information;

(f) liaison with all sections within the Office in connection with leakage of information matters - e.g. D.4, Regional Control and the R.S.L.O.s and the Operations Section.

The section worked in particularly close touch with S.L.B. and it was the task of the latter to advise as to the handling of various enquiries and in particular to ensure that these enquiries were made in such a way as to render it possible for criminal proceedings to be taken against offenders when necessary under either the Official Secrets Acts 1911-1939 or Regulation 3 of the Defence (General) Regulations 1939.

On May 1st 1943 the Director General transferred the work of B.1.K. to a new section of S.L.B. called S.L.B.2. under Lt. Colonel Cussen. Mr. Machell was transferred to other duties and Miss Small joined Lt. Colonel Cussen. The Director General in making this change had in mind the expansion of work in connection with leakage of information which was bound to arise during the course of the preparations for the invasion of Europe and its execution. It was clear that a good deal of executive action would be required and he desired to consolidate the investigation side with the legal side. It was laid down that all sections of the Office should refer every suspected case of leakage of information to S.L.B.2., who would be responsible for investigating the case, stopping the leakage and, where necessary, for reporting the case to the Director of Public Prosecutions. The Home Office issued a circular to all police authorities requiring that before any proceedings were taken under D.R.3. the case should be referred to the Director of Public Prosecutions.

The Director sought the advice of the Security Service through S.I.B.2. before authorising or taking proceedings. This step was necessary, first in order to secure uniformity of treatment for these cases and second, in order to prevent proceedings being taken even in camera in those instances where the strict secrecy of the information in question would be further jeopardised by the hearing of a charge.

The section also became responsible for advising, and in grave cases for investigating, the loss of secret documents as this was one of the most dangerous sources of leakage.

In order to carry out an investigation the section called for the assistance of the following: the C.I.D. officers attached to the Security Service under Major Burt (B.5 section), the R.S.L.O.s and S.C.O.s and the various police forces through the R.S.L.O.s.

The investigating officer who is called upon to deal with a case of leakage of information must, if he is to do his work successfully, know the true facts about the subject concerned. If an army officer is said to have told his girl-friend the date for the invasion of North Africa, the investigating officer cannot handle the case unless he himself knows the date or sometimes the approximate date.

The section therefore worked in hourly contact with the Operations Section. This latter section assessed the gravity of the leakage from the operational point of view and considered with the leakage of information section the type of investigation required and the measures necessary to "close" the leakage. The investigating officer selected by S.L.B.2. was then fully briefed on the subject in question. It was the practice, where all highly secret matters were concerned, to entrust the investigation to a B.5. officer unless it was desirable for a particular reason that Lt. Colonel Cussen should deal with the case himself - e.g. where a high civil servant was concerned.

There is always a proper place for the "specialist" in investigation work, and experience showed that this is true where leakage of information is concerned. Not only was the leakage of information section enabled frequently to dismiss a case as a mere repetition of a 'canard' or rumour, but also, to the advantage of its work, it gained experience in differentiating between those who recklessly and dangerously revealed official information which they had and those who did so in an unguarded moment and in all innocence. The type of treatment required in each case was of course quite different. In addition the section acquired its own technique in conducting investigations. It learned that in almost every case it was essential to take statements in writing from informants in a formal way, and then to proceed back along the track indicated. As a general rule this resulted in the persons responsible for the leakage being confronted with such abundant proof of their misdeeds that they were prepared to admit them under caution.

It might also be mentioned that very valuable results were obtained time and time again by the imposition of a telephone check on informants and suspects who were about to be interviewed. They very often filled in gaps in the information by telephoning their friends and associates.

This brief survey can perhaps best be concluded by giving one or two examples of leakages or loss of documents which were investigated:-

    (a) A high Admiralty official leaves a copy of the plan for the invasion of Sicily in a train. Investigation made by Lt. Colonel Cussen and Special Branch Metropolitan Police. Documents found by another passenger within three hours. Investigation completed within seven hours. A.D.N.I., who participated, concurred with Security Service in reporting to Chiefs of Staff Committee that the operation was not "compromised".

(b) An engineer employed on Operation Pluto (the oil pipeline to Europe) tells an army officer about its details in a hotel. The case investigated by a B.5 officer. Proceedings taken under D.R.3. in camera.

(c) An American naval officer tells those present at a private dinner party the main features of the plan for invading Europe. Case investigated by Lt. Colonel Cussen and G-2 CI SHAEF. Leakage effectively closed within twenty-four hours. Naval officer "returned" to the U.S.A.

(d) Two days before D-Day an accredited correspondent then on board a landing craft sends a message to his newspaper giving certain details as to the forthcoming landing. Owing to an error by SHAEF Censorship a number of such messages were allowed to reach their destination. Case investigated by Lt. Colonel Cussen and G-2 CI SHAEF and B.5. Censorship procedure corrected and advice given to Supreme Commander that any other remedial action would do more harm than good.

Renegades (S.L.B.3). From the commencement of the war the Security Service acquired information from various sources as to the activities of those British subjects who were in enemy and enemy-occupied territory and who were engaged in assisting the enemy in various ways.

So far as civilians were concerned the information was handled by the section of B Division dealing with Fascist activities and after the re-organisation of the Security Service by F.3.

Prisoners of war who had gone over to the enemy were the subject of reports by M.I.9. and these were dealt with by a section of B Division, B.4.A. under Major Whyte and later under Lt. Colonel Seymer, both of whom were assisted by Miss Barnes.

As the time for the invasion of the Continent drew near, consideration was given by the Home Office, the Law Officers and the Director of Public Prosecutions to the question as to how renegades should be dealt with. At a meeting presided over by the Attorney General the Security Service was asked to be responsible for the collection of evidence about these persons and to undertake the reporting of their cases to the Director of Public Prosecutions.

Once France was overrun it became apparent that although the Security Service had provided the armies in the field with a "Warning List" containing the names of British renegades who should be apprehended, the burden of detail involved was too great for the Army Intelligence personnel, nor did their training equip them for preparing cases for prosecution in the British Courts.

At the request of Major General Strong, Assistant Chief of Staff, G-2 (SHAEF), the Director General established an M.I.5. Liaison Section attached to SHAEF who were charged with the duty of investigating British renegade cases and collecting evidence in the field. The Director General at the same time amalgamated the section F.1, which by this time had relieved F.3 of civilian renegade work, with B.4.A., which was still dealing with prisoners of war. These two sections, together with the M.I.5. Liaison Section, were merged into a new section, S.L.B.3, which took over all renegade investigation both civilian and Service under the direction of Lt. Colonel Cussen.

Civilian cases have been dealt with by a sub-section under Mr. Shelford and, after his resignation, under Major Hughes; and Service cases by Lt. Colonel Seymer and latterly Major Patterson.

This work is still in progress and it is not possible at the present time to give a complete picture of what has been achieved. It may perhaps suffice to say that two civilians have been convicted of treason (Joyce and Amery), five civilians have been convicted of offences against Regulation 2(A) of the Defence (General) Regulations 1939, nineteen British, Colonial and Dominion Service personnel have been convicted of offences against the Army Act 1940, three British Service personnel have been convicted of offences against the Air Force Act 1940, and one soldier has been convicted of an offence against the Treachery Act 1940 (Schurch).

In addition a vast number of investigations have been made which will enable the Security Service in due course to present a comprehensive report on the whole of the suspected British renegades on the Continent.

Operations Section. The Operations Section was first formed in the autumn of 1940 as part of W Branch and its original charter was "to receive secret information particularly in regard to operations of the fighting Services through liaison officers and to examine communications with this object; also to test the security of Service establishment in which special work of operational value was being undertaken". At this time security relations between the operational authorities in the three Services and the Security Service were not satisfactorily integrated. Machinery was still being improved, one of the component parts of this machinery being the Inter-Services Security Board on which there was a Security Service representative in the person of Major Lennox, who was at that time in charge of Room 055 at the War Office. The Inter-Services Security Board was responsible, under the direction of the J.I.C., for the security of military operations and the prevention of leakages in that connection. The Security Service was concerned if a leakage was suspected; and it was necessary for the Security Service to know the true facts regarding any matter in connection with which a leakage was alleged to have occurred in order that it might make enquiries on appropriate lines.

The main function of the Operations Section was one of liaison between the authorities responsible for Service operations of all kinds and different parts of the Security Service. The object was to keep the Security Service informed as and where necessary about operational matters and to keep the operational authorities informed as and where necessary of the results of measures of an investigational or preventive nature taken by the Security Service. These essential functions did not change although a new charter was drawn up to define them more exactly when the Security Service was re-organised in the summer of 1941 and this charter was revised in January 1942 and again in June 1944. The revisions were made to conform to developments in the war situation and to accord with the wishes of the J.I.C.

In the final charter it was stated that the Operational Sections would keep the Director General informed of those operational plans which had a security interest; operational being used in its widest sense and including not only military operations of war but cover and deception plans, military exercises, secret tests, trials and experiments and also the journeys of V.I.P.s (Very Important Personages). At the same time the duties of the section in giving information to the Director B Division, S.L.B.2. (the section dealing with leakages), other B Division sections, A.D.D.4, E Division and F Division were laid down. These instructions formalised practices which had developed since the previous charter had been framed.

The Operations Section occupied a special position in that it represented S.I.S. as well as the Security Service on the Inter-Services Security Board. It became responsible for liaison with S.I.S. on secret operational matters generally and was also put into direct touch with S.O.2. (later S.O.E.) to carry out the same duties as it was performing for S.I.S.

An unexpected development arose from the position thus created. "Combined Operations", the Admiralty, the War Office, the Air Ministry and S.I.S. were all engaged independently in minor operations which were conducted with great secrecy by all of them and without information being exchanged. The result was that the Security Service Operations Section came to be the only part of the machinery to which the possibility of clashes between these minor operations became known; and it was therefore asked to undertake the responsibility of seeing that such clashes did not take place. Arrangements were therefore made to ensure that the Operations Section was kept systematically informed by all parties. A secret map was prepared showing exactly all future operations which were being planned as well as a secret project list which showed in geographical order all projected secret operations throughout Europe and Africa which were planned in this country or about which information was available here. Three copies only were made and they were distributed every week to the head of S.I.S. and the head of the security branch of S.O.E., the third being retained in the Operations Section for use within the Security Service. These lists did not cover detailed military plans but all minor raids and airborne expeditions up to and including major operations such as the landings in North Africa and the final invasion of Normandy. It did not include normal bombing operations against the Continent.

The section was also responsible for seeing that any information coming to the knowledge of the Security Service or S.I.S., which might have operational significance, should be communicated promptly to the Intelligence Staff of the Service or Department concerned.

When raids were planned on enemy-occupied territory the Operations Section was responsible for communicating to the Service or Department concerned any operational objectives of interest to the Security Service or S.I.S. such as the location of enemy intelligence stations or centres of communication. By this means arrangements were made to deal with objectives thus designated and to obtain information of interest to the Security Service and S.I.S.

The section was concerned as a liaison section with security arrangements connected with the development of plans for the "Overlord" operation and with the security arrangements for the various journeys abroad made by the Prime Minister.

In view of the detail involved in the various changes in the charter it is necessary to refer to the sectional report for a full statement of the work done by this section.

Research. In October 1941 the Director General formed "Research" as part of his staff and posted Mr. Curry to the appointment. The reports on the German Secret Services already mentioned were prepared in 1942 and 1944. Miscellaneous papers on South African problems and the security of Allied Secret Service operations in occupied Europe were written in 1943. After the report on the German Secret Service, 1942 had been compiled Mr. Curry suggested that arrangements should be made to bring together all the officers who were doing research work and to collate the results. It was intended to include not only those in the various parts of the Security Service such as B.1.A., B.1.B., B.1.C. and B.1.D., but also some in Section V, G.C. & C.S. and R.I.S. In consequence of the difficult relations with Section V which existed at that time this proposal was dropped after discussion with Colonel Vivian.

In 1943 the Director General lent Mr. Curry to S.I.S. to form Section IX on the condition that he continued the work of compilation in "Research". In the meanwhile Mr. Aikin-Sneath had temporarily joined "Research" and produced his report on the Enemy Alien Population in the United Kingdom (vide Bibliography No. 24).

Agents and the Press Section. (MS and MS/PS). It has always been the practice for a certain number of agents to be controlled by the officers of sections in B Branch or, later, B Division, but from the time when he joined the Security Service in 1931 and onwards Mr. Maxwell Knight specialised in the recruitment and direction of agents employed to penetrate the Communist Party of Great Britain and other Communist organisations in this country. From 1934, when B Branch became specifically responsible for investigating Fascist movements, the M Section (as this organisation is now called) was engaged in penetrating the British Union of Fascists and other Fascist bodies on similar lines. Early in 1938 the M Section was also entrusted with the employment of penetrative agents to obtain information about pro-German societies and groups in this country which had come under the influence of German propaganda and Nazi ideology. At the same time an attempt was made to employ M agents to obtain information about the sources of German intelligence which appeared to be associated with the organisations affiliated to the Auslands Organisation of the NSDAP established on British territory. All these desirable developments were seriously handicapped by lack of adequate finance. Until the late summer of 1939 the M Section consisted of one officer and one secretary and it employed fourteen agents, although six is regarded as the maximum number of agents to which an officer can give sufficient attention to produce good results. Shortly before the outbreak of war two further officers, one of whom had no experience, joined the section. Even after the outbreak of war Mr., now Major, Maxwell Knight was unable to obtain all the funds he thought necessary to enable him to cover the whole field allotted to him. In addition to penetrating the political organisations and movements mentioned above, he was expected to be in a position to provide agents to get into contact with individuals or groups of individuals suspected of being engaged in espionage.

In 1940 when B Branch, to which he then belonged, was overwhelmed with routine enquiries, Major Maxwell Knight improvised a body of five officers, one of whom was a woman officer, with experience in private life which made them suitable for dealing with some of the various interviews which arose out of these enquiries. They were frequently employed in connection with delicate cases in preference to reference to the Police. The experiment proved a success and the number of officers employed on this work was increased, but as the Security Service gradually settled down and obtained an ascendancy over the mass of work with which it had had to deal, they were gradually released after playing a valuable part in filling a gap in a difficult period.

At the time of the re-organisation in 1941 the M Section was left in B Division, but seventy-five per cent of its agents were engaged in the work assigned to the newly formed F Division. The main development of B Division, virtually restricted as it now was to dealing with the Abwehr and its agents, was on lines which generally speaking diverged from those on which the 'M' type of agent could be employed. The separation of the M Section from B Division therefore followed - not illogically - in 1942.

Major Maxwell Knight, who has special qualifications and aptitudes and has devoted great care and attention to this very exacting branch of the work - the running of agents - has set down his views on the methods which should be adopted in the M Section (vide the sectional report S.F.50-24-44(8A)). They embody the results of long experience and are based on a number of successes in a highly specialised field. They therefore deserve study by other officers who may be concerned in this type of work. He stresses the importance of co-operation with the Police and of a full understanding of the differences of outlook between the Police and an intelligence department, as well as a comprehension of each other's difficulties.

Among the very large number of cases which have been dealt with in MS it may be mentioned that information was supplied which was directly responsible for the detention of forty-three individuals under Regulation 18B. Of these thirty were members of the B.U.F. and thirteen were cases of aliens suspected of activities prejudicial to the war effort. In addition information produced by MS was almost solely responsible for the discovery of the activities of Anna Wolkoff and Tyler Kent, Molly Hiscox and Norah Briscoe, Mrs. Sybil Nicholson, Mrs. Irma Stapledon and Rogeiro Menezes.

All these cases, except that of Mrs. Nicholson, ended in conviction and in all of them the Law Officers of the Crown commented favourably on the agents concerned - not only on their work as agents but on the manner in which they gave their evidence in Court. An account of the Anna Wolkoff and Tyler Kent case will be found in the sectional report. It is one of the most important on account of the nature of the information obtained by Tyler Kent from the American Embassy. This information was, in the main, not concerned with the domestic affairs of the United States, but could be of the greatest value to the enemy and cause incalculable harm to the Allies. Captain Ramsay and his Right Club, William Joyce and the Secretary of the Belgian Embassy were all, more or less incidentally, involved. Anna Wolkoff and Tyler Kent were sentenced to seven and ten years penal servitude respectively.

Major Maxwell Knight has emphasised the importance of long-term planning in dealing with the Soviet Intelligence Service which is remarkable for its thoroughness, patience and its own long-term work; and offers more serious problems than those with which the Germans have confronted us. This is a point of first-class importance for the future, with special reference to the conditions of counter espionage work in peace-time.

The sectional report contains two especially instructive accounts: the case of Percy Glading and that of Werner Osterwald, a pre-war German agent. The former has been mentioned in Chapter III above; the latter is a useful model to illustrate how results can be achieved by co-operation between a head office section directing the use of shadowers and other routine methods and the M Section employing an agent to make contact with a suspect.

In 1940 Mr. John Maude suggested to the Deputy Director of B Division that arrangements might be made for the systematic introduction of agents as domestic servants. The question was examined and it was found that this could most usefully be done in the case of foreign embassies and legations in London. After careful preliminary work a section for dealing with the subject was started in April 1941 under Mrs. Gladstone and Mr. Dickson, of whom the former had, in the meanwhile, examined the possibilities of working though [...]. By July 1941 the section was in effective working order. It was developed with great skill and ingenuity and proved to be a valuable weapon in the hands of the Security Service for the purpose of obtaining information in a variety of ways for counter espionage work. The section worked in very closely with the B.1.G. and B.1.B. sections at Head Office dealing with the [...] Embassy and [...] Embassies and Legations with a view to countering the work of the German Secret Service.

An important principle followed by the section was to avoid suborning or seducing old employees. In preference to doing so they arranged that trained domestic servants of good character who had been recruited by us as agents should obtain employment in places of especial interest to us. These agents were not merely used to overhear conversations or to obtain the contents of diplomatic wastepaper baskets. They assisted in obtaining, or in putting other agents into a position which enabled us to obtain, documents and keys to ciphers.

Details regarding the South American Embassies and Legations covered by this section have been given in Chapter V, Part 1 (iv), (B.1.G.).

The representatives of other neutral countries also received close attention. Some of the [...] cases brought out the fact that our agents worked for patriotic rather than mercenary motives and were willing to live under very unpleasant conditions - even in a filthy [...] kitchen - in order to achieve the results desired of them.

At one time the war situation provided reasons for making it desirable to obtain access to the [...] diplomatic cipher. The elaborate arrangements by which this operation was successfully carried out are described in the sectional report. They involved the identification of the cipher clerk through a domestic servant, arrangements to induce him to strike up a casual acquaintanceship in a cafe and the long-drawn out cultivation of this acquaintanceship in order to exploit his indulgence in the pastime of swimming which gave opportunities for the employment of a highly technical process of duplicating the keys. As a result of a series of intricate and ingenious arrangements, the Security Service was placed in the position of having access to the cipher whenever it might be considered desirable to do so as a matter of policy.

It is a tribute to the reputation of this section that it received more demands from other sections for arrangements to place agents than it was able to meet in spite of every effort, within reason, to expand its capacity.

The sectional report is of great interest, if only because it shows how a clear idea in planning and thoroughness in execution were combined with creative imagination, humour, irony and restraint to produce an unusual and very important piece of work.

The Press Section under Captain Tangye was responsible for the distribution of Press cuttings and, as a corollary, for obtaining information from and about journalists and about their sources of information on matters which appeared in the Press when they had a bearing on the work of sections of the Security Service. The work consisted of obtaining certain types of intelligence and did not usually fall within a strict definition of counter espionage or security. Some of the reports were furnished to the Cabinet Offices to whom they were of interest from a political point of view - for instance, when they supplied information about criticism of Government measures which was being voiced without being published. In that sense they were not far removed from security in war-time in the widest sense of the term. The position was a delicate and difficult one and could only be maintained as a wartime measure.

Another aspect of security relations with the Press was dealt with by Mr. S. Sheppard who was also Personal Assistant to the Deputy Director General. He was responsible for liaison with the Press Censorship through the Military Advisers to Censorship for the purpose of preventing the publication of anything which the Security Service considered undesirable. Press censorship was voluntary and neither the Security Service nor the Censorship had the power to stop the publication of anything; but they could recommend against publication and the Military Advisers were ready to accept our recommendations provided they were based on good security grounds and to ask the censors to advise the Press accordingly. These arrangements worked well in practice. Subjects dealt with included espionage cases, prosecutions under the Defence Regulations or the Official Secrets Act, internment cases, escapes and escape routes from enemy-occupied territory and rumours. Special precautions had to be taken to prevent the appearance of anything but the authorised facts about the arrival, arrest and trial of enemy agents.

Room 055, War Office. First under Major Lennox and later under Mr. Orr, Room 055 served as a liaison section between parts of the Security Service and the War Office in certain respects. It was also used as a convenient point for contact with the public where individuals wrote to the authorities about subjects coming within the sphere of the Security Service, or for other interviews with members of the public, if and when appropriate, by officers of the Security Service who were thus able to act under cover of the War Office.

Overseas Control. The term 'Overseas Control' which had come into use in September 1941 refers to control over administrative arrangements in London for the staff abroad, i.e. the Defence Security Officers in the Colonies. It does not imply any executive control over intelligence work done in colonial territories by the local authorities. The section is also responsible for liaison with the Dominions Security and Police Services.

At the outbreak of war in September 1939 the permanent establishment of the Security Service overseas consisted of six officers located at Gibraltar, Malta, Cairo, Aden, Singapore and Hong Kong. Each officer was provided with a small staff of military personnel loaned from the local Military Command and had built up in the years prior to the war considerable records concerning local personalities and organisations of security interest. Reports on these subjects and on the general state of internal security were forwarded to the Security Service in London, where they were distributed according to their content to the appropriate sections. In addition to this permanent overseas staff a system had been established whereby security information was exchanged between the Security Service and established honorary correspondents in the Dominions and Colonies, and it was customary for the Colonial Secretary or the Chief of Police to act in this capacity. From the administrative angle, however, the direction required and given from London entailed little work and required the part-time services of only one officer, who was also engaged in the administration of the Security Service staff in general.

For the first ten months of hostilities security measures in the Colonial Empire remained on a peace-time basis; and, although Colonial Governments were able to provide themselves with legislative powers under the Colonial Emergency Defence Regulations, generally equivalent to those obtaining in the United Kingdom, it was noticed that administrations were loath to recommend the taking of active preventive measures to secure their territories from enemy activities.

Following upon the success of enemy operations in Europe and the establishment of enemy submarine bases on the Atlantic seaboard, the likelihood of an intensification of the campaign against Allied shipping and the possibility of enemy agents being landed on Empire territory became matters of considerable concern to the Dominions and Colonies. It was therefore decided, after an approach by the Colonial Office, to increase the direct overseas representation of the Security Service. An immediate result was the appointment of a Defence Security Officer for East Africa in June 1941, and this step was followed by a steady increase in personnel so employed until the end of August 1945, when the totalnumber of Security Service officers stationed overseas was twenty-seven, together with twenty-one secretaries despatched from London.

This increase in establishment led to both a considerable increase in the volume of administrative work handled by London and also in the number of enquiries of a general nature from overseas which could not be appropriately passed to London sections for action. At the time of the re-organisation in the summer of 1941 the section in the administrative branch of the Security Service under the Director A Division was given a charter by the Director General which read as follows:-

> "In view of the increasing importance of security work in the Dominions and Colonies it is more than ever necessary that this work should be efficiently co-ordinated. For the guidance of officers, the following is a general summary of the responsibilities and functions of the Overseas Section of A Division:-
>
> (a) To be responsible for the general administration of Defence Security Officers (i.e. for those paid by the Security Service) in the Colonies - changes in personnel, finance, office details, etc.
>
> (b) To be the normal channel for liaison on general matters with Security Service links overseas (Dominions and Colonies); but not on investigations (which are conducted from beginning to end by the appropriate section of the Security Service).
>
> (c) To publish a periodical "Overseas Security Bulletin" giving D.S.O.s and links, S.C.O.s in the United Kingdom (through D.4) and I(B) officers serving overseas news of such events in the United Kingdom - legislation, action against subversive bodies or individuals and the like - as have a strictly security aspect and may therefore be taken as likely to "inform" Overseas officers. These Bulletins to include contributions from the D.S.O.s themselves or from Security Service links, as received from time to time, and to collate pertinent reports derived from Overseas Intelligence Centres.
>
> (d) To be the channel for liaison on <u>Dominion and Colonial security matters</u> with the Dominions and Colonial Offices, but not so as to affect any existing liaison between the Director "B" and those departments.
>
> (e) To represent the <u>Security Service</u> at relevant conferences with other departments, accompanied by, or representing the views of, those specialists

within the Office whose work may be concerned with, or affected by, the terms of reference of such conferences.

(f) To be up-to-date as to the state of Field Security Sections in the Colonies in liaison with M.I.11.

(g) To "see", but not to take action on, correspondence with Dominions and Colonies on security matters, to be subsequently dealt with by the appropriate section, with a view to keeping a finger on the "pulse" of security work overseas.

(h) To keep the Empire security machinery under review and, in frequent consultation with B Branch, to submit recommendations to the Director General on Security Service requirements based on reports received from all sources, and to keep Director "C" and "D" informed in the same way that Director "C" and "D" submits military security requirements to the War Office and keeps A.5 informed.

(i) To pass at once to Director "C" and "D" any reports on intelligence of military interest received by the Security Service from Defence Security Officers overseas.

(j) To maintain the closest touch with D Division on all matters pertaining to the development of security enterprises outside the United Kingdom, whether they are taking place in a theatre of operations or not."

In April 1943, in consequence of the development of overseas work and the increasing number of policy questions requiring his decision, the Director General attached Overseas Control to his personal staff.

The staff of the section in 1939 was one officer on part-time duties and the final strength was three officers and two Grade 1 assistants with a proportionate increase in secretarial staff.

Prior to the war a routine liaison was in operation between the administrative and investigation branches of the Security Service and the Colonial Office. With the development of the Security Service in the Empire and the consequent increase in the number of reports received both on the operation of security control and on political and general matters it was obvious that the contacts hitherto established should become appreciably closer.

Such matters as the coincidence of cables sent by the Colonial Office to the Governors and by the Security Service to their representatives, finance and selection of staff all had to be jointly considered and it was found possible as a result to produce joint statements on security matters at inter-departmental meetings which thus carried greater weight and achieved more satisfactory results.

Naturally with the close day-to-day contact established by Overseas Control with the Defence Department of the Colonial Office a stage was reached when it was found possible, without any jeopardising of the security of information, to exchange our views and material of mutual interest and thereby for the Security Service to have considerable forewarning of the likely official views of the Colonial Office on impending points of concern to ourselves and other departments with which the Security Service had joint interests. It cannot be too strongly stressed that this liaison was one of the most valuable means by which we were able to ensure the acceptance, even if not always in full measure, of the considerable number of policy recommendations made to the Colonial Office throughout the war period.

Following upon the withdrawal of the Defence Security Officer, Jamaica and a concurrent vacancy in the Defence Department of the Colonial Office with which the Security Service conducted its liaison, the Colonial Office asked us to assist them in filling their vacant appointment, and in view of his qualifications our former representative was selected. It is also interesting to note that following the resignation of this officer we were again approached with a view to providing a security trained officer, preferably with experience as a Defence Security Officer; unfortunately no such officer was immediately available.

Following this close contact it was also learnt that the information supplied by the Defence Security Officer was in fact of considerable value to the departments of the Colonial Office concerned with the individual territory and that an increase in the flow would be welcome since the Colonial Office did not feel that it would be a proper course for Governors, whose secretariat's security was not always of the highest order, to despatch reports on these matters to the Colonial Office. Consequently our representatives were invited to consult with their Governors as to the most suitable method of despatch to London of information of this nature and security cover was at the same time ensured in the Colonial Office.

The Colonial Office also, being impressed by the achievements and future possibilities of security and realising that the retention of Defence Security Officers on a war-time basis would not long be a practicable possibility, came to the conclusion that the early training of suitable candidates for post-war security work under the Colonial Commissioner of Police was advisable. Arrangements were therefore made by the Colonial Office with the Security Service, the Home Office Immigration Branch and the Metropolitan Police under which selected officers would be given a course of training in the United Kingdom to fit them for security work. On the return of these officers to their territories their functions on behalf of security would be generally guided by a Security Service Officer located at some geographically convenient point in the area, who would be in close touch with London on the development of technique and general matters of security interest. The first steps in this scheme have been taken with the training of a member of the Trinidad Police Force, and it is hoped that on the return of Colonial Administrations to their peace-time basis this scheme will become a permanent arrangement.

With the progress of the war and the despatch of Defence Security Officers successively to East Africa, West Africa, Bermuda, Trinidad, the Leeward and Windward Islands, Ceylon, Jamaica, British Guiana, Newfoundland, Bahamas, British Honduras, the Islands Area of East Africa and, on their re-occupation, Burma, Malaya and Hong Kong, the duties which fell upon their shoulders became both greater in general scope and more specialised on counter espionage and counter sabotage matters.

Towards the end of 1941 a number of reports received by the Security Service and other departments in London connected with the lack of security precautions in South Africa, taken in conjunction with the rising number of sinkings of merchant ships routed round the Cape, proved the need for special security arrangements and advice by a trained Security Officer. It was therefore agreed that an experienced Port Control Officer from the United Kingdom should visit the Union and advise the Union Departments on measures necessary to ensure the security of ports and harbours and to prevent the leakage of information. As a result of this officer's recommendations the Union Government requested the Director General to provide an officer who, while nominally on the staff of the British Military Mission, would be available to them to initiate a port control organisation and to advise them on matters of security intelligence in general.

The detailed record of relations with the different Dominions and Colonies will be found in the Sectional Report (vide S.F. 50-24-44(11)).

(v) The Director General's review of the war period.

From December 1943 Mr. Eden became personally responsible for the Security Service. This change was made as the result of a suggestion by Mr. Duff Cooper when he relinquished the appointment of Chairman of the Security Executive, to the effect that it should be attached to one of the great Departments of State and specifically to the Foreign Office. Accordingly, when it became clear that the Allied Expeditionary Forces had been landed in Normandy without the enemy obtaining intelligence of the exact nature of the strategically plan employed against him or of the timing of the operation, the Director General addressed a letter to Mr. Eden on the 26th June 1944 in which he reviewed the part played by the Security Service from the beginning of the war and of the part which it still aimed at contributing towards its completion.

At this early date Sir David Petrie was able to mention that there was good reason to believe that the deception carried out through the controlled double agents was having the effect of pinning down and keeping in situ German forces which would otherwise have been concentrated against the Normandy bridgehead. He added that the completeness of the German confidence in these agents had been recently shown by a strong recommendation for the reward of the Iron Cross to one of these men who was the third of those under our control to be so "honoured". In conclusion he made the following remarks:-

> "It is now considered by the Imperial General Staff that there is clear evidence to show that 'the timing of our attack on Normandy was a complete surprise to the enemy'. This has resulted from the combined

efforts of the various Services and Agencies which have been working hard and long on the security side of the operation. The role of the Security Service has been peculiarly important and peculiarly difficult. In the end security has meant the prevention of the enemy's getting advance information of our plans. His most likely means was his spy organisation and it has failed him. If it had not, it would have been on the Security Service that the chief responsibility would have rested. If their work had been bad, no amount of good work in other quarters would have compensated for it. It must be made clear, however, that the contribution they have made to Overlord security is not the result of a recent intensive effort. Rather it is the crown and reward of sleepless and unflagging vigilance during the whole long course of the war. It is now fully evident that for many months past these islands have been swept clean, and kept clean, of enemy agents. This has been an initial and incalculable advantage in the working of the whole of the security system devised to protect the security of Overlord.

In doing what they have done, the Security Service has done no more than its duty. It is only fair to them, however, to recognise that their job has been an exceptionally difficult and chancey one and that they have done it supremely well. It is very desirable that this should be remembered, since it is one of the discouragements inseparable from security work that the better it is done the less there is to show for it.

It is not too much to say that the contribution of the Service to the nation during the defensive stage of the war has been an asset of the highest value. The Service is not without its critics and detractors, though it is but rarely that any of them is other than ill-informed. It has special duties and functions which can be performed only by itself, or by some similarly constituted service, although in not a few outside quarters the idea is held that this is not so. Therefore whatever innovations may be thought of after the war, it should not be forgotten that the Service, throughout a long period of national emergency, has done the work for which it exists and has done it with complete success. It has been tried and not found wanting.

I trust that no part of my testimony in favour of the Security Service will be discounted as being that of the present Head of it and so of no unbiased witness. As a matter of fact my position is one of almost complete detachment. I had retired from Government service before I joined it and as a "dug-out" have no official future in the Service after the war has been won. In the course of re-organising it and directing it for three and a half strenuous years, I have perhaps said more hard things of the Service than almost anyone else. Before I disappear, therefore, I would like to place on record that the Security Service has deserved well of the Nation, which, as coming from one circumstanced as I am, may be accepted without the least suspicion of bias."

Events during the subsequent course of the war until VE Day on 8th May 1945 confirmed the validity of these general conclusions and showed that the Security Service could make further important contributions as has been described above in the sections dealing with B.1.A. and its double agents and with the War Room and its service to the G-2 CI Staff of SHAEF. The War Room linked the Security Service directly with the complementary organisation in the field which shared its responsibilities for combating the enemy Secret Services and their agents. The successes achieved by the Security Service before and after the Normandy landing were made possible by the denial of intelligence to the enemy and by the fact that he was unable to establish a single good agent in a position to give him the essential information which might have enabled his General Staff to retrieve errors imposed on them by their own and Hitler's confidence in the reports prepared under the instructions of the Allied Staffs and transmitted to them through B.1.A.

If these successes were in the main ensured by the interception of the enemy's communications (by R.S.S. and G.C. & C.S.) supported, interpreted and enlarged by information obtained by interrogation (at the ports, the L.R.C. and Camp 020) they were made doubly sure by the thorough and elaborate measures taken to cover every possible loophole through which the enemy might have infiltrated or otherwise have obtained vital intelligence; that is by the security measures taken over a long period both in the Security Service and by other authorities.

(vi) The lessons from the past.

It may be a trite saying that the successes and failures of the past should serve the purposes of instruction for the future, but they enforce the lesson that effective counter espionage is far less easy to achieve in time of peace; and they indicate that the Security Service faces, after the successes achieved against Germany, one of the most difficult periods in its history. The immediate future would seem to call for a compact organisation, based on a sound allocation of functions, with a clear conception of its objectives and the means of reaching them. Above all it must be able to turn to the appropriate authority for crucial decisions on policy and to present its case effectively in times of crisis.

If it is to avoid unnecessary friction and the consequent waste of time, energy and talent, it must be remoulded, as occasion demands, in accordance with the principles applicable to all creative work. It must obey the laws of the conservation of energy and abide by the cardinal principle of Occam's razor - entia non sunt multiplicanda praeter necessitatem - which governs all scientific investigation as well as the production of a work of art. It must employ to the best advantage its human material and put its square pegs in square holes. The principle of the allocation of functions must be applied both internally and externally. Internally there must be a proper balance and a full understanding between the parts responsible for investigation, prevention, deception and organisation. The same principles of balance and understanding hold good in respect of the relations between the executive in its dealings with foreign agents; research and analysis in the presentation, in the most suitable ad hoc form, of the records about those agents and the instruments of the foreign powers employing them; and the more mechanical structure of the Registry as a vehicle of intelligence. Externally the Security Service must find its proper place in the machinery of government under the Minister of Defence to enable it to play its part in an integral process in conformity with the requirements of this Age of Science.

It would not be appropriate to attempt a detailed plan for the future as an appendage to this record of the facts; but in order to explain the question of the practical application of the principles just mentioned more clearly it is desirable to describe in outline the general nature of the organisation which seems to be prescribed by the lessons of the past.

To enable the Director General to discharge his responsibilities with the greatest possible degree of efficiency the internal form and external relations of the organisation should be based on the principle of the "simplicity postulate". This suggests the following proposals:-

1) The whole of the machinery under the Director General charged with responsibility for counter espionage, i.e. for combating an enemy secret service, should consist of three Divisions, each under a Director, with responsibilities for -

    (a) maintaining the Security Service as an efficient instrument to enable it to perform its functions (A Division);

    (b) the investigation of cases against individual agents, for obtaining intelligence about the organisation behind them and for using all the products for the purposes of deception (B Division); and

    (c) prevention in the fullest sense of the term, including all the present functions of C and D Divisions and internment policy (but not the investigation of the cases of individual internees or candidates for internment in wartime - as this falls to B Division), i.e. prevention, including measures to restrict opportunities for espionage (and sabotage) by all feasible means (C and D Divisions).

2) The Director General should be directly responsible to the Permanent Secretary to the Cabinet and to the Assistant (Military) Secretary and Chief of Staff to the Minister of Defence and through them to the Prime Minister, with the recognised function of taking or recommending measures to ensure co-ordination, <u>within the sphere of his own responsibilities</u>, between the organisation under the Chiefs of Staff on the one hand and the Home Office, the Foreign Office and other interested Services and Departments on the other.

3) The functional relations between the Security Service and S.I.S. should be governed by the following principles:-

    (a) All counter espionage intelligence should be recorded, carded and indexed by one Registry under the control and direction of the Director of A Division of the Security Service.

(b) The function of Section V of S.I.S. should be to obtain from abroad all the intelligence required by the Security Service for counter espionage purposes by other than open means, including the penetration of organisations in foreign countries. (To assist in this Section V should access to all the intelligence at the disposal of the Security Service).

The Passport Control Officers abroad should cease to be employed for S.I.S. purposes. Their passport and visa work is an essential part of the defensive machinery of the Security Service and it places them in a good position to act in liaison between it and the Security Services of friendly governments to which they are accredited. Clandestine work by S.I.S. should be conducted through an entirely separate agency.†

(c) The Director General of the Security Service should have facilities for and control over all measures for developing the interception of enemy (or potential enemy) communications, including wireless; and the financial powers to develop the necessary resources in accordance with the requirements arising out of his responsibilities. Under present circumstances this could best be provided by his having a seat on the "Sigint" Board with an effective voice in the control of grants allocated for interception for counter espionage purposes.

(d) It should be the function of an officer (or officers) under the Director General to collate all 'straight' intelligence available in British territories as obtained by different sections, to co-ordinate measures for obtaining it, to communicate it to S.I.S. for collation, and to communicate it to the Foreign Office and other interested Services and Departments. (This should include intelligence such as that obtained by a Security Service agent inside the German or other Embassies in London and intelligence about the organisations and instruments of foreign powers on British soil such as the - extinct - Auslandsorganisation of the NSDAP or the British Communist Party as a section of the Comintern, or Mosley's B.U.F. as the subsidised agency of Mussolini).

4) The functional relations between the Security Service and the I(B) Staff in the field are governed by the fact that - while the detection of enemy agents in the zone of operations and in British territory are complementary parts of an integral process which must be based on the Security Service records and its trained

---

† The fact that some foreign security services will not exchange information as freely with S.I.S. as with the Security Service is a strong practical reason for the liaison being direct and not through S.I.S. in such cases.

staff - the staff in the field must be subordinated to the Commander in Chief of the operations.

Above all it should be laid down, if necessary with the authority of the Committee of Imperial Defence - who have not formally reviewed the position since 1908 - that the Security Service is not a secret political police, but it primarily an instrument for military purposes under the control of the Defence Minister and the Chiefs of Staff and subject to the direction, within their respective spheres, of the Secretaries of State for Home and Foreign Affairs and other members of the Cabinet. It is not, in this capacity, a purely advisory body, but has executive functions and responsibilities not covered by any other part of the executive machinery. It is not concerned with British political parties or "subversive movements" as such, but it is concerned when they are the instruments of foreign powers or are financed or subsidised by, or use conspiratorial methods in collusion with, the agencies of such powers in action which may be directed in furtherance of their political or military aims. (As a corollary, it should not investigate other matters or movements, such as the Trotskyists, except with the express approval of the Minister of Defence and the Home Secretary).

These latter - enquiries about British political parties as instruments of foreign powers - are its secondary purposes. They are those of an intelligence organisation and generally speaking involve action of an advisory nature. They are matters of 'straight' intelligence as well as of measures for countering foreign secret service organisations.

Once the functions and responsibilities of the Security Service had been clearly defined and its place in the machinery of government had been recognised in a positive form on these lines, the maintenance and application of these principles would be the day-to-day work of the Directorate whose task would become simpler with each step taken to define and clarify its position.

THE END

APPENDICES

APPENDIX I
LIST OF DIVISIONAL AND SECTIONAL REPORTS

S.F.50-24-44
- (1) PA/DDG - Press Censorship.
- (2) Secretariat.
- (7) Operations Section.
- (8A) M.S. (Agents).
- (8B) M.S. Domestic Agency.
- (11) Overseas Control.
- (12) B Division Representative in Canada and U.S.A.
- (15) A.D.A. - Administrative Services.
- (16) Women's Establishment.
- (17) Regional Organisation.
- (18) Registry.
- (23) B.1.A. - Double Agents.
- (24A) B.1.B. - ISOS Material and Counter Espionage Methods in Gibraltar.
- (24B) B.1.B. - Mr. Hart's Reports.
- (26) B.1.B. - Diplomatic Section.
- (28) B.1.B. - Financial & Currency Enquiries.
- (30) B.1 Information.
- (31) B.1.C. - Counter Sabotage.
- (32) B.1.D. and B.1.D. - U.K. - L.R.C.
- (34) B.1.E. - Camp 020.
- (35) B.1.G. - Spain, Portugal & S. America.
- (36) B.1.H. - Ireland.
- (37) B.1.L. - Counter Espionage among Seamen and the Personnel of Air Lines.
- (40) B.3.C. - Suspected Communication with the Enemy.
- (41) B.3.A. and B.3.D. - Censorship.
- (42) B.3.E. - Signals Security.
- (43) B.4.B. - Enemy Espionage in Industry & Commerce.
- (45) B.6. - Shadowing Staff.
- (47) B.10. - Preliminary Investigation of Cases of German Espionage in the U.K.
- (50) C Division - Vetting.
- (53) D.1.- Security Measures.
- (54) D.2. - Liaison with the Admiralty.
- (55) D.3. - Liaison with the Air Ministry & M.A.P.
- (56) D.4. - Port and Travel Control.
- (57) D.5. - Liaison with the War Office.
- (58) D.6. - Protected Places and Areas.
- (59) Arrangements for compiling the History of D.1., D.2., D.3., and D.6.

- (60) E Division - Alien Control.
- (61) E.1.A.-F. - French Nationals.
- (62) E.1.A.-B. - Belgians.
- (63) E.1.A.-S. - Norwegians, Danes & Dutch.
- (64) E.1.A.-U.S.A. - Americans.
- (65) E.1.B. - Alien Seamen.
- (66) E.2.A. - Finns, Poles & Baltic states Nationals.
- (67) E.2.B. - Hungarian & Balkan Nationals.
- (68) E.3. - Swiss and Swedes.
- (69) E.4. - A.W.S. Department.
- (70) E.5. - Germans, Austrians and Czechs.
- (71) E.6. - Italians.
- (74) F Division - Subversive Activities.
- (75) F.-M.A. - Internal Security in H.M. Forces.
- (76) F.2.A. - Communism, Trotskyism and other British Left Wing Subversive Activities.
- (77) F.2.B. - Comintern Activities & Communist Refugees.
- (78) F.2.C. - Russian Intelligence.
- (79) F.3. - Fascist, Pacifist & Nationalist Movements.
- (81) The C.I. War Room.

APPENDIX II
ORGANISATIONAL CHARTS
JULY 1941

DIVISIONAL ORGANISATION

Director General's Staff

Legal Advisers (S.L.)
Mr. Pilcher (S.L.A.)
Mr. Hale
Lt.-Col. Hinchley-Cooke (S.L.B.)

Operations (O.P.)
Maj. Lennox
Room 055 W.O.
Mr. Orr

Director General (D.G.)
Brig. Sir David PETRIE.

Deputy Director General (D.D.G.)
Brig. O. A. HARKER.

Secretariat (SEC.)
Mr. Abbot

A. Division — ADMINISTRATION AND REGISTRY
Director (D.A.) Lt.-Col. Butler
Dep.Dir. Organisation (D.D.O.) Mr. R. Horrocks
Asst.Dir. (A.D.A.) Maj. Cumming

B. Division — ESPIONAGE
Director (D.B.) Capt. G. Liddell
Asst.Dir. (A.D.B.1.) Mr. D.G. White
Asst.Dir. (A.D.B.3.) Major Frost

C. Division — EXAMINATION OF CREDENTIALS
Director (D.C.) Brig. Allen
Deputy C (Dy.C.) Major Bacon

D. Division — SECURITY AND TRAVEL CONTROL
Director (D.G. & D.)
Deputy (Dy.D.) Lt.-Col. Norman

E. Division — ALIEN CONTROL
Dep.Dir. (D.D.E.) Mr. T. Turner
Asst.Dir. (A.D.E.1.) Maj. Younger

F. Division — SUBVERSIVE ACTIVITIES
Dep.Dir. (D.D.F.) Mr. J.H. Curry
Asst.Dir. (A.D.F.) Mr. R.H. Hollis
Asst.Dir. (A.D.F.3.) Mr. Aikin Sneath

A. DIVISION
ADMINISTRATION AND REGISTRY

Director: Lt.-Col. Butler

ADMINISTRATIVE SERVICES AND MALE ESTABLISHMENTS	ACCOUNTS AND FINANCE	WOMEN'S ESTABLISHMENT	REGIONAL CONTROL	REGISTRY AND ORGANISATION
Asst.Dir: Maj.Cumming	Miss	Lady Superintendent Miss Dicker	Mr. MacIver	Dept.Dir.: Mr.Horrocks Registry: Mr.

A.1. Camp Commandant, Security and Defence. Maj.Marshall

A.2. Billets, Catering, Home Guard, Male Applicants. Capt. Heywood

A.3. Transport Lt.-Col.Baxter

A.4. Supplies, maintenance, Secret Documents, Printing. Lt.Dawson-Cusack

A.5. Overseas Services, Organisation and Administration. Sir A. Jelf

A.6. Scientific Section and G.S.C. Photographic Section Mr.Smith

A.7. Miscellaneous Services Mr.Stewart
 {A.7.A. Cipher and Passes
 {A.7.B. Photostat (Country)
 {A.7.C. Teleprinters

R.1. Receipt and Despatch
R.2. Indexes
R.3. File Connecting
R.4. Filemaking and Extracting
R.5. Carding
R.6. Vacant
R.7. Policy Index and Registration
R.8. Communist Recording

Transit

B. DIVISION

ESPIONAGE

Director: Captain G.M.Liddell

B.1	B.2	B.3	B.4

B.1 ESPIONAGE
Asst.Dir.: Mr.D.G.White

- B.1.A. Special Agents — Maj.Robertson
- B.1.B. Espionage Special Sources — Mr.Hart
- B.1.C. Sabotage and Espionage Inventions and Technical — Lord Rothschild
- B.1.D. Special Examiners — Mr.Bingham
- B.1.E. Latchmere House — Lt.-Col.Stephens
- B.1.F. Japanese Espionage — Mr.
- B.1.G. Spanish, Portuguese and S.American Espionage — Mr.Brooman White
- B.1.H. Ireland — Mr.C.Liddell

B.2 AGENTS
Maj.Maxwell Knight

B.3 COMMUNICATIONS
Asst.Dir.: Maj.Frost

- B.3.A. Censorship Reception Analysis Distribution of material Preliminary Investigation
- B.3.B. Illicit Wireless Investigations. R.S.S. Liaison.
- B.3.C. Lights and Pigeons — Flt.-Lt.Walker

B.4

(Under control of Dir.B.
B.5. Investigation Staff — Supt.Burt
B.6. Watchers — Mr.
P.S. Press Section — Capt.Tangye)

B.4 ESPIONAGE
(Country Section)
Major White
(Officer-in-Charge)

- B.4.A. Suspected cases of Espionage by Individuals domiciled in United Kingdom. Review of Espionage cases. Espionage in British possessions abroad. — Maj.Whyte
- B.4.B. Espionage Industry and Commerce. — Mr.Crauford
- B.4.C. Leakage of Information.

C. DIVISION

EXAMINATION OF CREDENTIALS

Director: Brig. Allen
Deputy C.: Major Bacon

C.1 CO-ORDINATION OF CREDENTIAL EXAMINATION

Capt. Strong

C.2 EXAMINATION OF CREDENTIALS OF MILITARY PERSONNEL EMPLOYED IN MILITARY ESTABLISHMENTS

Capt. Stone (London)
Capt. Johnston (Country)

C.3 EXAMINATION OF CREDENTIALS FOR CIVIL DEPARTMENTS

Mr. Sams

D DIVISION

SECURITY AND TRAVEL CONTROL

Director: Brig. Allen
Deputy Dir.: Lt.-Col. Norman

Deals also with:
- Policy on Military Security
- Control of Photography
- Protected Areas and Places
- Advice on Passes, Permits
- Special Enquiries re Individuals

D.1
SECURITY AND DEFENCE IN FACTORIES, FIRMS AND ESTABLISHMENTS. LIAISON WITH MINISTRY OF SUPPLY

Major Brock

D.2
NAVAL AND SHIPPING SECURITY AND ADMIRALTY LIAISON

Captain Bennett, R.N.

D.3
AIR MINISTRY AND MINISTRY OF AIRCRAFT PRODUCTION LIAISON AND SECURITY

Group Capt. Archer

- D.3.A. Credentials. Travel.
  - Sq.-Ldr. Pettit
- D.3.B. Security of RAF civil controlled oil and petrol stocks
  - Mr. Mackay
- D.3.C. Liaison with Ministry of Aircraft Production Security in Factories Sabotage.
  - Sq.Ld. Bathurst.

D.4
SECURITY CONTROL AT SEA AND AIR PORTS TRAVEL CONTROL

Lt.-Col. J.H. Adam

- D.4.A. Exit Permits
  - Maj. Mays
- D.4.B. Traffic Control and Security at Ports
  - Maj. Burne
- D.4.C. Vacant
- D.4.D. Visas. Control of entry into U.K.
  - Lt.-Cdr. Cazalet R.N.,

Military Travel Permit Office.
(Located elsewhere)
- Col. Steward.

D.5
COMMISSIONS FOR M.I.5. G.S. BRANCH OF SECURITY SERVICE. INSPECTION AND ADMINISTRATION OF PORT SECURITY SECTIONS

Lt.-Col. Pearson

B DIVISION
ALIEN CONTROL

Dept. Director: Mr. Turner
Asst. Director: Major Younger

{ Lindley Committee
Aliens on Suspect Lists.
— Mr. Harvey.

Mr. Mitchell Officer in Charge

Asst. Dir.: Maj. Younger

E.1

- **E.1.A.** Nationals of Western Europe
  - French
  - Belgians
  - Czechs
  - Dutch
  - Scandinavians
  - Danes
  - ....

- **E.1.B.** Seamen
  - ....

- **E.1.C.** Aliens, Special Enquiries, Registry, Accounts
  - ....

E.2

Maj. Alley
Mr. Caulfield

- **E.2.A.** Nationals of Baltic, Balkan and Central European countries
  - Finns
  - Baltic States
  - Hungarians
  - Rumanians
  - Bulgarians
  - Turks
  - Yugoslavs
  - Albanians
  - Armenians
  - Poles
  - Greeks

- **E.2.B.** U.S. citizens
  - ....

E.3
Camp Administration and Intelligence
— Mr. Renton

E.4
A.W.S. Permits
— Col. Ryder

E.5
German & Austrian Subjects
Mr. Denniston

E.6
Italians & Swiss+ Subjects
Miss Weeks

+ temporarily

F. DIVISION

SUBVERSIVE ACTIVITIES

Deputy Director: Mr. Curry

F.1
INTERNAL SECURITY IN H.M. FORCES AND GOVT. ESTABLISHMENTS BELONGING TO H.M. FORCES

Lt.-Col. Alexander

F.2
COMMUNISM AND LEFT WING MOVEMENTS

Asst. Dir: Mr. Hollis

- F.2.A Policy Activities of C.P.G.B. in U.K. — Mr. Clarke
- F.2.B Comintern Activities generally. Communist Refugees. ....
- F.2.C Russian Intelligence — Mr. Pilkington

F.3
RIGHT WING AND NATIONALIST MOVEMENTS — BRITISH UNION, SCOTS NATIONALISTS, GERMAN AND AUSTRIAN RIGHT ORGANISATIONS, etc. PRO-NAZI INDIVIDUALS

Asst. Dir.: Mr. Aikin Sneath

F.4
PACIFIST MOVEMENTS: PEACE PLEDGE UNION, PEACE AIMS GROUP, etc. NEW POLITICO-SOCIAL AND REVOLUTIONARY MOVEMENTS

Mr. Fulford

APPENDIX II
ORGANISATIONAL CHARTS
APRIL 1943

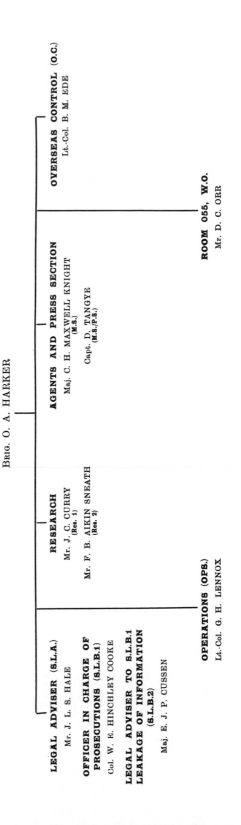

DIVISIONAL ORGANISATION

Director General (D.G.)
BRIG. SIR DAVID PETRIE

Deputy Director General (D.D.G.)
BRIG. O. A. HARKER

SECRETARIAT (SECTT.)
Mr. D. C. H. ABBOT

PRIVATE SECRETARY TO D.G. (PS/DG)
Mr. R. BUTLER

D.G. STAFF
See separate Chart

A. DIVISION
ADMINISTRATION AND REGISTRY

Director (D.A.)
Col. A. C. P. BUTLER

Dep. Dir. Organisation (D.D.O.)
Mr. R. HORROCKS

Asst. Director (A.D.A.)
Lt.-Col. M. E. D. CUMMING

REGIONAL CONTROL
Lt.-Col. A. S. MacIVER

REGISTRY
Mr.

LADY SUPT.
Miss M. I. DICKER

ACCOUNTS AND FINANCE
Miss

B. DIVISION
ESPIONAGE

Director (D.B.)
Capt. G. M. LIDDELL

Dep. Director (D.D.B.)
Mr. D. G. WHITE

Asst. Director (A.D.B.3)
Maj. M. A FROST

C. DIVISION
EXAMINATION OF CREDENTIALS

Asst. Director (A.D.C.)
Lt.-Col. H. H. BACON

D. DIVISION
SECURITY LIAISON WITH SERVICE DEPTS.; TRAVEL CONTROL

Director (D., C & D)
Brig. H. I. ALLEN

D.1 FACTORY SECURITY
Lt.-Col. R. G. G. BROCK

D.2 ADMIRALTY LIAISON AND SECURITY
Capt. A. C. M. BENNETT, R.N.

D.3 AIR MINISTRY AND M.A.P. SECURITY AND LIAISON
Grp.-Capt. J. O. ARCHER

D.4 TRAVEL AND PORT CONTROL
Asst. Director (A.D.D.4)
Col. J. H. ADAM

D.5 MILITARY PERSONNEL
....

D.6 PROTECTED PLACES, ETC.
Lt.-Col. H. A. WARING
Adviser
Lt.-Col. E. H. NORMAN

E. DIVISION
ALIEN CONTROL

Asst. Director (A.D.E.)
Capt. S. P. BROOKE BOOTH

F. DIVISION
SUBVERSIVE ACTIVITIES

Asst. Director (A.D.F.)
Mr. R. H. HOLLIS

A DIVISION

ADMINISTRATION AND REGISTRY

Director (D.A.)—Colonel A. C. P. BUTLER

ADMINISTRATION SERVICES AND MALE ESTABLISHMENTS

Asst. Dir.: Lt.-Col. M. E. D. CUMMING

- **A.1 External Services**
  Camp Commandant, Transport, Maintenance. Passes
  Maj. T. S. B. MARSHALL
- **A.4 Internal Services**
  Supplies, Printing, Gestetner, Teleprinter, Photography, Secret Documents, Library, Property Room
  Capt. A. C. DAWSON CUSACK
- **A.5 Special Section**
  Mrs.
- **A.6 Scientific and G.P.O. Photographic Section**
  Mr.
- **A.7 Cypher Section**
  Miss
- **A. Representative London**
  Mr. J. G. MOORE (A.Rep/L)

ACCOUNTS AND FINANCE (Acs.)

Miss

- **Acs. 1** Tax Assessor
  Military Accounts
  Mr.
- **Acs. 2** Billet & Transport Accounts
  Maj. C. P. SMITH

London Representative
Miss D. M. OWEN

WOMEN'S ESTABLISHMENT (W.E.)

Lady Superintendent: Miss M. I. DICKER
Asst. Lady Supt.: (London Office)
Mrs.

REGIONAL CONTROL (R.C.)

Lt.-Col. A. S. MacIVER

Enquiries re suspected espionage by persons domiciled in U.K.
Mr. J. E. BADELEY

REGISTRY AND ORGANISATION

Dep. Dir.: Mr. R. HORROCKS
Registry: Mr.

- **R.1** Receipt, ... Country
  Miss .... —London
  Mrs. J. M. RAE
- **R.2** Indexes
  Miss C. S. WELDSMITH
- **R.3** File Connecting
  Miss
- **R.3.Y** Special Files
  Miss
- **R.4** File Making, Extracting and Carding (B. and F. Divisions)
  Miss
- **R.5** File Making, Extracting and Carding (A., C., D., E. Divisions)
  Miss
- **R.7** Policy Index and Registration
  Miss J. MOTT
  Miss .... London
- **R.8** Communist Recording
  Miss
- **R.9** Destruction of Files
  Mrs

Registry Examiners
Mrs.

B. DIVISION

ESPIONAGE

Director: Capt. G. M. LIDDELL
Deputy Director: Mr. D. G. WHITE

Under control Dir., B.:
B.5 Investigation Staff Supt. L. BURT
B.6 Watchers Mr

B.1.A Special Agents
Lt.-Col. T. A. ROBERTSON

B.1.L Espionage through Merchant Shipping Crews & Personnel of Air Lines
Mr. J. R. STOPFORD

B.1.B Special Sources Case Officers
Mr. H. L. A. HART

B.1.C Sabotage and Espionage Inventions and Technical
Lord ROTHSCHILD

B.1.D London Reception Centre
Maj. H. J. BAXTER

B.1.E Camp 020 and 020R.*
Lt.-Col. R. W. G. STEPHENS

B.1.G Spanish, Portuguese and S. American Espionage
Mr. R. BROOMAN WHITE

B.4.B Espionage, Industry and Commerce
Mr. J. G. CRAUFURD

B.1.H Ireland
Mr. C. LIDDELL

B.3.A Censorship
Reception Analysis
Distribution of Material
Preliminary Investigations
Mr. R. E. BIRD

B.3.D Censorship Liaison
Mr. A. GROGAN

B.4.A Escaped Prisoners of War and Evaders Identification & Interrogation
Maj. J. R. WHYTE

Asst. Director:
Maj. M. A. FROST (A.D.B.3)

B.3.B Illicit Wireless Investigations
R.S.S. Liaison
Mr. R. L. HUGHES

B.3.C Lights and Pigeons
Flt.-Lt. R. M. WALKER

* For administrative matters the Officer in charge Camps 020 and 020R is responsible directly to D.A.

C. DIVISION

EXAMINATION OF CREDENTIALS

Director: Brig. H. I. ALLEN

Assistant Director: Lt.-Col. H. H. BACON

C.1
CO-ORDINATION OF CREDENTIAL EXAMINATION

Maj. S. C. STRONG

C.2
EXAMINATION OF MILITARY CREDENTIALS

Maj. H. C. M. STONE (London)

Capt. A. JOHNSTON (Country)

C.3
EXAMINATION OF CREDENTIALS FOR ADMIRALTY, AIR FORCE* AND CIVIL DEPARTMENTS

Mr. H. W. H. SAMS

* R.A.F. and M.A.P. cases are dealt with in conjunction with D.S.

D. DIVISION

SERVICES, FACTORY AND PORT SECURITY. TRAVEL CONTROL.

Director: Brig. H. I. ALLEN

D.1 — MILITARY
SECURITY MEASURES IN FACTORIES CONTRACTING FOR MINISTRIES OF SUPPLY, FOOD AND HEALTH. LIAISON WITH WAR OFFICE AND MINISTRY OF SUPPLY

Lt.-Col. R. G. G. BROCK

D.2 — NAVAL
SECURITY MEASURES IN FACTORIES AND SHIPYARDS ON ADMIRALTY CONTRACTS. LIAISON WITH ADMIRALTY

Capt. A. C. M. BENNETT, R.N.

D.3 — AIR
SECURITY MEASURES IN FACTORIES ON AIR MINISTRY AND M.A.P. CONTRACTS. LIAISON WITH AIR MINISTRY AND M.A.P. PETROL AND OIL SECURITY

Group-Capt. J. O. ARCHER

- **D.3.A.** Liaison with Air Ministry and M.A.P. Credentials
  Mr. C. H. SARGANT
- **D.3.B.** Petrol and Oil Security
  Mr. S. M. MACKAY
- **D.3.C.** Factory Security
  Country: Ft.-Lt. G. C. LAWS
  London: Sq.-Ldr. N. GATEY

D.4
SECURITY CONTROL AT SEA AND AIR PORTS AND OF SHIPPING. TRAVEL CONTROL

Asst. Dir.: (A.D.D.4.)
Col. J. H. ADAM

- **D.4.A.** Travel Control. Visas. Exit Permits. Military Permits
  Maj. W. S. MARS
- **D.4.B.** Distribution and Collation of Intelligence received at Ports. Exit and Entry of Seamen. Shipping Security. Travellers' Censorship
  Mr. B. H. SMITH
- **D.4.C.** Administration. C.S.W. Black Lists. Service Travel. Protected Places at Ports
  Maj. A. P. NOBLE
- **D.4.D.** Inspection
  Lt.-Col. C. C. CARTER
  Lt.-Col. J. G. E. ROBB

  Military Permit Office
  Col. G. R. V. STEWARD

D.5
MILITARY PERSONNEL ADMINISTRATIVE MATTERS. INSPECTION OF PORT F.S. SECTIONS

D.6
PROTECTED PLACES AND AREAS. CONTROL OF PHOTOGRAPHY. IDENTITY DOCUMENTS AND PERMITS. DISTRIBUTION OF SECURITY INTELLIGENCE TO MILITARY. MILITARY SECURITY CASES

Lt.-Col. H. A. WARING

Attached to D.6.
CONSULTANT AND ADVISER ON FACTORY AND MILITARY SECURITY. RESEARCH

Lt.-Col. E. H. NORMAN

E. DIVISION

ALIEN CONTROL

Assistant Director: Capt. S. P. BROOKE BOOTH

E.1.A.	E.1.B.	E.2	E.3	E.4	E.5	E.6
	SEAMEN		SWISS, SWEDES	A.W.S. PERMITS	GERMANS AND AUSTRIANS. CAMP ADMINISTRATION AND INTELLIGENCE	ITALIANS
FRENCH	Mr. C. R. CHENEY	Maj. S. ALLEY	Mr. K. F. A. JOHNSTON	Lt.-Col. C. F. RYDER	Mr. J. D. DENNISTON	Mr. A. W. ROSKILL
Capt. C. A. W. BEAUMONT		E.2.A FINNS, POLES, BALTIC STATES				
BELGIANS		Maj. S. ALLEY				
Miss D. HOARE-NAIRNE		E.2.B HUNGARY AND BALKAN STATES				
NORWEGIANS, DANES AND DUTCH		Mr. W. T. CAULFEILD				
Mr. E. J. R. CORIN						
U.S.A.						
Mr. P. E. RAMSBOTHAM						

F. DIVISION

SUBVERSIVE ACTIVITIES

Assistant Director: Mr. R. H. HOLLIS

F.1
INTERNAL SECURITY IN H.M. FORCES INCLUDING NAVAL AND MILITARY ESTABLISHMENTS AND CIVILIANS EMPLOYED UNDER R.A.F. OFFICERS

Lt.-Col. W. A. ALEXANDER

F.2
COMMUNISM AND LEFT WING MOVEMENTS

F.2A Policy and Activities of C.P.G.B.
Mr. D. K. CLARKE

F.2.B Comintern Activities generally Communist Refugees
Mr. H. SHILLITO

F.2.C Russian Intelligence
Mr. H. SHILLITO

F.3
FASCIST, RIGHT WING, PACIFIST AND NATIONALIST MOVEMENTS PRO-GERMANS AND DEFEATISTS

Mr. T. M. SHELFORD

BIBLIOGRAPHY

1. 'A' Branch Report (Held A.4)
2. Die Auslands Organisation der N.S.D.A.P. by Dr. Emil Ehrich (Filed in O.F.22-1, volume 42, 1808x).
3. Note on the Auslands Organisation of the National Sozialistische Deutsche Arbeiter Partei - 1935 by J.C. Curry (Held A.4)
4. Additional Note on the Auslands Organisation of the National Sozialistische Deutsche Arbeiter Partei - 1937 by J. C. Curry (Held A.4).
5. Amt Auslandsnachrichten und Abwehr by G.C. & C. S. (Filed in S.F.50-24-44 Supp. B).
6. The British Union of Fascists - July 1941 by F. B. Aikin-Sneath (Held A.4).
7. The Betrayal of the Left - An examination and refutation of Communist Policy from October 1939 to January 1941 with suggestions for an alternative and an epilogue on political morality (Copy in Library).
8. Committee of Imperial Defence - War Emergency Legislation Sub-Committee - Handbook and Index of the principal British legislation and special powers for war and civil emergency December 1931 (Held A.4).
9. Report and Proceedings of a Sub-Committee of the Committee of Imperial Defence appointed to consider the Question of Foreign Espionage in the United Kingdom 1909 (Filed in S.F.50-15-26).
10. Committee of Imperial Defence - Joint Intelligence Sub-Committee. Nazi and Fascist Party Organisations and Activities in British Territory (Filed in S.F.66-U.K.-63A).
11. Communism in Great Britain To-day - June 1932 (Held A.4).
12. Communism (General Aspects) - April 1934 (Held A.4).
13. Communism (Organisation & Working) - December 1934 (Held A.4).
14. The Communist Party - Its Aims & Organisation - April 1945 (Held A.4).
15. History of the Communist Party of the Soviet Union (Bolsheviks) (Copy in Library).
16. Communist Party of Great Britain - Paper prepared for the Home Secretary to submit to the Cabinet - 1943 (Filed in S.F.91-1-2 link).
17. Communist Party of Great Britain - Minutes of the Meetings of the Central Committee (Held A.D.F.)
18. Short Thesis of the Comintern (included in 17 above).
19. Note on Information received in connection with the Crisis of September 1938 (Filed in S.F.50-24-44 Supp. B).
20. 'D' Branch Report (Held A.4).
21. Distribution of Duties - I.P. Book No. 9 November 1918 (Held A.4).
22. Draft Defence Regulations 1939 Code A (Held A.4).
23. Draft Defence Regulations 1939 Code AB (Held A.4).
24. Enemy Alien Population in the U.K. by F.B. Aikin-Sneath (Held A.4).
25. Enemy Sabotage Equipment (Technical) 1942 by B.1.C. (Held A.4).
26. 'E' Branch Report (Held A.4).
27. War Office Branch Memorandum on Espionage in time of peace - 1909 (Filed in S.F.50-15-26).
28. 'F' Branch Report (Held A.4).
29. Game Book (Held A.4).

30. 'G' Branch Report (Held A.4).
31. Manual on the German Secret Services and British Counter-Measures - June 1944 by J. Gwyer (Held A.4).
32. Report on the German Secret Service or Abwehr up to March 1942 by J.C. Curry (Filed in S.F.52/4/4/10 link)
33. The German Secret Service - August 1942 by J.C. Curry (Held A.4).
34. Supplement to the Report on the German Secret Service issued in August 1942 by J.C. Curry (Held A.4).
35. The German Intelligence Service - April 1945 by the War Room (Filed in S.F.50-24-44 Supp. B).
36. The German Police System as applied to Military Security in War - Compiled by the General Staff, War Office 1921 (Held A.4).
37. Grundlagen Aufbau und Wirtschaftsordnung des National Sozialistischen Staates (Copy in Library).
38. Summary of Information relating to German Propaganda in the United Kingdom (Filed in S.F.55-Germany-3A).
39. The German Secret Service - December 1940 by D.G. White (Filed in S.F.50-24-44 Supp. B).
40. 'H' Branch Report (Held A.4).
41. The Home Office by Sir Edward Troup, K.C.B., K.C.V.O. (Copy in Library).
42. Lord Hankey's Report on the Security Service - May 1940 (Filed in S.F.50-24-9).
43. Historical Sketch of the Directorate of Military Intelligence during the Great War 1914-1918 (Filed in S.F.51-30-8).
44. Note on the Organisation and Activities of the Italian Fascist Party in the United Kingdom, the Dominions and Colonies - 1936 (Held A.4).
45. Additional Notes on the Organisation and Activities of the Italian Fascist Party in the United Kingdom, the Dominions and Colonies - 1937 (Held A.4).
46. The Italian Intelligence Service by Section V dated 15th July 1943 (Filed in S.F.50-24-44 Supp. B).
47. Lectures by Sir Vernon Kell (Held A.4).
48. History of the Post Office Investigation Branch up to the end of the War 1914-1918 (Filed in S.F.50-24-44 Supp. B).
49. Work of the Registry - I.P. Book 11 (Held A.4).
50. Chronological List of Staff taken to 31st December 1919 - I.P. Book No. 39 (Held A.4).
51. The Search for Evidence of Secret Graphic Communication - November 1943 by Professor H.V.A. Briscoe (Held A.4).
52. Memorandum on the Possibilities of Sabotage by the Organisations set up in British Countries by the Totalitarian Governments of Germany and Italy (Filed in S.F.66-U.K.-63A).
53. Soviet Communism by Sidney and Beatrice Webb (Copy in Library).
54. The Unofficial Shop Stewards Movement - November 1941 (Held A.4).
55. Die Wehrpolitische Revolution des National Sozialismus by Von Major Walter Jost (Filed in S.F.50-24-44 Supp. B).
56. War Office War Book - 1939 (Held D.D.G).
57. War Office Emergency Legislation Committee - First Interim Report (Held A.4).
58. Wireless, Notes on the Detection of Illicit (Filed in S.F.50-24-44(39)).

INDEX

Note: WWI = World War I; multiple forms of address (e.g. Brig./Col.) reflect the textual references and are given to clarify where references are all to the same person; variant spellings and MI5 division and section titles reflect the text and the complex changes in the organisation over time.

A (Alien War Service) Branch (WWI) 72, 76
A Division (Administration and Registry) 99, 142, 201, 202, 368–81
  Administrative Services and Male Establishments 368, 369–74
  Officers Establishment 373–4
  Regional Control 328–32
  Registry and Organisation 375–81
  Scientific Work (Secret Graphic Communications) 371–2
  Technical Equipment 370–1
  Women's Establishment 374–5
Abadan railway 244
Abbott, Mr 172, 203
Abwehr 9, 15–16, 45, 78, 79, 80, 81, 124, 125, 126, 158, 201, 233–45
  see also German espionage
Abwehrstelle see Abwehr
Abyssinian War 113, 138
Adam, Col. J.H. 150, 156, 205, 313, 321, 322
Aden 396
Admiralty 64, 65, 66, 67, 142, 317–19
AEG 264
AEU 96, 186
Afghans 384
Africa 231, 397, 400
  see also North Africa
African colonies 114, 212
Aiken-Sneath, Mr F.B. 164, 202, 303, 305, 350, 392
Air Force Act 390
Air Ministry 19, 72, 317–19, 363
air-raids 175–6, 228
aircraft industry 81, 127
Aircraft Workers' Movement 187
airline personnel agents (B1L) 262–3
Alba, Duke of 275
Alexander, Lt.-Col. 350
aliens see enemy aliens
Aliens Act 134
Aliens Order; Arrival from British or Foreign Territory Order 52, 219–20, 229
Aliens Order (1920) 52, 156, 157, 217, 227, 229
Aliens Restriction(s) Act/Order 71, 73
Aliens War Service (AWS) Department (E4) and A Branch (WWI) 72, 76, 202, 307, 315
Allen, B.W. 323
Allen, Brig./Col. H.I. 159, 176, 202, 313, 314, 318, 324–5, 327, 328
Allen, W.E.D. 109

Allied Control Commission 370
Allied Governments 55, 162, 202, 222
Allied Intelligence Services 55, 76–7, 222, 383–4
Allied Security Services 228, 304, 307
Allied Staffs 52
America
  German espionage in 17, 74–5, 126, 128, 135–6, 137, 237, 267, 267–70
  intelligence liaison with 54–5, 114–15, 135–8, 237, 304, 383–4
  see also OSS; War Room
  Japanese espionage in 140–1
  Nazis in 114, 136, 137
American Communist party 185, 358, 360, 361
American Embassy 21, 54, 166, 304, 383, 394
American Military Intelligence Service 137
American Naval Review 66
American Office of Naval Intelligence 137
American ships 216
Amery (traitor) 314, 390
Anarchists 6, 59, 101
Anderson, Sir John 26(n. 61), 101, 102, 280
Anglo-German organisations 46, 123–4
Anglo-Russian Trade Union Unity Committee 93
Ansabona telegrams 133
anti-Blumites 118
Anti-Comintern Agreement 123
Anti-Comintern Organisation 131
Arandora Star 165
Archer, Col. Liam 27(n. 74), 134–5, 175, 277, 278, 279, 280, 281, 283
Archer, Gp.-Capt./Wg.-Comdr. 142, 153, 267, 319–20
Archer, Mrs 161, 174, 190, 192
Arcos raid 94
Argentine 213
Arkossy, Francis 237–8
Armed Forces, subversion within 3, 5, 48, 53, 91, 92, 93, 94, 107, 191, 350, 351–3
Armstrong, George 386
Army Act 390
Army Council 73, 325
Arnheim, Hans 153, 266
Asia see Far East
Aubert (French spy) 126
Auslands Organisation, see Nazi Party
Auslands Pressestelle 131
Australia 114, 141, 165
Austria 119, 120, 132, 164

Austrian Communists 185
Auswartiges Amt 131
Auxiliary Military Pioneer Corps 185

B Branch (later Division) see B Division
B Division 13, 50, 55, 94, 99, 142, 151–6, 161–3, 169–74, 201, 202
   B1 Information Section 297–302
   B1 (later RB and WR-H) Registry 180, 224, 297, 298, 299, 333, 335, 337, 339, 380
   B1B 228–33
   B18 (later B1C) Sabotage Section 154–6, 204, 312, 233–45
   BR (RSLO) 174–5
   liaison with BBC (B3B) 292
   liaison with Censorship (B3A and B3D) 286–7
   liaison with RSS (B3B) 287–92
   Lights and Pigeons (B3C) 292–5
   neutral embassies 17, 19, 20, 259–61
   Research 297–302
   Security Sections 292–97
   Shadowing Staff 50, 99, 143, 302
   Signals Security (B3E) 295–7
   Special Cases (B1C) 267–70
Bacon, Lt.-Col./Maj./Capt. 142, 313
Bacteriological Warfare Committee 243
Bagot, Miss 351, 358
Bahamas 400
Balkans 95, 242
Bardwell, Lt./Capt. T. 320, 321
Barnes, Miss 389
Barton, B.K. 323
Basle 66
Baxter, Col. 225
BBC 292
Beaverbrook, Lord 166
Beech, Charles 96
Beech, Dick 96
Belgium 148, 158, 162, 178, 219, 231, 237, 304, 310, 394
Bene, Otto 111, 117
Bennett, Gill 5
Benois, Nadia 8
Berlin 5, 179
Bermuda 400
Betteshanger Colliery 365
Bevan, Col. 247, 253
Bird, Mr 259, 301
Birkett Committee (Home Office Advisory Committee) 151, 152, 160, 161, 166, 309–10
BJs ('Blue jackets') 24 (n. 16), 260
Blackett, Prof. 354
Blenheim Palace 174, 176
Bletchley Park 15, 16
Blomberg, Werner von 112
Blum, Mr R. 334
Blunt, Maj. Anthony 7, 20–1, 259
Board of Trade 265
Bode, Dr Otto Bernhard 152
Boer War 3, 63
Boettiger 133
Bohle, E.W. 113, 122, 123, 124

Bolshevism/Bolshevist see Communist ...
Borodin, Mikhail Markovich 93
Boyle, Air Cdre. 247, 382
Brandenburger units 148
Brandes, Willy 108
Brandy, Mrs 126
Brazil 74, 103, 104–5
Bridges Report 326, 327
Briscoe, Prof. H.V.A. 371, 372
Briscoe, Norah 393–4
British Army of Occupation in the Rhineland 81
British Communist Party see CPGB
British Expeditionary Force 74
British Fascist movements 112, 115–16, 129–33, 139, 142, 308–13
   see also British Union of Fascists
British Guiana 400
British Honduras 400
British National Party 311
British nationality 129, 130, 152
British Revolution 5, 59
British Union of Fascists (BUF) 107, 110, 147, 181, 228, 404
   fifth column threat 48, 80, 109, 146, 155, 156, 164, 167, 174, 176, 308–13
   finance 8, 46, 59, 115–16, 124
Brooke-Booth, Capt. 306
Brooman-White, Lt.-Col. 259, 275
Brose, Maj. 63
Browder, Earl 360
Brown, Sir Harold 267
Brussels 64, 65–6
Brutus (code name) 254, 255–6
Bryan, Col. 281
BUF see British Union of Fascists
Burgess, Guy 7, 13, 21
Burma 58, 384, 400
Burne, Lt.-Col. C.H. 321, 322
Burt, Ch. Insp. 245
Burt, Maj. 388
Burton, Cdr. 321
Butler, Col./Lt.-Col./Capt. 142, 202, 368, 375
Butler, Mr R. 203

C Branch (later Division) see C Division
C and D Divisions 201, 202, 313–28
C Division (Examination of Credentials) 142, 325–7
Cabinet 44
Cabinet Offices 327
Cadogan, Sir Alexander 121, 275–6
Cairncross, John 7, 21
Cairo 140, 244, 396
Calvo, Luis 275
Cambridge University 7, 21–2
Camp 020 51, 52, 77, 155, 159, 176–7, 180, 206, 210, 212, 213, 222, 228–33
Campbell, J.R. 183
Campbell, Mr 135
Canada 17, 108, 114, 165, 166, 383
Canaris, Adm. Wilhelm 9, 120, 135, 209
Caribbean 95, 286

INDEX 433

Caroe, Capt. 279
Carter, Capt. C.C. 323
Cato Street conspiracy 60
Cayzer, Maj. 273
Cazelet, Cdr. 322
Cecil, Robert 23
Censorship 53, 73, 124, 150, 286–7
Census of 1911 69
Central Counter Intelligence Bureau 333
Central Registry (Security Service) see Registry
Central Security War Black List 217
Ceylon 17, 54, 237, 400
Chamberlain, Neville 9, 121–2, 182
Chapman, Edward Arnold 231–2
Childs, Sir Wyndham 5
China 93, 103, 104, 105, 360
Churchill, Sir Winston 13, 68, 163, 349
CICI (Combined Intelligence Centre Iraq and Persia) 54, 271, 272, 273, 274
CID see Committee of Imperial Defence
Citrine, Sir Walter 186
civil security 6
Clarke, Mr 187, 188, 351
Clausewitz, Karl von 45
Clay, Miss 241–2, 312
Clayton, Capt./Mr F.C. 273, 323
Cockerill, Brig.-Gen. 70
codebreaking see GC & CS; ISOS; RSS; SIGINT
Cohen, Samuel 353, 359, 360
Cold War 21
Collins, Mr S.W. 371
Cologne 125
Colonial intelligence services see Director-General's Staff, Overseas Control
Colonies, liaison with 48, 49, 53, 54
Combined Defence Security Service 102
Combined Operations 391
Comintern (Third Communist International) 55–6, 59, 82, 90–2, 95–6, 101, 103, 104–7, 108, 182–4
  bureaus 5, 95, 103, 104
  dissolution 84, 356, 359–60
  wireless system, interception 5, 7, 85, 103, 105–7, 143, 358–61
  World Congresses 91, 106–7
Comintern-Red Army Mission in China 104
Comites Departementaux de Liberation 360
commercial and industrial intelligence (B4B/B15) 75, 81, 108, 155, 263–6
Committee of Imperial Defence (CID) 44, 49, 143
  Foreign Espionage Sub-Committee 65–7, 68
  Joint Intelligence Sub-Committee (JIC) 112, 113, 327–8
  War Emergency Legislation Sub-Committee 149, 156
Communist fifth column 46
Communist International
  Fourth 364–6
  Second or Socialist 87, 103
  Third see Comintern
Communist Party Armed Forces Organisation 191, 350, 351–3
Communist Party of Great Britain see CPGB
Communist schools in Russia (Lenin, Wilson) 85, 98, 104, 106, 191, 358, 359
Communist University for Workers of the East 104
Companies Department 265–6
Competent Military Authorities 73
Competent Naval Authorities 73
Concrete Pump Co Ltd 128, 151
Congress of Germans Abroad 129
Constant, Miss 368, 375
Constitutional Research Association 311
Cooper, Mr Duff 355, 400
Councils of Action 93, 96
Couper, Maj. J.R. 323
Cowgill, Lt.-Col. Felix 16, 23, 180, 207, 208, 209, 210, 212, 246, 301, 333–4, 367, 382
Cox, Idris 354
CPGB (Communist Party of Great Britain) 5, 7, 18–23, 84, 86, 91, 92–4, 101, 103, 104–7, 108, 182–4, 188–9, 191, 349–57, 358, 361–4, 392
  leakages of information to 19, 20, 353–7
CPSU(B) (Communist Party of the Soviet Union Bolsheviks) 86, 89
Craufurd, Mr 259, 265, 267
Crocker, Mr William 13, 14, 146, 169, 172
Crome (German journalist) 130
cryptography see GC & CS; ISOS; RSS; SIGINT
Cumming, Cdr. 67
Cumming, Lt.-Col. 368, 372
currency enquiries 261–2
Curry, John Court (Jack) 162, 172, 181, 202, 206, 267–8, 270, 312, 349–50
  and B18/B1C Section 154–6, 312
  and Official History 1–3
  and Research 203, 350, 392
  and Section IX 23, 358, 360, 392
Curzon, Lord 24(n.16), 93
Cussen, Lt.-Col. 385, 387, 388, 389, 390
Custodian of Enemy Property 266
Customs 44, 65, 66
Cyprus 59
Czechoslovakia 86, 119–20, 147, 148, 162, 228, 259, 384, 405

D Day Landings 18, 21, 205, 254–6, 332, 389, 400–1
D Division (Security and Travel Control) 50, 149, 150, 315–25
D (Imperial overseas) Branch (WWI) 50, 72, 76–7, 142, 153–4
Daily Herald 4, 93, 96–8
Daily Mail 65–6
Daily Worker 106, 184, 353
Dale, Walter 97
Dalmuir Ordnance Factory 365
Dame, Maj. 63
de Gaulle, Gen., Free French 162, 360
De Havilland 231
De Valera, Eamonn 134, 277, 278–9, 282, 284

Defeatists (F3/B7) 308–13
Defence (of the Realm) Regulations (DRR) 51–2, 70, 71, 72–4, 149, 157, 219–20, 229, 310, 390
Defence of the Realm Act 43, 72, 73
Defence Security Officers *see* DSO
Defence Security Service 99
Delimitation Agreement 138
democratic centralism 90
Denmark 74, 304, 310
Denmark (code for 'Japan') 140
Dent, Dr C.E. 371
Deutsche Bund (Canada and America) 114
Deutsche Uberseedienst 81, 263
Deuxieme Bureau 54, 245, 383
Devonshire House B1D/UK 225
Dicker, Miss 368
Dickson, Mr 277, 394
Dieppe Raid 353
Dimitrov/Demitrov, Georg/e 106, 107, 182, 359–60
diplomatic traffic and bags, interception of 20, 21, 56, 328
Director-General's review of the war period 400–2
Director-General's Staff 384–400
   Agents and Press Section (MS and MS/PS or M Section) 392–6
   central administrative machinery 385
   leakage of information section (SLB2) 386–9
   Operations Section/Room 171, 203, 388, 390–2
   Overseas Control 54, 271, 396–400
   Prosecutions (SLB1) 385–6
   Renegrades (SLB3) 226, 389–90
   Research 203, 392
   Room 055, War Office 203, 396
Directorate of Military Intelligence (DMI) 6–7, 70–2
Directorate of Military Operations (DMO) 44, 64, 69–72, 73
Directorate of Special Intelligence 70
DNB (German News Agency) 135
domestic servants as agents 20–1, 260, 325
Dominions, liaison with 48, 49, 53, 54
Dominions intelligence services *see* Director-General's Staff, Overseas Control
double (cross) agents (B1A) 3, 10, 15, 16, 17–18, 21–2, 52–3, 76, 127, 159, 161, 180, 206, 215, 240–1, 245–57, 303
Dream Plan 252
Drohl, Ernst Weber 278
Dronkers, Johannes Marinus 227, 386
Drueke, Karl Theo 386
DSO (Defence Security Officers) 54, 141, 273, 396–400
Dublin NSDAP 134, 135, 278
Dudkin, Mr 94
Dulanty, Mr 134
Duncombe, Mrs 126
Dundas, Ian Hope 116
Dunkirk 228

Dunlop Rubber Company 124
Dunn, Mr 136
Dutch East Indies 141
Dutt, R.P. 182–3
Dyer, W. 323

E (Control of ports and frontiers) Branch (WWI) 72, 77, 156
E Division (Aliens Control) 55, 201, 202, 303–8
East Africa 114, 231, 397, 400
Eckersley, Mrs 314
Economic Warfare, Ministry of (MEW) 53, 265, 269–70
Eden, Anthony 18, 400
Edenhofer (German journalist) 130
Edmonds, Maj. Harry 311
Edmonds, Colonel J.E. 63, 64, 65
Edward VIII, King, abdication of 9, 60, 117
Edwards, Capt O.B. 323
Egypt 138, 140, 211, 237, 244, 271, 396
Eildienst 268, 269
Eire 6, 101
   Germans in 134, 135, 151, 153, 175, 236, 238, 378
   security service liaison 54, 134–5, 175, 277–86
El Alamein 242
embassies *see* American; German; neutral; Portuguese; Soviet; Spanish
Emergency Powers (Defence) Bill 149
enemy aliens, registration and internment of 10, 46, 50, 66–7, 69, 70–1, 73–4, 149–50, 164–5, 184–5, 216, 303
Enemy Aliens Tribunals 161
Engineering and Allied Trades Shop Stewards National Council 184, 187
English National Association 311
English Steel Corporation 186
Ercoli *alias* Toglatti 106–7
espionage 42, 43
   see also German espionage; industrial and commercial espionage; Italian Espionage; Japanese Espionage; Soviet espionage
Evans, Major Morton 289, 291
Evening Standard 8–9
Ewer, William Norman 96–7
exit permits 10, 157, 160, 216

F Division (Subversive Activities) 201, 202, 308–13, 350–1, 393
F (Preventive) Branch (WW1) 49–50, 72, 73
Fairweather, J.C. 323
Falkland Islands 54
Far East 72, 77, 95, 104
Far Eastern Trading Co Ltd 108
Fasci all'Extero 112, 129, 138, 139–40
Fascism
   see also British Union of Fascists; Italian Fascism; Nazi Party
   anti-fascism 103, 106–7
   in Britain (F3/B7) 112, 115–16, 129–33, 139, 142, 308–13

INDEX 435

FBI (Federal Bureau of Investigation) 54–5, 136, 137–8, 141, 237, 268, 286, 383
Fifth Column 10–11, 45–6, 48, 59, 80, 115, 148, 155–6, 160, 167–8, 171, 174, 176, 305–6, 308–13
Filson, J.T.W. 323
finance and currency enquiries (B1B) 261–2
Findlay, Archibald Garrioch 116
Finland 86, 93
First World War 3, 11, 45, 47, 49, 51, 78
Fischer Williams (*later* Hart), Jenifer 20
Fisher, Sir Warren 101
Fleetwood-Hesketh, Lt.-Col. 256
Floyd, Capt. F.R. 323
Foreign Office 8, 19, 20, 44, 48, 53, 85, 130, 166, 189–90
Fortitude cover plan 27(n.82), 254, 255
Fourth International 364–6
France 10, 11, 45, 74, 75, 103, 148, 162, 219, 230, 237, 242, 304, 360
  German espionage in 126, 128
Franco-Prussian War 44, 63, 64, 65, 78
Franklyn, General 281
Frederick the Great 65
French Communist Party 182, 184
French Fascist Party 313
Friends of the Soviet Union 103
Frost, Maj./Mr 169, 171, 179, 202, 292, 295

G1 and G2/C&D 316–17
G2 (US Army Intelligence Branch) *see* War Room
G (Investigation) Branch (WWI) 50, 72, 74, 86
Gada 108
Gaertner, Margarete 81
Gallacher, Willie 183, 186, 191, 349
Garbo (double agent Juan Pujol Garcia) 17–18, 248, 252, 254, 255–6
GC & CS (Government Code and Cypher School) 4, 15, 16, 56, 57, 143, 178, 206–15
GCHQ (Government Communications Head-Quarters) 4
Gee, G.C. 323
German Admiralty 78, 125
German American Bund 114
German Chamber of Commerce 112, 127, 264
German Communist Party 184, 185
German Embassy 8, 81, 116, 117, 118, 119, 130
German espionage
  see also Abwehr; Camp 020; LRC; RSS; SCO
  1930s 124–8, 135–6, 137
  First World War 3, 4, 50, 63–4, 69–72, 74–6
  Franco-Prussian War 44, 63, 64, 65, 78, 96
  Second World War 9–10, 15–16, 17–18, 20, 21, 54, 148–9, 175, 176, 180, 201, 217–18, 237, 267–70
German Foreign Office (Aussenpolitisches Amt) 113, 131
German Intelligence (Nachrichten Bureau/Branch) 63, 64, 75, 78, 125
German journalists 81, 122, 130–1, 132

German nationality 111, 114, 129, 130, 152
German News Agency (DNB) 135
German Police System 78–80, 110, 113, 124–5
German Propaganda Ministry 8, 121, 122, 123–4, 131
German Secret Service *see* Abwehr; German espionage; RSHA
German Security Service *see* Sipo und SD; RSHA
German Social Democratic Party 79
German-Japanese treaty 132
Germany
  hegemony 45, 110, 111
  and Russia 147, 192
    war with 9, 107, 117, 184, 192, 199, 201, 349
  and Spain 117, 213, 217, 218, 230, 231, 236–7, 239, 240–1, 242, 243–4, 274–5
Gestapo 79, 110
Gibralter 212, 236, 238, 239, 240–1, 243, 244, 396
Gill, Maj. E.W.B 178, 179
Glading, Percy 7, 107–8, 189, 361–2, 394
Gladstone, Mrs 277, 394
Gleichschaltung 109, 130
Gneisenau battleship 280
Goebbels, Joseph 120, 121, 122, 123, 124
Goering, Hermann 81, 132
Goerschen, H.W.K.R. von 266
Goertz, Hermann 278, 279, 283
Gordon-Canning, Robert 116
Government Code and Cypher School *see* GC & CS
Government/War Office War Book 149, 156
GPO *see* Post Office
GPU (Soviet Secret Police) 98
Graaff, Johannes de 220, 227
Gray, Olga 7
Greece 139, 215, 237, 304, 354
Greek nationalists in Cyprus 59
Greek Seamen's Union (NEE) 185
Green, Oliver Charles 351, 362
Greene, Graham 27(n. 69)
Greenland 230
Griffith, Sir Francis 155
Grigg, Sir James 169
Grogan, Mr 259
GRU (Soviet military intelligence) 21
GUGB (Russian Security Service) 190
Gwyer, Maj. 259, 297, 299, 301

H (Secretariat, Administration and Records) Branch (WWI) 72, 77, 152
Haldane, Lord/Mr 65, 67, 68
Hale, Mr J.L.S. 306, 385
Halifax, Lord 121, 129, 133
Hall, Miss 297
Hamburg 125, 126, 131, 149, 206–7
Handley Page 314
Hankey, Lord 278
Hankey Report 12–13, 48–9, 149, 158–60
Hansen, George 98

Hardinge, Sir Charles 65
Hardt, Paul 108, 189, 190
Hardy, Mr 382
Harker, Brig. A.W.A. ('Jasper') 6, 13, 20, 99, 102, 142, 163, 169, 172, 192, 203
Harris, Tomas 17–18, 254, 255
Hart, Herbert 28(n. 90)
Hart, Jenifer (née Fischer Williams) 20, 28(n. 90)
Hart, Mr 301
Haston, Jock 365
'Haw-Haw, Lord' (William Joyce) 8, 109, 168, 292, 314, 390, 394
Haylor, Maj. 225, 272
Heinemann, Margot 354
Held, Stephen Carol 278, 279
Helmuth, Osmar 213
Henry, Sir Edward 65, 67
Hensky, Sir Maurice 101
Hernie (MV) 222
Heywood, Maj. M.B. 322
Higgins, Dr 372
Hill, Kurt Wheeler 135
Hill, Mr 259, 265, 268, 269, 270
Himmelmann, Herr 133
Himmler, Heinrich 45, 120, 132, 235
Hinchley-Cooke, Lt.-Col. W.E. 136, 161, 385
Hindenburg, Paul von 109
Hinsley, Sir Harry 2, 3
Hiscox, Molly 393–4
Hitler, Adolf 48, 192, 312, 349
   character 121
   Mein Kampf 112, 122, 123
   policy and preparation for war 48, 109–24, 192
   reference to Chamberlain 9, 121–2
Hitler Jugend 111, 122
Hoare, Sir Samuel 129
Hobbes, Thomas 312
Holland, Alice 105
Holland 74, 75, 103, 115, 120, 148, 153, 158, 162, 178, 219, 230, 304, 310
Hollis, Sir/Mr Roger 23, 202, 350, 351, 358
Holloway Gaol 229
Holt-Wilson, Lt.-Col./Capt. Sir Eric 12, 67, 72, 99, 142, 149, 151, 156, 159, 163–4, 263, 313, 314–15, 327
   quoted 6–7, 102
Home Defence Security Executive *see* Security Executive
Home Office 44, 47, 48, 53, 85, 130, 166–7
Home Office Warrants *see* HOWs
Home Ports Defence Committee 66
Home Secretary 42
Homer (codename for Donald Maclean) 7, 21
Hong Kong 54, 141, 396, 400
Hoover, J. Edgar 136, 268
Hornfjell (MV) 222
Horrocks, Reginald 15, 169, 170–1, 304–5, 368
   report by 375–81
Hove, Josef/Joseph Jan van 22, 227, 386
Howard, Sir Michael 18

HOWs (Home Office Warrants) 9, 68–9, 75, 97, 110, 115–16, 124, 126, 143
Hugenberg (German industrialist) 81
Hughes, James McGuirck (aka P.G. Taylor) 8
Hughes, Maj./Mr 259, 390
Humphry, Maj. E.S. 323
Hungary 92, 93, 119
Hunter, Mr 259
Hurst Committee 166
Husky operation 289
Hythe, Kent 65

IA (Intelligence) staff 70
IB (Security) staff 58, 70, 301, 404–5
Iceland 212, 231
ICI (Imperial Chemical Industries Ltd) 124
IG Farben Industie AG 264
Immigration Officers 218–19, 220, 399
Imperial Chemical Industries Ltd (ICI) 124
Imperial Fascist League 308
Incitement to Disaffection Act 107
Incitement to Mutiny Act 94
India 1, 48, 54, 72, 153
Indian Political Intelligence (IPI) 384
industrial and commercial espionage (B4B/B15) 75, 81, 108, 155, 263–6
Industrial Revolution 87
Information Index *see under* LRC
Inter-Services Security Board 390, 391
International Brigade 85, 358, 362, 364
International Class War Prisoners Aid 103
International Juridicial Association 103
International Union of the Revolutionary Theatre 103
International Union of Revolutionary Writers 103
internment 10, 46, 50, 66–7, 69, 70–1, 73–4, 149–50, 164–5, 184–5, 216, 303
Invergordon incident 107
investigation branch (WWI) 50, 72, 74, 86
IPI (Indian Political Intelligence) 384
IRA 27(n. 74), 135, 278, 279
Iraq 244, 271, 274, 286
Ireland *see* Eire; Northern Ireland
Ironside, Field Marshal Sir (*later* Baron) Edmund 11
ISBA 211
ISK (Intelligence Service Knox) 28(n. 98)
Isle of Man 303
ISOS (Intelligence Service Oliver Strachey) 16, 178, 206–15
Italian Communist revolt 93
Italian espionage 59, 138–40, 165–7, 366–8
Italian Fascism 8, 59
   Fasci all'Extero 112, 129, 138, 139–40
   Partito Nazionale Fascista 113, 138–40, 142, 165, 166–7
Italian Fascist Secret Intelligence Service 138–40, 142
Italian Fascist Secret Police (OVRA) 165
Italian nationality 129
Italy 119, 237, 240, 242, 244

INDEX 437

Jakobs, Josef 22
Jamaica 399, 400
Japanese Communists 360
Japanese espionage 50, 136, 140–1, 142, 255, 259, 368
Jeff (codename) 249
Jefferson, Jean 358
Jehovah's Witnesses 59
Jelf, Sir Arthur 323
Jersey 231
Jews 79, 164, 167
JIC see under Committee of Imperial Defence
Job, John Oswald/Oswald John 220, 386
Jodl, Alfred 256
Johannsen's Bureau in Hamburg 131
Johnson, Mr Herschel 137
Jones, Col. Idwal 323
Jones, Lt. 262
Jordan, Mrs Jessie 126, 136
Joyce, William ('Lord Haw-Haw') 8, 109, 168, 292, 314, 390, 394

Kaltenbrunner, Ernst 338
Kamenev/Kamaneff, Lev/Leo 4–5, 93
Karlowa, Herr 133
Keitel, Wilhelm 209, 256
Kell, Maj.-Gen. Sir Vernon 6, 8, 9, 10, 12, 13, 48, 49, 60, 67, 69, 70, 80, 99, 102, 110, 130, 131, 142, 146, 149, 161, 163–4
Kellar, Mr 259, 270, 273, 274
Kellogg Pact 95
Kelway, Capt R.S. 323
Kemble, Lt.-Col. P.B. 323
Kendal, Sir Norman 217
Kenny, John 282
Kent, Tyler 166, 393, 394
Kerensky, Alexander 86, 88, 89
Kerrigan, Mr 354
Key, Jose Estella 386
KGB 7, 20
Kieboom, Charles Albert van den 386
King, John Hubert 189, 190
Kirchenstein, Jakob 96
Klishko, Nickoli 93
Knight, Maj. Maxwell ('Uncle Max') 7, 20, 312, 392, 393, 394
Knox, 'Dilly' 28(n. 98)
Kordt, Dr Theodor 8, 133
Krassin, Leonid 93
Krivitsky, Gen. Walter 161, 190–2, 361, 362
KRO (Kontre Razvedupr) 191
Krupps 81
Kuchenmeister, C.W. 151, 267, 268, 269, 270
Kun, Bela 93
Kuo Min Tang 93, 360

Labour Party/movement 5, 7, 96, 356, 365
Lachmann, Dr 314
Laureyssens, Joseph August 218, 286, 306–7
League against Imperialism and for National Independence 103, 107–8
League of Nations 106, 138

Lease Lend Act 269
Lee, Col 136, 137
Lees-Smith, Mr 353
Leeward Islands 400
Left Wing movements see Communist ...
Lenihan, Joseph 280
Lenin, Vladimir Ilyich 45, 87, 88, 89, 90, 91, 103, 183
Lenin School 98, 104, 106, 191
Lennox, Maj. 203, 390, 396
Liberty Restoration League 311
Liddell, Mr Cecil 27(n. 74), 175, 259, 277, 278, 280, 281, 283
Liddell, Capt. Guy 6, 13, 110, 130, 131, 134, 136–7, 141–2, 161, 162, 169, 172–3, 174, 175, 176, 181, 190, 192, 202, 204, 205, 250, 253, 258, 267, 270, 278, 279, 280, 281, 284, 384
lights (signalling to enemy) 11, 168, 294
Link, The 123
Litvinov, Maxim 84
Lody, Karl Hans 74
Loeringhoven, Freiherr Freytag von 81
London 71, 77, 153
London Controlling Section (LCC) (operational cover plans) 253
London Reception Centre see LRC
Loraine Committee 166
Low Countries 10, 11, 242
LRC (London Reception Centre) 51, 52, 55, 77, 159, 180, 204, 206, 212, 217, 219, 220, 221–8, 244
 Information Index 51, 221, 223, 224, 225–6, 299, 301
Ludendorf, Erich von 45, 79–80
Ludwig, Otto Karl 130, 131, 132
Luftahrtministerium 131
Luftwaffe 11
Luxembourg 178
Lydd, Kent 65

M/MS Section (originally SIS agency) 7, 101, 107, 143, 181, 277, 392–6
McCartney, Wilfred Francis Remington 98
Machell, Mr 386, 387
machine tool industry 127, 156, 267–70, 319–20
MacIver, Lt.-Col. 174
McKenna, Gen./Lt.-Gen. 281–2
McKenna, Mr 65
Maclean, Donald (codename Homer) 7, 21
Macphail, Capt. A.J. 323
Maffey, Sir John 278, 281, 284
Magnificent Five 7, 21
Mahr, Dr Adolf 135
Malaya 141, 400
Malone, Cecil Lestrange 93
Malta 396
Mammut expedition 274
Manchuria 104
Manuilski, Dmitri 104–5
MAP (Ministry of Aircraft Production) 319

Mariott, Mr 247
Markmann (German industrialist) 151
Mars, Capt. W.S. 321, 322
Marty, Andre 182
Marx, Karl 16
Marxism 84, 87, 365
Mason, John 186
Master of Sempill 140
Masterman, Maj. J.C. (chairman of XX Committee) 17, 53, 247, 254
Mata Hari (Margeurite Zelle) 4
Mathews, Col. S. 323
Maude, Mr John 386, 394
Maunsell, Brig. 271, 272
Maurer (Abwehr officer) 120
Mauritius 54
Maxwell, Sir Alexander 150, 186, 353
Mayer, Franz 274
Mayers, Colin 140
Mediterranean 113, 138
Meier, Carl Heinrich 386
Melland, Lt.-Col./Maj. 214, 215
Melville, W. 50
Menezes, Rogerio de Magalhaes Peixoto de 275, 276, 386, 393–4
Menshevik Party 87, 360
Menzies, Sir Stewart 23
Mercantile Marine 154, 362
Merchant Navy 14
Metropolitan Police *see* Scotland Yard; Special Branch
MI1C (MI6) *see* SIS
MI5, as title of Security Service 6, 102
MI5 Registry *see* Registry
MI6 *see* SIS
MI8 143, 144
MI14 58
MI19 58, 143
microphotography 53
Midas plan 252
Middle East 77, 113, 138, 139, 140, 166, 211, 238, 240, 242, 244, 304
  Section B1B 270–4
Milices Patriotiques 360
Militant Workers 365
Military Permit Officers 54
Military Permit Offices 71, 77
Military (Port) Control Officers 54, 70, 77
Miller, Capt. 141
Miller, Peter 96
Miller, Tom 96
Mills, Major A.F. 323
Mills, Mr 383
Milmo, Mr 229, 232–3
miners 5, 93
Ministry of Air 19, 72, 317–19, 363
Ministry of Air Production (MAP) 319
Ministry of Economic Warfare (MEW) 53, 265, 269–70
Ministry of Information 353
Ministry of Labour 185–6, 217
Ministry of Shipping 154

Minority Trade Union Movement 93
MO5 44, 69–72
Molotov, Vlacheslav 84
Monckton, Sir Walter 152
Mongolia 360
Monie, Cmdr. 142
Morrison, Herbert 167, 310
Morrison, William 106
Morton, Desmond 27(n. 85)
Mosley, Sir Oswald 59, 115, 116, 164
  see also British Union of Fascists
Moss, Louis 353
Mountbatten, Lord Louis 247
Mulberry 354
Munich Crisis/Agreement 9, 120, 121, 133
Murphy, J.T. 96
Mussert Party 162, 310, 313
Mussolini, Benito 8, 48, 59, 109, 113, 115, 119, 139, 165, 404
Mutt (codename) 249

Nachrichten (Intelligence) Bureau/Branch 63, 64, 75, 78, 125
Napoleon 44, 65, 66
National Liberationist Alliance (Brazil) 105
National Minority Movement 5, 93
National Socialist League 308
National Socialist Parties 112, 115, 129
Nationalists (F3/B7) 308–13
Nazi (NSDAP) Party and Auslands Organisation 8–10, 48, 109–15, 122, 124, 129, 131, 152–3
Near East *see* Middle East
Nelson, Lord 173
Nesbitt, Lt. T. 321
Neukermans, Pierre Richard Charles 386
Neurath, Baron Konstantin von 131
neutral countries 54, 75, 76, 77, 162, 216, 270–86
neutral embassies 17, 19, 20, 259–61
New Propellor 184
New York 54, 71
New Zealand 114
Newbold, J.T. Walton 93
Newfoundland 400
Nicholson, Mrs Sybil 393, 394
Nicolai, Colonel 45, 77–8, 79–80, 122
Nidda (German journalist) 130
'night of the long knives' 110
NKGB 21
NKVD (Soviet Home Office) 20, 21, 190
Noble, Maj. A.P. 322
Noble, Mr 265
Non-Intervention Committee 118
Nordic League 308
Norman, Lt.-Col. 142, 316
Normandy Landings 18, 21, 205, 254–6, 332, 389, 400–1
North Africa 153, 205, 215, 218, 230, 237, 238, 240, 242, 353
Northern Ireland 277, 280
Norway 45, 74, 115, 162, 164, 180, 216, 230, 231, 236, 304, 310

Noulens, Hilaire 104
NSB Party (Holland) 115
NSDAP see Nazi party
Nuntia Bureau 81

Obed (saboteur) 238
Observation section (shadowing) 50, 99, 143, 302
Odbor (Council) of Yugoslavia 360
Office of Strategic Services see OSS
Official Secrets Act 43, 52, 66, 67–8, 130, 134, 140
OGPU (staff of Russian Security Service) 190, 191
Ohlendorff, Otto 338
Oka (Japanese Naval Attache) 140–1
OMS (Otdyel Mezhdinarodnoi Svyazi) 191
Operation Husky 289
Operation Overlord 254–5, 281, 283, 284, 332, 400–1
Operational Staffs 53
Operations Section/Room 171, 203, 388, 390–2
Oratory Schools 227
O'Reilly, John Francis 282
Orr, Mr 203, 396
Osborne, Mr 307
OSS (Office of Strategic Services) 18, 58, 285, 334
Ostdienst 81
Ostend 66
Osterwald, Werner 394
Ottawa 54, 136
Overlord deception plan 254–5, 281, 283, 284, 332, 400–1
Overseas Control see under Director-General's Staff
Overseas Defence Committee 141
OVRA (Italian Fascist Secret Police) 165
Owens (agent) 178

Pacifists (F3/B7) 59, 86, 111, 203, 308–13
Palestine 59, 273
Palmer, Mr 206, 207, 212, 214–15, 298
Pan-Pacific Trades Union Secretariat (PPTUS) 104
Panama 216
Paris 54, 71, 77, 178
Passenger Traffic Order (1939) 220
Passport Control Officers 55, 162, 404
Paton-Smith, Miss 158
Patterson, Maj. 390
People's Common Law Parliament 311
permanent revolution 91, 95
Persia 242, 244, 271, 274, 286
Peruvian spy 74
Petersen, Carl 135
Petrie, Sir David 11, 13–15, 18, 146, 179, 182, 199, 201, 328–9, 373, 400–1
 and Curry's History 1, 2, 3, 12–13, 16–17
Petrograd (St Petersburg) 88, 89, 91
Pfeiffer, Eric/h 136, 338
Pfister (BUF member) 109

Philby, Kim 7, 16, 21, 23
Philips, Maj. 99
Phipps, Maj. 386
Pieck, Hans Christian 189–90
Piepenbrock, Oberst Hans 120
pigeons 11, 12, 293–4
Pilcher, Mr G. St.C. 203, 309, 385
Pirelli 166
Plan Dream 252
Plan Fortitude 27(n.82), 254, 255
Plan Midas 252
Pluto (Pipeline Under The Ocean) 354, 389
Poland 45, 46, 147, 162–3, 182, 228, 266, 304, 360
police forces 42, 44, 48, 53–4, 59, 60, 64, 65, 76, 86
Pollitt, Harry 183, 191, 349
Port Control (D Division) 49, 50, 320–5
port and travel control 49, 50, 54, 70, 77, 149, 150, 156–7, 204, 215–21, 320–5
Portugal 216, 217, 218, 230, 231, 259, 275–6
Portuguese Embassy 21, 212, 259, 275–6
Post Office (GPO)/Postal Censorship 10, 44, 65, 66, 68–9, 73, 124, 143, 144
Potter, Mr H.H. 375
Pozo, Miguel Piernavieja del 275
PPTUS (Pan-Pacific Trades Union Secretariat) 104
Praetorius, Dr Friedrich Karl 251
Press, control of 66, 241, 292, 395–6
Prestes, Luis Carlos 105
Pretoria 114
preventive branch 49–50, 72, 73
Price, Capt. V.M. 323
Prime Minister 45, 49, 86
Prinz Eugen cruiser 280
Prioleau, Lt. 322
Profintern (Trade Union section of Comintern) 96, 187
Prohibited Places 68
proletariat 82, 90, 107
propaganda 45, 48, 53, 79, 80, 133
Protected Places 157
Pry, Gabriel 227
Purcell, Alexander 93
Putlitz, Wolfgang zu 8

Quisling, Vidkun 45, 313
Quisling characters 80, 199, 310
Rada (Council) of Poland 360
Radio Intelligence Section see RIS
Radio Security Intelligence Conference (RSIC) 288–9
Radio Security Section see RSS
RAF (Royal Air Force) 135, 138, 353
Rainbow (codename) 246
Rakovsky (Soviet Legation) 97
Rambaur, Lucien 227
Ramsay, Captain 309, 394
Razvedupr (GRU) 21
Red Army 88, 93, 96, 98, 104
Red Guard (workers' army of Petrograd) 88, 89

Redfern, Mr 386
refugees 219–20, 221–8
Regional Security Liaison Officers *see* RSLO
Registry
 B1 (later RB and WR-H) 180, 224, 297, 298, 299, 333, 335, 337, 339, 380
 Central 12, 15, 49, 55, 56, 77, 157, 160–1, 169, 170–1, 172, 176, 202, 224, 299, 375–81
 LRC Information Index 51, 221, 223, 224, 225–6, 299, 301
 SIS (Section V) ISOS Registry 23, 56, 106, 224, 299, 300, 301, 333, 358
Reichsbank 264
Reichsicherheitshauptamt (RSHA) 79, 206, 235
Reichskanzlei (Hitler's Bureau) 123
Reichstag Fire Trial 106
Reichswehrministerium 131, 132
Reid, Sir Edward 259, 262
Reilly, Mr 211
Research Section 297–302
Revolutionary Communist Party (Trotskyist Movement) 365, 366
revolutionary defeatism 84, 183–4, 185, 187, 188, 189
Revolutionary Socialist League 364
Rhineland 112, 120, 131, 148
Ribbentrop, Joachim von 8, 9, 117, 118, 119, 120, 122, 123, 124, 131–2
Ribbentrop, von (son of Joachim) 9
Ribbentrop Bureau (Dienststelle) 118, 122, 123, 131–2
Richter, Karel Richard 22, 386
Right Club 308, 309, 394
Right Wing movements (F3/B7) 60, 308–13
RIS (Radio Intelligence Section) (formerly SIS Section VW) 56, 57, 209, 212, 290, 298
Robb, Lt.-Col./Maj. J.G.F. 322, 323
Robertson, Lt.-Col./Maj./Capt. T.A. 161, 162, 171, 180, 204, 205, 246, 247, 272, 273, 287, 289, 334
Robson, R.W. 352, 353
Robson-Scott, Mr 305
Rolls Royce 365
Rome 54, 71
Room 055, War Office 203, 396
Rosenberg, Alfred 122, 124
Roskill, Sir Ashton 13, 15
Rothschild, Lord 155, 156, 176, 215, 233, 237, 239, 244, 259, 265, 267, 268, 270, 273, 312
Royal Artillery 135
Royal Canadian Mounted Police 114, 136
Royal Tank Corps 135
Royal Ulster Constabulary 277
RPS (Royal Patriotic Schools) 180, 204, 217, 221
RSHA (Reichsicherheitshauptamt) 79, 206, 233–45
RSLO (Regional Security Liaison Officers) 52, 54, 168, 174–5, 226, 328–32
RSS (Radio Security Service/Section) 9–10, 15, 16, 56, 57, 143–4, 161, 177–80, 206–15, 287–92
Rule of Law 42
Rumania 147, 179
Rumrich, Gunther Gustav 126, 135–6
Rundstedt, Gerd von 256
Russia *see also* Communist ...; Soviet ...
Russia, Czarist 74, 96
Russian Revolution 47, 86–90
Russian Trade Delegation *see* Soviet Trade Delegation
Russo-Polish War 5
Rust, W. 182
Ruter (German agent) 152
Rutland, Frederick Joseph 140–1
Ryder, Lt.-Col. 202, 307

sabotage 42, 43, 81, 107, 112, 113, 129, 138, 139, 148, 154–5, 166, 204, 233–45
St Petersburg *see* Petrograd
Sample, Miss 382
Scandinavia 75, 103
Scharnhorst battleship 280
Schellenberg, Walter 338
Schulenburg, Friedrich Werner Count von der 120
Schuster Committee 149
Schutz, Gunther 246, 278
Sclater, Lt.-Col. 259, 295
SCO (Security Control Officers) 157, 204, 215–21, 320–5
Scotland Yard, Directorate of Intelligence 92, 101
Scott, Sir Russell 8, 110, 115
Scott-Ford, Duncan Alexander Croall 14, 386
Scottish Nationalists 59
SD (Sicherheitsdienst) (German Security Service) 45, 132, 206–15
seamen agents (B1L) 262–3
Seamen's Union 96
Seckt, General von 192
Second Front 84, 245, 355, 365
Second or Socialist International 87, 103
Secret Service Bureau 6, 66, 67
Secret Service Committee 4, 5, 6
secret writing 53, 76
Section IX *see under* SIS
Section V *see under* SIS
Security Co-ordination, New York 138
Security Executive (Home Defence) 13, 49, 52, 53, 253, 327, 385
Security Service
 advisory capacity of 52–3
 functions and structure 41–61
 internal organisation 47–50, 141–4, 169–74
 liaison 53–8
  see also America; BBC; Censorship; Colonies; Dominions; Eire; RSS; Service Intelligence Staffs; SIS; SOE
 powers 51–2
 reorganisation (1931 and 1941) 6–8, 92, 101–4, 181–2, 201–3, 349–50
 scope 58–61

INDEX 441

...iet espionage within 19–20
...f numbers 5–6, 10, 14, 98–9, 142, 323–4,
   ...3
...men in 77, 374–5
...rity Service Intelligence Centre 146, 171,
...r, Cmdr. 382
...ce Intelligence Staffs, liaison with 48, 58
...er, Lt.-Col. 389, 390
...owing Staff 50, 99, 143, 302
...EF (Supreme Headquarters of the Allied
   ...editionary Force) 57, 58, 200, 301, 332–41
...ghai 54
...non Hydro-Electric scheme 135
...han, Mrs 363
...ord, Mr 390
...pard, Mr S. 395
...ds, James 354, 358
...to, Mr 351, 362
...ch, Baldur von 111
...Stewards' Movement 96, 187–8
Sicherheitsdienst see Sipo und SD
Sicily 205, 388–9
Siemens Schukert 135, 156
SIGINT (Signals Intelligence) 4, 15, 16, 17, 21, 28(n.99), 105–7
signalling to enemy (lights) 11, 168, 294
Sikorski, Gen. 239
SIME (Security Intelligence Middle East) 54, 58, 211, 238, 240, 271–4, 304, 367, 368
Simkins, Anthony 2–3
Simoes, Ernesto 276
Simon, Sir John 130
Simpson, Lt.-Col. 9, 143, 177–8, 180, 287–8
Sinclair, Maj. 161, 245–6, 386
Singapore 54, 141, 396
Sipo und SD (German Security Service) 45, 132, 206–15
SIS
  and Allies and neutral countries 54, 55
  relations with MI5 2, 5, 6, 22–3, 55–8, 101–4, 138, 403–4
    see also under Section V below
  three-mile limit 6, 102
  and RSS 10, 16, 179, 180
  Section IX 22–3, 83–4, 358, 392
  Section V 58, 85, 101, 103, 104–5, 202, 358
    ISOS Registry 23, 56, 106, 224, 299, 300, 301, 333, 358
    MI5 liaison with 7, 16–17, 55–6, 208–12, 381–2
    VW (later RIS) 56, 57, 209, 212, 290, 298
Skorzeny, Otto 235, 338
Slocombe, George 97
Small, Miss 386, 387
Smith, Mr H.L. 371
Snow (codename)/agent [...] 103, 116–21, 135, 147, 148, 151, 153, 161, 206, 236, 246, 247
Social Revolutionary Party 87, 360
Socialist International, Second 87, 103
Society for Cultural Relations with Soviet Russia 103

SOE (Special Operations Executive) 19, 222, 226, 238–9, 353, 354
  liaison with 382–3
South Africa 114, 231, 400
South America 95, 104–5, 259, 276–7, 286, 358, 395
South-Eastern Europe 132
sovereignty 86, 113, 129
Soviet Embassy 19, 21, 94, 364
Soviet espionage 4, 7–8, 18–23, 47–8, 50, 53, 59, 96–8, 107–8, 189–92, 203, 361–4
Soviet funding for strikes/*Daily Herald*, CPGB etc 4–5, 7, 93, 94, 103, 105–7
Soviet Government 56, 59, 83, 84, 93, 95, 96, 103
Soviet SIGINT 4, 21, 28(n.99), 105–7
Soviet Trade Delegation 5, 19, 93, 94, 96, 97, 108, 362, 364
Soviet Trade Unions 93, 94, 96
soviets, system of 90
Spain 74, 230
  and Germany 117, 213, 217, 218, 230, 231, 236–7, 239, 240–1, 242, 243–4, 274–5
Spanish Armada 66
Spanish Civil War 85, 117, 118, 129
Spanish Embassy 21, 259
Spanish ships 216
Spartacus struggles 93
Special Branch 3, 4, 5, 6, 47–8, 50, 51, 60, 101
Special Intelligence Bureau 66, 67, 68, 69
Special Operations Executive see SOE
Springhall, D.F. 18–19, 182, 184, 351, 352, 354, 356–7, 363
Squid weapon 354
SS *City of Lancaster* 249
Stalin, Joseph 83, 84, 86, 89, 95, 103, 161, 190, 191, 192, 349, 364
Stalingrad 242
Stapledon, Mrs Irma 393–4
Stephens, Col./Maj. 176, 180, 230, 232
Stephen's *Digest of the Criminal Law* 66
Stephenson, Maj. 272
Stewart, Sir Findlater 247, 253, 258, 261, 284–5, 296
Stewart, Robert 358–9, 361
Stinnes (German industrialist) 81
Stopford, Mr 259, 262–3
Strachey, Oliver 16
Stratton, Capt G.L. 323
strikes 5, 59, 86, 93, 94, 183–4
Strong, Maj.-Gen. 339, 340, 390
Sudetenland 148
Suez Canal 139
Suner, Serrano 275
Supreme Headquarters of the Allied Expeditionary Force see SHAEF
Suspect Lists 310–11
Sweden 162
Swinton, Lord 13, 14, 15, 49, 145–6, 179, 180, 199, 218, 219
  reorganisation by 181, 182, 201, 202, 385
  and Security Executive 13, 49, 168, 171, 385

Switzerland 162, 269–70
Syria 240, 241, 244

Taanevik (MV) 222
Tanganyika 114
Tangye, Captain 395
tank production 81
Tanner, Jack 96
Tate (codename) 251, 252, 257
Taylor, F.L. 323
Taylor, Lt.-Gen. Sir Maurice 267
Taylor, P.G. (James McGuirck Hughes) 8
TED (Trading with the Enemy Department) 265, 266
telephone bugging 20
Theatre Intelligence Section 301
Theseus ship 178, 179
Thomson, Sir Basil 11, 51, 76, 92, 217
Thomson, Raven 109
Thor Corporation 153
Thyssen (German industrialist) 81
Timmerman, Alphons Louis Eugene 386
Todan Maatschappij 153
Toglatti (Ercoli) 106–7
total war 45, 77–80, 111, 129, 147
Trade Unions 5, 93, 94, 96, 103, 186–8
travel control, port and 49, 50, 54, 70, 77, 149, 150, 156–7, 204, 215–21, 320–5
Treachery Act 43
Treasure (codename) 248
Treasury 48
Treaty of Versailles 81, 263
Trevor-Roper, Captain Hugh (later Lord Dacre) 13, 178, 206, 207, 212, 290
Tricycle (codename) 251
Trinidad 212, 213, 231, 400
Trotsky, Leon 83, 86, 87–8, 89, 91, 95, 358, 364
Trotskyites 59–60, 364–6
TUC (Trades Union Congress) 103, 186
Turkey 238, 240, 241, 273, 286
Turner, Mr 202, 304–5, 307–8
Turrou, Mr 136
Twenty (XX) Committee (sub-committee of W Board) 17, 52, 53, 247, 253
Tyneside Shipyard Apprentices 365

U-boats 257
Unilever 124
United Front organisations 96, 103–4, 106, 188
Unland, Werner 153, 278, 286
Uren, Desmond 19, 351, 354, 357, 363
Uruguayan spy 74
USA *see* America
USSR *see* Russia; Soviet ...
Ustinov, Jona ('Klop') 8
Ustinov, Peter 8–9

Vansittart, Sir Robert 101, 115–16, 129, 130
Velasco, Alcazar de 275
Venona Soviet decrypts 28(n. 99)
vetting (examination of credentials) 10, 19, 50, 73, 160
Vickers Armstrong 140, 365
Vile, Capt. T.H. 323
Vivian, Col./Maj. Valentine 7, 16, 23, 82, 96, 103–4, 106, 158, 190, 358, 359, 392
Voegler (German industrialist) 81

W Board 52–3, 253
W Branch 146, 169, 171, 172, 179, 390
Wadeson, Miss 225, 382
Waldberg, Jose 386
Walker, Flt. Lt. 259, 292, 293
Walshe, Mr 134, 282, 285
Walti, Werner Heinrick 386
War Office 3, 6, 10, 47, 64, 65, 66, 67, 69, 142, 317–19, 396
  Room 055 203, 396
War Office War Book 149, 156
War Room 58, 242, 301–2, 332–41
  Registry (WR-H) 380–1
Warschauer, Ludwig 266
Webb, Sydney and Beatrice 86, 90
Webster, W.H.A. 323
Wehrpolitik 112
Wellington, Duke of 65
Welsh Nationalists 59
Weltheim, Eriski 93
West Africa 400
Westminster School 8
Wethered, Maj. 382, 383
Wheeton, Stephen James 105–6
White, Brig./Mr/Sir Dick 7–8, 15, 17, 20, 161, 162, 176, 180, 200, 202, 203–4, 205, 222, 225, 272, 288–9, 302, 332–3, 339, 340, 384
Whyte, Maj. 389
Wightman, Maj. O.N. 323
Wilkie, Helen 190
Wilson, Horace 13
Wilson School 358, 359
Windward Islands 400
Winsor, Col. B.R. Benyon 323
Winter, Franciscus Johannes 386
Wirtschaftspolitische Gesellschaft 81
Wodan Handel Maatschappij 266
Wolf, Frau Johanna 133
Wolkoff, Anna 166, 393, 394
Woolwich Arsenal 7, 108, 361–2
Workers' International League (WIL) 365, 366
Workers' International Relief 103
World Committee against War and Fascism 103
World Revolution 83, 84, 86, 91, 96, 191
Wormwood Scrubs 175
Wright, Peter 28(n. 102)

XX Committee *see* Twenty Committee
Younger, Maj. 202, 305, 306
Yugoslavia 119, 242, 304, 360
Zell/a Mehlis code typewriters, Thuringia 151
Zelle, Margeurite (Mata Hari) 4
Zigzag (codename) 249
Zinoviev, Grigori 95
Zinoviev letter 5, 93